# Beneath Another Sky

# NORMAN DAVIES

# Beneath Another Sky

## A Global Journey into History

ALLEN LANE

*an imprint of*

PENGUIN BOOKS

ALLEN LANE

UK | USA | Canada | Ireland | Australia
India | New Zealand | South Africa

Allen Lane is part of the Penguin Random House group of companies
whose addresses can be found at global.penguinrandomhouse.com

First published 2017
002

Set in 10.2/13.87 Sabon LT Std by Jouve (UK), Milton Keynes
Printed in Great Britain by Clays Ltd, St Ives plc

A CIP catalogue record for this book is available from the British Library

ISBN: 978-1-846-14831-6

www.greenpenguin.co.uk

MIX
Paper from
responsible sources
FSC® C018179

Penguin Random House is committed to a
sustainable future for our business, our readers
and our planet. This book is made from Forest
Stewardship Council® certified paper.

*To*
*JOHN MARTIN*
*and*
*IAN LINDSEY*

*Who conferred to save the author*
*and thereby saved the book*

# Contents

# List of Illustrations

## PLATES

# List of Maps

# Introduction

## The Golden Road

My mother's most treasured reading was John Bunyan's *Pilgrim's Progress*.[1] The book sat on her bedside table for years, silently rebuking the levity of my father's favourite, *The Count of Monte Cristo*, which lay beside his pillow on the opposite side.[2] The two heroes epitomized my parents' contrasting frames of mind. I have every reason to suspect that the 'The Pilgrim' and 'The Count' presided discreetly at the launch of my own career.

Despite an obligatory pilgrimage to his birthplace at Elstow in Bedfordshire, aged seven or eight, I never really warmed to Bunyan. He was a Puritan and a preacher, earnest to a fault. Yet it was from him that I learned the wonderful allegory that presents life as a journey, that describes its 'Sloughs of Despond' and its 'Delectable Mountains', and promises a 'Celestial City' at the end. In school assembly we would all sing Bunyan's stirring hymn with gusto:

> He who would valiant be
> 'Gainst all disaster,
> Let him in constancy
> Follow the Master.
> There's no discouragement
> Shall make him once relent
> His first avowed intent
> To be a pilgrim.[3]

The metrical melody by Ralph Vaughan Williams greatly adds to the impact.

I was brought up to sing hymns. I can still sit down at the piano and play scores of them from memory. And there's none to beat *Cwm Rhondda*, the 'Prayer for Strength', sung in a sonorous A flat major, which is the ultimate girder-of-loins:

Guide me O Thou, Great Redeemer,
Pilgrim in this barren land.
I am weak, but Thou art mighty;
Hold me with Thy powerful hand.
Bread of Heaven! Bread of Heaven!
Feed me till I want no more.
When I pass the banks of Jordan
Bid my anxious fears subside.
Death of death, and Hell's destruction
Bring me safe to Canaan's side.
Songs of Praises! Songs of Praises!
I will ever give to Thee.[4]

Whenever a 'Slough of Despond' is looming, one or two quick bursts of *Cwm Rhondda* suffice to dispel it.

Once or twice a year my son Christian (who was named in part after Bunyan's hero) takes me to the Millennium Stadium in Cardiff, both to watch the rugby and to listen to the singing. There, the Welsh words soar even higher:

*Arglwydd, arwain trwy'r*
*Fi berein gwael ei wedd*
*Na does ynof nerth na bywyd*
*Fel yn gorwedd yn y bedd:*
  *Hollaluog! Hollaluog!*
  *Ydyw'r Un a'm cwyd i lan*
  *Ydyw'r Un a'm cwyd i lan.*[5]

Both my father and my mother lost elder brothers in the Great War. Most of the popular songs in their repertoire were drawn from that period, and would resurface for my benefit in the 1960s in Joan Littlewood's brilliant show *Oh! What a Lovely War*. Themes of loss and longing predominated:

There's a long, long trail a-winding
Into the land of my dreams
Where the nightingales are singing,
And a white moon beams.
There's a long, long night of waiting
Until my dreams all come true,
Till the day when I'll be going down
That long, long trail with you.[6]

Few modern pop songs possess either the melody, or the mood, or the message.

In the third or fourth form at school we all read William Hazlitt's 'On Going a Journey' as a classic example of English essay-writing. It was a revelation to me that someone could calmly dissect his own thoughts and feelings with such fastidious precision. Hazlitt (1778–1830), who had a miserable life, advocated the joys of solitude and the therapeutic benefits of travelling. The essay is best known for one sentence: 'It is better to travel than to arrive.' But it contains other gems, too: 'I am never less alone than when alone' and 'Give me the clear blue sky over my head and the green turf beneath my feet, a winding road before me, and a three hours' march to dinner – and then to thinking!'[7]

To my eternal advantage several of my schoolmasters shared Hazlitt's philosophy, and took us on numerous outings with much green turf beneath our feet. Before I was far into my teens, I had climbed the Lakeland hills (starting with Helvellyn), explored the Peak District (starting with Mam Tor), strolled through the glades of the ancient New Forest from our encampment in the Queen's Bower, trekked across the wastes of Dartmoor, and pitched my tent below the battlements of a Highland castle, serenaded by the Laird's piper.

Another schoolmaster who had a profound effect in a short time was David Curnow, later Professor of English Literature at the American University of Beirut. Newly graduated from Cambridge, he had the near-impossible task of injecting literary sensitivity into the blockheads of a group of sixth-formers who had already dropped English as a main subject. Tall and elegant, he played his part sporting a Teddy Boy quiff, a foppish cravat, and an immaculately pressed pair of cavalry twills. His technique was to sidle quietly into the room, hands in trouser pockets, to ignore the hubbub, and to take a piece of chalk and write a few lines of verse on the blackboard. He would then spin around, face the blockheads, say nothing, and wait for a response:

> Ah Sun-flower! weary of time,
> Who countest the steps of the Sun:
> Seeking after that sweet golden clime
> Where the traveller's journey is done.
> Where the Youth pined away with desire,
> And the pale Virgin shrouded in snow:
> Arise from their graves and aspire,
> Where my Sun-flower wishes to go.[8]

The effect was electric. The hubbub subsided. And silence fell onto a roomful of adolescent youths, all 'pined away with desire', who realized that William Blake was speaking directly to them about life, death, sex, and spiritual travel.

Around that time, almost by accident, I discovered the world of travel books. Wandering around Bolton municipal library, I hit on an unusually large travel section, mainly of Victorian vintage. Memorable titles included Arthur Young's *Travels in France* (1792), Alexander Kinglake's *Eothen* (1844), George Borrow's *Wild Wales* (1862) (which aroused my curiosity about family roots), R. L. Stevenson's *Travels with a Donkey in the Cévennes* (1879), which fed a fascination with rural France, and Joshua Slocum's *Sailing Alone Around the World* (1900). My undoubted favourite, though, was William Cobbett's *Rural Rides* (1830), which combined detailed descriptions of horseback journeys around pre-industrial England with trenchant political and social opinions. Long before I went up to Oxford, Cobbett had told me what to expect:

> Upon beholding the masses of buildings at Oxford, devoted to what they call '*learning*', I could not help reflecting on the drones that they contain and the wasps they send forth! However malignant as some are, the great and prevalent characteristic is *folly*: emptiness of head, want of talent, and one half of the fellows, who are what they call *educated* here, are unfit to be clerks in a grocer's or mercer's shop . . . And I could not help exclaiming to myself: 'Stand forth, ye big-wigged, ye gloriously feeding Doctors! Stand forth, ye rich of the Church whose poor have given them a hundred thousand pounds a year . . . Stand forth and face me, who have, from the pen of my leisure hours, sent among your flocks . . . [more] than you have all done for the last half century![9]

No less inspiring for a growing boy were works of fictional travel. I was whipped into a white heat by Jules Verne's *Twenty Thousand Leagues under the Sea*, Arthur Conan Doyle's *The Lost World* and Rider Haggard's *King Solomon's Mines*. I read H. G. Wells's *The Time Machine* when confined to bed with mumps or measles, and it only added to the delirium. In my mind I invented my own machine that could recover the light rays emitted by historical events and thus, by setting the dials to a particular place and a particular date – such as Thermopylae at –480, or Hastings at +1066 – could reconstruct a picture of the relevant scene. 'There are really four dimensions,' Wells wrote, 'three which we call the three planes of Space, and a fourth, Time.' And it stuck. Arduous journeys through Time and Space would be rewarded with limitless knowledge, untold marvels and the secrets of the Earth.[10]

Today, I am struck by the fact that supposed experts who draw up lists of their ten or twenty 'Best Travel Books of All Time' almost always ignore the foundations of the genre.[11] Most contemporary commentators appear blissfully unaware, for example, of Goethe's *Italian Journey*, one of the pillars of the canon. Goethe toured Italy for two years immediately before the French Revolution, but only published his diaries of the journey more than three decades later, having expanded them with extensive reflections and commentaries. At first sight, his work looks similar to the innumerable descriptions of the Grand Tour that well-heeled Europeans had been producing for centuries. In fact, it was highly innovatory. Goethe convinced himself that the highest purpose of travel was self-discovery; travel was *eine Schule des Sehens*, 'a school of seeing'; he wanted, he said, 'to discover myself in the objects I see'. By confronting new landscapes, works of art, and people, he was gauging his own reactions, and learning about his personal tastes, preferences, and opinions. He did so in large measure by what has been called his 'Discovery of the Antique' – the realization that the Greeks and Romans had left behind living traditions, not merely piles of ruins. He was engaged, in fact, in an experiment, one that was both psychological and cultural.[12]

Goethe's work was anything but a simple chronicle. Although based on diaries from 1786–8, the overlayering of later elaborations gave it a strangely ambiguous quality. It was, he wrote in a letter to a friend, 'both entirely truthful and a graceful fairy tale'. His love for the land beyond the Alps was lasting:

> *Kennst du das Land? wo die Zitronen bluehn*
> *Im dunkeln Laub die Gold-Orangen gluehn,*
> *Ein sanfter Wind vom blauen Himmel weht,*
> *Die Myrte still und hoch der Lorbeer steht.*[13]

(Know you the land where the lemon-trees bloom?
Where golden oranges gleam in dark foliage?
A gentle wind blows from the blue Heaven.
The myrtle is still, and the laurel stands high.)

The opening line of *Italian Journey* is, famously, '*Et in Arcadia ego*'.

I believe that the late Margaret Higginson, headmistress of Bolton School, who dared to lead a party of pubescent boys and girls to

Venice, Florence, and Verona in the Easter vacation of 1956, was moved by the same sort of ideas. For reading on the long train journey, she recommended a small book on classical literature called *Poets in a Landscape*.[14] I was hooked for life. What I did not know then is that the book's author, Gilbert Highet, a Scots professor of classics who made his name in the United States, had earlier produced the subject's 'bible' – *The Classical Tradition*.[15] 'The world is quite small now,' Highet wrote in yet another book, *People, Places and Books*, 'but history is large and deep. Sometimes you can go much farther by sitting in your own home and reading a book of history, than by getting into a ship or an airplane and traveling a thousand miles.'[16]

Aged just eighteen I went abroad for the first time on my own. Having passed the Oxford entrance exams, I went to Grenoble in the Dauphiné, to learn to speak French fluently and to test my survival skills. I dreamt the expedition up for myself, determined to follow in the footsteps of a favourite cousin, Sheila, who had studied there before the Second World War. My choice of destination was strongly influenced by the vicinity of the Alps. I attended classes at the university, while taking a room with the family De La Marche at 5, Rue du Lycée (long since demolished). I gained much from the kindness of my widowed landlady, 'Madame La Baronne', made friends with her sons, Christian and Bernard, and, though not funded for skiing, took to the hills whenever possible. One of the best ways of learning French, I found, was to help the boys' sister, Marie-Louise, with her homework and to repeat the exercises in her textbook. Marie-Louise, then twelve or thirteen, was known in the family as 'Choupette'. One day she was given a sixteenth-century sonnet to learn by heart:

> *Heureux qui, comme Ulysse, a fait un beau voyage*
> *Ou comme cestuy-là, qui conquit la toison,*
> *Et puis est retourné, plein d'usage et raison,*
> *Vivre entre ses parents le reste de son âge.*
>
> *Quand reverrai-je, hélas, de mon petit village*
> *Fumer la cheminée, et en quelle saison*
> *Reverrai-je le clos de ma pauvre maison,*
> *Qui m'est une province, et beaucoup davantage?*
>
> *Plus me plaît le séjour qu'ont bâti mes aïeux*
> *Que des palais Romains, le front audacieux:*
> *Plus que le marbre dur me plaît l'ardoise fine.*

*Plus mon Loir gaulois, que le Tibre latin,*
*Plus mon petit Liré, que le Mont Palatin*
*Et plus que l'air marin, la douceur angevine.*[17]

(Happy is he, like Ulysses, who has made a good journey
Or like the other one, who conquered the Golden Fleece,
And has then returned, full of experience and good sense,
To live among his kin for the rest of his days.

When, alas, shall I see my little village again,
Its smoke rising from the chimney? and in what season
See once more the enclosure of my poor house,
Which is a province for me, and much more besides?

The shelter that my ancestors built pleases me more
Than the palaces of Rome, with their bold facades;
And fine slate is more pleasing than hard marble:

I prefer my Gaulish Loire to the Latin Tiber,
My little Liré to the Palatine Mount
And the gentleness of Anjou to [harsh] sea air.)

The author, Joachim du Bellay, had made the long journey from his native Anjou to Rome, and was suffering from a bout of homesickness, as I did occasionally in Grenoble. Where, I wonder, is Choupette now?

Ulysses, of course, was the Roman name for the Greek Odysseus, the archetypal European wanderer. Homer had made him the hero of European literature's second founding classic. Odysseus, whose name means 'Trouble', a veteran of the Trojan War, was kidnapped by the predatory nymph Calypso, and only returned to his native Ithaca after a decade of adventurous travels. Homer's epic treatment of the story runs to 12,110 lines of dactylic hexameters. My own copy, in an English prose translation, was bought at a time when I was being pressed to apply for the school's elite Greek set. The translation, alas, struck me as less than exciting. 'All the survivors of the war had reached their homes by now,' it began flatly, 'and so put the perils of battle and of the sea behind them.'[18] My enthusiasm might have been greater had someone told me about the much earlier translation by George Chapman (1559–1634), a contemporary of Shakespeare, who was born only one year before Du Bellay died, or about the white-hot enthusiasm of John Keats's 'On First Looking into Chapman's Homer':

> Much have I travelled in the realms of gold,
> And many goodly states and kingdoms seen;
> Round many western islands have I been
> Which bards in fealty to Apollo hold.[19]

The object of Keats's enthusiasm was composed in ingenious rhyming couplets, each of two, ten-syllable lines:

> The Man (O Muse) informe, that many a way
> Wound with his wisedome to his wished stay;
> That wanderd wondrous farre when He the towne
> Of sacred Troy had sackt and shiverd downe.
> The cities of a world of nations,
> With all their manners, mindes and fashions,
> He saw and knew; at sea felt many woes,
> Much care sustaind, to save from overthrowes
> Himselfe and friends in their retreate for home.
> But so their fates he could not overcome,
> Though much he thirsted it. O men unwise,
> They perisht by their owne impieties,
> That in their hunger's rapine would not shunne
> The Oxen of the loftie-going Sunne,
> Who therefore from their eyes the day bereft
> Of safe returne. These acts, in some part left,
> Tell us, as others, deified seed of Jove.[20]

With Greek foolishly spurned, my classical education was confined to Latin, whose dignified cadences and superb grammatical motor I learned to admire. I soon progressed enough to be introduced to Virgil and his *Aeneid*, which I read more with reverence than with effortless mastery. And I frequently resorted to a parallel crib:

> *Arma virumque cano. Troiae qui primus ab oris*
> *Italiam fato profugus Laviniaque venit*
> *litora - multum ille et terris iactatus et alto*
> *vi superum, saevae memorem Iunonis ob iram,*
> *multa quoque et bello passus, dum conderet urbem*
> *inferretque deos Latio – genus unde Latinum*
> *Albanique patres atque altae moenia Romae.*[21]

> (This is a tale of arms and of a man. Fated to be an exile, he was
> the first to sail from the land of Troy and reach Italy, at its

Lavinian shore. He met many tribulations on his way both by land and on the ocean; high Heaven willed it, for Juno was ruthless and could not forget her anger. And he had also to endure great suffering in warfare. But at last he succeeded in founding his city, and installing the gods of his race in the Latin land: and that was the origin of the Latin nation, the Lords of Alba, and the proud battlements of Rome.)[22]

The impact of such writing on Western literature was permanent. Foremost among the many heirs and successors of Homer and Virgil was Dante Alighieri (1265–1321), whose divine *Divina Commedia* still awaited me, and which would provide the centrepiece of my Special Subject, 'The Age of Dante', during my studies at Oxford. Dante's spiritual journey through the afterlife was based on a Christian vision that pagans such as Homer and Virgil could not have shared. Even so, the Florentine belongs to the great triumvirate of spiritual journey-makers. He called Virgil *lo mio maestro e 'l mio autore*, 'My master and my author', choosing him as his guide on the first stage of the road to Paradise.

Through all of this, I became increasingly aware that there was more to travelling than simply going from place to place. Education, in fact, draws partly on class-teaching and book-learning, but equally on the formative effects of putting the learner into new and stimulating surroundings. At first, I willingly subscribed to the apparent axiom that 'travel broadens the mind'. I would have agreed with Mark Twain, himself a globetrotter, who wrote 'Travel is fatal to prejudice, bigotry and narrow-mindedness . . . charitable views of men and things can not be acquired by vegetating in one little corner of the earth all one's lifetime.'[23]

Nowadays, I am less sure. In a world where travel has lost many of its mental and physical exertions, one meets people who fly thousands of miles to do a bit of shopping in Dubai, to lie on a beach in Bali, or to watch a cricket match in Adelaide. 'I have been to the Galapagos Islands three times,' a well-heeled American lady told me on one long-distance flight, 'and can't think where to go next.' What do such people learn other than variations in temperature and the techniques of negotiating airports? Some travellers travel enormous distances and keep all their preconceptions intact. The mind, alas, is not broadened automatically. 'Travel makes a wise man better and a foolish man worse', as the proverb puts it.

Only recently did I read that one of the earliest pioneers of travel writing, the Italian poet Petrarch, reached the same conclusion nearly 700 years ago. In 1336, and uniquely for the time, Petrarch climbed Mont Ventoux in Provence with his brother, and recorded his impressions. He took a copy of St Augustine's *Confessions* with him, and read a relevant passage on the summit. 'People are moved to wonder by mountain peaks,' St Augustine wrote, 'by the waves of the sea, by waterfalls and oceans, and by the revolution of the stars, but not by themselves.' This mountain-top moment has been described as the 'opening day of the Renaissance'.[24] Petrarch, moreover, was thoroughly disgusted by a group of colleagues who had refused to join him on the ascent. In his words, they displayed a *frigida incuriositas*, a 'frigid lack of curiosity'.[25]

The full name of Bolton in Lancashire, the former County Borough where I was born and raised, is Bolton-le-Moors, which derives from its designation as such as a mediaeval parish. (Its takeover by Greater Manchester was hardly more justified than Putin's recent annexation of Crimea.) I spent many happy days as a youth wandering those moors, feeling the strength of my legs, finding my bearings in the mist and rain, and wondering about life's directions.

On a fine summer's evening one could stand on the edge of the moors at Rivington Pike, and watch the setting sun over the distant Irish Sea. The spike of Blackpool Tower, forty miles away across the flat Fylde, was usually visible; and, if the angle of light and the humidity were right, the shadowy outline of the Isle of Man would peep above the horizon. That, for me, was the West. Beyond the horizon lay Ireland, beyond Ireland, the Atlantic, and beyond the Atlantic – America. For many years, though, I was never tempted to cross the western sea. And I have yet to set foot on the Isle of Man.

My perch at the top of the Pike, sitting beside the Beacon Tower and watching the fire-red sun as it slowly sank from sight, also supplied an occasion for reviewing my own place in the galaxy. The obvious temptation, which had deluded mankind for millennia, was to think that the Sun was moving, and that I, the Beacon Tower and the Pike itself were stationary. Yet somewhere in my school lessons I had been taught the Copernican principle about the Earth rotating around a static Sun. Indeed, the Earth was not only revolving around the Sun at a mean 30 kilometres per second; at the same time, it was spinning on its own axis, giving rise to the phenomena of nights and days. And it was spinning at one hell of a rate. At roughly 53°N, Rivington Pike (together with me, the whole of the Earth's surface and the atmosphere around it) was cruising along at a cool 600 mph. One couldn't feel it. But the breeze in one's face betrayed the atmospheric drag, and by closing one's eyes it was not difficult to imagine what was actually happening. Despite its apparent movement, the Sun was hanging still, whilst the Pike and its surroundings were hurtling up and away in a huge elliptical arc. Without being able to perceive it directly, I was riding a colossal, planetary double thrust, one larger and the other smaller. The only thing to which it could be compared was the complex motion of the merry-go-round at Bolton's annual New Year Fair, where the great carousel revolved in its orbit round the central pillar and the individual 'whirler' cars spun simultaneously on their own axial track.

Far more frequently, however, I was drawn not to the West but in the opposite direction, and would plunge into the wild, mysterious moorlands on the inland side. Standing on the eastern scarp of Winter Hill, I could easily pick out the Peel Tower on Holcombe Hill above Ramsbottom, and further off the dark line of Blackstone Edge on the frontier of Yorkshire. In the era before motorways, Yorkshire, 'the Land of the Tykes', was a strange and inaccessible country, where people spoke in graveyard tones and always drove down the middle of the road. That, for me, was the exotic East. Beyond Yorkshire lay the North Sea, and beyond the North Sea, I knew, mainland Europe. So if 'the Pike' was the temple of the sunset, Winter Hill's scarp was the belvedere of the sunrise. One could sit among the heather and tufted grass, listen to the skylarks and curlews, and watch the growing sunlight as it illuminated the ridges and valleys of England's Pennine backbone.

Such was the wonderland of my youth. There was no better place to orient oneself in time and space, and it was on our doorstep. I would take the 19 or 20 bus to Doffcocker, or higher up to Montserrat, and stride along the old Chorley road, hugging the fence of the sheep fields and looking down to where several million souls were squeezed into a great industrial conurbation. In front the open sky beckoned, the breeze off the hills, and blessed emptiness. After a mile or so, I would cut up the quarry track opposite the 'Jolly Crofters' at Bottom o'th Moor, push on between the dry-stone walls, and, panting with expectation, step onto the high, windblown heathland – lord of all I surveyed.

I was aware from an early age that my freedom to roam the moors was a privilege that had not existed during my father's boyhood, and indeed that my own youthful roamings were technically illegal. Until the early twentieth century, the good people of Bolton were forced to stay at home and stifle in their own coal-fired pollution because the Bridgeman Earls of Bradford, the owners of the moors, would not grant access to territory reserved for grouse and partridge. It was a topic close to the heart of William Cobbett. In his day, men could be transported to Van Diemen's Land for stealing a game bird and executed for resisting a gamekeeper; he boiled with righteous indignation:

> It is said, and I believe truly, that there are more persons imprisoned in England for offences against the game laws than there are persons imprisoned in France (with more than twice the population) for all sorts of offences put together. When there was a loud outcry against the cruelties committed on the priests and the seigneurs . . . of France, Arthur Young bade them remember the cruelties committed on the people [of France] by the game laws, and to bear in mind how many had been made galley-slaves for having killed, or tried to kill, partridges, pheasants and hares.[26]

After the Game Act of 1831, which introduced both the registration of gamekeepers and the closed season for shooting, protests moved onto issues such as the right of access to land and the law of trespass.

I am proud to say that my Uncle Don – Donnie Davies, who was killed in the Munich air disaster of 1958 – played a prominent role in the mass protests that finally opened our section of the Pennines to the public. In 1910 he and his fellow conspirators invented a spurious pretext for erecting a historical memorial on the ancient track across Winter Hill. They found the records of a Scottish tinker called George Henderson, who had been 'foully murdered' on Rivington Moor in November 1838, and then gained permission to erect a monument to his 'eternal memory'. Policemen and gamekeepers were on hand as the commemoration party struggled up the steep path from Belmont with a donkey cart carrying the heavy iron caisson. But once 'Scotchman's Stump' had been fixed in its base and the unveiling ceremony started, hundreds of determined 'mourners' appeared over the brow of the moor, completely swamping the forces of order. A handful of protesters were fined for trespass. But all attempts to bar access to peaceful walkers were henceforth abandoned. Elsewhere in England the campaign persisted much longer. The biggest of all mass trespasses was organized on Kinder Scout in Derbyshire in 1932. The legal 'right to roam' was not finally established before the Countryside and Rights of Way Act of 2000.

Rambling round the moors, I also gained the habit of digging out local history, honing perhaps a latent detective instinct. Wherever I went, it became second nature not only to ask 'What can I see?' but also to wonder about everything that can no longer be seen at first sight. I became intrigued by the things that used to be there, but were no longer easily visible.

Roman Britain, with which the English feel an imperial affinity, left few sites in Lancashire. Manchester's origins begin with the Roman fort of *Mancunium*, whence stone roads radiated northwards. My father once drove us over to Affetside to inspect the meagre remains of one of them, locally known as Watling Street. Twenty miles further north, an important military settlement at *Bremetannicum Veteranum* (now Ribchester) lay on the banks of the Ribble. A silver cavalry helmet found there is now displayed in the British Museum.[27]

The Roman legions left in AD 410, but the subsequent wave of 'Anglo-Saxon' invaders did not reach our western coast with any great speed. I mistakenly took a tiny place near Bolton called Anglezarke, which is now surrounded by reservoirs, as proof of the Angles' early arrival. I was wrong about the derivation of the name, but right to assume that they and their culture did eventually arrive.

Since both Romans and Angles were immigrants, I was long puzzled by the identity of Lancashire's indigenous inhabitants. If they didn't speak either Latin or Old English, who exactly were they? With a Welsh surname like Davies, I ought to have guessed. The clues lie with a couple of hills, one called Pendle and another, just across the Yorkshire border, called Pen-y-Ghent. *Pen-* means 'Head' or 'Peak' in Welsh, and the names reveal that Lancashire's pre-Roman and pre-Anglo-Saxon 'aborigines' were Celtic 'Britons'. The native Lancastrians belonged to Wales before they belonged either to England or to Lancashire. Lancaster bears a name that can be traced to the Brythonic appellation of the River Lune; and it is entirely possible that large parts of the future county once lay within the bounds of the Clyde-based 'Kingdom of the Rock'.[28]

The supposedly fearsome Vikings always attracted me; my own first name means 'Norseman'. Their dragon-prowed longboats appeared in the ninth century, after which they settled in Ireland, in northern Scotland (which they called their 'Sutherland'), in York, and in Cumbria. At some point, I learned that 'Anglezarke' derived from the Old Norse *Anlafserg*, meaning 'Anlaf's Hill Pasture'. (There once was a Viking king of York called Anlaf Guthrisson.)

The Normans, who conquered England in 1066, were also 'Norsemen' in origin. They had arrived in France a few generations previously. Their French-speaking knights divided up the English land, and one of them, Harvey de Walter, a companion of 'The Conqueror', built a castle atop a hill not far from Bolton. His descendants thereon took the surname of De Hoghton. I once dragged my mother to Hoghton Tower on a trip involving many buses; there was nothing to support the rumour that Shakespeare had once taken refuge there, and the visit of King James I in 1617 when (as legend has it) he knighted the 'Sir Loin', was the sole national historical event with which it was connected.

The people of mediaeval England, therefore, were not quite as English as we were led to believe. Bolton's existence was first recorded in 1185 under the name of 'Boelton', but I could never work out what language or languages the original Boltonians might have spoken. The town's oldest building, a half-timbered inn called Ye Olde Man and Scythe, dates from 1251, but the name was unlikely to have been in place when the first drink was served.

The Protestant Reformation was a capital moment in English history, and I was greatly moved by the melancholy sight of the ruined monasteries dissolved by Henry VIII. I used to collect the brochures of the Ministry of Works, which was responsible for their upkeep, and would write off to the Ministry in London to obtain them. The magnificent ruins of Bolton Abbey, which we visited, are located in Yorkshire. But Furness Abbey was ours. I learned that Lancashire had been one of the centres of the Pilgrimage of Grace and of Catholic recusancy. A biography of the martyr St Edmund Campion undermined the myth that England was by nature a tolerant country.[29]

The Elizabethan Age, the last before Britishness set in, is much loved by the English. There are few signs of it in Bolton, except for parts of Smithills Hall, a beautiful half-timbered Tudor mansion. Beacon fires were lit in the summer of 1588 on Rivington Pike and elsewhere to warn of the Spanish Armada.

By the time of the Civil War, however, Bolton was firmly under the control of Cromwell's puritanical parliamentarians. In May 1644 it was the scene of a horrific massacre in which two thousand townsfolk were cut down by Prince Rupert's royalist cavalry. After Cromwell's victory, the leading local royalist, James, Earl of Derby, paid for the massacre with his life. Before his beheading, he took his last refreshment in Ye Olde Man and Scythe. Our Junior School class listened to the tale, standing awestruck beside the Churchgate Cross.

The Industrial Revolution turned Britain into a world power, and Boltonians are convinced that it was they who started it. Samuel Crompton (1753–1827), inventor of the 'spinning mule', who worked as a weaver in the old black-and-white timbered manor house at Hall i' th Wood, was the local hero. When we toured the house as schoolchildren, we learned that the town grew rich from Crompton's invention, whilst the inventor died a pauper.

My mother's family, whose surname was Bolton, clearly had older links to the town than my father's. My maternal grandfather, Edwin Bolton, was a stonemason and builder, who went bankrupt in the Great Depression of the 1930s. His wife, Elizabeth Isherwood, came from a family whose past was only discussed in whispers. As the family historian, I eventually rooted out the truth in the Census Return for 1861, when Major James Slater was living under the same roof as a serving girl, Betty Isherwood, in the Slaters' manor house at Egerton (the birthplace, incidentally, of Bolton Wanderers). Their son, James Slater Isherwood, was well educated and trained as a lawyer, but drank himself to an early death; hence my mother's lifelong dedication to the Temperance Movement, to godly living, and to John Bunyan.

The origins of my father's family, the Davieses, were more obscure still. My paternal grandfather, Richard Samson Davies (1863–1939), was allegedly a Welsh-speaking orphan, who walked into Manchester at the age of sixteen with a halfpenny in his pocket and a head full of myths. In the Congregational Chapel at Pendleton, he met and married Ellen Ashton, the child of a miner's unmarried daughter, with whom he lived happily for forty years and produced nine offspring. In the spring of 1901 they walked the ten miles from Pendleton to Bolton, pushing a handcart loaded with their worldly goods and surrounded by their five oldest children. Their sixth child, Richard, my father, was born shortly afterwards in a tiny, terraced cottage (now demolished) in Ash Street.

Yet, despite the hard beginnings, the Davieses prospered. Grandpa rose to the lofty status of general manager of Hodgkinson and Gillibrand's Globe Hosiery Works in Lower Bridgeman Street, and bought a detached house, which he called 'Wigmore' after the orphanage that had once sheltered him; it was considerably grander than anything that I was later able to afford. His eldest daughter, Lydia – my Auntie Sis – attended Cambridge, and his eldest son, Don, attended Bolton's long-established Grammar School (founded 1514).

Both the Davieses and the Boltons, like most British families, were sorely stricken by the First World War. My father's second brother, Norman Davies, was killed in September 1918, a nineteen-year-old pilot. My mother's eldest brother, James Bolton, an infantryman with

the Lancashire Fusiliers, died on the Western Front on the morning of
11 November 1918.

In addition to Bolton's grandiose Town Hall (1873), Bolton Wanderers
Football Club was a premier source of municipal pride. Together with
our neighbours, Blackburn Rovers, it was a founding member of England's Football League. In the decades before television, its stadium at
Burnden Park formed a weekly, male-only mecca. My Uncle Don, an
amateur international, played there before moving to Stoke City. (One
of his earlier teams was the 'Northern Nomads'.) My grandpa, Richard
Samson, claimed to have scaled the walls of Wembley Stadium in London to see the Wanderers win the Cup Final of 1923. I arrived on the
terraces post-1945, to watch all the 'greats' of the era – Stanley Mat-
thews, Tom Finney, and Wilf Mannion. Bolton's fearless centre
forward, Nat Lofthouse, who worked down a local coalmine before
joining the club, was my boyhood hero.

Many aspects of early twentieth-century Bolton were overshadowed
by the activities of its most illustrious son, the industrial magnate
William Lever (1851–1925), later Lord Leverhulme and founder of the
multinational Unilever corporation. The noble lord funded both the
Congregational Church on St George's Road, which my parents
attended, and the re-founded Bolton School, where I was educated. He
was born in a small house on Wood Street, similar to my father's birthplace, and laid the foundations of his fortune by making and selling
Sunlight Soap. As schoolchildren, we were all dutifully taken by coach
to the model village of Port Sunlight near Liverpool, where his main
factory was located and where a tanker fleet landed coconut oil from
his African plantations. Less known is Lord Leverhulme's extravagant
country house or 'bungalow' and its Japanese Garden overlooking the
reservoir at Anglezarke. The bungalow was burned down in 1913 by
militant suffragettes, and never rebuilt. Forty years later, when I was
roaming around, one could still hack into the overgrown shrubbery,
and collect handfuls of the former garden's exotic oriental blooms. If
ever there was a lesson in the transience of human fortunes, this was it.

As I progressed up the school, the scope of our expeditions became ever
more ambitious. While the annual camps of the 19th Bolton Scout Troop
had been held within Britain, the Senior Scouts were customarily sent
abroad. Our journeys do not compare with the school trips of the jet age,
which routinely despatch boys and girls to Nepal, to Namibia, or to

Patagonia, but they were no less exciting or challenging. In a short space of time, I found myself camping in Luxembourg, where we unearthed rusting helmets from the Battle of the Bulge; canoeing down the River Loire, where we inspected the chateaux from midstream: trekking in the Carinthian Alps on the frontier of Yugoslavia; and mountaineering in the Tyrol, where the alpine guide who led us across the Dachstein Glacier at dawn had only recently been released from Soviet imprisonment. This sturdy Austrian mountaineer told us his story as we munched a meagre breakfast at the glacier's edge, and my eyes were opened to the other, hitherto unfamiliar side of the Second World War. Still a teenager like us, he had been conscripted by the Wehrmacht, captured at Stalingrad, and worked to the brink of death in a Siberian camp where most of the prisoners perished. He was saved by a strong physique and by survival skills learned in boyhood in a more extreme environment than that of Winter Hill.

In those same years, I started to keep a notebook in which I recorded my favourite quotations. All the formative influences are there – Shakespeare, Hobbes, Michelet, Macaulay, Milton, Vidal de La Blache (the founder of human geography), Bacon, Plato, Aristotle, Gibbon, St Augustine, Blake, Byron, Shelley, Keats, Lamartine, Donne, Gray, Carlyle, Mill, Hazlitt, and many others. One of the first entries, dated August 1955, is a quote from Cobbett:

> God has given us the best country in the world; our brave and wise and virtuous fathers . . . gave us the best government in the world, and we, their cowardly and foolish and profligate sons, have made this once-paradise what we now behold![30]

The last entries were noted down on completing Gibbon's *Decline and Fall*:

> If the Christian apostles, St Peter or St Paul, could return to the Vatican, they might possibly inquire the name of the Deity who is worshipped with such mysterious rites in that magnificent temple.[31]

Both authors seemed to be telling me that the world always goes downhill.

My eclectic collection of poetry inevitably contained numerous items connected with journeys and life journeys. On this, as on most things, Shakespeare's observations are incomparably exact:

> Weary with toil, I haste me to my bed,
> The dear repose for limbs with travel tired,
> But then begins a journey in my head,

> To work my mind when body's work's expired.
> For then my thoughts (from far where I abide)
> Intend a zealous pilgrimage to thee,
> And keep my drooping eyelids open wide . . .[32]

Here, three hundred years before Rainer Maria Rilke, was Rilke's insight that 'the only journey is the one within'. Rilke, whom I encountered much later, wrote eloquently about the effect of travel on the traveller:

> My eyes already touch the sunny hill,
> going far ahead of the road I have begun.
> So we are grasped by what we cannot grasp;
> it has it: inner light, even from a distance –
> and changes us, even if we do not reach it,
> into something else, which, hardly sensing it,
> we already are . . .[33]

Robert Louis Stevenson (1850–94), whose *Treasure Island* and *Kidnapped* were standards of my youth, was a traveller who journeyed so far that he never came home. He is buried in Samoa. Distant lands filled him with childlike joy:

> I should like to rise and go
> Where the golden apples grow;
> Where below another sky
> Parrot islands anchored lie,
> And, watched by cockatoos and goats,
> Lonely Crusoes building boats;
> Where in sunshine reaching out
> Eastern cities, miles about,
> Are with mosque and minaret
> Among sandy gardens set,
> And the rich goods from near and far
> Hang for sale in the bazaar . . .
> Where are forests hot as fire,
> Wide as England, tall as a spire,
> Full of apes and cocoa-nuts
> And the [native] hunters' huts;
> Where the knotty crocodile
> Lies and blinks in the Nile,
> And the red flamingo flies
>     Hunting fish before his eyes . . .

Where among the desert sands
Some deserted city stands,
All its children, sweep and prince,
Grown to manhood ages since,
Not a foot in street or house,
Not a stir of child or mouse,
And when kindly falls the night
In all the town no spark of light.
There I'll come when I'm a man
With a camel caravan . . .[34]

Charles Baudelaire (1821–67) – like Stevenson a lifelong invalid – was a magical wordsmith too. I heard of his literary prowess during my student days from girlfriends – Margaret, Helen, and Jenny – who all were reading Modern Languages. His poetic collection *Les Fleurs du Mal* (1857) put him in court for 'offending public morals', and as a youth he had been sent by his stepfather on a long voyage to India, to cure his alleged indolence. The experience did not change his wayward habits, but he recalled it with delight:

*Pour l'enfant, amoureux de cartes et d'estampes,*
*L'univers est égal à son vaste appétit.*
*Ah! que le monde est grand à la clarté des lampes!*
*Aux yeux du souvenir que le monde est petit! . . .*
*Dites, qu'avez-vous vu?*[35]

(To a child who is fond of maps and engravings
The universe is the size of his vast appetite.
How immense is the world in the light of a lamp!
In memory's eyes how small the world becomes . . .
One morning we set out, our brains aflame,
Our hearts full of resentments and bitter desires,
And we go, following the rhythm of the wave,
Cradling our infinite in the finite of the seas . . .
But the true voyagers are the ones who only leave
Just to be leaving; hearts light, like balloons,
They never turn aside from their fatality
And, without knowing why, they always say 'Let's go!' . . .
Our soul's a three-masted ship searching for Icaria;
A voice resounds on the bridge: 'Open your eyes!'
From the Crow's Nest, a voice, ardent and wild, cries:

'Love – Glory – Happiness' Damnation! it's only a shoal . . .
Astonishing voyagers! What splendid stories
We read in your eyes that are deep as the seas!
Show us the treasure chest of your rich memories,
Those marvellous jewels made of ether and stars . . .
And tell us, what have you really seen?)[35]

I was one of those boys 'in love with maps and engravings', and I was as eager as anyone to hear the 'splendid stories' from the travellers' 'treasure chest'.

When I eventually came to the *Divina Commedia* at the age of twenty, I found to my surprise that Dante firmly places Ulysses, the archetypal wanderer, in the eighth circle of the Inferno, where he is permanently encased in a burning flame. In Dante's scheme, a pagan could not gain access to the cleansing realm of Purgatory, still less to Paradise. But, as a famous figure of Antiquity, one feels, he might have been treated more leniently. Dante's severe judgement, therefore, has provoked lengthy scholarly debates. It turns out that the luckless Ulysses was not condemned for his travels but rather for the earlier part he played in the stratagem of the Trojan Horse. For this he was cast into the company of 'fraudulent counsellors', and tied within the flame to his co-conspirator, Diomedes. Dante had to rely exclusively on Latin sources, which were traditionally pro-Trojan and anti-Greek. (The Romans believed themselves to be Trojan descendants.) In their view, and Dante's, the Trojan Horse was an example of despicable and dishonourable tactics.

Nonetheless, once the reason for Ulysses' misfortune has been explained, Dante allows him a long and eloquent speech in which he recounts his voyages and his motives for setting sail. He was driven, above all, by 'the ardour for becoming an expert in the world, and in human vices and virtue':

> ne dolcezza di figlio, ne la pietà
> del vecchio padre, ne il debito amore
> lo quale dovea Penelope far lieta
> vincer poter dentro da me l'ardore
> ch'i' ebbi a divenir del mondo esparto
> e delli vizi umani e del valore
> ma misi me per l'alto mare aperto
> sol con un legno e con quella compagna
> picciola da la qual no fui diserto . . .

(Not fondness for my son, nor any claim
Of reverence for my father, nor love I owed
Penelope, to please her, could overcome
My longing for experience of the world,
Of human vice, and virtue. But I sailed out
On the deep open seas, accompanied
By that small company that still had not
Deserted me, in a single ship . . .)[36]

To 'become an expert of the world' is no mean ambition.

Further on, after reaching the Pillars of Hercules, Ulysses tells of the half-time pep talk that he gave to his crew to stop them losing hope:

O frati, dissi, che per cento milia
perigli siete giunti all'occidente . . .
Considerate la vostra semenza:
fatti non foste a viver come bruti,
ma per seguir virtute e conoscenza.

('O brothers who have reached the west,' I began,
'Through a hundred thousand perils, surviving all . . .
Consider well your seed:
You were not born to live as a mere brute does,
But for the pursuit of knowledge and the good.')[37]

One could not put it more plainly: we travel to seek virtue and knowledge and to be more human.

After these forays into Romance languages that I had learned at school, I gradually turned eastwards and began a long Slavonic journey that is still in progress. I have often wondered whether it happened by instinct or by choice. It nearly began at the age of eighteen, when, on registering for compulsory National Service, I opted to join the Royal Navy, having learned that the Navy was running intensive Russian language courses. But I never made it into the Navy, because National Service was abolished before I could be called up. Instead, after arriving in Oxford, I found that beginners' Russian courses were available for students at the Oxford Polytechnic (now Brookes University), where they were sponsored by the rogue publisher and MP Robert Maxwell, for the benefit of his firm, Pergamon Press. Maxwell, born in Czechoslovakia as Jan Ludwig Hoch and later known as the 'Bouncing Czech', was involved in all manner of dubious deals, many of them behind the Iron Curtain. He was using Pergamon Press to re-publish scientific and technological books and journals translated from Soviet Bloc sources, and he occasionally invited the budding linguists across the road for drinks at his home, Headington Hill Hall. In this way, I took my first steps along the Slavonic trail, which after numerous twists and turns and stops and starts would eventually lead me to a second degree, in Russian Studies, at the University of Sussex.

Meanwhile, during my first long vacation at Oxford, I joined three of my former Boltonian classmates, who had bought a second-hand US Army jeep, and planned an overland expedition to Turkey. I had been reading Gibbon, and was eager to see the Theodosian Walls of Byzantium for myself. Europe was newly divided by the Iron Curtain, and the road to Istanbul ran right across the Soviet Bloc. It was an unforgettable (and risky) experience to drive east out of Vienna on an empty road, to notice that all the signposts to Budapest had been removed, to negotiate the triple line of tank traps, watchtowers, and barbed-wire fences, and then to hear the huge metal gates clanking shut behind us. We could easily have disappeared without trace. As it was, after 'a hundred thousand perils', we somehow completed the journey unscathed, returning home with the knowledge that the eastern half of our continent was filled with fascinating, forbidden historical fruit.

In the spring of 1962, having signed up for a student trip to Moscow (which was abruptly cancelled by the Soviet authorities without explanation), I found myself by default in Poland, a country of which I was hitherto blissfully ignorant. The great Faculty of Modern History at Oxford had taught us absolutely nothing about Poland's thousand-year past, and I began to mug up the basic elements from sheer shame. This inauspicious start led eventually to a PhD from the Jagiellonian University, to a lifetime of close personal and family links with Poland, and to a writing career, which began with Polish subjects.

I finally made it to Moscow after a year's delay. Our group arrived on the morning after Stalin's remains had been secretly removed from the mausoleum on Red Square. Lenin's mummified corpse, with its green skin and bright orange beard, had been left *in situ*, like that of some ghoulish Italian saint. But anyone could see that the sandstone plaque over the entrance bearing the late leaders' names had been crudely altered. We had reached the world capital of historical jiggery-pokery.

Russians, of course, possess both the largest country in the world and a magnificently rich language in which to describe it. Their literary and musical traditions are as wonderful as their political habits are deplorable. Their national poet, Alexander Pushkin (1799–1837), was passionate, fiery, and politically dissident. 'I was not born to amuse the Tsars,' he once said. He fought no fewer than twenty-nine duels, and died in the aftermath of the last one. Yet his formative influence on modern Russian was comparable to Shakespeare's on English or Goethe's on German. One poem that figures in almost every anthology is *Zimnii Put'*, or 'Winter Road', which is all about mood, and the tedium of a long, night sleigh ride.[38]

One might think that Pushkin's sublimely simple cadences are easy to translate. Yet the briefest of internet searches produces some hilarious results, where weird vocabulary, contorted grammar, ponderous word order, and artless rhythms defeat all attempts to cope with even the first stanza:

> Through the cool and wavy hazes
> Cuts the moon her slow way;
> On the glades of sadness, endless,
> Her distressing light she spays.

Or:

> Breaking thro' the waving fogs
> Forth the moon is coming,
> And on the gloomy acres
> She gloomy light is shedding.

Or again:

> Through the rolling, wavy fog
> The moon is making its way
> Sadly shining its light,
> Shining onto the sad glade.

Or even:

> Through the murk the moon is veering,
> Ghost-accompanist of night,
> On the melancholy clearings
> Pouring melancholy light.

Here is the strongest argument for learning Russian.

Poland's national poet, Adam Mickiewicz (1798–1855), was Pushkin's exact contemporary and, during exile in Russia, a personal friend. Like Pushkin, he wrote poetry that is filled with Romantic sentiments and classical restraint in equal measure, confounding the classifiers. He is forever associated with the opening lines of his epic *Pan Tadeusz*: 'Oh, Lithuania, my homeland! Only he who has lost you can gauge your true worth!' Yet he wrote everything from epics and sonnets to dramas and academic lectures. My own particular favourite, *The Steppes of Akkerman*, was written during his journey through the boundless expanses of southern Ukraine:

> *Wpłtynąłem na suchego przestwór oceanu . . .*

> (I have sailed onto the expanse of a dry ocean.
> The wagon plunges into greenery, and, like a boat, wanders
> Through the prairie's rustling waves, gliding through flowers.
> I pass coral islets of rank vegetation.

> Already dusk is falling. No road here, no dolmen.
> I look up, seeking the stars, my ship's couriers.
> There, afar, a cloud gleams in the sky. The morning star glimmers.
> There lies the glistening Dniester! There the pharos of Akkerman!

> Halt! How still! I can hear the flight of cranes
> Which are invisible even to the falcon's stare.
> I listen to a butterfly snuggling in the grassy lanes,

> And to a smooth-breasted snake nestling in the clover.
> In such silence, my curious ear strains
> To catch a voice from Lithuania . . . Drive on! No one's there.)[39]

Eastern Europe is a rich hunting ground for travel writers, inviting the same sort of 'orientalism' that has often been directed at the Middle East. Count Jan Potocki (1761–1815) was the great pioneer, often known, since he wrote in French, as Jean Potocki. An ethnographer, Egyptologist, and philologist, as well as a wealthy aristocrat, his journeys stretched from Mongolia to Morocco, and were described in numerous published accounts, but his collection of fictional stories, *Manuscrit Trouvé à Saragosse* (1815), is most celebrated.[40]

Juliusz Słowacki (1809–49) – pronounced 'Slow-Vat-Ski' – who vies with Mickiewicz for Poland's national laurels, was another traveller-bard forced to emigrate. His epic poem, *Podróż na Wschód* ('Journey to the East') was written in 1836–8 on a tour that took him to Greece, Egypt, Syria, and the Holy Land.[41] Part 1 contains his brilliant thumbnail sketch of 'Europe':

*Jeśli Europa jest nimfą – Neapol*
*Jest nimfy okiem błękitnem, – Warszawa*
*Sercem, – cierniami w nodze Sewastopol,*
*Azow, Odessa, Petersburg, Mitawa; –*
*Paryż jej głową, a Londyn kołnierzem*
*Nakrochmalonym, a zaś Rzym . . . szkaplerzem.*

(If Europe is a Nymph
Then Naples is her bright blue eye
And Warsaw her heart; Sebastopol,
Azov, Odessa, Petersburg are the thorns
In her feet; Paris is her head;
London, her starched collar,
And Rome – the scapular.)

He then related his departure from Italy:

*I ruszyć w podróż, bo się pieśń przewlecze*
*Niejedna jeszcze przerwana ideą.*
*Jutro kurierem wyjeżdżam do Lecce,*
*Jutro więc zacznę śpiewać Odysseą,*
*Albo wyprawę o Jazona runach*
*Na nowej lutni i na złotych strunach.*

([I must] make a start, for the song drags on
With yet another interrupted idea.
Tomorrow I take the stagecoach for Lecce,
Tomorrow I shall start to sing of the Odyssey
Or of Jason's search for the Golden Fleece
On a new lute, and with golden strings.) [42]

A Romantic poet from Europe's eastern periphery was summoning up the selfsame classical precedents as Joachim du Bellay three hundred years earlier.

My youthful forays into travel books did not stretch as far as Słowacki. But Bolton's library was well stocked with items connected with Central Asia and the Great Game, such as Fred Burnaby's *Ride to Khiva* (1876), Lord Curzon's *Russia in Central Asia* (1889), and Frank Younghusband's *Heart of a Continent* (1896). I also lapped up the work of the great travelling orientalist-illustrators, such as Edward Lear and David Roberts. From there I graduated to more modern books like Peter Fleming's *Travels in Tartary* (1941) and Heinrich Harrer's *Seven Years in Tibet* (1952). Patrick Leigh Fermor had yet to cross my path. But Rebecca West's *Black Lamb and Grey Falcon* (1941) and Fitzroy Maclean's *Eastern Approaches* (1949) were more than sufficient to fire an appetite. The East was firmly planted in my head long before I got there.

In that same era I was strongly reminded of the rapidly accelerating rate of travel. On one occasion, by complete accident, I ran into the world's first cosmonaut, the smiling Yuri Gagarin, who was visiting the Earls Court Show, and who, to my amazement, shook my hand. On another, I was taken by my French friend Henri to the airport at Le Bourget to see the world's first transatlantic airliner, a Pan American Boeing 707 parked on the tarmac.

My father's second elder brother, by contrast, did not live to see either jets or space rockets. Uncle Norman, in whose memory I was to be named, left school in the New Year of 1918 to join the newly formed RAF. After a few weeks of training, he received an officer's commission and, still a teenager, flew with his squadron to the Western Front in France. It was to be his one and only international flight. As I would duly learn, he was nevertheless a true globetrotter – but one of the kind who trots the globe in mind only. He was a passionate stamp collector.

The family stamp album started its career under Uncle Norman's guidance in about 1912, when he was thirteen years old. It is a wonderful repository not just of postage stamps but also of political geography and of period charm. Entitled *The World Postage Stamp Album, Revised & Enlarged*, it was compiled by T. H. Hinton – a member both of the International Philatelic Union and the Société Française de Timbrologie – and, sometime early in the reign of Edward VII, was published in London by E. Nister & Co., 24 St Bride Street, EC. It contains one page or more for every country in the world; and the head of each page is illustrated by a line of stamps. It is undated, but the latest stamp to be shown was issued in Transvaal in 1902.

The album is divided into six parts: I British Empire, II Europe + European Colonial Possessions, III Asia, IV Africa, V America, and VI Oceania. Underneath the illustrations, neatly separated by dotted lines, were spaces for thirty stamps per page. With 224 pages, there was room for 6,720 stamps. A note inside the cover, '3/0', indicates that the album cost three shillings.

Once the album was purchased, Uncle Norman further adorned the inside of the front cover with a large, flowing monogram of his initials, 'ND', beautifully drawn in blue ink. Sometime later, however, he was joined, willingly or unwillingly, by his younger brother Richard (my father), who was innocently known to the family as 'our Dick'. Presumably to prevent any more of the Davies brood from muscling in, young Richard wrote an open declaration beside Norman's monogram: 'This book is the sole possession of N and D Davies', and he added the family address: 'Wigmore, The Haulgh, Bolton, Lancashire'.

In due course, further inscriptions appeared. They included their elder brother's signature – 'Donny Davies, International Outside Right', 'Lancashire XI, Old Trafford', and 'Queen's Scholar, Cambridge' – a copperplate depiction of the word 'Philately', a cryptic insult in pencil reading 'Toshi, the One-eyed', and a fragment of someone's French homework: *'Comment vous-portez vous? Je vais tres bien!'* Was 'Toshi' Uncle Norman's nickname? And did he ever have the chance to practise his French in France? I doubt it. At all events, Uncle Don never followed his sister to Cambridge. After winning his scholarship, he was called up for service in the Royal Flying Corps, crashed his plane behind enemy lines, and spent the rest of the First World War in a German POW camp.[43]

The inside pages of the back cover were used for recording running totals for the collection as a whole, broken down into 'European', 'Australasian', 'American', 'African', 'Asiatic', and 'Others'. The earliest entries in the series read 'over 500 on Nov 2 1914' and '1980 on May 5th 1915', indicating an average increase of over 200 per month and 7 per day. Beyond that, the calculations are hard to follow. Written in pencil, many have become illegible, and many, I suspect, were the product of creative accounting.

Since the boys' father was a mill manager, it is reasonable to suppose that the cotton trade brought in a regular flow of commercial correspondence and with it a ready supply of foreign stamps. Yet the cotton trade does not explain the very substantial number of stamps from offbeat places such as Persia, Uruguay, Haiti, Mozambique, and the Ottoman Empire. How on earth did a couple of Lancashire schoolboys lay hands on so many exotic items? They would obviously have been swapping stamps with their friends in the playground. But in 1915 Dick fell into disgrace, through slacking at school, and was ordered by his father to work in the mill. It's hard to believe that Norman's pocket money and Dick's meagre wages permitted much extravagance. Even so, there are tell-tale signs of professional contacts. One yellowing packet contained five superb pieces from New Zealand showing the young Queen Victoria on the country's very earliest issue from 1852. How did those stamps reach them?

For thirty years, after Uncle Norman's death, my father never added to the collection; it was probably too painful for him. He occasionally brought it out of the cupboard to show his wife and children and to tell them that it was their 'insurance policy against a rainy day'. He only set his reluctance aside when paternal duty prompted him to teach the rudiments of philately to me. For my ninth birthday I was given a copy of Stanley Gibbons' *Simplified Stamp Catalogue* (Fourteenth Edition, London 1948); and Uncle Norman's hallowed album was placed in my hands with the words: 'This is what your uncle really loved.'

My strongest recollection, however, is one of confusion. Searching through the album's 224 pages, I couldn't find the countries for some of the stamps that I had already collected. My Auntie Ivy's lodger, whom I knew as 'Uncle Joseph', had given me some unusual stamps from his native CZECHOSLOVAKIA. (He was a wartime refugee from Prague.) And my Auntie Doris had a mysterious connection with a missionary, who wrote to her from SOUTHERN RHODESIA. But where had 'Southern Rhodesia' come from? It was in the catalogue but not in the album.

Turning to my father, I learned that many countries had been freshly created in the decades since the album was published, and others had ceased to exist. Czechoslovakia, for example, came into being in October 1918, barely one month after Uncle Norman's last flight. And Southern Rhodesia was created in 1923 after the break-up of an entity that appears on p. 24 of the album as BRITISH SOUTH AFRICA (RHODESIA). And there were lots of others – ADEN (where my cousin Peter was serving in the RAF), ALGERIA, EIRE (where Peter's girlfriend, Vera, came from), FINLAND (where my sister had a penfriend), JUGOSLAVIA, LEBANON, LITHUANIA, LATVIA, POLAND, SYRIA, VATICAN CITY, and quite a few others.

At which point, my father made a momentous decision. Uncle Norman's album, no longer fit for purpose, would have to be replaced. He bought a new, expandable, loose-leaf *Pacific Stamp Album*, and a large packet of loose leaves. We then set about the laborious task of writing out the name of every country in the catalogue onto a separate page of the new album, together with their capital cities. The operation took weeks, if not months. After that, we started on the still more laborious task of transferring the stamps from the old album to the new one. This was the burden that broke my will as a stamp collector. One, two, three years passed, and sometime in 1950 or 1951 I just gave up. I packed the *World Album*, still half-full, into a box, and put the *Pacific Album* on top of it, still half-empty. Instead of sticking in stamps, I turned to kicking a ball.

By the time that I returned to the unfinished task, nearly sixty years later, I was preparing to write a book called *Vanished Kingdoms*. The book's theme was based on a simple historical observation: that all political states – whether kingdoms, empires or republics – have a finite lifespan. Like human beings, they are born, they live for a longer or shorter time, and then they die. I now see that my early brush with 'timbrology' played a distinct part in planting the theme in my head.

So, remembering Uncle Norman's album, decades later, I took it out of its box and began to check its contents. The album's largest section, pages 6–88, was devoted to the BRITISH EMPIRE – an entity that had now completely vanished. The second section, on 'Europe', pages 89–162, contained relatively more survivors, from BELGIUM and BULGARIA, to SPAIN, SWEDEN, and SWITZERLAND. But the AUSTRIAN, GERMAN, RUSSIAN, and OTTOMAN EMPIRES had all gone up in smoke. A very long list of COLONIAL POSSESSIONS OF EUROPEAN POWERS had ceased to exist, and no fewer than seventeen German states, from BADEN, BAVARIA, and BERGEDORF, to PRUSSIA, SAXONY, THURN AND TAXIS (NORTH AND SOUTH), and WURTTEMBURG, had disappeared without trace. The island of CRETE, though an independent state, was described as being 'under the joint administration of Great Britain, France, Russia and Italy'; it declared union with Greece shortly before Uncle Norman started his collection. The DANISH WEST INDIES were sold to the United States in 1917, while the Davies brothers were still at school, and have been known ever since as the 'US Virgin Islands'. MONTENEGRO, described as a 'Principality', became a Kingdom in 1910 only to be cruelly annexed by Serbia in 1918 – the only Allied state to be destroyed by the First World War.

In Asia, most of the former sovereign states, such as CHINA and JAPAN, have hung on, though most have seen their regimes transformed, and several have changed their names; PERSIA became Iran, and SIAM became Thailand. KOREA, which is classed in the album as 'under the administration of Japan', has since split into two. In Africa, LIBERIA and MOROCCO are still intact, as is ABYSSINIA, now renamed as Ethiopia. In the map of the Americas, North and South, there have been no changes at all, except for the Venezuelan port of LA GUAIRA, which issued postage stamps from 1864 to 1869 for use on the ferries steaming to Curaçao. In the album's section on Oceania, the Territory of HAWAII was presented as a 'US Protectorate', although the United States had already annexed it. Its incorporation as the 50th State of the Union occurred in 1959.

*Vanished Kingdoms* took up five years of my life. When it was finished, I was at a loss. I had passed the milestone of 'three score years and ten'; thanks to the brilliant Birmingham hip-surgeon, Derek McMinn, I had regained mobility; and I had won a literary prize, which could be spent on long-distance travel tickets. So, while waiting for my publishers to make up their minds about what I should write next, I took matters into my own hands and organized a global tour.

*Vanished Kingdoms* drew its examples exclusively from Europe. Now, after poring again over Uncle Norman's album and contemplating my own circumnavigation, I began to realize that vanished kingdoms can be encountered at all ends of the Earth. I also saw that human history is a tale not just of constant change but equally of perpetual locomotion. Ever since the first specimens of *Homo erectus* stood up some 1.9 million years ago, almost certainly in East Africa, their descendants have ceaselessly moved on: from one abode to the next, from continent to continent, and from the mainlands to the islands. By the time that prehistory was merging into recorded history, they had reached most parts of the globe, except Antarctica. Like their creators, the creations of humankind develop from nothing, flourish, perish, and are replaced. And, like the individuals who make up the crowd, the species as a whole was born to move: to crawl, to walk, to run, and then to falter and pass the baton on. Throughout the ages, people have decamped from place to place, endlessly seeking the greener side of the hill. They may pause for a while, even for centuries, but sooner or later they will always gird up their loins for the next stage. They wander and explore, climbing and descending; they lead or they follow; they flee disaster or forage for new pastures; they stick together or split up; they advance or retreat, arrive or leave; they steer a steady course or they stray; they diverge, divide, detach, and disperse; they converge, collide, coalesce, and cohabit; they stir, flit, or drift, roam, rove, or ramble, spurt, scuttle, or scamper, plod, trudge, or tramp, rush, saunter, or slouch; they hasten or dawdle, walk, sail, ride, or fly, constantly migrating, emigrating, immigrating, populating, settling, colonizing; sometimes competing, clashing, conquering, or capitulating, and necessarily interacting, adapting, and evolving. They sally forth as solitary souls or wend their way in family groups or tribal masses. Like the

Mongol horsemen, they may race across the steppes and prairies, or like the Boers and Mormons trek through the wilderness in their winding wagon trains. They have crossed the oceans in style in first-class cabins, in the squalor of the steerage deck, in the agony of slave-ship holds, in great Viking longships and Polynesian canoes, in coracles and carracks. Like the Roman legions, they may march in orderly step, or, like the ancient barbarian hordes and modern twenty-first-century migrants, they may burst the borders through sheer weight of numbers. And all the while, in order to survive, they everywhere instinctively breed and reproduce, thereby keeping up the flow.

The world today is the net product of all these accumulated movements. Thanks to humankind's elemental drive, the Earth is filled with a profusion of races, religions, cultures, tribes, societies, linguistic families, ethnicities, nations, states, political groupings, and power blocs. A multitude of good neighbours, bad neighbours, allies, rivals, and enemies have proliferated. And I, a solitary traveller intent on making my own journey, was about to plunge into the profusion.

It all started with an invitation to give the keynote speech at a 'Third of May' event in Melbourne. My wife and I were happy enough about going to Melbourne but not about the prospect of a 24-hour, non-stop flight. The obvious solution was to fly to Australia by easy stages – via Dubai, Delhi, and Singapore. The longest stay would be in Tasmania, where friends were waiting to entertain us, and whence my wife would return home. Next came the realization that, with little extra effort, the return journey could be made by continuing eastwards – via New Zealand, Tahiti, and the United States. But there was no hurry, and no point in going to faraway places only to leave each country after a lightning guided tour, a quick, bland meal and sleepover at some anonymous airport hotel. Taking time was essential, and extra destinations could be added at will. Hence, Baku, Kuala Lumpur, Mauritius, and Madeira joined the growing itinerary. All were magical names on the map of places I had never seen and was unlikely to see again. Most definitely, as the day of departure approached, the frisson of excitement swelled. And I was determined not to be outdone by our son, Christian, who, suffering a similar fit of *Reisefieber*, had taken off – as young people do these days – for the Central Asia that I had known only from books. Instead of the usual banal greeting, his postcard to his parents carried the four stunning lines of a stanza that could well stand as the Wanderers' Watchword:

> We travel not for trafficking alone:
> By hotter winds our fiery hearts are fanned:
> For lust of knowing what should not be known
> We make the golden journey to Samarkand.[44]

What my exact motives were for embarking on a circumnavigation of the globe, therefore, I can't exactly say. I certainly didn't prepare myself by studying the many theories of why people need to travel, I submitted to the primeval urge to get up and go. I don't belong to the class of travellers who, in Baudelaire's words, 'leave just to be leaving'. Nor was I setting out, like Bunyan, on a high-minded pilgrimage. My goal was probably closer to Goethe's 'school of seeing' – to test my powers of observation, to spot the recurring themes and catch the fleeting details, and then to tell the story. I hoped that the telling of this impulsive adventure would have a touch of Cobbett's caustic wit, a feeling for Hazlitt's 'blue sky above my head and the green turf beneath', and the hint of Goethe's 'truthful and graceful fairy-tale'. Perhaps, like the ageing Ulysses of Lord Tennyson, I was just another 'gray spirit', who was yearning for one last adventure:

> Death closes all: but something ere the end,
> Some work of noble note, may yet be done,
> Not unbecoming men that strove with Gods.
> The lights begin to twinkle from the rocks:
> The long day wanes: the slow moon climbs: the deep
> Moans round with many voices. Come, my friends,
> 'Tis not too late to seek a newer world . . .
> [For] my purpose holds
> To sail beyond the sunset, and the baths
> Of all the western stars, until I die.
> It may be that the gulfs will wash us down;
> It may be we shall touch the Happy Isles,
> And see the great Achilles, whom we knew.
> Tho' much is taken, much abides; and tho'
> We are not now that strength which in old days
> Moved earth and heaven, that which we are, we are;
> One equal temper of heroic hearts,
> Made weak by time and fate, but strong in will
> To strive, to seek, to find, and not to yield.[45]

# I

# Kerno
*The Kingdom of Quonimorus*

'Charity,' says the proverb, 'begins at home.' So, too, do most journeys; travellers and circumnavigators set out by crossing their own doorsteps.

The first of my many visits to the very beautiful county of Cornwall in what the English call their 'West Country' was on a boyhood family holiday. The English perspective on this geography is promoted by any number of guidebooks, holiday brochures, and travelogues whose purpose is to perpetuate the acceptable face of the present. For the English, a successful imperial people, are taught to love their world as it is, lest the same things happen to them that they once inflicted on others. With the help of the English Heritage organization, Truro, Penzance, Newquay, and St Ives compete to attract the hordes of trippers, surfers, craft shoppers, teenage bingers, and beach-bums, who flock in to enjoy the seaside, fill the hotels, and boost the economy, but not to rock the status quo.

English Heritage was set up in accordance with the United Kingdom's National Heritage Act of 1983. It operates in all the counties of England, managing historical sites, preserving monuments, and promoting cultural events.[1] (It has its counterparts in other parts of the UK – in Wales, Scotland, and Northern Ireland.) In Cornwall, however, it has run into trouble because the Act does not specify whose national heritage it is authorized to support. In 1999 a group of protesters tore down a large number of English Heritage signs on the grounds that the sites where the signs were located belong to Cornwall's heritage, not England's. Their campaign was code-named Operation Chough, and they were said to be acting on behalf of an organization called The Cornish Stannary Parliament. Their activities eventually led to a court case on 18 January 2002 at Truro Crown Court where three men – Hugh Rowe, Rodney Nute, and Nigel Hicks – were put on trial for 'conspiring to cause criminal damage'; they had been caught by police carrying a large signboard from Pendennis Castle on the roof

Kerno (Cornwall)

ATLANTIC OCEAN

Portbud○
(Bude)

Ryskammel ○
(Camelford)

Lannstevan ○
(Launceston)

Lannwedhenek ○
(Padstow)

**KERNO
(CORNWALL)**

Bosvenegh ○
(Bodmin)

Lyskerrys ○
(Liskeard)

Tewynblustri ○
(Newquay)

Essa ○
(Saltash)

Sen Ostel ○
(St Austell)

Porth Ia
(St Ives)

Resrudh
(Redruth) ○

Truru (Truro)

Pennsans
(Penzance)

Kammbronn
(Camborne)

Aberfala
(Falmouth)

*The Channel*

○ Hellys
(Helston)

Penn an Wlas
(Land's End)

DEWNANS (DEVON)

N

○    10    20 km

of their car, and faced custodial sentences. The judge classed the defendants' motives as 'political', and expressed his intention of denying them 'publicity'. He handed down a heavy fine of £4,500 in total, and bound them over to keep the peace. The prosecution, which had introduced a Public Immunity Certificate to block information concerning unpublicized ownership deals between English Heritage and the Duchy of Cornwall, dropped the more serious charges. In justification of their campaign, the defendants had circulated a letter stating their opinion in no uncertain terms. It reads: 'The signs have been confiscated and held as evidence of English cultural aggression. Such racially motivated signs are deeply offensive, and cause distress to many Cornish people.'[2]

Marcus Quonimorus was a Romano-British king, otherwise *Margh* or Mark, who lived during the fifth to sixth century. His name has survived on an ancient wayside tombstone at Menabilly near Fowey, which seems to indicate that he was the father of 'Drustans' – almost certainly the Tristan from the mediaeval legends of Tristan and Isolde.[3] According to a fragile consensus of experts, the badly eroded inscription on the tombstone reads: DRUSTANS HIC IACET CUNOMORI FILIUS (Here lies Tristan, son of Quonimorus). The sixteenth-century antiquary, John Leland, maintained that the original text included an additional line: CUM DOM OUSILLA. This 'Dom[ina] Ousilla' can reasonably be equated with Queen Iseult, who invariably features alongside King Mark in the legends. In later versions of the story, Tristan is King Mark's uncle rather than his son, but this piece of the puzzle does not preclude the possibility that the one was named after the other. Every single point is contested. Nonetheless, the juxtaposition of three key names gives strong grounds for concluding that the Menabilly Stone records a historical reality out of which legendary embellishments subsequently grew.[4]

The historicity of Marcus Quonimorus is more soundly based than that of his supposed contemporary, 'King Arthur', though not entirely definite, offering the perfect playground for historical pedants. Yet, if there was a king, it is equally reasonable to suppose there was a kingdom, even if it cannot be properly named or precisely conscribed. A contemporary Welsh account mentions a king of Dumnonia called 'Cynmor', meaning 'Sea Hound', of which Cunimorus or Quonimorus is an evident transposition. The Frankish chronicler, Gregory of Tours, mentions a Breton ruler from the same era with a very similar name – King Cunomorus, who died in battle with the Franks around 550, and who is described as a Frankish vassal – '*Cunomorus tyrannus, praefectus Francorum regis*'. The word 'tyrannus' raises an echo, coinciding as it does with strong rumours that the villainous monarch might be the source for the scary tales of 'Bluebeard'.[5] Visitors to the château of Camors in Morbihan are shown round 'Bluebeard's Castle', which is attributed to a local Dark Age ruler variously named as Konomor or, in French, Comorre.[6] Cunomorus also features in an episode described by Gregory of Tours in the early life of St Malo (520–621):

Chanao [Conan], Count of the Bretons, killed three of his brothers, and also wished to kill [his fourth brother], Macliavus [Malo] . . . whom he kept in prison loaded with chains. But [Malo] was freed from death by Felix, Bishop of Nantes. After this, he swore to be faithful to his brother, but for some reason . . . became inclined to break his oath. Chanao began to attack Macliavus again, [forcing him to flee] to another count of that district, Chonomor by name . . . [who] hid him in a box underground . . . leaving only a small airhole so that he could breathe. When his pursuers

came, [it was said] 'Here lies Macliavus, dead and buried' ... And his
brother took the whole of the kingdom. For since the death of Clovis the
Bretons have always been under the dominion of the Franks and their
rulers have been called counts, not kings. Macliavus rose from the underground, went to the city of Vannes, and there received the tonsure and
was ordained bishop.[7]

It was an eighth-century Breton monk with the magnificent name of
Wrmonoc, author of the *Vita* of St Pol-de-Leon (d. 564), who first
explained that 'King Mark's other name was Quonimorus'.[8]

Of course, nobody can assume that the king's name could only have
been used by one person, or that one single realm was at issue. The
Marcus who was Lady Ousilla's husband and father or nephew to
Tristan, could either have been a king of *Cornovia* (the Latin adaptation of the Celtic *Kerno* (Cornwall); or of a *Dumnonia* (Devon), which
had different boundaries from today; or perhaps of a federated *Corno-
Dumnonia*, or even of something more extensive. The French historian
Léon Fleuriot floated the plausible hypothesis that Marcus Quonimorus ruled over a unified Breton-Brythonic kingdom on both sides of
the 'Celtic Sea'.[9]

Marcus Quonimorus would not have been a king in the familiar
modern sense. His tomb has no regal connotations, and his kingly status was the product of the later legends. Like the Irish or Welsh 'kings'
of the period, the Breton counts and the earliest Anglo-Saxon monarchs, he was probably little more than a local or regional chieftain; the
Latin *rex* simply meant 'one who ruled'. Yet the important thing,
beyond judicious doubt, is that he was a man of flesh and blood. He
and his kingdom do not belong with the mythical, legendary or fictional realms of Atlantis, Lyonesse, Camelot or Avalon. Together with
St Patrick and St David, they belong to the world of real-life post-
Roman rulers and of Celtic saints. They have the same right to star in
the 'Island Story' as do some of their better publicized Anglo-Saxon
contemporaries.

The Menabilly Stone, however, is not unique; it is but one of the better known specimens from a score of such Cornish relics, many of them
inscribed in both Latin and in Irish ogham script. The Selus Stone, for
example, now housed in the parish church of St Just-in-Penwith, records
the death of a putative Cornish king variously known as Selevan,
Levan, 'Salomon', or, in Welsh, 'Selyf'; its inscription reads SELUS IC
IAC-T (Here lies Selus) and is accompanied by a Christian Chi-Rho

cross. The St Kew Stone, in the church of the village of the same name, reads simply 'IUSTI', meaning '[The Grave] of Justus'. The Lewannick Stone I is equally spare, reading IGENAFIMEMOR, 'In Memory of Igenavus'. The so-called Worthyvale Stone I at Slaughterbridge near Camelford is particularly significant, partly because it is well preserved and partly because it is widely publicized as 'King Arthur's Stone' – though its inscription (LATINI [H]IC IACIT FILIUS MAGARI, '[The Grave of] Latinus: Here lies the son of Magarus') has no known connection with King Arthur.[10]

The fantasies of the Arthurian industry present a major obstacle to clarifying historical evidence from the post-Roman period. They are very prevalent in Cornwall, which was chosen by Thomas Malory for the setting of his *Morte d'Arthur* (1485), and in Victorian times by Alfred, Lord Tennyson for his twelve-part poem *The Idylls of the King* (1859–85). By sheer force of enthusiasm, they overshadow all other promising locations in Britain – such as Glastonbury, Clydeside or even the Scottish Borders – in the unending 'search for Arthur'.[11]

At Slaughterbridge in north Cornwall a mini-theme park called 'The Arthurian Centre' has grown up, offering exclusive access to the Worthyvale Stones:

> Visitors can walk through the fields where King Arthur and Mordred met for their last battle . . . Unravel fact from fiction. What links King Arthur to Star Wars, Lord of the Rings, Harry Potter and Shrek? . . . [Visit] the location [of the battle], which ended the fellowship of the Round Table in 537.[12]

The business, which is a Cornish counterpart to 'Bluebeard's Castle' in Brittany, is based on the flimsiest of assumptions: among them, that modern Camelford can be identified either with ancient Camlann or with Camelot, and that the name of Slaughterbridge records the site of an Arthurian battle. Unfortunately, the Old English word 'slaughter', unlike its contemporary homophone, inconveniently means 'a swamp or marsh'. Archaeological finds indicate that some sort of battle did occur there. But the link with King Arthur seems to belong entirely to the realm of invented tradition.

Antiquarians aiming to compile a list of Cornish kings, therefore, face insoluble problems. They usually divide them into the purely legendary – like Corineus (*c.* 1100 BCE) – and those attested in documentary sources. Of the latter, there are only five – Mark, Salomon, Dungarth, Ricatus, and 'Huwal of the West Welsh', who is mentioned in the

*Anglo-Saxon Chronicle* under AD 927. Arthur does not feature anywhere in those lists: he is absent both from Gildas, the only near-contemporary chronicler, and from Bede, and is not named before the *Historia Brittonum* of Nennius, from the last decade of the eighth century.[13]

Importantly, the realm of Quonimorus belonged to the category of maritime 'sea kingdoms' rather than to the territorial, land-based states that developed with the advance of the Anglo-Saxons.[14] Looking at a standard modern atlas, which emphasizes the ground contours, the roads, rivers, and network of settlements, the most striking feature appears to be the long, solid landbridge that joins Cornwall to Devon, and one is easily beguiled into thinking of Cornwall simply as a promontory of England. If, on the other hand, one pores over a coastal chart, one soon realizes that ancient Kerno lay at the focal point of 'the Celtic Sea'. It was by sea that the Celtic saints and traders travelled. In this light, the crucial feature becomes the network of sea lanes linking Kerno with Wales, Ireland, Brittany, and even with distant Galicia.

Thanks to these old-established sea lanes, a substantial group of post-Roman Britons were able to migrate from Kerno and Dumnonia to Gaulish Armorica, so establishing the land of 'Brittany'. Their migration was known to the Byzantine historian, Procopius of Caesarea, who died *c.* 560. Procopius was in the middle of writing his 'Gothic Wars' when a Frankish delegation arrived in Constantinople and told him of events in Europe's far north-west:

> Three very populous nations inhabit the island of [Britain], and one king is set over each of them. And the names of those nations are Angles, Frisians, and Britons who have the same name as the island. So great apparently is the multitude of these peoples that every year they migrate in large groups with their women and children and go to the Franks.
>
> And they are settling them in what seems to be the more desolate part of the land, and as a result they are gaining possession of [it].[15]

Procopius wrote in the present tense, indicating that the migration was still in progress. He was not aware either of the hostility between Britons and Angles or of the fact that it was only Britons who were migrating to the continent. But the overall picture was clear. Shiploads of migrants from Britain were sailing across the sea every season, and were wresting Armorica from its previous inhabitants. One district of south-west Brittany now bears the name of *Cornouaille* – in Breton, *Kerne*. Another on the northern coast called *Domnonée* was once the

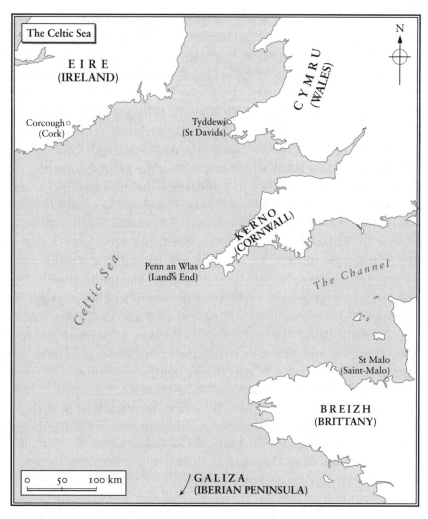

The Celtic Sea

EIRE
(IRELAND)

N

Corcough o
(Cork)

Tyddewi o
(St Davids)

CYMRU
(WALES)

KERNO
(CORNWALL)

Penn an Wlas o
(Land's End)

The Channel

Celtic Sea

St Malo
(Saint-Malo)

BREIZH
(BRITTANY)

0      50     100 km

GALIZA
(IBERIAN PENINSULA)

realm of King Conomor, mentioned by Gregory of Tours. Several historians suggest that 'Conomor the Cursed' of Domnonée and Marcus Quonimorus were one and the same person.[16]

Although the regnal dates of Quonimorus cannot be specified, it is clear that he reigned sometime in an early phase of the long era which followed the collapse of Roman rule but preceded the establishment of Anglo-Saxon hegemony. As yet, there was no England, and no Scotland; 'Wales', meaning the land of the Celtic Britons, still covered most of Great Britain. The Celtic people of Kerno, known to the Anglo-Saxons as 'the western Welsh', were closely related to the Britons elsewhere in the island, and as yet not strongly differentiated. They would have thought of themselves as the Cornovian branch of Britons, proud to possess a language, culture, and history completely separate from the Germanic newcomers. In all probability, Marcus Quonimorus held sway in the decades preceding the Battle of Dyrham near Aquae Sulis (Bath) in 577, whereby the Anglo-Saxons pushed on into the south-west and cut off the western Welsh from their compatriots on the northern side of the Severn.

This was also the era of Christianization, first by the Celtic Church and after 597 by the mission of St Augustine of Canterbury from Rome. Among the western Welsh, it saw the golden age of the Celtic saints, who criss-crossed the ocean in their coracles and curraghs, bringing the Christian Gospel to a largely pagan society. Few of those saints were to work and die in the land of their birth, and a great part of their legends and hagiographical *vitae* are taken up with seaborne adventures. St Perrin or Piran, who became the patron saint of Cornish tin-miners, was an Irishman known in his native land as Ciaran or Kieran. Having sailed from Ireland to found the Cornish abbey of Lanpiran, he also gave his name both to the 'Church of St Piran in the Sands' at nearby Perranzabuloe, and to Kerno's black-and-white flag.[17] St Petroc or Pedrog (d. 564), son of a Welsh prince, studied in Ireland and worked in Brittany before founding a monastic community at Bodmin.[18] (*Bos Menegh*, meaning 'House of the Monks', is the original form of Bodmin's name.) St Samson of Dol (d. 564) was another Welshman from Glamorgan, who founded the abbey of Dol in Brittany, and reportedly excommunicated King Conomor of Domnonée. St Brendan 'the Voyager' (d. 575) has been credited with one of the great voyages of discovery that took him on a seven-year journey from Ireland to Iceland, Greenland, and possibly to North America.[19] He was accompanied by the Briton, St Aaron, who later retired to the island of Cesabre in Brittany to which his Welsh disciple, Malo, later lent his name.

No Celtic saint would be complete without a string of miracles. St Petroc floated across the Celtic Sea with a millstone chained round his neck. St Budoc sailed in a barrel and St Ia, an Irish princess and founder of St Ives, went one better by riding the waves on a leaf. The list is almost endless – St Austell, St Blazey, St Cai, St Goran, St Just, St Kew, St Laudus, St Levan, St Mabyn, St Nest, and St Pol.[20] Their Pan-Celtic world was one. And its hub, not its remotest point, lay at *Penn an Wlas*, otherwise Land's End, which, from the Celtic perspective, was not the western periphery, but the dead centre.

Many of those who write about early Kerno make little effort to disentangle the mythological from the historical. None of us succeed in the task completely, but some gaily mingle fragile fact with seductive fiction until the two are almost indistinguishable:

> The story of Arthur is curiously interwoven with that of another Cornish king, who may have been Arthur's contemporary or successor. Mark, or Marcus, was a king of Cornwall during the sixth century or earlier, and his fortress was at Castle Dor, once the stronghold of the chief Gorlais. In the Arthurian legend, Gorlais is murdered, and Igraine his wife is seduced by Uther Pendragon and becomes the mother of Arthur. Later, when Arthur is chief or king, his wife Gwinevere is herself seduced by Lancelot, a knight at Arthur's court ... This theme of seduction and betrayal belongs also to King Mark, who sends his nephew Tristan to bring him an Irish bride, the princess Iseult. The story of the love-potion, given to the pair by Iseult's handmaiden, Bronwyn ... of their hopeless passion and the jealousy of King Mark, is known the world over, more famous even than Arthur's love for Gwinevere.[21]

Or more poetically:

> For he that always bare in bitter grudge
> The slights of Arthur and his Table, Mark
> The Cornish King, had heard a wandering voice,
> A minstrel of Caerleon by strong storm
> Blown into shelter at Tintagil, say
> That out of naked knightlike purity
> Sir Lancelot worshipt no unmarried girl
> But the great Queen herself ...[22]

\*

I am no expert on the seductive land Kerno, but I begin with it here because I was to re-encounter many of the issues that its history raises during my journey round the world. The early history of Kerno/Cornwall is a good example of the worldwide and continuing problem of indigenous peoples and of their struggles against rapacious conquerors, intruders, and exploiters. Far-fetched as it may seem to some, it illustrates the insidious historical process now widely recognized as 'cultural genocide'. The concept was the creation of Raphael Lemkin, the lawyer who coined the term 'genocide' in 1944, although the wider cultural extension of the term was not formally adopted by the UN Declaration on the Rights of Indigenous Peoples until 1994. Yet the practice to which it refers is almost as old as humanity. In our own time it has been publicized by the Dalai Lama, and by a growing awareness of the present-day fate of Tibet. The Tibetans are now facing the prospect that once faced scores of European peoples from the Cornovians to the ancient Prussians.[23] It will do the English no harm at all to consider their role in comparison to that of the Han Chinese in Central Asia.

'Cultural genocide', which smacks of political sensationalism, is not perhaps the best term to describe the phenomenon. Since 'genocide', and its synonym, 'ethnocide', belong to a group of nouns that refer to the most heinous crimes – from matricide to infanticide – their use in conjunction with culture is easily equated with cheap political posturing. Yet they refer to a historical reality that went unquestioned for centuries precisely because its habitual forms of violence stop short of wholesale exterminatory killing. Indeed, it was long considered 'natural', in the same Darwinian sense that the extinction of animal species was thought natural, and it is dangerous because the effects are only achieved gradually. It deserves to be exposed for what it is: a form of coercion exercised by the strong over the weak.

Such attitudes were deeply entrenched in the minds of nineteenth-century imperialists, and of twentieth-century totalitarians, both Communist and Fascist. Typically, cultural genocide has been embraced by people who believe that the spread of civilization can be equated with their own interests and enrichment, and they flourish wherever a powerful collective encounters a weaker one, whether on the plains of North America, in the outback of Australia, or in the disputed territories of Europe and Africa. The end results do not vary. The lands and resources of the weaker group are expropriated. The stronger group sends in soldiers, settlers, administrators, traders, and educators in overwhelming numbers. The indigenous people lose control of their property and their children. Their language disappears, along with the historical memories that every language conserves. Their culture lapses, and their separate identity is submerged. In the ultimate indignity, the country's name will vanish, too.[24] It is no accident, when newly liberated ex-colonies win back their independence, that they frequently insist on restoring their names; New Spain became *Mexico*; Ireland became *Eire*; Indochina dissolved into *Laos*, *Cambodia*, and *Vietnam*; Southern Rhodesia turned into *Zimbabwe*, the Dutch East Indies into *Indonesia*, and Burma into *Myanmar*.

The time spans of the process can stretch over centuries. The Anglo-Saxons established a dominant position in Kerno in the course of the ninth century, though the decisive steps were taken by King Athelstan, the *Rex Totius Britanniae*, who delineated the frontier between Devon and Cornwall on the Tamar in 936 and expelled the British community from Exeter. It is unlikely that Athelstan had any intention of transforming the culture of his Celtic subjects; the biggest prize were the tin mines, which were to flourish for a thousand years. Thereafter, however, the country's Celtic name steadily sank beneath that of its derogatory English replacement – 'Cornwall', meaning the land of the 'Cornovian Foreigners'. In 1337 a sizeable chunk of its territory, measuring 135,000 acres and including most of the Scilly Isles, was set aside to form the Duchy of Cornwall, whose income has been used ever since for the comfortable upkeep of the English monarch's firstborn son. Nevertheless, subdued and exploited, the sinking country put up a stout rearguard action in repeated rebellions, notably in 1497, when the rebels were defeated at Deptford Bridge on the outskirts of London, and later during the Reformation, when the English Bible and Anglican prayer book were imposed by the Tudor government. The last rumblings of revolt were provoked in 1688–9 by the imprisonment of the Cornish Bishop of Bristol, Jonathan Trelawney, one of seven Anglican prelates who defied the ordinances of King James II. His defiance made him the hero of 'The Song of the Western Men', sometimes called Cornwall's national anthem:

> A good sword and a trusty hand!
> A merry heart and true!
> King James's men shall understand
> What Cornish lads can do!
> And have they fixed the where and when,
> And shall Trelawney die?
> Here's twenty thousand Cornishmen
> Will know the reason why.
> And will Trelawney live?
> Or will Trelawney die?
> Here's twenty thousand Cornishmen
> Will know the reason why.

These words, composed long after the event, contain a heavy dose of poetic licence. They bypass the facts that the bishop was acquitted, that the 'twenty thousand Cornishmen' did not have to march anywhere, and that the nascent revolt did not actually materialize. If anything, they better reflect the events and emotions of the Anglo-Cornish War of 1549, the so-called 'Prayer Book Rebellion', which drove a Cornish army to capture Plymouth and besiege Exeter, and which involved the bishop's grandfather.[25] Nonetheless, they embody the spirit that inhabits the hearts of the non-English element of Cornwall's population, and has been their rallying cry ever since. Of course, they have their Cornish equivalent:

> Verow Trelawny bras
> Verow Trelawny bras?
> Mes igens mil a dus Kernow
> A woffeth oll an kas.[26]

The decline of the Cornish language – *Kerneweg* – followed the loss of political autonomy, although the critical moment was long delayed by a curious turn of fate. After 1066, William the Conqueror gave much of the land in Cornwall to the numerous Bretons in his entourage. As a result, as can be seen from their heraldic mottoes, the mediaeval aristocracy were accustomed to speak the same language as the common people, and English was long held at bay. *Kerneweg* was the traditional idiom both of the tin-miners and of the mediaeval Stannary Parliament, which met at Lostwithiel from 1204; its powers were not suspended until 1496, and not completely abolished until 1753. The rot only really set in, therefore, under the Elizabethan regime that forcibly anglicized both church services and church-based schools, removing the possibility of an autonomous Cornish script, orthography, grammar, and textbooks. Deprived of the standard tools of linguistic conservation, Cornwall's last native speakers were artificially confined to the oral tradition, and finally succumbed in the late eighteenth century.[27] The fate of *Kerneweg* well illustrates the contention that 'languages don't die naturally; they are killed.' And it was a precursor of the three thousand endangered languages that are expected to disappear worldwide in the twenty-first century.[28]

Of course, if you really think about it, none of the so-called 'indigenous peoples' is truly indigenous. Modern DNA studies have established the fact that the human race made its way round the globe in a series of prehistoric migrations that took it to all the earth's continents from one single starting point, probably in East Africa. The British Celts are no exception. Although some of them complain of Anglo-Saxon oppression, they, too, at some point must have been invaders, who suppressed and replaced the previous inhabitants of the Isles. The ethnicity of the builders of Stonehenge has never been established, though they were certainly neither Celtic nor English.[29] The name by which Britain's greatest prehistoric stone circle was originally known has equally been lost without trace. In the last resort, we are all the offspring of immigrants, and the concept of a Native Land belongs exclusively to the imaginary reconstruction of the Past.

What happens is that each new wave of migrants, who achieve a dominant position, grow emotionally attached to the territory and begin to think of it as their 'native land', their *patria*. The one-time immigrants become the new 'natives', and elaborate a new brand of patriotism, ignoring or deprecating everything that went before. In the case of Kerno/Cornwall, once English dominance was secure, new generations of Cornish-born Englishmen professed their love for the county of their birth and celebrated its role in the growth of England's diversity. The Nestor of the movement in modern times was Sir Arthur Quiller-Couch (1863–1944), known as 'Q' – Shakespearean scholar, Cambridge don, compiler of *The Oxford Book of English Verse*, and author of some thirty Cornish novels.[30] His most assiduous successor was A. L. 'Leslie' Rowse (1903–97), Fellow of All Souls College, Oxford, and one of the most opinionated and self-congratulatory figures in the history of learning. 'This filthy twentieth century,' he once opined, 'I hate its guts.'[31] Rowse was as prolific as he was antipathetic, publishing over one hundred books, many on Shakespeare in the footsteps of 'Q', though vastly more eccentric, but still more inspired by his Anglocentric view of Cornwall. The titles included *Tudor Cornwall: Portrait of a Society* (1941), *The Spirit of English History* (1943), *A Cornish Childhood* (1944), *The Contribution of Cornwall and the Cornish to Britain* (1969), and *The Little Land of Cornwall* (1986).[32]

The novelist Daphne du Maurier (1907–89), who lived most of her life there, greatly expanded Cornwall's literary repertoire. All of her best-selling novels – *Jamaica Inn* (1936), *Rebecca* (1938), *Frenchman's Creek* (1941), *My Cousin Rachel* (1951), and *The House on the Strand* (1969) – have a Cornish setting; for her and her readers, they portray a land of smugglers, ship-wreckers, secrets, and 'sinister tales'. The genre that she created was pursued and embellished by her only slightly lesser-known contemporary, Winston Graham (1908–2003), whose twelve 'Poldark' novels have twice enjoyed success as TV serials.[33] Both du Maurier's *Rebecca* and one of her short stories, 'The Birds' (1952), were turned into psycho-films by Alfred Hitchcock, as was Graham's *Marnie* (1961). Du Maurier's speciality, however, was jealousy, and she wrote in her own variety of poetical prose. *Rebecca*'s famous opening sentence, 'Last night I dreamt I went to Manderley again' is a perfect iambic hexameter; its closing line is almost as good: 'And the ashes blew towards us with the salt wind from the sea.' 'People who travel,' she wrote, 'are always fugitives.'[34]

Du Maurier's last novel, *Rule Britannia* (1972), took an entirely new and, some would now say, a strangely prescient line. It was a political satire set several decades in the future, and has become uncannily relevant to the Brexit era. Britain's imaginary relations with the European Community have broken down. The government is in disarray. A referendum returns a popular vote for 'Leave', as hyperinflation and social unrest accelerate. The country is divided, and a State of Emergency declared. To resolve the impasse, American forces invade by invitation to create a new state called 'USUK', pronounced 'You Suck'. The Queen and the American president are appointed joint heads-of-state. And Cornishmen rise again to lead the resistance.[35]

The red-billed Cornish chough is a species of the crow family. It is designated by ornithologists as the *Pyrrhocorax pyrrhocorax*, to distinguish it from the yellow-billed Alpine chough *Pyrrhocorax graculus*. In Western Europe, its habitat lies on rocky coastal cliffs from Ireland to Brittany (where it is known in French as the *crave à bec rouge*), and northern Spain. Further east, it lives on mountainous terrain in Eastern Europe and Central Asia, and has even been sighted on the slopes of Mount Everest. It acquired its Cornish moniker through being adopted as the mediaeval Duchy's emblem, surmounting Cornwall's coat-of-arms. In Cornish it is known as the *palores*, or 'digger bird', presumably from its habit of digging into the earth for worms and insects.[36]

The *Pyrrhocorax pyrrhocorax*, however, is an endangered species; it features on the Amber List of the Royal Society for the Protection of Birds (RSPB). Several hundred pairs still breed in various parts of the British Isles, but after long decline it completely disappeared from its native Cornwall. A last solitary pair was observed on the county's northern coast in the late 1960s. When the female died, the lone widower was left patrolling the cliffs until he, too, expired in 1973. His departure inspired a conservation project called Operation Chough, which is based at Paradise Park at Hayle on St Ives Bay and which aims to rear the birds in captivity before reintroducing them to the wild.[37] In its turn, the ornithological project inspired the name of the second Operation Chough, which challenged the pretensions of English Heritage.

Nothing better illustrates the parallel that can be drawn between the worldwide movement to preserve indigenous cultures and the belated rise of ecology and environmentalism. So long as the planet's resources appeared to be limitless, little concern was shown for self-sustaining consumption or biodiversity. In the same way, little interest was shown in the importance of humano-diversity or the survival of endangered human species. As late as the 1970s, the children of Australia's 'Stolen Generations' were being forcibly taken from their aboriginal families for their 'betterment'.[38] In Canada, a parallel policy of forcing the children of the country's 'First Nations' to undergo assimilation courses in residential schools continued until 2007.[39] Canada, in consequence, is one of the countries where the concept of 'cultural genocide' is best understood.

The good news is that culture, being non-material, possesses a strong potential for an afterlife. So long as the carriers and their records are not completely destroyed, something of their previous culture will always be transmitted into the cultural flora of the subsequent era. The Irish prove this truth better than anyone. Having largely lost their own language, they then produced a galaxy of masters of the English language. The Welsh, too, while cherishing the *Cymraeg*, sustain a parallel tradition of Welsh literature written in English. The Welshness of Dylan Thomas, for example, shines triumphantly through his English words.

Although *Kerneweg*, the Cornish language, died out, it is now being resurrected.[40] Its revival has been fostered both by scholars such as Henry Jenner, whose *Handbook* was published in 1904, and by patriotic enthusiasts who use it for everyday purposes and for teaching their children.[41] In 1928 the *Gorsedh Kernow*, or 'Court of Bards', was established in imitation of the Welsh Eistedfodd; a large helping of invented tradition has not stopped it from going from strength to strength. 'One generation has set Cornish on its feet,' declared Morton Nance, the first Grand Bard of modern times; 'it is now for another [generation] to make it walk.'[42]

The exhortation has been heeded. The Cornish Language Partnership, Maga, promotes study, and evangelizes.[43] The Cornish Stannary Parliament, which purports to be a reincarnation of the county's mediaeval legislature, and which was responsible for the demonstration against English Heritage, has been active since 1974 as a cultural pressure group.[44] And strong efforts have been made to bring Cornwall into the wider Celtic Revival. Recent book titles include *Celtic Cornwall*, *The Celts in Cornwall*, and *West Britons: Cornish Identities and the Early British State*.[45] Distinctly Cornish perspectives on Cornwall's identity are multiplying.[46]

Nor need the Cornish Revivalists worry anymore about being an isolated group of eccentrics. Linguistic rescuscitation is a worldwide phenomenon inspiring a new academic discipline called 'revivalistics'. The prime example is Modern Hebrew, a language that had not been spoken as a secular tongue for over a thousand years but which has been successfully brought back to life by the Zionist movement and is now the official state language of Israel.[47] Hawaiian, too, has been rescued. In 1980 it was prematurely pronounced dead, having been banned for nearly a century by American educational authorities, but which in reality was merely hibernating in what linguists call a 'comatose' state.[48] One of the pioneers of revivalistics, the anthropologist Mark Turin (b. 1973), manages both the Digital Himalaya Project at Cambridge University and the First Nations and Endangered Language Program at the University of British Columbia (UBC) in Vancouver.[49]

A corollary of linguistic revival is the realization that monolingualism is an artificial and outdated imposition enforced by misguided officialdom. Plurilingualism or multilingualism represents a much older and more natural state of affairs. Official policies of bilingualism, as introduced in Wales (and elsewhere, for example in Canada) since the 1960s, promise to bring an end to the age-old 'language wars'.

On many fronts, therefore, progress is being made. In 2011 the Cornish Pasty received the status of an *appellation contrôlée* under the European Union's PGI directive concerning Protected Geographical Indications, putting it on a par with champagne and Parma ham. And in April 2014 the separate nature of Cornwall's cultural heritage was officially recognized by the British government: 'The proud history, unique culture, and distinctive language of Cornwall', read the announcement, 'will be fully recognized under European rules for the protection of national minorities.'[50]

This decision was already far removed from the attitude of the magistrates who handed out those drastic fines to Cornish activists only fifteen years earlier. It was accompanied by a significant government grant to the Maga organization.

No less surprisingly, the ageing Leslie Rowse mellowed. Eventually leaving All Souls, he retired to Trenarren in mid-Cornwall, agreed to join the *Gorsedh Kernow*, which he had formerly ridiculed, and began to study the rudiments of *Kerneweg* grammar:

> This was the land of my content.
> Blue sea and feathered sky,
> Where, after years away, at last
> I came home to die.[51]

The Cornish chough also symbolically returned home. In the early twenty-first century, Kerno's national bird has resumed residence, having re-crossed the sea from Brittany.[52]

So there are many ways of remembering. There is no one path for rescuing a departed culture from oblivion. Many people believe that the soul or spirit of a lost culture lingers on in the elusive *genius loci* of the places where it once flourished.

Daphne du Maurier, for example, whose ancestry was both Cornish and Breton, talks little about the Celtic spirit, but obviously believed in its existence; she waxed eloquent over the witness of the stones:

> There is in the Cornish character, smouldering beneath the surface, ever ready to ignite, a fiery independence, a stubborn pride. How much of this is due to the centuries of isolation after the Roman conquest of Britain ... and how much to the legacy of those dark-haired invaders with their blue beads and their circlets of gold, heirs of a civilisation existing long before Rome was even named, is something the Cornish can argue for themselves. As an outsider ... I like to think that the two races, facing an Atlantic seaboard blown by identical gales, washed by the same driving mists, share a common ancestry, along with the Irish further west.
>
> Superstition flows in the blood of all three peoples. Rocks and stones, hills and valleys, bear the imprint of men who long ago buried their dead beneath great chambered tombs and worshipped the earth goddess ... The stones, like the natural granite cast up from the earth by nature, defy the centuries. To stand beside them, whether on the heights of West Penwith [or] amongst the bracken of Helman Tor ... is to become, as it were, an astronaut in time. The present vanishes, centuries dissolve, the mocking course of history, with all its triumphs and defeats, is blotted out. Here in the lichened stone is the essence of memory itself.[53]

The Cornish poet Norman Davies, who writes in English, specializes in capturing those same fleeting sensations. As he wanders along the cliff path to Morvah, or through 'the wounded silence' of Bodmin Moor, he hears the ancient echoes:

> Pines darkened, dank
> in bracts mystery,
> stand rank on rank
> like – History ...
> Pipit and lone Bunting
> scurry in low scrub.

Buzzards go a-hunting.
Merlin – perching stab
holds a view of conquest
Birds of prey may share.
History holds no inquest –
neither here, nor there.
Morvah soon emerging,
sapphire blue St. Just,
Whitesands ever surging
As the ocean must. –
These are but the gleanings,
Lyonesse ablaze.
Cornwall's hidden meanings
Lost in Kernow's haze.[54]

# 2

# Baki – Baku

*Flame Towers in the Land of Fire*

As the crow flies, or the jet plane, the western shore of the Caspian Sea lies exactly 2,713 miles from Land's End. It marks one of Europe's territorial extremities, just as Land's End marks another. The direct line of flight passes over the English Channel, Paris, Bavaria, Austria, Hungary, Romania, the Black Sea, Georgia, and Azerbaijan.

The fine, crescent-shaped city of Baku is the place where Europe ends, or travelling westward, where it begins. It occupies a superb location on the Caspian shore, looking straight into the sunrise. To the north, on the left, lies Russia and the mouth of the mighty Volga. To the south, on the right, lies Iran. To the west, at one's back, lie the Caucasian countries of Georgia, Armenia, and Azerbaijan. And to the east, straight across the shimmering waters, lie the Central Asian republics that line the route of the ancient Silk Road. The local Azeris call the city Baki. It was Russians, arriving later, who gave their version of its name to the rest of the world.

The Caspian is the largest stretch of enclosed water on the Earth's surface; a great lake rather than a sea, it is roughly five times bigger than America's Lake Superior or Africa's Lake Victoria. Replenished by the inflow from the Kura, Volga, and Ural rivers, its semi-saline contents have no exit, and Baku lies nearly 100 feet below sea level. Less degraded than its neighbour, the smaller Aral Sea, which has dried up almost completely, it, too, is threatened by pollution and evaporation. The 'Caspian' name was invented by ancient Greeks after a local tribe. But the Turks, the Turkmen, and the Azeris all call it the *Hazar Denizi*, 'the Sea of the Chazars', after its rulers between the seventh and tenth centuries.

Not everyone agrees that Baku is European. Some say it belongs to Asia. Most argue that it lies at a point where Europe and Asia overlap. The tourist ads talk of 'European charm in an oriental setting'. Yet the geographers who drew the intercontinental line between Europe and

Asia in the late eighteenth century, fixing the main Eurasian divide on
the ridge of the Urals, projected it southwards towards the Caucasus
and the Bosphorus, following the Ural River, the Caspian's north-
western river, and the Kura River Basin. By their reckoning, Baku and
northern Azerbaijan lie inside Europe, while everything below the
Kura lies in Asia.[1]

Nowadays, Baku is the capital of the sovereign Republic of Azerbaijan, a full member of the United Nations since 1991, and a non-
permanent member of the Security Council. At 86,000 square kilometres and with 9.5 million inhabitants, Azerbaijan is larger than a dozen
states of the European Union: similar in size to Portugal or the Czech
Republic, and part of the ex-Soviet sphere. Its citizens – Azerbaijanis –
are also, overwhelmingly, Azeris – that is, speakers of the Turkic Azeri
language. Five defining adjectives apply: 'ex-Soviet', 'Turkic', 'Muslim',
'Caucasian', and 'oil-rich'.

Baku is not the easiest place to reach. Azerbaijan's post-Soviet bureaucracy confronts the would-be traveller with an obstacle course
reminiscent of the Cold War. According to the official website express
visas can be issued in three days.

'Express visa, three days?' I ask at the consulate in London.

'Yes,' the voice replies, 'on presentation of your invitation from the
Ministry in Baku.'

My invitation is not from the Ministry. 'So what do I do?'

Deadly silence. After numerous twists and turns, the visa finally emerges on the seventeenth day. I have two days to join a flight from Frankfurt. Then, having left the consulate, I see the catch. Although the officials had checked my flight booking for the 21st of the month, they had issued the visa for the 22nd.

All applicants for visas are made aware of another problem:

> Due to a state of war with Armenia, the Government of Azerbaijan bans the entry of Armenian citizens, as well as [people] of Armenian descent ... Without prior consent ... the Government of Azerbaijan strictly bans any visit to the separatist region of Nagorno-Karabakh ... [and] its surrounding territories ... which are de jure part of Azerbaijan but under the control of Armenia. Foreign citizens who enter these occupied territories will be permanently banned from Azerbaijan, and will be [added to] the list of persona non grata.[2]

Visitors to Azerbaijan, therefore, cannot make a side trip to the aforementioned 'separatist region'. The most they can do is to read about it, and try to master the complications. The region known to the world by its Russian name of 'Nagorno-Karabakh' is known in Azerbaijan as just Karabakh, 'The Black Garden', and by its Armenian inhabitants as Artsakh. My erstwhile colleague at London University, David Lang, claimed that the name of Artsakh derives from King Artaxias I of Armenia (r. 190–159 BCE).[3] Today, it is ruled by the autonomous 'Republic of Artsakh', otherwise the Republic of Nagorno-Karabakh, which is linked with Armenia. The ongoing conflict that surrounds it goes back to 1918, as I will discover.[4]

At Frankfurt airport, the automatic check-in machine tells me to confirm that I possess a visa. It then requests the date of the visa's expiry, but not its start date. I tick a box to accept the dire financial consequences of supplying Lufthansa with false information – and duly receive a boarding card. But I hesitate. The flight will land at 21:00. The visa will only become valid at midnight. Is that an offence?

My fellow passengers fall into three distinct groups. The first look like standard Europeans: executives, tourists, ex-pats, students. The second group are obviously foreigners: Chinese and Japanese and Indians. But the third group, the majority, possess remarkably uniform features: jet-black hair, jet-black eyes, jet-black brows, aquiline noses, and pale skins. These, I think, must be the real Caucasians, not what the American government imagines to be Caucasians. Among the women there are a few head-scarves, but no abiyahs or burkhas.

My guidebook lists many prohibitions. Don't chew gum. Don't raise your voice. 'A stupid man,' says an obscure Azerbaijani proverb, 'is known by his laugh.' Don't point your fingers. Don't touch people. Don't lift your feet to show the soles of your shoes. Above all, don't mention Armenia. And don't pass comments on the ruling Aliyev dynasty. Idle words can put you onto the next plane home.[5]

Walking onto the tarmac at Heydar Alijev International, I am hit by a blast of warm air, the sight of a golden moon, and strong doubts. Three hours divide me from safety. Should I try to hang around in the arrival hall, or play it by ear?

I am last in the queue. The weary passport officer looks me lazily in the face, gazes at my out-of-date visa for Russia, tells me to look at the camera, and stamps my passport for entry. But just as he is handing it back his eye catches sight of the number 22. He wakes with a start:

'Your visa is not valid for today, sir; today is the 21st.'

'Really? It was issued by the Azerbaijani Embassy.'

'Your visa is valid for tomorrow, not today. Don't move.'

The officer leaves with my passport. I look round anxiously to see whether the embassy has sent someone to meet me, as they sometimes do, and glance at the departures board to see if any more flights are due to leave before midnight. There's one last flight heading for Ashkabad in Turkmenistan at 10.30 p.m. A more senior officer appears:

'Your visa is not valid today, sir.'

'I don't understand. Your visa section saw my travel tickets.'

'Your visa is valid for tomorrow, not today. Don't move.'

'Yes, I know. But it has already been stamped.'

The officers go into a huddle amidst looks of consternation. One points towards me, another to the exit. My eyes follow his finger, and raise my hopes. A group of diplomats are bidding farewell to a colleague, and are still standing by the barrier. I am fortunate that I can count on diplomatic support during foreign trips, usually at the cost of a 'meet the author' talk, and, having two passports, I can also vary which diplomatic service to call on. I hope this might be the welcoming party I had been told could be there.

The officers stroll over to deliver their verdict, and to my amazement the ambassador himself swoops:

'Good evening, gentlemen. This passenger is my guest. Can I help?'

'Good evening, Excellency. The passenger's visa is not valid for today.'

'Exactly, Officer. Very commendable of you to notice. Could you possibly accept my personal guarantee of his good behaviour for the next couple of hours?'

The gate swings open. I could easily have been despatched to Turkmenistan.

The ambassador announced that an appointment with the president was unlikely but not impossible.

'If it happens,' he says, 'someone will ring, and we report to the palace within the hour.'

My first impressions at night from an airport limousine suggest an old-fashioned oriental city in the throes of super-speedy modernization. New SUVs vastly outnumber the old Ladas, cruising past trendy boutiques on tree-lined boulevards, and jockeying with incongruous London cabs. Imperial Russian buildings alternate with Islamic façades, minarets, metro stations, and skyscrapers. The three brand-new, hilltop, neon-lit, glass-clad skyscrapers, the curvaceous 'Flame Towers', dominate the skyline. They are visible from my hotel balcony in the ancient Inner City, where I settle into a comfortable room with Persian rugs on the floor and a heavy embroidered coverlet on the bed. Over the washbasin a large blue notice informs: THIS WATER IS SAFE TO DRINK.

An orientational walk takes up the next morning. The steep streets of the Inner City, the Isheri Sheher, are still guarded by battlemented walls that surround a maze of cobbled alleyways, overhanging balconies, mosques, markets, and museums. The sturdy, circular twelfth-century Maiden Tower, the Qiz Qalasi, built from close-fitting limestone blocks, overlooks the bay. The nearby palace complex of the Shirvanshahs, in contrast, is being rescued from ruin by repair works. The seat of a ruling dynasty from the fifteenth to the eighteenth century, it would not rate highly in the league table of Islamic architecture. Among religious buildings, the Djuma Mosque is the finest, and the eleventh-century Muhammad Mosque the oldest. The latter was half-destroyed in 1723 by a Russian cannonball. According to the brochure, the attacking fleet was promptly sunk by a storm.

Souvenir stalls and antique shops crowd every corner. Buyers are scarce; the merchants doze in their chairs and their wares look forlorn. Trinkets and postcards dangle from strings; carpets are piled high; silk scarves billow in the breeze, and hand-beaten copper trays cover the cobbles. Red Army hats, helmets, epaulettes, and medals are on sale for a song; and replicas of the pointed 'Tatar Caps', as used by Bolshevik soldiers, are available on every stall. My only find was a framed share

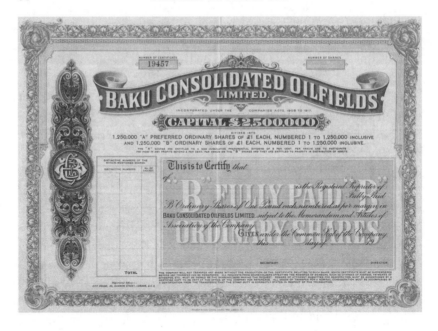

certificate from 1919, finely printed on green and white paper. The certificate, issued in London, had presumably languished in someone's attic for seventy years or more.

Descending the hillside steps, one reaches Baku's longest thoroughfare, the Neftçilar Prospekti, 'the Oilmen's Boulevard'. Eight lanes of zooming and hooting traffic have to be crossed by the marble underpasses that lead to the seafront Bulvar. Completed in 1910 as the preserve of the Russian imperial elite, the Bulvar is now a national park and the favourite promenade for all and sundry. Three parallel lines of magnificent gardens stretch for a dozen kilometres along the huge curve of the bay, starting from the giant Flagpole and ending in the distant gantries of the port. They are crammed with sub-tropical flowerbeds, cactus enclosures, and imported rare trees: cherry, magnolia, palms, and baobabs, in whose shade the crowds can stroll and soak in the ozone. We pass the musical fountains, the ferry terminal, the Dolls Theatre, and the Carpet Museum, and in a central position, the Azerbaijani Government House. Built between 1936 and 1952 during the Stalinist era, in pseudo-Moroccan style, this oversize edifice used to be the Dom Sovetskii, the seat of Soviet power, overseen by a long-gone statue of Lenin. The recently completed Heydar Aliyev Cultural Centre (2012), designed by the Iraqi-born British architect Zaha Hadid, is set back behind the seafront. Dazzling in pearl-white ceramics and glass, its flowing lines are a wonder of 'extreme architecture'. Together with the Flame Towers, the Eurovision Crystal Hall, and the Olympic Stadium, it marks just one year's increase to the city's collection of striking buildings.

My guide is a young woman graduate by the name of Nazaket, meaning 'Pleasance'. She has jet-black hair, jet-black brows, jet-black eyes, jet-black lashes, a good command of English, and a disconcerting posture of deference.

'I saw your brothers on the plane,' I say in a misplaced joke, to no effect.

'What do you want to see?' she asked repeatedly, as if I was the one with the knowledge. Eventually, towards lunchtime, I say 'a restaurant'. We sit in an open octagonal courtyard, where the tables looked out from shady recesses onto a central fountain.

'What do you want to eat?' Nazaket asks.

'Anything but meat,' I reply. Thereon, a whole stuffed pike is served up cold, its head and tail overhanging the table. Nazaket declines to join in, as I chomp my way through perhaps a quarter of the fish.

A solo evening stroll before bedtime is less stressful. The golden moon reappears, lighting up the Casbah's winding streets. Stray cats whine, grandmas peer down from the balconies, and washing flaps overhead. Round and round one goes, and down and down, until battlements loom and one walks through a narrow gateway straight into the twenty-first century. A romantic Russian film is being projected onto an open-air screen in the Philharmonic Gardens. Young couples hold hands, defying the rules. Others sit under the trees, sipping fruit juice and watching the swirling, coloured lights of the Flame Towers dancing on the skyline. It's warm, but also windy; it's not just a sea breeze, but a heavy, thumping wind, whose gusts shake the branches. The guidebook says that the mediaeval city's Persian name was Badkube, meaning 'Wind Strike'.

'Fountains Square' on the edge of the Inner City is Baku's favourite meeting-place by day and a well-publicized rendezvous point by night. Formerly known as the Parapet, it is filled in the evening by strolling crowds and solitary individuals, all seeking the cool air spread by a dozen plumes of tumbling water:

> For the first-time male visitor, a quarter of an hour sitting outside on Fountain Square, can be quite a surprise. Not only are Azeri women stunningly beautiful, many a young woman will promenade herself

wearing clothes that would be bold by European standards. Even the country's First Lady, Mehriban Aliyeva, likes to show herself as a 1960s femme fatale . . .

In Azerbaijan, traditional values were never fully eclipsed . . . A lot of the women that you see live with their parents, and have to obey strict curfew orders . . . [Outside the cities], you can expect to see much more conservative ways, and even some pockets of Islamic tradition . . . Marriages are very often arranged between families, and in rural areas marriage by kidnapping is not uncommon.[6]

Night life centres on nearby Abdulkarim Ali-Zadeh Street, and the guidebooks flag up warnings about the subterranean and euphemistically named 'Disco Clubs'. The Chevalier Bar in the Grand Europe Hotel is an upmarket equivalent.

This week's edition of *Azernews* – 'Azerbaijan's Number 1 Newspaper' – serves up a well-worn fare of presidential engagements and the war with Armenia:

President Ilham Aliyev and his wife, Mehriban Aliyev . . . attended the opening of a genocide memorial built in the northern town of Guba to honor victims of massacres committed in the area by Armenian and Bolshevik forces in 1918.

The Azeris are clearly not to be outdone by strident Armenian claims of genocide:

Tens of thousands of Muslims, as well as local Jews, were killed between March and September 1918 . . . in Baku and the regions, including Guba, Shamakhi, Goychay, Karabakh, and Lankaran. Nearly 167 villages were destroyed in Guba region alone.

The memorial complex has been built near a mass grave . . . discovered during construction of a stadium in 2007 . . . President Aliyev and his wife planted apple trees outside the memorial . . . President Aliyev said that Armenians committed similar crimes just twenty years ago. They destroyed everything, including mosques and other historical monuments . . . during the 1991–94 war. 'Those who committed those crimes are now trying to pass themselves off as civilized people,' the President said. The President warned that Azerbaijan will have to use force to regain control of its territory should Armenia continue its occupation. 'Today we are strong enough' . . . 'Today Azerbaijan has the mightiest army in the Caucasus Region . . . Azerbaijan's military spending exceeds Armenia's overall state budget by 30–50 per cent.'[7]

A second article described preparations for 'Oil Workers Day' on 20 September. The day marks the signing in 1994 of 'the Deal of the Century', whereby a consortium of thirteen international oil firms invested a total of $57 billion in Azerbaijan's offshore oil- and gas-fields. Official sources do not explain that 'the Deal' was closely linked to the end of the fighting against Armenia over Nagorno-Karabakh. So long as the fighting continued, the consortium had been unwilling to invest. Hence, despite an unfavourable military position, Azerbaijan called a ceasefire to ensure the deal's signature. Twenty years later, the president can boast that the state's oil revenues have given it the military superiority previously lacking; GDP has more than tripled.[8] Furthermore, Azerbaijan has secured access to international pipelines that transport its products to ocean-going terminals. One of the pipe-lines, the BTC (Baku–Tbilisi–Ceylan), opened in 2006, takes oil to a Mediterranean terminal in Turkey. The other, the TAP (Transadriatic Pipeline), now under construction, will carry gas along the Southern Gas Corridor to the European Union via Greece, Albania, and Italy. The state oil company, SOCAR, has invested $60 billion since inde-pendence in 1991.

A third article celebrates the achievements of the Azeri poet, Said Mahammad Hussejn Behzhat Tabrizi (1906–88), popularly known as 'Shahriar'. The title of his epic poem, *Heydar Baba Salam* ('Greetings to Old Man Heydar'), refers to a mountain near Tabriz in Iran, where he passed an idyllic rural childhood. For promotional purposes, it could also be taken as a favourable reference to the strongman of Soviet Azerbaijan, Geydar Aliyev. Published in 1954, the work became an instant classic on both sides of the frontier. 'Shahriar' was an Iranian Azeri, who also wrote in Farsi, and his continuing favour with official-dom shows how post-Soviet Azerbaijan values the cultural links with Iran's large Azeri population, hinting at eventual unification with (Ira-nian) 'Southern Azerbaijan'.

Duly warned about the dubious nature of official information, my next expedition took me to the headland on which the Flame Towers have been built, and which offers a panoramic view over the bay. My London cab roared up the hairpins, and for the grand sum of 2 manats 54 gapiks (about £1.20) deposited me beside a newly built mosque at the summit. This is where Baku's sacred sites are concentrated. On one side, behind the parliament, lies the Fexri Xijabani Cemetery enclosing a Soviet-style Avenue of the Distinguished, in which the mausoleum of the late president, Heydar (or Geydar) Aliyev, now stands. Lower down, three long avenues have been laid out – one for the graves of victims of a Red Army massacre in 1990, a second for soldiers killed in the Armenian War of 1987–94, and a third for the fallen from the Army of Islam of 1918. Flowers and portraits of the departed abound. There is even a new British monument commemorating the dead of the First World War. A slender Islamic tower rises over the Eternal Flame of Remembrance.

Nothing indicates what stood here until twenty years ago. The answer is an oversize, false-heroic statue of Sergei Kirov, the Bolshevik leader who headed the Communist Party of Azerbaijan from 1921 to 1926, and was later promoted to Leningrad. Kirov's murder initiated Stalin's purges in 1934. To mask his crime, Stalin shamelessly promoted the cult of Kirov's none too savoury personality.[9] Similarly, there is nothing to indicate the whereabouts of the monument to the 'Twenty-Six Commissars', the founding martyrs of Soviet Azerbaijan, which occupied a prominent site until its demolition in 2006. The techniques of selective memory, as perfected by the Soviets, are now used against them. Nonetheless, traces of the past always remain. Although the Kirov statue has gone, some of the accompanying sculptures have not. Scrambling down a cliffside path below the Eternal Flame, one finds a sandstone bust of Lenin, defaced but intact.

Better armed with every outing to understand what was around me, I was ready to pay the 10-manat fee and to hire a guide to show me round the Milli Azerbaycan Tarixi Muzeyi, the 'Museum of National History'. Housed in the late nineteenth-century Taghiyev Mansion, the exhibition is a modified version of its Soviet-era predecessor, and takes the visitor on a relentless journey from the dinosaurs to the present-day. My new guide, Ilaha, was gearing up for the full marathon of the nation's history; her face fell when I interrupted her gushing description of Azerbaijan's oldest fossilized tree, asking whether we could move fast forward to more modern times. She gracefully deferred, leaving me enough energy to relish the twenty top-floor rooms devoted to recorded history. The emphasis was placed in the classic period on so-called Caucasian Albania (see below), on the local mediaeval khanates, and more recently on the late nineteenth-century oil boom. Parts of the Taghiyevs' opulent residence have been preserved to illustrate capitalist decadence, though their philanthropy was not forgotten. In the complex period after the collapse of Tsarist Russia, Azerbaijan's first Democratic Republic is given the limelight, but not the Republic's Bolshevik and British opponents. No portraits of Baku's Bolsheviks, such as Stalin or Kirov, are on show.[10]

Next on the list, the Nizami State Museum of Azerbaijani Literature, the self-styled 'Temple of the Word', offers a surreal experience.
For the price of 10 manats and a compulsory pair of galoshes, one is
taken on a personalized tour of an exotic oriental palace completely
devoid of guests. As one passes from hall to hall, female attendants
spring into action, switching the lights on as one enters, and off as one
leaves: a journey from darkness into light and back, fifty times over.
The museum was planned in anticipation of the 800th anniversary of
the birth of the great Azerbaijani poet Nizami Ganjavi (1141–1209),
and opened in 1945 in conjunction with Soviet victory parades. Azerbaijan's literary age is taken to start with the Avesta, the sacred book
of Zoroastrianism, and in the span of three thousand years to encompass four thousand poets, each of them categorized as 'great', 'famous',
or 'outstanding'. Original artworks in the heroic Soviet spirit were
commissioned to illustrate every step of the way. One of them portrays
Nizami in the company of his peers – Virgil, Dante, Shakespeare,
Goethe, Victor Hugo, Pushkin, Tolstoy, and Gorky. As the guidebook
informs, 'This is a holy place. All immortals that are our pride are
here.'[11] The fact that Nizami wrote in Persian is glossed over. And one
should be careful not to confuse him with his famous compatriot,
Imadeddin Nasimi (1369–1417), who was skinned alive in Aleppo for
adopting the false doctrine of Khurufism.

Very appropriately, the museum's Soviet-era guidebook is still on sale.
'The museum's collection mirrors Lenin's words,' it says, 'telling us in colourful language about the century-old path of the Azerbaijainian people
towards their present-day heights of culture.' Did Lenin ever say anything
about Azerbaijan?[12] Not to worry. The guidebook provides information
on several writers, such as the distinguished J. Jabarli (1899–1934), who
has since fallen from favour. He is presumably in the basement.

After three full days in Baku, therefore, I felt sufficiently briefed for
an evening in the company of four Azerbaijani scholars invited by the
ambassador. We met in a rooftop restaurant beside the Maiden Tower,
the sea shining beyond the plate-glass windows. Dr Gulshan Pashayeva
was a presidential adviser on strategic affairs. She had been in Belfast,
looking for clues to a settlement of Nagorno-Karabakh. 'Is the St
Andrews Agreement really working?' was her first testing question.
Professor Farda Asadov was a mediaevalist from Chazar University,
acting, where necessary, as a brilliant translator and mediator in
the trilingual exchanges. Dr Arum Bati was an engaging lawyer and
historian, a British Indian now resident in Baku.

Yet the undoubted star of the evening was Professor Camil Hasanli – aka (in Russian) Dzhamil Gassanly – the country's leading twentieth-century historian. He came hotfoot from a television debate on the forthcoming presidential elections, and spoke Russian by preference – a convincing talker and a practised disspeller of myths. In half an hour he both consumed a hearty supper and disentangled for my benefit the intricate shifts of power in Baku between the Tsar's fall in March 1917 and the Soviets' final entry in 1920. It was quite untrue, Hasanli said without being asked, that the Twenty-Six Commissars were murdered by the British. The doughty professor does not pull punches. Not long before, in a speech at London's Chatham House, he had condemned the president's failure to honour promises of reform, and openly charged him with corrupt practices. The people do not want spectacular Flame Towers and Cultural Centres, but 'justice, a better health service and a fairer distribution of income'. After Hasanli left, the ambassador said:

'He's standing in the presidential election, as an anti-corruption candidate.'

One of the others guests added, 'He's a brave man.'

Next day, I looked at Hasanli's books in the academic bookshop. I found one on Soviet–Turkish relations, another on Soviet–Iranian relations, a third on the politics of Soviet Azerbaijan, and a fourth on Soviet policy toward Iran, 1941–6.[13] His bibliography lists twenty-eight books – in Azeri, Russian, Farsi, Turkish, and English.

Portraits of the two Presidents Aliyev, father and son, are everywhere. So, too, is their devotion to 'Education, education, and education'. At the brand-new ADA University, formerly the Diplomatic Academy, which teaches exclusively in English, I was surprised to meet numerous Oxbridge graduates, who had returned home to work. At the University of Slavic Languages, I was pleased to talk to a class of a hundred studying Polish. And at the University of Foreign Languages, the country's main training ground for international relations, the rector treated me over coffee to a long exposé of Azerbaijan's strategic difficulties.

'We come under enormous pressure,' he said, mentioning no names, 'both from the South and from the North.'

'South' means Iran, 'North' means Russia.

If we are to believe human-rights watchers, Azerbaijani citizens also come under much pressure. In the estimation of the US-based Freedom House organization, Azerbaijan, like Russia, is 'Not Free', whereas neighbouring Armenia and Georgia are judged 'Partly Free'.[14] On the 'Corruption Perception Index' of Transparency International, Azerbaijan is 119th on the list of 168 countries – a score in the same bracket as Russia and Belarus.[15] In 2011 Amnesty International presented an award to the Azeri journalist Eynulla Fatullayev, who spoke of his battle for free speech in a country where the press is constantly gagged.[16] In 2012 protesters who demonstrated during the Eurovision Song Contest were violently dispersed, and the choice of Baku as the host for an internet freedom forum was widely mocked. 'Azerbaijan's ruling elite have used their wealth,' wrote the *Guardian*, 'to establish a repressive regime where police constantly monitor people ... and peaceful protests are violently broken up.'[17]

Not long ago, a grotesque incident lifted the lid on prevailing conditions. An Azerbaijani soldier, Lieutenant Ramil Safirev, who had been sent to a NATO conference in Hungary, was imprisoned for life there for murdering an Armenian colleague with an axe. He was extradited to Azerbaijan to serve out his sentence in jail. Yet his return became an occasion for national celebrations. He was pardoned by the president, promoted, awarded eight years' backpay, and allotted an apartment. Suspicions were aired that the Hungarian prime minister, Viktor Orban, only agreed to the extradition in return for the equivalent of a multi-million dollar payment.[18]

This was all very relevant to the upcoming presidential elections. Monitors had noticed a peculiar situation: neither of the two leading candidates was actually campaigning. The president's spokesman explained: 'The president has no need to campaign; he is standing on his record.' The leader of the opposition REAL movement, Ilgar Mammedov, was lingering in jail, accused of inciting violence, and another opposition candidate was barred for possessing dual Azerbaijani and Russian citizenship. That's why Professor Hasanli entered the ring. He was, the ambassador had said, 'a whale among plankton'. In order to thwart him, the 'President's Apparatus' filled the hustings with a shoal of pseudo-oppositionists, and persuaded the Board of Caucasian Muslims to dissociate itself from him.[19]

I heard often that phrase, the 'President's Apparatus'. It referred to an all-embracing machine of political control. The president's New Azerbaijan Party, for example, which holds 70 of 123 seats in parliament, has a permanent majority and a stranglehold on legislation. The president's relations and confidants hold a near-monopoly on directorships and appointments – just like the old Communist nomenclatura.

And all the services of public order – army, police, and security agencies – operate at the president's behest. As in the former USSR, a democratic facade fronts a brutal dictatorship. No living Azerbaijani has ever known otherwise.

As a mere visitor, I did not expect to catch sight of the 'President's Apparatus'. But one day, as I left the Literature Museum, I walked into a totally gridlocked one-way street. A large black SUV full of plain-clothes agents was forcing its way down the street in the wrong direction. Someone was demonstrating who was boss.

The standard history of Azerbaijan, issued in Russian by the Azerbaijani Academy of Sciences, is clearly a modified version of an earlier Soviet edition. Covering the whole sweep from the Stone Age to the advent of Soviet power, it takes contemporary state territory as the stage for all events, and retains much of the original Marxist language. Part III, on 'Feudal Society', for example, begins neatly in AD 226 with the arrival of the Persian Sassanid dynasty and ends with the Russian takeover in 1828. But significant changes have been made. Although the February Revolution in March 1917 is still described as 'a bourgeois-democratic revolution', the events of October 1917 are downgraded to a *perevorot*, a 'political coup'. It may be a coincidence, but the general editor of the series is Academician Igrar Aliyev.[20] (Half the modern population seems to be called Aliyev, or 'kinsman of Ali', the Prophet's son-in-law and the holiest name in Shia Islam.)

Only passing reference is made to a Roman inscription that was discovered in 1948 near Qobustan (Gobustan), 40 miles or so to the south of Baku:

<IMPDOMITIANO CAESARE AUG[USTO] GERMANIC[O] L-IULIUS MAXIMUS LEG XII FUL>

(Domitianus Caesar Aug[ustus] Germani[cus] being Emperor, L[ucius] Julius Maximus, [Centurion of] the XII Fulminata Legion, [laid this monument.])[21]

In the nationalist mindset, foreign inscriptions are incidental to a nation's story. Even so, the most easterly Roman inscription ever recorded serves as an important signpost in time and space. Whatever the centurion's mission was, it took place during the Emperor Domitian's Persian wars between AD 84 and 96. Coming from the XII Legion's base at Phasis, now Poti on the Black Sea coast some 450 miles distant, Julius Maximus had entered the territory of a state then known as 'Albania'. He had probably been sent on reconnaissance, or as a liaison officer with local rulers. Almost certainly, he would have encountered Zoroastrian fire-worship, but in no way either Azeris or Muslims. The preceding history of the region had been bound up with the comings and goings of Medes, Persians, Parthians, and ancient Greeks. The conquest of Alexander the Great in 331 BCE had provided a key moment. One of Alexander's defeated adversaries at the Battle of Gaugamela (Atropates, meaning 'Protected by Fire', an ally of Darius) subsequently ruled a state known as Media Atropene. Hellenistic civilization would still have been in the ascendant for the Roman centurion to appreciate.

Zoroaster or 'Zarathustra' was a philosopher of the first or second millennium BCE (his dates are completely uncertain) who founded the dominant religion of Persia from ancient times until the arrival of Islam. His teachings encouraged a dualistic view of the world, in which Light contends with Darkness, inspiring both an established state Church and a network of fire-temples.[22] Thanks to the presence of inflammable natural gas, the Caspian area has always attracted fire-worshippers. The etymology of Azerbaijan's name is 'Land of Fire'.

The ancient kingdom of Caucasian Albania occupied territory to the west of the central Caspian, and existed as a vassal state of the Persian Empire for much of the first millennium AD. It was known in Old Persian as Arran – a name that lingered on after the kingdom's demise. The state language belonged to the Lezgic linguistic group and possessed its own alphabet, similar to Georgia's. Its rulers adopted Christianity from Armenia at an early date, and their Albanian Orthodox Church maintained its autocephalous status from AD 313 to 705.[23] A handful of sixth- or seventh-century church buildings have survived. The state overlapped with parts of modern Armenia. Its capital was established at Partaw (Barda), and Khazars exerted a major influence.[24] Without much justification, modern Azerbaijani nationalists take Caucasian Albania to be the ancestor of their modern nation state.

The Caucasian Albanians lived through an era that saw the rise and fall of successive regional powers – the Sassanids, the Arabs, and the Seljuks – and were the real founders of the settlement that later became Baku. From its origins in third-century Iran, the Sassanid Empire – sometimes labelled 'the Neo-Persian Empire' – expanded until it embraced most of the modern Middle East from the Mediterranean to Afghanistan. The Arab armies of the Prophet, who destroyed the Sassanids in AD 633, installed Islam throughout the same area, creating

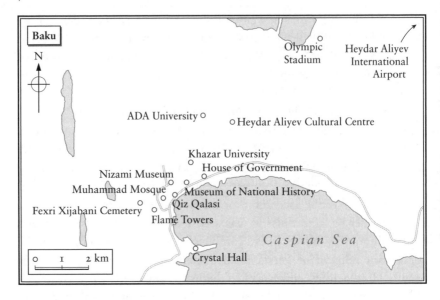

the first Caliphate. Not surprisingly they encountered resistance from both Christians and Zoroastrians, and could introduce Islam only gradually. (They arrived in the same period as the semi-nomadic Turkic Khazars, whose similarly vast realms were centred on the northern end of the Caspian.) For their part, the Seljuks were descended from a Turkic war-leader, Seljuk (d. 1036), who started his career as a Khazar governor, and whose descendants, at the head of the Oghuz Turks, overran the eastern Arab world, setting themselves up as champions of the Caliphate in Baghdad. The Great Seljuk Empire held sway under eighteen sultans before splintering around 1300.

The crystallization of a distinct Azeri-speaking community reached its critical point during that Seljuk period, when Turkic tribes from the mountainous Altai region of Central Asia were migrating westward, bringing their western or Oguz branch of the Turkic linguistic family with them. Turkification, like Islamicization, was prolonged. Genetically, the natives of modern Azerbaijan share more with their neighbours in Georgia and Armenia than with Turks or Iranians; but religiously, they were incorporated into the Muslim world by the Arab invasions, and were added to the linguistic Turkic fold by the tribal migrations somewhat later. This complex nation-building process was well advanced before the country was partitioned between Persia and Russia in modern times.

The short-lived but shattering irruption of the Mongols in the thirteenth century accelerated the disintegration of the Seljuk Empire, leaving numerous small khanates in its wake. Baku became the strong-point of the Khanate of Shirvan. But commercial progress was not obstructed. Mediaeval Baku was a fortified city of perhaps one square mile, with a double line of walls. The hillside palace of the Shirvan-shah, the 'Ruler of Shirvan', and the Maiden Tower overlooked a port filled with scores of anchored ships. Little in this picture had changed by the time of the famous 'Panorama of Baccu' engraved by the German traveller (and graduate of the Jagiellonian University in Kraków), Engelbert Kaempfer, in the late seventeenth century.[25]

A period of relative political stability returned with the Safavid dynasty, who reigned over a revitalized Persian Empire between 1501 and 1736. The Safavids, who originated in Ardabil in north-west Iran, were leaders of a Sufi sect that gained mastery over the whole empire. They were also Shias, and were responsible for the forcible conversion of their subjects to the brand of Islam that pertains to the present day. Their court language was Azeri; their capital moved to Isfahan; and their architectural legacy is unsurpassed. 'Isfahan,' says the proverb, 'is half the world.'[26]

The shadow of Russian expansion had lain over the Caspian ever since Ivan the Terrible's capture of Astrakhan, the former capital of Khazaria, in the mid-sixteenth century. But it was Peter the Great who founded Russia's Caspian Fleet and who in 1722–3 launched the first Russo-Persian War. Peter's depredations were resisted and reversed, however, and it was only in the early decades of the nineteenth century that the key advance was made. In 1828, by the Treaty of Turkmen-chay, Russia forced Persia to cede the most northerly territory of its empire, including Baku. Provincial nomenclature was notoriously fluid, but with time Russian officialdom established three governates: those of Shirvan or Baku, of Yelizavetpol for inland Karabakh, and of Yerevan further west. The name of Azerbaijan was reserved for the Persian province centred on Tabriz to the south of the new border.

The Tsarist province of Baku was of little consequence before oil was discovered. It formed part of the imperial Transcaucasus region, whose nationalities were far more intermingled than today. At the time of the Russian takeover, Yerevan, the future capital of Armenia, pos-sessed a predominantly Muslim-Azeri population, while the inhabitants of Baku included large numbers of Christian Armenians and Tats, or 'Transcaucasian Persians'.

An oil well drilled at Bibi-Heybat near Baku in 1847 claims to be the oldest anywhere. Decrees issued in 1872 offered land grants by auction

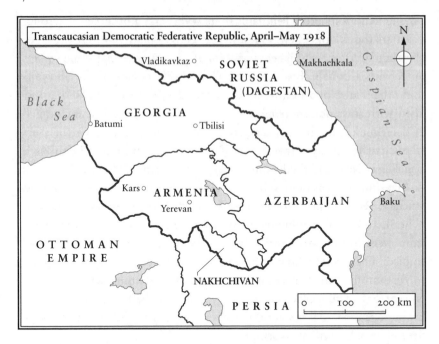

and the prospect of tax-free investment. A stampede ensued, briefly turning the Baku oilfields into the world's largest producer by the end of the century.[27]

The 'Era of the Oil Barons' was fronted by a score of individuals who struck it rich. Some of them, like Azadullayev or Meylamov, were locals, and were among the first to adopt Russified versions of their Muslim surnames. Others, like the Swedish Nobel brothers, Robert and Ludwig, or the French de Rothschilds, Edmond and Alphonse, came from abroad. Founded in 1876, when oil barrels were still being hauled to the harbour by donkey cart, the Nobels' firm Branobel – an acronym for 'Nobel Brothers' – adopted the image of a Fire Temple as the company logo. Two years later, the world's first oil tanker, Branobel's SS *Zoroaster*, was plying between Baku and the railhead at Astrakhan. By 1909, when the Moscow Chamber of Commerce marked Emanuel Nobel's birthday with the gift of a silver and diamond-encrusted Fabergé clock, the company had branches and depots all over Russia. The family lived in their grand Villa Petrolea, and their workers were housed in the Petrolea model village.[28]

None of the Baku barons, however, was half as famous as Haji Zeynalabdin Taghiyev (1823–1924). Born the son of a poor shoemaker from the Isheri Sheher, he never finished school, and worked as a semi-literate stonemason. But in 1873 he bought a part-share in a plot of land on the Aspheron Peninsula, where initial failures prompted his partners to sell out. Then, suddenly, he found himself the sole owner of the Caspian's biggest gusher, and a tycoon on the scale of John D. Rockefeller or Clint Murchison, Sr. Yet Taghiyev's lasting reputation owed less to his fabulous wealth than to the way he spent it. He became Baku's greatest philanthropist. He built the paved road from Baku to Bibi-Heybet, and the city's theatre and opera house; he funded the municipal tramways, the waterworks, the fire stations, factories, a printing works, and the leading newspaper, *Kaspy*. He poured his generosity into educational schemes. Hundreds of youths were sent to study in Russia's best universities; he founded the first Muslim Girls' School, and, despite opposition from the clergy, sponsored the translation of the Koran into Azeri.[29] Nor was Taghiyev's generosity confined to his homeland. His biggest benefaction went to the Madreseh School in Teheran. He paid for Armenian orphanages, Orthodox churches, the Muslim Charitable Society in St Petersburg, and the repair of Astrakhan's Mosque. 'All my work has been directed to one goal,' he said, 'that my nation will attain happiness.'[30]

Legends featuring Taghiyev abound. One tells how Baku's fishermen were hit by a dearth of fish. Taghiyev went down to the dock, took a valuable ring off his finger, placed it on a fish's tail, and cast it into the sea. Next day, the waters off Baku were filled with shoals of fish.

Baku in its prime, like San Francisco after the Gold Rush, was a boom town attracting entrepreneurs, professionals, and fortune-seekers from all ends of the empire. It had excellent communications by rail and sea, and in addition to oil refineries possessed tobacco, chemical, and textile factories. Russian officials presided over a cosmopolitan collection of Azeris, Armenians, Poles, Jews, Tats, and Georgians, and over a tiny plutocracy, a prosperous bourgeoisie, and a large, restless proletariat. Great industrialists topped the social pyramid. Poles, like the engineer Zrębicki, who pioneered offshore drilling, or the architect Gocławski, were prominent professionals. The oil workers themselves were mostly insecure, migrant wage-earners from all over the Transcaucasus. In 1904–5 riots erupted; refineries were burned; Muslims and Christians clashed, and Cossack troops restored order with brutality. Thanks to its large industrial proletariat, Baku was one of the few places in the Tsarist Empire where revolutionary socialism made sense. After 1905, it was seething, and the secretive Bolsheviks were one of several groups stirring up ferment. The so-called 'Caucasus Trio' of Stalin, (Sergo) Ordzonikidze, and (Anastas) Mikoyan were all active there. It was in Baku that Stalin's first wife, Kato Svanidze, died, poisoned, it was said, by environmental pollution. 'Baku was the place,' Stalin would confess, 'where I lost all feelings of humanity.'[31]

During the First World War, Baku lay to the rear of the Russo-Ottoman campaigns in the Caucasus, but in 1917, when the Russian armies dispersed, it became a target for rival forces aiming to seize its wealth. The rivals included Tsarist loyalists or 'Whites': Bolshevik and other socialist 'Reds', Turks, Islamicists, Azeri autonomists, Armenian 'Dashnak' socialists, and the British, who were advancing from Mesopotamia. The outcome was a protracted game of political musical chairs.

Popular historical works often make the false assumptions that the Bolsheviks overthrew the Tsar or that the Soviet Union was established by the October Revolution of 1917. What actually happened was markedly different. Firstly, in February 1917, Tsardom was overthrown by a variety of political opponents, who established a pro-Allied, constitutional and republican government headed by the democratic socialist, Alexander Kerensky. Secondly, that same summer, Russian armies fighting Germans in the west and Ottomans in the east began to break up, creating a dangerous emergency. Thirdly, in October 1917 in Petrograd, the Bolsheviks overthrew Kerensky's government, establishing the RSFSR (the Russian Soviet Federative Socialist Republic), or 'Soviet Russia' for short. Then, since Soviet Russia failed to gain recognition from most parts of the late empire, a score of independent regions and national republics came into existence. Soon, to consolidate their power, the Bolsheviks were obliged to fight a long series of military campaigns against the breakaway states, initially in the so-called Russian Civil War of 1918–19 and subsequently, from 1919 to 1923, in each of the former empire's non-Russian regions. In some of these conflicts – in Finland, Poland, and the Baltic States – they were defeated. But elsewhere – in Ukraine, Central Asia, and the Caucasus – they emerged victorious. Yet, before the second half of 1922, they were in no position to think of creating a Union of Soviet Socialist Republics (the USSR), which was not formally launched until 1 January 1923. Understanding those turbulent six years, 1917–22, is essential to a full appreciation of early Soviet history.

The political contortions are well illustrated by events in Azerbaijan. In 1917 Baku province had belonged to the Tsarist Empire for nearly a hundred years, and its oil wealth was coveted by all of the Tsar's would-be successors. The Bolsheviks were not alone in seeing it as a prize beyond price. 'Without Baku's oil,' Lenin said, 'the Soviet state cannot survive.' Yet few Azerbaijanis joined the Bolshevik cause, or showed enthusiasm for the Communist-dominated Baku Commune, the *Bak-Sov*, which emerged in the autumn of 1917.[32] Political power was contested by numerous interests: by Caucasian federalists, Azeri nationalists, Islamic fundamentalists, conservative Christian Armenians, Pan-Turkic idealists, reactionary ex-Tsarist generals, by assorted non-Marxist socialists and syndicalists, and by the small British 'Dunsterforce' of General Lionel Dunsterville (1865–1946), which set out from Baghdad to protect Baku from the 'Germano-Turks'. The charismatic Dunsterville, a personal friend of Rudyard Kipling, was the original 'Stalky'. In his eyes, all Russians and pro-Russians, with the exception of the Bolsheviks, were regarded as friendly.[33]

In March 1917 Kerensky's Provisional Government in Petrograd, foreseeing regional autonomy, had set up a Special Transcaucasian Committee. But it also pursued the unpopular policy of keeping Russia in the war. Later in the year, therefore, the Special Committee was pushed aside by a so-called Transcaucasian Commissariat, based in Tbilisi, which contained Georgian, Armenian, and Azeri representatives, all seeking to distance themselves from Russian control. In December the Commissariat endorsed an Armistice with the Ottomans, and on 24 February 1918 it established its independence through the formation of a Transcaucasian Democratic Federative Republic (TDFR). Peace came shortly after with the Treaty of Brest-Litovsk, which ended formal hostilities both on Europe's Eastern Front and in the Caucasus. The Treaty handed various cities, including Batumi, to Ottoman control. It also prompted a peace conference at Trabzon, which was attended by a delegation from the TDFR. But it could not calm the havoc in Baku.

For the Bolsheviks of the *Bak-Sov*, with their government of dictatorial Commissars, wanted no truck with the TDFR, still less with growing Ottoman-Muslim influence. What they wanted was union with Soviet Russia, from which they were now cut off.[34] Yet developments were not moving in their favour, and in desperation, in March 1918, they unleashed a wave of 'Red Terror'. With the help of armed Armenian nationalists, they massacred over 10,000 Azeri Muslims as a prelude to the declaration of the Communist-run *Bak-Sov* Commune. The blood of the victims of those 'March Days' gave the impulse to what is now seen as Azerbaijan's own independence movement.

At the end of May 1918, however, the Transcaucasian Federation fell

apart, the interests of its three constituent countries proving incompatible. The Georgians and Armenians, being Christians, rejected
rapprochement with the Ottoman Empire, while the Azeris were in
dire need of Ottoman assistance to deal with the *Bak-Sov* Commune.
After Georgia and Armenia had split off, Azeri leaders, having
announced the formation of the Azerbaijani Democratic Republic
(ADR) on 28 May, moved from Tiflis to Yelizavetpol (Ganja), and laid
plans for an attack on Baku. A friendship treaty between the ADR and
the Ottomans paved the way for the so-called Army of Islam, which
was commanded by Nuri Pasha and formed at Ganja by the merger of
two professional Ottoman divisions, the local Muslim Corps and Dagestan volunteers.

One thing was shared by all warring parties, not least the British
and Americans: the hope of capturing Baku's oil.[35] The Ottomans plot-
ted to take over a strip of southern Georgia to build a railway line for
oil export; the Azeris had to stick with the Ottomans, because Batumi,
the new railway's intended terminal, was in Ottoman hands. The Baku
Bolsheviks were promising their masters in Moscow that the oil could
be permanently secured if greater assistance were given. The Soviet
government even offered a deal to Germany whereby 25 per cent of
Baku's oil would go to Germany in return for help in winning it. But
the Bolshevik camp was riven with factions. The comrades in Baku
begged Stalin, now their Commissar in Tsaritsyn, for food and troops.
When he refused, they protested in vain to Lenin in person.

The battle for Baku was shaping up into a three-sided contest. Bolshevik units left Baku to skirmish in the direction of Ganja, burning
Muslim villages as they went. The Army of Islam counterattacked.
Dunsterforce was moving up through northern Persia towards the Caspian port of Anzeli. The British, who had set out from Baghdad before
the rise of independent Azerbaijan, knew how fast things were changing. But no one foresaw the next surprise.

On 26 July the *Bak-Sov* was overthrown by a coup mounted by an
assortment of Social Revolutionaries, Mensheviks, and Armenians. At
stake was whether or not to appeal for British assistance. The Bolsheviks, never in complete control, lost the argument and resigned. Their
successors set up a regime called the 'Central Caspian Dictatorship'.
The leadership was new, but the forces at their disposal under General
Dukacheev were unchanged. They consisted of 6,000 infantry in the
so-called Baku Battalions, mainly Armenian: a Cossack contingent,
and an artillery park of forty guns. Unfortunately, the Bolshevik

Commissars, fearful of arrest, had decamped, taking the city's main arsenal with them.

The departure of the Bolsheviks removed the last barrier to inter-religious and inter-ethnic strife. The atheist Bolsheviks, ruthless and repressive, had nonetheless kept religious conflicts to a minimum. But now the Army of Islam was out to avenge the victims of the March Days. And the Armenians were not short of Christian militants. In this way, the last battle on the Great War's Caucasus Front may also be regarded as the first salvo in the long-running Azeri-Armenian struggle.

The Army of Islam took up positions on the ridge overlooking Baku four days after the Central Caspian Dictatorship was formed. Yet it made no haste to unleash a decisive attack, thereby creating a lull during which the first British troop-carrying ships sailed into the bay from Persia. Dunsterforce, which was in place by late August, increased the firepower of the defenders – a battery of field artillery, a machine-gun section, three armoured cars, and two Martinsyde reconnaissance planes – but added only 1,000 men to their overall strength: two British infantry battalions from the Warwicks and North Staffordshires, and an assortment of Indians, Australians, and New Zealanders. It spent two to three weeks strengthening fortifications and training local irregulars. The RAF single-seater biplanes, nicknamed 'Elephants', circled the city constantly.

The fall of Baku occurred in two stages. One mass attack on 13 August was halted amidst heavy losses. A second during the following night brought the Army of Islam into the city centre. Having lost about two hundred of his officers and men (whose graves now lie in the Fexri Xijabani Cemetery), General Dunsterville sounded the retreat. The remnants of his force scrambled onto their boats, and sailed for whence they came – Persia.[36]

The local Armenian population, however, could not escape. Panic-stricken and driven into the port area, they were set on by bands of Muslim soldiery who had been given the traditional two days' licence for rape and pillage. By the time Ottoman regulars restored order, between 10,000 and 20,000 Armenians lay dead. The 'September Days' had repaid the 'March Days' amply.

The fall of Baku also sealed the fate of the fugitive Bolshevik Commissars. They had never reached their intended destination of Bolshevik-held Astrakhan. Instead, their ship was commandeered by hostile elements, and they were handed over to the mercy of Russian 'Whites' at Port-Petrovsk. From there they were sent as prisoners back across the Caspian to Krasnovodsk, where all but one were sentenced to death on the orders of an anti-Bolshevik Committee. On 20 September the 'Twenty-Six' were lined up on a railway embankment outside Krasnovodsk and shot. Their deaths provided the impulse to a favourite legend of Bolshevik propaganda, which blamed a British officer, Captain Teague-Jones, for the massacre.[37]

Only one item of Bolshevik decision-making from 1918 stayed in place. In July, when the Armenian National Council in Nagorno-Karabakh declared its autonomy and its wish to join Armenia, the Bolsheviks backed it. The decision was agreed by both the *Bak-Sov* and Stalin, in his other role as Soviet Commissar for Nationalities. For the moment, during the heyday of the ADR, it could not be implemented, but would have lasting consequences.[38]

On paper, the Azerbaijani Democratic Republic, which moved its capital to Baku in late September 1918, was one of the most liberal and progressive states on earth. It claimed to be the first democratic republic in the Muslim world; it was dedicated to universal education; and in matters such as women's suffrage it was well in advance of Britain or the United States. It hosted a full range of political parties, encouraged ethnic reconciliation, held early parliamentary elections, and published a constitution. The parliament met in December, confirming the first constitutional government. The prime minister in 1918–19, a lawyer and former member of Russia's state Duma, was Fatali Khan Khoyski (1875–1920).[39]

Khoyski's government made strenuous efforts to gain international recognition. It remained neutral between 'Reds' and 'Whites' in the Russian Civil War, and sent a delegation to the Paris Peace Conference, where, in January 1920, it was belatedly recognized de facto by the Allied powers. It was granted de jure status by several fellow post-Russian states such as Poland, Ukraine, and Finland. But Persia stalled at the name of Azerbaijan. To calm Persian objections, the ADR called itself 'Caucasus Azerbaijan' on the international stage.[40]

Nonetheless, despite achievements especially in the educational field, where it launched the University of Baku and founded many schools, the ADR struggled to keep afloat throughout the twenty-three months of its existence. Its tiny political elite, many educated in Moscow or St Petersburg, were separated by a cultural chasm from the devout and often illiterate masses, and 'the idea of an Azerbaijani nation-state did not take root'.[41] Territorial disputes persisted with Armenia over Nagorno-Karabakh and Nakchivan, and with Georgia over Balakan and Zaqatela. The oil trade, which had stalled, could not be properly restarted. And violent social unrest broke out, notably in the southern city of Lankaran. Worst of all, two major powers, Britain and Russia, could not keep their imperialist fingers out of the pie.

Less than two months after General Dunsterville's hasty retreat, a much larger British force of some 5,000 troops from the Indian Army landed in Baku under the command of Lieutenant-General William Thomson. It was sent after the Armistice of Mudros that had ended hostilities between the British and Ottoman Empires in Mesopotamia, and which stipulated, among other things, that Ottoman units within the Army of Islam should leave Baku. General Thomson acted as if the ADR wasn't there, neither fighting it nor supporting it. He pulled down the Azerbaijani flag, raised the Union Jack, appointed himself Military Governor, and declared martial law. If one could have asked the British what they were doing, they would probably have replied that they were acting in trust for their wartime Russian allies. 'The Allies cannot return home,' General Thomson declared, 'without restoring order in Russia and [putting] her in a position to again take her proper place among the nations of the world.'[42] The general clearly thought that he was in Russia.

This second British expedition, apart from keeping the Bolsheviks out of Baku, was handed two specific objectives. Firstly, it sent detachments to bolster Azerbaijani forces in Nagorno-Karabakh, where the ADR's governor and Minister of Defence, Major-General Khosrov Sultanov, was hard pressed by the Armenian separatists. Secondly, it had orders to link up with his British comrades in Batumi in Georgia, thereby securing the Baku–Batumi railway line. General Cooke-Collis landed in Batumi a couple of weeks after General Thomson's arrival in Baku. Together they aimed to reboot and protect the oil trade until the Russian Civil War ended.

General Thomson's force – which rarely features in general accounts of the country's history – stayed in Baku from November 1918 to August 1919. During those months he made only unofficial contacts with the ADR, and watched with dismay as the 'Reds' steadily gained the upper hand in Russia's civil war. Trotsky's Red Armies were drawing ever closer to the Caucasus. Independent Armenia went to war against Turkey, and independent Georgia, run by Mensheviks, trod a precariously neutral line between Istanbul and Moscow. Furthermore, a strong Turkish national movement was emerging from the Ottoman ruins. Britain's isolated outpost in the Caucasus was becoming untenable. General Thomson's troops, badly needed in an unstable Iraq, duly returned to Mesopotamia.

As soon as the British turned their backs on Baku, the ADR came
under threat in the best Leninist style 'from without and from within'.
Unlike Georgia or Armenia, it was vulnerable to a seaborne invasion –
as the British had twice demonstrated – and Bolshevik strength in the
north Caspian area was recovering rapidly. In 1919 Red forces hung on
to Tsaritsyn, where Stalin was making his name, and reasserted control
over the lower Volga. Sergei Kirov suppressed a workers' revolt in
Astrakhan, the home of the Caspian Fleet, and the 'Whites' were
expelled from Port-Petrovsk (Makhachkala) on the coast of Dagestan.
A *dessant* or amphibious landing from that direction grew more and
more likely. Moscow repeatedly called on the ADR's leaders to co-
operate, implying retribution for non-compliance. Agitation, strikes,
and protests stirred up in Baku by the Azerbaijani Communist Party
further undermined the democratic leaders' resolve.

In the early months of 1920 the wider Bolshevik cause entered a
phase of excessive euphoria. Lenin convinced himself that the time had
come to spread the Revolution abroad and to topple the European
strongholds of capitalism. Bolshevik theorists had long argued that the
Revolution could not survive in backward Russia if not supported by
the workers of Europe's more advanced, industrial states; they always
assumed that the Red Army would march westward as soon as Russia
itself had been stabilized. Trotsky, the Commissar for War, aware of the
Red Army's shortcomings, had an alternative plan. 'The road to Berlin,'
he declared, 'lies through Calcutta.' His objections were overruled by
Lenin, however, and a million-strong 'Western Army' was ordered to
concentrate on the Berezina. The young Mikhail Tukhachevsky, the
Red Army's most brilliant commander, was earmarked to take charge.[43]
Before that, Trotsky had one other task for him to accomplish – the
conquest of Baku.

Tukhachevsky's operations in the Caspian in April 1920 were soon to
be overshadowed by the more sensational campaign that followed in
the west, but they were pursued with skill and success. Three elements
were involved: first, a political coup in Baku to disrupt the ADR's government; second, a land invasion of Azerbaijan by the XI Red Army
from the north; and third, a *dessant* to secure the oilfields. The plan
was finalized for 21 April.

The leaders of the ADR, alerted to the imminent attack, did not
measure up to the challenge. The few troops at their command were
mainly deployed on the Armenian border, and their passivity was compounded by an inability to stop the Communist plotters in their

midst. Neither Mirza Davud Huseynov (1894–1938), chairman of the Soviet Revolutionary Committee and the son-in-law of former prime minister Khoyski, nor his comrade, Nariman Narimanov (1870–1925), educated on a Taghiyev scholarship, were seen as dangerous. When Parliament met to debate whether to welcome the Red Army or not, it passed a nonsensical resolution favouring the 'full independence of Azerbaijan under Soviet power'. It was, states a neutral historian, 'an act of abdication'. The 'overthrow of the republic was amazingly easy.'[44]

The consequences flowed swiftly. Tukhachevsky arrived in Baku by armoured train on 28 April, unopposed. Government ministers were rounded up by the Cheka. Four million tons of oil were seized, and all the leading officials and company owners arrested. The re-established *Sovrevkom* (Soviet Revolutionary Committee) invited the 'workers' to sack the homes of the 'blood-sucking bourgeoisie'. During the previous period of Bolshevik rule, in 1918, private oil companies had merely been supervised by so-called Workers Councils; this time they were closed down. By 30 April 1920 the Azerbaijani Soviet Socialist Republic was in business.

One person who vividly recalled the Soviet takeover was Zuleykha Asadullayeva, born in 1914, the daughter of an oil baron, who had lived a comfortable life of servants and governesses in their home (now the Iraqi Embassy) on Samad Vurgun Street, and in their seaside house at Mardakan. The family spoke Russian, not Azeri, and the women did not wear a veil or chadar:

> I was 6 years old when the Red Army entered Baku. Few people knew that [it] was coming; everyone thought it would be the Turks . . . Its government leaders did not want everyone to panic. Parliament met for three days deliberating . . . Finally, they did [surrender] after receiving promises that the Bolsheviks would harm no-one . . . What poor judgement!
>
> I'll never forget the scene . . . My mother and father [Khalef Meymalov] stood in the dining room, looking out of the window . . . The streets were full of rough, dirty Red Army troops. My father turned sadly to my mother. 'We're finished,' he said.
>
> We organized to leave home immediately. At six o'clock that afternoon two coaches whisked us away to stay with a friend, and then, after a week, to our country place . . . Both my parents were arrested. My mother was eventually released, but Father was imprisoned for twelve months. [The Cheka] was executing 50 people every day . . . He was probably executed, too. We don't know what actually happened.[45]

The mother and children escaped with some delay after bribing Soviet officials. Robbed of their valuables at the frontier, they took refuge in Turkey. Zuleykha later emigrated to the United States. Her sister-in-law, Leyla, a Taghiyev, committed suicide. And her husband, Ali Asadullayev, ended up supporting the Russian Fascists.

Soviet rule in Azerbaijan lasted from April 1920 to December 1991 – a total of nearly seventy-two years. From the start it imposed a Russian-led, dictatorial system, but not direct incorporation into Soviet Russia. The outward form of state institutions passed through different stages, but the system's central feature, the so-called 'dictatorship of the prole-tariat', the subordination of all political and administrative bodies to the iron control of the ruling Communist Party – the Russian Social Democratic Labour Party (Bolsheviks) or 'RSDLP (b)' for short – did not change. Every decision regarding Azerbaijan was subject to orders coming from the Kremlin in Moscow.

After an initial period, when the Red Army was completing its conquest not only of Azerbaijan but also of neighbouring Armenia and Georgia, the Bolsheviks merged the three conquered countries in 1921 into the Soviet Federation of Transcaucasia. They exercised their control through the ruling party's *Kavbiuro* or Caucasian Bureau, where their key man was Joseph Stalin, the Commissar for National-ities. Stalin condemned all opponents to the federative scheme as 'nationalist deviationists', and suppressed them without mercy. Faced by continuing ethnic strife, one of his most urgent tasks was to enforce a series of territorial settlements. In Azerbaijan, Bolshevik planners carved out two territorial enclaves. One of them, Nakchivan in the south-west, which was surrounded by Armenian territory though largely inhabited by Azeris, remained under Azerbaijani control. But Karabakh/Artsakh, largely inhabited and run by Armenians, was set up as the Autonomous Soviet Republic of Nagorno-Karabakh, nominally attached not to Armenia but again to Azerbaijan. This mis-chievous arrangement ensured that tension between Armenia and Azerbaijan persisted, and that Moscow could act as the eternal arbiter between them.[46] Political name-changing was running riot. The auton-omous republic's capital, whose local names were Khankendi in Azeri and Vararakn in Armenian, was officially renamed 'Stepanakert' – in honour of Stepan Shumyan, one of the murdered Commissars.

By 1922, when Stalin succeeded Lenin as General Secretary of the Communist Party and most of the former Tsarist Empire had bowed to

Bolshevik rule, preparations could begin for launching the Soviet Union. Together with Soviet Russia, Soviet Ukraine, and Soviet Belarus, the Soviet Federation of Transcaucasia would be one of the USSR's four founding members.

For health reasons, the popular Russian lyrical poet Sergei Yesenin (1895–1925) lived for long spells in Baku in the early 1920s, together with his scandal-seeking wife, the American-born dancer, Isadora Duncan, eighteen years his senior. Whether from conviction or conformity, Yesenin wrote the propagandistic and officially promoted 'Ballad of the Twenty-Six':

> I recall how the British shot our men from Baku,
> Those twenty-six brave men and true . . .[47]

Newlyweds and schoolchildren in Baku were henceforth encouraged to rend the poem and to have their photographs taken beside the dead Commissars' grandiose memorial.

From the outset, according to popular sources, 'all the private oil companies were nationalized', and the country's oil industry passed under the control of the state-owned Soviet monopoly, AZNEFT. It comes as a surprise, therefore, to discover that several of the supposedly liquidated companies continued to function abroad for decades, and that some outlived the Soviet Union itself.

BAKU CONSOLIDATED OILFIELDS LTD (BCO), for example – of which I am the proud owner of a worthless share certificate – had operated since 1908 from registered offices at 48, Cannon Street, London EC4. It merged in 1919 with Russian Imperial Petrol Ltd, in response to the growing Bolshevik threat. BCO's investments in Baku were estimated at £85 million, far outpacing those of Rothschilds Bank with £25 million and Royal Dutch Shell with £20 million.

Thanks to political instability, Bolshevik decrees could not be enforced in Baku until the arrival of Tukhachevsky's XI Red Army. Even then, though the company's physical assets – the oilfields, the oil stores, the buildings, ships, and equipment – were seized, the company itself, and its huge financial capital, lay far beyond the Bolsheviks' reach. BCO was free to continue trading outside the USSR, and it never abandoned the struggle for compensation. The date of its dissolution, amazingly, was 21 August 1997. It outlasted Lenin, Stalin, Krushchev, Brezhnev, and even Gorbachev.

Branobel, too, enjoyed a similar post-Revolutionary afterlife. Founded in 1876, it was not dissolved until 1959 – a run of eighty-three

years compared to BCO's eighty-nine. Its Russian assets had been estimated in 1914 at 30 million roubles, and it was saved from looming
ruin by a deal clinched in early May 1920 between Ludwig Nobel
and J. R. Rockefeller Jnr, the owner of Standard Oil (New Jersey), who
reportedly bought out half the company. The seller was eager to offload
his shares before the Bolshevik axe fell; the buyer was keen to scoop
them up because he mistakenly counted on 'anti-imperialist' American
entrepreneurs being welcomed by the Bolsheviks. The residual Branobel firm, meanwhile, set out on a forty-year campaign to achieve
liquidation on favourable terms. It was finally closed down by its last
president, Ludwig Nobel's grandson, Nils Nobel-Oleinikov, in the age
of the sputniks.[48]

The repercussions of the Bolshevik seizure of Azerbaijan's oil passed
through several phases – some optimistic, some pessimistic. In April
1921, for example, the Anglo-Soviet Trade Agreement, the brainchild of
the British prime minister, David Lloyd George, aimed to end the block-
ade of Soviet Russia and to restore full relations. It coincided with the start
of Lenin's New Economic Policy (NEP), which shelved some of his
more extreme ideological doctrines, and was driven by the misconception that the Bolsheviks, if treated reasonably, would respond reasonably.
It was notable for being the first occasion when the Soviet government
was officially recognized by a major power.[49] Yet it could not have been
signed without a clause promising negotiations over Soviet Russia's
repayment of debts. One segment of those debts originated in loans
extended to the Tsarist government; another derived from the seizures
of British property, including nationalized oil assets. The Bolsheviks
were perfectly willing to talk, but not to repay a penny.

The history of Soviet debt negotiations, therefore, is one of intrigue,
and sheer bad faith; they led absolutely nowhere over nearly a dozen
years. As soon as they started, the Soviet negotiating team raised astronomic counterclaims for the alleged costs of so-called 'Allied
Intervention': that is, of Britain's support for its wartime allies, who
had been removed by the Bolsheviks. Complications also arose through
the adventures of American businessmen, such as Harry Ford Sinclair,
who before being jailed for corruption, was planning a unilateral deal
with Stalin, including large investments in Baku.[50] In 1923 Lord Curzon nearly brought talks to a halt by demanding the immediate release
of Father Budkiewicz, a jailed Catholic priest.[51] And in 1927, after the
Arcos Raid in London, where British police broke into the premises of
the All-Russian Co-operative Society, seeking evidence of subversion,

Anglo-Soviet diplomatic relations were suspended for two years.[52] In December 1932 a British MP was still trying to ascertain what, if anything, was going on:

> SIR WILLIAM DAVISON asked the Secretary of State for Foreign Affairs what action had been taken by HMG with regard to the confiscation without compensation, by the Russian Soviet Government, of the properties, tanks, plant and oil belonging to the British company known as 'Baku Consolidated Oil Ltd', of the estimated value of L 4,000,000.
>
> MR. EDEN. The circumstances under which the Anglo-Soviet debts and claims negotiations were terminated on 27 January last, have been explained to the House ... No further action has been taken.[53]

Soviet Azerbaijan remained part of the Soviet Transcaucasian Federation until 1936; and from then to 1991, as the Azerbaijan SSR, was one of the USSR's fifteen constituent republics. But it was not a free country. In the late 1930s it suffered terribly from Stalin's purges and the Great Terror, when some 80,000 Azeris, including Communist activists, were killed. To add insult to injury, the city of Ganja was renamed Kirovabad.

During the Second World War, Baku's oil once again became a great prize. Thanks to the Nazi–Soviet Pact, oil from Baku fuelled the Luftwaffe in the Battle of Britain, and the RAF came very close to bombing the Caspian oilfields. Then, in June 1941, Operation Barbarossa changed everything. In 1942–3 Baku was named as the Wehrmacht's principal target. Adolf Hitler's generals served him an iced birthday cake, which displayed a map of the Middle East; the central point, where the cake knife made its cut, was at Baku. After the Battle of Stalingrad, however, the danger passed, and the Germans' failure to capture the oilfields spelled disaster for them.

In August 1941, fearing the machinations of a pro-German Shah, Stalin had agreed to a joint Anglo-Soviet protectorate over Iran, which brought the Red Army into 'South Azerbaijan', and gave the Americans a route for ferrying vast amounts of military aid through the 'Persian Corridor'. In 1945–6 he declared a bogus People's Republic in Tabriz, anticipating annexation, but then decided against it, deferring perhaps to American pressure.[54]

Exactly at that time and place a young Soviet security officer from Nakhchivan, Geydar Aliyev (1923–2003), was winning his spurs in 'South Azerbaijan'. He was destined to become the head of Baku's KGB, the head of Azerbaijan's ruling Communist Party, and from 1969 to

1982 one of the very few Muslims, or ex-Muslims, ever to serve in the central Soviet Politburo. (At the time his Muslim identity was hidden or denied.) Much of his authorized biography, now on sale, is devoted to recriminations against President Gorbachev, who dismissed him.[55]

Those immediate post-war years also saw mass population transfers such as Stalin enforced elsewhere in the USSR. Some 100,000 Azeris or more were deported from Armenia to Azerbaijan, and similar numbers of Armenians from Azerbaijan to Armenia. The violence inevitably stoked the ethnic hatreds that would later erupt.

Despite economic mismanagement and intervals of horrific oppression, Soviet rule brought some progress. It introduced universal education for girls as well as boys; it recognized the Azeri language, which passed through phases of using the Arabic, Cyrillic, and Latin scripts; and it established a secular state. The Islamic authorities were cudgelled and cowed, but not decimated like the Orthodox clergy in Russia. A popular handbook from the 1960s presents a typically bland description:

> Azerbaydzhan, a country comprising eastern Transcaucasia and north-western Persia . . . mountainous in the north and south, with the Kura River lowland in the centre . . . There are rich deposits of oil, also iron, copper, lead and zinc . . . Area 33,400 square miles; population (1959) 3,698,000 (48 per cent urban), chiefly Turkic-speaking Azerbaydzanis (67 per cent), Russians (14 per cent) and Armenians (12 per cent). Azerbaydzhan has the third largest oil industry in the USSR, and also textile, engineering and food industries. There is cotton-growing, sericulture, horticulture and viniculture; sheep, buffalo and horses are raised; and old crafts (silk and carpets) are still practised. Principal towns: Baku (capital), Kirovabad, and Sumgait . . .[56]

The handbook fails to mention any of Stalin's numerous crimes. Today, visitors to Baku wonder why so many of the ubiquitous memorial tablets end with the unexplained date of 1938.

One man who must have followed Azerbaijan's progress with interest was Anastas Mikoyan (1895–1978). An Armenian by birth, he was one of Stalin's original associates, and thrived at the summit of Soviet politics for decades, serving in 1964–5 as Head of State. (His younger brother was the co-designer of the MiG fighter plane.) He himself was the supreme political escapologist. 'Mikoyan could walk across Red Square in a thunderstorm,' it was said, 'and dodge the raindrops.' Mysteriously, he was the sole Baku Commissar who had avoided execution, and in April 1920 he commanded Tukhachevsky's armoured train. As Foreign Trade Minister in the 1930s, he imported American ice cream to Russia; Stalin commented ominously: 'Anastas Ivanovich loves ice cream more than he loves Communism.' But he didn't touch him. He and Mikoyan used to drink a toast: 'To Hell with all those Russians.'[57]

In 1987, during Gorbachev's era of 'Glasnost', the frozen conflict in Nagorno-Karabakh re-erupted after seven decades. Crowds of demonstrators in Stepanakert demanded union with Armenia. The government in Baku tried to impose direct rule, but was confronted by a popular referendum that transformed the ASR of Nagorno-Karabakh into an independent but unrecognized republic supported by Armenia. Moscow fatally hesitated. Military conflict was inevitable.[58]

Some of the worst atrocities were perpetrated while the USSR was still intact and Gorbachev still in power. Scattered Armenian communities were again especially vulnerable. The 'Sumgait Pogrom' of February 1988 sparked further attacks elsewhere,[59] including the 'Pogrom of Kirovabad' in November and the 'Baku Pogrom' of January 1990, which preceded a wholesale Armenian exodus. At Kirovabad, Azerbaijani troops were photographed destroying Christian cemeteries, thereby incurring accusations of cultural 'cleansing'.[60]

The renewed ructions between Azerbaijanis and Armenians showed that the Soviet system was breaking down. And, just as Azerbaijan's first republic came about through the collapse of Tsarist Russia, so the second independent republic came about through the collapse of the Soviet Union. No one was prepared. Tensions rose steadily in 1989–90. A Popular Front appeared, demanding national independence, even unification with the Azeris of Iran. Conditions in Nagorno-Karabakh went from bad to worse. President Gorbachev, whose grasp of nationality questions was feeble, declared a state of emergency, sent in the Red Army, and watched as a massacre of protesters ensued on 19 January 1990. He later admitted to 'Black January' being his 'worst mistake'.

Independence was declared in October 1991 while the USSR was theoretically intact. Azerbaijan's affairs thereon descended into chaos. The first president, in 1991–2, Ayaz Mutalibov, former General Secretary of the local Communist Party, tried to assume dictatorial powers without genuine support. He presided over the outbreak of open war with Armenia. The second president, in 1992–3, Abulfaz Elchibey, former dissident and leader of the Popular Front, mobilized democratic support but then mishandled both the economy and the Armenian war. Confronted by rebellious troops, he fled.

The military operations of 1991–4 can only be described as a 'dirty war'. The Armenian side was bolstered by Russian tanks, artillery, and mercenaries. Azerbaijani forces were stiffened by Afghan and Chechen mujahadin. Both sides resorted to Yugoslav-style ethnic cleansing. The Azeri population disappeared from Karabakh, and the Armenians from large areas of Azerbaijan. Villages were torched. Land mines were sown. Tens of thousands were killed, and half a million refugees took flight. But the Armenians prevailed on the ground. By the ceasefire of May 1994, they controlled all of Nagorno-Karabakh, together with seven contiguous districts.[61]

Throughout those years Geydar Aliyev had been lying low, and he now timed his comeback to perfection. Since 1988 he had been running his home district of Nakhchivan. He returned to Baku at President Elchibey's invitation, accepted the post of parliamentary speaker, then coolly announced, with constitutional precision, that the absent Elchibey had forfeited his office. His masterly manoeuvre must have filled his KGB cronies with pride, and was backed by a national referendum. He won 99 per cent of the vote in a stage-managed presidential election in 1993. Over the next decade he forged everything that Azerbaijan has since achieved, including the 'Deal of the Century', which restarted the country's oil industry.

Geydar Aliyev's official biography takes great pride in his meteoric career in the KGB. Pictures of his humble origins in Nakhchivan are contrasted with photos of him dressed as a KGB captain, colonel, and finally major-general. Presidential shots show him talking to the Pope, to George Bush Jnr, and to Vladimir Putin. The closing passage, therefore, is somewhat unexpected for a man who had served atheist Communism for fifty years. 'He died convinced that he had fulfilled his mission predestined by Allah,' it says, and 'He liked to read in his spare moments these lines by [the Soviet Azeri poet] Samad Vurgun':

> Death won't have reason to rejoice! It won't
> Capture those who loved their Native Land.
> And those who lived with love and died beloved
> Will be revered by custom and the world.[62]

Geydar Aliyev's son, Ilham (b. 1961), once a gambler, playboy, and security official, stepped smoothly into his father's shoes, burnishing the ubiquitous cult of Geydar's personality. Ilham's own cult soon followed. His critics maintain that he lives lavishly from secret foreign bank accounts, hides property under his infant son's name, and holds court in a Dubai castle. It is difficult to ascertain whether any of this is true or not.

In Karabakh-Artsakh nothing much has changed since the ceasefire of 1994, least of all the recriminations. Azerbaijan claims that 20 per cent of its territory is 'occupied', demanding unconditional Armenian withdrawal and the right of return for refugees. It has obtained four unenforced United Nations resolutions. The breakaway republic of Nagorno-Karabakh continues to function, and the United States, pressurized by a vociferous Armenian lobby, recommends a referendum. Representatives occasionally meet under the auspices of the Organization for Security and Co-operation in Europe (OSCE) 'Minsk Group' and its 'Prague Process', where hope, trust, and progress no more apply than in nearly thirty years of Israeli–Palestinian stalemate.

The glittering waterfront at Baku, therefore, does not tell half the story. Azerbaijan is a country whose remarkable economic success cohabits with dismal politics. The continuing and formally unended state of war with Armenia fuels arguments for maintaining 'a strong hand' at the helm, and a repressive regime faces few challenges either from its own citizens or from foreign countries that benefit from its oil. The admirable Professor Hasanli seems very much like a voice crying in the wilderness.

Azerbaijan does not shrink from using raw cash to safeguard its interests and improve its image. It pays the British government to hire SAS troops for secret security training.[63] It shells out large sums to screen sugary publicity slots on CNN. It spent a fortune hosting the Eurovision Song Contest in 2012, and has bought its way into top-level football, where the players of Atletico Madrid now run around incongruously in shirts emblazoned with the words 'Land of Fire'.[64]

Even so, Azerbaijan does not sit easily with its newfound identity. A virulent form of narrow nationalism has replaced Marxism-Leninism as the official ideology, and encourages a range of excesses, from ethnic homogenization to historical fantasies. People and places have been repeatedly forced to change their names over the last century, and the trend continues.[65] One recent proposal in Parliament is that the former Russification of surnames should be reversed by dropping endings such as -ev and -ov; President Aliyev would become 'President Ali'.[66] Another proposal promotes the idea that the state's name should be changed to 'Northern Azerbaijan', implying that 'Southern Azerbaijan' is illegally occupied by Iran.[67]

Given these preoccupations, the regime has little inclination to invest in badly needed social development. Endemic poverty has been reduced, especially in rural districts, and prestige projects abound, but there is limited substance behind the window-dressing. The boutiques are as empty as the National Literature Museum. Dreary, decaying, Soviet-era housing blocks dominate the outer suburbs, and beggars drift in the backstreets. Affluent Azeris go to Iran for medical treatment, while the refugee camps remain full. The gap between rich and poor is widening.

Above all, in the international arena, Azerbaijan's room for man-oeuvre is very restricted.[68] It fears that the ayatollahs of Iran are plotting to undermine its traditionally secular stance, and locks up Azeri clerics who travel for religious study to Qum or Isfahan. Within the Caucasus region, it displays only minimal solidarity with its Armenian and Georgian neighbours.[69] Relations with Turkey are less warm than Geydar Aliyev once hoped, speaking as he did of 'One nation, two states'. Economic ties thrive, but the long-projected Turkic Council struggled to take off, and a Mutual Assistance Pact was only signed in 2010. Moscow continues to pull many strings, perpetuating the stalemate over Nagorno-Karabakh. It continues to support Armenia, while happily selling arms to Azerbaijan. Overall, Aliyev's regime most nearly resembles the fictional 'Tazbekistan' as satirized in the comedy show *Ambassadors*.[70] For a high-income state, Azerbaijan's performance in the Good Country Index measuring 'contributions to the common good of humanity' is abysmal: it ranks 122nd out of 125, trailing all except Iraq, Vietnam, and Libya.[71]

Vladimir Putin's visit to Baku in August 2013 was described as a 'working session'. Flanked by Foreign Minister Sergei Lavrov, and the presidents of Rosneft and Lukoil, he came with two warships of Russia's Caspian Fleet, which is presently being revamped. At the end of a five-hour pow-wow with President Aliyev, an agreement for sharing pipelines was announced. Putin said that Russia's good offices were always available. Aliyev said that Russian weapons were the 'best in the world'.[72] Two years later, Russian cruise missiles were fired from the Caspian into distant Syria.

For all we know, President Putin may also have advised on electoral management. Immediately before the presidential election, the Azerbaijani Electoral Commission inadvertently published the results, giving President Aliyev 74.8 per cent of the vote. He eventually claimed victory with 84.6 per cent, against 5.5 per cent for the luckless Hasanli. OSCE observers declared the elections 'seriously flawed'.[73]

By that time, news had arrived that the president of the United States, after three decades of silence between the leaders of both countries, had spoken to Iran's new president by telephone. A momentous breakthrough was hailed. In August 2016 Vladimir Putin returned to Baku for a trilateral meeting with the presidents of both Azerbaijan and Iran.[74] The international weathervane was shifting. The wind in Baku had veered once again.

On the eve of my departure, an invitation reached me to attend Queen Elizabeth II's birthday party: a regular event in the calendar of all British embassies abroad but not for wandering historians. The venue was the grand ballroom of the Fairmont Hotel in the Flame Towers complex. A thousand guests descended from their limousines, and passed through the security gate to be presented to the British ambassador, together with Lady Penelope and the scarlet-liveried military attaché in attendance.

We then proceeded into a glittering hall bedecked with red, white, and blue balloons, and fitted out with two monster screens. Huge placards publicized the theme: 'This is GREAT Britain'. I walked in with the British-Indian barrister I met a few days previously.

'What will happen to the word "Great",' he asked, 'if the Scottish referendum is lost?'

The choir of the British School breaks into the British and Azerbaijani anthems. Speeches are drowned out as hungry hordes besiege the food tables. Loudspeakers blast out 'Crown Imperial' and Handel's 'Zadok the Priest', and the screens light up with a film of the Queen's coronation in 1953.

'I watched all that live,' I tell a nearby US Marine colonel for small talk, 'the first TV I ever saw.'

The leading guests circulate. The Israeli ambassador, Mr Harpaz, squeezes the flesh.

'Have you been to my country?' he asks hopefully.

Israel and Azerbaijan are surprisingly close; they both fear Iran. The Fairmont's manager, Mr Ellis, has a word.

'We do birthday parties like this all the time,' he begins, 'especially for one-year-old boys.'

'Circumcision parties,' a voice explains. 'Exactly, 220 dollars a head.'

A Yorkshireman in a kilt bends my ear. He is manager of the company that is filling Baku with London cabs.

'It was the President's idea,' he says, 'but we undercut the locals: 16 manat for the airport trip instead of 30.'

He has a thousand vehicles on the road, and is aiming for three thousand. They are all painted purple.

'The locals call them *badimçan*,' he tells us, 'aubergines'.

A Russian admiral in an ill-fitting jacket greets the American colonel with a demonstrative show of false jollity. He leaves, so I ask the American, 'Is it all hunky-dory with the Ruskies nowadays?'

'We try our best,' he grins, 'but they don't think like us.'

One can say that again.

Not everyone thinks of the former Soviet republics as victims of imperialism and colonialism, but that is exactly what they are. They were all conquered, usually twice – once by the Tsars and then by the Bolsheviks. They were overrun by foreign armies, officials, and settlers; their elites were forced to collaborate; their culture was diminished, and their economies were constructed in the interests of a foreign power.[75] So they are all now struggling with this blighted legacy.

A whiff of that legacy engulfed me as I left Azerbaijan. I passed through two control points at the airport, but very nearly fell at the third hurdle. The female passport officer sat in her glass cage wearing a smart green uniform, long permed golden curls, a peaked cap, and an array of medals on an ample bosom. She checked my passport, told me to look at the camera, and was handing back my documents when her eye caught sight of the number 22. Her face contorted in a mixture of horror and elation:

'You are leaving Azerbaijan early, sir. Why is that?'

'I don't think so. My flight tickets have always been for today, the 30th.'

'You arrived on the 22nd. Your visa is for nine days. Don't move.'

'No, I'm sorry; my plans haven't changed. My tickets were checked.'

She counted on her fingers, before calling over a colleague amidst looks of deep concern. People with nine-day visas were supposed to leave after nine days. I could not reveal that I had actually arrived on the 21st. I bit my lip.

'You are leaving early,' she resumed. 'It's not permitted. You leave tomorrow. Don't move.'

'I don't understand. I'm the ambassador's guest.'

'The ambassador must know: your departure date is the 31st, not the 30th.'

Her eyes narrowed. Her fingers tapped the counter. What she saw on the screen did not match the stamp in my passport. Either the computer had been hacked or the stamp had been forged. Or both. In any case, who, but a spy, or an Armenian, might want to leave early? And would this early-leaver cause trouble? It was a close call.

'This time you can go,' she said severely. 'But next time, it's not permitted!'

# 3

# Al-Imarat

*Mountains of Money and Gulfs of Misunderstanding*

The trip from Azerbaijan to the United Arab Emirates (UAE) involves no more than a hop towards Teheran, a skip across the mountains and deserts of Iran, and a jump over the Persian Gulf. Direct flights scheduled by Azerbaijani Air or by Emirates Airlines cover the space in less than three hours. The direction is south-south-east, and destinations are either Abu Dhabi or Dubai. In a thousand miles one is transported from the Turkic to the Arab world, from the realm of Shia Islam to that of the Sunnis.*

During the flight, my attention was drawn to the extraordinary importance that the Emirati government extends to higher education, and in particular to educating foreign students. An in-flight magazine sings the praises of Abu Dhabi's universities. 'The diverse student life in Abu Dhabi,' it purrs, 'is in a class of its own.'[1] Five institutions are listed, most of them offshoots of Western ones:

University of Abu Dhabi: Aviation Science, Civil Aviation, Architecture
Paris-Sorbonne Abu Dhabi University: Languages, Marketing, Economics
New York Film Academy, Abu Dhabi: Short Film Courses, Acting
Alliance Française, Abu Dhabi: French Language at all levels
New York University, Abu Dhabi: Liberal Arts, Social Sciences, Humanities.

But Abu Dhabi is only one of seven Emirates, in which a hundred further universities flourish.[2] The strategy is not hard to fathom. Prestigious foreign sponsors are persuaded to set up an overseas campus, and fee-paying students are then recruited from around the world to work for

* The Islamic world has been divided since the first century of Islam between Sunnis and Shias. Both branches claim to be the descendants of the Prophet Mohammed: legitimacy is the fundamental point at issue rather than doctrine. The Sunnis are the majority; the Shias, led numerically by Iran, are the minority.

degrees that promise to give access to the 'global workforce'. Tuition in English, a 'multinational milieu', competitive prices, and 'tailor-made, innovative courses' are all laid out before them.

As you descend to land in Dubai after sunset, the flares of offshore oil rigs flicker over the waters of the Gulf. The watchers at the planes' windows have been tipped off to look for something else, too. And as the plane banks on its approach, a sharp spike appears far below, illuminated in green and gold. As we overfly Dubai City, manoeuvring to land from the inland side, the *Burj Khalifa* or Sheikh Khalifa's Tower, the world's tallest building, is still far below; then, as we land, it stands to one side, soaring far above us. Yet another sight makes even more of an impression. As the plane makes its pass over the airport, it descends through the glare of city lights before plunging again into total darkness. For three or four minutes, making its turn, it moves over a silent void: neither a lamp nor a road disturbs the brutal blackout. The desert below us is a vast expanse of emptiness right beside the narrow lighted strip of civilization. In the Gulf, the desert is never far away.

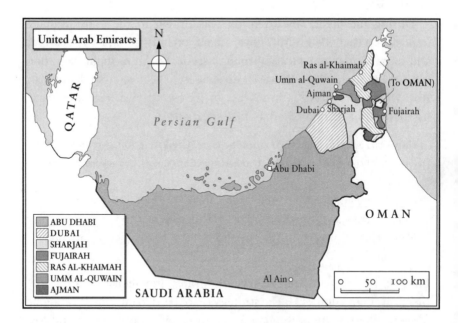

The Terminal Building at Dubai International is cavernous, marble-floored, and puzzling. There are two separate arrival halls, Hall A filled with a heaving mass of weary men, and Hall B with orderly lines of both men and women, mainly Europeans, who move steadily towards the long line of glass immigration booths. I am waved into the second hall with no questions asked. The bearded passport officer, dressed in immaculately ironed robes and pure-white *ghotra*, greets me in Arabic. I present a letter of invitation, and receive a visa stamp on the spot. None of the nonsense inflicted in Baku.

Expecting to be met by a driver, I pass out through the revolving exit doors, only to be hit by a blast of roasting air and a crowd of humanity pushing and shoving amidst piles of bags, cases, baskets, and trunks. I retreat into the air-conditioned zone, where the driver finds me. This country is made up of compartments, mainly invisible, and you have to know where you belong. 'Welcome to the Emirates!' the driver says, adding quizzically, 'Why did you go outside?'

A night drive to the hotel takes us out of Dubai City into the surrounding desert. The limousine speeds past signs to 'International City' and 'Academic City'. The former is 'a low-cost housing project'. Holding his nose, the driver says: 'They suffer from the sewage plant.' Academic City, still incomplete, is destined to be a 'super campus' for a score of foreign academic partners, including the American University, the British University, and the Mahatma Gandhi University.

'Soon,' the driver says, 'there'll be 40,000 students there.'

The moon and the stars shine brightly. The sand blows across the empty road. We pass police posts that look like frontier checkpoints. On the horizon, a line of fast-moving lights appears, rhythmically rising and falling.

'What's that?' I ask.

'Camel-racing,' says the driver. 'They train in the cool of the night.'

My luxury hotel is built like an oasis. The central glass-covered foyer contains full-size palm trees and high-spewing fountains, around which twenty storeys of bedrooms and conference halls are laid out in a circle. The Arab guests congregate inside on easy chairs, sipping coffee and enjoying the cool of the fountains; the westerners lounge outside in the stifling heat beside a string of swimming pools. The Arabs are covered from head to foot, the men in white, the women, two steps behind them, in black. The westerners seem to possess nothing between business suits and beachwear, wandering through the lobby barechested in Bermuda shorts, or in bikinis and flip-flops. The hosts pretend not to notice.

Arab headdress is a statement not just of fashion but of identity. The male *keffiyeh* or *ghotra*, a headscarf, is worn over a white *taqiyah* or skull-cap and held in place by a black *agal* or quoit. Emiratis and Saudis prefer scarves in red-and-white check, though some keep to pure white. Palestinians prefer black-and-white check, and Jordanians often sport tassels. For women, the *hijab*, or 'screen', which covers head and chest but leaves faces fully visible, is obligatory and matches their full-length black *abayah* or gown. Only a small minority of Emirati women wear the Saudi-style *niqab* or 'face mask'.

The food in the hotel restaurant reflects the variegated make-up of its guests and personnel. The buffet, divided into Middle Eastern, Euro-American, Indian, Far Eastern, and African sections, groans with worldwide delicacies. The waiters and managers display similar variety. The smiling, sari-clad beauty who shows me to my seat is a Filipina. The managerial trainee is a young woman from Glasgow. Over the next few days I am served in turn by an Afghan, a Nepali, a Singhalese, a Sudanese, a Colombian, an Iranian, a Ukrainian, a Mongolian, a Malagasy, and a Mauritian, but never by two persons of the same nationality. Someone seems to be taking precautions against a backstairs mutiny.

The hotel's TV is dominated by international channels. On CNN I see another lavish educational advertisement, this time for the UAE's 'Higher Colleges of Technology'. Students carrying piles of books walk purposefully towards ultra-modern white and glass buildings. The HCT's self-description on its website pulls out all the stops:

> Founded in 1988 by Federal Decree, Higher Colleges ... [has] a well respected reputation for innovative learning. Over 18,000 students attend seventeen modern men's and women's campuses in Abu Dhabi, Al Ain, Dubai, Fujairah, Madinat Zayed, Ras al-Khaimah, Ruwais and Sharjah ... Students learn in a sophisticated e-learning environment that encourages independent and life-long learning.[3]

Separate campuses for men and women doesn't sound especially 'innovative'.

According to some sources, the name of Dubai is derived from an Arabic word connected with 'Locusts'. The posters proclaim 'SUN, SAND AND SHOPPING', and for my money there's far too much of all three. The midday sun blazes down without mercy, bringing insufferable summer temperatures between 40 and 50 degrees Celsius; the all-time high, in 2002, reached 52.2 Celsius or 126 Fahrenheit. The sand, for the most part, is not the gentle sort, on which you can sit or lie comfortably, but the hard and gritty variety that sticks in hair, mouth, ears, clothes, and shoes. And shopping is almost compulsory since the huge, air-conditioned malls offer unrivalled asylum from the outside heat. There is something grotesquely inappropriate about these himalayas of merchandise on sale in a supremely artificial setting. Both the goods and the swarming bargain-hunters are imported. International brands empty the pockets of the brainwashed and fill the coffers of the ruling sheikhs.

Up close, the *Burj Khalifa* is so big that no one can photograph it whole without sailing out to sea or hiring a helicopter. Some visitors love the stomach-churning lifts that travel to the top at 10 metres per second; others stick to the shopping malls. They walk endless marble floors, ride aimlessly on gleaming elevators, breathe in the recycled air, stare at stingrays and sharks in the aquarium behind the world's largest piece of acrylic, or (absurdly) head for the artificial ski-slope.[4] Whatever they do, they make a major contribution to global warming.

The most fashionable and expensive places to stay in Dubai are the Burj Al-Arab Hotel[5] and the Palm Island Resort. The former, which has its own helipad, claims to be 'the world's most luxurious'; the latter was dredged from the sea in 2001–6 in the form of palm fronds encircled by a breakwater.[6]

For those who can brave the heat, there are better sights to see. The Jumeirah Mosque, for example, now forty years old, is reputedly the most photographed object in Dubai, and one of the few mosques to welcome infidel visitors. Its pale, yellow-grey stone, its sturdy domes and slender minarets stand out against the azure sky, pleading for the shutter to click.[7] The nearby Roundhouse, guarded by an enormous flagpole, is where the assembled sheikhs determined on 2 December 1971 to form the UAE. There are bustling Iranian and Indian quarters. The Old Al-Fahidi Fort, once the home of the ruling dynasty but now the city museum, best illuminates the contrast between today and yesterday. Built in the eighteenth century from mud-baked bricks and coral stone, its crenallated walls and round towers are set off by an ancient two-masted, high-prowed dhow, which stands on a high pediment. Despite appearances, the 'old days' were not very long ago. Before the early 1960s, when the oil began to flow, scattered inhabitants lived in primitive conditions amidst the sands of the desert shore. Barely fifty years ago, there were no paved roads, no electricity, no fresh water, no secular schools, and no registrations of births and deaths in a population less than 5 per cent of that today. The Old Fort guarded the tiny harbour with antique cannon; graceful dhows plied the Gulf's blue waters; fishermen and pearl-divers huddled in reed cabins; and pirates abounded. Bedouin tribes from the interior rode past on their camels; the odd British warship dropped anchor, and the RAF maintained a string of sand-strips on the imperial air-route from Iraq to India.

North of Dubai, five smaller Emirates crowd the triangular Arabian Peninsula, which stretches to the Strait of Hormuz, the 'pinchpoint' of Gulf shipping through which 20 per cent of the world's oil passes. (The mountainous tip of the Peninsula, overlooking the Straits, is an enclave belonging to Oman, the UAE's eastern neighbour.) Sharjah has a reputation of religious conservatism. Ajman, an enclosure within Sharjah, is the smallest of the Emirates. Umm al-Quwain, further north, is the least populous, but houses a major tourist attraction, the Dreamland Aquapark. Ras Al-Khaimah, meaning 'Top of the Tent', has valuable iron mines.[8] Mountainous Al-Fujairah, home of the Sharqiyin tribe, lies on the east coast, on the Gulf of Oman.

The Emirate of Sharjah, or Al-Shariqa, offers a pleasant contrast to Dubai; it is less busy, less commercial, less flashy, and has a special ethos of its own. Indeed, since Sharjah City is no more than a short taxi ride from Dubai International, it provides a convenient refuge. At the very first roundabout within Sharjah, signs point to Islamic institutions such as the SUPREME COUNCIL OF FAMILY AFFAIRS and the SHARJAH ISLAMIC BANK.

The Al-Hamra Hotel, a category or two below my previous abode, is modest and welcoming. (Its name, meaning 'The Red One', is the same as that of the Alhambra Palace in Granada.) Much of the entrance hall is taken up by a maroon-coloured Bedouin tent replete with carpets, curtains, and cushions. The reception desk is overshadowed by a large portrait of the 'Sheikh Dr Sultan', that is, Sultan bin Muhammad Al-Qasimi, the ruler of Sharjah. A notice in the lift says: PLEASE WEAR RESPECTABLE CLOTHES; bare knees and bare shoulders are banned. The swimming pool is only available for single-sex sessions: two for men, and one for women. Through a tiny window I spy a small public garden with lawns and flowerbeds: a minuscule local mosque, one palm tree, and the Al-Britannya Grocery Store. In my room, a large green arrow marked QIBLA fills half the dressing table. *Qibla* means 'Direction', and indicates the compass point for Mecca, to which the faithful pray five times each day according to the law of *Salat*.

The local newspaper prints exact prayer times. They differ from

emirate to emirate to reflect slight variations in the natural times of
sunrise and sunset:

|          | Fajr (Dawn) | Dhuhr (Noon) | Asr (p.m.) | Maghrib (Sunset) | Isha (Twilight) |
|----------|-------------|--------------|------------|------------------|-----------------|
| Abu Dhabi | 05.14 | 12.07 | 15.19 | 17.37 | 19.07 |
| Al-Ain | 05.09 | 12.02 | 15.14 | 17.32 | 19.02 |
| Dubai | 05.09 | 12.02 | 15.14 | 17.32 | 19.02 |
| Fujairah | 05.05 | 11.58 | 15.10 | 17.28 | 18.58 |
| R.A.K. | 05.05 | 11.58 | 15.10 | 17.28 | 18.58[9] |

Instructions about the prayer ritual are to hand. After the necessary
ablutions, the faithful 'Servant of God' faces Mecca and stands in silent
contemplation. A series of prescribed movements follows, each accompanied by the recital of a *rakat* or 'holy text': one, a declaration of
God's greatness, 'Allahu Akbar', with open palms raised beside the
head; two, an opening prayer spoken with folded arms; three, an invocation to Allah made with a deep bow and hands on knees; four, a
longer recital in upright stance; five, six, and seven, threefold kneeling
in the *sajdah* position, hands and forehead touching the floor; eight,
sitting back on one's heels; nine, turning one's head to the right (to
address the benevolent angels), and ten, to the left (to defy the evil
ones). Each performance takes five to ten minutes. Prayer occupies a
minimum of half an hour each day.

Breakfast at the Al-Hamra is not as expected. The television is
switched to a Russian channel for the benefit of a noisy group of tourists from Moscow; an Orthodox Patriarch is celebrating a saint's day
and denouncing *propaganda protiv Boga*, 'Propaganda against God'.
The clock shows that Moscow Time is the same as Gulf Time, under-
lining that what westerners call the 'Middle East' is perceived by
Russians as the 'Near South'. Another group consists of players and
officials from Kuwait's Al-Yarmouk football club. (Their team's name
recalls a mediaeval battle between Arab Muslims and Byzantine Christians.) They, like the Muscovites, ignore the rules and sport bare knees.
A breakfasting Saudi family, the mother draped in full *abayah* and
*burkha*, look the other way. A wall map describes the Gulf not as
Persian but as Arabic.

Sharjah is built abreast a creek that opens into the Gulf. Its pride and joy is the Corniche, a long promenade running along the creek for a couple of kilometres from the marina to the Al-Seef Mosque. Lined with trees, flowering shrubs, and shady benches, it is the perfect place to take the morning or evening air, and to watch the Emirati world stroll by. Saris and turbans mix with *abayahs* and *dishdashes* or *thawbs* – the standard, long-sleeved, ankle-length robe worn by almost all adult men. But there are no religious policemen checking up on the correct attire: this is not Saudi Arabia.

The morning's press can be comfortably perused from a tree-shaded bench on the Corniche. Two English-language newspapers are on sale – *Gulf News* and *The Gulf Today*: the former from Dubai, the latter published in Sharjah itself. Both offer wide foreign coverage, but both are palpably cautious in tone. Each gives the date in dual style – Sunday, January 19, 2014/Rabi Al-Awwal 17, 1435. Shia Iran is viewed with suspicion, as is the Arab Spring. Egypt's military regime, which has just suppressed the Muslim Brotherhood, is praised, and Israel is condemned. A front-page article in *The Gulf Today* reports congratulations sent by the UAE to 'the people of Egypt'.[10] *Gulf News* leads with 'No Ties with Israel before Peace Deal'.[11] The contradictions of American foreign policy are examined. Football matches played in the English Premier League by Arsenal (sponsored by Emirates Airline) and by Manchester City (sponsored by its rival, Etihad) claim acres of newsprint. And UAE government policies attract grovelling deference.

Almost nothing is said about the Syrian civil war, which by now has been in progress for almost three years. Silence surrounds the eccentric activities of the UAE's neighbour, Qatar. But in the foreign as distinct from the local press, numerous references point to the clandestine involvement of several Gulf States, including the UAE, in support of groups fighting the Syrian government. This policy is driven partly by distaste for the Assad regime, partly by a sense of solidarity with the Syrian Sunnis, and partly by the hope of restoring stability. And it seems to be spreading to the conflicts in Libya and Yemen. One suspects that it is having the opposite effects from those intended.[12]

By 11 a.m. the heat is driving everyone indoors, and the magnificent Museum of Islamic Civilization, which stands beside the Corniche, offers a cool and satisfying retreat. Opened in 2008, the museum is housed in a long elegant building of honeystone surmounted by a golden dome; it aims not only to present the achievements of worldwide Islamic culture, but also, and more ambitiously, to explain and illustrate the religion's principles in a restrained and non-triumphal manner. Bilingual captions in Arabic and well-translated English assist my steep learning curve. The word 'Islam', for example, means 'Submission to God'. A section devoted to the 'Five Pillars of Islam' claims to introduce 'the world's fastest growing religion'; it takes the visitor through the basic elements of Islamic practice – *shahadah* or 'belief in the One God and His Prophet', *salat* or 'fivefold daily prayer', *zakat* or 'compulsory alms-giving', *sawm* or 'fasting', and *Hajj* or 'Pilgrimage to Mecca'. It is accompanied by a display of stunningly beautiful handwritten copies of the Koran, and large-scale replicas of the world's greatest mosques, from Morocco to Jakarta. Another section presents an outline of mediaeval Islamic science and technology, which, as Western specialists now appreciate, greatly advanced astronomy, mathematics, chemistry, cartography, medicine, and agriculture. Visitors can interact with working models of astrolabes, irrigation screws, paperworks, distillation machines, and even an elaborate copper and glass distillery to produce rosewater. The hours tick happily by. Upstairs four more enormous galleries are laid out with vast displays of ceramics, carpets, textiles, metalware, weapons, and musical instruments. 'To him, who pursues the path of knowledge,' the Prophet said, 'Allah will show the road to Paradise.'

One leaves the Museum of Islamic Civilization with one's head filled by beautiful images and unanswered questions, but also noticing that almost all the non-religious objects relating to the 'Golden Age of Islamic Civilization' – comprising the five centuries after the Prophet's death – are replicas. For over a thousand years the followers of Islam seem to have passed the time either neglecting or destroying their heritage.

Oil money is now pouring in to rescue the cultural sites that had been left to wrack and ruin. The old City Wall of Sharjah has been completely rebuilt, with gates and towers, to enclose a designated cultural district. Restoration work on the Emir's Old Fort proceeds in the middle of a street lined with skyscrapers.

The Museum of Calligraphy is one of the gems that benefits from the current renaissance. I had it all to myself, except for the guard-cum-curator who pressed me to sign the visitors' book. Calligraphy – literally 'beautiful writing' – is called *khatt* in Arabic, meaning 'design', and it gained importance through the ban on all forms of figurative art; mediaeval Islam suffered a heavy dose of what appears in the Christian tradition as *iconoclasm*, literally the 'smashing of images'. So creative and decorative impulses were channelled into the laborious copying of religious texts, principally of the Koran. There are two basic forms: 'angular' and 'cursive'. The former developed first, in the seventh century, in a style known as Kufic after the Iraqi city of Kufa. The latter, which came to the fore in the tenth century, comes in four major variants known as *thuluth*, *naskh*, *riq'ah*, and *muhaqqaq*. Important regional styles emerged in Persia, the Ottoman court, and western China. All are written on paper or parchment with a *qalam* or reed pen, and all have been adapted to writing on tiles, textiles, and coins. 'Calligraphy,' it has been said, 'is the flower of a man's soul.'

Fortunately, no great expertise is required to appreciate the beauty of Islamic calligraphy, whether the elegant severity of the Kufic style or the ornate ingenuity of the cursive varieties. One soon learns to recognize the *Basmala*, the four-word text of 'In the Name of Allah, the Most Gracious and Most Merciful', which can be fashioned into thousands of different inventive and evocative shapes. Calligraphy, moreover, is a living art; many of the museum's exhibits are by present-day artists working in all the world's continents.

Commercial calligraphers can be found in all the main souks and shopping centres, offering visitors beautiful souvenirs made to order. One of them is Amir Hossein Golshani in Dubai's Khan Murjan Souk. Another is the Iraqi artist Uday al-Araji, who advertises his wares and his philosophy on the internet: 'As Uday Araji defines Arabic calligraphy, it is a kind of fine art, including shapes, colors, space, golden ratio etc. [He] uses all the elements of the art to reach out to Visual Beauty, [and] is fluent in all kinds of Arabic calligraphy ... All [his] works are handmade ... on special paper.'[13]

Islamic banking is another subject that repays a little investigation. It is easily spurned abroad since Sharia law has been unfairly stereotyped as a barbaric code that merely encourages beheadings for apostasy or stoning to death for adultery. Yet, in the wake of the disgraceful record of many Western bankers, it is refreshing to find a financial system apparently based on ethical principles. Islamic banking shuns the concept of a free market; it rejects speculative finance, and opposes excessive interest. Instead, it promotes the concept of financial fairness, by which the strong are prevented from exploiting the weak, and where risk is shared between lenders and borrowers. The Sharjah Islamic Bank, founded in 1975 as Sharjah's National Bank, pioneered the sector in the Emirates.

Shopping in Sharjah is best done in the cool of the evening. Stallkeepers in the souks are delighted to fit out a lady tourist with an all-concealing black *abayah* or a gentleman with an all-white, full-length *dishdash*. Unlike the spoiled shopkeepers of the air-conditioned malls of Dubai, they have time to chat with their customers and to flatter them with personal attention. I was caught by one standing in the shade outside the Souk Al-Arsa and smoking a cigarette. He beckoned to me to come over, led me inside by the arm, and fussed and joked as he produced a selection of *dishdashes*, meticulously checking their size and length. For good measure, I even bought a red-and-white *keffiyeh*, together with the accompanying *agal* and *taqiyah* or skullcap. I presume that they are all made in China.

A gentle walk home along the Corniche is not to be missed. Dhows and motorboats compete on the creek. Couples come out to stroll, and children have not yet been sent to bed. The setting sun bathes the minarets of the Al-Seef Mosque in pink, before the lights are turned on and neon transforms it into a vivid mauve and green. The day ends with a solo swim in the hotel's rooftop, moonlit pool.

Abu Dhabi, 75 miles down the coast to the west of Dubai, and 100 miles from Sharjah, is both the capital of the UAE and much the largest of the Emirates. The preferred translation of its name comes out as 'Rich in Gazelles', perhaps because of an ancient watering hole. For several decades Abu Dhabi stayed in the shadows, while Dubai pioneered the strategy of using oil money to foster international partnerships, which in turn fuel innovation, expansion, and inward investment. The tempo was dramatic: as someone put it, 'two or three Manhattans in a quarter of the time'. In the first decade of the twenty-first century, the trading bloc operated by the Gulf Co-operation Council (GCC) attracted over $30 billion of inward investment.[14] But during the Great Recession of 2008 Dubai's wonder machine was nearly derailed: several government enterprises were facing unrepayable debts; and it was Abu Dhabi that rode to the rescue. The *Burj Khalifa* project, for example, originally the *Burj Dubai*, was bailed out on condition of the name change. The world press talked of 'Dubai's spectacular fall', more recently of its 'road to recovery'.[15] Dubai's Strategic Economic Plan was revised.[16]

Abu Dhabi, meanwhile, was embarking on its own vertiginous climb. Its oil reserves are estimated at 97.8 billion barrels – the equivalent of a century's production. Its airline, Etihad, founded in 2003, is fast chasing Dubai's older Emirates. The senior principality is now

moving into advanced defence manufacturing and nuclear energy production. Accounting at present for about 40 per cent of the UAE's
GDP, it will soon control a commanding share. The centrepiece of its
ambition is embodied in a planning document called *Abu Dhabi Vision
2030*, which, alongside forecasts of breathtaking economic growth,
envisages four colossal projects.[17] One of these, Khalifa Port, is already
entering the construction phase on a reclaimed offshore island.[18] The
second, the Khalifa Industrial Zone (KIZAD), spanning 417 square
kilometres of coastal land, is set to become one of the world's largest.[19]
The third, on Saadiyat Island,[20] is creating cultural partnerships with
the Guggenheim Museum in New York, the Louvre in Paris, and the
British Museum in London; and the fourth, Masdar City, due for com-
pletion in 2020–25, is rising in the desert beyond Abu Dhabi's airport.
Self-confidence on this scale is a rare commodity. The spectacular
Marina on Yas Island has hosted Formula 1 motor-racing since 2009.

Masdar City is described as an 'arcology project'. Arcology, it
appears, is a hybrid term uniting Architecture and Ecology in a concept
pioneered by the Italian visionary Paolo Soleri (1919–2013), who built
the experimental town of Arcosanti in the Paradise Valley of Arizona
in the 1970s.[21] Masdar City follows closely in Arcosanti's steps.
Designed by Norman Foster, it aims to create a self-sustaining urban
environment that will both overcome and exploit its hostile natural
surroundings. Sheltered from the desert winds by a perimeter wall,
cooled by a giant air-turbo system, which will lower street temperatures to 15–20 degrees Celsius, and powered by a field of 88,000 solar
panels, it will be home to scientific institutes, commercial companies,
and 50,000 comfortable people devoted to 'clean tech' and alternative
energy. There will be no cars, no skyscrapers, no urban sprawl, no car-
bon emissions, and no air pollution.[22]

Still more ambitious technological projects are sponsored by the
UAE government. They include a 'rainmaking mountain', four nuclear
power stations, and an unmanned mission to Mars, due to be achieved
by 2021.[23]

Abu Dhabi's proudest monument, however, is already built, and a
visit to the Sheikh Zayed Grand Mosque is essential to understand
both the intellectual climate that is driving development and the role of
so-called 'moderate Islam'. This splendid building, finished in 2008, is
a religious showpiece to outshine all the secular towers, malls, and
palaces put together. It proclaims that success is the product of God's
providence. Its proportions are grandiose; the nave floor is covered by

the world's largest seamless carpet. But the curvaceous lines of its minarets and courtyards are warm and elegant, and the interior's massed floral motifs have a fresh, childlike quality. Elevated on a bluff, and floodlit in a pale shade of green against the black night sky, it exudes mystery and spirituality. Yet it feels neither triumphant nor threatening. Non-believers are welcome. Visitors come and go, and even in this holy place, women wear the *abayah* and cover their heads, but do not hide their faces. They roll up with their friends and families, laugh, chatter, and scold their husbands, and drive out of the car park on their own.

The man to whom the Grand Mosque is dedicated, Sheikh Zayed bin Sultan Al-Nahyan (1918–2004), was the UAE's founding father. (*Sheikh*, meaning 'Elder', is the generic name of Bedouin chiefs, often used in place of the more formal *Emir* or 'Prince'; *Zayed* or *Zaid*, meaning 'Abundance', is a common first name; *bin Sultan*, meaning 'Son of Sultan', is the patronymic; and *Al-Nahyan* is the name of the clan that has ruled Abu Dhabi throughout modern times.) Born in the pre-modern era, Zayed was largely brought up in the desert among his Bedouin kinsmen. He had little formal education, and survived the assassinations both of his father, Sheikh Sultan of Abu Dhabi, and of his father's successor, Sheikh Saqr. Zayed lived in the shadow of an elder brother for decades, before succeeding to the throne in 1966, just as the oil boom began.

Sheikh Zayed's forty-year rule is remembered for three achievements: firstly, the creation of the UAE, after five years of tortuous manoeuvring with the British; secondly, the policy of 'turning the desert green' through oil-financed welfare and development projects; and thirdly, an unprecedented period of internal and external peace. Zayed was no liberal, but a devout Muslim with four wives, and an unchallenged despot. He once told *The New York Times*, when asked about prospects for a democratic parliament: 'Why introduce a system that engenders dissent and confrontation?' But he was a skilful conciliator, a generous benefactor, and an active proponent of regional stability. First elected UAE president by his fellow sheikhs in 1971, he held the position until his death.[24]

Unlike the Grand Mosque, the seven-star Emirates Palace Hotel in Abu Dhabi is uninhibitedly devoted to Mammon. For ordinary mortals, its jaw-dropping opulence is hard to comprehend. A top-floor suite overlooking the Gulf costs $11,000 per night; the restaurant lists a St Émilion red at $17,500 per bottle; and the hallway contains a 'Gold to

Go' machine, which dispenses miniature bullion bars at $5,000 a shot. Overhead, workmen patiently apply gold leaf to the ceiling around the Swarovski chandeliers, and tourists creep surreptitiously into the washrooms just to feast their eyes. The English footballer, David Beckham, stayed here while purchasing a villa on Palm Island; the rest of the properties reportedly sold out within a week.

Yet the Emirates Palace does not rest on its laurels. A permanent exhibition in the hotel's basement offers sensational displays of the planned Cultural Quarter on Saadiyat Island, replete with futuristic scale models of the forthcoming Zayed National Museum, the Guggenheim AD and the Louvre AD, all of which will be surrounded by seawater. The National Museum will soon be the centrepiece; it will consist of five stainless-steel towers in the shape of bees' wings – somewhat reminiscent of the Flame Towers in Baku – which will act as a natural 'thermal solar' cooling system. The design of the Guggenheim envisages a similar cluster of asymmetrical structures, this time in concrete, linked by massive tube-chutes in opaque glass. The Louvre complex will be made up of numerous houses and palm gardens all covered by a free-standing 'flying saucer' roof. This future, as conceived by *Vision 2030*, is scheduled to become reality in little more than a decade. 'When Man makes plans,' goes the Arab saying, 'God chuckles.'

The architectural daring of Abu Dhabi's vision has received critical acclaim, but the motives behind it have raised eyebrows. Some think it the product of lucre-fuelled vanity; others discern a passion for nation-building. Within living memory, the Emiratis and their forebears were desert nomads; they now have to be convinced that their civilizational space ride is more than a mirage. Similar projects are afoot in neighbouring Qatar, the world's richest state; and, in the view of *The New York Times*, the aim in both instances is 'to re-shape national identity', 'to re-vamp the Arabs' tarnished image', and 'to find a balance between modernisation and Islam'. 'Sheikh Khalifa and his government want to instill national pride into a new generation of Emiratis, while providing the tools, both intellectual and psychological, for living in a global society.'[25]

In its present mood, therefore, Abu Dhabi is more interested in the future than the past. The city's historical Fort is far less significant than Dubai's; and the modest Heritage Village, out on the Marina Spit, which aims to underline the differences between today and yesterday, is easily missed. Outside it, youths in traditional Arab dress lounge on the sea wall, dirtying their immaculate robes and cheering on their pals, who are putting powerboats through their paces in the harbour. One can sit on a nearby bench, gaze across the water to the show-off skyscrapers on Abu Dhabi's version of a Corniche, and reflect that a few decades ago this was just an empty beach.

A trip to the oasis of Al-Ain, 'The Eye' or 'The Spring', requires a two-hour drive along the empty, sand-blown road to the south of Abu Dhabi City. On the way one passes the perimeter fence of the Al-Dhafra Air Base, where the Emiratis' F16 fighter jets are based, and the Americans share facilities. Once an oasis claimed by Saudi Arabia, Al-Ain is now a substantial town hosting several universities, research centres, and manufacturing enterprises. But it is also a settlement with surprisingly ancient antiquities.

In the heat of the day, I am the sole visitor to the Hili Archaeological Park. The eager guide sets off on an exhausting tour of every single prehistoric mound, barrow, and burial chamber in sight. My Australian bush hat barely saves me from sunstroke. 'Mad dogs and Englishmen,' I mutter. Surprisingly, the Hili people lived here seven millennia ago. A stone lion in bas-relief on the Grand Tomb from 5000 BCE stirs the imagination, as do tales of prehistoric copper mines, of camel caravans crossing Arabia, and of the sea trade with Mesopotamia. The Park was a better choice for a visit than the adjacent Hili Fun City.

The central area of the oasis offers an extensive network of premediaeval irrigation works and some welcome shade. Over 100,000 date palms flourish thanks to the *falaj* system of water channels that flow from level to level over 3,000 acres. For the Bedouin, the taste of juicy dates and the gentle sound of clean running water is balm to the soul.

Yet the town's prize exhibit is undoubtedly the Al-Jahili Fort – a wonderful mixture of pure *Beau Geste* and vintage *Biggles*. Its baked beige walls are surrounded by a sea of dunes; the gateway opens onto a cobbled courtyard and a collection of low, white-washed buildings that house the local museum. It was once the regional governor's residence, and the headquarters of the Trucial Oman Scouts (see below). An elderly waiter – a relic of the British Empire like me – pours sweet Arabic coffee from the long spout of an engraved bronze jug.

'The TOS pilots,' he begins, 'used the fort as an air base. They would land their biplanes on the sand beside the walls and stride in here for a drink.'

My biggest surprise, however, came from poking my head round the door of a museum room devoted to the British writer and explorer, Sir Wilfred Thesiger. I knew a bit about Thesiger. Like me, he had been an alumnus of Magdalen College, Oxford, and I had read his classic *Arabian Sands*. I had always taken him for a Victorian, a wayward eccentric in the mould of Richard Burton or C. M. Doughty. A magnificent photograph of him filled a wall of the memorial room. Standing on a high rock, and dressed in Bedouin clothes, he carried a carbine, a tangle of cartridge belts, and a haughty smile. He was dirty, deeply sun-tanned, and thickly bearded. Beside him stood the two Bedouin boys who wandered with him for five years round the 'Empty Quarter'. Yet it was the date that surprised me. Having crossed Arabia on foot, Thesiger walked out of the desert into the Al-Ain oasis in 1959. His appearance, however, suggested 1859.

Returning to the coast, the lower road from Al-Ain leads through the oasis of Al-Wathba, the mecca of camel racing. This is the Newmarket of camel fanciers, and the site of the annual Sheikh Zayed Grand Prix Festival, where, for five days in January, some 10,000 camels compete for lavish prizes. In the off-season the resort is used for cycle racing and equestrian events.

To the non-initiated, the *Camelus dromedarius* is an ugly, ungainly, and smelly beast. Its face is adorned with three eyelids and incongruously long eyelashes; its back extends into a weird hump; it ruminates noisily like a cow, and farts with great potency; when provoked, it spits with venom;* its urine has the consistency of syrup; and, uniquely, it mates in a sitting position. But for the Bedouin it is a lifesaver: a beast of burden, an unrivalled means of desert transport, and a staple source of meat, milk, leather, hair, and dung fuel; and for the modern Emiratis, an embodiment of their heritage. They love it as many Europeans love horses. By racing them, they commune with their past. Moreover, despite its splayed feet and flailing legs, the camel can outsprint the average racehorse – and can maintain 25 mph for long distances. To be ridden, it requires a special saddle perched on the back of the hump; and jockeys have to be small and light, usually boys. They cling on precariously with their knees, and are prone to accidents: having twice as far to fall as a horse jockey, they often suffer severe injuries.

Gambling is forbidden in the Islamic tradition; it is the 'Fourteenth Greater Sin' and 'the handiwork of Satan'. Sharia law prescribes harsh penalties, including flogging. In the UAE there is no lottery, and there

---

* Camel spit does not consist of saliva, but of semi-digested food from its upper stomach.

are no betting shops. Fortunately, the Prophet ruled that placing bets on archery contests, horses, and camel races was permissible. 'Angels,' it is said, 'are present at camel-races.' Consequently, the racecourses are awash with cash. Top camels cost up to $500,000. Rich Emiratis vie to bet indecent sums, and salve their consciences through the Prophet's other injunction – to give generously to charity.

Yet angels rarely frequent the stables where boy-jockeys live and work. According to Human Rights Watch, cruelty and exploitation are rife. Most of the boys are unpaid captives, bought in India or Pakistan, and quietly trafficked without questions being asked. If maimed or overweight, they can be ruthlessly cast aside. In 2002 UAE law banned their importation and robot jockeys have been introduced as an alternative, but the old abuses continue. Anti-Slavery International has taken up the case of underage camel jockeys.[26]

Human rights organizations equally condemn the draconian laws against homosexuality, which in some instances is punishable by death.[27] Female Genital Mutilation flourishes in traditional tribal communities, where the federal prohibition of the practice is ignored.[28]

Al-Wathba Jail lies beyond the tourist trail, but its name was splashed round the world in 2011, when an Australian woman wrote of her maltreatment there. Yvonne Randall was incarcerated without trial, nominally for not paying her hotel bill. In her version, her bill was not paid because her employer had stolen her credit card when she tried to leave his employ.[29]

All of which seems incompatible with another attraction at the oasis, the Al-Wathba Wetland Reserve. Freshwater lakes are a great rarity in the Gulf countries, even more the concept of a refuge for flamingos. Nonetheless, Emiratis feel a strong bond with desert creatures. They particularly revere the wild oryx – the *Oryx leucoryx* or Arabian oryx – a magnificent tall-horned, white-coated antelope, which was once on the verge of extinction, and is now the state's official animal. It can go for months without drinking, and thirsty Bedouin believe that by following the sound of underground water, it will always lead them to a spring. They call it *al-Maha*. The Ancient Egyptians used it for sacrificial offerings; and Aristotle held it to explain the myth of the unicorn. It was hunted to the edge of extinction before the formation of the UAE, and has gradually been revived by the work of dedicated conservationists. The last four wild specimens were rounded up in 1968, and a breeding herd was established on one of Sheikh Zayed's private islands. Today its numbers are 500 and rising. It can best be seen either at the Al-Maha Reserve in Dubai, or at the Sir Bani Yas wildlife park. It is the 'species that came back from the dead'.

In view of the extreme climate and the absence of any substantial population, the history of the southern shore of the Persian Gulf makes only a meagre tale. It consists of the rise and fall of sheikhdoms large and small, of rivalries over trade and shipping, and of relations between local rulers and regional powers. In the nineteenth and early twentieth centuries the sheikhdoms were both obscure and inoffensive, occupying a remote coastal area between the Ottoman lands and the Kingdom of Oman. Ruled by Sunni Muslims, they feared Shia-ruled Persia across the Gulf, yet valued their independence from the Ottomans, whose domain stretched from Mesopotamia to the promontory of El Katr (Qatar). So their association with Britain at the start of the nineteenth century was based on mutual interest. The treaty of 1820, which created a loose political entity called the Trucial Coast – commonly known as the Pirate Coast – was nominally directed against marauding pirates, but aimed to preserve the status quo. The British sought to protect the approaches to India, and the sheikhs to gain shelter from external intrusions. The Treaty of Perpetual Maritime Peace of 1853 established British naval control over the Gulf, creating a Residency at Bushire (Bandar Bushehr) in Persia.[30] The Treaty of 1892, which created the more formal Trucial States, left the sheikhs in full control of internal affairs, while handing the management of foreign policy to Britain. The British Resident sought to act when necessary as mediator between the sheikhs, but had few forces at his disposal.[31]

All the ruling families have an ancient lineage, and all are descended from, or related to, wider clans or tribes. In popular usage the 'ten families' refers to the clans that have ruled the independent Arab states of the Gulf since their foundation. They are:

| | |
|---|---|
| the Al-Sabah of Kuwait, | the Al-Nuaimi in Ajman, |
| the Al-Khalifa of Bahrain, | the Al-Sharqui in Fujairah, |
| the Al-Thani of Qatar, | the Al-Nahyan in Abu Dhabi, |
| the Al-Maktoum in Dubai, | the Al-Said in Oman, and Zanzibar |
| the Al-Qasimi in Sharjaj | the Al-Mu'alla in Ras Al-Khaimah, Umm al-Quwain |

Both the Al-Nahyans and the Al-Maktoums are descended from the same Bedouin Bani Yas tribe from the Arabian interior. The former have ruled Abu Dhabi since 1761; the latter took hold of Dubai in 1833, when eight hundred Bani Yas tribesmen invaded the coast. The Al-Nuaimis of Ajman claim to be *Quarashi*, that is, direct descendants of the Prophet. The Al-Qasimi tribe are content with their descent from Imam Ali, the Prophet's son-in-law. One of their descendants, Sultan bin Muhammad Al-Qasimi, the present ruler of Sharjah, was portrayed in the reception of my hotel; another, Saud bin Saqr Al-Qasimi, is Emir of Ras al-Khaimah. Their forebears led the pirates of the Gulf in the eighteenth century, thereby coming into conflict with the Omanis, and later with the British. It was the naval war between these families and the British that was ended by the treaty of 1820.

Whether or not the Trucial States formed part of the British Empire is an open question. The British usually assumed that their protectorate in the Persian Gulf belonged to the imperial network, if only in associated fashion. The sheikhs probably assumed that they were Britain's partners but not its subjects. Yet neither the *Encyclopaedia Britannica*'s authoritative eleventh edition (1910–11) nor Uncle Norman's stamp album makes any reference to the Trucial States. The encyclopaedia treats the region under its voluminous entry on 'Arabia', where a map clearly marks it out as part of Oman. Only three places are named – Abu Dhabi, Sharja, and Birema (Al-Ain). Along the Pirate Coast the word 'Jewasimi' is printed, referring no doubt to the lands of the Al-Qasimi.[32] The encyclopaedia's article on Oman repeats the assertion that the Al-Katr promontory in the Ottoman province of El Hasa forms Oman's northern boundary.[33] One suspects that the editors' information was slightly out of date.

The economic potential of the region was recognized during the interwar period, but not exploited. In 1932 a purpose-built fortress was erected near Sharjah to protect the airstrip of British Imperial Airways; and a subsidiary of the Iraq Petroleum Company, the Petroleum Concessions Ltd (PCL), was set up to secure options on future development. All the concessions were signed with local rulers, greatly increasing their importance.[34] The Japanese invention of cultured pearls in the early twentieth century spelt disaster for the traditional pearling industry.

The Trucial States were not afflicted by military action during the Second World War, though normal trade was disrupted and acute shortages occurred. Those who were children at the time still remember the hardships:

My grandparents lived in Hamriyah near the sea. During [the war], ships stopped coming from countries like India, and people went hungry. My grandfather caught fish and my grandmother cut the fish into pieces and distributed it. They later moved inland to Dhaid, and lived on a farm. There were no stores or markets, and they would have to go to Sharjah by camel to stock up on things like sugar. It would take a whole day to go there, and another day to get back.

When I was little, I used to go with my grandfather to the farm, and he milked the camels. The milk was frothy, and he joked that it was camel ice cream. We took the milk, put freshly made *ragag* (wafer thin bread) into it, and poured honey over it. We thought it was delicious.[35]

The education of those wartime children was still limited to three or four years in one of the *Mutawwa* or 'Teacher Schools'. They sat under an awning on the sand, listened to a turbaned instructor intoning the sacred texts of the Koran and the *Hadeeth* (The Sayings of the Prophet), learned to memorize the key passages and the responses of Islamic rituals, and, if they were lucky, to master the basics of writing and calligraphy. They had no maths, no science, and no English.[36]

The strategic raison d'être of the protectorate dissolved, however, after Britain lost its Indian Empire in 1947 and began the retreat from 'East of Suez'. The British Residency was moved from Bushire, an Iranian port on the Gulf, to Bahrain in 1946. Yet the dispositions of the treaties lingered on for a quarter of a century before definitive political changes were made amidst the inexorable spread of the Middle Eastern oil industry.

Visitors were rare in those days, and few descriptions are extant. But a Middle Eastern trader, Munir Al-Kaloti, who was destined to become one of the Emirates' richest men, has talked of the era before oil and independence:

[My] visa . . . came from the British Consulate in Amman, Jordan. There was nothing like the UAE at that stage. You could not travel freely between Abu Dhabi and Dubai . . . There was no asphalted road, no building over one floor . . . It was the very, very beginning . . .

The first thing I found were very nice people, very welcoming, very poor . . . They had nothing. There was no electricity connection at all. I stayed with some friends who only had a generator for the lights . . .

I would go to Zabeel to see Sheikh Rashid [Dubai's ruler]. He used to sit outside his palace so that everyone who had a request or a problem could go in his turn. He would be sitting there on the wooden seat, smoking his famous pipe . . . And he would see everybody.

Around the time of Ramadan each year, Sheikh Rashid would buy huge quantities of meat for his people's Iftar meals and Eid celebrations.

The people lining up in front of the palace would petition for a certain quantity of livestock, and the Sheikh would strike a bargain. They love goats here because of . . . the lean meat; you can't eat fat in the heat . . .

Sitting next to the Sheikh was an official, [called] Khamal Hamza. He would say to me: 'OK, you are going to [buy] the livestock. And then the bargaining would begin.'[37]

Originally formed in 1951 as the Trucial Oman Levies, the Oman Scouts were officially engaged in patrolling the frontier and keeping an eye on the Bedouin, who would arrive without warning from Arabia's nearby 'Empty Quarter'. Unofficially they were charged with suppressing the slave trade and with contesting Saudi attempts to infiltrate. By 1957, the force was commanded by about 150 British officers and manned by around 1,000 soldiers drawn from Jordan's Arab Legion and from desertion-prone local levies.

A veteran of the RAF's Air Despatch Squadron recounts the realities of his military service:

In 1961, I was seconded as a *Sharwish* (Sergeant) to the Trucial Oman Scouts . . . At one period we were putting patrols into the Empty Quarter [and] I was detailed to supply them . . . They gave me a Twin Pioneer aircraft, one WO1 Master Pilot (who liked a drink) and a navigator.

The pilot used to perform an exercise he called 'Dune Hopping', in which he flew at 200 feet . . . one hand holding a flask of (laced) coffee and one hand on the control column . . . The supplies were petrol, oil, lubricants (POL) etc., and goats. I was then asked if I could drop this lot [from the air], as [landing] was difficult! I duly explained that free dropping live animals could pose a problem . . .

[After loading the petrol, oil, POL etc.,] I put a large tarpaulin into the fuselage. The goats were then delivered, and myself, the pilot and the navigator proceeded to tie them up. Eventually we took off, [but] about an hour into the flight, eight of the goats broke free. The pilot and navigator locked themselves in their cabin, and left me to it. I spent the next hour-and-a-half trying to pin the animals down. They, of course, were peeing and crapping everywhere . . . And dune hopping did not help.

We landed, and the door was opened from outside. Fourteen goats, frightened out of their wits, escaped into the desert, followed by one badly traumatised Sergeant, smelling and looking exactly like the goats. It took two weeks and many, many scrubs with potions and lotions before anyone would come within 25 yards of me . . . NIL SINE LABORE.[38]

Wilfred Thesiger arrived on the scene in the nick of time to record traditional life before it disappeared. His fame rests on his deeply empathetic
descriptions of pre-modern peoples, particularly the Marsh Arabs of
Iraq and the Bedouin of Arabia. On his first journey to the fringes of
the Empty Quarter, he had learned 'to adapt himself to Bedu ways' and
'to the rhythms of their life'. Morning in a Bedouin campsite in the desert was governed by age-old practices:

> My companions were always awake and moving about as soon as it was
> light. The cold kept them from sleeping, for they had little other than the
> clothes they wore ... Still half asleep, I would hear them rousing the
> camels, [which] roared and gurgled as they moved, and the Arabs shouted
> to each other in their harsh, far-carrying voices. The camels would shuf-
> fle past, their forelegs hobbled to prevent them from straying, their breath
> white on the cold air. Then someone would give the call to prayer:

>> God is great.
>> I testify that there is no god but God.
>> I testify that Muhammad is the Prophet of God.
>> Come to Prayer!
>> Come to Salvation!
>> Prayer is better than sleep.
>> God is most great.
>> There is no god but God.

> The lingering music of the words ... hung over the silent camp ... I
> would watch old Tamtaim, who slept near me, washing before he
> prayed ... He washed his face, his hands and his feet, sucked water
> into his nostrils, put wet fingers into his ears, and passed wet hands
> over the top of his head. [He] swept the floor in front of him, placed
> his rifle before him, then prayed towards Mecca. He stood upright, bent
> forward on his knees, and bowed down till his forehead touched the
> ground. He performed these ritual movements several times, slowly and
> impressively ... Sometimes, after his prayers, he would intone long pas-
> sages from the Koran, and the very sound of the words had the quality of
> great poetry. [Yet] many of the Bedu knew only the Koran's opening
> verse:

>> In the name of God, the Compassionate, the Merciful,
>> Praise be to God, lord of the worlds!
>> The Compassionate, the Merciful!
>> King of the Day of Reckoning!

A little later I would hear the bell-like notes as someone pounded coffee in a brass mortar . . . I would get up. In the desert, we slept in our clothes, so all I had to do was to adjust my head-cloth, pour water over my head, splash it onto my face, then go over to the fire and greet the Arabs: '*Salam alaikum*' (Peace be on you). And they would stand up and answer '*Alaikum as salam*' (On you be peace) . . . If we were not in a hurry, we would bake bread for breakfast; otherwise we would eat scraps from our meal the night before. We would drink tea, sweet and black, and then coffee, which was bitter and very strong. The coffee-drinking was not to be hurried. The server poured a few drops into a small china cup, handing it to each in turn and bowing as he did so . . . It was not customary to take more than three cups.

The camels which these Bedu rode were females. In the Sudan, I had ridden on bulls, since there the females are kept [exclusively] for milk. Throughout Arabia, however, females are ridden from choice. Nearly all the male calves are slaughtered at birth, though [some males are used] as pack animals . . . Bull-camels to act as sires are consequently very rare. Later, when I travelled to the Hadhramaut, I was accompanied by a man who rode one. We were constantly pursued by tribesmen with females to be served. We could not protest. Custom demanded that this bull should be allowed to serve as many females as were presented. No-one even asked the owner's permission. They just brought up a camel, had it served, and took it away.[39]

His notoriety stemmed from his frankness about the importance to him of male companionship. Such discussions were still taboo in the 1950s; today they fuel a branch of academic literature:

In Arabia, Thesiger recruited two particularly close companions. One was a 15-year old goatherd, Salin bin Kabina. '*We were watering camels in a wadi and I remember he came up wearing this red loincloth and . . . this long hair. He asked if he could come with me. I asked the Sheikhs, who said 'Yes, if he could get a rifle and a camel.'*

Thesiger considered bin Kabina an assistant . . . '*There was no question of bin Kabina being a paid servant. He wouldn't have risked his life for me under those circumstances. The last thing I wanted was a master–servant relationship with the Bedu*' . . . Thesiger's photos show a lean, taut young man with fine features, and shoulder-length hair . . .

Thesiger's other close companion in Arabia was Salim bin Ghabaisha, Bin Kabina's cousin. '*He was no more than 15 or 16, with an unusually husky voice and the spare, linear, almost feminine figure that Thesiger*

*admired. He had a grace and quiet dignity that contrasted with the*
*boisterously energetic Bin Kabina, although a stronger, more staid and*
*more ruthless character. In* Arabian Sands, *Thesiger waxed over his*
*appearance, likening him to Antinous when first seen by Hadrian*
*in the Phrygian Woods.'*[40]


One might think that the British blundered badly by pulling out at the
very time that the production of oil and gas was coming on-stream. But
London viewed it differently. For one thing, the first well drilled in
1950 at Ra's Sadr near Abu Dhabi produced not a single drop of oil; the
scale of the subsequent oil bonanza was not predicted. For another,
British civil servants guided every move, expecting that British firms
would play a central role in all future petroleum developments, however they turned out. Britain hoped to cut its costs while continuing to
reap whatever economic benefits were to be had.

In the mid-1960s, when political arrangements were already under
review, oil production spiked dramatically: the years 1962–4 were particularly dramatic, as exports began to flow from the Jebel Dhanna
terminal. But growth in the Emirates was not yet comparable to that in
Saudi Arabia or Iran, both of which had a head start, and overall
reserves had not been assessed.[41]

In 1968, however, the British government announced its intention of
withdrawing from the region completely within three years. The news
provoked what have been described as 'frenzied negotiations' – not
only between the ruling sheikhs and the British but also among the
sheikhs themselves.[42] The British favoured the creation of a unitary
state. The sheikhs' Trucial Council was extremely cautious. From
1968 to the summer of 1971 both Bahrain and Qatar participated in
the negotiations, and only last-minute objections prevented them from
joining the Federation of Emirates that emerged. The UAE's founding
document was signed at the Dubai Guest House, now 'Union House',
on 2 December 1971.[43] It created the *Dawlat al-Imarat al-Arabiyah*
*al-Muttahidah*, or *Al-Imarat* (The Emirates) for short. The British
Political Agency was transformed overnight into the British Embassy.

Since then, political changes have been minimal, whilst economic,
financial, and demographic expansion has been volcanic. Crude oil
production has risen steadily from 1.146 million barrels per day in
1984 to 2.804 million in 2012.[44] Sovereign wealth funds have grown

out of all proportion. The Abu Dhabi Investment Authority (ADIA) founded in 1976 now possesses holdings valued at $773 billion, second in the world only to Norway's and representing a capital sum equivalent to $839,305 for each inhabitant. It dwarfs both the sovereign fund of Dubai and the UAE Federal Investment Authority.[45] Economic enterprises, public and private, have proliferated wildly, and the population has rocketed. In 1971 the UAE's uncounted population was perhaps 100,000; its present estimate stands at 9.479 million. Abu Dhabi and Dubai used to be small ports, each harbouring 20,000–30,000 souls; they now house respectively 603,000 and 1,137,000. Sharjah City tops half a million.[46]

Problems are inevitable. Territorially, the UAE was long disturbed by Saudi incursions into border oases, and feels aggrieved by Iran's occupation of three Gulf islands: Abu Musa and the two Tunbs. The disputed islands lie smack in the middle of the shipping lanes of the Strait of Hormuz, and Iran has unilaterally built an airstrip on Greater Tunb.[47]

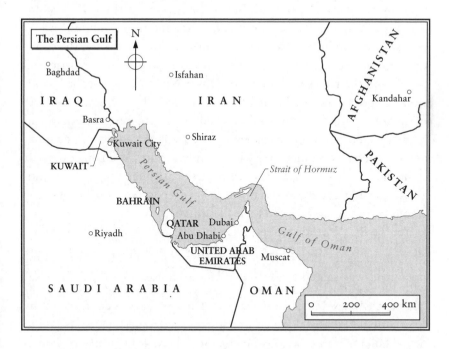

In the political sphere, as Sheikh Zayed knew only too well, absolute regimes are vulnerable to rifts within the ruling courts, and Sharjah in particular has suffered from repeated turbulence. In 1972 Sheikh Khalid was killed by a cousin, and Khalid's younger brother, Sultan, was raised to the throne amidst tribal warfare. But resentments lingered, and in June 1987 Sultan himself was overthrown in his absence by an older brother overlooked fifteen years earlier. The usurper, Sheikh Abdul Assiz, was commander of the National Guard, and his Baluchi mercenaries closed the airport, arrested newspaper editors, and barricaded themselves into the Royal Courthouse. He complained of financial mismanagement. For three or four days it looked as if he had succeeded; the ruler of Dubai was alone in lodging a public protest. But the UAE Council voted to restore Sheikh Sultan. Abdul Assiz backed down, agreeing to be named Crown Prince and Deputy Ruler.[48]

In 1991 the UAE was rocked by the forcible liquidation of the British-based Bank of Credit and Commerce International (BCCI), of which the government of Abu Dhabi was a 77 per cent shareholder. BCCI was the brainchild of a Pakistani financier, Agha Hasan Abed, who had built it up to be the seventh largest bank in the world with assets of $20 billion. On the surface it appeared respectable; its central office in London was audited by Price Waterhouse Cooper, and regulated by the Bank of England. But investigations in the United States over the affairs of a BCCI subsidiary, First American Bank, uncovered widespread fraud. BCCI's clients included Saddam Hussein, the dictator of Iraq, Manuel Noriega of Panama, the Palestinian terrorist Abu Nidal, and the rogue CIA operator Oliver North. The so-called Sandstorm Report concluded that BCCI was driven by secrecy, deliberate obfuscation, bribery, arms running, and drug trafficking. International regulators moved in simultaneously; BCCI was forced into liquidation, and its managers pleaded guilty in a London court. Abu Dhabi was left suing the Bank of England in a hopeless case that dragged on until 2005. The liquidators, who claimed to have recovered 45 per cent of the creditors' lost money, closed their files in 2012.[49]

Yet the BCCI affair has left a lasting scar on the UAE's reputation. Despite a law of 2002 which made money laundering illegal, rumours persist that banks in the UAE, and in Dubai in particular, continue with the malpractices that made BCCI notorious. Headlines such as 'Corrupt Money Hides in Dubai' or 'Dubai's Dark Side Targeted by International Financial Police' are far from welcome.[50] Dubai is said to be the hub for Iran sanctions-busting, for filtering the profits of Somali piracy, and for the operations of Russian mafia bosses. Bank accounts can still be opened with no questions asked; residence permits can be bought; and no curbs are placed on the movement of funds. 'Russians carrying suitcases of cash buy apartments which they never live in.'[51]

The Norwegian-born French magistrate Eva Joly, who specializes in financial crime, is insistent that Dubai remains the 'world centre' of money laundering. She has linked it not only to French scandals, such as Elf, but also to the Magnitsky Case in Moscow and to the Bank of Kabul, whence $1 billion of American aid money went missing.[52]

Something about this aspect of the UAE can also be learned from the murky career of the Indian businessman, Naresh Kumar Jain, aka Patel, who was known as the 'World's *Hawala* King' and operated from Dubai for twenty years. (A *hawala* is an agency dealing in international money transfers.) Jain's organization was allegedly a front for illegal transfers that were said to have reached the level of $2 billion per day. Suspected of using the so-called 'layering technique' – legal transactions covering more dubious ones – it allegedly attracted the custom of international drug smugglers, 'white slave' traffickers, and, reputedly, terrorist groups including Al-Qaeda. Jain, who denies all charges, fled the United States in 2007, jumped bail in Dubai in 2009, and was then arrested and held in Delhi. But he has never been convicted.[53]

Yet one cannot suggest that all that glitters in the UAE is criminal. The transparent career of another businessman from Dubai, Munir Al-Kaloti, shows exactly the opposite. A Palestinian born in Jerusalem, Kaloti came to Abu Dhabi in 1968 as a refugee from the Arab-Israeli conflict. After various ventures in the food trade – he was the man who bought 20,000 goats for Sheikh Rashid – he hit on the idea of clearing up the scrap metal left behind by the oil prospectors, and of smelting it down into a saleable commodity. He then moved into second-hand jewellery.

'Dubai was much more open than the surrounding countries,' he recalls, 'no taxes, no controls, and flights from all over the world. Before long, people were flying in with scrap gold from mines in Africa or Asia, and were asking, who can handle this?'

He started with one kilo of gold bought for 40,000 Deutschmarks. He then opened an assaying laboratory, a specialized gold forge, and a chain of up-market stores. His original bullion factory is still operating in Sharjah, turning out $30 billion-worth of gold bars per annum. Kaloti International has offices in Hong Kong, Singapore, and Surinam. In 2015, when a new refinery outside Dubai started production, it was expected to triple the firm's output.[54] As for Kaloti himself, they call him 'the alchemist'. 'Only in the UAE can a scrap man end up with a factory filled with gold.'

A still larger organization in the UAE, the Al-Ghurair Group, has similar humble origins. Ahmad Al-Ghurair and his son Saif came from a family of Dubai pearl divers, who by 1960 had accumulated enough cash to diversify. They built the Emirates' first sugar refinery, the first cement works, the first steel mill, and the first shopping mall. To these they added the country's largest bank, the Mashreq (formerly the Bank of Oman), and a host of other concerns. The Al-Ghurairs now sit comfortably in the Forbes list of billionaires.

The Federal Constitution was originally intended to be provisional, pending further negotiations with prospective members, but was eventually declared permanent. Its 151 articles promise equality for all citizens, universal education, a customs and monetary union, joint armed forces, and a 'comprehensively democratic regime' for an 'Arab and Islamic society'. The flag is made up of three horizontal stripes of green, white, and black, with a vertical red bar on the left. The emblem is a stylized eagle. The currency is the *dirham* (UAD) currently standing at 1 = US $3. Islam is the official religion, Arabic the sole official language, and 2 December the National Day. The National Assembly, which has an advisory function, consists of representatives from all member states in proportion to population. The Executive Council is made up of the seven heads of the seven member Emirates. The rulers of Abu Dhabi and of Dubai possess the right of veto; the five others – Sharjah, Ajman, Ras al-Khaimah, Umm al-Quwain, and Fujairah – do not. The Council appoints a president from among its members, and a prime minister to run the federal government. It keeps its own competences to a minimum, thereby upholding the traditionally unshackled powers of each sheikh within his own domain.[55]

As in the four Gulf States that do not belong to the UAE – Kuwait, Bahrain, Qatar, and Oman – political power remains concentrated in the ruling families, and is upheld by elaborate regulations, fierce law enforcement, and a deep-rooted culture of deference. There are monarchies and constitutions, but nothing resembling a constitutional monarchy, let alone the comprehensively 'Democratic Regime' promised by the Constitution.[56] The sheikhs in their sheikhdoms enjoy despotic rights; and the Federation, which depends on consensus among the sheikhs, is weak. All decisions are made by decree. The courts and the police, staffed largely by foreign mercenaries, answer directly to the top. Unauthorized gatherings are banned; both formal and informal censorship is in force; and the ancient idea of equating outspoken criticism with sedition is only diluted by the ancient custom of sheikhly pardons.

Abject deference to the rulers, however, is ubiquitous; it finds its way like the dust of the desert into the nooks and crannies of all social groups and institutions. Every success has to be attributed to the personal genius of the appropriate ruler, to whom words of admiration and gratitude must be expressed on all occasions. In December 2011, for example, the UAE celebrated its fortieth anniversary under the slogan 'SPIRIT OF THE UNION'. A gala concert was staged by the Royal Oman Symphony Orchestra under the British conductor Neil Thomson. The programme started, predictably perhaps, with Verdi's *Il Forza del Destino*. The opening lines of the evening's anniversary brochure attributed the success of the orchestra to 'the gracious directions' and 'sublime taste for classical music' of His Majesty Sultan Qaboos bin Said.

Each of the seven men who rule the UAE is equally the direct controller of all the financial and economic organizations that manage his wealth. In the words of their own, unfree press, they are 'the Titans of Government and Business'. The most influential of them, Sheikh Khalifa bin Zayed Al-Nahyan, aged sixty-seven, is simultaneously the ruler of Abu Dhabi, the chairman of the ADIA, and president of the UAE. The second in the pecking order, Sheikh Mohammed bin Rashid Al-Maktoum, is simultaneously the ruler of Dubai, chairman of Dubai Holding, and UAE vice-president and prime minister.

The only political constraints that such men face come from the numerous members of their extended families. For, above everything else, they are tribal chiefs; they are the sons of fathers who kept multiple wives and begat large broods of children; they owe their birthright to unwritten rules of precedence laid down by previous sovereigns, favourite wives, and competing mothers. Family politics are conducted in secrecy behind the closed flaps of the tribal tent, and are never explained.

In consequence, the 'decision-making process' – as political scientists would call it – is maximally opaque. Every plan, proposal, or provisional arrangement has to be passed up for approval by the ruling family, and the outcome is consistently uncertain. Diplomats and businessmen talk of the 'black hole' or the 'black box': that is, the private and secret sphere within which all executive decisions are taken. Little has changed since petitioners would whisper through the door of the ruler's tent, and hope for a reply.

Institutionalized nepotism is an essential adjunct to the system at every level. The late sovereign of Abu Dhabi, Sheikh Zayed, had

thirteen sons, and all them would have expected a position commensu-
rate with their status. The present Crown Prince, for instance, General
Sheikh Mohammed bin Zayed bin Sultan Al-Nahyan, is the present
ruler's half-brother; he is also the Deputy Supreme Commander of the
UAE's armed forces, and chairman of the Emirate's primary investment company, Mubadala. The Foreign Minister is Sheikh Zayed's
fourth son, and the Minister of the Interior his sixth. The CEO of
Mubadala, on the other hand, Khaldoon Khalifa Al-Mubarak (aged
twenty), belongs to the family's younger generation. As a sideline, he is
also chairman of Manchester City FC. Sisters can rarely compete with
brothers. Fatima Al-Jaber, Chief Operating Officer of the Al-Jaber
Group and the first female director elected to the Abu Dhabi Chamber
of Commerce, is exceptional. Her title of COO (instead of CEO) suggests that she still works under male supervision.

The social scene is almost as unbalanced as the political one. Barely
20 per cent of the population are Emirati nationals, in other words
resident citizens; the overwhelming majority are foreign migrants or
temporary workers. Some of the latter are highly paid consultants and
managers; many more are domestics, clerks, taxi-drivers, and labourers. None of them have any rights beyond what is written into their
contract or their visas, and none of them can hope to gain Emirati citizenship except by marriage. Every institution in the UAE has to be
headed by a native Emirati director, and every corporation is bound by
law to keep at least 51 per cent of its shares in Emirati ownership. In
consequence, the public has been prevented from developing any sense
of equal citizenship. The roads are crowded with expensive vehicles;
the streets are thronged with people from all the continents; and the
multicultural mix can appear perfectly prosperous and harmonious.
But each and every one has to know their place, and deep-seated prejudices persist. Slave-trading was not suppressed until the 1960s, and
the ancient concept of 'head money', which sets a tariff on the value of
different groups, is alive and well. Europeans can walk onto a pedes-
trian crossing with confidence, knowing that their life insurance is
worth 200,000 dirhams or more; the lives of Asians and Africans are
valued at about 40,000 dirhams apiece. Mentalities change slowly.

Emirati citizens enjoy unwaveringly preferential treatment over foreigners in all internal matters. They alone possess full property rights.
They benefit from state-provided health care from cradle to grave, subsidized housing, priority in employment, low-interest loans for all
young families, and not least free education. (A modern curriculum,

including maths and English, came into being in the 1970s; after independence a full set of textbooks and exams followed in the 1980s.) These lavish welfare provisions makes nonsense of official statistics that put the average income per capita at a mere $48,000.

At the other end of the scale, the lot of migrant labourers is particularly harsh. They form the largest population group and are typically young males from the subcontinent, forbidden to bring their families, and obliged to live in substandard, barrack-style accommodation, often six or eight to a room. Not understanding Arabic, they are entirely at the mercy of unscrupulous employers, contractors, and middlemen. They work on construction sites, often in the open in broiling temperatures, and – by Emirati standards – are paid a pittance. They are not permitted to change employers or to negotiate pay and conditions. Their one hope is to send a remittance home for the support of their wives or parents. To this end, all thoughts of complaint, let alone of protest, are suppressed.

International monitors have noted all manner of abuses. As in Bahrain and Qatar, many of the poor migrants to the UAE become indebted to loan sharks and to the very agents who imported them in the first place. On arrival many are given less than favourable contracts, which they can't read and which they accept for fear of being sent home. As a result, they are driven into unredeemable levels of debt, toiling from dawn to dusk essentially as slaves or indentured servants. In 2006 the government of India launched an investigation into suicides among its nationals in the UAE. Workers at the *Burj Khalifa* site in Dubai rioted, and others at Dubai Airport staged a sympathy strike. In 2007 some four thousand strikers were arrested.[57] In 2010 workers constructing the NYU-Abu Dhabi campus alerted American authorities to abuses.[58] International pressure is growing for the UAE to sign up to the various human-rights and labour conventions, including the UN Convention on Torture.

One form of social pathology, of course, encourages others. The presence of disproportionate numbers of single men has led to a rise in prostitution, human trafficking, and sex tourism, especially in Dubai. Russian and Ethiopian women are said to be in high demand, and foreign-based gangs, who have mastered the art of well-placed bribes, operate with impunity.

Huge economic progress, therefore, has been achieved at the cost of huge social ills, particularly among migrants. For practical purposes, each of the three main groupings in the UAE lives in its own cocoon.

The indigenous Emiratis have little in common either with the hordes of migrant workers, who greatly outnumber them, or with the expats, on whom they depend to run all the main institutions and businesses in the state. Casual visitors from the West, like myself, are automatically channelled into the company of other westerners. It is difficult to see how this statistically wealthy society, based on a form of apartheid, can continue to prosper without far greater degrees of equality and elementary justice. It is simply not sustainable that 80 per cent can toil and suffer indefinitely for the comfort of the 20 per cent. Pre-Revolutionary France comes to mind.

I was shown around Dubai by a couple who had been teaching English there for the last two decades, and around Abu Dhabi by a talented young computer programmer from Poland. I enjoyed invitations to diplomatic receptions. But I made no contact either with the migrant workers, whom one sees on every occasion, or with ordinary Emirati families. To discover their perspective, I consulted the experience of others more enterprising than myself. A visitor from New Zealand, for example, has posted an account of his conversation with boatmen who were plying the ferry on the Dubai Creek:

> I stopped and chatted to the Pakistani crew . . . Their life was so starkly different from mine: different, but showing pics of our kids to each other was pretty universal. [They were] so friendly, and obviously enjoyed chatting to a Kiwi from the land of famous [cricketers] . . . Time and again, I talked to men who had not seen their sons and daughters for a year or even three, in their free choice of waged shackles. Their rare visits home [only] served to re-kindle their homesickness . . .[59]

A resident British journalist, on the other hand, investigated why expats don't integrate with Emiratis. 'The reality in Dubai,' she reported, 'is that most of us live in an expat bubble. Yes, our friends may come from two hundred countries – but do we have many Emirati friends? Unlikely.'[60]

Another journalist documented the Emirati side of the coin. The first person she interviewed was the writer Abdel Khalek Abdullah: 'Emiratis are starting to lose much of their identity,' the writer said; 'the presence of so many expats leads to unacceptable behaviour that does not conform to our traditions.'[61]

The chronicle of 'unacceptable behaviour' is headed by the case of the British couple who were expelled in 2008 for copulating in broad daylight on the beach. But scanty foreign female dress and alcohol abuse also fuel the feeling of 'being swamped' and the tendency of citizens to entrench themselves in exclusive suburbs on the city outskirts. A lady academic from the UAE university, Professor Ibtisam al-Ketbi, was particularly outspoken: 'We have become a minority [in our own country],' she lamented, 'and Arabic is no longer the first language. We are surrounded by foreigners, and live in constant fear for our children because of the spread of drugs and the rise in crime rates . . . We are practically living in reservations . . . In twenty years' time, we'll end up like the American Indians.'[62]

Religious tensions add to other existing divisions. The Emirates has long enjoyed the reputation of being the most moderate state in the region. It is certainly not in the same repressive category as the austere Wahhabi kingdom of neighbouring Saudi Arabia. In his day Sheikh Zayed took flak from conservatives for insisting that all 'peoples of the Book' should enjoy their places of worship. A variety of Christian Churches – Catholic, Protestant, Orthodox, and Coptic – are therefore tolerated; and several smaller denominations, such as the Mormons and the Pentecostals, function without restriction.

Yet by Western standards the bounds of Emirati tolerance are narrow. Neither Buddhists, nor Hindus, nor Sikhs are free to open their temples, and no foreign missionaries are admitted. The authorities are reluctant to accept that Islam itself contains pluralities. Official censors routinely monitor the content of sermons in mosques, and Sharia law dominates the largest judicial sector, especially with respect to family affairs and criminal offences. Both alcohol and pork meat are on sale (except in Sharjah), but Muslims and non-Muslims alike are subject to Sharia-based penalties. Floggings are commonplace, and antediluvian definitions of adultery or of domestic violence prevail. Muslim men are free to marry women 'of the Book', in other words Christians or Jews; but Muslim women are not free to marry non-Muslims. The Emir of Ajman offers cash rewards to any convict who succeeds in memorizing the whole of the Koran.

The Shias, in particular, are trapped. They constitute 15 per cent of Emirati citizens, and over 40 per cent of residents. They are classed as Muslims, but have no influence in the institutions governing Muslim practice. Their mosques can only function as private bodies. What is more, they are politically suspect, being regularly denounced for admiring Iran or for supporting Hezbollah. In 2013–14 some four thousand Shiites were summarily deported from the UAE, their work permits withdrawn without notice. The only government to protest was that of Pakistan.[63]

Within the Shia community, the Ismaili sect enjoy better conditions. The Ismaili leader, the Aga Khan, is a friend of the Sheikh of Dubai, and in 2008 an elegant Ismaili Centre was opened to foster good relations. A glaring anomaly persists, however, with regards to Judaism. As a 'people of the Book', and founders of the Abrahamic tradition, Jews ought logically to enjoy the same rights as Christians. But no public synagogue exists. Internet chat rooms debate the issue. 'Is there a synagogue or not?' 'Yes, in the Scroll Room of the liner *Queen Elizabeth II* [now moored as a tourist attraction in Dubai Harbour].' Attitudes towards Israel complicate the issue. Emiratis often justify their reservations about Judaism by citing Israel's maltreatment of Palestinians.

Sheikh Zayed attempted to improve matters, but he must have been dismayed by the consequences. He created the Zayed Center for Co-ordination and Follow-Up in Abu Dhabi, as a think tank and forum for dialogue.[64] And he donated a large sum to Harvard Divinity School to establish a chair of Islamic Studies.[65] Both initiatives failed. The Zayed Center, after hosting prestigious guests such as ex-presidents Clinton and Carter, was targeted by militant critics who accused it of promoting Holocaust denial. At Harvard, protesters denounced Sheikh Zayed as a slave-owner and sponsor of anti-Semites. The Zayed Center was abolished in 2003, and the donation to Harvard rescinded.

The proliferation of universities, therefore, sits uneasily alongside a rigid, dictatorial system and a bleak, not to say barren, social and intellectual landscape. Dubai alone, amidst its skyscrapers and metro lines, hosts seventy-nine universities – compared to 109 in the whole of the United Kingdom. Three of them have 'American' in their title, others having 'British', 'Canadian', 'French', or 'Russian' labels. Tuition fees range from 22,000 dirhams to 90,000 dirhams per annum; courses in Business Studies cost over 100,000 dirhams, and in Dental or Medical Schools up to 250,000 dirhams. There are parents willing to pay. But how do they distinguish the decent from the dodgy? Perhaps they go through the list on the internet and test their instincts: Aga Khan University, Atlanta University, Bharathiar University, Calicut, Duke, Exeter, Fuqua, Griggs, Heriot-Watt, Indira Gandhi National, Jazeera, Kidville, London Business, Murdoch, Nottingham, Online, Philippine, Quaid I Azam, Richford, Strathclyde, University of Dubai, Vellore,

Wollongong, Zayed International . . . All of them advertise online, and all have plausible mission statements:

> The University of Jazeera responds to national, regional and international changes by embracing diversity and nurturing innovation in learning, teaching, research and community service. UOJ is dedicated to developing a community of scholars that promotes ethical behaviour and disseminates knowledge to UAE society and throughout the world.[66]

But *caveat emptor.* Kidville University belongs to an international chain of nurseries. Phantom universities, which may happily take financial deposits but operate only in the virtual sphere, undoubtedly exist.

Nonetheless, Emirati rulers are clearly putting their faith in higher education. Sheikh Zayed's handsome benefaction to the London School of Economics may be taken as a signal of his good intentions.[67] Much is said about a 'knowledge-based economy', and Emirati planners refer to the buzz term frequently in their efforts to escape from dependence on oil. Yet the pursuit of knowledge can hardly be justified on economic grounds alone; the meaning and purposes of knowledge are central to all educational matters. UAE leaders are pouring in thought and resources, and on paper at least, their priorities are clear:

> Today, the UAE offers a comprehensive education to every male and female student from kindergarten to university; [it is] free at all levels to the country's citizens . . . Much has been achieved but there is a deep awareness that more needs to be done . . . Education remains a top government priority, [and is receiving] a 21 percent or Dh 9.8 billion allocation in the 2014 federal budget; [of this] Dh 3.8 bn is being spent on academic excellence programmes in local universities.
>
> To implement government policy, the UAE Ministry of Education has developed . . . a series of ambitious 5-year plans designed to bring significant qualitative improvement . . . especially in the way teachers teach and students learn.[68]

The key phrases are 'academic excellence' and 'significant qualitative improvement'. The Emirates College for Advanced Education was launched to pursue those ends. 'We are like those who climbed a mountain and reached the top,' said Sheikh Zayed; 'when we look down, we want to go higher still.'

A lecture at Al-Ain gave me a taste of this much-vaunted educational system. I was introduced by the Provost, a genial, silver-haired Canadian, who had been brought out of retirement to run the university;

and I was honoured by the presence of the Rector, a sombre black-robed matron, who was said to be an aunt of 'the Sheikh'. The lecture room was fitted with all the latest remote-controlled devices for raising blinds, dimming lights, video-recording lectures, and projecting PowerPoint presentations. The plush red seating would not have been out of place in an opera house. Gentle currents of calibrated coolness wafted inaudibly from ceiling vents. Thirty or forty members of staff, overwhelmingly European, sat together in the central section. Three female students, in their black abayas, sat on the extreme right side, resolutely resisting the Provost's pleas to move into the centre.

Tea and dainty cakes were served afterwards. As I chatted to a group of English professors, the Provost herded the three brave female students towards me. Their heads were covered but not veiled. Only one of the three was relaxed enough to speak, and asked to do so in French. She was Algerian, and my two minutes of polite conversation with her constituted the sum total of my interaction with the student body. Just as businessmen confront the 'black hole', so short-term visitors come up against the 'glass wall' that inhibits ready interaction with the locals.

Then I was taken on a tour of the sun-drenched campus. My white-robed guide drove me in a golf buggy from one magnificent building to the next. A gigantic mural portrait of Sheikh Zayed beamed down from the gable end of a crescent-shaped administrative centre. The Olympic-class swimming pool and sports hall faced trim, student residences and science laboratories newly built in fine, red brick. The shelves of the vast new university library were hardly weighed down with books, but the wired-up reading cubicles were spacious and well lit, and the central book-delivery area was fully computerized. Uniformed attendants stood around eager to help.

I was slow to see what was missing. There were no swimmers in the pool, no researchers in the labs, no readers in the library. All facilities were empty. It was Thursday afternoon; all the students, I was told, had been bused out to join their families for the Muslim weekend on Friday and Saturday.

'What I've shown you,' the guide announced, 'is the women's campus; women make up 80 per cent of students, but since no one's here we can drive round freely. The men's campus is on the other side of The Crescent.' He explained how the library worked. Men and women have separate entrances on opposite sides of the building; they collect their books from separate counters, and read in separate reading rooms. The strict separation of the sexes, and the guardianship of men over women, are immutable principles of Emirati life.

On my last evening, I am invited to supper by three friendly American academics, all employed in the UAE in what they called 'Edubiz', two of the three being specialists in 'QDoubleA' – Quality Assessment Analysis. They are high-earners, freely admitting to salaries significantly higher than they had enjoyed in North America.

The conversation starts with politics.

'Are there any dissidents in this country?' I begin.

'You bet!' one of them replies. 'Thousands and thousands of them. The trouble is, anyone who speaks their mind is knocked on the head so hard that the rest are scared to death.'

Only recently, five people had signed a letter proposing that membership of the National Assembly should in part be organized by election. The signatories were immediately arrested, and threatened with trial for sedition.

'Sedition, for God's sake; that's like treason,' he continues.

'It reminds me of the Communists in Eastern Europe,' I reply. 'They couldn't tell the difference between constructive criticism and armed rebellion, so they just sat tight until everything collapsed.'

'Yeah, that's it,' he goes on. 'Though these guys are rampant liberals compared to their Saudi neighbours, they still believe their authority derives from Allah.'

'The Divine Right of Kings?' I suggest.

'Exactly, and Allah doesn't negotiate!'

'So what of the Islamists?' I continue. 'There can't be a Muslim country without Islamists!'

'Of course not. We've lots of them, and they come in fifty-seven varieties. But the problem's the same as with secular dissidents. The authorities can't tell the difference between cranks and extremos. There's a group called *Al-Islah*, which means "Reform". One of their stars, a Yemeni woman, won the Nobel Peace Prize.* Yet the government is treating them all as subversives, and accusing them of plotting to seize power.'

The trial of ninety-four Al-Islah associates took place in Abu Dhabi in the middle of 2013. The defendants were berated for belonging to the

---

* Tawakel Karman, founder of 'Women Journalists without Chains'. Nobel Peace Prize, 2011.

Muslim Brotherhood at a time when Mohamed Morsi, a member of
the Brotherhood, was serving as Egypt's first democratic president. The
group's link with the Brotherhood was no secret; it had been formed in
the 1970s by Egyptians fleeing from Colonel Nasser's regime. Fifty-six
people received jail terms; eight were sentenced in absentia; and twenty-
six were acquitted.[69]

'So can the sheikhs keep the lid on the bottle?' I enquire.

'Jeeze, I wish I knew. They are sure trying; they are giving a lot of
attention to controlling the internet.'

The UAE's main server, ETISAT, routinely blocks unwelcome internet sites and monitors everyone's tweets and Facebook entries.

'Dead right,' someone confirms. 'There was a critical blog written by
some joker on the staff at UCT, you know, and that was shut down.'[70]

As the talk turned to education, I was taken aback by my interlocu-
tors' continuing frankness. None of these professionals doubted that
something was seriously rotten in the system for which they were working. They didn't blame the government, though they moaned about the
'black hole', and they weren't accusing their expat colleagues, though
they hinted at a few bad apples. What was bugging them was the
ingrained Emirati culture of teaching and learning.

'The main obstacle,' one said, 'is a bone-headed, static view of
knowledge, which they don't seem to associate with thinking.'

'All the teachers want to do,' said another, 'is to present a PowerPoint
summary of any given subject, so that the students can regurgitate it.'

'Independent thinking, forget it!'

'Cutting-edge research, they don't have a clue.'

They then bore down on the 'crazy gender ratio'.

'Women study mainly as a means of escaping the supervision of their
husbands and brothers.'

Many, it appears, are mothers before they enrol; and the majority
will start raising a family as soon as they graduate. Relatively few can
pursue an academic or professional career. But attitudes are a bigger
barrier than circumstances.

'It's a nightmare trying to persuade Emiratis to do a PhD,' the third
academic explained. 'They can't see the point; they have no concept of
"pushing the boundaries" or "breaking new ground". Some say that
they're lazy. I don't think that's it. We can't get them to enter research
programmes requiring "an original contribution to knowledge"
because they see it as a contradiction in terms.'

The consequences are dire. 'Emiratization' has been in place in academia for twenty years, but is not bearing fruit. The goal was to train up the locals and to replace the imported professors.

'But we can't give anyone a chair if they've never done a PhD.'

Tempted to criticize, Europeans and Americans must remember both the flaws of their own systems and the immense time span over which modern educational culture has matured in the West. The Islamic world is not alone in producing people with a static view of knowledge. When Francis Bacon was writing his classic work on *The Advancement of Learning* (1605), his contemporary, Galileo, was being cast into a dungeon for questioning the Church's view of the cosmos. That was four centuries ago. The Emiratis are trying to catch up in decades.

Everyone knows that university rankings are not the product of an exact science, and that English-speaking schools, which invented the practice, have an inbuilt advantage. At the time of my visit to the UAE they were ranked in the following order: Cal Tech (1), Harvard (2), Stanford (3), Oxford (4), Princeton (5), and Cambridge (6). Yet the lowly placements of Arab universities were embarrassing. Despite lavish funding, only four of them could be found in the top 1,000. Many shortcomings visible in the UAE appear endemic to the region. The top Emirati institution, the United Arab Emirates University at Al-Ain, though rated eighth in the Arab world, ranks only 1,157 overall. The University of Sharjah stands at 1,694, the American University of Sharjah at 1,922, and the much-lauded Higher Colleges of Technology, which 'encourages independent and life-long learning', at 2,074.[71] One view holds that Arabs are suffering a hangover from religious methods of learning, which emphasize memorization and ritualistic quotation. Another blames the dead hand of despotic regimes that repress critical thought.

Yet Emiratis need to ask whether advanced learning and research can be traded like any other commodity. Can they really expect to buy knowledge? Their American friends may be inclined to say 'Yes', though many think the answer more complicated. Educational standards are partly the product of good educators, who can be trained or hired; but they are largely the outcome of fruitful interactions between the teacher and the taught. If the students in a class are badly prepared or poorly motivated, they would not benefit from the presence of Albert Einstein himself. The nature of the soil is as crucial as the quality of the seed. Time may hold the key. Education is a great oak that grows slowly over generations; no one can speed its rhythms, least of all by saturating it with money. It is the principal transmission mechanism of culture. And culture is stronger than money.

To be fair, many thoughtful Muslim educators are aware of the deficiencies. They all quote the Prophet's statement that 'the pursuit of knowledge is incumbent on all Muslims, men and women', and repeat His question: 'Are those who know equal to those who don't know?' They point to the fact that the Prophet's own wife, Aisha, was a learned person, and draw comfort from the expansion of girls' education in many, though not all, Muslim countries. In this regard, the UAE, like Iran, would be among the leaders, whereas Yemen, Jordan, and Sudan would be among the back-markers. These educators' newfound interest in the achievements of mediaeval Muslim civilization serves to remind them of their relative backwardness in today's world, enjoining them to bemoan the rift that was allowed to develop between religious and secular education. In short, they readily accept the concept of a Great Divergence. All they want is that the gap should be closed quickly.[72]

Not all Emiratis are enamoured of the drastic but imperfect transformation of their native land. Quite apart from anxieties concerning migrant workers and expats, many older people, who experienced the transition from desert tent to air-conditioned tower block, share a sense of nostalgia for the 'good old days' of communal solidarity:

> We did everything together. We cleaned together, we fished together, we made things together. We shared our food . . . The children were not just the parents' child, they were the neighbourhood's child. After finishing work, we would sing songs together. We hardly did anything alone. Life was harder than it is now, but it was . . . a beautiful life. It was simple, and everyone stuck together. Now everyone is scattered . . . and looking only to their own affairs.[73]

It would be hard to argue that the Emirates have a major colonial legacy to overcome. The British can rightly be accused of imposing themselves on much of the Arab world for political ends, and of pulling out before a stable democratic system was introduced. But, unlike Palestine or Iraq, no serious attempt was made in the Trucial States to establish a full-blown imperial regime. The worst effects of the British protectorate in the Gulf were to perpetuate an antiquated patriarchal society, legitimize the divine right of the Sheiks, and help exclude the 'winds of change'.

As I prepared to leave, therefore, the figure of 80 per cent was ringing in my mind. Some 80 per cent of the population are denied basic citizen's rights, and are underpaid by at least 80 per cent of average earnings; 80 per cent of graduates have no prospect of equal treatment or of governing their own lives. Even the affluent natives are restless. It looks like a socio-political time bomb. Fairly soon perhaps, there's an 80 per cent chance of it exploding.

Unlike Cornwall or Azerbaijan, or many countries that I was to visit, the Emirates have few ancient roots. They are the creation of recent decades, witnesses to the dizzying pace of contemporary change. The teeming crowds that one sees in Dubai or Abu Dhabi are all made up of migrant newcomers. The so-called 'natives', the Emirati Arabs, the children and grandchildren of the Bedu that Thesiger describes, left the neighbouring desert only two or three generations ago. The members of the multinational labour force, which is numerically dominant, are both the beneficiaries and the victims of an aggressive globalizing economy. And the army of expats is the product of the jet age. Their predicament is at once enviable and unenviable. One cannot help wondering whether the boom may not end as suddenly as it began.

# 4

# Dilli – Delhi

*Dalits, Temples, and Gun Salutes*

From Dubai to Delhi is the same distance as that between Baku and Dubai, though in a slightly confusing direction. Emirates Flight 380 takes off over the Gulf, crosses the Strait of Hormuz, and follows a bearing east-north-east over Pakistan. One forgets that northern India pushes so far into the Himalayas, and consequently that the Indian capital sits on a higher latitude than either the Strait or Karachi. To the left is the North-West Frontier and the Khyber Pass, to the right the province of Sind and the deserts of Rajasthan. In a mere three hours the flight makes the transition from one major region of Asia to another, from the Middle East to the Subcontinent.

'The Indians,' said the ambassador emphatically, as we ride in his limousine away from the airport, 'take NO real interest in Europe. They're not encouraged to. They look to America, they increasingly fear China, and they're paranoid about Pakistan. The European Union is simply not in the picture.'

'Surely not, Your Excellency.'

'Oh yes,' he continues. 'The European nations may be here in force individually, especially the British. But they operate as competitors, as rivals; they don't show any solidarity; they don't present themselves as Europeans.'

Prime ministers do indeed arrive with vast delegations in tow. Trade ministers descend on Delhi surrounded by swarms of businessmen. Industrialists do the rounds, selling cars or aeroplanes or ships.

'The British, the Germans, the French, even the Belgians – they all do it,' says the ambassador. 'They jostle each other, vying for arms deals, investment projects and political favours. And that's what the Indians see.'

The conversation continues next morning over breakfast.

'But surely, Your Excellency, the EU now has its own ambassador to India, and is deeply involved in joint trade talks.'

'That's true. The new EU ambassador, a Portuguese, has a PhD from Oxford.'

'And the trade talks? I thought that a trade agreement was in the offing.'

'The talks have been dragging on for years and years. Would you like porridge? I'm sure our Indian chef can oblige. And by the way, I've arranged an interview for you with Vickram Bahl, the TV anchorman. He's extremely pleasant.'

Jostling, whether diplomatic or physical, sums up Delhi's way of life. 'Delhi is supposed to have 16 million inhabitants,' the butler says, 'but they can't really count them.' Bombay and Calcutta have more. And it feels as if they're all out on the street together. When the ambassador ventures from his compound, he travels in convoy. The cars line up, the chauffeurs jump to attention, the passengers brace themselves for take-off. The flag on the bonnet flutters, the Indian soldier on the gate salutes, and the metal grilles swing open.

Outside, most of the cars are small, nippy Japanese saloons – Toyotas, Nissans, and Martui Suzukis. The most popular motorbike, a black-painted 250cc, is named Passion. The older, second-class taxis are painted black, green, and yellow: they are Ambassadors, the much-loved Indian copy of the Morris Oxford, just as my father drove in the 1950s. Yet the lords of the road are the ubiquitous scooterized rick-shaws, the tuk-tuks, which dominate by sheer numbers; Delhi has 100,000 of them. They canter rather than race: switch lanes without warning, and hold up a tail of vehicles straining to overtake. In Delhi, they are painted bright green and carry a yellow hood; in Bombay they are black. At the rear, they display a square registration plate starting with DL, the letters CNG to indicate Gas-fuelling, and a series of warnings to tailgaters such as STOP, KEEP DISTANCE, or POWER BRAKE.

Our white-painted pilot car acts as pathfinder, surging into the shoal, and scattering the small fry as it goes. I felt almost as if I had dived head first into the aquarium tank in Dubai – the great swirls of fish, large and small, cruising along in aimless circuits, never slowing, occasionally taking fright, but rarely colliding. The ambassadorial lim-ousine clings to our back bumper like a limpet; and the cars behind, despite their CD plates, struggle to keep up. The view from the side window resembles that from the porthole of a submarine cruising past a coral reef. The mobile mass is made up of scooters, motorbikes and tuk-tuks, interspersed with taxis, private cars, and brightly painted

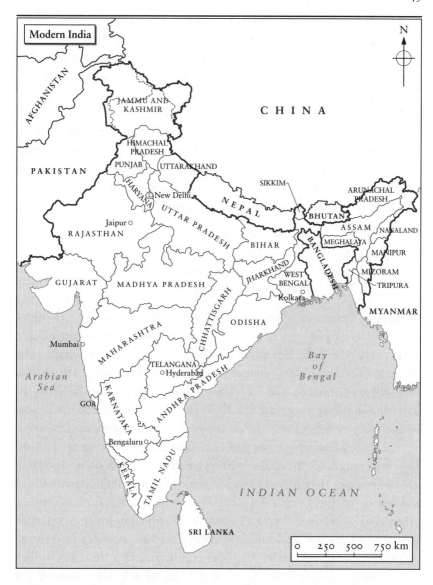

Modern India

AFGHANISTAN

PAKISTAN

JAMMU AND KASHMIR

CHINA

HIMACHAL PRADESH

PUNJAB

UTTARAKHAND

HARYANA

New Delhi

SIKKIM

ARUNACHAL PRADESH

BHUTAN

NEPAL

ASSAM

NAGALAND

Jaipur

RAJASTHAN

UTTAR PRADESH

BIHAR

MEGHALAYA

MANIPUR

BANGLADESH

MIZORAM

GUJARAT

MADHYA PRADESH

JHARKHAND

WEST BENGAL

TRIPURA

Kolkata

MYANMAR

CHHATTISGARH

ODISHA

MAHARASHTRA

Mumbai

Bay of Bengal

Arabian Sea

TELANGANA

Hyderabad

ANDHRA PRADESH

GOA

KARNATAKA

Bengaluru

KERALA

TAMIL NADU

INDIAN OCEAN

SRI LANKA

0 250 500 750 km

trucks. The red buses of the Delhi Transport Corporation, which pull out regardless, are the fearless sharks. Commercial vehicles carry advertisements front, back, and sides. A van from the All-Asian Services Corp glides past; among the advertised services is FRIDGE FOR DEAD BODY.

The art of Delhi driving demands a gap of several inches between each vehicle, plus generous blasts on the horn whenever the gap drops to almost nothing. The pandemonium of horns plays in counterpoint with the screeching of brakes and the drumming of hot tyres. We over-take a goggled scooter-rider leaning low over the handlebars, his grey-haired grandmother perched side-saddle on the pillion in her orange sari. His ashen face, eyes half-closed, sways within a finger's breadth of my window. Our driver hoots. The All-Asian Services Corp is closing in on its next client.

Delhi's road signs act as an eye-opener to India's omnivorous language scene. Traffic signs, for 'One Way' or 'No Entry', use British-based visual symbols. But the directional signs, and the names of streets, are quadrilingual. Leaving the highway, the signboard for Shanti Path, the 'Peace Road', displays four lines of text:

> Hindi name (in Devanagari script)
> SHANTI PATH (in Latin capitals)
> Punjabi name (in Gurmukhi script)
> Urdu name (in Persian script)*

Reputedly, India as a whole has 122 major languages and 1,599 minor ones. Some 75 per cent of citizens speak Indo-Aryan languages, and 20 per cent one of the Dravidian tongues, such as Tamil or Telugu.[1] The Constitution recognizes eighteen 'scheduled languages' for use in regional governments, and six 'classical languages', including Sanskrit. The 'national languages' are Standard Hindi and English. A law passed in 1963 to phase English out over fifteen years was never implemented.

The British Embassy is located near the government quarter of New Delhi, so we escape from the traffic shoal and embark on a tour of an area of the city that was designed in the early twentieth century as the showpiece of the British Empire. The architect, Sir Edwin Lutyens (1869–1944), was well known for stylistic fusions; in India he invented a blend of Classical and Oriental styles and gave it expression in the city's ubiquitous red sandstone.[2] The buildings, as harmonious as they are colossal, are distributed over a wide expanse of lawns, avenues, and flower-filled gardens. The largest of them, the Viceroy's domed resi-dence (now the *Rashtrapati Bhavan* or Presidential Palace), is raised on a ridge. The surrounding collection of ministries is adorned with

---

* Hindi, Punjabi, and Urdu are related languages from the northern Indo-Aryan linguis-tic group, but all use different alphabets. Hindi and Urdu are both variants of the Hindu-stani language, which have diverged since the Partition of 1947. Devanagari and Gurmukhi are both variants of the ancient Brahmic script, and are recognizably similar. Persian was the language of the court of the Moghul emperors. English was introduced by the East India Company in 1830.

similar domes, columns, and porticoes, protected by enormous iron railings and stone elephants. Further official residences are scattered round the hillsides, forming what was known as the Lutyens Bungalow Zone or 'LBZ'. Below them, in a spacious park, the India Gate, reminiscent of the Arc de Triomphe (but even bigger), was designed as a partner to Lutyens' Cenotaph in London; it is dedicated to the 90,000 Indian Army soldiers who fell in the First World War.

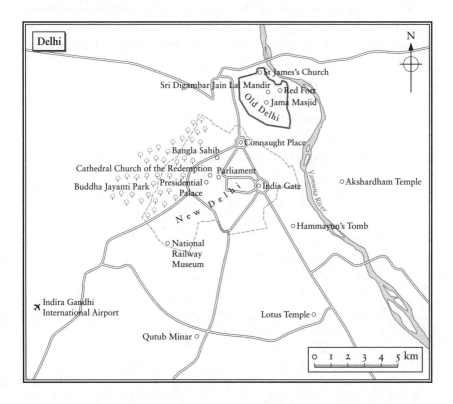

The plans for India's new capital were announced by the King-Emperor, George V, at the Delhi Durbar in 1911, and realized by 1931 at astronomic cost. When the empire evaporated a mere sixteen years later, Lutyens' urban masterpiece was handed to the Indian Republic for free – a gracious haven amidst the jostling.

The Coronation *Durbar* or 'Court' staged at Delhi from 7 to 16 December 1911 had marked the symbolic pinnacle of British rule in India. It was a week-long ceremonial extravaganza at which Emperor George and Empress Mary, dressed in exotic regalia and seated on elevated thrones, received the obeisance of all the Indian princes. Bejewelled elephants paraded. Ostentatious wealth was flaunted.

Gaudy turbans dripped with rubies and sapphires. Diamond tiaras flashed in the sun. Patronage was traded for sycophancy. No fewer than 28,702 gold and silver commemorative medals were struck. And 'God Save the King' was played incessantly. Alone among his peers, the Gaekwar of Baroda, one of the richest princes, staged a symbolic act of defiance. Dressed in a simple tunic without medals, he made a curt bow to the imperial couple, before turning his back – a conspicuous insult.[3]

That very same week, on 11 December 1911, the Bengali philosopher-poet Rabindranath Tagore (1861–1941) composed a patriotic song, the 'Jana-Gana-Mana', which he offered as an alternative to 'God Save the King':

> *Jana-Gana-Mana-Adhinaayaka, Jaya He!*
> *Bhaarata – Bhaagya – Vidhaata*
> *Punjab, Sindhu, Gujarata, Maratha,*
> *Draavida Utkala Banga,*
> *Vindhya Himaachala Yamuna Ganga . . .*

> (Thou art the ruler of all people's minds;
> Thy name rouses the hearts of
> Punjab, Sindh, Gujarata, Maratha,
> In Dravida, Orissa, and Bengal.
> It echoes in the hills of the Vindhayas and Himalayas,
> Mingles with the music of Yamuna and Ganga
> And is chanted by the waves of the Indian Sea.
> They pray for the blessing and sing thy praise.
> The salvation of all people waits in thy hand.
> Thou dispenser of India's destiny,
> *Jaya He! Jaya He! Jaya He!* Victory, Victory, Victory to Thee!)[4]

The words were ambiguous. Some took the word 'ruler' to refer to Mother India; others thought it referred to George V. But the ambiguity served a purpose. The song was soon adopted by the Indian National Congress, which was founded in 1885 as a loyalist forum for dialogue with the British, but which evolved into a political movement for Home Rule and later for independence. In 1950 the song became India's national anthem.

At the foot of the slope below the President's Palace lies the huge circular building of the *Sansad Bhavan*, India's Parliament, yet another of Lutyens' designs and opened in 1927. It contains two chambers: one, the *Lok Sabha* or House of the People, for 545 members, the other, the *Rajya Sabha* or House of the States, for 250 regional representatives.

Today, the *Sansad Bhavan* is surrounded not only by palm trees but by machine-gun nests too.

Outside the Parliament stands an oversize statue to Shaheed Bhagat Singh (1907–31), a Marxist Sikh, who, crying '*Inquilab Zindabad*', 'Long Live the Revolution', exploded a bomb inside the building in protest against imperial rule. The bomb failed to kill anyone, but the bomber was hanged for an earlier assassination. To balance the imagery, a statue to Gandhi was added in 2015.

High above the Parliament's dome, India's national tricolour flutters proudly. Together with the peacock, the lotus flower, and the 'immortal' fig tree, the *Tiranga* or 'Three Colours' is one of the country's most treasured emblems. Its horizontal stripes of saffron, white, and green are surmounted in the middle by the twenty-four-spoke *chakra*, the Wheel of Righteousness, an ancient symbol copied from the Lion Capital of Ashoka, from the holy city of Sarnath on the Ganges.[5] The semi-legendary and 'sorrowless' Emperor Ashoka (r. 268–232 BCE), who converted to Buddhism, is said to have ruled the whole of the subcontinent in a spirit of tolerance, non-violence, and harmony.[6]

Such are the myths on which the new India was born nearly seventy years ago. Practice can be rather different. Leaving New Delhi, we head to a panel discussion on 'Democracy and Culture' at the Indian International Council. The Council's chief benefactor, Syed Haider Raza (b. 1922), a Muslim artist who has lived most of his life in Paris, sits at the front in his wheelchair. The chairman, Ashish, a poet, has just produced an anthology of Polish verse in Hindi, without knowing Polish; he talks of 'Indian democracy's crisis', and says there is much more to democracy than elections alone. Aluk, an artist, says the arts are 'a vehicle for democratic persuasion'. Risking to raise the name of Winston Churchill, I expound on the saying that 'Democracy is the worst of all systems of government – except for all the others.' The last speaker, Rajiv, an eloquent academic, rails against a panoply of present ills. Next day, a *Times of India* headline reads 'Is India now an Illiberal Democracy?'

My arrival in Delhi coincided with the annual celebrations of the social reformer B. R. Ambedkar (1891–1956). Full-page announcements by the Ministry of Information appeared in the press, and poster portraits hung in the streets. I had previously had no idea what a titan of a man he was.

Known as *Babasaheb*, or Honourable Master, Bhimrao Ramji

Ambedkar or 'B.R.A' was the first 'untouchable' Indian to be fully educated and to assume a prominent position. One of the 'Fathers of the Nation', his popularity rivalled Gandhi's; in a 2012 poll he was voted 'the Greatest Indian'. His parents had worked for the British Army, but as a boy he was not allowed to sit in class with other pupils, and listened to lessons through the window; he could only have a drink if the water was poured into his glass from a balcony. Nonetheless, having finished grammar school, he graduated in law from the University of Bombay. A scholarship from the defiant Gaekwar of Baroda then took him to Columbia Law School in New York and to the London School of Economics where he was awarded a PhD in 1922. Four years later, as a barrister, he successfully defended a trio of professors who had been prosecuted for criticizing the caste system. After that, he began a campaign to open the public water supply to untouchables, and was brought into the limelight alongside Mohandas Gandhi. His milestone book *Annihilation of Caste* appeared in 1935.[7] 'B.R.A' parted company with Gandhi over his demand for untouchables to be declared an electoral class, and the two were only reconciled with difficulty. (Gandhi, while aiming to reduce inequalities, thought the castes were a source of social orderliness.)

In 1947 the *Babasaheb* became India's first Minister of Law and served in the key role of Chairman of the Constitutional Commission. Near the end of his life he converted to Buddhism, whose advocates have given him the status of *Buddruati* or 'saint', and as his second wife, he married a Brahmin. His career shows how the national independence struggle went hand in hand with social liberation.

The caste system, the *Chaturvarnya*, against which 'B.R.A' fought so tenaciously, originated many centuries ago as a hierarchy of trades – priests and scholars on top, warriors and governors next, merchants and craftsmen in the middle, and workers at the bottom. But it wasn't just an ancient system of social order. It was driven from the beginning by the mystical Hindu principle of *karma*, whereby a person's current predicament was determined by past deeds, including those enacted in previous lives before reincarnation. As a result, it encouraged the dubious idea that high social status was the product of innate virtue and that less privileged people deserved their misfortune. What is more, it was always mixed up with irrational assertions of purity and pollution, where the upper social layers were assumed to be 'clean', and the lower ones 'defiled'. Since no one could know what commendable actions or despicable offences they might have performed in their earlier incarnations, they were all taught to accept their lot with fatalistic humility. In practice, the upper echelons were tempted to surround their good fortune with inordinate pride, and to defend it to the hilt, whilst looking down on the less fortunate with contempt.

Under British rule the caste system hardened into a more rigid and universal hierarchy, where the four *varnas* or caste groupings pre-determined everyone's social status, and where equivalents of Hindu castes were replicated among Muslims, Buddhists, and Sikhs.[8] The *Brahmana* or Brahmins were 'the enlightened ones'; the *Kshatriya* or Protectors could hold senior military or civilian positions; the *Vaishya*, literally 'the Settlers', were engaged in economic tasks as traders, farmers, artisans, or money-lenders; and the *Shudra* or 'servants' performed services to fulfil their superiors' needs. The upper castes – the *Brahmins*, the *Kshatriya*, and the *Vaishya* – considered themselves to be specially favoured by the gods, and to be *dvija* or 'twice born'. To mark the spiritual rebirth that was assumed to accompany their physical reincarnation, they were initiated as youths by the ceremony of the 'sacred thread', which was wound round their body, entitling them (and only them) to embark on the study of the Vedas. Everyone else was inferior.

These broad divisions, however, were only the beginning of it. Each of the four *varnas* was divided into *jatis* or sub-groupings, and each *jati* into sub-sub-groups. The sub-castes of the Vaishyas, for example, included the Agraharis, the Barnwals, the Gahois, the Kasuadhans, the Khandewals, the Maheshwaris, and many others. The Brahmins comprised about one hundred sub-groups. As a result, the full 'List of Castes' was over four thousand strong.[9] Great diversity also prevailed among the lower castes. The Shudras, the most numerous of the *varnas*, were divided between the *Sat-Shudra*, who were considered 'clean', and the despised *Ati-Shudra*, who were not. Below them lived a broad swathe of *avarnas* or 'non-*varna* castes', and below them, the people who belonged to no caste at all. The latter were classed in English as the 'outcastes' or 'untouchables', although they again were divided between the 'un-approachables', the 'untouchables', and the 'unseeables', who were not supposed to be even seen by others. In imperial parlance, the 'outcastes' were named 'the depressed classes'. In Gandhi's terminology they were the *Harijan* or 'Children of God'. One also encounters the term *Pan-chama*, meaning 'the Fifth Estate'. But among themselves, and in the steps of Ambedkar, they have adopted the name of *Dalit*, the 'oppressed'.[10]

'B.R.A' himself belonged to a sub-group called *Mahar*, descendants of the indigenous people of Maharashtra state. Over time, the Mahars came to be regarded by the superstitious populace as 'polluted' and were not permitted to set foot in Hindu temples. They were forced to wear a spittoon around their neck to prevent them spitting onto the ground, and to carry a broom for erasing their footprints.[11] In southern India, particularly in the region of Madras, the *Paraiyan* caste – from which the English word 'pariah' derives – formed a substantial sub-group, whose sometime middling status fell to become the lowest of the low. Their name means 'drummer', but, after losing their original occupational designation as court entertainers, they ended up as domestics, gravediggers, scavengers, and slaves.[12]

To complicate matters further, in addition to their designated caste, many Indians belonged to genealogical clans called *gotras*, each supposedly descended from the same, male ancestor; these, too, had their senior and junior lines. In short, every single person in India was placed at birth into a series of social pigeonholes, from which it was all but impossible to escape.*

Nowadays, discrimination based on the former castes is banned by law, and, in theory, strict penalties await anyone who abuses a person from a lower or despised category. The main social groupings that function in contemporary India, not least in electoral politics, are based either on religious communities, economic classes, regional identities, or extended families. The time has gone when the lower orders faced insuperable barriers to advancement. The first untouchable to break the taboo was K. R. Narayanan (1920–2005), who rose to the positions of ambassador to Thailand, Turkey, and China, and then of President of the Republic from 1997 to 2002.

Ever since the 1950s the government of India has been engaged in policies of positive affirmation. In order to do so, it set up an official catalogue of Scheduled Castes (SCs) and Scheduled Tribes (STs), together with a category that the bureaucracy designated, inimitably, as the Other Backward Classes (OBCs), representing about 40 per cent of the population.[13] It also sets quotas for the employment of disadvantaged groups. The Supreme Court has ruled that all educational bodies must

* There were also regional variations. In South India, for example, instead of the four *varnas*, only three caste-groupings were recognized: the Brahmins, the non-Brahmins, and the Untouchables. A powerful kinship group called Reddy, headed by warriors and landowners, cut across caste barriers, and still plays a prominent role in the state of Andhra Pradesh. In Bengal, the influential *Baidya* caste, literally 'physicians', were partly classed as Brahmins and partly not.

reserve a quarter of their places for disadvantaged applicants. Needless to say, 'disadvantaged' often proves to be a thin cover for *Dalit*, and the principles of equality and meritocracy by which the new India is supposed to operate are often observed in the breach.

Indeed, the whole issue of caste remains a very touchy subject. For one thing, Indian surnames are often linked to a family's former caste. Sharma, for example, meaning 'priest', clearly indicates Brahmin origin; so does Jha or Chakravarti. Gupta, meaning 'Ruler', is a *Kshatriya* name, while Bazigar, meaning 'gypsy acrobat', and Nat, meaning 'dancer', have Dalit overtones. Indians forever try to guess what a person's caste background may be, especially when a name can be pinned to a craft or occupation:

| | | |
|---|---|---|
| Achari = carpenter | Dubashi = translator | Bania = merchant |
| Darzi = tailor | Gandhi = perfume-seller | Majumdar = scribe |
| Desai = landlord | Nehru = canal dweller | Patel = village headman |
| Sirkiband = basket-weaver | Chamar = tanner | Mochi = shoemaker |

(Agrawal, Bahl, and Mittal, in contrast, are names derived not from castes but from clans.) People wishing to shed their caste identity often adopt the artificial surname of Kumar, which inevitably arouses suspicions.

'B.R.A' contested yet another item of social pathology, namely the ill-treatment of the Scheduled Tribes. The government's list or 'Schedule' of such tribes contains no fewer than 461 communities totalling 83 million people and including indigenous peoples, such as Muncha, Karbi, and Naga, that are in danger of extinction.[14] (The long-running conflict between central government forces and the 'indigenous' people in Nagaland on the Burmese frontier, for example, remains unresolved.) India is not a country readily associated with racial or aboriginal abuse, but it happens.[15] The dark-skinned Dravidians of southern India often risk being mistakenly equated with Dalits. Some of the *Paraiyan* have now adopted the prouder title of *Adi-Dravida*, 'the indigenous Dravidians'.[16]

The severest critics maintain that 'casteism' and other forms of collective discrimination are thriving. 'Democracy hasn't eradicated the caste system,' writes the novelist Arundhati Roy; 'it has entrenched and modernised it.' She quotes Ambedkar, whose works she has edited, saying 'For the Untouchables, Hinduism is a chamber of horrors.' And she supplies the damning statistics. The ex-Brahmins who make up 3.5 per cent of India's population hold 70 per cent of all senior government posts. The former Vaishyas dominate economic life in a similar way. Nine out of ten of India's richest men belong to the traditional *Bania* merchant caste. (The Ambani family, whose patriarchal father died in 2002, has been counted among the world's three wealthiest families.) In contrast, nine out of ten of the street-sweepers and sewage workers employed by government departments are Dalits. Roy's article on this subject is entitled 'India's Shame'.[17]

Most glaring, however, is the low status and rooted maltreatment of women, especially women of the lower castes. Female infanticide is said to be rife in rural areas, and the trafficking of girls, for either prostitution or domestic servitude or forced marriage, has made international headlines. Nepal is one of the main suppliers and Delhi one of the main markets. India's gender ratio is seriously skewed, and superstitions persist. 'Two girls are a sign of sin,' they say, or 'a boy is an asset, a girl a liability.' Almost all the least attractive jobs are reserved for women. Thousands and thousands of them work every day carrying baskets of human excrement on their heads, as they clean out the village latrines all over rural India. Dalit women are doubly vulnerable. Haryana State, next to Delhi, whose name means 'God's Abode', has an unenviable record of sexual violence.[18]

Men, too, have problems. Their chances of finding a wife are less than even; brides can be priced at 15,000 rupees upwards; and youths are drawn into a culture of disrespect and gang rapes. Press reports routinely refer to the victims of 'rape' as 'underprivileged women'. The euphemism is a device for overriding some very ugly realities. The word *Dalit* does not mean 'untouchable', as the higher castes often call them; its literal meaning of 'oppressed' has overtones of 'broken' or 'crushed', and hints at continuing and widespread practices of systematic harassment and persecution. In 1989 the Indian government passed a law with the remarkable title of 'The Scheduled Castes and Scheduled Tribes (Prevention of Atrocities) Act'. Among the offences that the Act sought to prevent was forcing Dalit people to eat or drink obnoxious substances (such as urine and excrement); assaulting Dalit women; using a position of dominance to exploit a Dalit woman sexually; and fouling the water source of a Dalit village. Such outrages, apparently, are still prevalent. Every single week, thirteen Dalits are murdered; five Dalit houses are burned down; six Dalits are abducted; and twenty-one Dalits are raped.[19] A crime against Dalits occurs every eighteen minutes, yet many officials refuse to enforce the legislation. According to an international report, Dalit people are barred from entering police stations in 28 per cent of rural villages; public health workers decline to enter Dalit homes in 33 per cent of villages; Dalits are not permitted to eat at the same table as non-Dalits in 77 per cent of villages; and 48 per cent of Dalit villages lack their own source of water. Who can say, therefore, that caste has been eliminated in India? According to the International Dalit Solidarity Network, 'Dalit women experience triple discrimination based on caste, economic situation, and gender.' And 'Violence is used . . . as a social mechanism for humiliating entire Dalit communities.'[20]

The sheer savagery that Dalits can face is exemplified by the tragic case in 2006 of Surekha Bhotmange and her family. An educated Buddhist and Dalit married to an illiterate husband, Surekha had bought a plot of land in the upper-caste village of Khairlanji in the region of Nagpur. The village council repeatedly refused her permission to construct a brick-built house, and she angered her neighbours by giving information to the police about a local crime:

> On September 29 2006, Surekha Bhotmange (45), her daughter Priyanka (17), and her two sons Roshan (21) and Sudhir (23) were brutally killed in a planned attack by a group of non-Dalit villagers . . . [The father] was away . . . The four victims were dragged to the village centre, strapped to a bullock cart, stripped, paraded naked, tortured and maimed, [attacked] with bicycle chains, axes, daggers and sticks . . . Men from the entire village of some 150 families gathered . . . even as their womenfolk looked on . . . They [tried to] force the sister and one of her brothers to copulate, and [having failed] crushed Sudhir's genitals. They then gang raped Ms Priyanka, thrusting the sticks into [her]. After hiding the bodies in houses, they [threw] them into the canal. This was celebrated like a festival. Later, a village meeting was called, and everyone present was ordered not to mention the massacre to any outsider.[21]

After lengthy investigations, the perpetrators escaped the death sentence.[22]

Yet the treatment of Dalits forms only part of the problem. In 1988 the Indian government also outlawed the *Devadasi* system. The *devadasis* or *joginis*, literally 'serving-girls of the Gods', go by a variety of names, most usually translated into English, unkindly, as 'temple prostitutes'. Female babies have been sold to Hindu temples since time immemorial. They undergo an elaborate ritual at puberty, after which they provide all manner of ceremonial, artistic, and sexual services. In practice, they are slaves, and, if they escape, are regarded as unmarriageable renegades. Although most common in southern India, they are common enough in Delhi, where their numbers are estimated at 50,000–60,000.[23]

Growing interest in women's rights recently provoked a hunt for the first Indian woman to have contested her rape publicly. The heroine was identified as Mathura, an orphaned member of the Ghand tribe, who had been raped in a village police station in Maharashtra State on 26 March 1972. Her ordeal began when her brother took her to the station, complaining that a neighbour was pressing her into a forced marriage. The police concluded that the girl was guilty of causing the dispute, locked her up, and then attacked her. The higher authorities, however, decided to prosecute, and a legal saga was played out over six years. The policemen were successively acquitted, convicted, and re-acquitted on appeal. The judge of appeal ruled that Mathura had consented to her misfortune. She received no justice. But her case inspired both press reports and public protests. Forty years later, selling baskets in her native village, she was amazed to be sought out by a CNN news team.[24]

Some months after I left, Delhi was the scene of a horrendous crime that became world news.[25] A young woman, a trainee physiotherapist, was walking along a main street with her boyfriend after an evening at the cinema. They boarded a bus, thinking it a regular service, only to find themselves trapped and attacked by half a dozen men. The girl's companion was beaten senseless; she was dragged to the back of the bus and repeatedly raped. But that's not the worst. She was assaulted internally with an iron rod with such violence that her intestines were ripped out of her body. The victims were then dumped by the roadside. Somehow the man recovered, but, despite surgery, the young woman died. The press called her Damini, 'Lightning', after a film heroine. Speculation raged as to whether or not she was a Dalit; she was not. The trial of the perpetrators began in March 2013: a reminder of aspects of Indian life that casual visitors don't see, but which confirm a recent assessment of the country as 'An Uncertain Glory'.[26]

So far, most of my time in Delhi had been spent at the top end of the social scene: chatting to diplomats, eating in revolving restaurants, taking tea at the art deco Imperial Hotel, and racing round the tourist circuit. One brief taste of 'the other side' happened on the day that I visited the Red Fort. Having rested to let the midday heat subside, I hired a rickshaw to take me round the adjacent quarter of Old Delhi.

This was not a motorized tuk-tuk, and Old Delhi is not New Delhi. As soon as you plunge into the sprawling tangle of alleyways to the west of the Red Fort, you jump straight from the First World into the Third. The press of sweating humanity is oppressive. The rickshaw-wallah, groaning with the effort, stands on the pedals to get traction; in tricky sections, he dismounts and pushes. He has no gears, no bell, and only one rudimentary brake. He yells aloud continuously to keep the crush at bay. For the traffic shoal here is packed like sardines, and moves on feet as well as wheels. We weave and squeeze and graze and jockey. There is no chance of turning against the flow. If we slow for a pothole, or a bottle or a mangy dog, we are instantly bumped from behind. Cycles in front and alongside are strapped high with bales of cotton or drums of oil or building beams. Young men and women carrying boxes on their heads dodge in and out, and skip over the foul-smelling gutter; a crippled beggar, dust-caked and wide-eyed with fright, sows pandemonium as he crawls across the street on all fours. Overhead, scores of ancient electric cables strung between buildings sag to head height. Unprotected wires dangle, threatening to spark. Gaunt old women squint between the washing on the high balconies. People of all sizes and ages sit, stand, stroll, and sell as best they can on litter-deep pavements. Open booths serve as shops, workshops, or eating parlours. Bystanders just gape as the tide surges past. In a dark corner, a family of destitutes lies in the filth; a girl with infested hair clings to a blank-staring mother; a naked baby boy, covered in sores, crawls over his prostrate father . . .

I said something to the rickshaw-wallah about the film *Slumdog Millionaire*, and touched a raw nerve.

'This,' he assured me, shouting over his shoulder indignantly, 'is *not* a slum; it is a respectable district that fell on hard times. No, not a slum; you don't find beggars in a slum.'

Old Delhi is a cut above the *jhuggi jhopris*, the hutments or slums.

'They are completely different,' he continues. 'They're elsewhere. You can go on a tour, if you want.' They are down at the Yamuna Pushta, on the riverbed. They imply shanties and hovels and open sewers and mountains of decaying rubbish and gangs of wild children, the real slumdogs, who roam the tips.

'Old Delhi is just a place with too many people,' he says.

Human life is packed cheek-by-jowl with nowhere to breathe. India's population is growing by 18 million every year. Prime Minister Rajiv Gandhi, before his murder in 1991, proposed mass sterilization.

'Too many people' sums it up. The newspaper carries an article about 'Delhi's Unending Search for Water'.[27] The Yamuna River is dead. Supplies from the hydro-electric dams in nearby Himachal Pradesh are insufficient. Not a drop is saved from the annual monsoon downpours. And the Delhi Jal Board's Master Plan is constantly delayed. Thirst looms.

That evening, I was invited with a friend from the British Embassy to have supper with one of the academics we had met at the democracy seminar. Our host was a prominent member of India's liberal elite, and lives in a gated precinct. He is an active secularist, staunchly opposing the mixing of religion and politics, and is extremely knowledgeable about maltreatment of minorities around the globe. He regaled us with details of the Bulgarian Communist Party's policy, which he had witnessed in the 1980s, of forcing Turks to slavicize their names.

Indian politics is not a subject for the faint-hearted. But, since the professor was familiar with Eastern Europe, it was natural to ask him about India's brush with communism, and her long association with the Soviet Union.

'In the days before Independence,' I ventured, 'communism must have had its supporters in the struggle against colonialism, poverty and the caste system.'

'Of course it did,' he replied, 'but it never really took root; the comrades quarrelled, and we now have dozens of communist parties.' After 1947, India's links to the USSR were driven by fears of China, not by a love of communism. 'Indians don't take to foreign ideologies.'

Scores of parties competed in the democratic arena, nearly all based on race, religion, caste, or tribe. The only Indian communist known to me, M. N. Roy (1887–1954), was a Brahmin married to a Californian.

At that time, India's government, under the left-of-centre United Progressive Alliance, had been holding power for nearly a decade.

'These days,' the professor said, 'it's not parties that have the upper hand, but multi-party alliances.'

Nehru's Congress Party, which ruled the roost for decades, had split into quarrelling factions, and its Oxbridge-educated, upper-caste leaders, headed by the Gandhi dynasty, looked increasingly out of date.*

---

* Although Pandit Nehru was undoubtedly of Brahmin descent, doubts have been expressed about his successors. Indira Nehru, Pandit's daughter, married Feroze Gandhi, a Farsi Zoroastrian, in contravention of the Brahmin code. Strictly speaking, therefore, neither

After the election of 2004, Sonia Gandhi handed the premiership to a gentle, turbaned Sikh, Manmohan Singh, a long-serving bureaucrat.

'The whole point about our PM,' the professor explained, 'is that he doesn't belong to the former ruling circles, and doesn't offend anybody.'

The ladies, meanwhile, were talking about the wave of gang rapes that was plaguing India.

'The Dalit women are most at risk,' one said. 'No one defends them.'

'In the rural villages,' another added, 'there are no toilets, or running water. Women traditionally go out into the fields after dark to relieve themselves; and that's when the gangs strike.'

'Are these crimes really more prevalent,' someone asked, 'or are women less reticent about protesting?'

The parliamentary opposition was run at the time by another coalition, the right-of-centre National Democratic Alliance. The party that drives it is the Hindu nationalist Bharatiya Janata Party (the BJP), whose central concept, *Hindutva*, is variously translated as 'integral humanism' or 'cultural nationalism'; but its opponents accuse it of violence. In 2002 ethnic riots in Gujarat left two thousand dead, and many more, mainly Muslims, displaced. Gujarat's Chief Minister, Narendra Modi, was charged with complicity. He cleared his name legally, and made his state blossom. 'Modi is heading for the national scene', we were told, 'and he's from the Other Backward Classes.'

In the national elections of May 2014, Narendra Modi did indeed sweep to a landslide victory. Enjoying an absolute majority, his party could rule without a coalition. The agency wires buzzed. Some said that he was a formidable manager, who would run India as efficiently as he ran Gujarat. Others said he was a barely disguised Hindu firebrand, waiting to set India alight. But everyone commented on his being a member of a sub-caste of the *Ghanchi*, one of the OBCs. This information was equivalent to knowing in Britain at what school a politician was educated. The Ghanchis, literally 'sellers of vegetable oil', are not at the bottom of the caste list, but they are not even close to the top of the bottom half. Modi's father had been a tea-wallah at a railway station, and he had employed his son to hand out drinks and wash up cups. Entering his official residence at No. 7 Race Course Road, the new prime minister was the first of his kind to cross its threshold.[28]

---

Sanjay Gandhi, who died in an air crash in 1980, nor Rajiv Gandhi, who was assassinated in 1991, nor Rajiv's Italian-born widow, Sonia, can be counted as Brahmins.

Perhaps the biggest secret of Modi's background, however, emerged as a result of details on his electoral registration form. For fifty years Modi had presented himself as a bachelor, and, in the tradition of Hindu ascetics, had regularly praised the virtues of celibacy. But now, pressed by the media, he confessed not only that he had been married but also that his wife was still alive. He and Jashodaben Chimanlal had been forcibly wed as teenagers by their families. They had separated after three years, he to join a Hindu sect and she to train as a primary schoolteacher. Jashodaben confirmed everything. She was living in a one-room apartment in a rural village with no bathroom. And she was content with her role as a class teacher – mainly of Muslim girls.[29]

Shortly before that election, the High Court in Delhi upheld the death sentences passed on four men convicted of Damini's rape and murder. (One of the suspects had already killed himself in jail.) Justifying the sentences, the judge declared, with manifest inaccuracy, that the case represented 'the rarest of rare crimes'. Thanks to the public outcry in 2013–14, an avalanche of unreported past crimes was coming to light, together with growing evidence of police negligence and complicity. No fewer than seventy serving police officers in Delhi were now facing rape charges.[30]

But shortly after the election, yet another horrendous gang rape hit the headlines. Two teenage cousins, aged fourteen and sixteen, who had gone out after dark, were raped, strangled, and hanged in Katra village in Uttar Pradesh – their bodies left dangling on a mango tree.[31] Their gruesome fate further underlined the fact that the maltreatment of Indian women is often attended not just by sexual violence but (as also in the case of Damini) by depraved sadism.

The caste question lurked behind almost every issue. After our supper, the professor's wife, who was born in Punjab, laughed as she explained how she had learned 'to emit false signals' about her social origins. If directly challenged, she would counter a question with a question: 'What do YOU think that my background is?' And the busybody would always get it wrong.

Yet the professor told how confusing signals could also lead to trouble. He usually dresses in the national garb of *kurta* and *pajama*, whilst sporting a trimmed beard as adopted when a student in Europe. His dress signals 'Hindu', but his beard does not. One day, when showing relatives round a temple, an attendant ordered him to leave.

'Get out,' the attendant cried, 'you're a Muslim.'

'I assure you, my dear man, I am not.'

'Yes, you are; you have a beard! You are a Muslim.'

So the professor had to correct the man severely. 'BULLSHIT!' he roared. 'BULLSHIT. I'M A BRAHMIN.'

All the guidebooks talk of the seven successive cities on which Delhi was built. But it is no less instructive to think of seven successive religions or civilizations. To understand the immense diversity of India's capital, one useful strategy is to explore those religions – one for each day of the week.

**Hinduism** is as old as India. Its European name was invented in the eighteenth century to encompass a vast and diverse collection of traditions and beliefs, to which Indians most commonly refer, not as Hinduism, but as the *Sanatana Dharma*, 'the ancient teachings'. It is replete with countless gods and goddesses, legends, doctrines, rituals, festivals, and holy Sanskrit scriptures, and customarily consists of four major sects: *Shaiva* (for devotees of the god Shiva), *Vaishnava* (for devotees of Vishnu), *Shakta* (for devotees of Shakti), and *Smarta* (for those for whom the supreme deity is the abstract but omnipresent Brahman). Some Hindus recognize a godly 'Trinity' – Shiva, Vishnu, and Brahman; others claim that each god offers a different road to the same goal. The Hindu scriptures comprise both the *Shruti* or divinely 'revealed texts' and the *Smriti* or 'remembered texts': the former include the Vedas and the Upanishads, the latter the sacred epics of *Mahabharata* and *Ramayana*.[32]

A multitude of guides and websites, each more convoluted than the next, attempt to expound the principles of 'the world's oldest religion'. At the risk of oversimplification, one can concentrate on one god, 'the Lord Shiva', whose shrine can be found in most temples, and on the 'Nine Beliefs' that most Hindus hold. Shiva, who threatens death, decline, and destruction, needs to be appeased. The nine core beliefs form 'the ties that bind':

1.  an all-pervasive Supreme Creator exists, lord of the seen and unseen
2.  the four Vedas are divinely inspired
3.  the universe passes through endless cycles of creation, growth, and dissolution
4.  *karma*, the law of cause and effect, ties man's destiny to his deeds
5.  the soul is constantly reincarnated until attaining *moksha* or 'liberation'

6. temple worship enables people to contact the unseen world
7. the aid of a *satguru* or 'master' is vital to knowing the Absolute Transcendent
8. all life is sacred, demanding the practice of *ahimsa* or 'non-violence'
9. all the world's religions lead towards the same Divine Light.

Many tourists in Delhi are directed to the Swaminarayan Akshardham, founded in 2005, the capital's most modern temple. Standing beside the Yamuna River, this enormous edifice was built in a mix of pink sandstone and white marble and is covered in carvings of flowers, fauna, musicians, dancers, and deities. Containing 20,000 statues, 234 lifesize stone elephants, multiple IMAX screens, and a musical fountain, it was entered in the *Guinness Book of Records* for being 'The World's Largest Comprehensive Hindu Temple'.[33]

I am advised, however, to give Akshardham a miss. There are countless smaller, more authentic temples in Delhi. So I jump into a taxi with my guide of the day, jostle through the traffic, then screech to a halt amidst a cacophony of honking horns in the middle of a roundabout, where our chosen temple is inconveniently located. The colour scheme is garish. Visitors are required to shed their shoes and sometimes their socks. A labyrinth of stairways and tunnels leads along an obstacle course of caves, cellars, and side-chapels all filled with glowering gods and fantastical beasts. The symbolic *Shiva Lingam*, or Shiva's Stone, lies in a central area. Ringing the brass bell to announce our presence, we offer a donation to the priest, and receive a spot of holy oil on the forehead, a red prayer mantra on the wrist, and a teaspoon of water to drink. (Westerners fearful of bacteria can pour the water on their hair.) A cross-legged priest sits behind a glass screen, reading the holy texts into a microphone.

**Jainism** grew out of Hinduism. Known to its followers as *Jaina dharma*, it was founded sometime in the second millennium BCE, when the Vedic tradition was already ancient. Rishaba, the first *tirthankara* or 'propagator of the faith', cannot be dated; the second, Parshva, belonged to the ninth century BCE, and the third, Mahavira, the main one, to the sixth century BCE. Mahavira's disciples called him *jina*, 'the conqueror', which refers to the conquest of one's self.[34]

Jainist doctrines, evolving from earlier Hindu ones, place special emphasis on *ahimsa* and *karma*. The Jains accused the Hindus of laxity, and instituted a system of vows to heighten the degree of self-control to which devotees can aspire. Ordinary lay people take the so-called 'lesser vows'; dedicated monks and ascetics adhere to the five 'greater vows':

1. *ahimsa*, 'non-violence', which demands doing no harm to any living creature
2. *satya*, 'truth': always speaking the truth, except when it leads to violence
3. *asteya*, 'self-denial', which regards enriching oneself as a form of theft
4. *brahmacharya*, 'abstinence', especially sexual abstinence
5. *aparigraha*, 'detachment', involving the renunciation of property and family.

The Jainist interpretation of *karma* has led them to a very specific understanding of the workings of the soul. In its pure state the soul is thought to be capable of infinite knowledge, infinite bliss, and infinite energy. In reality, however, it is full of impurities, just as gold is; and the lifetime task of Jains is to purify 'the bondage' of their souls in the same way that gold is refined.

Jainist theory and practice, therefore, demand dedicated study. Nonetheless, certain features are easily grasped. One is the strict adherence of the Jains to a vegetarian and non-dairy diet. In their eyes the preparation of meat, milk, cheese, and even root vegetables involves unacceptable degrees of violence. The Jains also cultivate special attitudes to human limitations. Their concept of *anekantavada* or 'pluralism', for example, holds that no single viewpoint ever expresses the absolute truth, thereby demanding a diversity of opinions. They tell the tale of the blind men and the elephant: one man feels its trunk, a second its ear, and a third its foot. The only way to comprehend the beast in full is for all perspectives to be pooled.

No visitor to Delhi should miss the main Jain Temple, the Sri Digambar Jain Lal Mandir, which stands in the city centre in the Chandni Chowk district. Built in 1656 by a Muslim Emperor who wished to humour his Jain financiers, it is popularly known as Lal Mandir, the Red Temple, and is immediately recognizable from its three soaring, mitre-shaped towers in luminous red brick. In order to enter, one passes a high *manastambha* column. In the entrance hall visitors hand over not only their shoes but all other leather items: handbags, belts, watch straps, and camera cases. (Leather, to a Jain, is the relic of a murdered animal.) One then crosses the courtyard and climbs the stairs to the devotional area. The main shrine is devoted to the Lord Mahavira, who is presented sitting in the lotus position, surrounded by the statues of *tirthankaras* or 'lesser luminaries'. Jain art is fond of symbols, such as the swastika and the wheel-in-hand; it also favours standing male nudes, which derive from the prehistoric Indus Valley Civilization. The atmosphere of calm contrasts with a Hindu temple's bustle. People come and go, leaving offerings of fruit, grains, rice, and candles, their faces reflected in the warm glow emitted by gilded paintwork and the flames of butter lamps.

**Buddhism** is in many ways a partner to Jainism. The Lord Buddha, the Master of Perfection, was a contemporary of the Mahavira, and probably knew of him. Both were high-born princes who renounced their inheritance; both promoted habits of deep philosophical reflection; and both gained followings that have thrived for 2,500 years.

Born *circa* 563 BCE, Siddhartha Gautama was brought up in a ruling family in present-day Nepal. Realizing that luxury and power did not guarantee happiness, he plunged into the study of religion, and at the age of twenty-nine declared that he had found 'the middle path' between self-denial and indulgence, and had thereby become enlightened. When asked who he was, he replied, 'I am awake' – *buddha* meaning 'awake'; and the appellation stuck. The implication is that his previous state of consciousness resembled a deep sleep. Like Jesus Christ, he left no written testimony. Moreover, he often maintained 'the noble silence', thereby obstructing the task of his disciples who wanted to know his thoughts. The ideas and sayings directly attributed to him were recorded centuries after his death, and organized into the threefold scriptures known as the *Tripitaka*: the *Sutra* (direct sayings), the *Vinaya* (monastic rules), and the *Abhidharma* (on psychology and philosophy).

By then, two main Buddhist schools were emerging. One, the *Hinayana* or 'Little Raft', developed mainly in Ceylon, Burma, and Indochina, and emphasized individual self-perfection; the other, the *Mahayana* or 'Big Raft', from Tibet, China, and Japan, emphasized compassion and service to others.[35]

The clearest summary of Buddha's teaching is to be found in accounts of the sermon that he delivered on emerging from six years in the forest and declaring his enlightenment. It contains many famous sayings, such as 'Be lamps unto yourselves', which suggests that we should not submit to external authority, or 'Each of us is the sum total of what we have thought.' It also lists three 'noble truths' and 'the eightfold path' to self-fulfilment. The first truth is the inevitability of *dukkha*, usually translated as 'suffering' or 'adversity'. The second, *tanha*, condemns the excessive pursuit of private desires. And the third expounds the need for overcoming one's cravings and desires. The 'Eightfold Path' systematically outlines the methods whereby the adept can reach *nirvana*, the perfect mental state. It includes Right Knowledge, Right Aspiration, Right Speech, Right Behaviour, Right Occupation, Right Effort, Right Mindfulness, and Right Concentration. The last two subjects point to *raja yoga*, the 'royal road' of meditation, which lifts people above their daily round.

Unlike Hinduism or Jainism, Buddhism was widely exported beyond India. Starting in Nepal and Bhutan (where today it is the official religion), it crossed the Himalayas into north-east Asia, and also travelled to the south-east, into present-day Indonesia. Focused as it is on people's inner lives, it disdains prevailing cultures, social norms, or political systems, and aspires to universal appeal.

Not surprisingly, Delhi possesses numerous Buddhist temples, schools, and study centres. All the main, international branches – Tibetan, Chinese, Zen, and others – are represented. Fearing temple fatigue, I was content to stroll in the Buddha Jayanti Park in the New Delhi suburbs, created for the 2,500th anniversary of the Master's enlightenment, and opened in 1993 by the Dalai Lama. It is a place where one really does feel awake. A fine golden statue of the Buddha sits under a stone canopy on a small island in the lake, surrounded by water lilies and goldfish. A sapling from the holy Bodhi fig tree stands nearby. Garden birds flit among the bushes. Warm spring sunshine floods in. Perhaps the Lord Buddha is to Asia what St Francis of Assisi is to Europe, only more so.

The city of Delhi, originally called Dillika, was founded in the days of the Rajput emperors in the eighth to ninth centuries. Its earliest remains are located in the modern suburb of Mehrauli. In those days, the Hindu religion had no serious challenger. Jainism had declined from an earlier peak, and Buddhism was the main alternative. In Europe, the Byzantine Empire was approaching its apogee, and the short-lived Frankish Empire of Charlemagne dominated the West. Shortly, the Hindu world, like that of the Christians, would be shaken by a new and militant religion, sprung from the sands of Arabia.

**Islam**, following several minor incursions, reached the subcontinent in the last decades of the twelfth century. It was but the latest of several such civilizational invasions, and was brought in the saddlebags of wild tribesmen from Persia and Afghanistan, who rode into the lush valleys of the Indus and the Ganges, overthrowing everything in their way. It was a religion with a mission: to proclaim the invincibility of Allah and His Prophet, to spread the word of the Holy Koran, and to crush the Infidel. Its advocates had already been pursuing these aims for half a millennium, taking control of a vast swathe of the earth's surface from Iberia to Central Asia, and moving still further afield into East Africa and the East Indies. Its severe, warrior precepts bore little relation to those of the comfortable civilizations that it now encountered, and its turbaned horsemen must have stared in wide-eyed wonder when they first saw a Shivan temple or a gilded statue of the Buddha. The Hindu guru or Buddhist monk must equally have scratched their heads in amazement on learning from the newcomers that there was only one God.

The ruler most usually credited for the Muslims' advance into India was Sultan Muhammad of Ghor (1150–1206), often known as Ghori, whose power base lay in north-west Afghanistan. Nominally subordinate to the Abbasid Caliph in Baghdad, he and his ancestors spent the best part of a century warring with their Turkic neighbours to the east, the lords of Ghazna. In the course of these wars they razed the city of Ghazna by fire, thereby earning the epithet of *Jahansuz* or 'world burners'; they also became involved in a dispute over the district of Multan in Punjab, on the far side of the Khyber. Ghori assembled an army of 120,000 mamluk slaves, led the first of four expeditions into 'Hindustan' in 1175, and gained a decisive victory at the Second Battle of Tarain in 1192. His chief commander during the battle, Qutb-ad-Din, a Kipchak-Cuman slave, proceeded to conquer Delhi and to serve as Ghori's deputy.

Ghori, however, had no offspring, and had trained his slave-commanders to be his successors. When he was assassinated, therefore, his empire was divided among them, and Qutb-ad-Din, surnamed *Aibak*, assumed the title of Sultan, and started the first independent reign of the Slave Dynasty of the Delhi Sultanate. In this way the Indian population of the far-flung Sultanate mingled with their conquerors, thereby launching the rich fusion of Hindu and Muslim elements in the hybrid civilization of subsequent centuries.[36]

The second city of Delhi, located in the modern western suburbs, was created in the early thirteenth century by successive rulers of the Slave Dynasty. Its centrepiece is the amazing *Qutub Minar*, 'The Tower of Qutb-ad-Din'. Assembled from massive blocks of red sandstone, it is densely decorated with elaborate, abstract carvings, and at 73 metres was the world's tallest building in its time. It provided me with an unforgettable afternoon, mixing with local trippers and pondering the vast expanses of Indian history. I was shown round the site by an official guide wearing a wide-brimmed, bright yellow sunhat and speaking a flowery brand of subcontinental English.

I sat in the shade of the ruins with my telephoto lens, snapping the details of the carved sandstone against the pure blue backdrop of a cloudless sky. I then noticed an even more colourful sight. The trippers were lining up, family after family, to take their group pictures against the most exotic section of the ruins. I could snap away from a distance taking pictures of the picture-takers. Indians are handsome people at the worst of times, but in relaxed mood and surrounded by their ancient heritage they assumed a special level of photogeneity. The saris, turbans, and parasols shone in every hue of the rainbow, mixed with baseball caps, sunglasses, jeans, trainers, and jet-black hair. Proud parents held up their infants to the lens or iPhone. Venerable elders stood with grandchildren and great-grandchildren, telling them no doubt about Ghori and the Minar's builders. Everyone was smiling.

The Sultanate of Delhi lasted through five dynasties until 1526, when it was overthrown by yet another Muslim invasion, from Afghanistan. The new rulers, the Moghul emperors, set up court in Agra. But when they moved their capital to Delhi in 1648, the brand-new, purpose-built city of *Shahjahanabad* awaited them beside the Yamuna River. At its heart, the *Lal Qila* or Red Fort, another outsize sandstone masterpiece, gave rise to the city's modern name, which derives from the Hindustani *dehali*, meaning 'gateway' and pronounced 'Dilli'. (The inhabitants are 'Dilli-wallahs'.) You line up beside the moat to pass the security check, males on one side and females on the other. You then climb the stairs towards the battlements. The midday sunlight dazzles, and the sunbaked stone walls exude heat like a stoked furnace.

I could have made the almost obligatory pilgrimage to the Taj Mahal in Agra, in the company of many others, but decided instead to stay in Delhi to see another magnificent Moghul mausoleum. Humayun was the second Moghul Emperor (r. 1530–56), and his tomb was constructed by his successor, Akbar, who was followed later by Shah Jahan (r. 1628–58), the Taj Mahal's patron.

Humayun's Tomb betrays a mix of Persian and Indian styles, and provided the model on which the taller Taj Mahal was based. Its solid orange-red stone is lightened by generous expanses of white marble. Its frontal view is dominated by a bottom row of small honeycombs, by a middle section of handsome oriental arches, and high above by a superbly proportioned, white-tiled dome. The surrounding park of 400 acres is irrigated and dotted with cypresses, and further tombs of Moghul dignitaries adorn the periphery. Although it can't compete with the romantic love story of Jahan and Mumtaz Mahal at Agra, it does have a storyline of its own. Humayun, 'The Lucky One', was once the owner of the Koh-i-Noor diamond, whose name means 'Mountain of Light'. Three hundred years after Humayun's death, the very last Moghul Emperor, Bahadur Shah II (r. 1837–57), hid in the mausoleum from the British. But his luck ran out. He was arrested by the gallant Captain Hodson, and the fiction of Moghul rule ended. (His demise created the political vacuum within which Disraeli could declare Queen Victoria Empress.)

Mosques, both Sunni and Shia, abound in Delhi, where roughly one-third of Muslims are Shia. The Quwwat-ul-Islam or Might of Islam (1193) is the oldest mosque. The Jama Masjid (1650) is the largest, holding 25,000 people, and overshadowing the nearby Shia Jama Masjid. The Lal Masjid or Red Mosque (1754), in Bara Bazaar, must be the busiest. Yet none in my view compares with the sublime Sheikh Zayed Grand Mosque in Abu Dhabi.

**Sikhism** is sometimes described as a synthetic religion, drawing on elements of Hinduism, Buddhism, and Islam. This may be true, but the description underplays the great originality and vigour of the movement, which arose in the Punjab during the fifteenth century and evolved towards its final form in the eighteenth century. Its founder was Guru Nanak (1469–1539), a teacher of Hindu origin, who made five great journeys, including one to Tibet and another to Mecca, and laid the foundations of the *Gurmat Sikki*, the 'Way of the Guru'. His most famous saying was 'There is no such thing as a Hindu or a Muslim'; he insisted on belief in the omnipotent One God; and he started the Sikhs' strong tradition of social justice, where work, worship, and charity formed the three pillars of a good life. The word *Sikh* means 'student', and *Sikkhi*, the religion, 'the Study'.[37]

Sikh doctrines and practice are based on the teachings of the Ten Gurus – of which Guru Nanak was the first – and on the text of the *Adi Granth* or 'First Volume', the Sikhs' most holy book, to which each of the ten gurus made contributions. Nanak's successor, the scholarly Guru Angad Dev (d. 1552), standardized the unique Gurmukhi script, in which all Sikh scriptures are written. Guru Amar Das (d. 1574) established the community's organizational structures, creating the *manji* system of 'parishes' and 'dioceses' and prescribing ceremonies for birth, marriage, and death. Guru Ram Das (d. 1581) turned Amritsar into the Sikhs' holy city and the Golden Temple there into their holiest shrine; he also founded the hereditary principle, whereby all subsequent gurus were his direct descendants. Guru Arjan Dev (d. 1606), through his persecution and death at the hands of the Moghuls, inspired the martial spirit of the Sikhs, and supervised the compilation of the earliest version of the *Adi Granth*. Guru Hargobind (d. 1644) formalized the Sikhs' executive council, the *Akal Takht* or 'Timeless Throne', together with the institution of binding decrees, the *gurmata* or 'guru's intentions'. The achievements of Guru Har Rai (d. 1661) escape me, and the boy Guru, Har Krishan (d. 1664), died young. Guru Tegh Bahadur (d. 1675) was executed by the Moghul Emperor for protecting Hindus facing forcible conversion. Gobind Singh (d. 1708), the most influential of all Gurus, completed the scriptures, organized the *Khalsa* or 'Army of God', built a Sikh Empire in northern India, and announced himself to be the last guru to appear in human form.

When complete, the holy Sikh Scriptures were named the *Guru Granth Sahib* or 'Book of the Gurus' Mastery', but are often referred to as 'the Eleventh Guru' or just 'The *Granth*'. They were written down in the Gurmukhi language, an antiquated concoction of Hindi and Punjabi with its own script: over 5,000 poems, hymns, aphorisms, and stories divided in thirty-one *ragas* or chapters. They condense the wit and wisdom not only of the Ten Gurus, but also of the fifteen *bhagats* or 'wise men' from Namdev to Kabir; and make frequent reference to Punjabi folk music, and the need for joyful singing. The opening lines are those of Guru Nanak's *Mul Mantra*, which all Sikhs learn to recite by heart:

> *Ik oangkar sat nam karta purkh nirbha'u nirvair akal murat ajuni saibhan gur prasad.*
> 'The One of which everything is, and is continuously, the eternal creator personified, without fear, without hatred, the image of timeless being, beyond birth, self-existent, by the Guru's Grace.'[38]

Nonetheless, the Sikhs today come across as a supremely practical and orderly people. Highly distinctive in their customs and dress, especially the men's turbans, they observe the seven prohibitions:

1. Do not cut a hair of your head
2. Do not touch alcohol, tobacco or drugs
3. Do not commit adultery
4. Do not crave material possessions
5. Do not observe superstitious rituals, fasting, veils, pilgrimages or circumcision
6. Do not sacrifice animals
7. Do not emulate yogis, monks, beggars or celibates

While following simple, positive precepts, Sikhs are open to different opinions and cultures. The injunction for them to work well has produced many fine craftsmen and engineers. The injunction for them to worship well requires regular attendance at the *Gurdwara* or Temple (literally 'Doorway to God') and knowledge of the *Granth* and *Panth*. And the injunction to be charitable leads them constantly into projects for feeding the hungry, caring for the sick, and helping the poor. They are trained to approach life through the concept of *chardi kala* or 'optimistic resilience'. All Sikh males are surnamed *Singh*, meaning 'lion': all females *Kaur*, meaning 'princess'. Women enjoy equal rights and are entitled to lead communal prayers. Men are urged to adopt a dignified, martial bearing, and to emulate the 'soldier-saints'. Both men and women are brought up to observe the 'Five Ks' – *kes, kanga, kara, kirpan*, and *kacchera*: that is, to wear uncut hair, and to carry a wooden comb, an iron bracelet, a dagger, and a special undergarment.

The chance to visit a Sikh temple, therefore, is not to be spurned, and Delhi's principal temple, the *Gurdwara* of Bangla Sahib, beckons strongly. Built in 1783 in white marble, it possesses a high central tower capped with a golden dome, and is framed by a large artificial lake. I am accompanied as guide by a man from the British Embassy's consular section who has written a thesis on Sikhism. We leave our socks and shoes in numbered boxes near the entrance, and walk on bare feet through a cleansing stream of water. We then climb the carpeted steps to a higher level to be greeted by a huge, smiling, and bearded Sikh dressed in a pure white gown and bright red turban. Standing beneath a canopy, he urges us to feel at home, and to ask questions. He then offers us small cakes on a silver tray as a gesture of welcome, and kerchiefs to cover our heads. Further food is available, he tells us, in the Langar Hall. (*Langar*, the custom of free hospitality, proffered to Sikhs and non-Sikhs alike, was introduced by Guru Nanak.) We are now free to join the throng of men and women who are circulating in a clockwise direction round the central, covered shrine. The Holy Book, the *Granth*, in a richly jewelled cover, lies open in a raised glass case under a super-structure of burnished gold. Three turbaned servitors take turns in reading the scriptures with the aid of a microphone. Some people sit cross-legged on the carpet, repeating the texts under their breath; others recite 'the holy name' or huddle in family groups or lean against a pillar; but most just saunter along, soaking in the atmosphere. There is no set service, no collection boxes, no seats or pews, and no sense of compulsion. After a while we return to the sunshine and stand on a balcony to watch a second throng of people as they stroll round the lake in the cool and quiet, before landing back in the din and jostle of motorcycles, street stalls, smoke, and hawkers beyond the exit. A printed portrait of the Guru Nanak makes a fitting souvenir.

**Christianity** accounts for 2 per cent of India's population. It arrived in the far south with the Nestorian Church in the fifth century, was reintroduced by the Portuguese in Goa in the sixteenth century, and later expanded through British missionary activity, which focused on the conversion of the lower castes. Arundhati Roy, a Christian born in Kerala State, has described her village church where 'Parayan priests preached to an Untouchable congregation.'[39] Protestant and Catholic missions toiled competitively among the masses. Most Indians stayed largely indifferent, while the white Sahibs and Memsahibs drove in their landaus to attend church and to thank God for the empire. The landmarks of that era are still present in Delhi. Half a dozen churches are still in use. The Central Baptist Church (1814) is the oldest; St Stephen's (1862), founded by the SPCK (Society for Promoting Christian Knowledge), is the most attractive; and St James's (1836) is architecturally the most ambitious. Two cathedrals were designed by Henry Medd as spiritual adornments to the government quarter in New Delhi. The Cathedral of the Redemption (1927) is Anglican. The Cathedral of the Sacred Heart (1929), now fronted by a huge portrait of Pope John Paul II (who visited Delhi in 1986 and 1999), is Catholic. Some of the missions, convent schools, and hospital foundations still operate.[40]

Nothing is more redolent of past glory than the Cathedral of the Redemption; it is one of the few places in Delhi where one is in danger of catching cold. Bulky and boastful on the outside, it is dim, damp, and dismal on the inside. Once patronized by the Viceroy, it now serves as the headquarters of the Anglican Church of North India, a handful of whose officials, exclusively Indian, sit at tables in a corner of the apse. The chairs in the nave look abandoned, and decades must have passed since the walls shook to the sound of organ, choir, and congregation belting out 'Now thank we all our God! With hearts and hands and voices.' I sidled round seeking traces of former worshippers. The most modern item on display was a memorial to an RAF officer killed in 1940.

The **Baha'i** faith claims a similar number of adherents in India to those of Christianity, though its presence in Delhi is more prominent. Like many other religions, it owes its existence to the revelations of one man, who defied persecution and gained a following. That man was Mirza Husayn Ali Nur (1817–92), a Persian nobleman from Teheran. Dismayed by the sectarian divisions of Islam, pitting Sunni against Shia, and attracted by a contemporary heresy called Babism, he sought a universal faith that would unite all human beings. Taking the name Baha'u'llah, meaning 'Glory of God', he renounced his wealth, enraged the authorities in his native Persia by making a public declaration (essentially 'a plague on both your houses') in Shiraz in 1844, and was driven into a life of exile.[41]

According to the official Baha'i website, unity is the central idea – the unity of the One God, the unity of all religions, and the unity of all human beings. 'All religions,' it states, 'represent different stages in the revelation of God's will and purpose for all humanity.' Further, 'for a global society to flourish, it must be based on certain fundamental principles, which include: the elimination of prejudice, full equality between the sexes, the recognition of the essential oneness of all religions, the elimination of extremes of poverty and wealth, universal education, the harmony of science and religion, a sustainable balance between nature and technology, and the establishment of a world federal system based on collective security and the one-ness of humanity.'[42]

These principles may seem impossibly utopian, but they are embodied in the beautiful Lotus Temple that has risen on Delhi's southern outskirts. Opened in 1986, 'the Lotus' is, more correctly, the Baha'i House of Worship, and, more poetically, 'the Dawning-Place of the Mention of God'. Like all Baha'i temples, the ground plan is a nonagon, from which twenty-seven marble-clad petals thrust elegantly upwards in threefold clusters. Under the noonday sun, the petals shine radiantly white; against a fiery sunset, they appear black; and illuminated at night, they turn to silver. Inside, the open space below the petals is uncluttered: no statues, no images, no pulpits, no altars. It is no accident that the Lotus has become one of the most visited sites in the world. Among others, it acts as a magnet to devotees of the Hindu goddess Durga. At the very least, it is a sensationally successful piece of architecture, one that is uncannily appropriate to its Indian setting.

One last shrine awaited. Born as I was within a stone's throw of the line where George Stephenson's Rocket opened railway history, and raised in the age of steam and train-spotting, I knew in advance that Delhi's Railway Museum was a mecca for the faithful. And it doesn't disappoint. Like all other places of worship in Delhi, it deserves a week rather than half a day; and for the post-imperialist, British visitor it is redolent of a sense of redemption. British railway engineers secured our good name to a degree that Victorian missionaries did not.

Whenever the subject of subcontinental locomotion is raised, one turns to the classic survey, *The Development of Indian Railways* (1930) by Nalinaksha Sanyal.[43] This book, which started life as a PhD thesis at the London School of Economics, contains all the facts, maps, statistics, cost charts, and stories that one might wish to know. The author describes the state of overland transport in the early part of the nineteenth century. 'Over thousands of miles wheeled carriage was unknown,' he writes, 'and merchandise could only be carried inland . . . on buffaloes, camels, and pack bullocks at enormous costs (from 6*d.* to 1*s.* per ton per mile).' And he lists the obstacles put before the governor-general in 1845, when the East India Company submitted its first railway project:

1. Periodical rains and inundations
2. The continued action of violent winds and of a vertical sun
3. The ravages of insects and vermin
4. The destructive growth of spontaneous vegetation upon earth and brickwork
5. The difficulty and expense of securing the services of competent engineers
6. The unenclosed and unprotected country through which railroads would pass
7. The fear that over large areas passenger traffic would not be substantial.[44]

Nonetheless, the Great Indian Peninsula Railway opened the first section of track over 20 miles from Boree Bunder to Thane near Bombay on 16 April 1853. It then grew exponentially over 71,000 miles of track and 7,500 stations.

The National Railway Museum confronts visitors with a choice. The

air-conditioned main building contains a fantastic jumble of photographs, maps, artefacts, and railway paraphernalia. The sweltering
park outside offers scores if not hundreds of old steam locomotives in
varying stages of grandeur and decay. I make instinctively for the locomotives; they belong to the sort of history that you can see, smell, and
touch. My old heart races, and my legs won't carry me fast enough. The
camera clicks and clicks. Every imaginable type and design, every conceivable livery, any number of vanished but once proud companies are
lined up for inspection. A tiny 0-6-0 tank engine from the 1890s is
painted in blue, black, white, and red, and shows off its tall, tapering
chimney and bulbous, brass valve case. Towering beside it, a giant black
4-8-2 express from the 1930s sports a front-mounted searchlight, an
eight-pointed star on its boiler door, and a curvaceous, latticework cow-
catcher. One can clamber onto the footplate or sit on the buffers without
hindrance. The BOMBAY, BARODA AND CENTRAL INDIA and the
RAJPUTANA-MALWA rub shoulders with the KOHILKHUND AND
KUMAON, the BENGAL-NAGPUR, the SOUTHERN MAHARATTA, the
DARJEELING-HIMALAYA, and the DELHI-UMBALLA-KALKA – magic
to the eyes and music to the ears. And a small metal plate, hidden
under the pistons of an exhausted monster, catches my eye: L&YR –
HORWICH-1891. It was through Horwich, on the outskirts of Bolton,
that I passed to reach the lovely moorlands of my boyhood. Here, as the
Buddha would agree, is the path to *nirvana*.[45]

Visiting India's Golden Age of Steam, I was inevitably reminded of the
view of British India as presented by Uncle Norman's stamp album. In
those days, the subcontinent possessed two separate and parallel political systems. One, since 1860 directly under the Indian government,
ruled thirteen great provinces. The other, in the hands of hereditary
princes, controlled hundreds of native states, large and small, scattered
around the Peninsula. The *World Postage Stamp Album* reflected this
division. Pages 22–3 were given over to 'THE BRITISH EMPIRE –
INDIA': pages 24–9 to 'the BRITISH EMPIRE – INDIAN NATIVE
STATES AND PRINCIPALITIES'. This latter section, occupying six
whole pages, exceeded the five-page section for 'GREAT BRITAIN'.
Each page was headed by images of Victorian or Edwardian-era stamps,
plus a list of the names of the relevant states: from 'ALWAR' to
'WADHWAN'. No fewer than forty-two 'native states', as the British
called them, possessed their own private postal services.
     Postal issues from the native states, however, fell into two

categories – the 'conventional' and the 'feudatory'. The former were issued by states that had signed a postal convention with the British Empire, permitting their stamps to circulate anywhere in India: the latter were reserved for internal use. The convention states were just six:

| | | |
|---|---|---|
| CHAMBA | GWALIOR | NABHA |
| FARIDKOT | JIND | PATIALA |

The feudatory states were many times more numerous. Their exotic, often mellifluous and evocative names can still cast their spell:

| | | |
|---|---|---|
| ALWAR | DHAR | MORVI |
| BAMRA | HYDERABAD | NEPAUL |
| BARWANI | IDAR | NOWANUGGUR |
| BHOPAL | INDORE | ORCHHA |
| BHOR | JAIPUR | POONCH |
| BIJAWAR | JAMMU | RAJASTHAN |
| BUNDI | JASDAN | RAJPEEPLA |
| BUSSAHUR | JHALAWAR | SCINDE |
| CASHMERE | KASHMIR | SIRMUR |
| CHARKARI | KISHANGAR- | SORUTH |
| COCHIN | LAS BELA | WADHWAN |

'Chimborazo, Cotopaxi' runs the famous line of W. J. Turner's *Romance*, 'had stolen my soul away.' So, too, did Bijawar, Kishangar and Travancore.[46]

The forty-two Indian native states listed in the stamp album, therefore, formed less than 10 per cent of the 575 such states that were functioning within British India in the early twentieth century. In that period the map of the subcontinent was made up of a crazy patchwork of territories, in which the thirteen imperial provinces were interspersed with scores of princely states large and small, where native rulers maintained a large measure of autonomy under the guidance of a British resident officer. The vast majority of those mini-states used the imperial postal service. But their distribution was uneven. Punjab, for example, encompassed numerous native states. In other regions such as Bengal or Madras, imperial provinces dominated, and native states were relatively sparse.[47]

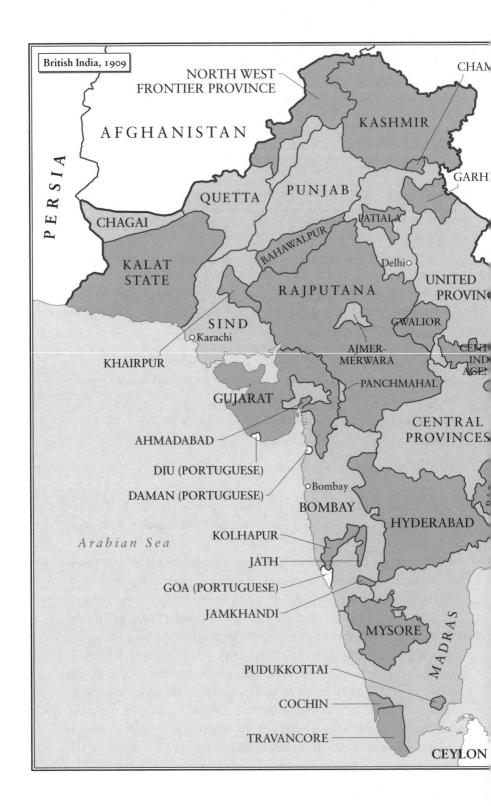

British India, 1909

NORTH WEST
FRONTIER PROVINCE

AFGHANISTAN

KASHMIR

CHAM

PERSIA

QUETTA

PUNJAB

GARH

CHAGAI

PATIALA

KALAT
STATE

BAHAWALPUR

Delhi○

RAJPUTANA

UNITED
PROVIN

SIND
○Karachi

GWALIOR

CENT
IND
AGE

KHAIRPUR

AJMER-
MERWARA

PANCHMAHAL

GUJARAT

CENTRAL
PROVINCES

AHMADABAD

DIU (PORTUGUESE)

DAMAN (PORTUGUESE)

○Bombay

BOMBAY

HYDERABAD

Arabian Sea

KOLHAPUR

JATH

GOA (PORTUGUESE)

JAMKHANDI

MYSORE

MADRAS

PUDUKKOTTAI

COCHIN

TRAVANCORE

CEYLON

British India
princely states

N

TIBET (CHINA)

COOCH BEHAR

SIKKIM

EPAL

BHUTAN

ASSAM

RAJSHAHI    KHASI

BIHAR                    MANIPUR

BENGAL

Calcutta

BURMA

ORISSA

TRIPURA

ANGUL

SIAM

Rangoon

Bay
of
Bengal

INDIAN OCEAN

0    250    500 km

Uncle Norman's stamp collection from the Indian native states was not among his best. He had five stamps from Gwalior, four from Indore, four from Jind, three from Travancore, two from Cochin, and just one solitary example from Chamba – a '3 pies grey'. Yet the excitement that must have raced through his mind as he stuck that lone stamp from Chamba State in the top left-hand corner of page 26 can only be imagined. Could he have known where Chamba was? By what fantastic combination of transport – bullock-cart, train, and merchant ship – did the '3 pies grey' find its way to Bolton? And what did he make of a currency that appeared to be counted in meat pies? His album does not reveal what currency or currencies were then used in the native states. He may or may not have known that 12 pies = 1 anna, and 16 annas = 1 rupee.

The stamp from Chamba was printed in 1911, the year of the Delhi Durbar, the lowest valued item in the first Indian series of George V's reign. It was headed 'INDIA POSTAGE', and depicted the bearded king-emperor in left profile, wearing his coronation crown and ermine stole, and placed in an oval frame surrounded with foliage. The nominal value of 'THREE PIES' was written out in English at the bottom, and attached in numerical form as '3 p' to two lateral shields. The colour is a pleasant shade of mid-grey, neither charcoal nor poplin. The black overprint in capital letters, 'CHAMBA STATE', was stamped on it, when it was put into circulation in 1913. The exemplar, which found its way to my uncle's house at The Haulgh, Bolton, bears no postmark, but has lost its gum and is therefore classed as 'fine used'; it looks as if it was soaked off an envelope, having escaped franking. It was a worthy herald of the peace and order that Chamba enjoyed.

Further information was readily available had Uncle Norman sought it out. At about the time that he began collecting, the *Encyclopaedia Britannica*'s magnificent 11th edition appeared, presenting substantial entries on each of the Indian states; and it is very likely that his school library in Bolton possessed a copy:

CHAMBA, a native state of India, within the Punjab, amid the Himalayas, and lying on the southern border of Kashmir. It has an area of 3216 sq. m. Pop. (1901) 127,834 ... Chamba is entirely mountainous; in the east and north, and in the centre, are snowy ranges. The valleys in the west and south are fertile. The chief rivers are the Chandra and Ravi ... The principal crops are rice, maize and millet. Mineral ores of various kinds are known, but unworked. Trade is chiefly in forest produce. The capital of the state is Chamba (pop. 6000), situated above the gorge of the Ravi. External communications are entirely by road. The state was founded in the 6th century, and [later], though tributary to the Mogul empire, always practically maintained its independence. Its chronicles are preserved in a series of inscriptions, mostly engraved on copper. It first came under British influence in 1846, when it was declared independent of Kashmir. The line of the rajas of Chamba was founded in the 6th century A.D. by Marut, of an ancient family of Rajputs. In 1904 Bhuri Singh, K.C.S.I., C.I.E., an enlightened and capable ruler, succeeded.[48]

Bhuri Singh (r. 1904–19) must have been sitting on the throne when Uncle Norman fixed the stamp from his realm into the album.

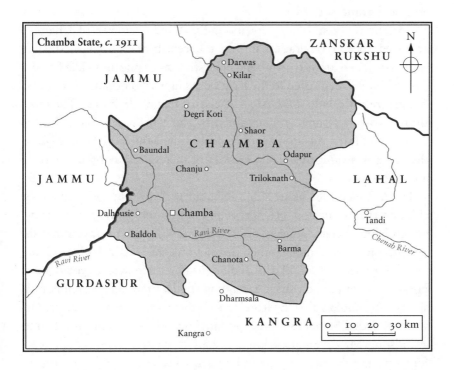

The ruling House of Chamba, of immense antiquity, boasted an unbroken line of sixty-seven rajas or princes, who ruled their hereditary dominions between AD 500, when the dynasty was launched by Raju Maru or Marut, and 1948, when it was merged into the Republic of India. In terms of duration, the dynasty puts Queen Victoria's Saxe-Coburg Gothas (later, the Windsors) completely in the shade. The

average length of the Rajas' reigns was twenty-two years. Their original seat was at Bharmour, but a new capital was built in AD 920 and
named after Raja Sahila Verma's daughter, Champavati. The state was
traditionally divided into five mandalas or districts – Chamba, Bharmour, Bhatti, Churah, and Pangi. It held out in its Himalayan
stronghold for 1,400 years, outlasting all the successive empires of the
region – Afghan, Moghul, Sikh, and British.[49]

As from 1846, under British rule, Chamba served as a base for Britain's Indian Army during the Sikh Wars, and subsequently flourished
as a protectorate of the empire. The post office, from which Uncle Norman's stamp would probably have been posted, was built in 1863. Raja
Sri Sham Singh Bahadur (r. 1873–1904) constructed roads, opened
schools, subsidized an imposing Scottish Presbyterian Church, and
erected a grandiose palace.

Thanks to their remote location, the Hindu temples of Chamba
acquired special veneration during the centuries of India's Muslim
supremacy, and are still attracting huge streams of pilgrims. The Champavati Temple, dedicated to the Raja's daughter who became a goddess,
is a centre for Hindu *Shaktism*, the cult of female divinities. The Lakshmi Narayan Temple is maintained by the Vaishnavite Sect. During
two annual fairs, the Suhi Mata Mela and the Minjar Mela in August,
the town is swamped by vast crowds of merchants, bargain-hunters,
and sightseers.

H. H. Raja Sir Sri Bhuri Singh Bahadur took over in 1904, when his
elder brother abdicated. His accession photograph shows him wearing
a high white turban, a heavy black moustache, and an array of medals
and decorations. Among other distinctions, he was a Knight Commander of the Order of the Indian Empire. He was devoted to a
programme of public works, extending roads, funding a museum, and
sponsoring India's first hydro-electric scheme for Delhi's benefit. He
was succeeded by his son, Sri Ram Singh (r. 1919–35), and then by his
grandson, Major Sri Lakshman Singh (1925–71). Today, Chamba
forms part of the Indian state of Himachal Pradesh. The former Rajas'
descendants live on as private citizens, but have lost all political authority. And pilgrims travel to the temples in helicopters – invented in the
same year that Uncle Norman's Bristol fighter crashed.[50]

Together with their princely peers, the Rajas of Chamba participated
in British India's extraordinary system of precedence based on the
number of gun salutes with which each was entitled to be greeted. The

pecking order was precisely calibrated by an 'Official Table of Gun Salutes'. At the top of the list, entitled to a twenty-one-gun salute, stood the Nizam of Hyderabad, the Gaekwar of Baroda, and the Maharaja of Mysore. In 1917, in recognition of distinguished war service, the Maharajas of Gwalior and of Jammu and Kashmir were promoted to the first class. The second class, entitled to a nineteen-gun salute, included the Maharajas of Indore and Travancore, and the Maharana of Udaipur. The third and largest group consisted of middle-ranking rulers allotted salutes varying from seventeen to eleven guns. The sub-classes within the group were headed by the Maharao of Kotah (seventeen), the Maharaja of Dholpur (fifteen), the Maharaja Raol Sahib of Bhavnagar (thirteen), and the Nawab of Janjira (eleven). The fourth class, entitled to a nine-gun salute, was headed by the Maharaja of Baria. At the very bottom of the Official Table, the Raja of Bashahr was entitled to nine guns, but only on his private estates. British officialdom was subject to a parallel table of ranks:

13 guns: Consuls-General, Rear Admirals, Maj-Generals, AVMs
15 guns: Lt-Governors, Vice-Admirals, Lt-Generals, RAF Marshals
17 guns: Provincial Governors, Generals, Admirals, RAF ACMs
19 guns: Ambassadors, Field Marshals, Admirals of the Fleet etc.
31 guns: the Viceroy, and members of the Royal-Imperial Family
101 guns: the King-Emperor.

The details of these hierarchies were constantly changing, but when Indian independence finally came, the Raja of Chamba stood in the 63rd position among 122 named 'Salute States' – sandwiched between no. 62, the Pathan Nawab of Cambay, and no. 64, the Maharaja of Charkhari. A mid-Table ruler, the Raja of Chamba was addressed as 'Highness', greeted by eleven-gun salutes, and enjoyed equal status with chargés d'affaires, brigadiers, commodores, and air commodores. This was obviously far from the highest rank of imperial India, but he could take encouragement that he was not classed among the 443 rulers of 'Non-Salute States', who were not greeted by a single gun.[51]

After independence in 1947, the Official Table of Gun Salutes was retained for formal occasions, and as a social lubricant in the transition between empire and republic. The Nizam of Hyderabad, who was a Muslim and had refused to recognize the republic, was demoted from the top spot in the Order of Precedence and stripped of the honorific style of 'Exalted Highness'; he was replaced by the Hindu Maharana of

Udaipur. The system finally came to an end in 1971, the same year that saw the death of the very last Raja of Chamba.

So now the maharajahs and their gun salutes have gone, and with them one of the many pillars around which a common Indian identity might have been formed. Since then, India, like all new states with a diverse population, has been wrestling with the problem of how to create and strengthen a belief in national unity. In 1782 the nascent United States adopted the old Latin motto widely used by the Austro-Hungarian monarchy – *E pluribus unum*, 'One out of many'. The USA has succeeded. Austria-Hungary ultimately failed. What chance has India? As Rabindranath Tagore stated almost a hundred years ago: 'India is many countries packed into one geographical receptacle.'

In 1947, having thrown off the British Empire and separated from Pakistan, many Indians were content to think that they were no longer British. But negative definitions could hardly suffice, and the leaders of the newborn republic, headed by Pandit Nehru, adopted the mission of forging a form of 'secular nationalism', basing it on a shared view of the past, common civic values, and an array of national symbols from the flag, anthem, and emblem to the bird, flower, tree, and river, and even to the 'national fruit' – the mango – and the 'national aquatic animal' – the dolphin.[52] Nehru's ideas contained a strong dose of British Fabian socialism, and were summarized in his book *The Discovery of India* (1946), which he had written in prison.[53] They dominated the first two decades of independence.

The particular view of the past favoured by Nehru and his entourage centred almost exclusively on the heritage of Sanskrit, the language once used in all the classical texts of Hinduism, Jainism, and Buddhism. It encouraged a refined and scholarly but elitist culture, completely inaccessible to the illiterate masses – the equivalent of Latin-based classical studies in Europe. The cult was so strong that the 'national song' adopted by the Indian National Congress in 1931, as a rival to Tagore's Bengali 'Jana-Gana-Mana', had been composed in Sanskrit:

> *Vande Mataram!*
> *Sujalam, suphalam, malayaja shitalam,*
> *Shasyashyamalam, Mataram!*
> *Vande Mataram!* . . .
> (I bow to Thee, O Mother!
> Richly watered, richly fruited

Cool with the winds of the south,
Dark with the crops of the harvests,
Our Mother! / Her nights rejoice in moonlit glory,
Her lands are dressed with flowering trees,
Sweet of laughter, sweet of speech,
Mother! Source of blessings, giver of bliss.)[54]

Indian patriots singing 'Vande Mataram' in Sanskrit were a close equivalent of European students singing 'Floreat Etona' or 'Gaudeamus Igitur'.

From the start, however, this rarefied concept of Indianness was challenged from below by a variety of populist voices. One group of dissenters were the so-called 'Hindi-wallahs', who sought to develop national consciousness through promotion of the Hindi language. Their efforts seemed to be bearing fruit until 1951, when language riots erupted in the south, especially in Tamil Nadu, confirming the opposite policy of linguistic plurality, including English. Another, more militant group, the Rashtriya Swayamsevak Sangh (RSS) or National Patriotic Association, crystallized around the concepts of Hindutva, 'Hinduism', and Hindu Rashtra, 'the Hindu Nation'. 'India belongs to the Hindus,' one member said; 'it is Hindustan.' Founded in 1925, the RSS is the parent organization of Prime Minister Modi's Bharatiya Janata Party (BJP); it has repeatedly been banned, both by the British and by post-independence governments. Its paramilitary volunteers conduct campaigns against Muslims, Christians, and secularists, lobbying for religious-based education, defacing road signs, attacking the sacred sites of 200 million non-Hindus, and inciting war against Pakistan. One of its early leaders, M. S. Golwalkar, admired both Adolf Hitler's Third Reich and the State of Israel. Another, Nathuram Godse, assassinated Mahatma Gandhi on 30 January 1948. Former 'Volunteers', Atal Bihari Vajpayee (b. 1924) and Narendra Modi (b. 1950), have become India's tenth and fourteenth prime ministers respectively.[55]

The view of the past favoured by the nationalists centres on the idea of oppression, both political and social.[56] Their narrative cites '1,200 years of slavery', meaning two centuries of British rule preceded by a thousand years of Muslim rule. In this construction, India's subordination began with the invasion of an army of the Umayyad Caliphate, in AD 711, and ended with India's adoption of a republican constitution in 1950. The prevalence of mass poverty and the caste system is seen as a by-product of foreign rule. Much resentment is directed at upper-class, foreign-educated politicians, such as Nehru and the Gandhis, and there is much irate criticism of rival historical interpretations. A book by an American author dedicated to an inclusive approach to India's past, Wendy Doniger's *The Hindus: An Alternative History* (2009), was withdrawn by the publishers following threats and a lawsuit in an Indian court.[57] The nationalists are enemies of diversity and pluralism in both the past and the present.

Back in the ambassador's residence, I relaxed in an armchair with *The Times of India*. It is still printed in the font invented by its parent paper in London. The front page discusses domestic politics. International affairs are kept for the inside pages.

Delhi's view of the world, however, is far removed from London's. Despite Mahatma Gandhi's precepts, India is a nuclear power that has refused to sign the Non-Proliferation Treaty but proclaims a 'no first use' policy. Her first atomic device, in 1974, was code-named 'The Smiling Buddha'.[58] The supreme preoccupations are with India's two immediate neighbours: Pakistan and China. Both, like India, possess nuclear weapons; both are regarded in New Delhi as incorrigibly unfriendly; and both are apt to combine against Indian interests. A state of semi-active war has persisted between India and Pakistan since 1947 over Kashmir. A state of undeclared war continues with China over the territory of Arunachal Pradesh, which the Chinese claim to be 'southern Tibet'. Further tensions are driven by events in Nepal, where the royal government was recently overthrown by Maoist rebels. No one in Delhi believes that the Maoists were not encouraged by China's communist regime.

Relations with Pakistan were seriously disrupted by terrorist attacks on Mumbai in November 2008. The Indians refuse to believe that the terrorists, from the militant Lashkar-e-Taiba movement, were not equally linked to Pakistan's intelligence services. President Manmohan Singh, who was born in Gah, in present-day Pakistan, made conciliatory gestures, and the two countries have entered a more favourable phase. But the conflict over a divided Kashmir goes on, as do complications with Bangladesh. Prime Minister Modi made a lightning stopover in Lahore in December 2015; his counterpart served him a vegetarian meal washed down with Kashmiri tea.[59]

Relations with China, in contrast, have worsened. On 19 April 2012 India test-fired an Agni-V ICBM, which soared out of Wheeler Island in the Bay of Bengal to a point in the southern ocean midway between New Zealand and Madagascar. (Agni is the God of Fire.) Indian pride overflowed. 'On Thursday morning', wrote *The Times of India*, '[The God of Fire] came into his own to hurl a potent fireball across the Indian Ocean at over twenty times the speed of sound.' Editorial comment rejoiced that India was becoming the sixth member of 'the super-exclusive intercontinental ballistic missile club'. The Chinese press was less impressed. 'Delhi should not be so arrogant . . .', wrote *The People's Daily* in Beijing. 'India doesn't stand a chance in a nuclear arms race.' China's Foreign Ministry was still calling India 'a co-operation partner, not a rival', but elsewhere in Beijing the Agni-V was condemned as a 'political missile'. It emerged that the head of the 300-strong team of scientists who worked on the rocket's research and development is a woman. Ms Tessy Thomas, aged forty, is a Roman Catholic from Kerala, a graduate in engineering, the wife of a navy commodore, and the mother of a student son. 'Science has no gender,' she is quoted as saying. The Indian press have named her *Agniputri*, 'Daughter of Fire'.[60] Since the missile test, President Xi and Prime Minister Modi have exchanged visits. But tranquillity is threatened by Beijing's plans for a 'Maritime Silk Road' in the Indian Ocean.[61]

India's relations with Russia are less matey than previously with the Soviet Union. But a residue of sympathy remains, especially among the many Indians with leftist leanings and in India's defence sector, which relies heavily on Russian arms. Russia and India have no common frontiers, and no ongoing disputes. Equally, they have no strong cause for closer ties. Delhi and Moscow smile at each other from a distance without rushing to embrace.[62]

After tepid relations during the Cold War, India is moving slowly towards a relationship of mutual admiration with the United States, much strengthened by the visit to Delhi in 2006 of President George W. Bush, who announced a US–Indian 'strategic partnership'. The Americans praise 'the world's largest democracy'; and the Indians equate American rhetoric with a willingness to counterbalance the rise of China. Yet the United States has to walk a tightrope between India and Pakistan, whilst the Chinese easily take fright at Indo-American rapprochement. When Delhi cosies up to Washington, Beijing pours scorn on India's participation in the West's 'anti-Chinese policy of containment'. Most Indians liked President Obama, while Obama, who has visited Delhi three times, likes India. Prime Minister Modi has visited Washington twice.[63] Will the populist Modi now see eye to eye with the populist Trump?

*

The anchorman arrived with a camera crew of three, a broad smile, and a sprained ankle.

'I want to talk about Europe,' he said as he limped in. Vickram Bahl is a star television interviewer and editor-in-chief of ITMN; his *Insight* programme attracts about 20 million viewers, and has run for years.[64] His precise, clipped English betrays a period of study in England. He recently interviewed President Putin. Today's interview is scheduled for 11 a.m. in the ambassador's Garden Room. Outside the long, circular windows, banks of tall yellow foxtail lilies line the immaculate lawn. Gardeners on ladders are trimming the hedges. Red sandstone elephants surround the fishpond; a peacock struts down the path lined with palms, fig trees, and eucalyptus, and a monkey swings through the overhanging branches.

Ensconced in a deep armchair, and smiling beneath his bald pate, Bahl kicks off.[65]

'I want to ask you about Europe,' he repeats. 'We hear that you look beyond the beaten track. What do you make of this euro-crisis? Is it serious, or are the media just scare-mongering?'

'I am a historian,' I protest feebly, 'not an astrologer.'

'Of course,' the anchorman persists, 'but historians can stray into the future.'

I succumb, and hold forth for half an hour in this unlikely setting on my views of multiple European crises.

'Oh dear! I'm terribly sorry, I haven't poured the tea. Please excuse me. Wasn't it Walter Scott who asked "What would the world do without tea?"'

'Or Mr Gladstone. He said he was glad not to have been born before teatime.'

'Yes, but do you know where tea came from?'

'From China perhaps?'

'Well, it was from the Lord Buddha. After falling asleep as he tried to meditate, he angrily plucked off his eyelids to stay awake. His eyelids fell to the ground, took root, and grew into the very first tea bush.'

It is a soothing conclusion to the kaleidoscopic, troubling, overwhelming experience of India.

# 5

# Melayu

*Amuck or Amok at the Muddy Confluence*

In the old days, ships sailing east-by-south out of India would hug the coast of the Bay of Bengal for three or four weeks before rounding the tip of the Malay Peninsula and turning either north-east towards China or due east towards the Spice Islands. Leaving the estuary of the Hugli River at Calcutta at 22° N, they would call at the ports of Chittagong, Rangoon, Jung Ceylon (now Phuket), and Malacca, and would pass the shores of five different present-day countries – Bangladesh, Myanmar (Burma), Thailand, Malaysia, and Singapore – before reaching their critical waypoint on the equator. Dropping anchor in what was then called the *Tanah Melayu*, 'the Land of the Malays', they would have covered over 2,500 sea miles, or 5,000 kilometres of ocean.

Nowadays, commercial jetliners cover those same sea miles in five or six hours. Even so, the distances involved are surprisingly substantial. Flying from Delhi to Kuala Lumpur, for example, is no less than 2,384 miles. The distance is much greater than that between London and Moscow, or between Los Angeles and Miami on opposite coasts of the United States. It crosses only a tiny slice of the world's greatest continent, but the new destination offers radically different human and cultural scenery from that which was left behind. The Malay Peninsula lies at the far end of a qualitative as well as a quantitative leap from India.

Kuala Lumpur International Airport (KUL) is a showpiece of mega-modern architecture: full of light and pale blue glass, extravagantly spacious, and reminiscent of a make-believe jungle whose canopy is supported by slender, steel branches. A space-age Aerotrain whisks passenger between terminals. Barely twenty years old, it embodies the message that Malaysia is prosperous, ultra-innovative, and attractive. Over the entrance, one reads *Lapangan Terbang Antarabangsa Kuala Lumpur*. One of the words presumably means 'airport'.[1]

'KUL' or 'LTAKL' is a long way from Kuala Lumpur. Like London

(Gatwick) or London (Stansted), which are closer to Brighton or Cambridge respectively than to London, it was evidently designed for the convenience of the political and business elite and is much closer to the country's modern capital, Putrajaya, and to the super-modern, high-tech city of Cyberjaya. It is located close to the coast on the southern edge of the Greater Klang Valley Conurbation, not too far from ancient Malacca. Passengers for Kuala Lumpur face a drive of 72 kilometres.

LTAKL is also the main hub for the country's national carrier, Malaysia Airlines; 'Moon-Kite' logos, red-blue-white colours, and smart uniforms are ubiquitous. In 2013 the company was still basking in its 5-Star Skytrax rating – one of only seven such elite airlines. In sixty-eight years of operation it possessed a near-perfect safety record, suffering only two fatal incidents, one a kidnapping.

Yet 2014 was an unparalleled *annus horribilis* for Malaysia Airlines. In March, Flight MH370 bound for Beijing took off from LTAKL and inexplicably vanished into the night. In July, Flight MH17, bound for LTAKL from Amsterdam, was destroyed over eastern Ukraine by a surface-to-air missile. In total, 537 passengers were lost. Public relations were mishandled. The company's reservations and share price plunged and its image collapsed. In August the same year it submitted to a renationalization plan.[2]

Since the planned monorail link with the city centre was never built, an airport coach serves instead. Traffic drives on the left; clearly the British were here. The six-lane highway is almost empty and lined with acacia trees, palm groves, and dense jungle. Green-painted, monolingual road signs are written in the Latin alphabet, but, as in Estonia or Malta, they convey little to non-natives. There is plenty of time to guess what IKUT KIRI or TAMAT or KECEMESAN may stand for.

As the coach starts up, a balding gent dressed in a pale-green, palm-printed shirt climbs aboard, wreathed in false smiles. Speaking through a mike, he claims to work for the Luxury Travel Corporation. He distributes snack boxes, then proceeds to deliver a pep talk.

'Bad things can happen,' he announces ominously, 'to people who lose their embarkation cards.'

He sidles up to my neighbour.

'Where are you from, sir?' he asks. 'Egypt? Ah, a very nice country. I can answer your questions,' he offers, adding coyly, 'but I'm not supposed to talk politics.'

No one was trying to talk politics.

After about an hour, the coach pulls into the Lucky Garden *Ristoran* for a stop. Thirty yards separate us from the glass doors of the shopping area, and we walk through a wall of heat to get there. I buy an English guidebook and a couple of local newspapers – one in Chinese, the other in Malay. The stallholder shrugs, guessing correctly that I can't read them. TANDAS obviously stands for 'Toilets'. But does PEREMPUAN mean 'Gents' and LELAKI 'Ladies', or vice versa?

Back in the bus, I pick at the papers and at the lunchbox of rice cakes, pickles, and mixed tropical fruit. The box is marked: 'Consume by 12.31.' Leave it until 12.32, and who knows what might happen? The colourful Chinese newspaper, the *Sin Chew Daily*, is full of pictures and artistic pictographs. The front page is topped by a photo of heavily armed police carrying a multilingual banner:

BERSURAI!
KALAU TIDAK KAMI TEMBAK
DISMISS!
IF NOT WE SHOOT.[3]

Below it, a huge advertisement for Swiss Rado watches features Andy Murray.

The Malay newspaper is called *Utusan*, and *Selasa* has to mean 'Tuesday', to match today's date; other decipherable words include *status*, *sentral*, *konflik*, *parlimen*, *presiden*, and, probably, *kapsul*. The main headline reads: '10 syarikat dilupus – Najib'. As a photo shows, Najib is a man, but it escapes me what he has been up to. The front page also carries a colour portrait of a handsome woman wearing a full-sleeved robe, a headscarf in shocking pink with silver trimmings, and a Mona Lisa smile. Her name appears to be Sri Wani Choo Abdullah. Inside pages reveal the editors' geographical horizons; they show illustrated stories from Vietnam, Taiwan, the Philippines, Burma, Sudan, China, Australia, and France, but not Britain.[4]

The guidebook, which contains a large chapter on 'Values and Attitudes', is more revealing. 'Conformity and Harmony', 'Deference and Respect', 'Consensus', 'Face', and 'Politeness' all receive separate sections. 'In Malaysia,' the author advises, 'individual interests tend to be subordinated to the needs of the wider social group', and 'deviation from social norms is difficult'. Or again, 'hierarchy or inequality' is 'a social principle', and 'the associated attitudes of deference and respect' are 'pervasive'. The foreign visitor is warned: 'The crucial principle in adapting to Malaysian cultural ways is to avoid public embarrassment. Openly displaying what you think or feel is not appreciated.'[5]

Morning in Kuala Lumpur begins with the call of the muezzin from a nearby mosque; while calling the faithful to prayer, the amplified voice is reminding everyone else that this is a predominantly Muslim country. At 5.45 it is completely dark. Barely one degree north of the equator, the days and nights here are of equal length; dusk and twilight don't really exist. The infidels roll over. Shortly, however, birdsong erupts with the same high decibel level as the muezzin: a full-throated chorus of squawks, clicks, and whistles. By 6.30 morning has emphatically broken; the tropical sun is streaming through half-closed blinds, and any further attempt to rest is quickly defeated by the roll-call taking place in the courtyard of an adjacent Chinese school. Armed with a megaphone, a teacher is reading out the pupils' names with military precision, her voice reverberating with each triple volley: 'Chang Lim Wei! One-Two-Three! Chong Khoo Hi, Chung Bai Lo . . .' All schools in Malaysia start early to miss the noonday heat.

After breakfast, I sally forth to find my bearings. Downtown Kuala Lumpur is reminiscent of a second-rank American city such as Atlanta or St Louis: far too much concrete in a jumble of skyscrapers, flyovers, and high-rise condos. The heat forces you to move around by air-conditioned car or taxi. My first taxi-driver says *Kuala* means 'Delta' and *Lumpur* 'Muddy'. After subsequent taxi rides, 'delta' changes to 'estuary', and 'estuary' to 'confluence'. I decided on 'Muddy Confluence'. It was founded, I learned, by a party of tin-miners, who set up camp in the Klang Valley in 1862. Most of them died, but the survivors

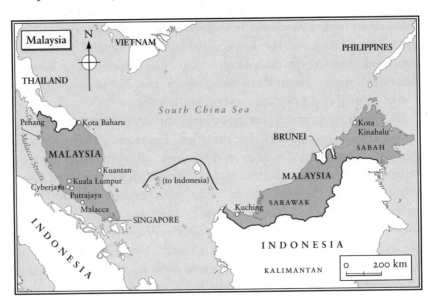

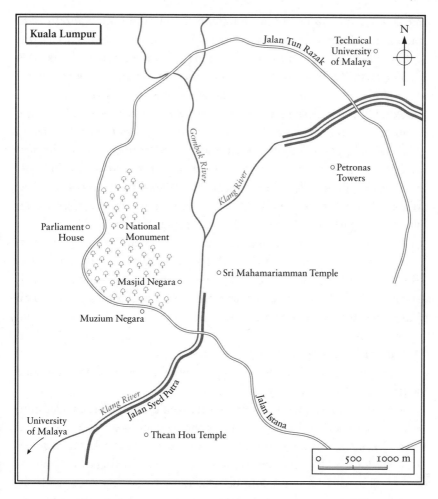

hung on. The town then gained prominence as the capital of the Sultanate of Selangor. The sultanate's honorific name, *Darul Ehsan*, means
'Sincerity's Abode'.[6] What a romantic kingdom, not yet vanished!

Kuala Lumpur's streets are thronged with people from three instantly
recognizable racial groups. The majority Malays are short and stocky
with milk-brown skins. They are Muslims; the men wear a loose-
fitting, collarless shirt, the *batik*, and sometimes a fez-like black hat,
the *songkok*; the most traditional accessory is the *sampin*, a sarong
worn round the hips. The women wear headscarves combined with
shawls, knee-length blouses called *baju kuning*, and silk skirts. They
all like simple, bold colours. The Chinese, the largest minority, tend to
wear simple Western-style clothes. Chinese women favour the
*cheongsam*, a high-collared, one-piece dress. The Indians are mainly

dark-skinned Tamils. As in India, they wear the cotton *kurta* with matching trousers or *pajama*. Their women are wrapped in elegant, colourful saris. Everyone can see at a glance who everyone else is.

The twin Petronas Towers act as a magnet for anyone with a camera. Until overtaken by the Khalifa's Tower in Dubai, they were designated the tallest in the world. Yet they somehow make a more sympathetic impression than their Emirati rival. Built in the 1990s by Malaysia's largest oil company, they are joined halfway up by a bridge, and their circular shapes are broken up by strong horizontal lines at each storey, giving them the appearance of soaring columns of silver rings. They are extremely photogenic, especially when snapped from the nearby park on a foreground of flowering jacarandas.[7]

By now, I have acquired a guide, Karolina, a delightful young European woman who is working in Malaysia on some sort of internship. She is well informed, energetic, and very good at explaining the difficulties that she herself had encountered. For a start, she takes me to an Indian bar for tea. The waiter asks:

'Milk and sugar?'

'No milk, no sugar,' I reply.

In a couple of minutes he comes back with a mug of plain tea loaded with sugar. Perhaps it's my Lancashire accent.

Outside the cosmopolitan city centre, Kuala Lumpur is divided into ethnic neighbourhoods: mosques mark the predominance of Malays, and several Chinatowns contain Buddhist shrines. There is a Little Korea as well as a Little India; and some of the less salubrious districts are inhabited by migrant workers, especially Bangladeshis. Cruising round suburban Kuala Lumpur, we call in at the hilltop Buddhist shrine of *Thean Hou* or 'Queen of Heaven'.[8] Climbing hundreds of steps, and shedding our shoes, we enter into the presence of a gigantic, golden Buddha, who smiles enigmatically amidst pungent yellows, blues, violets, and greens. Lighting a scented candle, we retreat down the steps to be greeted in the car park by the statue of a jovial Confucius. Given Malaysia's threefold ethnic divide, one really ought to follow up with visits to the *Masjid Negara* or 'National Mosque'[9] and the *Sri Mahamariamman* Hindu temple.[10]

In British times, the Malays thought themselves to be the downtrodden victims of imperialism, but they now rule the roost. The standard word for 'Malay' in the Malay language is *Melayu*, and one comes across the phrase *Ketuanan Melayu*, meaning 'Malay Dominance' or 'Malaya for the Malays'.[11] But since this ethnic group and their language can be found over a wide area beyond the Malay Peninsula, including eastern Sumatra and coastal Borneo, the alternative and more nationalistic term of *Bumiputra*, meaning 'Son of the Soil', has been promoted over the last half-century by the Malaysian authorities.

The Chinese have controlled business for centuries, migrating south from the fifteenth century onwards. The biggest outflow followed the Opium Wars of the mid-nineteenth century. Their native languages are not Mandarin but Hokkien, Cantonese and Hakka, which often drives them to communicate with each other in English.

The Indians were a more recent imperial import, brought in by the British as contract labourers from southern India and Ceylon to work the tin mines and rubber plantations. They mainly speak Tamil or Telugu, and are clearly at the bottom of the pecking order.

The time comes to have a haircut. The hairdresser is a dainty young Chinese woman in floral blouse and tight black trousers. When I say 'Trim, please', she hesitates, then says 'Tim, yes.' Within seconds, she is hacking off the longer hair on the side of my head, which I carefully cultivate to hide big ears. 'Wonderful,' I say as I leave, puzzled. What did I do wrong?

Next day, Karolina and I meet again and take a taxi to the University of Malaya in the outer suburbs.

'How long?' she asks.

'About thirty minutes,' the driver replies.

'Do you know where it is?' she persists, seeking reassurance born of experience.

'Yes, yes,' he replies, 'Ya, ya', and sets off with a roar. After forty-five minutes we are going round the same roundabouts for the third and fourth time. We arrive at the campus of a totally different university. The driver is crestfallen. Karolina saves the day, pulling out a street map to fix our location.

'How much?' I ask the driver on arrival.

'Nothing,' he says, 'nothing'.

'What is it?' I ask Karolina. 'It's not just a language problem, is it?'

'No, it's not; not at all, it's Malaya,' she replies. 'It is a mixture of deference, etiquette, and above all the fear of losing face.'

The guidebook's adjective 'pervasive' comes to mind. The waiter understood 'No milk, no sugar' alright, but he probably felt a bit mean for putting nothing extra into a foreign guest's tea, so he added the sugar to be on the safe side. The hairdresser may have been embarrassed by not understanding 'trim', so she pressed on regardless. Since her task was to cut hair, she guessed that the client would be best pleased if she cut off more rather than less. And the taxi-driver perhaps felt inhibited to ask his passengers to repeat a destination that he had not fully understood. So he set off in the hope of working it out as he went along. He drove three times round that suburban block while try-ing to decide between the University of Malaya or the Technical University of Malaya. He plumped for the wrong one, covered himself in shame and refused to take a cent. Everyone says 'Yes', it seems, just to be polite, even when they mean 'No'.

Thanks to the taxi-driver's meanderings, my arrival at the Univer-sity of Malaya was seriously behind schedule.

'Don't worry,' Karolina said, 'people here have a very flexible view of punctuality. They call it "rubber time".'

The guest lecture produced another surprise. I had been listened to without contestation in Baku, Abu Dhabi, and most recently in Delhi. But now I faced a questioner with real spirit. The young woman was wearing a maroon-coloured Muslim headscarf, and speaking flawless English.

'We are very angry,' she began, 'at the conduct of the imperialists.' She was also upset at the way that I had been 'diminishing their guilt'. A few minutes into the tirade the chairman asked whether she had a question.

'How does the Professor defend himself?' she asked.

So I tried my best. (The accusation was not specific, but it was driven, I think, by a reluctance to consider the sufferings of Europeans as equivalent to those inflicted by Europeans on others. I had stepped inadvertently into the quagmire of 'cultural misappropriation', and had not 'positioned myself' clearly.)

'I believe that we should condemn *all* inhumane conduct,' I replied, 'and by describing unjust events that occurred elsewhere I am in no way diminishing the injustices that were inflicted on Africa or Asia. Com-parison is part of the historian's stock-in-trade, and in order to evaluate phenomena, we have to compare one with another.'

With that, the questioner had to be satisfied. But I noticed that she didn't behave like a local, and did not heed the guidebook's advice about 'avoiding public embarrassment at all costs'. Was she perhaps from Brixton or Bradford?

Afterwards, one of my professorial hosts treated me to cakes and tea, accompanied by a beginner's lesson in the workings of Malaysian government.

'Is it a democracy?' I opened naively. He pulled a face. 'I mean, are the democratic structures just a facade? Entering the country a couple of days ago, I had the uneasy feeling that I was entering a police state.'

'Hm,' the professor pondered. 'The lower house of parliament is elected by universal suffrage, and the "King", too, is elected; he's chosen for a four-year term from the nine sultans of the country's nine provinces.'

That was a start.

'But in practice,' he went on, 'the system does operate like a one-party state, and the upper house is appointed. There's no formal dictatorship, but the country's ethnic majority always votes as a block for the same party [the United Malays National Organization or UMNO] and can always translate their numerical advantage into legislative decisions.'

In other words, a 'tyranny of the majority' bolsters *Ketuanan Melayu*.

'Does the term "ethnocracy" fit?' I asked.

'I suppose it does,' he replied. 'The opposition, drawn mainly from Chinese parties, is very weak and parliament rarely objects to oppressive measures.'

Here perhaps was the key information. If the legislature is packed with representatives trained from birth to be deferential, the executive does whatever it wants. Law 179, it transpired, which provides for the summary arrest and unlimited detention of political suspects, and which the British introduced in the early 1950s to fight the Anti-Communist Emergency, had never been repealed. It was suspended in 2011, but remains in reserve. Expecting a Malaysian MP to oppose a government Bill, I concluded, may not be very different from asking a waiter for tea without sugar.

We also discussed the long-standing language issue. Under the British Empire all the main schools had taught in English, yet after independence, almost everyone expected English to be replaced. The problem was, replaced with what? Malaysian nationalists assumed that Malay, the language of the majority, would be adopted exclusively by all state institutions. Unfortunately, neither the Chinese nor the Indians spoke Malay. Nonetheless, in 1969, after years of frustration and intercommunal rioting, the advocates of compulsory 'Malayicization' decided to press on regardless.

My informant described the fiasco played out at the University of Malaya in the academic year of 1970–71. Without warning, the authorities ordered that courses should be taught in Malay, even if there were no course materials, no suitable books in the library, and no competent instructors. The old English textbooks were being badly translated in haste by amateurs, and professors with no command of Malay were reading out notes prepared for them by their students. The experiment inevitably collapsed amidst great bitterness. Most of the non-Malay staff left to set up private, English-based universities that have thrived ever since, and the standing of the state universities slumped.

The preferred form of speech of many Malaysians, however, is neither pure Malay nor standard English, but an extraordinary linguistic concoction that mixes up all the country's languages and that can vary from speaker to speaker. In Malay, the concoction is known as *Bahasa Rojak*, literally 'mixed speech', but it is more widely labelled *Manglish* – or 'mangled English'. *Slanga* and *Fusion Talk* are further names. The dictionary definition of *Manglish* as 'an English-based pidgin or creole' is not entirely satisfactory, because it fails to convey the idiom's unprecedented fluidity. It is used in songs and films as well as in everyday conversation. One of its characteristics is 'code-switching', a habit whereby the base language is constantly shifting. It is perfectly possible, for example, for the first part of a sentence to be based on English (with a few Chinese, Tamil, or Malay words thrown in) and for the second part to be based on Chinese or Malay (with a few English words added). Such gymnastics form one of the attractions of *Manglish*. Linguisticians distinguish *Manglish I*, which was developed on the basis of English, and *Manglish II*, in which the Malay element predominates.[12]

Native English-speakers, of course, cannot expect to follow *Manglish* with any high degree of comprehension. English words, when they occur, are usually pronounced eccentrically, and even *Manglish I* is far removed from anything spoken in Britain or the United States. One hears people being addressed as *Boss* – just as Cockneys address all and sundry as *Guv*, for 'Governor'. The word *Got* stands out, meaning 'There is' or 'There are'. So, too, do the ubiquitous *Can*, meaning 'Yes' or 'Sure', and *No Can*, meaning 'Sorry' or 'Not possible'. And one can hardly miss the affix *lah*, which is hitched to the end of every other sentence. *Lah* means nothing in particular, but imparts a casual, relaxed tone to whatever precedes it. *Let's go yum cha* means 'Let's go and drink some tea'; but *Let's go yum cha lah* would have to be translated by something like 'Wouldn't it be cool to drink some tea!' *That's why lah* is common *Manglish* for 'That explains it.'

Given Malaysia's marked ethnic divisions, the world of insults is especially rich. The Indian-derived P-word – standing for *pariah* or 'outcaste' – is officially banned; and attempts are now being made to stop non-Malays from being categorized by the derogatory *kafir* or 'infidel'. The incorrect K-word for an Indian in Malay is *keling* or *kling* or 'darkie'. Malaysian Indians classify Chinese as *manjatholi* or 'yellow skins' and Malays as *valiangkati* or 'loafers'.[13]

One cannot expect national monuments and national museums to be anything other than nationalistic, but my visit to Kuala Lumpur's Heritage Park, which lies in a hilly section of the city's western suburbs, gives a powerful insight into the identity that state officialdom currently promotes. The *Tugu Negara* or 'National Monument', built in 1966, takes the form of a complex of linked buildings – a cenotaph, an elegant ring of oriental pavilions, a large bronze statue, and a spacious reflecting pool. The Iwo Jima-style statue presents a group of soldiers wearing Australian hats and planting their standard on a conquered summit. It is dedicated, on the left and in English, to 'THE HEROIC FIGHTERS IN THE CAUSE OF FREEDOM – MAY THE BLESSING OF ALLAH BE UPON THEM'; on the right is an inscription in Arabic. A pamphlet informs that the Monument guards the memory of the fallen 'in two World Wars and the Emergency'; it does not reveal that most of those who fell were serving in the British Army.[14]

The nearby *Muzium Negara* or National History Museum is built in the shape of a traditional longhouse. Fronted by fountains, and by large, ceramic panels depicting arts and crafts, the entrance approach is dominated by a full-colour, life-size portrait of Malaysia's royal couple, only recently enthroned. The *Yang di-Pertuan Agong* – literally, 'He who is made Lord' – is generally referred to in English as 'the King'. He stands in the portrait dressed in a black and gold suit, exotic headgear, and resplendent sash and star. Beside him is 'the Queen' wearing a pale gold robe and tiara. He is Abdul Halim Mu'adzam Shah, aged eighty-four, the hereditary Sultan of Kedah, who at the time of my visit was entering the fourteenth five-year reign of Malaysia's unique, rotating monarchy. He is an Oxford-educated jazz enthusiast, an important symbol of unity, and the only monarch to have served two terms.*

The museum's exhibition is divided up into four galleries, each corresponding to one of the four main eras of Malayan history:

A.  Geology and Prehistory
B.  The Mediaeval Malay Kingdoms
C.  The Colonial Era, 1511–1957
D.  Independent Malaysia since 1957

---

* By the time this book went to press in late 2017, Abdul Halim had been replaced by Muhammad V of Kelantan.

No trouble has been spared in filling the showcases with ancient musical instruments, fine period costumes, and historical reconstructions supported with excellent maps and bilingual charts. And every gallery has its highlighted key moments. Gallery B presents a full-scale reconstruction of the scene in 1415, when Arab emissaries converted the Sultan of Malacca (Melaka) to Islam. Gallery C highlights the arrival of the Portuguese adventurer Diogo Lopes de Sequeira, in 1509, and Gallery D the departure of the British in 1957, and the raising of the Malaysian flag by Prime Minister Tunku Abdul Rahman. Nonetheless, the largest space is devoted to the Victorian and Edwardian eras. Nostalgic photographs reveal colonial Georgetown in its prime, and the Royal Navy's massive battleships at anchor in the bay. Modern British visitors are but a poor shadow of those self-confident gents in their bowlers and spats and their wasp-waisted ladies with their bustles and parasols.[15]

The abiding reflection, though, concerns 'alternative history' – what might have been but wasn't – as a way of understanding the contingency of history. Many historical experiences were shared by the progenitors of both Malaysia and Indonesia, and the supposition is that a single 'Malay nation' might well have emerged. After all, there was a common root language; standard Malay and Indonesian are still mutually comprehensible. And there was a common way of life, fired by Islam and by maritime trade. The long history of the Malay Peninsula is one of intimate interaction with its neighbours, especially with Sumatra, Java, and Borneo. The present-day differentiation of Malaysia from Indonesia was by no means inevitable; it was only produced by the former's 160-year subjection to the British and the latter's 400-year relationship with the Dutch.[16]

As often happens, historians need to start as near to the beginning as they can. One of the subjects not prominently expounded at the National Museum was that of Malaysia's *Orang Asli* or 'Indigenous Peoples'. A museum dedicated to them exists somewhere outside of Kuala Lumpur, but is hard to find. Yet the long-neglected aboriginals of the Peninsula, though their numbers do not exceed 150,000, are attracting increasing attention. They live in eighteen registered tribes, and are conventionally divided into three sub-groups – the Semang or Negritos, the Senoi, and the Proto-Malays. The Negritos, regarded as the country's oldest inhabitants, live in the north. The Senoi, the most numerous, include agriculturalists and live in the centre. The Proto-Malays, who are seen as the ancestors of the country's majority group, live in the south. They all cling to remote mountainous areas, where they traditionally practise animist religions and avoid contact with outsiders. In past centuries they were the target of slave-traders, and more recently of Christian and Muslim missionaries. Since 1950, they have been placed under the state Department of Aborigines.[17]

One might imagine that new nations would be sensitive to the interests of vulnerable minorities. But this does not follow. Not long ago, a Malaysian prime minister could protest against what were the perceived privileges of the *Orang Asli*. 'They are not entitled to more rights than Malays,' he wrote, 'even though they are natives.' It is only very recently that the present prime minister has introduced the concept of 'One Malaysia', and is pressing for the aboriginals to be called not *Orang Asli* but *Orang Kita*, 'Our People'.[18] But care is needed. If one goes back far enough, all indigenous people came from somewhere else.

After all, the Malays themselves were once migrants. Their language, Malay, belongs to the Austronesian group, which has branches as far afield as Madagascar and Polynesia, and they are thought to have landed in stages on the peninsula that now bears their name sometime between 2500 and 1500 BCE. The main controversies rage over their provenance. One theory prefers Yunnan, a second New Guinea, and a third pre-Chinese Taiwan.[19]

The long period of the ancient Malay kingdoms, therefore, covers two or three millennia, and an area far broader than the Malay Peninsula. Bygone states can often be compared to those fascinating Russian dolls, the *matryoshki*, where one wooden doll conceals others that are hiding inside it. In South-East Asia, behind the better-known historic states such as the Majapahit Empire or the Sultanate of Malacca, an older and more venerable entity had been hiding until rediscovered by modern scholars. It was the state of *Sri-vijaya* – the Sanskrit for 'Happy and Glorious' – whose home base was in southern Sumatra, and whose life extended from the seventh to the late fourteenth century.

A French orientalist, Georges Coedès (1886–1969), the director of Thailand's National Library after the First World War, has been credited with two signal achievements: one is a theory about the 'hinduization' of early South-East Asian states; the other the 'rediscovery' of Sri-vijaya.[20] Before Coedès, confusion had reigned about the political order of the region during the second half of the first millennium. Scholars had struggled in a fog of conflicting names and dates.

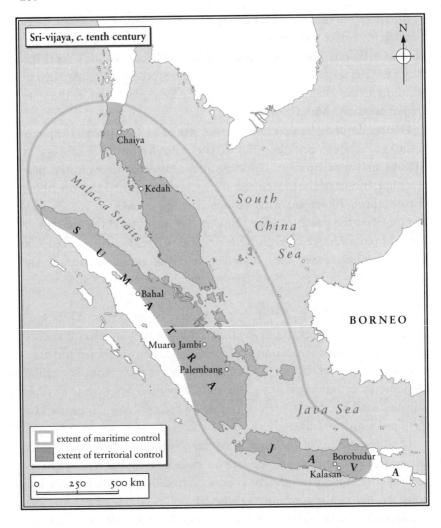

The Chinese had talked of a country called 'San Fo Qi' (*San-fo-tsi*), Sanskrit sources of 'Yavadesh', and the Arabs of 'Zabag'. Coedès noticed the close resemblance of these names with the nomenclature of Malay-language sources, and postulated the previously unsuspected idea that they all referred to one, single state based at Palembang in Sumatra.

In the years since Coedès, the jigsaw puzzle of Sri-vijaya has been pieced together by archaeologists, epigraphers, and mediaevalists from many countries. Very little physical or textual evidence has survived, and the identification of Palembang as the imperial capital was not confirmed until 1993.[21]

According to the so-called Kedukan Bukit Inscription dated 605 Saka (AD 683),* the Sri-vijayan state was founded by a warlord, who arrived with 20,000 men to capture and occupy the district around the Musi River estuary. A port was built, from which ships could command the adjacent Straits. Valuable gold deposits ensured the growth of lucrative trade, especially with China.

Further information can be gleaned from the treatise of Yi-jing (I-Tsing), a Chinese Buddhist monk who visited the nascent state in 688–95 and studied there. Yi-jing's forty chapters focus on Buddhist teaching. But many details can be learned *en passant*, among them the geographical nomenclature of the era.

One must not confound what I-Tsing calls the 'Islands of the Southern Sea' (*Nan Hai*), explains the editor, 'with what we know today as the South Sea Island':

> By the term *Nan Hai*, [I-Tsing] meant the South China Sea and the Malay Archipelago . . . There, he tells us, were more than ten countries, and all under the influence of Buddhism . . . [Mo-lo-yu Country (*Malayu*), otherwise known as Shih-li-fo-shih (*Sribhoga*) was the second of those ten countries] . . . Sribhoga seems to have been a flourishing country in the time of our author, who went there twice and stayed some seven years, 688–95, studying and translating the original texts, either Sanskrit or Pali. In his works, he uses 'Bhoga' and 'Sribhoga' indiscriminately . . . When the kingdom became great and extended as far as Malayu . . . the whole country received the name of 'Sribhoga' . . . The change of name . . . must have happened just before I-Tsing's time.[22]

In short, Sri-vijaya was not yet Sri-vijaya. Further details can be extracted:

- Bhoga, the capital, on the Bhoga River, was the chief trading port with China.
- The distance from [Chinese] Kwantung to Bhoga was almost 20 days by a favourable wind, or sometimes a month.
- Malayu was 15 days' sail from Bhoga.
- The King possessed ships . . . sailing between Bhoga and India.
- The capital, a centre of Buddhist learning, [housed] more than a thousand priests.

* The Saka calendar (now the official calendar of the Republic of India) is based on the Saka Era, which is taken to begin in the year equivalent to AD 78 in the Gregorian calendar.

- [The form of] Buddhism was chiefly what is called *Hinayana*, represented for the most part by the Mulasarvastivada School.
- Gold seems to have been abundant. People would offer flowers made of gold to the Buddha.
- Other products included *pinlang*, nutmeg, cloves and camphor. The people used fragrant oils on their bodies . . . and made sugar balls by boiling the juice of fruit and plants.
- In the country of Sribhoga, in the eighth month and also in the middle of spring . . . a standing man casts no shadow at noon.
- The local language was known as 'Kun-lun', i.e. Malay, not Pulo Condore.[23]

By the end of the seventh century a ruler known as Dapunta Hyang Sri Jayanasa led an expedition into western Java before overrunning many of the adjacent coastal regions. It is doubtful that he had the ability or desire to dominate interior districts, but few ports or trading centres escaped his grasp. Beyond the Straits, large parts of Thailand were annexed, especially the Pan Pan kingdom, which lived from trade across the isthmus. The Sri-vijayan practice of taking over rival commercial networks brought them into Indochina; and in the early ninth century an expedition was sent across the Indian Ocean to colonize Madagascar. (The Malagasy language, long a philologist's riddle, is now firmly linked with its Malay roots; as DNA testing shows, much of Madagascar's population is directly linked to the thirty 'founding Sri-vijayan mothers'.)[24]

Sri-vijayah's links with countries as far afield as Vietnam and Madagascar show that seapower, and the seaborne trade, which it protected, was a central feature of the state's existence. It also explains how rivalry could arise with distant countries such as India or China.

In this early period the rulers of the Sri-vijayan Empire were closely connected with the Shailendra Dynasty from central Java (Shailendra in Sanskrit means 'Lord of the Mountain'), and it is likely that a joint state was created. Several royal marriages certainly took place to cement the link. Dewi Tara, the daughter of Jayanasa's son, Dharmasetu, married the Shailendran king Samaratunga, and around 792 Samaratunga mounted the Sri-vijayan throne. There is reason to believe, therefore, that the great Buddhist Temple of Borobudur, reputedly the world's largest, was built during Samaratunga's reign.

Candi Borobudur stands on an elevated site between two volcanoes in central Java, and was probably constructed around AD 800. To say that its dimensions are colossal is an understatement; 55,000 cubic metres of stone were taken from a nearby quarry to build it. Admirers compare it to Angkor Wat in Cambodia. Four levels linked by circular terraces take pilgrims round a winding route from the foot of the temple to the *chattra* or 'parasol' at the pinnacle. Every terrace is lined with carved stone panels, and adorned by statues of the Buddha. The massive panels, which depict everyday life as well as Buddhist mythology, number 2,672; the statues number 504. Inscriptions, cut into the stone in Old Malay, Old Javanese, or Sanskrit, abound. One of the most famous displays the image of a fine eighth-century sailing vessel, a high-prowed, triple-masted double outrigger, an indication of the empire's seapower.

Borobudur's later history is obscure. The site was repeatedly buried by volcanic ashfalls, and the exact circumstances of its demise are unknown. Sir Stamford Raffles rediscovered it in 1814, when governor of Java. Fully unearthed in 1835 and later restored, it is Indonesia's prime tourist attraction.[25]

The zenith of the Sri-vijayan Empire is usually placed in the tenth century, when the hostile kingdom of Medang in eastern Java was destroyed and Sri-vijayan influence reached as far as Manila. The Khmer Empire in Vietnam reputedly paid tribute. Relations with China in the era of the Tang and Song dynasties were particularly good. Contact was maintained with the court of the Arab Caliphs in Baghdad. An Arab account states that the Sri-vijayan realm was so vast that the swiftest vessel would not be able to sail around it in under two years.

Art and culture were closely allied to the promotion of the Vajrayana variant of Buddhism. Temple architecture clearly flourished, though few prime examples survive. The temples of Sumatra such as Muaro Jambi or Biaro Bahal were built in red brick; in Java, at Kalasan or Borobudur, they were constructed in stone. A fine pagoda in Sri-vijavan style is still extant at Chaiya in Thailand. Many fine statues of the Buddha have been found, in both bronze and stone. Sri-vijava continued to be home to a large school of Buddhist scholars, attracting pilgrims and visitors from abroad. The eleventh-century Bengali scholar Atisha (Atiśa) was a successor to I-Tsing. He studied under a Sri-vijayan master, and later, being summoned by the ruler of Tibet, played a key part in the development of Tibetan Buddhism.

The lingua franca of Sri-vijaya was Malay, in the form now classed as Old Malay, the common ancestor both of modern Malay and of Indonesian. It spread along the trade routes throughout the Indies, and was widely used on official inscriptions, supplying a rich source for contemporary philologists.

Decline set in from the early eleventh century, prompted by the depredations of Rajendra Chola, the 'God-King' of Coromandel in southern India, who descended on the city of Kadaram (Kedah) in either 1017 or 1025, carried off huge quantities of booty, including the city's bejewelled 'War-gate', and occupied sections of the Malay Peninsula. Commerce was interrupted, and piracy increased. Sedimentation in the Musi River cut off Bhoga (today's Palembang), which was replaced as the capital by Jambi. Religious conflicts pushed northern Sumatra and eastern Java out of the Sri-vijayan orbit: the province of Aceh in Sumatra adopted Islam, and the Javanese maharaja of Kediri reverted to Hinduism, creating a new power-centre that absorbed all the archipelago's easterly parts as far as Timor and Papua.

Nonetheless, the stricken empire limped on, its economic prosperity less damaged than its political strength. The end came in 1288, when a Javanese expedition under Singhasari, successor to Kediri, conquered southern Sumatra and suppressed the residual authority of Jambi and Palembang. Within five years Singhasari's successor, Majapahit, had established himself as the regional hegemon and launched the new political enterprise that bears his name.

Sri-vijaya's legacy does not impress latter-day nationalists in Malaysia or Indonesia, who base their identity on different criteria. But the political entity whose memory Coedès rescued, thanks above all to his palaeographical work, did exert a significant influence on subsequent events. It was largely responsible, for example, for the spread of the Malay group of languages, which form a prominent aspect of the region's cultural make-up. It was responsible also for the establishment of the spice trade, which dominated the region's economy for centuries to come. Whenever Europeans hear the nose-twitching names of camphor, aloes, cloves, nutmeg, sandalwood, and cardamom, they should applaud the long-lost empire that first sent those spices to Europe.

Lastly, the fall of Sri-vijaya spawned a company of noble and royal princes, who would long contest Majapahit power. One of them, Sang Nila Utama (d. 1347), crossed from Sumatra to the strategic island of Temasek, where he founded what became the city of Singapore.

Like Sri-vijaya, the Majapahit Empire (1293–c. 1500) expanded far and fast from its original district, and was thalassocratic, that is, dependent on seapower in general and on control of the Straits in particular.[26] The founder of the empire's political fortunes, Raden Wijaya, a Javanese potentate, was crowned in Trowulan on the day equivalent to 10 November 1293, having outwitted and defeated a punitive expedition sent to Java by Kublai Khan, Emperor of China. One of his successors, Rajasanagara Hayam Wuruk (r. 1350–89), brought the growing empire into its golden age: apart from Java, his possessions embraced Sumatra, the Malay Peninsula, parts of Borneo, Sulawesi, the Moluccas, New Guinea, and the Philippines. A visiting Italian monk, Odoric of Pordenone, was dazzled:

> The king of Java has seven crowned kings subject to him. His island is populous, and is the second best of all the islands that exist . . . [He] has a truly marvelous palace. For it is very great, the stairs of the interior are coated with gold, even the roof is gilded. The Great Khan of China engaged in war many times with this king but was always vanquished.[27]

The empire's court language was Javanese; its main religious and scholarly language, Sanskrit. Hinduism and Buddhism were practised in parallel. The administration was centred on the twelve provinces of the *Negara Agung* or 'Core State', which was surrounded by the *Nusantara* or 'vassal kingdoms', the *Mancanegara* or 'tribute states', and the *Mitreka Satata* or 'allied states' in places as distant as Myanmar, Siam, Cambodia, and Annam. This system is often described as the 'mandala model', after the Sanskrit word for 'circle'; it implies a central core and peripheral rings of descending influence.

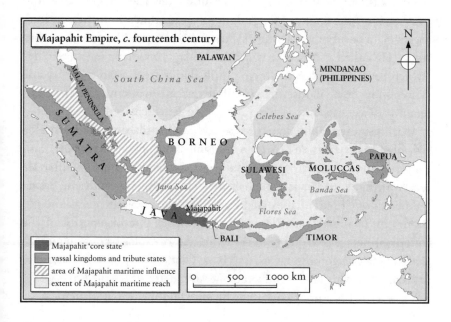

As from the late fourteenth century, however, decline set in and was accelerated by civil war. Majapahit proved impotent in face of the rising Islamic sultanates, and of Malacca in particular; the empire's shrinking rump held out on Java until its last ruler was defeated by the Sultan of Demak in 1527.

Yet Majapahit's history is well known, partly from an abundance of local sources, such as the *Pararaton* or 'Chronicle of Kings', and partly from the researches of Dutch historians, who were eager to discover the origins of their colony in the East Indies.[28] Although Majapahit vanished, its memory and legacy never did. The modern Indonesian flag, the *Dwiwarna* or 'Bi-colour' of red and white, is an exact copy of Majapahit's royal standard.

The Sultanate of Malacca was founded in 1402 by a Hindu prince, Maharaja Parameswara, the great-grandson of Sang Nila Utama of Temasek, and thrived under the founder's heirs and successors until captured by the Portuguese in 1511.[29] Parameswara came from a dynasty of rulers whose domain lay in the *Sri Tri Buana* or 'Three World Realm' made up of Palembang in Sumatra, Bintan Island, and Temasek (Singapore). He himself claimed to have been the last raja of Temasek, but, driven out by a raid from the Sumatran Majapahit, he fled to a district on the western shore of the Straits. Here, as legend relates, Parameswara was resting under a melaka tree when he saw a tiny mouse-deer that one of his hunting hounds had trapped on the shore. Instead of submitting to the dog, the deer fought back and pushed it off the bank, so that it landed upside down in the water. Recognizing a good omen, Parameswara decided to build a fort there and then. He called it Melaka, which in Malay stands for the tree under which he had rested, but which Tamils derive from a word for 'upside down'. The brave mouse-deer is still featured prominently on the city's coat of arms.

Parameswara's kingdom prospered, not least because the prince adopted Islam, the title of Sultan, and the name of Iskandar Shah, joining a string of similar states that were extending Muslim influence eastwards. Secondly, it established a close alliance with the Ming emperors of China, thereby stemming the threat from expansive neighbours in Thailand and Vietnam. And thirdly, it took control of the intercontinental trade route to the Moluccas or 'Spice Islands' which lie halfway between the Sulawesi and New Guinea. One of the Portuguese adventurers who later conquered the sultanate is recorded as saying: 'Whoever is Lord of Malacca has his hand on the throat of Venice.'[30]

For more than a century, Malacca functioned efficiently, supported by sound administration and a well-ordered economy. The sultans held absolute power, but were guided by two written law codes, one civil – the *Undang-Undang Melaka* or 'Laws of Malacca' – and the other maritime – the *Undang-Undang Laut* or 'Laws of the Sea'. Ten reigns covered 128 years:

| | |
|---|---|
| 1400–1414 | Parameswara (Iskandar Shah) |
| 1414–24 | Megat Iskandar Shah |
| 1424–44 | Muhammad Shah |
| 1444–6 | Abu Syahid Shah |
| 1446–59 | Muzaffar Shah |
| 1459–77 | Mansur Shah |
| 1477–88 | Alauddin Riayat Shah |
| 1488–1511 | Mahmud Shah I |
| 1511–13 | Ahmad Shah |
| 1513–28 | Mahmud Shah II |

The principal officers of state, drawn from any social class, were divided between the secular and the military. The *bendahara* was equivalent to the Sultan's chief adviser; the *laksamana* or 'admiral' commanded the fleet and organized the defence of the realm. The legendary warrior Hang Tuah, master of the martial arts in the late fifteenth century, was the most famous *laksamana*. A portrait of him in bronze stands in the National Museum. He is credited with the defiant war-cry, now a staple of Malaysian nationalism: *Takkan Melayu Hilang di Dunia* ('Malays will never vanish from the earth').[31]

The alliance between Malacca and China gave rise to diplomatic missions, at least one royal marriage, and an invaluable description of the sultanate in its prime. Parameswara famously visited China in person, receiving an official Letter of Friendship from the emperor, and the Muslim-Chinese admiral Zheng He (Cheng Ho) made return visits to Malacca. A royal marriage was arranged between Sultan Mansur Shah and the Ming princess Hang Li Po. The description of Malacca can be found in *Xingcha Shenglan* ('The Starry Raft') (1436), an account composed by the Chinese writer and translator Fei Xin, who had accompanied Admiral Zheng He on his voyages.[32] It shows that the Malays, 'whose skin resembles black lacquer' and whose hair is dressed in 'mallet-like chignon style', were seen as exotic foreigners by their

Chinese visitors. It also reveals interest in the sultanate's entrepôt trade and its tin-mining industry. Malacca's unique currency consisted of tin ingots; ten one-pound ingots made a unit called 'a small bundle'; forty made 'a large bundle'.

In the course of the century the conversion of the ruling house to Islam was followed by the conversion of the whole population. Hinduism, Buddhism, and the animist beliefs of the hill tribes were all suppressed. The process was certainly rapid, and possibly ruthless:

> The intolerance of Muslim rulers, Sufis and Ulama of Southeast Asia regarding the infidels was, in all likelihood, more heightened than in India. This was because the Shafi laws that they followed accord mandatory death or conversion to the polytheists, [whereas] the Harufi laws as practised in India accord them a more tolerant dhimmi status ... Shafi laws give exactly four months for the infidels to convert, while other schools give up to a year ... The Malacca Sultanate was in existence for only a century. This suggests that greater coercion was most likely applied in the conversion of the Hindu, Buddhist and Animist infidels of Malaya, Indonesia and the Philippines.[33]

The Portuguese arrived in 1509. Admiral Diogo Lopes de Sequeira put on a friendly face and invited the Sultan to be Portugal's representative east of Goa. But friction arose between Catholics and Muslims; some Portuguese were killed, and an attempt was made to seize their ships. So two years later a Portuguese fleet under Afonso de Albuquerque set sail from Goa to seize Malacca by force. The result was a seventeen-year war. The port and fort were taken by storm. The Sultan fled first to Pahang, then to Bintan, and finally to Sumatra. Skirmishes continued until his main base on Bintan was razed to the ground in 1526. Shortly afterwards the exiled Sultan died. One of his two sons went north to found the Sultanate of Perak; the other went south to found the Sultanate of Johor. Malacca remained a Portuguese colony, until the Portuguese were replaced by the Dutch in 1641, and the Dutch by the British in 1824.

None of which suggests that memories of the Sultanate of Malacca fell into oblivion. On the contrary, both Perak and Johor are constituent states of present-day Malaysia; and both look back in admiration to their common Malaccan progenitor. On this point the National Museum in Kuala Lumpur is emphatic: it names the Sultanate of Malacca as the 'first national Malay state'.

Portuguese dominance in the East was challenged by the Dutch as a result of the Portuguese-Spanish union in 1580. Already in revolt against Spain, the Netherlands henceforth regarded all of Portugal's possessions as fair game. A Dutch fleet sailed for the 'Spice Islands' in 1595; the Dutch East India Company (*Verenigde Oost-Indische Compagnie* or VOC) was founded in 1602; and Dutch supremacy at sea gradually forced the Portuguese out. The VOC's headquarters on Java at Jayakarta (Batavia) was set up in 1619, and a chain of fortified trading posts established to link it with Europe. Malacca was annexed in the early 1640s, when the Portuguese were distracted by the Restoration War against Spain. Dutch rule in Malaya was marked by a determination to exclude foreign powers and by the exercise of only nominal overlordship over the local sultans. It came under threat from the mid-eighteenth century onwards from Britain's conquest of India and the ever-expanding reach of the Royal Navy. It collapsed following the occupation of the Dutch Republic by the armies of revolutionary France in 1795.[34]

British influence infiltrated the Malay Peninsula over some forty years. Beginning in 1786, when the Sultan of Kedah leased the island of Penang to a subsidiary of the British East India Company, it increased greatly during the Napoleonic Wars; the Dinding Islands were acquired, Malacca occupied, and the colony of Singapore founded on Temasek Island. This eclectic collection of territories was transformed by the Company in the 1820s into an administrative entity called the Straits Settlements. Linked only by its sea lanes, it used to house penal camps, thereby gaining the epithet of 'India's Botany Bay'. The principal city, Georgetown, was built on Penang, otherwise Prince of Wales Island.

In 1867, however, the Settlements became a British Crown Colony, subject to the rule of a governor and Legislative Council resident in Georgetown. (This is when the first Victorian postage stamps were issued.) In 1874 the Colony returned the Dindings to the Sultan of Perak, together with a slice of the mainland called Wellesley Province. (Nowadays, the grand harbour of the Dindings, renamed Majong, shelters the principal base of the Royal Malaysian Navy.) Yet expansion continued. One by one the independent sultans of the Peninsula were cajoled, persuaded, or otherwise compelled to accept British 'Residents' – essentially political minders who ensured that British interests were upheld. Four sultanates –Negri Sembilan, Perak, Pehang, and Selangor – joined up to form the 'Federated Malay States', while five others – Perlis, Kedah, Kelantan, Terengganu, and Johor – remained as separate, but British-protected 'unfederated states'. In 1895 all these

British Malaya, 1922

N

South China Sea

SIAM

PERLIS

KEDAH

PENANG

KELANTAN

TERENGGANU

PERAK

DINDING

PEHANG

SELANGOR

Kuala Lumpur □

NEGRI
SEMBILAN

Malacca Straits

MALACCA

JOHOR

SINGAPORE

Federated Malay states
Unfederated Malay states
Straits Settlements

0    50    100 km

sultanates were incorporated into the Straits Settlements, creating an entity commonly known as British Malaya.[35]

The manner by which Britain gained control over the sultans is well illustrated by the examples of Selangor and Perak. In the 1860s the central districts of the Peninsula were riven by gang warfare. Two Chinese secret societies, the Hai San and the Ghee Hin, were fighting over money and the booming tin mines. Thousands of recruits and mercenaries were imported from mainland China and Singapore, and violence grew to dimensions that the sultans could not handle. As a

result, at the end of the fourth so-called 'Larut War', the British were
called in to restore order, and in 1874, as part of the settlement, the
rulers of Selangor and Perak accepted Residents.

A central role in these events was played by a young British colonial
officer, Frank Athelstane Swettenham (1850–1946), a native of Belper
in Derbyshire. Starting as a junior clerk in Singapore, Swettenham
raced up the career ladder to become the first British Resident of Perak,
and then Resident in Selangor. He was instrumental in winning the
goodwill of the sultans, and in laying the foundations of the Federation
of Malay States. In 1901–4, Sir Frank reached the ladder's top rung by
serving as governor and commander-in-chief of the expanded Straits
Settlements.[36]

Swettenham was more than an administrator, however. He was a
formidable linguist, an author, and an amateur photographer, whose
work has left vivid images of British Malaya in his time. His *Vocabulary of the English and Malay Languages* (1882) paved the way for all
subsequent dictionaries, and his books – *Malay Sketches* (1895), *The
Real Malay* (1900), and *British Malaya* (1907) – are primary texts for
the period.[37] Yet his opinions were coloured by the ineffable prejudices
of an imperialist observing colonials from a lofty height. 'The leading
characteristic of the Malay of every class,' he opined, 'is a disinclin-
ation to work.' This was a roundabout way of saying: *Valiangkati!*

Nonetheless, Swettenham could wax eloquent, and the imperial
Resident's words introduced the wider world to the Malays:

Imagine yourself transported to a land of eternal summer, to the Golden
Peninsula 'twixt Hindustan and Far Cathay . . . : a land where Nature is
at her best and richest: where plants and animals . . . seem inspired with
a feverish desire for growth and reproduction, as if they were still in the
dawn of Creation.

And Man?

Yes, he is here. Forgotten by the world, passed by in the race for civilisation, here he has remained in his own forests, by the banks of his
beloved streams, unseeking and unsought . . . [Yet] this is the land of a
Race that has spread over a wider area than any other Eastern people.
Malaya, land of the pirate and the *amok*, your secrets have been well
guarded, but soon . . . the irresistible Juggernaut of Progress will have
penetrated to your inmost fastness, slain your beasts, cut down your forests, 'civilised' your people, clothed them in strange garments, and
stamped them with the seal of a higher morality.[38]

Believing, like many in his generation, that every nation was endowed with archetypal characteristics, he painted a picture of the 'Real Malay' that was sympathetic and critical in equal measure:

> The real Malay is a short, thick-set, well-built man with straight black hair, a dark brown complexion, thick nose and lips, and bright intelligent eyes. His manners are polite and easy. Never cringing, he is reserved with strangers, and suspicious . . . He is courageous and trustworthy . . . but he is extravagant, fond of borrowing money, and very slow to repay it. He is a good talker, speaks in parables, quotes proverbs and wise saws, has a strong sense of humour, and loves a good joke. He takes an interest in his neighbours, and is consequently a gossip. He is a Mohammedan and a fatalist . . . He never drinks intoxicants, and is rarely an opium-smoker. But he is fond of gambling, cock-fighting and other kindred sports, [being] by nature a sportsman, [taming] elephants and thoroughly at home in a boat. Above all, he is conservative to a degree . . . venerates his ancient customs and traditions, fears his *Rajahs*, and has proper respect for constituted authority . . . He is, however, lazy to a degree, is [lacking] in order and method of any kind, and considers time of no importance. His house is untidy, even dirty, but he bathes twice a day and is very fond of personal adornment in the shape of smart clothes . . .
>
> A Malay is intolerant of insult or slight . . . He will brood over a real or fancied stain on his honour, until possessed of the desire for revenge. If he cannot [punish] the offender, he will strike out at the first human being that comes his way . . . [in] a state of blind fury . . . the *amok* . . .
>
> The spirit of the clan is also strong within him. He acknowledges the necessity of carrying out . . . the orders of his hereditary chief, while he will protect his own relatives at all cost . . .[39]

Swettenham's priceless catalogue of characteristics discusses boys and girls, before launching into a description of the Real Malay woman:

> After marriage, a woman gets a considerable amount of freedom, which she naturally values. In Perak, a man who tries to shut his womankind up, or prevent their intercourse with others, and their participation in the fetes and pleasures of Malay society, is looked upon as an ill-conditioned person . . .
>
> The general characteristics of Malay women, especially those of gentle birth, are powers of intelligent conversation, quickness in repartee, a strong sense of humour, and an instant appreciation of the real meaning of those hidden sayings, which are hardly ever absent from their conversation . . .

They are generally amiable in disposition, mildly – sometimes fiercely – jealous, often extravagant, and evince ... an increasing fondness for jewellery ... In these latter days, they are developing a pretty taste for horses, carriages, and whatever conduces to luxury and display, though, in their houses, there are still a rugged simplicity and untidiness, absolutely devoid of all sense of order.[40]

Swettenham's insistence on the disorderliness of Malays sits uneasily with his other comments about courageous elephant-tamers and amiable, freedom-loving female conversationalists. It is, quite literally, gratuitous, and we recognize it today as a sign of the racist frame of mind that automatically denigrated colonial peoples in order to justify imperial rule. It has been challenged by post-colonial sociologists such as Syed Hussein Alatas (1928–2007), whose ground-breaking study *The Myth of the Lazy Native* (1977) was widely acclaimed for putting down Swettenham's original put-down.[41]

One feature of Malay life, which few visitors witness but Swettenham described, is the notorious phenomenon of 'running amok'. According to folklore, it is caused by the spirit of a tiger breaking free from the human in whom it was unwittingly imprisoned. According to modern socio-psychologists it could be a by-product of Islam's severe prohibition on suicide. (It is not peculiar to Malaya, of course. The act of 'going berserk' is well known in northern Europe, for example in 2011 in the terrible episode of mass murder by Anders Breivik in Norway. And random 'killing sprees' and 'school massacres' are a depressingly regular by-product of America's deplorable gun culture.) Captain Cook reported something similar from Polynesia, now classed as *cafard*. And in Indonesia it is known as 'The Dark Eye'. The *Shorter Oxford English Dictionary* summarizes the phenomenon under the heading of 'Amuck':

Amuck, a and adj; also amock, amok. 1663. [Malay, *amoq*, fighting furiously in homicidal frenzy.] 1. Orig. adj or sb a frenzied Malay. 2. To run amuck, to run viciously, frenzied for blood. 3. Fig. Wild or wildly.[42]

The surprising thing is not that English borrowed a word from Malay, but that it did so in 1663, over a century before the Straits Settlements were founded.

Frank Swettenham reported an incident in Perak in great detail:

Just before sunset on the evening on the 11th of February 1891, a Malay named Imam Mamat (that is, Mamat the Priest) came quietly into the house of his brother-in-law at Pasir Garam on the Perak River, carrying a spear and a *golok,* i.e a sharp-pointed cutting knife. The Imam went up to his brother-in-law, took his hand, and asked his pardon. He then approached his own wife and similarly asked her pardon, immediately stabbing her fatally in the abdomen with the *golok.* She fell, and her brother, rushing to assist her, received a fatal wound to the heart. The brother-in-law's wife . . . managed to escape . . .

Having secured two more spears in the house, the murderer now gave chase to the woman and her little children, and made short work of them. A tiny girl of four years old and a boy of seven were killed, while the third child received a blow to the back; a spear thrust disposed of the mother – all this within one hundred yards of the house.

The Imam now walked along the riverbank, where he was met by a friend called Uda Majid, rash enough to think that [he] could prevail over the other's madness. He greeted the Imam respectfully, and said, 'You recognise me. Don't let there be any trouble!' The Imam replied, 'Yes, I recognise you, but my spear does not', and immediately stabbed him twice. Though terribly injured, Uda Majid wrested the spear from the Imam, who again stabbed him twice, in the lung and the windpipe, and he fell. A man ran to the assistance of Uda Majid, and the Imam turned on the newcomer and pursued him. But seeing Uda Majid get up and attempt to stagger away, the Imam went back, and with two more stabs in the back, killed him . . . The murderer was then seen to rush along the river bank, to wade out twice into the water, and to return. He was then lost sight of . . .

For two days, a body of not less than two hundred armed men under the village chiefs made ceaseless but unavailing search for the murderer. Then suddenly, at 6 pm, Imam Mamat appeared in front of the house of a man called Lasam, who hardly had time to slam the door in his face, and fasten it. The house at that moment contained three men, five women, and seven children, and only one spear.

Lasam asked the Imam what he wanted, and he said that he wished to be allowed to sleep in the house. He was told that he could do so [if] he threw away his arms, and to this the Imam replied with an attempt to spear Lasam through the window. The latter, however, managed to seize the weapon with the help of his son . . . receiving a blow to the face from the *golok.* During this struggle, the Imam had forced himself halfway through the window, and Lasam, seizing his own spear, thrust it into the thigh of the murderer, who fell to the ground. In the fall, the shaft of the spear broke off, leaving the blade in the wound.

It was now pitch black, and a man went out from the back of the house . . . to call the village headman. On his arrival, the light of a torch showed the Imam lying on the ground with his weapons out of reach. So the headman pounced on him and secured him. The Imam was duly handed over to the police and conveyed to Teluk Anson, but he died from loss of blood within twenty-four hours . . .

Here is the list of the killed and wounded:

KILLED
Alang Rasak, wife of Imam Mamat aged 33
Bilal Abu, brother-in-law of Iman Mamat aged 35
Ngah Intan, wife of Bilal Abu aged 32
Puteh, daughter of Bilal Abu aged 4
Mumim, son of Bilal Abu aged 7
Uda Majid aged 35

WOUNDED
Kasim, son of Bilal Abu aged 14
Teh, daughter of Bilal Abu aged 6
Mat Sah aged 45
Lasam aged 45

It is terrible to add that both women were far advanced in pregnancy.

Imam Mamat was a man of over forty years of age, and I never heard any cause suggested why this quiet, elderly man of devotional habits . . . should suddenly, without any apparent reason, develop an inhuman instinct and brutally murder . . . his closest relatives and friends.[43]

Despite such unsettling episodes, the achievements of Swettenham's contemporaries in building the Peninsula's economy were very real.[44] Because British rule was indirect, administrative costs were low, while profits from tin mining and rubber production were extremely high. To encourage investment, British administrators developed a system of land concessions, which tempted the locals to dispose of land to the great benefit of London-based companies. They then organized the inflow of indentured labour, mainly of Indians from the Madras Presidency, but later of Chinese. Tin and rubber prices were notoriously unstable, however, and fluctuations caused social distress; Malaya would be particularly hard hit in the Great Depression of the 1930s. In this way the British colonial administration was responsible not only for designing the Peninsula's ethnic make-up but also for fostering conditions that eventually underlay the militancy of labour and the rise of a communist movement.[45]

\*

Both Christmas Island and the Keeling or Cocos Islands lie far out in the Indian Ocean on the far side of Sumatra. Christmas had valuable guano mines; the Cocos were the private domain of the Clunies-Ross family. Although British-occupied, they were unattached administratively until 1886, when they were placed under the governor of Singapore and became an adjunct of the Straits Settlements. Before the turn of the twentieth century, British Malaya had no connection with neighbouring Borneo, the world's third-largest island. Within Borneo, Labuan had been a British Crown Colony since 1848. Sabah belonged to the British Protectorate of North Borneo, and Sarawak had been ceded as a private fiefdom to the Brooke family, 'the White Rajahs', in 1841 and went its own way.[46] In 1906, however, the discontented settlers of neighbouring Labuan petitioned Whitehall to transfer them to the rule of the Straits Settlements. Their petition was granted, and the Settlements' expansion was complete.[47]

Uncle Norman's stamp collection contained more stamps from the Straits Settlements than from British India, displaying nineteen from Queen Victoria's reign, eight from the reign of Edward VII, and six from the early part of George V's reign, enough to fill one whole page. Unsurprisingly, it did not include the rarest of Straits Settlements sets – nine stamps from India marked EAST INDIA POSTAGE, but overprinted in 1867 with a crown and a new value in cents.[48]

Yet my uncle was not lucky with his postmarks. Numerous items show a partial postmark – -INGA, PEN-, -PORE, or -NANG – but only one shows a near-perfect postmark. It is a rose-coloured, Victorian issue for 32 cents from 1867, surcharged in 1885 with the words THREE CENTS and a thick bar. The circular postmark reads 'MALACCA', 'A' (for Central Post Office), and 'DEC 19'. Only the year of its posting is missing, but it must have been between 1885 and 1892, when the colony issued a new Victorian set.

Uncle Norman, like me, lived in an age when children were still taught world geography, and 'The Straits of Malacca' was one of many places whose names had to be memorized. Like Cape Horn, which commanded the sea routes to the Pacific, or the Cape of Good Hope, which linked the Atlantic and Indian Oceans, or the Strait of Hormuz, the Malaccan Straits formed a vital 'pinch point' for intercontinental trade. (It was only later, in the age of oil, that the Strait of Hormuz assumed a similar importance.) We were not taught anything about the region's nations and cultures; but as children of the British Empire,

despite having no internet, we had ready access to further sources of
information:

> MALACCA, a town on the west coast of the Malay Peninsula, in
> 2 degrees 14′ N and 102 degrees 12′ E, which, with the territory lying
> immediately around it, forms one of the Straits Settlements and gives its
> name to the Straits that divide Sumatra from the Malay Peninsula. Its
> name, more properly transliterated as *melaku*, is that of a jungle fruit, and
> is also borne by the small river, on the right bank of which the old Dutch
> town stands. The Dutch Town is connected by a bridge with the business
> quarter on the left bank, inhabited . . . by Chinese, Europeans and Malays.
>
> Malacca, now a somnolent little town [and] a favourite resort of rich
> retired Chinese . . . is visited by few ships, and is the least important of
> the three British settlements on the Straits . . . It has, however, a remark-
> able history. The precise date of its foundation cannot be ascertained,
> but . . . the Roman youth, Ludowigo Barthema, is believed to have been
> the first European to visit it, sometime before 1503 . . .[49]

Over 120 years, from 1826 to 1946, the Straits Settlements were served
by a total of twenty-seven governors; each held office on average for
four to five years. In the early period the governors answered to the
East India Company, and from 1867 to the Colonial Office. Many were
Scots, many former military men, and many the sons of Anglican vic-
ars. Almost all spent brief spells in Malaya between postings in other
far-flung outposts of the empire. The first governor, Robert Fullerton
(1773–1831), a Scot, had started his career in India and had previously
governed Penang. The last one, Sir Shenton Thomas (1879–1962), had
been governor of both Nyasaland and the Gold Coast before sailing
out to Malaya in 1934.

In December 1941 the Japanese Army landed on the shores of Kelantan, and quickly occupied the whole of the Malay Peninsula and
Singapore. For the next five years of Japanese occupation the Chinese
community was brutally oppressed, while the Malays were given to
believe that they had been liberated from British oppression. National
sentiment among the Malays was greatly strengthened, and towards
the war's end slogans of 'neither British nor Japanese' proliferated. But
in 1945 the empire of the Rising Sun collapsed.[50]

The Malayan Union was created in September 1945 as part of His
Majesty's government's reorganization of Britain's reinstituted South-
East Asian possessions. Separated from Singapore and North Borneo,

it was designed to be a modern, streamlined, and self-governing member of the Commonwealth. Yet, by sending the sultans into retirement and by offering equal citizenship to ethnic Chinese and Indians, it alienated Malay opinion. Protests were vociferous, and the Whitehall planners, facing both Communist and nationalist resistance, were driven back to the drawing board. They had underestimated rapidly changing attitudes that had arisen from the war.[51]

The politics of this period were complicated and inflamed. The Malayan nationalist UMNO party, carrying banners such as 'Britishers Out' and 'Malaya for the Malays', strove to gain the upper hand against the traditionalists, who wanted to restore pre-war norms, against the Communists, who enjoyed strong Chinese support, and against a pan-Malay movement, calling for the unification of Malaya and Indonesia. The outcome was for long uncertain.

Formally introduced on 1 April 1946, the Malayan Union lasted only twenty months. Formed from the former federated and unfederated states with a designated capital at Kuala Lumpur, it was publicly opposed both by forty colonial bigwigs, including Frank Swettenham, and by many Malays, who took to wearing white armbands in sympathy for the humiliated sultans. Self-evidently a dead duck, it was relieved of its misery on 31 December 1947.

The Federation of Malaya (1948–67) emerged as the result of the so-called British-Malay 'Pleno Conference' held during the existence of the ill-starred Union. Its territory was extended to include Sabah and Sarawak on Borneo, but not Singapore; and a separate Federal Territory was created at Kuala Lumpur (on the model of the Australian Capital Territory at Canberra). Its system of government reflected a compromise between the British and the sultans. A British High Commissioner was assisted by a Federal Executive Council and a Federal Legislative Assembly, while the sultans regained their traditional domestic roles within the constituent states. Strict limitations were put on the definition of citizenship.

A dozen years of the Federation's existence were taken up by the so-called Emergency, a protracted military conflict between the British Army and armed Communist rebels. Communist partisans had fought the Japanese with distinction, and treated the return of the British as an obstacle to their programme of social liberation. But they were hugely encouraged by the victory in 1949 of Mao-Zedong's Communists in China, and, having taken to the jungle, they could only be overcome by painstaking political and security operations. Britain's ultimate success was later hailed as a model of its type.[52]

'Emergency' was a term chosen to pacify the insurance companies, which baulked at paying compensation for war damage. The Malayan National Liberation Army's assassinations of officials, planters, and mine-owners were answered not only by bombings, defoliation, torture, village burning, and wholesale clearances, but also by strenuous efforts to strengthen the loyalty of Malay communities. The mastermind of the campaign was Field Marshal Sir Gerald Templer (1898–1979), Britain's 'greatest general' and author (or popularizer) of the phrase, 'winning hearts and minds'.[53]

Those same years saw the rise of the Federation's most prominent political figure, Tunku Abdul Rahman (1903–90), or 'Sir Tunku Abdul Rahman Putra Al-Haj ibni Almerhum Sultan Abdul Hamid Halim Shah'. Born the son of the twenty-fourth Sultan of Kedah, 'the Tunku' was a Cambridge-educated lawyer who had worked in the pre-war civil service of the Straits Settlements. Returning from England in 1939, he was employed in a local post under the Japanese occupation, but threw himself into national politics in the post-war era, promoting both Malay-Islamic identity and the concept of a secular state. He was president of UMNO – the United Malays National Organization, Malaysia's largest political party – from 1951, and as the co-ordinator of the national alliance, the architect of successive electoral victories. Chief Minister of the Federation from 1955 to 1957, he was the natural person to lead the country towards self-determination. Widely revered, he was to be rewarded with the epithet of 'Father of Independence'.[54]

Unfortunately, several deep-seated problems – ethnic, regional, and international – dogged the Federation's progress. The ethnic problem, of balancing the demands of Malays and non-Malays, was exacerbated by differences between militant and moderate Malay parties, insecurity among the minorities, and the British government's support for equal citizenship. North Borneo had been integrated since 1945 with Singapore, but the arrangement was not stable. Some groupings there wanted to merge with Indonesia, whereas others were counting on a closer relationship with the Federation. Singapore was not coping, and it looked for a new solution.

Indonesia had gained full independence from the Netherlands in 1949, and regarded itself as the chief anti-colonialist power in the region. It was opposed in principle to the return of British rule in the

Malay Peninsula, viewing both the Federation and Singapore with suspicion. Its possession of southern Borneo – Kalimantan – gave it the means to meddle in North Borneo.

Nonetheless, leaders of the main ethnic groups in the Peninsula established a strong enough consensus in the 1950s to press for radical change. The political vehicle for their aspirations was an electoral Alliance, supported by the Tunku's UMNO, the Chinese MCA (Malaysian Chinese Association), and the Indian MIC (Malaysian Indian Congress). Together with the British, they hammered out a new constitutional settlement, in which equal citizenship was accepted alongside an elected monarchy, Malay was the official language, and there was proportional representation in cabinet and parliament. The British then announced they were pulling out. The Tunku declared independence on 31 August 1957, assuming the post of prime minister.

One of the last (and perhaps least likely) colonial servants, who witnessed Malaysia's road to independence, was the British novelist and composer Anthony Burgess (1917–93).* Between 1954 and 1962 he worked as the director of English Studies at the Malay College at Kuala Kangsar in Perak state, and later in Brunei. Burgess once said that he wished to be known as 'a musician who writes novels' rather than 'a novelist, who writes music on the side'. As good as his word, he composed a *Sinfoni Melayu* fusing Western and Oriental musical styles. But he also learned Malay to a high level, including the ancient Jawi script; and it was in Malaya that he wrote his first novel, *Time for a Tiger* (1956). His biographer relates an incident in a restaurant where Burgess was bawling in Malay at a waitress, who patently understood nothing of what he said. His British companions took this as proof that Burgess's command of Malay was less than fluent. He then told them that the waitress was Chinese: he had been telling her in no uncertain terms that if a Mancunian could learn Malay, so could she! Burgess and his wife were well known for disregarding the stuck-up conventions of the colonial elite. 'Colonialism,' he wrote in his first novel, '[involves] the enforced spread of the rule of reason. But who is going to spread it among the colonisers?' After eight years in South-East Asia, Burgess was invalided out and sent home to Britain, where he started work on *A Clockwork Orange* (1962). Yet he always retained a fellow feeling for the Malays. 'We

* As a student at Manchester University, Burgess, like me later at Oxford, had been tutored by A. J. P. Taylor. On one of his essays, Taylor reportedly wrote: 'Full of bright ideas insufficient to conceal a lack of knowledge.'

only wear shoes,' says one of his characters, 'because the British built roads that hurt our feet.'[55]

Burgess scours late colonial Malaya for darkly comic possibilities. His characters, especially the British ones, are caught up in a fading system that is no longer taken seriously. One of his stories opens on the airport runway of Dahaga. 'The Malay State of Dahaga and its inhabitants,' the reader is told, 'do not really exist':

> The Chinese captain and the Malay second pilot worked stolidly through the check-list.
> 'Lap-straps, no smoking?'
> '*Sudah*' (Done)
> 'Hydraulic hand-pump?'
> '*Tutup*' (Shut)
> 'Carburetor heat?'
> '*Sejuk*' (Cold)
>
> It was Chinese New Year, the first day of the Year of the Monkey. The passengers had driven through the hot morning town to the airport, slowed or stopped by the Lion-Dance swaying through the streets. Young, slim-waisted Chinese had crashed gongs, looking Mexican in wide-brimmed hats, and the brisk, sweating dancer had leapt and run and bowed and advanced and retreated ... Into the open mouth of the Lion people had stuffed, for good luck, little red parcels or *ang pow* ...
>
> In Victor Crabbe's mouth a tongue was stuffed like a parcel, a *pow* by no means *ang*. In his head a Lion-Dance circled and thumped to loud gong-crashes. Last night he had been smothered by Chinese New Year hospitality. Bird's nest, shark's fin, sucking pig, boiled duck, bamboo shoots, beansprouts, huge staring fish, sweet-and-sour prawns, stuffed gourds, crisp fried rice and chicken wings. And whisky. Glass after glass of it, neat. *Kung Hee Fatt Choy.* That meant roughly, a Happy New Year. One mustn't lose face; one couldn't say 'No more whisky.' He lolled back, eyes closed, eyes closed, too, to his wife's quiet weeping.
>
> Fenella Crabbe sniffed into her handkerchief, and the Sikh traveller in the seat across the aisle smiled with sympathy. It was hard to leave old friends, a loved house, a known town. But duty was duty. Where the British were sent, there they had to go. That's how they had built their Empire, an empire now crashing about their ears ...[56]

Those near-prophetic words were written when the British were preparing to take themselves off from Malaya for ever.

*

The Malaysian leaders, in contrast, were looking to the future. The Federation's economic development was assured by two five-year plans, for 1956–60 and 1961–5. Rubber, tin, palm oil and iron ore had all restored their fortunes, and were valuable exports producing a regular financial surplus. But smooth progress in the 1960s was disrupted by international politics. When the Tunku raised the possibility of uniting the Federation with North Borneo and Singapore, President Sukarno of Indonesia denounced the project as a 'neocolonialist plot'. The government of the Philippines also objected. Indonesian infiltrators destabilized Sarawak, where another Emergency, known as the *Konfrontasi*, was contained with difficulty.[57] Pressed on all sides, therefore, the Tunku decided to forge ahead with unification and the creation of an expanded state to be called 'Malaysia'. Following a welter of commissions, inquiries, and referenda, the plan came to fruition on 16 September 1963.

In 1963–5, however, amidst stormy political seas, Singapore's shotgun wedding with Malaysia moved quickly towards a messy divorce. Although 70 per cent of Singaporeans had voted for the merger, the two years of cohabitation satisfied no one. Fresh Communist disturbances arose, this time on Singapore Island. New language laws caused offence, and in 1964 racial rioting erupted. Bills put before the parliament in Kuala Lumpur by Singaporean deputies were constantly blocked, and in the summer of 1965 the parliament voted 134:0 for Singapore's expulsion. Greatly relieved, Singapore became an independent republic within the Commonwealth. (See Chapter 6.)

Such as it exists today, therefore, the state of Malaysia came into existence in the wake of Singapore's departure. It retained the three provinces of North Borneo from the union of 1963, and the constitutional settlement of 1957. Relations with Singapore were restored, both sides accepting that they were better off as independent good neighbours. Their reconciliation was helped by the Indonesian civil war that broke out in the late 1960s.[58]

Since then, the wheels of government in Malaysia have turned pretty smoothly. Fourteen heads of state have reigned in rotation, drawn from the same circle of hereditary sultans and enjoying the title of *Yang di-Pertuan Agong*:

| | | |
|---|---|---|
| 1957–60 | Tunku Abdul Rahman | Negri Sembilan |
| 1960 | Sultan Hisamuddin Alam Shah | Selangor |
| 1960–65 | Tunku Syed Putra | Perlis |

| 1965–70 | Sultan Ismail Nasiruddin Shah | Terengganu |
| 1970–75 | Tunku Abdul Halim | Kedah |
| 1975–9 | Sultan Yahya Petra | Kelantan |
| 1979–84 | Sultan Ahmad Shah Al-Mustain Billah | Pahang |
| 1984–9 | Sultan Iskandar | Johor |
| 1989–94 | Sultan Azlan Muhibbuddin Shah | Perak |
| 1994–9 | Tunku Jaafa | Negri Sembilan |
| 1999–2001 | Sultan Salahuddin Abdul Aziz | Selangor |
| 2001–6 | Tunku Syed Sirajuddin | Perlis |
| 2006–11 | Tunku Mizan Zainal Abidin | Terengganu |
| 2011–16 | Tunku Abdul Halim, *secondo voto* | Kedah |
| 2016– | Muhammad V | Kelantan |

These elected monarchs cultivate a modern and unifying image that contrasts strongly with that of the ancient and hereditary monarchy in neighbouring Thailand. Under them, seven prime ministers, always drawn from the same Malay-dominated UMNO Alliance, have held office. The head of state appoints the prime minister, guided by the wishes of the parliamentary majority, and supervises the choice of cabinet ministers.

The 'Tunku', having served as Malaysia's first monarch, stayed at the helm as prime minister for a long third term, 1960–70, bridging the transition from Federation to Malaysia. The one issue that had not been settled before the British left, the language of state education, remained controversial, and the sole traumatic episode occurred in May 1969, when race riots broke out in Kuala Lumpur causing serious loss of life.

The spark that ignited the riots sprang from a disputed election in Selangor state. Both the UMNO and the opposition staged victory processions, leading to armed clashes, arson, and widespread murder. Official reports calculated the deaths at 198, but other sources put them at 600, mainly of Chinese. Soldiers and police restored order in a couple of days, but a National Emergency was announced and parliament was suspended for eighteen months. During this time Malaysia was ruled by a self-appointed National Operations Council, which published a document known as the *Rukunegara* or 'Statement of National Principles' (1970). Ever since, public readings of the document have been compulsory in all schools and public meetings. The stated principles are: 'Belief in God', 'Loyalty to King and Country', the 'Supremacy of the Constitution', the 'Rule of Law', and 'Courtesy and Morality'.[59]

After the Tunku's retirement, his successors have held to the custom of mixing dialogue with the threat of the iron fist. The public face of government is mild and modest, but the record on human rights is deficient. The six heads of government, who dominated the last half-century, have given priority to the continuity and stability that was lacking in the post-war years:

| | |
|---|---|
| Tunku Abdul Rahman | 1957–70 |
| Abdul Razak Hussein | 1970–76 |
| Hussein Onn | 1976–81 |
| Tun Mahathir bin Mohammad | 1981–2003 |
| Abdullah Ahmad Badawi | 2003–9 |
| Najib Abdul Razak | 2009– |

Nonetheless, the nationalist tone of politics increased after 1970. The Tunku's distaste for *Bumiputra* attitudes was abandoned, and the New Economic Policy linked modernization with affirmative ethnic action. The National Registration Department insisted that the race of every citizen be declared on their ID, thereby putting 'non-Bumis' at a lifelong disadvantage. Under Mahathir Mohamad, the longest-serving prime minister, an Islamic tinge was added to official nationalism, the government lost favour with Western allies, and the opposition leader was prosecuted on dubious charges of sodomy. The current prime minister, Najib Razak, the son of the second prime minister and nephew of the third, inevitably attracts accusations of nepotism in the ruling party. His government has been constantly wracked by scandals of corruption.[60]

Malaysia's performance in the international arena today may best be described as 'good to middling'. Once a pillar of the anti-Communist system, Malaysia has lost some of its shine in Washington's eyes, not least through its refusal to recognize Israel. It has maintained peace with its neighbours, but continues to have niggling territorial disputes with Thailand, Indonesia, and Singapore. It houses the Southeast Asia Regional Centre for Counter-Terrorism (SEARCCT),[61] but discovered through the leaks of Edward Snowden that its own leadership is under surveillance by American and Australian intelligence.[62] Prime Minister Najib Razak served as chairman of the ASEAN organization for 2015.[63]

The name of Najib Razak rings a bell. Well, I never! He is the man who appeared on the front page of the newspaper that I was trying to decipher on the airport coach. The salacious story about him was the time-honoured one of 'the minister and the actress'.[64] It's a sign that the press can't be completely shackled. And Sri Wani, thirty-seven, the lady in shocking pink, doesn't appear to be just an actress. Oh, my word! She was in the news because her husband had just applied to a Sharia divorce court, suspecting her to be a man.

Breakfast radio is popular the world over. In Britain it's the 'Today' programme on BBC Radio 4. In Poland it's Radio TOK FM, and in Malaysia 'The Morning Run' on BFM 89.9. The station describes itself as 'independent', 'uncensored', and 'focused on business and current affairs'. It has been on air since 2008, founded by a Malaysian once employed by Capital Radio in London.

Fearing rush-hour traffic as well as wayward taxi-drivers, Karolina urges an early start, so we set out soon after the muezzin has switched off and arrive in the suburbs at Petaling Jaya with plenty of time to spare. My interview is scheduled for 7.20. The producer offers coffee. I am there because he saw an article that I wrote for *The Financial Times* and has read my *Vanished Kingdoms*. Other staff members join in the pre-interview chat. They are eager to tell us that BFM, though independent, operates under strict government rules and is closely monitored 'by the Ministry'. They do not admit to censorship, but rather to being constantly warned to watch their step. The twenty-five-minute conversation passes off without a hitch. The questions are again about History as a guide to the future, and the permanence or otherwise of the European Union. The interviewer, called Khoo, seemed to be hoping for a dire prediction about China.[65]

For my last evening I am invited out to supper by a couple of postgraduates, who have expressed an interest in studying in Britain. To the question, 'What sort of food?' I answer 'Fusion'. If ever there was a country where fusion cuisine ought to flourish, this is it. But many of the Chinese and Indian restaurants look exactly the same as those in London. I am told that the solution is *Nonya-Baba*, a style of cooking developed by the 'Old Chinese', that is, by the emigrants who left southern China many generations ago; as befits Malaysia, it combines Cantonese with Malay and Indian elements. We start with *laksa*, a large bowl of thick noodle soup mixed with coconut milk, which is served with a side plate of sour fish, and is a meal in itself. Everyone uses chopsticks. Next, we receive a varied collection of Indian griddle cakes, called *roti*, which come in a variety of shapes and sizes, and are accompanied by a matching variety of sauces. You choose a cake, and then a sauce. The best was *roti chanai*, a thin slice of bread dipped in curried lentils. The feast is washed down with an unusually frothy and milky tea called *teh tarik*. Someone in the background is burping. In Malaysia, slurping and burping are regarded as signs of appreciation. People eat rice with their fingers, and waiters rush round with little towels and finger-bowls of warm water.

We are joined at the end of the meal by a professor from one of Kuala Lumpur's private universities. He is Chinese and blessed with a sunny temperament. He has seen the world, has worked in Europe, and is deeply involved in the theory and practice of innovation.

'Malaysia is going to be OK,' he declares, 'absolutely OK.'

We hear about Cyberjaya or 'Cyber City', the 'Silicon Valley of the East', which was launched under government sponsorship in the 1990s. The aim was to diversify Malaysia's economy and by 2020 to propel it into the ranks of 'fully developed nations'. Several leading high-tech firms, such as Dell, IBM, and Hewlett Packard, were persuaded to invest, and a new Multimedia University was established. The strategy, it was hoped, would lead to the creation of a pool of native cutting-edge expertise, which in turn would generate a stable of innovative Malaysian enterprises. For some reason the project's last stage has not yet met expectations, even though Malaysia has its own space agency, *Angkasa*, and a vibrant military technology sector.[66]

Freescale Malaysia is one of the high-tech Western firms that have set themselves up in the country. The offshoot of a Texas-based US parent company, it has its headquarters in Petaling Jaya – near BFM – and has recently celebrated forty years of operating there. According to the website, it is 'a modern semiconductor facility for assembly and testing of integrated circuits (IC)', that is, 'microprocessors, micro-controllers, digital signal processors, and radio frequency ICs'.[67] When it hit the headlines in 2014, persistent rumours held that the company was secretly engaged in the development of aviational 'stealth technology', in other words, methods of making aircraft invisible to radar.

The professor, however, makes light of such information, and brims with anecdotes. He disregards the guidebook's advice about being 'very careful about ethnic-based or political jokes'.

'Have you heard the one about Malaysia's space mission?' he begins.

'No, we haven't.'

'Well,' he continues, 'the Prime Minister of Malaysia was looking for a volunteer, who would fly a rocket to the moon. He first asked an Indian, who demanded $1 million to attempt the feat. "No can," he says, "no can." The PM next asked a Malay, who wanted $2 million. "No can," he says, "no can." Finally he asked a Chinese, who insisted on $3 million. "No can," the PM says, "no can, it's outrageous." "But one million is for you, Prime Minister," the Chinese replies. "Do you want the other two million for yourself?" "No, no, no, Prime Minister; you don't understand: a million for you, a million for me, and a million for the Indian to fly the rocket." '

I was advised to travel in comfort to Singapore by train, but the train runs only twice a week. So, once again, a coach ride awaited. The journey of 324 km takes six hours from Kuala Lumpur: one sees the same green signs, the same monolingual names, the same immaculate highway, and the same motley bunch of foreign travellers. I was conscious of rolling in the tracks of the Japanese Army, which came this way in 1942. The highway hadn't been built then, of course. But the Japanese commanders had the bright idea of bypassing the British defences, and of driving unimpeded right down the middle through the jungle (see pp. 254ff).

As luck had it, our bus was held up for longer than the Japanese were. When it reached the customs post before the Johor Causeway, Malaysian officials discovered a supposedly suspicious person in our midst. A young man of Middle Eastern appearance was taken away, and everyone else had to wait for a couple of hours while he was checked out. Unable to return to the coach, we stood around in the sweltering heat. My fellow passengers speculated whether he was an Arab, a Turk, or perhaps a Greek. It turned out that he was Iranian.

Finally, as our line shuffled forward towards Singapore Passport Control, I noticed that the sign, PLEASE WAIT AT THE YELLOW LINE, was written exclusively in English. Over the top in blue biro someone had scrawled the Malay equivalent. And underneath, in red biro, some-one else had scribbled the equivalent in Chinese letters. Then, as we passed into Singaporean space, a notice written in red capital letters

stood out: WARNING: DEATH FOR DRUG TRAFFICKERS UNDER
SINGAPORE LAW.

The frontier post is built like a grim fortress. Sniffer dogs circulate
as we stand in line with our cases to pass the security gate. The women
officers who doublecheck our passports are not under orders to smile.
I get a distinct whiff of the old German Democratic Republic: efficient
but not exactly brimming with friendliness, and not as advertised in
'Malaysia Truly Asia'.

Malaysia, in fact, is a 'not quite' country. It is colourful and relatively dynamic and affluent; its GDP (PPP) is higher than that of
neighbours such as Thailand, Vietnam, Indonesia, and China, but it is
not in quite the same top league as the so-called 'Asian Tigers'.[68] It
claims to be a land of multi-ethnic harmony, but its dominant Malay
community cannot quite bring itself to share power. It is a fairly stable
democracy, but the practices of the ruling party, which has held power
for sixty years, mean that it does not quite qualify for Freedom House's
'Fully Free' category.[69] It shook off its problematic relationship with
Singapore, but has not quite established a new, angst-free *modus
vivendi*. It has embarked on a strategy of high-tech development, but
has not quite achieved its ambitions. And under pressure one sees the
same 'almost, but not quite' stance in Malaysian psychology. When
flight MH370 disappeared, Malaysian officials could not quite overcome their inhibitions, and did not quite tell the world what they knew.

So, in trying to work out what I thought about Malaysia, I, too,
could not quite make up my mind. I felt like the taxi-driver, who set off
in the hope of reaching a state of certainty somewhere along the way,
but didn't quite succeed. *That's why lah.*

# 6

# Singapura

*Island-City of Lions and Tigers*

Singapore is often classed as a city-state. It might be better presented as an island-state, for it's not like Manhattan, where virtually all the land has been developed. The built-up area of Singapore occupies roughly half of the island's land surface, the rest being filled with parks, nature reserves, golf courses, military training areas, woods, patches of jungle, reservoirs, village remnants, and nondescript urban sprawl. It lies off the very tip of the Malay Peninsula, and is separated from it by the shallow waters of the Johor Strait. The total area, which incorporates sixty smaller islands, is 716 square kilometres or 276 square miles, significantly smaller than Hong Kong. The total population in 2016 was 5.729 million, compared with Hong Kong's 7.4 million.[1] The original mile-long causeway that links the island with the Malaysian state of Johor was built by the British in 1923, when both ends lay within the Straits Settlements colony. The independent state celebrated its fiftieth anniversary in 2015.[2]

My own point of entry, however, did not take me over the Johor Causeway, but over the *Linkedua*, the 'Second Link Bridge', which was built in the 1990s to relieve the traffic jams and which joins Malaysia to the north-west corner of the island. The coach pulls out of the fortified Customs, Immigration, and Quarantine complex, and drives up the ramp onto a winding two-kilometre six-lane dual carriageway held up by columns. The exhilarating view over the shining waters of the Johor Strait is heightened by the occasion's geographical significance. We are leaving behind the last tip of the vast, unbroken Eurasian landmass, across which one could walk or drive overland to India, Brittany or Norway, to Arctic Russia, Mongolia or China, or to the farthest reaches of Siberia. In front, looking south and east, there is nothing but oceans, seas, and a myriad of islands, of which Singapore is the very first: nothing, that is, as far as Ecuador. For a few moments we fly as if suspended between the continental mainland and the insular world.

The coach then rumbles along the Ayer Rajah Expressway to deposit its passengers at the downtown Golden Mile Bus Station. A five-minute taxi ride takes me to the Raffles Town Club. And within an hour of my crossing the frontier, the receptionist is handing me the key to room 301.

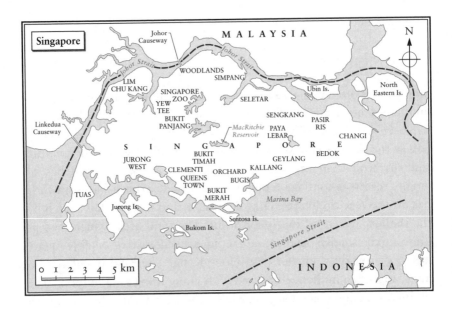

The Republic of Singapore is now the third richest country in the world – one of the marvels of our age. With a GDP per capita of US $51,855 (2015), it has in this respect far outstripped its former 'mother country'.[3] Seventy-five years ago it was the appendage to an underdeveloped colony, whose whole existence served outside interests, and the scene of Britain's most humiliating wartime defeat. It was poorly administered, racked by crime, and reportedly filled with gangs, thieves, prostitutes, and drifters. The dockside district was a slum, even though the commercial port facing Sentosa Island was active, and the Royal Navy operated the largest dry dock in the empire. But its spirit had been broken. It was a place where naval ratings would enjoy themselves ashore and then forget. In which context, one of the curious relics of the late colonial period is a label attached to a poorly publicized aspect of human life. The port's 'ladies of leisure', of whom there were many, developed a technique that gave them peerless renown in the eyes of their clients. Their accomplishment belonged to the intimate realm of vaginal gymnastics; through the flexing of internal muscles that most women never learn to exercise, it delivers unsurpassed levels of pleasure. Famed throughout the empire, it is the 'Singapore Grip'.[4]

Singapore's name has little to do with the city's modern connections. It comes from the Sanskrit words *Singha* and *Pura*, meaning 'Lion City', and was given in the late thirteenth century to the first tiny settlement on the island. At the time, Sanskrit was the principal court language of the Sri-vijayan Empire (see Chapter 5), and legend tells how a Sri-vijayan prince called Sang Nila Utama landed on the island during a hunting expedition. Spying a beautiful orange and black feline in a clearing, the prince was wrongly told that it was a lion. Almost certainly the beast was one of the many tigers that roamed the island until modern times. The tigers were known to be strong swimmers and could cross the Strait with ease, feasting on the wild pigs and deer that abounded in the virgin rainforest. Man-eaters were still common enough in the mid-nineteenth century for the government to pay a bounty of $100 dollars per pelt. Singapore's very last tiger was shot in 1902 from a balcony of the Raffles Hotel.[5]

As in Malaysia, the population of Singapore is ethnically mixed, except that the proportions of the tri-racial mix are different. Here, the Chinese represent almost 75 per cent, the Malays 13 per cent, and the Indians less than 10 per cent. The religious breakdown shows Buddhists at 33 per cent, Christians 18 per cent, Muslims 13 per cent, Hindus 5 per cent, and the rest proclaiming no strong affinity. Overall numbers have grown in step with economic expansion, swelled both by natural demographic growth and a flood of immigrants.

For fifty years and more, however, the city-state's immigration policy has been closely controlled. At first, the restrictions were strong enough to reduce the non-resident population in 1965 to a mere 2.9 per cent. From the 1980s the flow steadily increased so that by 2010 the percentage of non-residents had multiplied almost ten times to 25.7 per cent. Even so, low-skilled applicants, known as 'foreign workers', face barriers that do not apply to highly qualified entrants, known as 'foreign talents', or to international students. They are subject to a regime of work permits and a $5,000 cautionary deposit, and cannot obtain citizenship. The authorities have also taken care not to upset the existing ethnic balance. The majority of immigrants are Chinese either from Malaysia or China, while a substantial minority comes from India.[6]

Singapore's dominant Chinese community belongs mainly to the Hokkien-speaking group, whose ancestors originated in China's Fujian Province in the nineteenth and twentieth centuries.[7] They are closely related to the Taiwanese, less so to the Cantonese of Guangdong and Hong Kong, and least of all to the northern Han of Beijing. Nonetheless, the presence of other Hakka and Cantonese minorities has led, as in China itself, to Mandarin being introduced as the lingua franca. Clearly, the Singaporean Chinese are proud to be a self-reliant and self-confident community. At the same time they are conscious of belonging to the 50 million-strong Chinese diaspora, and retain residual sympathies with China itself. In this they share their compatriots' outlook in Thailand, Malaysia, Indonesia, and the Philippines, to whom they feel closer than to local Indians and Malays. The overseas Chinese have always been merchants, traders, and money-men. In the eyes of critics, their collective solidarity and control of key professions and activities have given them political clout beyond mere numbers.[8]

Singapore's linguistic and cultural kaleidoscope, therefore, is complicated. A huge variety of Chinese, Indian, and South-East Asian vernaculars are spoken in private, whilst four official languages fill the public sphere. English remains the most important because it bridges the intercommunal divisions, but Mandarin, Tamil, and Malay all enjoy protected status. For the foreign visitor the variety of street signs, alphabets, and voices is stunning, and the most common local patois, *Singlish* – Singapore's answer to *Manglish* – is incomprehensible to me.[9]

Singapore's determination to create an equal society from its ethnically diverse people was probably the underlying cause of her split with Malaysia. During the post-war years various political combinations were tried, and Singapore was formally united with the Federation of Malaya for only two short years. By general consent, however, the experiment of 1963–5 was a disaster. Independence followed immediately. To ensure a smooth transition, and to guard against a repetition of the violent disturbances that had occurred, the British government maintained a military garrison on the island until 1972.

Evidence of the British heritage is encountered on every hand. Here, only a stone's throw from the equator, they drive on the left-hand side of the road; they ride in London-style double-decker buses between miles of flowering azaleas and yum-yum trees; and their electric plugs have three square pins, exactly as in Britain. And the street names! Most Singaporean streets currently have oriental names. But there are enough of the old ones left to raise a strong whiff of nostalgia – Orchard Road, Fort Canning, Queensway, Cross Street (as in Manchester), Marymount Road, Marine Parade, and Normanton Park. On the MRT's East West (Green) Line, there are stops called Lavender,

Redhill, Dover, and Lakeside; on the North South (Red) Line – Admiralty, and Somerset: and on the North East (Violet) Line – Woodleigh, Clarke Quay, and Harbourfront.[10] In the published list of 'Ten Best Brothels' the well-established Orchard Towers competes with the Crazy Horse, the Naughty Girl, and the Blue Banana.[11] (Registered prostitutes work legally, though whether any of these establishments still practise 'the grip' is not specified.) And in Singapore's professional football league, the S League (founded in 1904), Geylang International competes with Courts Young Lions, Tampine Rovers, and the Warriors. This last club, formerly singapore Armed Forces AFC, is the most successful in the league's history. Most interestingly, Chinatown is still called Chinatown.

Sooner or later every visitor recognizes Singapore's obsession with triple-barrelled acronyms. One meets the CBD (Central Business District), the DTL Line (Downtown Metro), the URA (Urban Redevelopment Authority), the SIA (Singapore International Airlines), and the NUS (National University of Singapore), but then realizes that for Singaporeans the habit gives rise to much merriment. Officially, PAP stands for the name of the ruling party, but unofficially for 'Pay and Pay'; the Public Utility Board, PUB, for 'Pay Until Bankrupt'; and the Singapore General Hospital, SGH, for 'Sure Go to Heaven'.

Petty regulations make for another obsession. A popular, not to say subversive, T-shirt sums up the city's heavy-handed reputation. On the front, one reads the slogan SINGAPORE IS A FINE CITY, and on the back, a long list of the fines that the police can enforce:

| No smoking | No chewing gum | No monkey feeding |
| $1000 | $1000 | $1000 |
| No jay walking | No bird feeding | No homosexual acts |
| $500 | $1000 | 2 Years Jail |
| No water wasting | Not flushing the toilet | No littering |
| $1000 | $1000 | $1000 |
| No stealing of WiFi | No spitting | No dumping |
| $5000 | $1000 | $500 |
| No eating or drinking | No flammable goods | No flower picking |
| $500 | $500 | $1000 |

Possession of Drugs
DEATH

# Singapore MRT

Kranji **NS7**
Woodlands **NS9**
**NS10** Admiralty

**NS8** Marsiling

Yew Tee **NS5**

Ten Mile Junction **PB14** **11**

**Bukit Panjang**

Jelapang **PB12** — Segar **PB11**

South View **PB1** **PB2** Teck Whye **PB4** **PB5** **PB6** **PB13** Senja **PB10** Fajar

Choa Chu Kang **NS4** **PB1** — **PB2** — **PB3** — **PB4** — **PB5** Phoenix **DT1** **PB7** Petir

Keat Hong

**PB8** — **PB9**

Pending Bangkit

Cashew **DT2**

Hillview **DT3**

Bukit Gombak **NS3**

Beauty World **DT5**

King Albert Park **DT6**

Marym **CC1**

Caldecott **CC17**

**2**

**EW29** Joo Koon

Sixth Avenue **DT7**

Stevens **DT10**

Tan Kah Kee **DT8** **CC19** **DT9**

Bukit Batok **NS2**

**EW28** Pioneer

Botanic Gardens

Newtor

Lakeside **EW26**

**EW27** Boon Lay

**EW25** Chinese Garden

**NS1** **EW24**

**Jurong East**

**CC20** Farrer Road

Orchard **NS2**

**4**

**EW23** Clementi

Somerset **NS2**

**EW22** Dover

**CC21** Holland Village

Buona Vista **EW21** **CC22**

**Dhoby Ghaut**

**EW20** Commonwealth

one-north **CC23**

Queenstown **EW19**

Kent Ridge **CC24**

Redhill **EW18**

Clarke Quay **NE5**

**12**

Tiong Bahru **EW17**

**NE4** **DT19** China1

Haw Par Villa **CC25**

Outram Park **EW16** **NE3**

**DT18** Telol

Pasir Panjang **CC26**

Labrador Park **CC27**

Tanjong Pagar **EW15**

Telok Blangah **CC28**

**HarbourFront** **NE1** **CC29**

**6** **9**

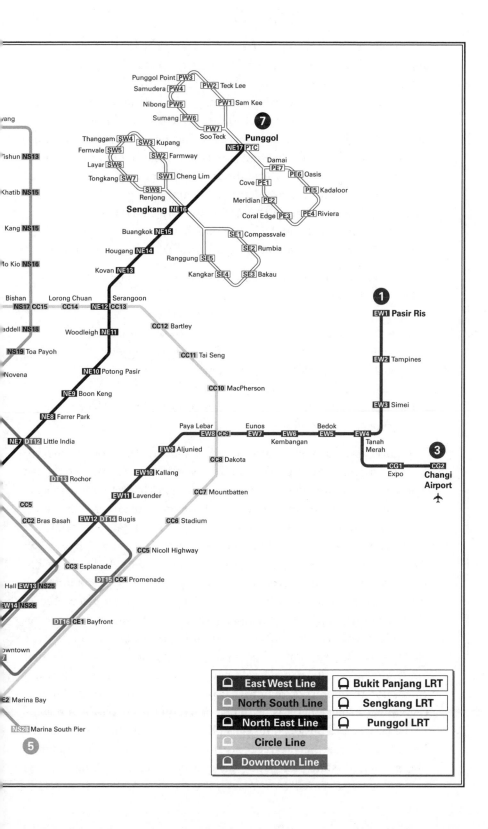

Punggol Point PW3
Samudera PW4          PW2 Teck Lee
Nibong PW5            PW1 Sam Kee
Sumang PW6
                     PW7
                   Soo Teck        **7**
Thanggam SW4  SW3 Kupang                    **Punggol**
Fernvale SW5                             NE17 PTC
Layar SW6      SW2 Farmway
                                    Damai
Tongkang SW7   SW1 Cheng Lim        PE7
               SW8                Cove PE1    PE6 Oasis
            Renjong                              PE5 Kadaloor
**Sengkang** NE16         Meridian PE2
                            Coral Edge PE3   PE4 Riviera
Buangkok NE15          SE1 Compassvale
Hougang NE14           SE2 Rumbia
            Ranggung SE5
Kovan NE13      Kangkar SE4   SE3 Bakau

vang

ishun NS13

Khatib NS15

Kang NS15                                                    **1**

o Kio NS16                                            EW1 **Pasir Ris**

Bishan    Lorong Chuan   Serangoon
NS17 CC15   CC14    NE12 CC13                          EW2 Tampines
addell NS18   Woodleigh NE11   CC12 Bartley
NS19 Toa Payoh              CC11 Tai Seng              EW3 Simei
Novena        NE10 Potong Pasir
         NE9 Boon Keng      CC10 MacPherson
         NE8 Farrer Park
                     Paya Lebar   Eunos      Bedok
NE7 DT12 Little India  EW8 CC9  EW7 EW6  EW5  EW4
                EW9 Aljunied    Kembangan    Tanah      **3**
     DT13 Rochor       CC8 Dakota          Merah
                                           CG1      CG2
         EW10 Kallang                      Expo   **Changi**
CC5                  CC7 Mountbatten              **Airport**
CC2 Bras Basah   EW12 DT14 Bugis                    ✈
         EW11 Lavender   CC6 Stadium
CC3 Esplanade   CC5 Nicoll Highway
      DT15 CC4 Promenade
Hall EW13 NS25
W14 NS26
      DT16 CE1 Bayfront

owntown

E2 Marina Bay

NS28 Marina South Pier

**5**

| 🚇 **East West Line** | 🚋 **Bukit Panjang LRT** |
| 🚇 **North South Line** | 🚋 **Sengkang LRT** |
| 🚇 **North East Line** | 🚋 **Punggol LRT** |
| 🚇 **Circle Line** | |
| 🚇 **Downtown Line** | |

Singapore's all-encompassing by-laws are legendary. One offence, applying mainly to men, bans urinating from a standing position after 11 p.m.; noise regulations insist that all law-abiding citizens are seated while passing water between then and 6 a.m. Disfiguring walls with graffiti carries a mandatory punishment of caning. 'Non-trivial littering' results in community service wearing a shame-provoking, bright-coloured jacket. Chewing gum is so feared that one needs a doctor's prescription to buy it. And disgusting habits such as defecating or urinating in public lifts are deterred by alarms and ingenious odour detectors, 'Urine Detection Devices' – otherwise UDDs.

Fortunately, Singaporeans love to laugh at themselves. They tell the story of the two men and one woman stranded on a desert island:

If they are Americans – one man shoots the other and grabs the woman.
French – they all make love together.
Thais – one man rents out the woman to his colleague.
British – the woman tells the other two to have sex without her.
Malaysians – the woman accuses both men of betraying her.
Indians – they all hold hands and meditate.
Chinese – they all plant rice.
Indonesians – they plant a flag, and claim the island for Indonesia.
Singaporeans – they all sit around and wait for orders.[12]

The governmental system introduced at independence owes much to British advice. It is a parliamentary, constitutional, and republican democracy, and provides for regular elections at all levels. Yet it appears to be more popular among the local voters than among the international political indexers, who tend to call it 'authoritarian' or 'semi-democratic' or even, like Malaysia, 'half-free'. Since 1959, when the British introduced internal autonomy, the People's Action Party co-founded by Lee Kuan Yew has been in power, and no alternations between ruling and opposition parties have ever taken place. Accusations against a supposedly 'one-party state' have inevitably arisen. Even so, there have been few hints of electoral impropriety, and Singapore's place on the Corruption Index is commendably low. So it seems that Singapore has a paternalistic political culture that suits both rulers and ruled, not an oppressive regime that imposes its will by force. There is certainly a strong emphasis on public order, on the far-reaching powers of the police, and on social responsibility. Draconian fines are imposed for trivial offences, civic freedoms do not meet European standards, and no welfare-state philosophy has ever been accepted. Singaporeans are required to make provision for their own health care from cradle to grave, and a world-class private medical system has developed in consequence. The government limits its role to ensuring a stable environment for private enterprise and family life. The one thing still to be fixed is the weather, which inflicts a year-long 32°C, and suffocating humidity levels. But the city planners are working on it, with air-conditioned streets and subways and glass-covered public spaces.

Singapore's head of state is an elected president. Unlike the parliament and government, the presidency has experienced numerous problems, but since the revision of the Constitution in 1991 it is subject to direct elections in which all citizens are obliged to vote. It now enjoys reserve powers raising it above its previous, purely ceremonial role. The president gives assent to parliamentary bills, manages the Corrupt Practices Investigation Bureau, oversees implementation of the Internal Security and Religious Harmony Acts, and participates in decisions to spend financial reserves and make senior state appointments. Since September 2011 the incumbent has been Tony Tan Keng Yam, a former maths lecturer, educational administrator, and cabinet minister. His residence is the grandiose *Istana* or Palace, set in a magnificent park. Built in 1869 on the site of a nutmeg plantation, the Palace, as Government House, was home to the governor of the Straits Settlements. Queen Victoria's statue still stands in the grounds.[13]

Singapore scores badly, too, on the question of censorship. A euphemistically named Media Development Agency (MDA) issues licences for all publications and performances in the press, theatre, concerts, recordings, videos, gaming, film, and internet, and its counterpart, the Media Corp, for broadcasts on radio and TV. The general tone is restrictive on virtually anything related to sex, violence, race, drugs, and politics. The MDA once notoriously banned the song 'Puff, the Magic Dragon' believing that it encouraged the smoking of marijuana. Film classification shields young people; films in the highest category of 'Restricted 21+' can only be shown in selected downtown cinemas. Pornography, even so-called 'soft porn', is banned.[14] A conservative populace appears to support governmental strictness, never having abandoned the strait-laced standards of colonial times.[15]

The Misuse of Drugs Act (1969) acts as the standard-bearer of another harsh government policy. Apart from classifying drugs and drug-related equipment in minute detail, it contains clauses about the detention of suspects without warrant, their presumed intent, and the collective responsibility of whole groups of people apprehended. The possession of drugs carries sentences that range from caning to life imprisonment, drug trafficking an automatic death penalty (as it says on the T-shirts). Police searches at ports and airports are ruthless and pre-emptive, and offenders from all over the world are regularly caught.[16]

The retention of capital punishment has repeatedly attracted the attention of Amnesty International.[17] Before recent amendments, Singapore had the second-highest execution rate in the world after Turkmenistan. Convicts are sentenced to death for murder, treason, and kidnapping as well as drug trafficking; they are allowed one appeal, and can beg for the president's clemency. Hangings take place at dawn on Friday mornings at Changi Jail. The Republic's Chief Hangman, Darshan Singh, started his career under colonial rule in 1959, and was still active half a century later. Attention was drawn to him by the Australian press during protests in 2005 against the execution of a Vietnamese-Australian heroin dealer; it emerged that the words he uttered to the condemned on the scaffold were: 'I am sending you to a better place than this. God Bless You.' A British author's book on the subject, launched in 2010 in Malaysia, was banned.[18] Government spokesmen maintain that capital punishment is reserved for 'very serious cases' and that the country is 'one of the safest places in the world'. The last statement is certainly true; Singapore's crime rate is extremely low. According to the international Numbeo database, Singapore occupies the 119th place among 120 countries surveyed for crime and safety indices. South Korea alone has a better record.[19]

This authoritarianism and social conservatism sit alongside Singapore's astounding economic success, which is all the more remarkable since the island has no natural resources of note. There is no oil or gas, no reserves of timber or minerals, no large internal market, and far too little productive land or water. All the basic goods and commodities have to be imported, and finished products re-exported. When independence arrived without warning, the Port of Singapore, therefore, had to expand dramatically. Vital, strategic decisions had to be taken and a large and skilled workforce assembled. The so-called 'Singapore Model' combined an open, free-market economy with central planning undertaken by the Economic Development Board (EDB) and with a low-tax environment attractive to foreign investors. High-tech industry was harnessed to the expansion of trade, and several specialized sectors such as oil refining, ship repairing, and biomedical products were targeted. Since then, some 10,000 corporations have set up their business in Singapore, mainly from the United States, the European Union, and

1. (*above*) 'A School of Seeing': Goethe's explanation of the value of travel is expounded in his *Italian Journey* (1816–17). Portrait by Tischbein, 1787.

2. (*left*) Dante and Virgil meet the shade of Ulysses, *Inferno* Canto 26. Dante's sublime *Divine Comedy* describes a spiritual journey from Hell to Heaven.

3. (*above*) Marcus Quonimorus Rex:
a post-Roman, Celtic ruler of Cornwall
and possibly of Brittany.

4. (*right*) The Tristan Stone, Menabilly:
a sixth-century tombstone marking the
putative grave of Marcus Quonimorus
and his son, Tristan.

5. (*below*) Cornish chough, *Pyrrochorax
pyrrochorax*: emblematic Cornish bird,
once thought extinct but now resurgent.

6. (*above left*) 'And shall Trelawny die?' Bishop Sir Jonathan Trelawny (1650–1721), hero of the 'Song of the Western Men'.

7. (*above*) Daphne du Maurier (1907–89), novelist of Cornish and Breton ancestry, long-term resident of Menabilly.

8. (*left*) 'Dolly' Pentraeth, fishwife of Mousehole, reputedly the last native speaker of Cornish, *c*. 1775.

DOROTHY PENTREATH of MOUSEHOLE in CORNWALL, the last Person who could converse in the Cornish language.

Printed for I.Hinton,at the Kings Arms,in Paternoster Row.

BACCU.
*eine Stadt in Meden, an der Caspischen See.*

*Die Caspische See.*

*a. Das Feld-Thor. b. die Meer Pforte. c. die Berg Pforte. d. der Marck. e. Spital.*
*f. Königl Schloß. g. Sultans Residenz. h. Kirch und Thurn. i. Monstroser Turn von Ziegeln.*

9. (*above*) Panorama of Baccu, 1683: an engraving of the Caspian port from the period of Safavid Persian rule.

10. (*below left*) Baku's iconic Flame Towers, completed 2012: the architectural fantasy of an oil-rich nation.

11. (*below right*) The Aliyevs, father and son, *c.* 2010: post-Communist dictators of Azerbaijan.

12. (*above*) *The Execution of the Twenty-Six Commissars*, September 1918: a prime example of Bolshevik propaganda.

13. (*below*) The British Dunsterforce, one of several contenders for control of the Caspian oilfields, marches into Baku, August 1918.

14. (*top*) Wilfred Thesiger, 1948: old-style explorer, author of *Arabian Sands*.

15. (*above*) The beach at Abu Dhabi, 1948: a few pearl fishers, the occasional dhow, and no modern amenities.

16. (*right*) Abu Dhabi Corniche, 2012. Arab boys on the waterfront with the Emirate's sensational skyline beyond.

17. (*top*) Sheikh Zayed Grand Mosque, Abu Dhabi, 2012: 'exudes mystery and spirituality'.

18. (*above left*) Dubai: Manhattan in half the time, an explosion of construction in the desert.

19. (*above right*) Gold to Go: a gold bullion dispenser at the Emirates Hotel, Abu Dhabi.

20. (*right*) Hindu Temple, Delhi: dedicated to Lord Vishnu and the goddess Lakshmi.

21. (*below*) Jama Masjid, the 'World-Reflecting Mosque' (1658), Delhi, built by the Mogul Emperor Shah Jahan.

22. (*bottom*) Lotus Temple (1986), Delhi, constructed from twenty-four free-standing 'petals', and reputedly the world's most visited shrine.

23. (*above left*) Delhi Durbar, 1913: King-Emperor, Queen-Empress and little Maharajas, British India's ruling elite.

24. (*above right*) Untouchables, 1890: the lowest of the low in the Indian caste system and a running sore that has not gone away.

25. (*left*) B. R. Ambedkar, the 'Honourable Master', India's most popular figure, and the first untouchable to reach high office.

26. (*above*) Chamba State, 3 pies grey (1911). The Raja of Chamba, 63rd in the princely ranking, was entitled to an eleven-gun salute.

27. (*above*) Malayan Durbar, 1897: sultans from the federated and unfederated states of Britain's Straits Settlement colony.

28. (*right*) Sir Frank Swettenham, Governor of the Straits Settlements, linguist and prolific author.

29. (*inset right*) Straits Settlements 32 cents rose (1867), surcharged THREE CENTS and posted in Malacca in 1885.

30. (*below*) *Running Amok* (1864): an alleged feature of the pathology of Malayans.

31. (*above*) Malayan Emergency, 1949: Chinese suspect, British officer, Malay soldier, a campaign for 'winning hearts and minds'.

32. (*left*) 'The Tunku', Sir Tunku Abdul Rahman, son of the 24th Sultan of Kedah and Malaysia's founding father.

33. (*below*) *Tugu Negara*, Malaysia's Iwo Jima-style National Monument (1966).

34. (*above*) Singapore Harbour, 1900: 'the appendage to an underdeveloped colony'.

35. (*below*) Singapore skyline today: 'the third richest country in the world'.

36. (*left*) Sir Stamford Raffles, 1817: botanist, linguist, historian, servant of the East India Company, Governor of Java and Singapore's founder.

37. (*below*) Raffles Hotel: home of the 'Singapore Sling', scene of imperial splendour and of Japanese *hara-kiri*.

38. (*bottom*) Lt.-Gen Arthur Percival and his staff march to surrender, 15 February 1942: 'Britain's most humiliating wartime defeat'.

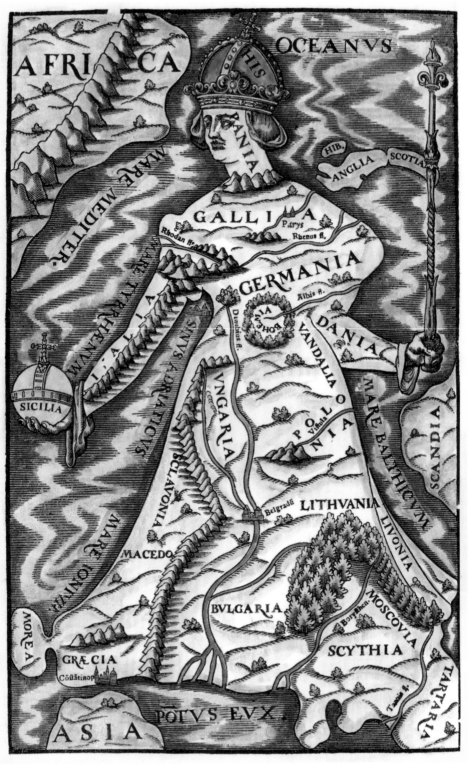

39. *Regina Europa*, 'Queen Europe' (1628), woodcut by Sebastian Münster, Basel.

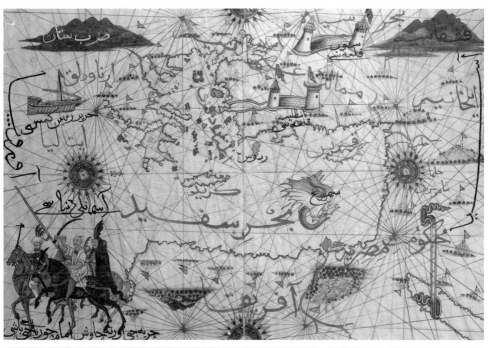

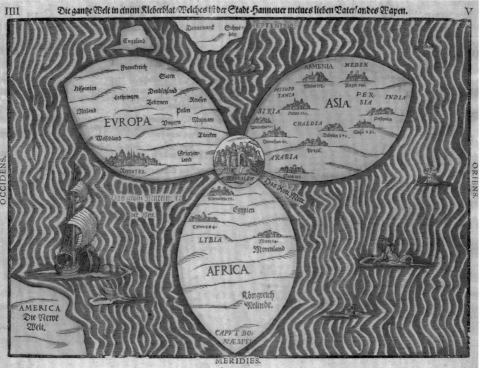

40. (*top*) The Arab Maghreb or 'West': a sixteenth-century Ottoman miniature.

41. (*above*) The Kleeblat Map: Europe, Africa and Asia. Woodcut from the *Itinerarium Sacrae Scipturae* by Heinrich Bünting, Magdeburg, 1581.

42. (*top left*) Hasekura Tsunenaga (1571–1622), Japanese diplomat, eastbound
circumnavigator and Roman nobleman.

43. (*top right*) Alexander Blok (1880–1921), Russian poet of 'We are the Scythians'.

44. (*above*) Burke and Wills, would-be explorers of Australia who lost their way.

Japan, and more recently from India and China. Nonetheless, the government keeps tight control over all major developments. The Republic's sovereign wealth fund, Temasek Holdings, which controls assets of around $200 billion, is fully owned by the Ministry of Finance, and holds a majority stake in many leading enterprises, such as Singtel, ST Engineering, Mediacorp, and Singapore Airlines. The Government Investment Corporation (GIC) manages foreign reserves. The results speak loud. Singapore is the leader of the four 'Asian Tigers'; it possesses the world's fourth-largest financial centre, the world's fifth most active port, and the highest percentage per capita (15.5 per cent) of dollar millionaires. Economic growth between 1960 and 1999 averaged 8 per cent per annum.[20]

Singapore has had its own currency since 1967. The Singapore dollar, $SGD, is regulated by the Monetary Authority of Singapore (MAS). Initially pegged to British sterling and to the Malaysian *ringgit*, it liberated itself by stages, adopting a (nearly) free-floating, market-based regime in the 1980s. One peculiarity is its interchangeability with the Brunei dollar. In late 2015 exchange rates were hovering around 1 $SGD = 70 cents US.[21]

From independence, systematic social policies were embraced to keep pace with the booming economy. Public housing, for example, was the subject of enormous effort. The Housing and Development Board (HDB), founded in 1960, adopted a series of five-year plans to eliminate existing slums and to meet rapidly growing needs. The old British policy of ethnically segregated neighbourhoods was abandoned, and flats in the new, city-centre estates were allocated in accordance with strict guidelines for ethnic integration. At the same time, the state-backed Central Provident Fund (CPF) provided subsidized credit for mortgages that in turn were linked to a compulsory savings scheme. The HDB's original estimate foresaw the annual construction of 147,000 units, an aim achieved both through high-rise estates in the city centre and high-density new towns, such as Queenstown or Woodlands, in outlying districts. New underground lines were built, and new stations opened, to meet burgeoning commuter demands. From the 1970s the emphasis shifted to provide more varied housing for all income groups, and to create smaller-scale, user-friendly, and self-sustaining neighbourhoods designated as 'precincts'. By the twenty-first century, no fewer than twenty-three new towns were operating, each divided into nine or ten neighbourhoods, and each neighbourhood into multiple precincts.

Modern health care is provided on the basis of two principles: 1) that all services must be paid for by patients, and 2) that public assistance makes private health insurance schemes affordable. In this way Singapore avoided the two extremes – one exemplified by the United States, where nearly half the population could not afford health care prior to 2011, and the other by the United Kingdom, where the spiralling costs of the National Health Service are building an unsustainable financial burden.[22]

World-class education, it seems, has been the secret weapon in Singapore's armoury. It was not rhetorically trumpeted to the housetops as in Britain, where Prime Minister Tony Blair repeatedly sounded off about 'Education, Education, Education'. But when comparative international results were first drawn up in 1995, Singapore gained first place in the world listings for maths and science teaching (while the UK came 25th and 10th respectively, and the USA 28th and 17th).[23] What is more, since English is the main language of instruction, Singapore is now moving fast into the $2 trillion international market for educational services, aiming to become 'the Global Schoolhouse'.[24] Its prospects are much better than those of the UAE.

As befits the Republic's present-day standing, the National University of Singapore (NUS) is a powerhouse of international higher learning. In 2015 at no. 12 in the world rankings,[25] it was placed higher than all other Asian universities – higher, in fact, than all other non-American or non-British schools. Forty years ago the majority of Singaporeans received no tertiary schooling whatsoever; the NUS, formerly a sub-branch of the University of Malaya, was growing from its merger with a small, British-founded medical school and with the humanities-based Raffles College; most would-be graduates had to study abroad, mainly in Britain. Yet after independence, higher education was made a priority. The government of the Republic recognized the link between research, technology, and economic performance, and the NUS has mushroomed beyond all recognition. It now has 30,000 students divided between two campuses: the old one at Bukit Timah Road, the new one at Kent Ridge, overlooking the harbour. Some 80 per cent of undergraduates are locals; 80 per cent of postgraduates come from abroad; and 60 per cent of the staff qualified overseas. In earlier decades, the emphasis was placed on the applied sciences. But the twenty-first-century NUS is a research-intensive institution offering comprehensive courses in all disciplines.[26]

At my lecture on the variety of perceptions of European history, a pointed question ended the session.

'Is it not true,' a woman mused, 'that this city's success was built on British foundations?'

'I always assumed,' I replied, 'that Singapore thrived because the British had left.'

All these issues need to be weighed in any attempt to assess the achievements of Singapore's 'Founding Father', Lee Kuan Yew (1923–2015), or 'Li Quan Yu', who occupied senior state positions for over fifty years. A fourth-generation Singaporean and shopkeeper's son, 'LKY' grew up in an English-speaking family of Chinese Hakka origin, won a scholarship to Raffles College, and, still known as Harry Lee, went on to win a Double Starred First in law at Fitzwilliam College, Cambridge, then to practise as a barrister in post-war London. Returning home in 1950, he set up a law firm with his brother, Dennis, dealing with trade-union affairs and adding Mandarin to his earlier knowledge of Japanese.

LKY's political career took off in the 1950s. His views had matured through contacts with the British Labour Party, then a broad church that combined a left-wing middle-class leadership with mass membership. The People's Action Party (PAP), which he co-founded in November 1954, followed the same pattern. It called itself 'socialist', but was run, in his words, by 'beer-swilling bourgeois', who recruited a large following among the Chinese working class. The leadership needed trade-union support to compete in elections, while militant trade unionists, often with Communist sympathies, needed people such as LKY to mask their real intentions. The matter came to a head in 1957. The militants took over the PAP by rigging party conference votes, and LKY was ousted. Fortunately for him, the British authorities were in no mood to tolerate Communist infiltrators, as they assumed they were. So Lee's political enemies were arrested, and he was restored to his position as the party's Secretary-General. Cured of leftist leanings, he never looked back.[27]

In the years that followed, Lee took the reins not only of the ruling party, but also of the nascent state. In 1961, already prime minister, he led a campaign to unite with the Federation of Malaya as a means of shaking off British control. He then switched direction, and took the lead in opposing Malay domination of the federation. Despite his sincere hopes for compromise, he found himself treated by Kuala Lumpur as a renegade. When he went on television on 7 August 1965 to announce Singapore's independence, he fought back the tears: 'Every time we look back on this moment . . . it will be a moment of anguish. For me it is a moment of anguish because all my life – you see, all my adult life – I have believed in merger and the unity of these two territories.'[28] Neither Lee nor his country, which had none of the appurtenances of statehood, was ready for the sovereignty that was rudely thrust upon them.

Singapore's predicament, however, and that of LKY were near unique. All aspects of state- and nation-building were forged from ground level under the direction and supervision of one man, who stayed at the helm for two whole generations. It was inevitable that the end product reflects the principles and characteristics of the long-term leader, who served as Prime Minister from 1959 to 1990 – a world record – as Senior Minister from 1990 to 2004, and as Minister Mentor from 2004 to 2011. What exactly those principles and characteristics add up to is the subject of numerous biographies and studies.[29] Apart from being intellectually capable, Lee Kuan Yew had both stamina and strategic foresight; he was certainly a democrat of sorts and a consensus-builder, instinctively avoiding the worst extremes, and mixing a conciliatory approach with a frequent hard line in both domestic and international relations. And he had a strong sense of communal welfare based on multiculturalism and racial equality. Yet it would be idle to deny that, like Tunku Abdul Rahman, he also had a strong paternalistic streak, with a tendency to ride roughshod over legal niceties and to maltreat his opponents. He was a lifelong advocate of corporal punishment, for example, which he encountered at his first, English-run school. And he did not hesitate to intervene in delicate matters such as birth control or marriage policy. In his later years, when human rights came to the fore, he even attracted criticism from liberal conservatives; and he became litigious, launching lawsuits against journalists at home and abroad who had accused him of corruption or nepotism. Nonetheless, his achievement was immense. No other modern politician can match him for the strength of the personal imprint that he left on his country.

One must equally marvel at the transitions that LKY made in the course of his lifetime. He started as an English-speaking colonial boy, climbing up the ladder of advancement in the British Empire. In his early career he worked as a regional politician, hoping to integrate Singapore with Malaya. Yet from mid-career to old age he was riding the sovereign Tiger with skill and success. In his memoirs he boasts of having learned to sing four national anthems. The first was 'God Save the King'; the second the Japanese *Kimigayo*; the third between 1963 and 1965 the Malaysian *Negaraku*; and the fourth the *Majulah Singapura*. According to the Constitution, this anthem, the Majulah, should be sung in its original Malay version, although approved English, Mandarin, and Tamil translations are also available.[30] It was composed in the 1950s in anticipation of self-government:

> *Mari kita rakyat Singapura*
> *Sama-sama menuju bahagia*
> *Cita-cita kita yang mulia*
> *Berjaya Singapura*
>
> *Marilah kita bersatu*
> *Dengan semangat yang baru*
> *Semua kita berseru*
> *Majulah Singapura*
> *Majulah Singapura!*
>
> (Come, fellow Singaporeans
> Let us all walk to happiness
> May our best aspirations
> Bring Singapore success
>
> Come let us all unite
> In a fine, new spirit
> Together we all proclaim
> Onward Singapore
> Onward Singapore!)

LKY's four anthems represent each of modern Singapore's main historical periods: the colonial, the Japanese, the post-war, and the independent. Each has its own special flavour.[31]

The colonial period lasted from the re-founding of the city in 1819 to the Japanese invasion of February 1942 – 123 years in all. It began in very unusual circumstances created by the Napoleonic Wars and exploited by the splendidly unusual figure of the British colonial administrator Sir Thomas Stamford Raffles (1781–1826).

Born aboard ship off Jamaica to a merchant family from Yorkshire, Stamford Raffles devoted his entire career from the age of fourteen to the East India Company. He never attended university, but possessed an insatiable thirst for knowledge, particularly in botany, zoology, anthropology, history, and languages. His first posting, in 1805, was to Penang, where he learned Malay, before moving on as British agent in the Dutch-ruled Sultanate of Malacca. He was already in place, therefore, when the Royal Navy began to exert control over Dutch colonial possessions to prevent them falling into French hands after the Netherlands were occupied by revolutionary France in 1795. His big promotion came in 1811, when he was appointed lieutenant-governor of the newly conquered island of Java. He spent much time exploring, collecting botanical samples, and establishing commercial contacts, substituting British links in place of existing Dutch ones. He became a distinguished tropical botanist, zoologist, and published historian, author of the first English history of Java, and a Fellow of the Royal Society.[32] Returning to London in 1815 to clear his name against hostile accusations, he stopped over on St Helena to visit the imprisoned Napoleon, whom he described as 'vulgar' and 'authoritative'. The Company kept faith with him, and he returned in 1818–26 to a second governorship in the Far East, this time at Bencoolen on the west coast of Sumatra. His travails were many. His first wife died on Java, his second on Sumatra. His consolation lay in scientific exploration and oriental learning.

In 1819 the island of Singapura offered what one of Raffles' biographers dubbed the 'golden opportunity'. It was not uninhabited, but had long since escaped the interest of local rulers. It had never been claimed by the Dutch, and, though nominally a possession of the Sultan of Johor, was not subject to any effective control. It had not even attracted Raffles' attention until he visited it in person and saw the possibilities for himself. From his Sumatran base at Bencoolen, he had long been scouring the Straits in search of a suitable site for a new naval station, and had previously favoured the nearby Riau Islands. But in the New Year of 1819 he took action. Using a pretender to the throne of Johor, Hussein Shah, who was handsomely paid to accede to the plan, and ignoring calls for restraint from London, he drew up a spurious treaty of secession, and on 6 February claimed the island in the name of the East India Company. The British flag was raised. A declaration was read out in English, Dutch, French, Mandarin, and Malay. And a small garrison was left behind to build a fort. Raffles left promptly, ordering safe passage to be given to all shipping in the Singapore Strait.

His thoughts were recorded in a letter sent to a relative in England less than a fortnight later:

> At Singapore I found advantages far superior to what Rhio* afforded, and . . . you will easily form a judgement of the value of what we have obtained. You only have to glance at the map of the Straits of Singapore . . .

* The Riau Islands.

to consider that we have another port at St. John's, close under which all the China trade must pass: this will convince you that our station completely outflanks the Straits of Malacca . . . It has further been my good fortune to discover one of the most safe and extensive harbours in these seas, with every facility for protecting shipping in time of war etc. In short, Singapore is everything we could desire . . . It will soon rise into importance, I would undertake to counteract all the plans of the Mynheer;* it breaks the spell; and they are no longer the exclusive sovereigns of the Eastern Seas.[33]

A couple of days after that, writing to the Duchess of Somerset, Raffles instructed her how to find the new acquisition on the atlas:

Follow me from Calcutta, within the Nicobar and Andaman Islands, to the Prince of Wales' Island, then accompany me down the Straits of Malacca, past the town of Malacca, and round the south-western point of the Peninsula. You will then enter what are called the Straits of Singapore, and in Marsden's map of Sumatra you will observe an Island to the north of these straits called Singapura; this is the spot, the site of the ancient maritime capital of the Malays, and within the walls of these fortifications, raised not less than six centuries ago, on which I planted the British flag, where, I trust, it will long triumphantly wave.[34]

Once established, the growing city expanded according to the Jackson Plan of 1822, designed by the resident engineer, and received constitutional statutes drawn up by Raffles himself. Schools, churches, and roads were built, and Christian missionaries invited. In the first phase of its existence, to 1858, Singapore was the easternmost link in the East India Company's chain of possessions; extremely isolated, it lay a full month's sailing time from India and three months from Britain. Important milestones were marked by the Anglo-Dutch Treaty of 1824, which delineated the definitive boundary between the British and Dutch empires; the formation in 1826 of the colony of Straits Settlements, to which Singapore was allocated; the creation of the Royal Navy's repair station in 1836; and Britain's lease of Hong Kong in 1842, which raised Singapore's importance as a communications hub. The first Commandant was Major-General William Farquhar, formerly Raffles' chief engineer. At the end of four decades, the population topped 50,000. The Fort Canning Reservoir supplied drinking water to town and navy; and annual income rose to £12 million.

* Mynheer – the Dutch lords.

In the second phase, from 1858 to 1867, the Straits Settlements including Singapore were transferred to direct rule by the India Office in London (see Chapter 5). In the third and longest phase, from 1867 to 1942, rule by the Colonial Office saw Singapore blossom into an international emporium and manufacturing centre. The opening of the Suez Canal in 1869 reduced the sailing time from Britain to forty days, and opened up a new route via Aden and Singapore to Australia and New Zealand. The arrival of the electric telegraph in 1871, through a cable laid from Bombay to Penang, put London into direct contact with the governor of the day, Major-General Sir Harry St George Ord and all his successors. And the shipment of a consignment of rubber-tree seedlings from Brazil in 1877, only twenty-two of which survived the voyage, was sufficient to launch the rubber industry throughout Malaya. Tin-smelting also began, and immigrant labour, mainly from southern China, was imported. From then on, Singapore acquired all the modern urban attributes – a city hall, a railway station, fortifications, and in 1922 an airport.

Many parts of old Singapore, like the notorious Bugis Precinct, were distinctly sleazy. But life for the wealthy and privileged British elite held many attractions. One of the very last to enjoy it, in the autumn of 1941, was the socialite Lady Diana Cooper, who accompanied her politician and diplomat husband, Duff Cooper, on a mission to inquire into the readiness of Singapore's defences. Lady Diana's biographer weaves her own hilarious and indiscreet reminiscences into his narrative:

> It was the city of her dreams: 'no trams ... or smoke and squalor of ports'. It was full of character and charm, with endless fascinating streets of indefinable period crumbling before her eyes. The street-restaurants 'smelt better than Prunier's', with succulent little baked crabs and delicacies in *sang-de-boeuf* bowls. The atmosphere was Sino-Monte Carlo with flashes and whiffs of Venice, 'most frail, tarty, and peasant-pompous: the working life of the Chinks going on down every street – coffin-making, lantern painting, and a tremendous lot of shaving. I never tire of strolling and peering and savouring.'
>
> She settled down to learn Malay so as to communicate with the servants, but since most of them were Indians or Chinese, the incentive to study hard was limited. Ah-hem, the *amah*,* could not speak to the cook, who in turn had no common language with the gardener. A police chauf-

---

* A wet-nurse.

feur called George, who looked like Genghis Khan and wore a red badge meaning that he could speak English, was the only link with the household. Sen Toy, the butler, was particularly hard to make contact with; once Duff asked for his driver and received a bottle of crème de menthe.

Diana had elegant lanterns painted with Chinese characters and hung them around her bedroom, but had no idea whether she was 'advertising trusses, or aphrodisiacs, or the price of a roger for all I know.' The house was delightful, a villa open to the winds with a rough garden of flowering forest trees and neatly clipped cypress and hibiscus hedges. All the walls seemed to fold back, and there was only a minimum of furniture. To complete the décor she bought a jade-green parakeet with scarlet cheek and nose. Diana would slip the ring of his chain onto a long bough of hibiscus and perch him on a flower-vase, where he glowed like a jewel.

One fearful night a 'brain-fever bird', whose speciality was uttering a single gloomy note at two-second intervals, settled on the tree outside the bedroom window. Duff was quickly hysterical with rage, and Diana, half in tears, was soon imploring him not to bombard the darkness with the Ming pieces which she had just lovingly acquired . . .

A trip across the Straits to Johore was considered in order, though [it] almost ended in disaster when the Sultan's baby elephant reached out with its trunk and tried to rip her skirt off. But things were different when it came to flying to Java in a Hudson bomber. 'No place for women,' said [the Air Vice-Marshal] firmly . . .

Diana had no illusions that Singapore would long survive their departure. 'The Germans don't look too healthy,' she told [her son], 'and we don't worry about the Wops, but those slit-eyed dwarfs from Japan are a pest.' The inhabitants would undoubtedly depart at the first opportunity.[35]

For the British, the name of Singapore must for ever be associated with one of the greatest of imperial calamities. For it was in Singapore, in February 1942, that Britannia lost her grip, as one might say, on a large part of her empire; and she did so in such a ridiculous manner that her credentials for holding on to the rest were seriously undermined. The island had been publicly declared 'an impregnable fortress'; it was 'the Gibraltar of the East', the hub of all the empire's main sea lanes. In the interwar years it had received the astronomical sum of £63,000,000 to be spent on its defences. It was guarded by the Army of Malaya with over 100,000 troops, by numerous RAF and RAAF squadrons, and by the Royal Navy's Far Eastern Fleet. In late 1941 its garrison was strengthened by two mighty capital ships – the 35,000-ton battleship *Prince of Wales*, and the 27,000-ton battlecruiser *Repulse*. It formed part of the still larger Allied British, Dutch and American Command (ABDACOM), whose headquarters were on Java under the allied commander-in-chief, General Sir Archibald Wavell. Yet, put to the test, it collapsed like a flimsy bamboo hut.[36]

The Malayan Campaign of 1941–2, like the French campaign of 1940, lasted less than two months, and was brought to a sudden close for exactly the same reason: no one had told the enemy that they were not supposed to deploy modern military methods or advance through glaring gaps in strategic defence lines. The defenders were led by an incompetent assortment of blimps and toffs, whose performance was later characterized as 'unexampled military bungling, administrative ineptitude, inter-service feuding, and plain ignorance'.[37] An American commentator summed it up as Britain's 'Lousiest Hour'.[38]

When the Japanese army landed on the north-east coast of Malaya, 400 miles from Singapore, on 7–8 December 1941 – simultaneously with the bombing of Pearl Harbor – the British Command did not imagine that the landings posed a mortal danger. On hearing the report of Lieutenant-General Arthur Percival, the OC (Commanding Officer) Malaya, the governor of Singapore, General Sir Shenton Thomas, remarked to his entourage: 'Well, I suppose that you'll shove the little men off!'[39]

In reality, the invaders possessed every sort of advantage except that of numbers. Within a week they had forced the British to abandon Penang on the west coast, exposing its population to a cruel fate. They enjoyed a monopoly of tanks, heavy bombers, modern fighter planes, and landing-craft, and a marked superiority in mobile artillery. They had developed an advanced capacity for combined operations, and completely new tactics for jungle warfare: their staff planners were inspired by the same sense of daring and enterprise behind German blitzkrieg in Europe. British counter-measures failed to materialize before the Japanese had cleared their landing zones; the foot-slogging British infantry were outpaced and outmanoeuvred by Japanese columns moving unopposed along minor roads and jungle paths. British strongpoints at small towns and railways junctions were repeatedly outflanked. The scene was observed by Lieutenant-Colonel Freddie Spencer-Chapman:

> The majority of them [the Japanese] were on bicycles, in parties of forty or fifty, riding three or four abreast, and talking and laughing as if they

were going to a football match. In fact, many of them were wearing football jerseys; they seemed to have no standard uniform or equipment, and
were travelling as light as they could . . . All this was in marked contrast
to our own frontline soldiers, who were equipped like Christmas trees
with heavy boots, packs, haversacks, water bottles, blankets, ground-
sheets and even greatcoats and respirators, so that they could hardly
breathe, let alone fight.[40]

The British commander, Lieutenant-General Percival, 'colourless and
toothy', refused to strengthen the shore defences of Singapore Island
because 'it would affect internal morale'. He confessed to the 'utter
weariness of . . . both officers and men'. 'To their physical fatigue was
added a mental fatigue brought about by the enemy's complete supremacy in air and sea and by a general air of futility.'[41] Within a month the
front was approaching the foot of the Malay Peninsula.

The British Army's discomfiture on land was compounded by the
Royal Navy's defeat at sea. On 8 December 1941 the newly promoted
Rear Admiral Sir Thomas Phillips, known to his men as 'Tom Thumb',
sailed out of Singapore aboard the *Prince of Wales* at the head of a
flotilla of five warships code-named 'Force Z'; he was heading for the
Japanese landing-grounds in northern Malaya, which he aimed to take
by surprise. (He should have been accompanied by the aircraft carrier
HMS *Indomitable*, which, though allocated to the Far East, was still
undergoing repairs in Britain.) His dilemma has been described by a
sympathetic naval historian:

> Should he steam into the Gulf of Siam and expose his ships to air attack
> from Indo-China, in the hope of breaking the enemy's communications
> with their leading force? He took the chance. With the Royal Air Force
> and the British Army fighting for their lives, the Royal Navy could not be
> true to its traditions by remaining idly at anchor.[42]

Unfortunately, Force Z had already left port when Phillips learned that
no land-based air cover could be provided, and he reached the middle
of the South China Sea before realizing that his flotilla had been picked
up by Japanese submarines and spotter-planes. Deciding to turn back
for Singapore he hoped to make his presence felt at the more southerly
landing zone at Kuantan. Tragically, since he was keeping radio silence,
he failed both to signal his exact position and to call for protection
from RAF 453 (Fighter) Squadron, which was standing by for such an
eventuality. At 11.25 a.m. on the morning of 10 December, therefore,

an airborne strike-force of thirty-four high-level Japanese bombers and fifty-one torpedo-carriers closed in on their prey. The first wave started a fire in the *Prince of Wales*'s hangar. The second wave knocked out her propellers, and tore open the *Repulse*'s decks and jammed her rudder. Within a few minutes the *Repulse* rolled over and sank, her guns still blazing. Some 508 men lost their lives. Three more torpedo attacks scored multiple hits on the flagship, which by now was a drifting and smouldering hulk. In a generous act the Japanese pilots radioed to the British destroyers giving them clearance to move in and take off survivors. Then, at 1.30 p.m., the *Prince of Wales* exploded and sped to the bottom, taking Rear Admiral Phillips and 326 others with it. RAF fighters arrived in time to watch the destroyer crews as they fished sailors and corpses from the oil-stained sea.[43] The scale of the disaster can only be compared to that of Tsushima thirty-seven years earlier, when the Japanese had first demonstrated Asia's military potential by demolishing a Russian fleet.[44]

The RAF performed no better. Its leader, Air Vice-Marshal Henry Brooke-Popham, complacent to a degree, had earlier sent a plan called 'Operation Matador' for London's approval; it assumed that no fighting would take place in Malaya, since the Japanese attack, if it came, would be directed against Thailand. He had not received the expected delivery of modern Beaufort bombers. The two squadrons based in Singapore – RAF 36 and RAF 100 – were equipped with outdated, open-cockpit biplanes, the Vickers *Vildebeest*, which Brooke-Popham had described as 'Good enough for Malaya'. The Malay motto of RAF 100 Squadron ran *Sarang tebuan jangan dijolok* ('Don't stir up a hornet's nest'). The spirit of the Battle of Britain was far, far away.

By mid-January 1942 the British prime minister, Winston Churchill, was contemplating the imminent fall of Malaya and the impending siege of Singapore. 'The vital need,' he told the regional commander, 'is to prolong the defence of the island to the last possible minute.' On 19 January, therefore, he was astonished to hear from Field Marshal Wavell that prolonged defence was impossible. 'All plans were based on repulsing seaborne attacks,' Wavell explained weakly. 'Little or nothing was done to construct defences on the north side [or] to prevent a crossing of the Johore Strait.' Churchill was, in his own words, 'staggered'. Describing a 'fortress' as 'a completely encircled strong place', he drew up a ten-point plan to defend Singapore 'TO THE DEATH'.[45]

The very next day an infuriated Churchill had to consider the strategic implications. Which was the more essential for the empire,

Singapore or Burma? On balance, the prime minister favoured Burma. 'As a strategic object,' he wrote, 'I regard keeping the Burma Road open [to China] as more important than the retention of Singapore.' An indication of his thoughts reached Canberra, letting the Australians know that they might soon be cut loose (as indeed they would be). An angry letter winged its way to London from the Australian Premier: 'After all the assurances we have been given,' John Curtin fumed, 'the evacuation of Singapore would be regarded here as an inexcusable betrayal. Singapore is a central fortress in the system of the Empire and of local defence. We understood that it was to be made impregnable, and in any event was to be capable of holding out for a prolonged period until the arrival of the main fleet.'[46]

In the meantime, RAF strength was decimated. Early in the New Year its resources had been concentrated at Palembang in Sumatra, where 225 Bomber Group (mainly Hudsons and Blenheims) and 226 Fighter Group (mainly Hurricanes) were assembled. Brooke-Popham, on the verge of a nervous breakdown, had been sent home and replaced. Shortly afterwards, the Japanese landed in Sumatra, launching a fierce attack on Palembang itself. On 26 January, 36 and 100 Squadrons were committed to action at Endau in Johor State. They were almost annihilated. Eleven of twenty *Vildebeests* were shot down, and both squadron leaders were killed. The remnants were withdrawn to Java. Singapore, which had already lost the core of its naval defence force, was now all but stripped of its air force, too.

Then came the issue of reinforcements. If Singapore were indeed to be abandoned, common sense dictated that any supply convoys heading east from Suez should be diverted. They were not. On 22 January the 44th Infantry Brigade landed with 7,000 men, and two days later an Australian battalion with 2,000. With the exception of some first-class Australian machine-gunners, the new arrivals consisted entirely of raw, untrained recruits. 'It would have been better,' commented one historian, 'if those two convoys had never set sail.'[47]

All organized fighting on the Malayan mainland ceased on 1 February. Major-General David Murray-Lyon (11 Indian Division) had been dismissed. Brigadier Gordon Painter (22 Indian Infantry Brigade) had surrendered. Major-General Arthur Barstow, known as 'Bustling Bill' (9 Indian Division), had been killed. Captain Patrick Heenan, Indian Army, was about to be shot for treasonable espionage. Heavy equipment was destroyed. A strategic bridge, vital for the retreat, was prematurely demolished. Telegraph lines were needlessly severed.

Luckless units such as the 22 Indian Brigade were cut off. Others, such as the 27th Australians, bravely charged the advancing enemy with fixed bayonets before pulling back. Lieutenant-Colonel Charles Anderson, an Australian and organizer of the fighting retreat of the so-called 'Muar Force', was awarded the Victoria Cross.[48] But nearly 50,000 Commonwealth troops had been killed or captured.

The race was on to reach the Johor Causeway before it, too, was blown up. The III Corps marched over from Johor Bahru intact. But at 8 a.m. on 2 February two pipers from the Argyll and Sutherland Highlanders led the final rearguard squad to safety to the tune of 'Hielan' Laddie'. As the skirl of the pipes died away, the dynamite under the causeway erupted and the seawater rushed in. Large sections of the infrastructure nevertheless remained intact.

The odds were loaded against the remaining defenders from the start. Food rations were totally inadequate. Ammunition and fuel reserves dwindled after the island's main depots were hit by enemy shells. No anti-tank ditches had been dug, and no suitable labour force remained to dig them. Above all, the water shortage was acute, and the mainland terminal of the pipeline under the causeway was in Japanese hands. The great, fixed gun emplacements possessed an arc of fire that could not be trained inland; in any case, they could only fire anti-naval, armour-piercing shells. Radar cover was minimal, and only one paltry squadron of Buffaloes and Hurricanes remained to deter incoming bombers. The telephone system disintegrated under mortar barrages launched from barges moored in the Strait. Demolitions and evacuations were carried out amidst incessant air raids. Two thousand people were dying every day. Armed looters were roaming the streets. The British Empire's largest floating dock was scuttled, the dockside cranes were hobbled, and the dockyard workers were sent to Ceylon. To avoid the scenes of mass rape and murder that had accompanied the Japanese entry into Hong Kong, all female personnel were sent to Sumatra. An armada of nearly one hundred small ships left the marina. One of these, a launch carrying Rear Admiral E. J. Spooner, ran aground on a sandbank, where half its passengers, including the admiral, perished from hunger and thirst.

Troops of the Japanese 5th and 18th Divisions came ashore from the mainland under cover of darkness during the night of 8–9 February. They were accompanied by swimmers, who carried their packs and rifles over their heads, and by scores of huge pontoons transporting tanks, trucks, fuel, and ammunition. The British searchlight system was sabotaged. The invaders had landed 23,000 men on the northern and western coasts by morning. Their arrival was followed by enormous artillery salvoes; long-range Japanese guns were firing from the mainland at targets 12 to 15 miles distant. Contrary to orders, the entrance area to the Johore Causeway was not manned, and the defensive 'Jurong Line' was penetrated. The one remaining airfield at Kallang near Singapore City was demoted to a forward landing strip, after all its planes were withdrawn to Sumatra.

Wavell, as the commander-in-chief, paid a flying visit, during which he was on the receiving end of a fine Churchillian message: 'The battle must be fought to the bitter end and at all costs,' the message read. 'Commanders and senior officers should die with their troops. The honour of the British Empire and of the British soldier is at stake ... The whole reputation of our country and of our race is involved.'[49]

As he left, picking his way in the dark down the steps to his waiting flying-boat, Wavell tripped and fell, knocking himself unconscious and breaking two bones in his back. It proved a symbolic moment.

On 12–13 February the inner defence lines began to crumble. The Japanese spearheads were led by tanks. Bukit Panjang village fell, followed by Bukit Timah. The road to Singapore City lay open. General Percival ordered his forces to regroup along a shorter perimeter. Driving to consult the governor, he found Government House hit by a shell, and empty. All stocks of banknotes were burned, and the mast of the radio station was toppled. Worst of all, the main conduit of the MacRitchie Reservoir was breached, sending thousands of gallons of drinking water to waste. The municipal engineer reported that the pipes would run dry within twenty-four to forty-eight hours.

On Saturday 14 February stout resistance was offered by the Singapore Volunteer Corps and the 1st Malaya Brigade – local Chinese units led by British officers. They were well aware of the horrors inflicted by the Japanese in China. But bravery was losing its rationale. By now, both the reservoirs and the central food stores had been captured. An Australian general, H. Gordon Bennett, wired his prime minister but not his immediate superiors that he intended to surrender, forbade his men to escape, then succeeded in escaping himself.

In the final scramble, many small ships loaded with refugees and would-be escapers surged out of Singapore's harbour. Most vessels were intercepted by Japanese patrols, and many were sunk. One of them, however, the gunboat SS *Vyner Brooke*, crowded with Australian nurses, reached the Sumatran shore only to find that Japanese parachutists had been dropped onto Sumatra the previous day. The nurses were lined up on the beach, driven backwards into the water at bayonet point, and machine-gunned. Only one, Sister Bullwinkle, left for dead, survived.[50]

On the morning of 15 February, when the final staff conference convened in Fort Canning at 9.30 a.m., it was 'Black Sunday'. General Percival argued that a protracted defensive posture could gain nothing; the choice lay between an improvised counterattack and immediate surrender. His colleagues held that to mount a counterattack was impossible. So the decision was taken to surrender. The Siege of Singapore had lasted thirteen days.

A delegation was sent to parley with General Tomoyuki Yamashita at Bukit Timah. When they arrived, he insisted that General Percival should participate in a capitulation ceremony in person, and that the flag of the Rising Sun should be raised atop the Cathay Building, Singapore's tallest. Although several massacres had already taken place, he guaranteed the lives of British and Australian civilians and military personnel. Hostilities were to cease at 8.30 p.m. Before that, the empire's representatives were to be ritually humiliated. A group of British officers were marched under guard to Bukit Timah, and were filmed as they marched. Guarded by two diminutive Japanese, they strode along wearing their regulation tropical kit: steel helmets, chinstraps, short-sleeved khaki shirts with epaulettes, knee-length shorts, and knee-high stockings. General Percival marched on the far left of the front row, looking straight ahead. An officer in the middle carried a large Union Jack on a long stick. Another beside him carried the white flag of surrender. The act of capitulation was signed by Generals Percival and Yamashita at 8 p.m. that evening.

Percival's war memoirs recount the capitulation scene in his customary self-apologetic style:

> I feel that my readers will not wish me to recount in any detail [those] painful events . . . The meeting with General Yamashita took place in the Ford Factory . . . There was not much chance of bargaining, but I did what I could to ensure the safety of both troops and civilians . . . He received more placidly than expected my statement that there were no ships or aeroplanes in the Singapore area, and that the heavier weapons, military equipment, and all secret documents had been destroyed on my orders.
>
> Little did I think at that time that later in the War I should myself be present at General Yamashita's capitulation – but so it was to be.[51]

In a final chapter, entitled 'Retrospect', Percival claimed that the Japanese forces had been five times as numerous as generally assumed, and he expounded on 'the usual British custom' of hunting for 'scapegoats'.[52]

A Japanese news agency put out its own version of events. It printed what purported to be the full text of the 49-minute conversation between the British and Japanese commanders:

> Yamashita [TY] – I will accept only unconditional surrender.
> Percival [AEP] – Yes.
> [TY] – Have any Japanese soldiers been captured?
> [AEP] – No, not a single one.
> [TY] – I want to hear whether you want to surrender or not [unconditionally].
> [AEP] – Will you give until tomorrow morning?
> [TY] – Tomorrow? I cannot wait.
> [AEP] – How about waiting until 11.30 p.m. Tokyo time?
> [TY] – If that is the case, Japanese forces will have to resume attacks. Will you say yes or no?
> [AEP] – [No answer]
> [TY] – I want to hear a definite answer, and I insist on unconditional surrender. What do you say?
> [AEP] – Yes . . .
> [TY ] – Rely on Japanese Bushido [Spirit of the Warrior].[53]

The maltreatment handed out both to citizens and to POWs once Singapore's garrison had capitulated defies description. Five thousand Chinese were slaughtered in the first few days, the initial cohort of some 50,000 victims to be killed before war's end. Women who had remained were raped en masse, and forced into Japanese Army brothels. Over 80,000 British, Australian, and Indian troops were captured, of whom one in three would perish from starvation, overwork, beatings, or disease.[54] The camp at Changi near Singapore was one of the deadliest and most infamous.[55] Governor Thomas, who had insisted on black ties at dinner until the very end, found himself among the captives. And in his misfortune he redeemed himself. 'It doesn't matter about us,' he lamented. 'It's the people I'm sorry for. It's their country – and somehow we let them down.'[56]

The consequences of 'the greatest debacle in the history of British arms' are not difficult to discern. Firstly, though the British returned for a season in 1945, they had irrevocably lost face in their subjects' eyes. 'The colonial edifice founded by the adventurer, Stamford Raffles, on an equatorial mud village'[57] was doomed. The 'imperial spirit', which Raffles himself personified and which had been cultivated for centuries, was doomed too.

Secondly, as part of a general revolt against European imperialism, the Asians were encouraged to take their destiny into their own hands. Although, as one writer put it, British imperialism was 'infinitely preferable' to its Japanese counterpart, the illusion that Europeans were born to rule and Asians to serve was shattered for ever. 'It was only a matter of time before the frenetic, humid and opulent port . . . ceased to be known as "Europe's Gateway to the East", but rather as "Asia's Gateway to the West".'[58]

Thirdly, by falling from their perch, the luckless British were opening the door to American power and influence. As one strain of Anglo-Saxons was bowing out, another, brasher and more powerful, was being ushered in. Here as elsewhere, the handover took some time to complete. But, as the People's Republic of China arose from the ruins of one section of the defunct Japanese domain, the United States appeared as the protector of all 'free nations' in South-East Asia and the Pacific. No country was quicker off the mark than Australia. In his New Year's Message for 1942 the Australian Prime Minister, John Curtin, made no bones about the strategic shift:

> We look for a solid and impregnable barrier . . . against the three Axis Powers, and we refuse to accept that the Pacific struggle must be treated as a subordinate segment of the general conflict . . . Without any inhibitions of any kind, I make it clear that Australia looks to America, free of any pangs as to traditional links or kinship with the United Kingdom . . . We shall exert all our energies, therefore, to the shaping of a plan, with the United States as its keystone.[59]

Such was the first fruit of 'the inexcusable betrayal'.

Winston Churchill was well aware of the shift from the outset. On 15 February 1942, the day of Singapore's fall, he made one of his periodic 'world radio broadcasts'. After reviewing events since the signing of the Atlantic Charter in the preceding August, praising Russian resistance to Nazi Germany, and denouncing Japan's 'criminal madness', he announced two great events. The first was 'the entrance of the United States into the war', [which] 'is a fact that cannot be compared with anything else in the whole world'. Only then did he tell his listeners of the second event:

I speak to you under the shadow of a heavy and far-reaching defeat. It is
a British and Imperial defeat. Singapore has fallen . . . Let us move forward steadfastly together – into the storm and through the storm.[60]

The Japanese occupation of 1942–5 would have lasted far longer but
for the American victory in the Pacific War. Yet to begin with, prior to
the decisive naval battles of the Coral Sea and Midway, the Allied cause
was sorely pressed. The triumphant Japanese aimed to transform Singapore into the southern showpiece of their new empire, renaming it
*Syonan-to* or 'Light of the South'. They imprisoned British soldiers,
officials, and residents, and began enforcing not just military decrees
but a systematic programme of imposing their own language, culture,
and education: they announced the demise of English as the lingua
franca; introduced Japanese paper money; changed the clocks to Tokyo
time, and brought in the Imperial calendar, in which 1942 became
Year 2062. They also subjected the Chinese community to cruel repres-
sions, though they claimed to be uniting all Asians against foreign
imperialism through *Nippon Seishin*, 'the Japanese Spirit'. In his very
first pronouncement on the afternoon of 15 February 1942, General
Yamashita laid out the objectives:

> We hope that we sweep away the arrogant and unrighteous British
> elements, and share pain and rejoicing with all peoples in a spirit of 'give
> and take' . . . we also hope to establish the East-Asia Co-prosperity
> Sphere, on which the New Order of Justice has to be attained under 'the
> Great Spirit of Cosmocracy'.[61]

Three years later, following his emperor's order to surrender, the commander of the Japanese 7th Army, General Itagaki, signalled his
readiness to obey, though he still had 70,000 men under arms. On the
evening of 3 September 1945 three hundred of his officers held a farewell *sake* party at the former Raffles Hotel before falling on their
swords 'to meet their ancestors'. The next day Itagaki surrendered
aboard HMS *Sussex* anchored in the bay. On 12 September Lord Louis
Mountbatten presided at a second ceremony of ritual surrender in the
city hall, humiliating the enemy who had once humiliated the Allies.
The British flag, which had accompanied General Percival to his capitulation at Bukit Timah in 1942, was flown aloft to emphasize the point.
    General Percival, meanwhile, newly released from a POW camp in
Manchuria, had made it in time to Tokyo, where he took part alongside
General Douglas MacArthur at the principal surrender of Imperial

Japan aboard the USS *Missouri*. He was then flown to Kiangan in the Philippines to be present at the surrender of the Japanese 14th Army, whose commander was none other than his old foe from Singapore, General Yamashita. Percival refused to shake his hand.

The wretched Yamashita suffered an unenviable fate. He stood trial for war crimes and atrocities committed by his troops in Singapore and particularly in Manila. Although brilliantly defended in court by an American military lawyer, who argued that no officer can be held responsible for crimes committed without his knowledge or against his orders, he was found guilty and executed. His death marked the launch of the so-called Yamashita Standard, the legal principle of 'Command Responsibility' that holds good to the present day.

Singapore's post-war recovery was not straightforward. The returning British had lost much prestige, and India's declaration of independence in 1947 was widely seen as the harbinger of more such events. Economic wheels soon began to turn again, but preparations for self-government were bedevilled by territorial complications. In their wisdom, administrators of the Colonial Office joined Singapore in 1945 not with the Malayan Union, but with the British colonies of North Borneo and Sarawak. Singapore's freedom of movement was restricted; and it was not until 1957 that it was able to shed responsibility for Christmas Island and the Cocos. One of the reasons for Singapore entering the Malaysian Federation in 1963 lay in the wish to share these regional burdens. Race riots between Chinese and Malays, fuelled by the tensions of federal politics, broke out in 1964. In this light, the decision to expel Singapore from the Federation can only be viewed as a blessing. North Borneo and Sarawak stayed in the Federation; Singapore left.

Independence reached Singapore, therefore, in less than ideal circumstances. Few preparations had been made, while the region was disturbed by civil war in Indonesia and cultural revolution in China. The founding fathers – who in addition to 'LKY' included Chinese such as Goh Keng Swee (1918–2010), Indians such as Devan Nair (1923–2005) and S. R. Nathan (1924–2016), and the redoubtable Baghdadi Jew David Marshall (1908–95) – can only have felt very vulnerable. Yet they forged ahead without major setbacks, taking care to seek advice and assistance from other small but affluent states. The Swiss were brought in to regulate the banking system; Dutch consultants organized urban and spatial planning; and defence and security services were set up in conjunction with the Israeli Defence Force and Mossad (whose officers arrived posing as Mexicans). The concept of 'Total Defence' – military, civic, economic, social, and psychological – was borrowed from Austria. Compulsory military service was introduced (the Singapore Armed Forces still maintain a permanent reserve of about 400,000 trained men), and above all, close co-operation with the United States was sought and has continued since the late 1960s.[62] There is no formal alliance, but a series of strategic agreements underlie a large measure of mutual understanding. Singapore buys advanced American equipment, and benefits from access to US bases and training schemes. In return, American forces use facilities in Singapore. USAAF fighter squadrons rotate at Paya Lebar Air Base, and the Changi naval yard accommodates American aircraft carriers. In 2012 the Singaporean Air Force possessed no fewer than seventy Lockheed Martin F-16 multi-role fighters, half held on standby in North America. Vigilance is the watchword, although the enemy is not specified. Every 15 February is 'Total Defence Day'. Sirens wail. Speeches are made. The Public Warning System (PWS) broadcasts an 'Important Message' on radio and television. Civil defence teams assemble. And all citizens are urged to take note. Singapore does not intend to fall into the slough of complacency that once scuppered the British.

A couple of free days in Singapore is the limit that most visitors can spare during their business trips or stopovers, but they would be well advised to stay longer. Their tactics will depend on whether they wish to brave the heat in the open, or take refuge in air-conditioned museums and galleries. If the former, they can explore some magnificent open-air destinations such as the Botanical Gardens, the National Orchid Garden, or the tropical Sungei Buloh Wetland Reserve; if not, they will have to decide between the excellent Museum of Asian Civilizations, the National Museum, the Singapore History Museum, or perhaps the new National Gallery in the old City Hall, which concentrates on contemporary oriental art. Those who opt, as I did in Delhi, to follow the religious circuit, can start with the Buddha Tooth Relic Temple, the Sri Mariamman Hindu shrine, the Malabar Mosque, and St Andrew's Cathedral. A secular tour would take them to the Chinatown Heritage Centre, to 'Little India', to the Malay Village, *Kampong Glam*, and to the sensational, ultra-modern development on the waterfront at Marina Bay.[63]

'BBB' stands for *Bras Basah Bugis*, usually condensed in English to Bugis Street, or just 'Boogie'. Originally named after the 'Bugis people' – mediaeval Indonesian pirates – it is situated near the main inlet

of Marina Bay, and was the traditional district of ill-repute, full of red
light areas, gambling dens, sailors' bars, fortune-tellers, strippers, grip-
pers, and transvestites – the Orient's answer to Place Pigalle or the
Reeperbahn. In the 1980s, however, the squalid streets and slum-
dwellers were swept away, and the district is now devoted to 'art and
heritage and shopping'.

Anyone with a historical bent will direct their steps to places where
history was made. The Landing Site beside the Singapore River in the
CBD (Central Business District) makes for a good start. Surrounded by
skyscrapers, motor boats, and planted palms, one has to close one's
eyes to imagine how it was nearly two centuries ago when the first British expedition stepped ashore. Novelists have already done so:

> The city of Singapore was not built up gradually, the way that most cities
> are, by a gradual deposit of commerce on the banks of some river or at a
> traditional confluence of trade routes. It was simply invented one morn-
> ing early in the nineteenth century by a man looking at a map. 'Here,' he
> said to himself, 'is where we must have a city, half-way between India and
> China . . .' This man's name was Sir Thomas Stamford Raffles.[64]

A white marble statue of the empire-builder is at hand. Nearby are the
financial quarter at Raffles Place, Raffles Hospital, and Raffles City.

The Old Ford Motor Factory on the Upper Bukit Timah Road, emits
similarly strong historical echoes. It contains the very room in which
General Percival surrendered on 15 February 1942, and has been filled
with pictures and documents from the National Archives. The nondescript site only heightens the event's magnitude. Much of the exhibition
is devoted to 'The Syonan Years', that is, Singapore under Japanese
occupation.[65] The resultant tragedy of Allied POWs is commemorated
at the Changi Chapel and Museum.[66] Sites of Japanese interest are laid
out for Japanese tourists.

The cool of a cinema is another good escape route from the climate,
especially if there's a chance to see Royston Tan's moving film *15*
(2003), which explores the depressing world of adolescent dropouts.
Teenage suicide, it appears, is far too common in Singapore.[67] An
extended ride on the superbly swift, silent, and soothing metro system,
the MRT, is also good for relaxing, for keeping cool, and for people-
watching.

Sightseeing, of course, is hungry work, and Singapore's cuisine caters
for many tastes. There are any number of high-class restaurants, but
the eating experience not to be missed is supplied by the ubiquitous

'hawker centres' or 'food courts' (now much imitated in Australia), where a ring of twenty or thirty food stalls surrounds a common dining area. Each of the stalls offers a different speciality, whether Chinese, Malay, Indian, or Western, and the hungry consumer can stroll round the counters buying whatever tickles the taste buds. The combinations of offerings are endless, and a local guide can be of great assistance in overcoming the gastronomic language barrier. But plunging in and following one's fancy is the quickest way to learn. Seafood is abundant, and a barbecued stingray served on a banana leaf with sambal sauce is very popular. Otherwise, one can compose a menu as one circulates. A plate of *bak kut teh*, the universal pork rib soup, could be followed by *chai tow kway*, 'radish cake', which either comes 'black' (with black soya sauce) or 'white' (without the sauce). For dessert, a serving of *durian pendek*, 'the King of Fruits', may please the stout-hearted; the custard-like flesh, which sits in its spiky shell, is pleasant enough, but the odour is so pungent that eating the fruit on public transport is banned. *Rambutan* or 'Dragon Fruit' is a less risky choice. The whole delicious repast could be washed down with a glass of soya bean milk or perhaps Tiger Beer. The one item that won't be found is 'Singapore Noodles', that is, fried rice noodles sprinkled with curry powder. This particular concoction has taken hold in Chinese restaurants in the United States, but not in Singapore itself.[68]

One of the gastronomic curiosities still extant is the old colonial habit of mixing oriental dishes with eccentric British food products. A popular offering is a Chinese pork chop in thick tomato sauce with frozen green peas. Fish and chips might be served up with spring rolls or chop suey. And a 'Horlicks Dinosaur', where Horlicks powder is piled high on top of the bedtime beverage, is enough to bring Auntie Doris to ecstasy. The tour de force, much loved by Australians, is deep-fried crab in marmite sauce.

Great care has to be taken ordering tea or coffee. If one says just *Teh* or *Kopi*, the drink will be served in best imperial fashion with condensed milk. *Teh-C* or *Kopi-C* summons up tea or coffee with evaporated milk, the C standing for 'Carnation'. In order to get a straightforward, ungarnished cuppa, it is necessary to order *Teh-O-kosong* or *Kopi-O-kosong*; the Malay word *kosong* means 'empty' or 'without'. The vocabulary dates from a time when the British brought essential supplies with them, and when, in the days before refrigeration, a tin of 'Carnation Milk' was highly valued in the tropics.[69]

Afternoon tea at Raffles Hotel lies at the opposite end of the scale of luxury from drinking *Teh-C* in a hawker centre. Opened in 1887, the Raffles rapidly became an iconic establishment in colonial times, its grand, white-painted facade resembling that of Government House. It originally overlooked the seafront, which has since receded through land reclamation. Its Tiffin Room claims to be Singapore's oldest first-class restaurant. Its Long Bar saw the invention of the famous Singapore Sling cocktail, and it was here, on 14 February 1942, that a last rousing chorus of 'There'll Always Be an England' was sung. The list of previous guests reads like an inventory of the artists and politicians of the *Grande Époque*. When Rudyard Kipling stayed in 1889, he was a struggling, little-known writer. 'Providence brought me to a place called Raffles Hotel,' he wrote in *From Sea to Sea* (1899), 'where the food is as excellent as the rooms are good. Let the traveller take note: feed at Raffles and sleep at Raffles.' The quotation has been used for the hotel's advertising ever since.

In the 1930s Raffles' owners fell into bankruptcy, and during the Occupation of 1942–5 the hotel was turned into a traditional Japanese inn. In 1987, however, it was declared a national monument, before undergoing complete refurbishment. In the 1990s (as I remember from an earlier visit) one could still take tea in the lobby, where a tall Sikh waiter wearing a pure white tunic and bright red turban served cream cakes on a silver tray. Sipping their Pink Garden (green tea with rose petals) or their Tibetan Secret (green tea with lemongrass), guests sank into a deep, flowery sofa, admiring the teakwood floors and the hand-made carpets, and watching as a member of staff hoovered the outside pavement.[70]

More recently, a sovereign wealth fund from the Gulf has gained ownership of the Raffles, and pushed its services beyond the pocket of ordinary visitors. A steak in the restaurant now costs $200 and tea is taken in the renovated Writer's Room. But the hotel museum on the third floor still recalls past glories. Among other things, one learns that the Hainanese barman who invented the Singapore Sling around 1910 was called Ngiam Tong Boon, and that his secret recipe, long hidden in the hotel safe, contained ten ingredients:

| | |
|---|---|
| 30ml | Gin |
| 15ml | Hering Cherry Liqueur |
| 120ml | Pineapple Juice |
| 15ml | Lime Juice |
| 7.5ml | Cointreau |

7.5ml    Dom Bénédictine
10ml     Grenadine
A dash of Angostura Bitters
One slice of pineapple, and
One cherry

Served in an extra-tall glass, the 'pink bombshell' should be consumed quietly, preferably to readings from former Raffles residents such as Ernest Hemingway, Somerset Maugham, or Kipling himself.[71]

Touring the globe today, with much greater speed and comfort than Raffles or Kipling, it is easy to forget the processes of globalization that have made it possible. Most people take them for granted. Yet a visit to Singapore, which in 2007 was rated the world's top country in the original Globalization Index,[72] should prompt the globetrotter to pause and reflect. For the astonishing rise of Singapore coincides almost exactly with the half-century of accelerated globalization that started around 1970 and which now, in the early twenty-first century, is beginning to cause something of a backwash, especially in Europe and America. Singapore has been one of the principal beneficiaries; the 'Rust Belt' of America's Midwest, or the textile towns of northern England, where I come from, are among the most obvious losers. Most of the striking political events of recent decades, from the collapse of the Soviet Bloc in 1989–91 and the emergence of China to the electoral earthquakes of the Brexit referendum in Britain and the unforeseen presidential triumph of Donald Trump in 2016, are, in various ways, closely connected.

The word 'globalization' is too recent to appear in my outdated copy of the *Oxford English Dictionary*, but it is widely taken to refer to 'the process of international integration arising from the interchange of world views, products, ideas and other aspects of culture'. It is measured, insofar as it can be, by the ratio between a country's share of world trade and its GDP. The phenomenon has in fact been hard at work for most of my adult life. Driven by startling advances in transport and communications, it is usually divided into economic, cultural, and political sectors.[73] Economic globalization is the sphere within which Singapore has been a star performer. It has been accompanied by the vast expansion of world trade, the supremacy of huge international corporations, and the prominence of neo-liberal economic theorists such as Friedrich Hayek or Milton Friedman. Its underlying facilitators include jet aviation, the computerization of commercial and financial transactions, the explosion of commodity trading, especially in oil, the internet, and the widespread dismantling of barriers to the free circulation of capital, labour, and knowledge. Countries like Singapore, which depend on maritime trade, owe much to the invention in 1956 of the standardized container and in the 1960s of the ultra-large class of oil tankers and container ships. The world's largest ever ship, the *Seawise Giant*, which weighed in at 564,763 DWT, passed an important phase of its unusual career in Singapore. Launched in Japan in 1981, and over ten times the size of the *Titanic*, the ULCC·* was sunk in the Persian Gulf by Saddam Hussein's air force during the Iran–Iraq War, and later salvaged and towed to Singapore for rebuilding. Relaunched two years later as the *Happy Giant* and frequently resold and renamed, it was entirely impractical, unable to navigate the world's major canals and shipping straits, and incapable of slowing down in less than five to ten miles. A relic of mindless globalization, it was finally broken up in 2010 in the Indian shipyard of Alang-Sosiya by a gang of 18,000 workers.[74]

Globalization remains a potent force in the world. By general consent it has generated both positive and negative consequences. An estimated 300 million people have been lifted out of poverty, many of them in China, while similar numbers elsewhere have been reduced to penury. Average growth rates have mounted in both developed and developing nations, but unhealthy social inequalities have arisen. The bloated incomes of a small international elite resemble the ludicrous proportions of the *Seawise Giant*, as do levels of both governmental and individual debt. Economic ministries around the world have adopted austerity programmes that hurt the most vulnerable classes. And voluble discontent is growing. Liberal democracy itself is said to be under threat. So the time has clearly come to review the consequences of globalization and to curb its excesses. The British economist Jim (now Lord) O'Neill, sometime chief economist at Goldman Sachs and government minister, and creator of the acronyms BRICs and MINTs, holds that 'fixing globalization' is the top priority.[75]

For Singaporeans, who have already engineered their economic miracle through globalization, the priority lies with the methods for sustaining it. They think no less about the future than the past; indeed, the Republic's very survival depends on the success of several colossal infrastructure projects. Land reclamation, for instance, is critical. It is

* Ultra-large crude carrier.

slow work, but over the last half-century it has increased the Republic's territory by over 20 per cent. One project at Jurong Island near the main harbour artificially amalgamated seven islets through landfill, and now houses an offshore industrial park, whose petrochemical products provide one-third of the entire manufacturing sector's income. It will soon host the world's largest complex of underwater oil stores.[76]

Water conservation demands similarly long-term schemes. Forty years ago the Public Utility Board launched a plan called 'The Four National Taps', which aims for self-sufficiency in water by the mid-twenty-first century. (The treaty governing imports of water from Malaysia is due to terminate in 2061.) Much of the island's drinking water is already supplied by seventeen storm-water catchment reservoirs. The island's first de-salination plant, SingSpring opened in 2005, followed five years later by an ultra-modern, reverse-osmosis plant, Tuaspring, which meets 10 per cent of total water needs. The present output of 30 million gallons per day is due to triple, and five further sites for de-salination have been identified.[77] Great progress is also being made with so-called 'NEWater', the brand name for Singapore's revolutionary recycled effluent scheme. Five separate plants have come on stream in the last fifteen years, producing ultra-pure water by UV disinfection of sewage and advanced membrane technology. Opinions differ as to whether NEWater is more 'potable' than a Horlicks Dinosaur.[78]

For my last evening I was invited to supper at the well-appointed Graduate Club by a professor from New Zealand and his Singaporean wife. The professor is a sixth-generation Kiwi whose ancestors had sailed away from the Cornish tin mines to seek their fortune in an antipodean gold rush; his wife is the daughter of Chinese migrants from Malaya who had worked in the British Civil Service. Since her father's and her mother's native languages were mutually incomprehensible, they had all spoken English at home, and were categorized, like LKY's family, as 'the Queen's Chinese'. The couple had met in Singapore, had lived for a period in Auckland, but now were back thanks to his posting as the Secretary-General of the Association of Pacific Rim Universities (APRU). Fish was on the menu: the soup was lobster bisque, and the main course oven-baked Chilean cod, which was clearly a migrant as well.

The fact that an intercontinental organization like APRU has its headquarters in Singapore – next to the Kent Ridge campus of the

NUS – says much about Singapore's geopolitical location. A network of nearly fifty centres of higher education as far apart as California, Central and South America, Australasia, and the Far East, accepts it as a natural focus. Like its older partner APEC (Asia-Pacific Economic Cooperation), APRU is US-inspired, and is a symptom of Washington's Pacific Turn.[79] In a globalized world, economic interests have to be dovetailed with those of science, research, and education.

Talk of the Pacific Rim leads naturally to reflections on Singapore's strategic position and about the *Pax Americana* that has replaced the old *Pax Britannica*. Ever since their victory over the Japanese in 1945, the Americans have consolidated their hold, using all means available – military, political, and economic – exercising a form of imperialism that is less direct than that of the British, but no less effective. They have fought two wars to defend their interests – one in 1950–53 in Korea under United Nations auspices, and the second in 1960–75 in Vietnam and neighbouring countries. They have established democratic regimes, granted independence to countries like the Philippines, encouraged the growth of free-market economies, pursued so-called 'de-colonization' schemes, and backed international organizations such as ASEAN (founded in 1967). But everything is done on the premise that the numerous bases of the US Navy, Air Force, and Marines are not disturbed. Singapore is a prime beneficiary of the system. In return for accepting American hegemony, it receives a degree of security that it could not possibly organize on its own.

One of the prominent features of American Pacific imperialism is the predilection for islands. Whereas old-fashioned imperialists would occupy and directly exploit substantial land areas, the Americans have been content to gain control of a chain of relatively small insular territories, from which their naval and aerial power can be projected. The US conquest of the Pacific began with the purchase of the Aleutian Islands, an extension of Alaska, in 1867 and the overthrow of the Kingdom of Hawaii in the period 1893–1900; it was extended by the Spanish-American War of 1898, yielding the Philippines and Guam, and by the partition of Samoa in 1899. Everything was cemented by construction of the Panama Canal in 1914. This all took place in an era when China was in eclipse, and Japan alone was strong enough to think of contesting it. Yet Japan's desperate counter-blow, in 1941, ultimately proved counter-productive. After 1945, America's hold was strengthened by bases in Japan and South Korea, by the treaty with Taiwan, and by US acquisitions in the Marshall Islands and elsewhere.[80]

Guam offers perhaps the clearest illustration of this strategy. Slightly smaller than Singapore Island, it is one of the Mariana Islands in the Western Pacific. Discovered by Magellan in 1521, it provided the Spanish Empire's principal staging-post for the Manila Galleons for over three centuries. During the eleven decades of American rule, Guam has evolved into an 'unincorporated, organized territory' of the United States, and the indigenous Chamorro people have been reduced to a minority in their own country. The majority, as in Singapore, are Asian immigrants, mainly Filipinos, whose votes prop up the status quo democratically. The American Naval Base at Sumay and a huge Air Force Base guarantee the prevailing order. American governors bask in their residence much as their British counterparts basked in Singapore's Government House, far from home but trusting in military might and dreaming of impregnability.[81]

In the post-war era, regional stability was maintained by the absence of a credible challenger to American hegemony. The People's Republic of China, which emerged in 1949 after generations of crippling civil war and occupation, rarely intervened abroad except through clandestine Communist movements. (The foray of the Chinese Red Army into Korea in 1951 was an isolated exception.) In the twenty-first century, however, China is moving rapidly to become the world's largest economy and it is hard to believe that its growing military muscle will never be flexed, particularly in the naval realm. Disputes with its neighbours over uninhabited islands in the South China Sea may well herald more serious conflicts to come. The status of Taiwan has never been settled, and the ripples caused by a paranoid client in North Korea could well suit its purposes. President Obama's announcement in 2012 that the American strategic centre of gravity would shift towards the Pacific rules out any chance of Uncle Sam retiring gracefully from the scene.[82]

In this context, Singapore has few strategic options. It has a special position on pan-Chinese horizons, and, though obviously sitting in the shade of the American umbrella, cannot seek an increase of US influence. Its relations with Malaysia and Indonesia are cool but correct. So it is left with just one country with which to forge a closer partnership. Both Australia and Singapore share feelings of horror at the way the Pax Britannica ended; both participate in the Five Power Defence Arrangements that the British left behind in 1971; and both enjoy healthy economies that happily intertwine. So Singaporeans and Australians increasingly look towards each other for succour and sympathy.[83]

In the era of Brexit, some delusional British Brexiteers have suggested that, by leaving the European Union, the United Kingdom could become 'a new Singapore'. They dream of a country unburdened by vexacious bureaucracy, which will become an international, free-trading powerhouse in full control of its borders, its laws, and its money. As Gandhi said of Western civilization, 'it would be a nice idea'. It is true, of course, that Singapore's sensational rise to prominence has been achieved by, among other things, a steady increase in population managed by an enviably efficient immigration system. Yet in the real world, the two countries differ so fundamentally in social culture, political institutions, collective psychology, educational performance, economic productivity, state indebtedness, size and location, and historical legacy, that all expectations of rapid convergence belong to the realms of cloud-cuckooland.[84]

I once started writing a novel whose opening scene was set at Changi Airport in Singapore. It was an identity thriller in which the two main protagonists, a Russian man and an American woman, meeting by accident, know nothing about their common genes. The narrator, a Sherlock Holmes-type figure, appears at first to be pursuing them, but in fact is secretly investigating his own complicated origins. The idea had potential, but the vertiginous somersaults of the plot soon lost credibility, and the author lost patience.

Nonetheless, the opening scene in Changi's main passenger hall was well conceived. It described the comings and goings of thousands of people from every continent and every country on earth: individuals from all races, all ages, countless cultures, and both sexes. They rush to and fro across the hall, or stand in lines, or saunter around aimlessly; bumps and near misses occur every minute. Watching closely, the narrator tries to guess the reasons for their journeys and the life-stories hidden behind their faces. He concludes that Singapore is a global microcosm, that 'Asians' are a fiction, and that life is a lottery, determined by random collisions or by unnoticed close shaves.

One group, however, stands out from the multitude. The Australians are as distinctive in their dress as in their lusty voices, their accents, their gestures, and their suntans. They flock to Changi in their thousands every day, making the first stop on the way to the rest of the world; and they stop over on the way back, drawing breath before the last leg home. For them, as it was to be for me, Singapore is the 'Barbican of Down Under'.

# INTERLUDE

# Oriens
*Facing the Sunrise*

There is a history of everything that exists; whatever it is, concrete or abstract, object or idea, it has a past, from which a historical narrative can be constructed. The daily task of 'finding one's way', therefore, is no exception; there is a history of 'finding one's way', that is, of orientation (including all the techniques and devices that aid it), and also of 'getting lost', that is, disorientation. Both are essential features of the human condition.

Historians, too, must find their way. Whatever their subject or period of interest, they have to navigate through Time and Space, establishing what happened at particular moments and places, and creating a chronological narrative. To alert their readers to the twists and turns of the journey, they use all manner of devices, from maps and diagrams to calendars, timeline charts and place names. And like anyone else, they, too, can lose their way.

When preparing my survey of Europe's past, *Europe: A History*, and its accompanying maps, I decided to abandon the convention whereby the top of the map points to the north. Instead, by turning the base clockwise through 90 degrees, I put the West at the top, East at the bottom, South on the left and North on the right. Thanks to this decision, both playful and serious, the familiar horizontal outline of the European Peninsula disappeared, and a strange vertical profile took its place. Iberia stood up like a human head; Italy stuck out like an extended arm; Northern Europe featured on the top right; and the broad expanses of Central and Eastern Europe occupied the lower half of the page. Unaware of the full implications, I was challenging a habit that helps people to know where they are, and strengthens their confidence about their place in the world.

The idea, of course, was by no means original. A sixteenth-century print of 'Europa Regina', which first appeared in the *Cosmographia* of the German-Swiss geographer and linguist Sebastian Münster

(1488–1552), is a well-known predecessor.[1] It shows a standing image of 'Queen Europe', whose crowned head is marked HISPANIA – the greatest power of the day – and whose wide, flowing skirts reach to the PONTUS EUX or 'Black Sea'. Her chest is marked GALLIA, and her midriff GERMANIA, below which a circular area, ringed with trees, is marked BOHEMIA. Her golden orb, SICILIA, is held at the end of the extended Italian right arm, while the sceptre, DANIA, is held by her left arm. UNGARIA and SCLAVONIA occupy the queen's right hip and thigh, correctly facing POLONIA and LITHUANIA on her left side. The hem of her robe is taken up by MOREA, GRÆCIA, BULGARIA, SCYTHIA (Ukraine), and TARTARIA. MOSCOVIA occupies a tiny strip between SCYTHIA and LIVONIA. The three kingdoms of the British Isles, ANGLIA, SCOTIA, and HIB[ernia], are ingeniously attached to the upper part of the sceptre, but are coloured brown, like AFRICA, ASIA, and SCANDIA (Sweden), implying that they did not really belong to Europe. Even so, the relationship of the parts to the whole are accurately preserved.

Münster's purpose, like my own, was to draw his readers' attention to the total make-up of Europe. In my case, I was setting out to challenge the tendency in some places to regard Western Europe as the only part of the continent worthy of consideration. Our mental maps of history and geography often derive from stereotypes and prejudiced perceptions, and it had become commonplace over the last couple of centuries for westerners to ignore the eastern part of our continent almost completely. Of course, by insisting on the inclusion of the East, I was not passing judgement on it. I simply wanted to emphasize that the nations of Eastern Europe exist, that they have a long history, and ought to form part of any comprehensive description. To this end, an unconventional map that forced readers to revisit their assumptions was not unreasonable.

Most of the critics and reviewers who commented on *Europe: A History* saw the point of my cartographic experiment. Together with the book's 'capsules', which introduced a mass of variously esoteric topics into the text, it was one of the features most frequently remarked upon. Yet a small number, mainly American, didn't like the maps one bit. Indeed, they did not confine themselves to mere expressions of doubt; they seemed to be outraged and offended that someone should dare to disfigure Europe's established orientation. They reacted as if my map had somehow undermined the very essence of Western civilization, opening the door to intolerance and chaos. They convinced me that their fervent attachment to 'the West', and by extension to a Western perspective on the world, was not just a mental habit. It derived from deep emotional bonds going to the roots of their identity and security. For many Americans, 'the West' is not just a location; it is a political and moral entity that confirms their supremacy in the contemporary world.

Surprisingly, one of the most strident critics was a historian with whom I shared a number of encounters, both positive and negative. He called the maps in my book 'silly', and likened their author to a small animal character from *The Wind in the Willows*. He even suggested that the map of Europe had been deliberately distorted in order 'to put Poland in the middle'. Oh dear! One can turn the map of Europe upside down or back to front or round and round, and one can love Poland or hate her, but the one thing you can't do is deny that the homeland of Chopin and John Paul II lies in the centre of Europe. It was a trivial but revealing incident, an instance of ancestral prejudice.[2] But it confirms something else: that the natural corollary of lionizing 'the West' is depreciating 'the East'.

Finding one's way round the world in the days before maps and compasses required a modicum of astronomical knowledge. The prime directional indicator was the sun, whose apparent movements are caused by the spinning of the Earth, and whose return to view opens every day at every spot on the Earth's surface. Of course, prior to Copernicus (1473–1543), most people held that it was the sun that circled the Earth and not vice versa. But the misconception did not alter the fact that the sun rose over the same sector of the horizon each morning, and sank below the opposite sector each evening.

For this reason, many languages use the same word for 'sunrise' as for 'East'. English is not one of them, but Latin is, as are several Slavonic languages. The Latin noun *Oriens*, formed from the present participle of *oriri*, 'to rise', stands for 'the East', 'the sunrise', 'the Orient', that is, the lands of the East, and also for a Roman sun god. In Christian practice, it is a synonym for Christ, 'the dayspring', who gives 'light to them that sit in darkness' (Luke 1:78, 79).

Once East is determined, the other cardinal directions automatically fall into place. If you face the sunrise, your extended left arm points to the North, and your right arm to the South; the West is directly behind you. South marks the point that the sun will reach at midday, and the West the direction of the evening sunset. For this reason, though not in

English, one word often stands both for 'the South' and for 'noon'. In French it's *le Midi/le midi*, and in Italian *il mezzogiorno*.

The cardinal directions, known since time immemorial, provide the basic information on which all journeys and voyages are made, and a series of technical devices from the astrolabe and the quadrant to the global positioning system (GPS) have greatly alleviated navigators' problems. The invention of the astrolabe (literally 'the Star-Taker') has been attributed to Hipparchus of Nicaea (*c.* 190–120 BCE), the 'Father of Trigonometry'. GPS was developed by the US military in the 1970s. Another crucial advance was made in ancient China by the discovery of the Earth's magnetic field. The Chinese invented a device with a magnetic pointer in the Han era (second century BCE), but long failed to recognize its navigational potential. Their use of lodestone compasses was picked up by Arab traders and transmitted to the Western world sometime in the eleventh century AD. The transportable compass supplied directional information by night as well as by day, on sea and on land, in fair weather and foul. It established one of the key prerequisites for what used to be called the Age of Discovery. Since its magnetic pointer always pointed roughly north, it probably inspired the convention of putting the North at the top of maps.

Cartography has a similarly lengthy history. The world's oldest known map was produced in Babylon in the ninth century BCE. Anaximander of Miletus (*c.* 610–545 BCE) is credited with Europe's oldest surviving map, which puts Greece at the centre of the world, surrounded by the three continents of EUROPE, ASIA, and LIBYA (Africa). Parallel achievements occurred in China and India. But progress was astonishingly slow. Ptolemy's *Ecumene*, a depiction of the 'Known World' from the second century AD, was still being produced in the fifteenth century. In the meantime, more than a thousand *mappae mundi* had been produced in mediaeval Europe. The much-reproduced *T-O Maps*, based on the *Etymologiae* of St Isidore of Seville (560–636), the 'last scholar of the ancient world', put the East at the top. So, too, does the magnificent *Mappa Mundi* from Hereford Cathedral dated to 1300. A Portuguese, Diogo Ribeiro (*c.* 1475–1533), is often cited as the first scientific cartographer. But it was left to the genial Gheert de Cremer, Gerardus Mercator (1512–94) (whose nationality is contested), the inventor of projections, to show that all maps inevitably involve distortions. Both Ribeiro's *Padrón Real* (1527) and Mercator's *World Map* (1569) have the Arctic at the top and the Antarctic at the bottom.[3]

Maps would be much the poorer without place names, which also possess a rich history. Yet the systematic study of place names – toponomy, or in German *die Namenkunde*, a famously fruitful field for fantasists – was a late developer. Its founder is usually taken to be the Danziger professor Ernst Förstemann (1822–1906); its first use in English is dated to 1876.[4] Förstemann had his counterparts in most European countries, such as Walter Skeat in England, William Watson in Scotland, and Auguste Longnon and Albert Dauzat in France, and there were some precocious pioneers in the United States enthused by Native American cultures, such as Henry Rowe Schoolcraft (1793–1864).[5] Early toponomists concentrated on the derivation of place names in their own countries. More recently, they have adopted global perspectives. Among them, one finds the American, George Stewart (1895–1980), author of *Names on the Globe* (1975), and the Australian, Marcel Aurousseau (1891–1983), coiner of the vital term *exonym*, 'a name given to a place by foreigners'.[6] (An obvious exonym would be 'Wales', a country whose indigenous name is *Cymru*.) The antonym of exonym is *endonym*.*

There's nothing like travelling round the world to sharpen one's sense of orientation. For our entire language of location – that is, the terms that describe where places are – is relative, not absolute. In my case, I had assumed that I was leaving England for the 'Middle East' and the 'Far East', and that next I would fly on to 'the Other Side of the World' in Australia and New Zealand; after all, that was what I was taught at school. It was fixed in my mind that New Zealand would be 'the Halfway Point', beyond which, if I kept on going eastwards, I would be heading for home. It was certainly a mind-stretching experience to cross the International Dateline and to realize that our concept of 'a day' is highly subjective and artificial.

Thanks to the journey, I also learned that my own orientational mindset was embarrassingly parochial. On reaching the Far East, I soon understood that for people who live in that region the far East lies in what Europeans might think of as the 'Far West' – that is, in California, or perhaps Mexico. If you think about it, every spot on Earth lies to the east of somewhere, and to the west of somewhere else. There is no such thing as an 'eastern country', except in the minds of its inhabitants or neighbours. Concepts of place are mobile for the simple reason that the Earth itself is both round and mobile.

---

* Some scholars prefer *xenonym* to exonym and *autonym* to endonym.

As everyone knows, or ought to know, the Chinese do not call their country 'China'. The Koreans do not talk of 'Korea' or the Japanese of 'Japan'. All these names are exonyms. Throughout the last thousand years and more, the Chinese have called their homeland *Zhong Guo* (中国), meaning the 'Middle Kingdom', or sometimes *Zhong Hua*, the 'Middle Nation'. One must ask, therefore, about what exactly China was in the middle of when the terms were coined? The short answer is 'the Known World' (as known, that is, to the ancient Chinese). They knew of Greece and Rome in one direction, and of the western Pacific islands in the other. But they were not adventurers, never finding either the Americas or Australia. Their 'seven great voyages' of the early fifteenth century were not voyages of exploration, but shows of strength along the well-known routes to India and Arabia.

Another name that the Chinese used for centuries was *Tian Chao* (天朝), meaning the 'Celestial Empire'. Like the Romans, they drew a clear distinction between the civilized world, of which they were the centre, and the barbarians beyond, against whom they built their Great Wall.

The Chinese character for East, *Dong*, has many important connotations. In its modern, simplified form, 东, it is not very expressive; but in its traditional form, 東, one can recognize the Sun, 日, shining through the Tree, 木 – in other words the sunrise. Its opposite, *Xi* (西), meaning 'West', can conceivably be identified as a sun descending – in other words the sunset.

*Dong* and *Xi* can often be found in close company. *Guangdong* (Canton) stands for 'Eastern Province'; its neighbour *Guangxi*, which borders Vietnam, stands for 'Western Province'. In the nearby Pearl River Delta, the *Xi Jiang* or 'West River' faces the *Dong Jiang* or 'East River'. The Chinese habitually refer to regions of the world as 'oceans'. Hence *Dongyang*, literally 'Eastern Ocean', would normally be translated as 'East Asia', and *Nanyang*, 'Southern Ocean', as 'South-East Asia'. *Xiyang* or 'Western Ocean' originally referred to India and Arabia, but later came to mean the 'Western World' in general.

According to political circumstances, Koreans call their country either *Hankuk* or *Choson*. Each of these alternative endonyms has a venerable pedigree, and each has been revived to suit contemporary purposes. *Hankuk*, used exclusively by the citizens of South Korea, means something like 'Great Domain'; *Choson*, as used in North Korea, derives from the name of a fourteenth-century dynasty, and thanks to a book published in 1885 it attracted the pretty but dubious translation of 'Morning Calm'.[7] Insofar as South Korean and North Korean officials talk to each other, they use the forms of *Namhan* and *Bukhan*, standing for 'South State' and 'North State'. Korean exonyms for Korea's neighbours include *Jungguk* (China), *Daeman* (Taiwan), and *Libon* (Japan).

According to context, the Japanese call their country either *Nippon* or *Nihon*, which is famously translated into English as 'the Land of the Rising Sun'. This wonderful, poetic image raises a question. Where do you have to stand for the islands of Japan to appear in the line of the sunrise? The answer is not in Japan itself, but on the mainland to the west, facing the islands. And this is the key to the name; it can only have been invented either by the ancient Chinese or by the ancestors of the Japanese before they sailed from the mainland. In the shared pictographic written language of China and Japan, *Kanji*, the two relevant characters, 日本, stand respectively for 'Sun' and 'Origin'. In the spoken languages, Mandarin-speakers would pronounce these characters as *Ri-ben*, while Japanese-speakers read them as *Ni-hon*, or more formally as *Ni-pon*. The Japanese often add a third word, *Koku*, meaning 'State' or 'Nation', thereby producing *Ni Hon Koku*, literally 'Sun-Rise-State'. Japan's national flag, variously known as *Ni-Shoki*, the 'Sun Mark', or *Hinomaru*, the 'Circle of the Sun', originated in these most ancient times.

As to exactly when and how the Japanese nation was formed, and adopted its famous name, much controversy rages. The islands had been inhabited from the Stone Age, and two ethnically distinct but indigenous peoples, the Ainu and the Yamon, have been recorded there. In the third century BCE, however, a third group, the Yayoi, began to arrive from the mainland, bringing rice-farming and bronze-working with them, and it is the Yayoi whom later Japanese national historians most frequently claim to be their ancestors. Their previous homeland has variously been identified either with central China below the Yangtze River or with southern Korea. By the time of the late Kofun period (AD 250–700), Yayoi culture had supplanted its predecessors; the country was known to the Chinese as *Wo* (meaning 'people who bow down') and was divided into five warring kingdoms. A strong united state with an emperor and a capital at Nara was created in the early eighth century. The origins of Japan's ruling dynasty are traced to that time.[8] So, too, is the poem on which the national anthem, the *Kimigayo*, is based:

*Kimi ga yo wa*
*Chiyo ni,*
*Yachiyo ni*
*Sazare-ishi no*
*Iwao to narite*
*Koke no musu made*

(May the reign of the Emperor
Last a thousand generations
Or more,
Until the pebbles
Grow into boulders
Lush with moss.)

One thing that Chinese, Koreans, and Japanese have in common is that all reject the Eurocentric idea that they live in the 'Far East'. Yet it is only recently that Europeans and Americans have woken up to the inappropriateness, not to mention the laughable side, of their language. On the other hand, one should not be too surprised if a label that dates from the twelfth century takes a while to drop out of circulation. A common-sense solution was proposed by two Harvard professors in 1964:

> When Europeans travelled to the East to reach Cathay, the Indies and Japan, they naturally gave those distant regions the general name of the 'Far East' ... For people who live there, however, the region is neither 'East' nor 'West', and certainly not 'Far'. A more acceptable term for the area is 'East Asia', which is more geographically precise and does not imply ... that Europe is the center of the civilized world.[9]

And East Asia it now is for all but the most geographically challenged.

Yet westerners have not been alone in their self-centred concepts. For ages, both the Chinese and Japanese were taught to think of Europe as *Taixi*, meaning 'Extreme West'. Pronounced *Taisei* in Japanese, the term originally referred to lands bordering the Middle Kingdom, but prompted by the late sixteenth-century Jesuit Mission of Matteo Ricci, it came to refer to the more distant Christian and European 'West'. Those Jesuits distinguished between the 'Little West' in India and the 'Great West' in Europe.

At the other end of Eurasia, more than five thousand miles away, the continental coasts mainly face west, not east; but just as the islands of the Rising Sun lay offshore from the Middle Kingdom, another group of islands of comparable size (Japan is slightly larger) lay off the northern coast of the Roman Empire. The Romans had crossed the strait, which they called *Oceanus*, in late republican times. But in AD 43 – or as they might have reckoned, in 796 AUC – they established their province of Britannia in the southern part of the largest island. The insular peoples whom they found there, the Hibernians and the Britons, were Celts. Then, in the same broad era when the Yayoi were already consolidating their empire of the Rising Sun, another people with similar maritime aspirations were preparing to make the same sort of move. The Angles lived originally on a continental peninsula, now called Jutland, in a district that still bears their name of *Angeln*. They were one of several such Germanic communities who regularly sent their longboats round the shores of the *Mare Germanicum*, and raided vulnerable settlements on the coast of Britannia. They and their allies are generally known to history as 'Anglo-Saxons' or as 'Angles, Saxons, and Jutes', though their collective undoubtedly included others such as Frisians and Batavians and mixed pirate gangs. Yet starting in the late fourth century AD they progressed from raiding to colonizing. They gained a foothold on 'the Saxon Shore' before the Romans left, and in the fifth century penetrated the interior, displacing or absorbing the native Celts, and embarking on the conquests that slowly led to the creation of 'England'.[10]

The direct sea crossing that separated Britannia from the invaders' bases in Germania Barbarica is similar in length to that which once separated the proto-Japanese from their destination in *Nippon*: about 200 kilometres or 120 miles. The one big difference lies in the direction. The proto-Japanese, dreaming of a future homeland, gazed into the sunrise; the proto-English gazed into the sunset. Many centuries later, the emerging English sailed into the sunset to conquer Ireland, marched into the sunset to conquer Wales, and in the guise of Pilgrim Fathers struck out into the sunset across the ocean to settle North America.

Not only in the period of the Anglo-Saxon conquest, but for many centuries afterwards, Latin was Western Europe's sole written lingua franca, and it is from Latin that Europe's basic directional vocabulary is derived. *Oriens* has an exact twin in *Occidens*, meaning the 'setting sun' and by extension 'the West', formed from the verb *occidere*, to 'sink or fall down', but also 'to perish'. (The image of the sun dying in its own blood was a common poetic metaphor.)

In AD 285 (1038 AUC), when the Roman Emperor Diocletian divided his empire into two halves, he raised his co-ruler, Maximian, to the rank of Augustus and 'Emperor of the West', while keeping the more populous and affluent East for himself. For more than a century two connected Roman Empires functioned in parallel: one the *Imperium Romanum Occidentale*, still based on Rome, and the other the *Imperium Romanum Orientale*, based on the new capital at Constantinople. In AD 395 the Emperor Theodosius divided the empire up in a different way, creating the four huge Praetorian Prefectures of Gallia, Italia, Illyria, and Oriens. The Prefecture of Oriens, centred on Constantinople, was the most easterly of the four, and was itself divided into five *dioeceses* or 'administrations', one of which was also called Oriens. The Diocese of Oriens, whose governor, the *Comes Orientis* or 'Count of the East', resided at Antioch in Asia Minor, consisted of fifteen provinces, stretching from Asia Minor and the island of Cyprus to Mesopotamia, Palestine, and Egypt. After AD 476, when the Western Empire collapsed and Rome itself was abandoned, the prefectures of Gallia, Italia, and Illyria ceased to exist, but the Prefecture and Diocese of Oriens survived, becoming the core of what historians would subsequently reinvent as the 'Byzantine Empire'.

Yet within the Byzantine context, as the reference point of Rome disappeared, the sense of *Oriens* shifted once again. The name of Oriens no longer suited the Eastern Empire as a whole, and was confirmed instead as a label for the Byzantines' eastern provinces, which they had inherited from the former Diocese of Oriens, and which from the seventh century became a battleground between Christian Byzantium and the expansive forces of Islam. In this emanation, the label stuck for a millennium and more. It gave rise in Europe to any number of vernacular equivalents, including in English 'the Orient', which became the regular mediaeval and early modern term for what is now known as 'the Near East' or 'the Middle East'. As from 1883, the famous railway train, the Orient Express, ran from Paris to Constantinople (Istanbul).

Another important change, prompted by the Roman Empire's centre of gravity moving to Constantinople, was that Greek replaced Latin as the main imperial language. As a result many Greek terms found their way onto the map. One of them was *Anatoli*, which became the standard name for the peninsula that the Romans had called Asia Minor. Lying across the Bosphorus immediately to the east of Constantinople, *Anatoli* means 'dawn' or 'sunrise'. It was taken up by the migrating

Ottoman Turks, when they drifted into the province in the twelfth and thirteenth centuries, and it emerged as Turkish *Anadolu* – yet another 'Land of the Rising Sun'. Latinized by westerners, it was turned into *Anatolia* and forms the heart of the modern Turkish republic.

The Greeks, one should note, possessed a long tradition of looking on the East with disdain. They habitually divided their own world from that of the 'barbarians', in other words, of primitive people who talked 'bla-bla-bla' instead of Greek. Yet when they came under attack in the fifth century BCE from the Persian Empire, the Greeks added the highly civilized Persians to their list of barbarians. Barbarity, in other words, was not just an attribute of linguistic difference; it was the mark of essential otherness.[11]

In due course, after Venice took control of mediaeval Europe's trade with the Orient, the Venetians introduced the Italian calque of *Oriens*, *il Levante*: one more term with a long lifespan. In a variety of vernacular versions – *le Levant* in French, *der Lewante* in German, and 'the Levant' in English, which received it in the late fifteenth century – it was a widely used partner term for the Orient and a geographical alternative to talking directly about the Ottoman Empire. The relevant adjective, 'Levantine', originally referred to any 'inhabitant of the Levant', but acquired the specific meaning of 'Latin rite of Christian living under Ottoman rule'. In the years before 1914, when several European powers opened branches of their own national postal services within the Ottoman Empire, the stamps were boldly overprinted LEVANT. It was a none too subtle way of announcing the fact that the sovereignty of the Ottoman Empire, 'the Sick Man of Europe', was being infringed.

In the meantime, the destruction of the Byzantine Empire had far-reaching consequences, which few westerners noticed; it legitimized the rise of Russia as Europe's new political 'East'. As Constantinople was swallowed up by the Muslim Turks, Moscow claimed the leadership of the defeated Orthodox Christians, and Muscovite ideologists proclaimed their *Tsar*, in other words their 'Caesar', to be the emperor of the 'Third Rome' – that is, the true successor to Augustus and Constantine. By so doing the Russians set themselves up as the permanent rivals of the Ottoman Turks, with whom endless wars were fought for control of the Black Sea and the Balkans. Moscow champions the cause of the Christian Slavs of the Balkans, like the Serbs and the Bulgars, to this day. Yet it also created a lasting antithesis between Russia and the 'West'. Generations of Russians were taught to believe, especially by their branch of the Orthodox Church, that they had all the virtues that 'decadent westerners' lacked: vigour, pure hearts, and allegiance to the true faith.

Modern Russian culture continues to be affected by these ideas. Deep divisions persist between the so-called 'westernizers', who believe that Russia should follow Europe's path of development, and the so-called 'easterners' or 'Eurasians', who cling to the opposite, namely that Europe is the ancestral foe, the source of enmity, deceit, and corruption. Nowhere is the easterners' case put more forcefully than in the poetry of Alexander Blok (1880–1921), the leading poet of the revolutionary era. Blok did not publicize the fact that he had been brought up in Warsaw, in the decadent West, preferring instead to shout defiance at the treacherous Western Powers, which were supposedly enemies of the Revolution. 'There may be millions of you,' he mocked, 'but we are тьмы, и тьмы, и тьмы – *i T'my, i T'my, i T'my* – hordes and hordes and hordes':

> You are but millions. Our unnumbered legions
> Are as the sands upon the sounding shore.
> We are the Scythians! We are the slit-eyed Asians!
> Try to wage war with us – and you'll try no more.
>
> Full centuries long you've watched our Eastern lands,
> Fished for our pearls, and bartered them for grain,
> Made mockery of us, while you laid your plans
> And oiled your cannon for the great campaign.
>
> O Ancient World, before your culture dies,
> Whilst failing life within you breathes and sinks,
> Pause and be wise, as Oedipus was wise,
> And solve the age-old riddle of the Sphinx.
>
> That Sphinx is Russia. Grieving and exulting,
> And weeping black and bloody tears enough,
> She stares at you, adoring and insulting,
> With love that turns to hate, and hate – to love.
>
> We shall abandon Europe, and her charm.
> We shall resort to Scythian craft and guile.
> Swift to the woods and forests we shall swarm,
> And then look back, and smile our slit-eyed smile.
>
> O Ancient World, arise! For the last time
> We call you to the ritual feast and fire.

> O peace and brotherhood! For the last time,
> O hear the summons of the barbarian lyre![12]

For many Russians 'the East' is not just a location; it is the source of identity.

After the Bolshevik Revolution of 1917, these 'Eurasian' ideas were preserved in the émigré 'White' community until they re-emerged in Russia after the collapse of the Soviet Union in 1991. Along the way, they were reinforced by some radical academic theorizing. One influential figure was Prince Nikolai Trubetskoy (1890–1938), a philologist of the Prague School, who argued that the phonology and tonal patterns of the Russian language, unlike its Indo-European grammar, derived from the speech patterns of the non-Slavic peoples of Central Asia. His insights were developed by his colleague, Roman Jakobson. Thirty years later another orientalist, Lev Gumilëv (1912–92), developed an intriguing theory that combined ecological, anthropological, and psychological elements to explain the Central Asian origins of a Russian 'super-ethnos'. The son of two dissident poets, Nikolai Gumilëv and Anna Akhmatova, he had spent fourteen years in the Gulag, where, by observing prisoners' behaviour, he formulated key concepts, including *passyonarnost'* or 'passionarity'. His sensational book *Ethnogenesis and the Biosphere of Earth*,[13] though written in the 1970s, lingered for decades in the underground while he was publishing obscure academic works on the steppe peoples, including the Khazars and the Xiongnu (Khunnu), sometimes taken to be the ancestors of the Huns. But his time came. At the turn of the millennium his work inspired an influential branch of Russia's neo-nationalism in the guise of Alexander Dugin's Eurasia Party, together with the popular slogan 'Embrace your inner Mongol'. It is also thought by some to represent an important strand in the ideology of Vladimir Putin.[14]

Yet Eurasianism, *Yevraziystvo*, has proved attractive not only in Russia but also among the post-Soviet dictatorships in Central Asia, especially in Kazakhstan. In 2014 a Eurasian Economic Union came into being as an adjunct to the so-called Commonwealth of Independent States and the Eurasian Customs Union.[15] In Astana, the capital of Kazakhstan, the 'Eurasian National University', founded in 1996, was dedicated to L. N. Gumilyov.[16]

Sailing east as opposed to sailing west has always been an option; but all the earliest circumnavigators of the world chose to leave Europe westwards. Their decision was largely determined by the fact that sixteenth-century west European sailors could not begin to make a significant move to the East before sailing along the whole length of Africa and rounding the distant Cape of Good Hope. The Portuguese Fernão de Magalhães, better known as Magellan, certainly planned his westbound route in 1519 on the basis of sound knowledge. Thanks to his predecessor, Vasco da Gama, who had pioneered the route to India via the Cape thirty years earlier, he would have known that sailing on eastwards beyond India offered one possibility for circling the globe. He rejected it partly because of the prohibitively long first leg and partly because he hoped and believed – as it proved correctly – that a similar route could be opened up round the tip of South America. Magellan himself died before he could return to Europe full circle; and the laurels for the first circumnavigation must go either to his deputy, Juan Sebastián Elcano, who brought the *Victoria* safely home, or more probably to Magellan's Malay slave, Enrique da Malacca, who is usually airbrushed out of the story.* Francis Drake also chose the westerly route, personally steering his vessel right round the world in 1577–80.

The annals of eastbound navigation, however, though less publicized, are no less remarkable. They involve memorable feats by men and women from several continents. One of the great pioneers was a Berber from Tangier, Ibn Battuta (1304–68), whose travels make his contemporary, Marco Polo, look like a stick-in-the-mud. Battuta did not circumnavigate the globe, but made numerous voyages and journeys whose total mileage must have easily surpassed the globe's circumference. He criss-crossed the Middle East and Central Asia, sailed to East Africa, and visited China, India, and the East Indies. The account of his travels known as the *Rihla* or 'Journey' was unknown to the Western world until modern times.[17]

The first eastbound circumnavigator is generally acknowledged to be the Spanish Franciscan Martín Ignacio de Loyola (c. 1550–1606), a close relative of the founder of the Jesuits. The intrepid friar had already completed a westbound circumnavigation before repeating the feat in the opposite direction in 1584–9. He made the journey in three stages,

---

* Enrique da Malacca had been Magellan's servant for several years, and had already made the voyage from the East Indies to Europe before joining the expedition of 1518–21. After Magellan's death in the Philippines, he took ship for Malaya well in advance of Elcano's departure, and, presuming that he made it to Malacca without accident, he would have completed a full circumnavigation at least a year before Elcano did.

sailing from Spain to China, from China to Mexico, and from Mexico to Spain. In his lifetime he was probably the most travelled human being in the world.[18] I, like all who travel in comfort in his wake, pay him homage.

Hasekura Tsunenaga (1571–1622), like Ibn Battuta, cannot be rated a circumnavigator, but earned a distinguished place in the chronicles of worldwide travel. A Japanese *samurai*, he was sent as an ambassador to the Vatican between 1613 and 1620, crossing the Pacific to Mexico and then the Atlantic. He was baptized in Spain and given the name of Francisco Felipe Faxicura. The main commercial object of his embassy did not bear fruit. He was the one and only Japanese emissary to visit Europe before the late nineteenth century.[19]

Although she was not a circumnavigator, Aphra Behn (1640–89), an extraordinary Englishwoman of the Restoration era, made her mark as a spy, a writer, and a long-distance traveller. She travelled far, but her achievements as a shipboard passenger were less remarkable that those in other roles. Born in Kent, the daughter of a barber and a wet-nurse, she was probably brought up under the name of Anne Johnson, though she later answered to 'Ann Behn', 'Mrs Bean', 'Agent 106', and 'Astrea'. Her international career took off when she married a Dutch merchant called Behn, and accompanied him to the Netherlands. Thanks to her knowledge of languages, she then became a valuable asset to the English government during the Anglo-Dutch Wars, and worked as an intelligence officer in Antwerp. If her word is to be believed, she sailed both to Surinam and to the Dutch East Indies. Returning to England in the mid-1670s, she then moved into the limelight of racy, Restoration literature, publishing a spate of dramas, novels, and poetry. Once famous for her wit and bawdy verse, she fell into lengthy oblivion until her recent revival as a feminist literary heroine:

> Her balmy lips encount'ring his
> Their bodies as their Souls are joyn'd
> Where both in Transports were confin'd
> Extend themselves upon the Moss.
> Cloris half-dead and breathless lay
> Her eyes appear'd like humid Light
> Such as divides the Day and Night
> Or falling stars, whose fires decay
> And now no signs of life she shows
> But what in short-breath-sighs returns and goes.[20]

If Charles II had thought fit to fund a Bad Sex Prize – just the kind of thing that might have amused him – Behn would have been a strong contender. Her alleged masterpiece is the novel *Oroonoko: or, the Royal Slave. A True History* (1688).[21]

Father Pedro Cubero (1645–97), a Catholic missionary from Aragon, was ploughing his furrow around the globe as Aphra Behn emerged as a writer. Cubero's journey between 1670 and 1679 started in Venice. He travelled overland via Warsaw, Moscow, and Isfahan to the Persian Gulf, where he boarded a ship for India. From Goa, he sailed to Colombo, Malacca, Manila, and Canton. He then crossed China to Peking, before retracing his steps to the Philippines, where in 1678 he joined the annual Manila Galleon bound for Acapulco. Traversing Mexico on foot, he headed home via Cuba. His *Peregrinación del Mundo* (1680) is rated one of the finest of all travel books; it tells of his capture by Malabar pirates, enslavement in the Maldives, imprisonment in Dutch-ruled Malacca (for propagating Catholicism), and brush with death during the great Philippine earthquake of 1677. He was reportedly one of only a handful of survivors aboard the Manila Galleon. The frontispiece of his *Peregrinación* presents a sonnet, describing him as 'Missionario Apostolico' (Apostolic Missionary), 'Sol que resplandece' (A Shining Sun), 'Explorador de tanta gloria' (An Explorer of Great Glory), and 'Luz al error' (A Light against Error).[22]

Giovanni Gemelli Careri (1651–1725), another circumnavigator and Vatican agent, followed much of Cubero's route, except that he reached Persia via Egypt and Armenia. Commercially astute, he made a 300 per cent profit from buying quicksilver in the East Indies and selling it in Mexico. His six-volume *Giro del Mondo* (1699), illustrated by fine maps and engravings, is an informational treasure trove. It tells, inter alia, of his visits to the Moghul Court in India, the Great Wall of China, and the Aztec ruins of Teotihuacan. He thought the Great Wall 'ridiculous', since it runs along steep, high mountains 'where neither Birds nor Tartar horses could climb'.[23]

By the eighteenth century, round-the-world journeys on established routes were becoming routine. Circumnavigations speeded up in the nineteenth century with the advent of steamships, and in the twentieth century with the help of aeroplanes. But 'firsts' could still be recorded. In 1889–90 Nellie Bly (Elizabeth Jane Cochran), a journalist sponsored by the *New York World*, circled the globe on the easterly circuit in seventy-two days. Kitted out in a checked tweed cap and ankle-length tweed suit, she carried no more than a small Gladstone bag. She stopped over in Paris to meet Jules Verne, author of *Around the World in Eighty Days*, before making for Italy, the Suez Canal, Singapore, Japan, and San Francisco. On the final stage across the United States, she was provided with a private train which ensured that she beat the eighty-day deadline. 'Energy rightly applied,' she primly commented on her return, 'can accomplish anything.'[24]

The 'Near East' and the 'Middle East' are overlapping, but not identical terms, and have different origins. The former was disseminated from the late eighteenth century, first alongside and then in place of 'Orient' and 'Levant'; it was the work of Europeans untroubled by imposing their own perspective. 'East' in this context clearly means 'East of Europe'; since Europe has no adjacent western landmass, its equivalent, the 'Near West', has never been coined. Needless to say, the idea of defining substantial regions of the Earth through their relationship with one's own region is highly patronizing. Only recently have more neutral names, such as 'the Arab World' or 'Western Asia', been adopted.

The 'Near East' came into vogue in the guise of the French *Proche-Orient* at the time of Napoleon's expedition to Egypt in 1799–1800. It was in widespread use by the second half of the nineteenth century, and it always implied that a 'Greater Orient' lay somewhere further away. It was often used alongside another alternative term, *L'Asie Antérieure*, 'Anterior Asia'. Its ill-defined partner, the 'Far East', sometimes referred to India, sometimes to the East Indies, and sometimes to China, Korea, and Japan. The distinction was encouraged by the fact that prior to the opening of the Suez Canal in 1869, European ships could sail through the Mediterranean to the Near East in a matter of days, whereas voyages to the Far East lasted weeks and months.

This pairing of locations, which are seen to be either 'near to' or 'far from' the point of reference, is extremely ancient. The Greeks of Alexander the Great talked of 'India on the Near Side of the Ganges' and of 'India beyond the Ganges'. The Romans of the same period called northern Italy *Gallia Cisalpina*, that is, 'the Celtic Lands on our side of the Alps', and *Gallia Transalpina*, 'the Celtic Lands on the Other Side of the Alps'. Their language was closely connected with power relations. A district or region described as 'Near' often had the connotation of 'somewhere that we control'. A place described as 'Far' could imply that it lay 'beyond our control'.

Under Vladimir Putin, the Russians have put a new twist on the old concept. By deploying the term *Blizhneye Zarubezhe* or 'Near Abroad', they have given notice that foreign countries are divided in their minds between those whose sovereignty is fully acknowledged, and those nearer home whose independence is questionable. Putin routinely talks of the former Soviet republics as belonging to 'Russia's sphere of influence'. Ukraine, for example, has been a sovereign state and a member of the United Nations since 1991; its frontiers are internationally guaranteed. But it is also a key member of the Near Abroad, and hence, in Putin's view, is 'not even a state'.[25] If Moscow so desires, therefore, Ukraine's territory can be invaded, its provinces, such as Crimea, plundered, and its rulers denounced as fascists and impostors.

The concept of the 'Middle East' can be dated exactly to 1902. British sources refer to an article written by a British author who was searching for a geopolitical term that would span the area between the Ottoman Near East and British India; American sources attribute the prize to the strategic author Alfred T. Mahan, who in the same year applied the term to the area 'between Arabia and India'.[26] The constituent countries, which both had in mind, were Persia, Afghanistan, Arabia, and the Trucial States – none of which formed part of the Ottoman domain. For a couple of decades, therefore, the 'Middle East' sat comfortably alongside its older neighbour, the 'Near East'. Yet in 1920, when the Ottoman Empire fell apart, the political rationale that had underpinned the concept of the 'Near East' collapsed with it, and the previously limited concept of the 'Middle East' expanded quickly to fill the vacuum. Henceforth, all the new, ex-Ottoman states – the Republic of Turkey, Syria, Lebanon, Palestine, Transjordan, Iraq, together with the British protectorate of Egypt and the nascent Kingdom of Saudi Arabia – were judged to have joined an enlarged Middle East. Pakistan and Israel, both created in 1948, were added after the Second World War; and since the evaporation of the Soviet Union in 1991, question marks have been raised whether or not five Central Asian republics should be included as well. All these countries have been profoundly affected by the dramatic rise of the oil industry, which was virtually non-existent when the concept of the Middle East was invented, but which today is closely linked to perceptions of the vital strategic interests of the Western Powers.

If one goes to the Middle East, of course, one finds that its inhabitants are extremely diverse – linguistically, religiously, historically, and politically. The Turkic peoples, the Iranic group, and the Arabs do not possess any strong degree of common identity. They happen to live in the same neighbourhood, but they don't belong to the same 'kith and kin', don't interact easily, and rarely display any strong solidarity. As shown by the current civil war in Syria, and by events in Syria's borderlands with Turkey, numerous ethnic minorities such as Kurds, Assyrians, and Yazidis are caught up in the general melee.

The Middle East was the birthplace of the three great monotheistic religions – Judaism, Christianity, and Islam. All three continue to be present, but none suggests any sense of coherence, let alone of mutual co-operation. Israeli society is rent by divisions caused by the rise and political clout of the ultra-orthodox. The Christian denominations still squabble over the Holy Places, and Christian minorities, such as the Coptic Church in Egypt, still suffer persecution. In the Muslim world, the conflicts between Sunnis and Shias are as bitter as resentments against the Infidels. Recent conflicts have drawn the world's attention to the existence of previously obscure religious minorities, including the Syriacs, the Alouites, and the Druzes.

To cap it all, the Middle East has also served as the playground of successive major empires – the Ottoman, Persian, British, French, and Russian – each of which has left its own inimitable legacy. In the twentieth century, the Americans were able to construct a far-reaching (though incomplete) hegemony for the simple reason that no united resistance could be offered.

What is more, it is doubtful if any of the so-called 'Middle Easterners' think of themselves as such. The national identities of Turks, Iranians and Arabs – indeed of Syrians, Iraqis and Egyptians, and of sects and factions within the larger groupings – are far stronger than any shared regional allegiance. The Arab world, in particular, is notoriously fractious, and pan-Arabism has been signally unsuccessful. The United Arab Republic, which joined Egypt to Syria in the late 1950s as conceived by Colonel Nasser, lasted all of three years.

Nonetheless, the Arabs possess their own mental framework of geographical locations. They traditionally take Egypt to be the centre, their 'Middle Kingdom', assuming thereby that 'the West' consists of Egypt's western neighbours and 'the East' of Egypt's eastern neighbours. For these purposes, they employ their own unique terminology. Egypt has been the civilizational heartland of the region for six or seven millennia, and in 1945 it was the natural place in which to found the Arab League. Yet it has not always been Arab, and present-day Egyptians do not call their country 'Egypt'. In the days of the Pharaohs, the language of Ancient Egypt was a semitic tongue that has only survived in the liturgy of the Coptic Church; its religion was made up of an astonishing collection of polytheistic beliefs and rituals that today attract millions of fascinated visitors to the temples of Thebes or to the funereal Valley of the Kings. In the Hellenic and Roman periods that followed, the language of the elite was Greek, and the principal religion, after conversion in Roman times, was Christianity. Alexandria, from the fourth to sixth centuries, was one of the foremost centres of Christian civilization. The Arabic language arrived in the company of Islam in the seventh century, since when no major changes have occurred. The pharaonic name for the future Egypt was *Kemet*, meaning 'Black Soil' (of the Nile); the Hellenic name was *Aegyptos*, whence the Latin *Aegyptus* and the English *Egypt*; and the Arabic name is transliterated variously as *Misr* or *Masr*. English attempts to translate *Misr* can differ, but the best one seems to be 'border country'. These linguistic progressions underline the impermanence of cultures and civilizations.

*Al-Maghrib*, the Arabic term for 'the West', refers to the area that most Europeans would call 'North Africa'. Its inhabitants, the Maghrebis, are the source of the French term *Maures* and the English *Moors*. *Al-Maghrib* is the product of Islam's lightning conquests in the seventh century, which stretched from Arabia to the Atlantic. Traditionally, it was applied to the coastal zones of Libya, Tunisia, Algeria, and Morocco, though the formation of the Arab Maghreb Union in 1989 has seen it extended to Mauretania and the Western Sahara. Its use is contested by members of the indigenous Berber population, who see themselves as the natives and propagate their own term, *Tamazgha*.

*Al-Mashriq*, the Arabic term for 'the East', is a companion concept with the Maghreb. It, too, derives from the early conquests of Islam, and at its greatest extent it comprises all the Arab countries between Egypt and Iran, namely Palestine and Israel, Jordan, Lebanon, Syria, Iraq, Saudi Arabia, Yemen, and the five Gulf States. *Al-Mashriq* may also be taken to include Sudan and even Somalia, but it has most frequently been associated with the so-called 'Fertile Crescent', the great arch of land stretching from the southern Levant to Mesopotamia. It has nothing whatsoever to do with Asia beyond the Gulf, and for political as well as cultural reasons it is something to which the Israelis do not subscribe.

Within the Mashriq or Mashreq, one encounters the name of *Bilad-al-Sham*, which is usually translated as 'Greater Syria' or 'the Lands ruled from Damascus'. It was the name given by the conquering Arabs to the former Byzantine Diocese of Oriens. Yet its literal meaning is 'the Land of the Left Hand', just as Yemen is the land of 'the Right Hand'. A person standing in Mecca, and facing east as the Koran prescribes, would have pointed to Syria with the left hand and to Yemen with the right. These terms are perfectly orientational in nature.

Few Western terms, in fact, coincide exactly with their Arab or Middle Eastern equivalents. In 1921, for example, when the British created the Emirate of Transjordan, the locals called the new state *Sharq Al-Ourdun*, literally 'East of the Jordan' – a precise description of the emirate's location within the Palestine Mandate. When the emirate gained its independence, however, it adopted the new term of *Jordaniya*, a more ambiguous term that hints at claims on territory on the West Bank as well as on the east.

Mediaeval Arabs were among the pioneers in the history of geographical concepts. The tenth-century historian and geographer Abu Al-Hasan Al-Masudi, for example, wrote a large treatise of 365 chapters and 3,661 paragraphs, the *Muruj adh-dhahab*, that aimed to describe the past of all the world's lands and peoples. Born in Baghdad around 896, he finished his treatise in 958 shortly before his death in Cairo after a lifetime of protracted travels and studies. The preface contains a warning:

> We have given the present work the title of *The Meadows of Gold and the Mines of Gems* . . . in order to excite a desire and curiosity after its contents and to make the mind eager to become acquainted with history . . . There is no branch of science, nor any object of interest, of which we do not speak, nor is there any important fact which we do not mention . . . Whosoever changes in any way its meaning . . . corrupts the lustre of its information, or makes any alteration, and whoever ascribes it to another author, may he feel the wrath of God![27]

Al-Masudi was familiar with Greek philosophy, Persian literature, Indian mathematics, and numerous languages in which he followed everything from astronomy to medicine. His great work, partly translated into English in 1841 and fully into French in between 1861 and 1877,[28] is a remarkable compendium of information about Europe, Asia, and Africa. In the West, he had heard of Britannia, and had obtained a list of the Frankish kings from Clovis to his own day; his description of the Maghreb included Cordoba, Granada, and Seville. He knew many intimate details of Byzantine life, having befriended the Muslim convert Leo of Tripoli in Syria; and he was well informed on the pagan Rus and their trading activities on the Black Sea. To the south, he had set foot in Ceylon and in East Africa, listed the Zagawa and Ghana kingdoms of West Africa, and estimated that the source of the Nile lay 1,000 *farsangs** below Aswan. To the north, where he had travelled widely, especially in Persia and Armenia, he was able to describe numerous Turkic peoples, both nomadic and sedentary, and to distinguish all the main ancient civilizations from Babylon and Assyria to the empires of Cyrus the Great and Alexander. In the East, he is fulsome on India and China, which he may have visited, less so on Japan. Beyond the 'Sea of China,' he writes, 'there is nothing'. He assumed that the space between China and 'the Sea of the West' (the Atlantic) was filled by unbroken ocean.

Most amazingly, five hundred years before Copernicus, Al-Masudi was well aware that he was living on a spinning globe, and understood longitude and latitude. He even attempted some basic calculations, reporting that people on the equator have 'days and nights of equal length'. The Earth, he reckoned, was thirty-seven times the size of the moon; its diameter was 12,100 *farsangs*, and its circumference 27,000 miles. 'The cultivated land from the Fortunate Islands to the extremity of China' measured 13,500 ½ miles and was 'half the Earth's circumference'. The distance between the Earth and the sun was put at 4,820,000 miles.†

*The Meadows of Gold* paid close attention to seas and oceans – their location, size, and properties. Al-Masudi even understood that 'seas change their place', having observed that continents now consisting of dry land had once been under water. The 'greatest [of the seas] in the habitable world' was 'the Abyssinian Sea' (the Indian Ocean):

And in 304 AH [AD 926], I made a voyage from the island of Kanbalu to Oman, in a vessel [of the brothers] Ahmad and 'Abd es-Samed . . . I passed then the spot where, subsequently, [their] vessel was wrecked, and where those two men and their crew perished. When I made my first voyage on this sea, Ahmad Ben Helal Ben Okht el-Kattal was Emir of Oman. I have frequently been at sea; as in the Chinese Sea, in the Sea of Er-Rum [the Mediterranean], in that of the Khazars (the Caspian), of El-Klozom (the Red

* The farsang or *parasang* was an ancient unit of measurement of Persian origin, first mentioned by Herodotus. It is often equated with the European 'league', but its length varied wildly.
† The Fortunate Islands are possibly the Canaries. By modern calculations, the length of the equator is 24,902 miles, and the median distance between the Earth and the sun 92,955, 807 miles.

Sea), and in the Sea of El-Yemen. I have encountered many perils, but I found the sea of the Zanj [Zanzibar] . . . the most dangerous of all.[29]

Al-Masudi was also intent on cataloguing all the rulers of the world, great and small, past and present, adding, wherever possible, a sketch of their personalities and policies. He worked his way through the Roman and Byzantine Emperors, the Kings of Persia, the Emperors of China and everything beside and between. Nearer home, he was deeply interested in the growth of the Islamic Caliphate, which, larger than the Roman Empire and set up after the Prophet's death, had been ruled since 750 by the Abbasid dynasty:

> Abu Ja'far Abd Allah ibn Muhammad ibn Ali . . . known as 'Mansur', was proclaimed Caliph while on the way to Mecca. His uncle, Isa ibn Ali, received the oath of allegiance . . . on Sunday, 12 Dhu al Hijja, 136 AH 754 AD. Mansur was then forty-one years old . . . His mother was a Berber slave girl called Sallama. He died on Saturday 6 Dhu al-Hijja 158 AH 775 AD, having ruled twenty-two years less nine days. He was again on the pilgrimage [to Mecca] when death surprised him at a place called 'The Garden of Bani Amir', on the high road to Iraq. He was then sixty-three years old. They buried him at Mecca, uncovered because he was wearing the *ihram** . . .
>
> They say that his mother Sallama said: 'When I was pregnant with Mansur, I saw in my dreams a lion, which emerged from my side, and crouched, roaring, his tail beating the ground, while from all around [other] lions appeared, and gathered about him, and bowed their heads to the ground.'[30]

The account is packed with colourful anecdotes, which sceptics may think apocryphal, but somehow resonate with the spirit of the time:

> According to Ibn Ayyash, known as 'Al-Mantuf', 'He Who Plucks His Beard', Mansur was sitting one day looking out over the Tigris from the audience hall of the Khurasan Gate in the new town which he had just built and which bore his name: *Madinat al-Mansur*, in other words Baghdad . . . [Suddenly,] an arrow shot from who knows where landed at his feet. Mansur was terrified. He picked the arrow up and began to twist it around in his hands. Between the two vanes he read these lines:
>    Do you expect to live to Judgement Day?

---

* *Ihram* – the uniform white clothing, consisting of two plain sheets, which all male pilgrims wear on the Haj.

> Do you imagine there will be no Final Reckoning?
> You will be asked to answer for your sins –
> And then questioned on the state of the Believers.[31]

The arrow had been fired on behalf of a man imprisoned unjustly by one of the Caliph's officials. The man was pardoned.

On another occasion, Mansur talked about his predecessors, the Umayyad Caliphs, whom he and his late brother, Abul Abbas, had overthrown. Mansur said:

> Abd Al-Malik was an arrogant tyrant . . . Sulaiman's only ambition lay in his belly and his balls. Umar ibn al-Aziz was like a one-eyed man among the blind. The only great man of the dynasty was Hisham. As long as . . . their conduct was not base, the Umayyads held the government with a firm hand . . . But then power passed to their effeminate sons . . . who chased after pleasures forbidden by Almighty God. They knew not that God works slowly, and believed themselves safe from His snares . . . Then God [took away] their power, covered them with shame, and deprived them of their worldly goods.[32]

Unlike the brief rule of the Umayyads, the Abbasids were to cling to power in the Caliphate for seven and a half centuries, first in Baghdad and to 1517 in Cairo. Their successors, the Ottomans, hung on in Istanbul until the Caliphate with its black flags was itself abolished in 1924. In their view and that of their followers, the Caliph was God's deputy on Earth, the Prophet's Successor, and 'Commander of the Faithful'. They would have been taken aback to hear that they were living in the 'Middle East'.

From the Russian perspective, of course – as mentioned earlier – the 'Middle East' is actually the Near South, and the role of the Russians in fixing global orientations cannot be underestimated. After all, starting in the twelfth century from the remote, landlocked principality of mediaeval Muscovy, they extended their dominions across Eurasia more forcefully than anyone else. The Cossacks, who in 1585 were sent across the Ural Mountains into Siberia by Tsar Feodor I, were riding into the sunrise, and they and their successors kept going across the taiga and tundra until they reached the Pacific over 6,700 miles and sixty years later. The port of Vladivostok, which means 'Lordship of the East', was founded in 1648, fifty-five years before a permanent foothold was gained on the Baltic at St Petersburg. Henceforth, Russian traders, adventurers, settlers, convicts, and military expeditions streamed into

Siberia, claiming the land, taming the natives, and building the biggest contiguous empire in world history. By pushing overland, they achieved what all the other European imperial powers undertook by sailing overseas. It was Empress Catherine the Great who took the advice of a Swedish surveyor in her service and in 1775 fixed the boundary of Europe and Asia on the Ural ridge. In 1784, during the same reign, the first Russian settlement was established in Alaska on the far side of the Bering Strait. And they still kept going. In 1812 a Russian outpost was set up at Fort Ross, barely a hundred miles north of San Francisco in California. By that time, the empire of the Tsars stretched from eastern Europe to north-western North America, with the whole length of Asia in between – a distance of over 9,000 miles. The overland, easterly distance between Moscow and Fort Ross was almost twice that between the same points travelling westwards.

Russian nomenclature is naturally determined by Russian experience. In Russian usage, *Dal'nii Vostok*, 'the Far East', has long referred not to China or Japan, but to the vast, Russian-ruled landmass between Lake Baikal and the Pacific coast. Until 1867, when it was sold to the United States for 2 cents per acre, Alaska formed part of this region. (So, too, until abandoned in 1846, three years before the Californian Gold Rush, did Fort Ross.) For a very long time, however, no clear distinction was made between Siberia and the Far East. The matter was only remedied in 2000, when a Far Eastern Federal District was created, covering nine sub-districts in an area of 6.2 million square kilometres. Unlike others, therefore, the Russians can't use the 'Far East' to refer to China, Japan, and Korea. Instead they have invented a unique term of their own; the non-Russian 'Far East' has been dubbed the 'ATR' or 'Asia-Pacific Region', the *Azyatitsko-Tikookeanskii Reghion*.

Russians have equally been past masters at changing geographical names for political purposes. Across the centuries, whenever they annexed a city or a country, they would replace local or historical names, thereby severing traditional associations. This subject is as vast as Russia itself, but a good example might be the invention of 'the Lesser Kuriles' to accompany the seizure of four Japanese islands off Hokkaido in 1945. Those islands had never previously belonged to the Kurile chain, but few observers noticed the toponymical sleight of hand that was used to mask the land grab.[33]

In modern times, Western-orientated geographical language has been greatly boosted by the rising influence of the Americans, who are largely of European descent, who speak and promote the universal lingua franca of English, and who are set to become the last-ditch defenders of 'Western Civilization'. Their Eurocentric attitudes were consolidated by the fact that for nearly two hundred years the original thirteen colonies built their sense of location by focusing their gaze on the sea lanes to Europe, and by turning their backs on the continental interior. Opportunities for opening up the inland 'Frontier' in a major way were not realized until the Louisiana Purchase of 1803. The key expedition of Meriwether Lewis and William Clark, who charted the interior all the way to the Pacific coast, did not take place until 1804–6.

Hence, the famous command, 'Go West, my boy', was almost entirely a nineteenth-century phenomenon. It is most usually associated with the Californian Gold Rush, but it symbolizes a sea change in American thinking. Tens of thousands of men and women climbed aboard their wagons, to seek their fortunes in the endless prairies beyond the sunset. Earlier frontiersmen had already crossed the Appalachians from Virginia and Carolina. But now a tidal wave of humanity spilled over all points of the Frontier into lands that were still the preserve of Indian tribes and buffalo herds. It was these pioneers, on reaching the central continental areas in the vast Mississippi-Missouri-Ohio Basin, who thought of their new homes as lying in 'the Mid-West'. They did not think of calling it 'Middle America'. All they had in mind was their own journey, which had taken them halfway from the old colonial base on the Atlantic coast to the ultimate Land of Promise in the West.

As things stand, America still lingers in the shadow of its Eurocentric past. The American press still discusses the 'Middle East' and more bizarrely but less frequently the 'Far East'. Americans have not yet adapted fully to the consequences of living on a new continent, whose logic demands a change of vocabulary. Americano-centric language would refer to China and Japan as 'the Far West', and to Europe as the transatlantic 'East'.

Yet it is not inconceivable that American thinking may be set to change. In 2012 President Obama announced that the predominant US strategic presence was going to move from the Atlantic to the Pacific theatre; and if such a geopolitical shift were to happen, the consequences could be far-reaching. For the first time since the United States began to project its military power around the globe, Europe would cease to hold pride of place in American considerations, and the 'Great Ocean' that Magellan 'discovered' would loom ever larger. The prospect of future conflicts in the South China Sea, or between the two Koreas, are inexorably pulling American resources westward to 'the Far East'. China's ambitions to establish maritime supremacy over the western Pacific, which leaders in Beijing regard as home waters, is challenging American hegemony for the first time since the defeat of the Japanese in 1945.

Barack Obama himself, who was born in Hawaii and went to school in Indonesia, belongs to a minority of Americans who see the spinning globe more realistically. Going to law school at Harvard in the suburbs of Boston could only have hardened his suspicions of the 'East Coast Establishment', and he spoke openly about the anachronism of the nation's capital being located on the Atlantic seaboard. The site of Washington and the District of Columbia was chosen in the mid-1780s at a time when the territory of the thirteen colonies ran north to south along the Atlantic shoreline, and when the Potomac River marked the halfway house between the northern and southern states. Ever since then, it has grown ever more eccentric.

Before he left office in 2017, therefore, one could have imagined the president making two announcements. Firstly, in his strategic review, he may have talked of concerns not in the 'Far East' but on the 'Western Pacific Rim'. Secondly, he could have set up a commission to consider plans for moving the national capital from Washington to a more centrally placed city. In explaining the decision, he might have talked of the attractions not of 'the Mid-West', but of 'the Nation's Heartland', the 'Strategic Fulcrum', and America's 'Dead Center'.

Reflections about the East and the Orient automatically lead into thoughts about Orientalism. In its origins, 'Orientalism' was a neutral, value-free term; it referred to the work of European artists and writers, orientalists, who found their subject matter in the Orient. Examples of such work would include Brighton's Indian-style Royal Pavilion (1787) in architecture, Robert Southey's epic *Curse of Kehama* (1810), Byron's magnificent 'The Destruction of Sennacherib' (1815), and Thomas Moore's *Lalla Rookh* (1817) in poetry, Flaubert's *Salammbô* (1862) in the realm of novels, and Verdi's *Aida* (1871) or Borodin's *Polovtsian Dances* (1887–90) in music. In scholarship, the long pedigree of Orientalism goes back to early studies of Hebrew, Sanskrit, Mandarin, Persian, and Arabic. Much of the literature was infused with an idealizing spirit of admiration and delight:

> Know ye the land where the cypress and myrtle
> Are emblems of deeds that are done in their clime,

Where the rage of the vulture – the love of the turtle –
Now melt into sorrow, now madden to crime?
Know ye the land of the cedar and vine?
Where the flowers e'er blossom and the beams ever shine
Where the light wings of Zephyr, oppress'd with perfume
Wax faint o'er the Gardens of Gul in her bloom,
Where the citron and olive are fairest of fruit
And the voice of the nightingale never is mute;
Where the tints of the Earth and the hues of the sky
In colour, though varied, in beauty may vie;
And the purple of Ocean is deepest in dye
And the virgins are soft as the roses they twine
And all, save the spirit of Man, is divine?
'Tis the clime of the East; 'tis the Land of the Sun.[34]

More recently, Orientalism has taken on a more judgemental connotation. Thanks to an influential book by the late Edward Said,[35] it has come to refer to the deprecatory or patronizing attitudes of many westerners, who are perceived to have treated oriental culture with contempt. According to Said and his many acolytes, the essence of their treatment is to fabricate a false image of oriental culture as static and backward, and to imply that Western culture is dynamic, progressive, flexible, and superior. In this interpretation, the colourful but primitive Orient sometimes seems to resemble a straw man invented to underline Western superiority.

Said's detractors have been as vocal as his admirers. In *For Lust of Knowing*, for example, the Arabist and novelist Robert Irwin was at pains not only to expose factual faults but also to decry many of Said's basic attitudes. '[Said] hates the Middle Ages [and] loathes the past,' Irwin railed; 'he does not have the ability to enter into the spirit of other ages.' Or again, '[*Orientalism*] is a long and persevering polemic . . . written far too quickly and carelessly.'[36] Yet the criticisms never quite struck home. They attacked the bricks but not the edifice. 'The most thought-provoking works inspired [by *Orientalism*],' wrote one reviewer, 'have not blindly accepted Said's propositions, but have expanded and modified them.'[37]

In the same decade as Said's main work, another influential study launched a still wider inquiry into the ways whereby scholars from one part of the world assess other cultures and civilizations. Talal Asad's *Anthropology and the Colonial Encounter* (1973) was less regionally specific than Said's *Orientalism*, and went deeper into issues such as the interaction of 'power structures' and 'the production of knowledge'. Written by a Saudi-born American anthropologist, the son of a famous Jewish convert to Islam, it blew apart Western assumptions about the 'civilizing mission' of imperial regimes and the supposed objectivity of studies that they had encouraged. It marked a major step on the road to postmodernism.[38]

Anyone who has been involved with Western studies of Eastern Europe will recognize similar, 'orientalist' attitudes in that field as well. The most extreme example must surely come from the *Osteuropa* pseudo-research centres set up by the Nazis, who recruited academic support for their view that the Slav peoples as well as Jews were subhumans fit only for expulsion or extermination. Such horrible racist nonsense underlay Hitler's policy of *Lebensraum* in the East.[39] Yet it was anything but new. German nationalists in the late nineteenth century were happy enough to proclaim the superiority of German *Kultur*, together with its corollary, the inferiority of all non-Germanic cultures. Their counterparts in Britain and France similarly cultivated the notion that English or French culture also belonged to a first-class, 'historic' category. They had a strong influence on their American contemporaries, who were trying to formulate the constituents of Western civilization, of which they themselves wanted desperately to form part. All too often the end product was a highly selective hotch-potch that idealized the achievements of imperial Western Europe while totally ignoring or marginalizing the cultures of Eastern Europe.[40] In describing this phenomenon, I once invented the slogan 'West is best, East is Beast.'[41]

Modernizing Jewish attitudes were affected by the same sort of trends. In the late nineteenth century, Jews were flocking out of Eastern Europe to Berlin, Breslau, and Vienna in search of education and social advancement. For those who succeeded, the Second Reich seemed a promised land of tolerance, freedom, and prosperity, and it was not uncommon for liberated German Jews not only to embrace German culture wholeheartedly but also to speak disparagingly about the religious communities of *Ostjuden* from which they had escaped.[42]

The Zionist movement, launched by Theodore Herzl in 1895, developed its own set of orientalist attitudes. The Zionists' prime objective was to persuade Europe's Jewish masses to abandon the places where they then lived – mainly under Russian or Austrian rule in the historic lands of Poland-Lithuania – and to migrate from there to their biblical homeland in *Eretz Israel*, in Palestine. To this end, they could never admit that life in Eastern Europe, at least for many Jews, was bearable, or that the causes of ethnic friction were complex. On the contrary, despite the fear of pogroms and deportations, they had a natural interest in exaggerating the prevalence of anti-Semitism and in propagating their views about the unrelieved hostility of the locals. Their strident denunciations, not too effective before 1939, became irresistible in the wake of the Holocaust. Few paused thereafter to reflect that the Nazi instigators of the Holocaust were not East Europeans, but supposedly highly cultured Germans. Independent Poland in particular, where the world's largest Jewish population had long been housed, was targeted.[43] And generalized accusations did not stop after 1945. 'Poles,' opined a Polish-born Israeli prime minister, 'imbibe anti-semitism with their mother's milk.'[44] He never talked of Germans or Russians in that manner. Hard-line Zionists think nothing good ever came out of Poland.

Finally, the negative effects of the Cold War should be considered. For two whole generations, from 1948 to 1989, the world was brutally divided between East and West. The division was not just physical, in the shape of the Iron Curtain or the Berlin Wall; it was deeply political, cultural, and psychological. The leaders of the West, in the United States, believed strongly that their system was the best; the leaders of 'the East', in Moscow, were trained to believe that the superior merits of Communism would triumph. Westerners were tempted to revive the older stereotypes about a poor, benighted East, while most of the captive Easterners idealized America and longed for their 'Return to Europe'. The conflict has ended, but the stereotypes persist.

Here, one must stress the importance of irrational and emotional factors: the elements of power, pique, prestige, and prejudice. To be placed at the centre of a gathering is to occupy a place of honour; to be pushed to the periphery is the lot of the unwanted guest. And similar things happen symbolically around placings on the mental map. If one were a Bismarck or a dyed-in-the-wool Germanophile, one would relish the concept of a German-dominated *Mitteleuropa*, and would hope to see it revived. Yet if you happened to be a European orientalist, holding your nose against a whiff of the supposedly inferior peoples of Eastern Europe, you would strongly object to a central position being occupied by the less worthy representatives of Western civilization. Yet Poland suffered the greatest humiliation of all. Thanks to the so-called Enlightened Despots, it was destroyed, dismembered, and dismissed from the map of Europe altogether; throughout the nineteenth century, when many of the familiar features of modern Europe were taking shape, it did not exist, even to be maligned. In short, maps are geographical creations, but not only geographical creations.

Fortunately, the Poles have their own perspectives. Today, despite the populist government installed in 2015, they are reasonably secure, members both of NATO and of the European Union. Contrary to official propaganda, they have largely forgiven the Germans, who in Nazi times officially classified them, alongside Jews, as *Untermenschen*. They are offended by Russian leaders, whom they suspect, probably erroneously, of consigning them to the 'Near Abroad'. And they are both baffled and offended by opinions that persist in presenting Poland not as a prime victim of the Third Reich, but as an incurable co-perpetrator of the atrocities. And they have their own stereotypes to battle the foreign ones. *Polska*, they say, *jest pimpkiem swiata*. ('Poland, like the Oracle of Delphi, is the navel of the world.')

It is Australia, however, that is now coming up over the horizon. Australia experienced a profound change of locational attitudes in the course of the twentieth century. Starting life in a British convict colony, its inhabitants had been led to believe that it was a slightly larger and hotter version of the Isle of Wight, tethered somewhere off England's south coast. An 'all-White' immigration policy was pursued, barring entry to all non-Europeans. Its children learned about the kings and queens of England in their history books, and about England's mediaeval wars with France in their studies of Shakespeare. No one cared to tell them about Australia's true location, about the history and cultures of the adjacent Asian countries, or about their native Aborigines.

An early signal that change was coming occurred on the eve of the Second World War. The Australian prime minister, Robert Menzies, in his very first radio broadcast, was talking about the country's geopolitical situation. 'What Great Britain calls the Far East,' Menzies declared, 'is for us the near North; and in the Pacific Australia must regard herself as a principal.'[45] He was challenging not only Australia's subservience to Britain but also the thought processes that underlay the subservience. In less than three years, following the fall of Singapore in 1942, Australia rebelled against British control, welcomed the advent of American power in the region, and began the long process of re-adjusting to her place in the world.

More recently, the process spread far beyond the domains of defence and foreign relations. The traditional 'White Australia' policy was

dumped in the 1970s; large numbers of Asian immigrants were admitted; and radically new educational objectives have made citizens aware
both of human diversity and of neighbouring Asian civilizations. Australia remains a valuable member of the political 'West', but in many
respects it has consciously joined 'the East'.[46]

No few chapters in Australia's past relate to the 'history of getting
lost'. There is the true story of the early seventeenth-century Dutchman
who claimed to have discovered the great South Land, but had actually
landed in Brazil, and there were many instances of ships being wrecked
off the coast of western Australia, having been blown off course by the
'Roaring Forties'.[47] Above all, the tragic episode of Robert Burke and
William Wills, who died in the attempt to cross the continent overland,
tells of the perils of disorientation. Having set out from Melbourne in
August 1861, it is not quite true to say that Burke and Wills 'lost their
way'. Every morning the pitiless Australian sun indicated their general
line of march – due north on the outward journey, and due south on the
return. And after six months they succeeded in reaching the coastland
of the Gulf of Carpentaria. Yet they soon became seriously disoriented,
constantly underestimating distances, floundering in unfamiliar
terrain – travelling both in summer heat and in tropical rains, and possessing few skills for living off the land. Most fatally, they spurned
assistance from the aborigines, whom Burke thought 'inferior'. At one
point, already in severe distress, he fired his pistol at some curious
locals, causing them to flee – the equivalent of a stranded alpinist shooting at the Mountain Rescue Team. The remnants of the expedition
succumbed at the end of June 1862 within striking distance of a remote
cattle ranch located, symbolically, at Mount Hopeless. One could say
that they had been 'culturally lost'. Modern research suggests that they
may have died less from simple exhaustion or dehydration than from
acute vitamin deficiency brought on by the toxic effects of eating ill-
prepared meals of the nandroo plant. The sole survivor of their
expedition was the camel-master, an ex-soldier called John King, who
was found and cared for by a tribe of the Yantruwanta People.[48]

None of which changes the fact that Australia, like Greece or California, is blessed with incomparable daylight, which enhances shapes
and the brilliance of colours; almost invariably, an Australian sunrise
is a sight to be behold:

The Morning Star paled slowly, the Cross hung low to the sea
And down the shadowing reaches, the tide came swirling free.

The lustrous purple blackness of the soft Australian night
Waned in the gray awakening that heralded the light.
Still in the dying darkness, still in the forest dim
The pearly dew of the dawning clung to every giant limb,
Till the sun came up from the ocean, red with the cold sea mist,
And smote on the limestone ridges, and the shining tree-tops kissed.
Then the fiery Scorpion vanished, and the magpie's note was heard
And the wind in the she-oak wavered, and the honeysuckles stirred.
The airy golden vapour arose from the river's breast;
The kingfisher came darting, out from his crannied nest;
And the bulrushes and reed-beds put off their sallow gray,
And burned with cloudy crimson at the dawning of the day.[49]

# 7

# Moris

*Land of Creole and Dodo*

In 1642, when the Dutch sailing captain Abel Janszoon Tasman was commissioned to search for the unknown southern continent, the *Terra Australis Incognita*, he was stationed at Batavia on Java, the capital of the Dutch East Indies. At that time, more than a century after Columbus, European navigators conventionally distinguished the 'Old' or 'East' Indies, which they reached by crossing the Indian Ocean, from the 'New' or 'West' Indies in the Caribbean, which they reached by crossing the Atlantic. England's East India Company, founded in 1600 as 'The Company of Merchants of London trading into the East Indies', had established its very first trading post at Banten, also on Java, some fifty miles from Batavia. The Dutch East India Company, founded a couple of years later as the 'United East India Company' (*Verenigde Oost-Indische Compagnie*, or VOC), was Tasman's employer. In the preceding decades it had been taking control of the 'Spice Islands' trade, while the centre of gravity of English interests moved to the Indian subcontinent.*

Judging Tasman's task from a modern perspective, one might have expected his expedition to have sailed south. After all – as we know but he didn't – Australia's nearest shores lay only 800 or 900 miles directly south of Java's eastern tip: in favourable conditions, the voyage would have required little more than a week's sailing.

Yet no one, except local fishermen, ever sailed south. Recent excavations on the coast of north-western Australia have revealed that Javanese sailors had long been accustomed to cross the intervening waters; they collected guano on the coastal cliffs, and, before returning home, camped on the beaches of what is now the Kimberley Region.[1]

* In seventeenth-century English terminology the distinction was also made between 'Hither India', meaning the subcontinent, and 'Further India', meaning Malaya and the 'Spice Islands' where, under Dutch influence, the concept of the 'East Indies' came to be focused.

But Europeans in Tasman's time had no incentive to follow their example. The map published by the Dutch East India Company before Tasman sailed, Willem Blaeu's *Indiae quae Orientalis dicitur* (1635), gives an excellent snapshot of existing knowledge.[2] It stretches from 'Indostan' to 'Corea' and 'Iapon', and from northern China to 'Iava' and 'Timor'. The central area of the map shows the Malay Peninsula, Borneo, and the Philippines with great accuracy. Singapore, of course, which did not yet exist, is missing. The string of islands below the equator – Sumatra, Java, Bali, Flores, and Timor – are prominently displayed. But, further east, the cartographers could not reconstruct the full outline of Papua New Guinea, and had difficulty placing a cluster of isolated locations discovered in the 1620s (now thought to belong to the Gulf of Carpentaria). At the bottom of the map, south of the East Indies, they presented nothing but a large expanse of open sea.

Empty seas, however, would not have deterred a seasoned navigator. In order to reach the East Indies in the first place, Tasman had confidently crossed many thousands of miles of open ocean, via the Atlantic and the Cape of Good Hope. The problem off Java was a notorious phenomenon similar to its counterpart in the Atlantic, 'the Doldrums': that is, a sub-equatorial expanse of ocean, where sailing ships could not rely on systematic wind patterns, and where they risked becoming becalmed. Modern geographers call it the 'Intertropical Convergence Zone' (ITCZ), which is plagued by feeble winds, violent electric storms, and unbroken cloud cover that obstructs the use of sun-based navigational instruments. The Timor Sea, which forms a stretch of the ITCZ between Indonesia and Australia, is frequently struck by cataclysmic cyclones.[3]

Tasman, therefore, adopted a manoeuvre that by the seventeenth century was commonplace in the Atlantic. To make the quickest passage from Europe to southern Africa, sailing ships would cross the north Atlantic, heading for Venezuela or Brazil to avoid the Caribbean doldrums, before changing course and recrossing the southern Atlantic to the Cape of Good Hope. First discovered by the mediaeval Portuguese, this dog-leg *Giro del Mar* greatly increased both the number of nautical miles travelled and the chances of reaching the desired destination on time. As Tasman and his patrons realized, its equivalent for a ship aiming to sail from Java to a point far to the south was first to head south-west across the Indian Ocean towards Africa before doubling back on an eastbound course at a higher latitude. Convinced that 'Australia' existed, somewhere between the Indian and Pacific Oceans but knowing nothing of its dimensions, he sought to enter the region by running before the prevailing westerly winds, the so-called 'Roaring Forties', that blew latitudinally on either side of the tip of Africa. Hence, on leaving Batavia, he first needed to position himself correctly for the start of the critical eastbound run across the southern ocean. To this end he would make use of a small Dutch-owned island, way to the west, where he could rest his crew and take on supplies. As it proved, his calculations were reasonably accurate, and late in 1642, after some 11,000 exhausting miles at sea, he finally set foot on the beautiful island that is named after him. After that, Australasia was no longer 'incognita'.

In the eyes of modern travellers, Tasman's route may seem eccentric, if not absurd. It is certainly not the one that is usually followed by anyone heading to Australia from south-east Asia today; people just board a plane at Singapore or at Jakarta (as Batavia is now called) and fly directly to Melbourne or Sydney. Yet for anyone who wants to feel how the world has changed, there is something to be said for following in the wake of the old pioneering navigators, and reliving the realities of sailbound travel. If one has time and patience for the roundabout route, one first leaves Singapore for Mauritius before going on from Mauritius to Western Australia.

In Tasman's day, Mauritius was a newly founded and terribly remote, but vital, staging-post for the Dutch East India Company's shipping. Measuring a mere 64 × 48 kilometres, or 2,040 square kilometres, it was a speck in the ocean and was largely uninhabited. More than a thousand miles off the African coast, it had not received its first permanent town and port until 1638, but was uniquely important in the period prior to the settlement of the nearby Île de Bourbon (Réunion) or distant Cape Town. Moreover, blessed with heavy rainfall, Mauritius possessed an abundant water supply fed by mountain streams. In those years, ships from Europe would frequently drop anchor in Table Bay, waiting for good weather before rounding the Cape of Good Hope. But, if they needed more substantial stores or refitting, they had to press on to Mauritius.

Even so, Mauritius was not marked by that name on the most widely used map of the era. Willem Blaeu's *Africae Nova Descriptio*, though published in the same atlas as his *Indiae quae Orientalis*, dated from 1617 and used the older name of 'I(sla) do Mascarenas', after one of the Portuguese pioneers of the route; it ignored the name given to it by the Dutch in honour of their Stadtholder, Prince Maurice of

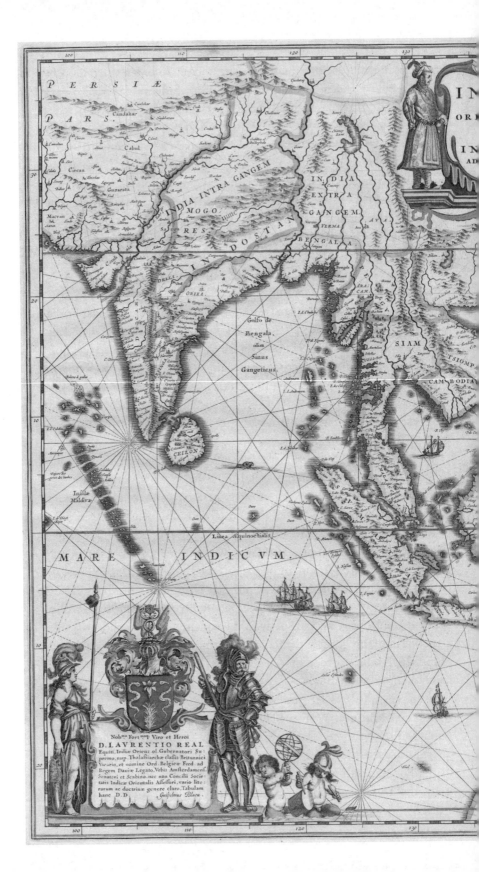

Orange – Maurits van Oranje – perhaps because the Stadtholder did not inherit the most senior position in his ruling house until a year after the map's publication.[4] Similarly, Blaeu's map did not use the formula of 'Indian Ocean'. It mentioned the *Mare Indicum* or 'Indian Sea' in the immediate vicinity of the subcontinent, while calling the greater expanse to the east of Africa the *Oceanus Orientalis*, the 'Eastern Ocean'. Everything was in a state of nomenclatural fluidity.

From Tasman's Journals,[5] the dates, times, and speeds of his voyage can be calculated exactly. He left Batavia on 14 August 1642, reaching Mauritius three weeks later on 5 September, his average speed over the 3,445 nautical miles a remarkable 6.5 mph or a little more than 4 knots. By the time he arrived his two ships, the *Heemskerck* and the *Zeehaen*, were not in good shape, and he spent the next month repairing their spars and rigging. He weighed anchor again on 8 October, with orders to sail south from Mauritius to latitude 52° S and only then to turn about for the long eastbound run. Fortunately, having trouble holding his course amidst the buffeting of the westerlies, Tasman decided to turn east much earlier and to follow the 44th degree of latitude. He was lucky. If he had stuck to his orders, he would have missed Australia completely, with no prospective landfall before Tierra del Fuego. As it was, he made it after forty-seven days at sea, sighting land on 24 November close to 42° S. The southernmost cape of the island that now bears his name, at Australia's southernmost extremity, lies at 43.6° S.

For the next two centuries Mauritius served as a major junction of intercontinental sea lanes. Before the opening of the Suez Canal in 1869, every European ship heading for India, the East Indies, or Australia had to round the tip of Africa before pushing on into the near-boundless waters of the Indian Ocean. Sailors who had spent weeks on a tiny rolling vessel would invariably look forward to the moment when they could drop anchor at the Grand-Port of Mauritius, stretch their legs on the sandy beaches, and drink pure running water before setting sail again on the final leg of their voyage.

The same sort of experience held good for the first seven or eight decades after Australia was settled by Europeans in the late eighteenth century. Australia's First Fleet, which sailed to Botany Bay in 1787–8, chose to make its halfway stop at Dutch-ruled Cape Town, rather than at Mauritius, which by then was in French hands. But the voyage on leaving the African shore was essentially similar for all who travelled round the world from West to East. As one of Australia's leading historians has put it: 'Before them stretched the awesome, lonely void of the Indian and Southern Oceans, and, beyond that, nothing that they could imagine.'[6]

One detail of Tasman's stay in Mauritius remains open to conjecture. Did he see the dodo? One can say for certain that the flightless wonder was running around the island, wild and free, when he landed, and it is hard to believe that he didn't meet it. In all probability, his crewmen joined those who entertained themselves by hunting it. One can say with equal certainty that by the time the First Fleet sailed past a century and a half later the Mauritian dodo was definitely extinct.

The flight from Singapore to Mauritius is longer than that from New York to London. Unlike Tasman's route, however, it follows a dead straight line, and once the coast of Sumatra is left behind, there is nothing to see for more than seven hours but sky, clouds, and seawater. Nonetheless, the drone of the engines eventually changes key, and the Air Mauritius Boeing 777 banks steeply, descending between volcanic peaks and towering thunderclouds to land among palm groves on the island's south-eastern seaboard. As it taxis to a halt at Sir Seewoosagur Ramgoolam International Airport, the tarmac is steaming from a recent tropical shower. (Sir Seewoosagur was prime minister in 1968, when the island gained its independence.) Over the terminal building flies a flag with four horizontal bands: red, blue, yellow, and green. The red, says a brochure, stands for the blood that was shed in the period of slavery and colonization; the blue for the all-surrounding ocean; the yellow for the sunshine (which was turned off on the day I arrived); and the green for the luxurious vegetation. Within an hour I was safely ensconced in a comfortable airport hotel. I threw the curtains wide to watch the sun set over the blue-purple head of the Mont du Lion, which soars over a strip of sandy beach and the waving fields of sugar cane. *Rouj, Ble, Jon e Vet. Les Quatre Bandes. Se vre!* For anyone who knows French, the spelling is strange, but the sense is perfectly clear. And a different interpretation of the national colours can be met. A Mauritian informant told me that many years ago his father had said to him that Red stood for the Indians, Blue for the Africans and Europeans, Yellow for the Chinese, and Green for the Muslims.

In the twenty-first century, Mauritius is on the road to nowhere special; it has lost its role as a major maritime destination. It forms part of one of the three archipelagos that lie off the eastern coast of southern

Africa: the first being Madagascar, the second the Seychelles, and the third the Maccarenes (Réunion, Rodrigues, and Mauritius). Despite its tempting offerings of a tropical paradise combined with old-world charm, it is visited only by the discerning few – by francophone tourists, by enthusiasts of extreme sports such as crater-running and kite-surfing, and by indefatigable globetrotters of all nationalities who have little else in the world left to see.

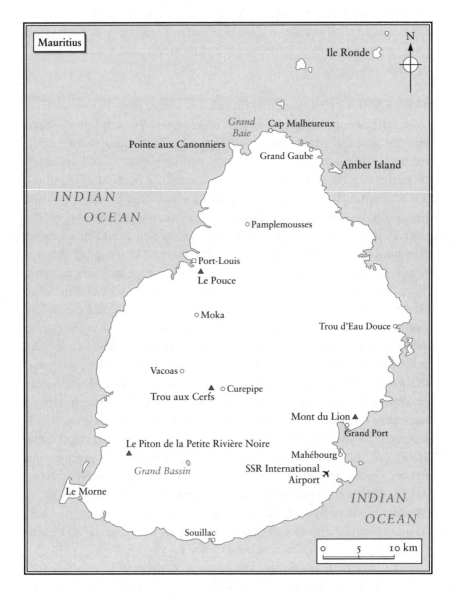

*

After a day recovering from travel fatigue and waiting for the two-day rainy season to ease, the time comes for a tentative expedition to the nearest village – Plaine Magnien. The local bus is run by the 'Noisy Travel Corp'; the stop is at the end of the hotel's driveway; the fare is two rupees; and the conductor gleefully cranks out tickets, turning the handle of a veteran ticket machine. The driver hollers to the chattering passengers, warning them to hang on as he roars round the tight corners of the winding country road. He screeches and jolts to a halt between a long line of shops. To the left is the PHARMACIE DODO, and opposite is the QUIN-CAILLERIE KASHMIR. The dark-skinned faces all look subcontinental, but the voices are not. The none-too-tidy shops hide behind piles of fruit and vegetable boxes, offering a range of services from chicken-roasting and dress-making to shoe repairs and second-hand cycles. A Hindu temple stands at the end of the row, its rafters adorned with mystical swastikas. A poster shows a matchstick figure dropping litter into a basket, and exhorts the populace to 'FER COM MWA' ('Do as I do!'). But the bus stop is firmly marked in English, and the policeman is wearing a British-style uniform embellished by a revolver. Then the next rattly bus arrives to drive us down to the nearby town of Mahébourg. It is run by a company called 'La Perle du Sud'. For three or four miles the sunken road winds between waving fields of sugar cane, before opening out suddenly to reveal a long, yellow-painted bridge that spans a broad river. A modest green mosque crouches beneath the trees on the approach to the bridge, and pastel-shaded houses cast their reflections in the river.

This is Mahébourg, named after its founder, the long-departed French governor, Bertrand-François Mahé de la Bourbonnais (1699–1753).* It could easily be in southern India. Coconut palms wave in the breeze, and the throng is dressed in white cotton shirts and bright-coloured saris. The city's pride is its magnificent seafront, which at one end overlooks the island's original harbour at Grand Port Bay. The rain has stopped. The clouds are clearing from Mont du Lion and a fresh balmy breeze is blowing. At the Pointe du Canon, which once housed the battery commanding the harbour entrance, a modern cultural centre has been built on the emplacement, and behind it a tall black granite obelisk surrounded by yellow-bloomed flame trees. The obelisk is inscribed '1835–1935', and was erected by the British on the centenary of the abolition of slavery.

---

* Not to be confused with his grandson, Louis-Charles Mahé de la Bourbonnais (1795–1840), the world chess champion, who was to die penniless in London and is buried in Kensal Green Cemetery.

Further along, at the angle where the Bay meets the Esplanade, another monument awaits, dated 1910. A memorial stone stands in front of a semi-circular, ceramic pictorial map, which presents a pretty picture of little sailing ships firing decorative broadsides. It commemorates the Battle of Grand Port of 1810, when the Royal Navy defeated the French and opened the way to the British takeover. But this is history emasculated. Sea battles of the Napoleonic era were not harmless affairs. Warships closed to point-blank range. Ear-splitting salvoes drove iron cannonballs through mighty timbers, and swept the decks with deadly grapeshot. The air above that fine harbour would have been rent by the crash of falling rigging, the crackling of fires, and the screams of maimed and dying sailors who would never see Brest or Portsmouth again.

Mahébourg's Esplanade, exuding faded colonial glory, has seen better times. The elegant stone walkway is still there, even if the wasp-waisted ladies with parasols and top-hatted gents in tow who once strolled here have passed on. A row of Victorian guest houses still awaits visitors, but a gold-plated Buddhist temple now dominates the fashionable North End, and beside it an outsize Buddha built from small stone tiles. A posse of saffron-robed monks offer their greeting of peace with clasped hands. Further on, the twentieth century intrudes with a cluster of box-shaped hotels, outdoor restaurants, and a recreation park. Still further, at the South End, the twenty-first century is represented by the self-contained, pseudo-primitive resort of Preskil (Presqu'ile) where global travellers are persuaded to live in grass huts. Beyond that is a yacht marina, though with very few yachts at their moorings. On one side of the marina is a large circular plaque dedicated (in English) TO THE FATHER AND MOTHER OF GOD, and on the other a tiny and ancient Catholic shrine perched precariously on the rocks. Protected by a quaint little roof and painted bright blue, it is dedicated to the Christian Madonna, *La Vierge*, against whose gender-specific claims the neighbouring plaque is presumably directed. Surmounted by a lopsided iron cross, it seems to protest: 'We, too, still have our place here.'

Anyone enquiring after the history of Mauritius could do worse than to compare Wikipedia's English-language entry with the French version. The latter is not only more detailed; it has attitude.[7] It denigrates the initial Dutch efforts to colonize the island, presumably to enhance the French takeover that followed. It is lenient in its description of the slave-based social system, introduced by the French in the eighteenth century, and remarkably indulgent to the advent of the British, who replaced the French in the early nineteenth century. The principal author, one presumes, is a person of conservative disposition, most probably a native Mauritian, who is troubled by the turbulence caused by the French Revolution. Elsewhere, there is no shortage of more critical historians to challenge such conservatism.[8]

The first recorded human birth on Mauritius, which took place at Grand Port on 14 November 1639, brought Simon van der Stel into the world. This was thirteen years before the foundation of Cape Town at a time when Mauritius still offered the sole safe harbour at the southern end of the Cape routes. The baby's father was a senior official of the Dutch East India Company; his mother was Javanese. The infant, therefore, was the product of *métissage*, a mixed-race union, which was to become the island's norm,[9] and he grew up to become governor of the Cape Colony.

The Dutch period, which lasted from 1598 to 1710, got off to a bad start and ended in a rout. In contrast to the much larger island of Madagascar, it was a land with no indigenous inhabitants. The consignment of African slaves that Admiral Wybrand van Warwyck brought with him in 1598 promptly escaped into the bush, rendering the first group of settlers stranded without a viable workforce. Subsequent efforts to set up a colony failed too, and it was not until 1638 that a permanent settlement could be established. Even though they developed the harbour of Grand Port, the Dutch made no serious efforts to exploit the rest of the island. After the rapid success of Kaapstad (Capetown) in South Africa, which was supported by a far more dynamic colony, the Dutch East India Company was not persuaded to pour comparable resources into Mauritius and the island declined. In 1710, in the middle of the War of the Spanish Succession, the Dutch of Mauritius found themselves plundered by pirates, deprived of supplies, plagued by rats, and battered by repeated storms. They packed their belongings and sailed off.

The French period lasted similarly for about a century. Established since 1642 on the neighbouring Île de Bourbon (now Réunion), some hundred miles distant, the French bided their time after the signing of the Treaty of Utrecht (1713) before sending over an expedition to Mauritius on 20 September 1715. The expedition's commander, Guillaume Dufresne D'Arsel, took possession in the name of Louis XIV:

> Étant pleinement informé, qu'il n'y a personne dans l'île, nous déclarons en vertu et l'ordre de Sa Majesté prendre possession de l'Île de Mauritius et islots, et lui donnons suivant l'intention [du Roi] le nom de 'Île de France'.

(Being fully informed that there is nobody on the island, we determine
by virtue of His Majesty's order to take possession of Mauritius and isles,
and according to the King's intention we named it 'Île de France'.)[10]

For ninety-five years the Isles of Bourbon and of France were to be
ruled as one entity.

Yet, unlike the Dutch, the French made strenuous efforts to develop
their new acquisition to the full. They founded the port and capital of
Port-Louis on the west coast to facilitate links with Bourbon, and in
1723 they issued Letters Patent to launch a comprehensive system of
slave-based land grants. In theory at least, life on the new plantations
was governed by Louis XIV's *Code Noir*, which since 1685 had regulated relations between colonial landowners and their slaves. The
Frenchmen who moved over from the Île de Bourbon in 1715 brought
Malagachi women and African slaves with them. They were the first
wave of permanent settlers, who in time gave rise to the 'franco-
mauritienne' landowning class. They were soon joined in 1723 by a
more substantial group of *concessionaires*, who had sailed out from
France to benefit from the royal land grants and launch the sugar industry. Larger concessions of 1,000 *arpents* or more were typically awarded
to noble families such as those of Sieur Chazal de Chamaret or the
Duchess de La Marque. Smaller concessions were handed to soldiers
and civil servants. Two-thirds of the island's land surface was distributed in this way.

The expansion of sugar plantations required the mass importation
of a larger labour force made up principally of black slaves from either
Madagascar or Senegal. These slaves quickly became numerically dominant, but were forbidden by the *Code Noir* to own property. Yet a high
degree of interracial marriage and concubinage combined with growing rates of manumission to nullify the designation of the landowning
elite as 'white'. People of mixed race were everywhere. And the label
'Créole' was attached both to *métis* as a group and to their language.

In 1766 France's royal government took direct control of the islands
from the Compagnie des Indes, and in the same era the legal division of
society into 'whites' and 'blacks' (slaves) was modified by the introduction of a third category of *libres* or 'freemen'. In 1789 on the eve of the
Revolution, 10 per cent of the population of 40,000 were white slave-
owners, 85 per cent were black and 5 per cent were freemen. Insular life
centred on the great sugar plantations and the commercial activities of
a handful of coastal towns.

News of the Revolution reached Port Louis on 31 January 1790, when Paquebôt no. 4 sailed into harbour ten weeks after leaving Bordeaux. The ship's captain, Gabriel de Coriolis, had witnessed the storming of the Bastille in person, and ordered the revolutionary tricolour to be flown at the mast. Red, white, and blue cockades were distributed on the dockside.

The next ship to arrive, *Le Stanislas*, in April, brought orders for the colony to form its own legislative assembly and to create self-electing municipalities in each of the island's quarters. In 1792, in line with events in France, the Assembly voted for the abolition of the nobility, and in 1794 for the abolition of slavery. Port-Louis was renamed 'Port-Nord Ouest', and Mahébourg 'Port-Sud Est'.

A sharp reaction was in store. The island's ruling class refused to implement the revolutionary decrees, and violent riots erupted. For several years the nobles did not know if they were still noble or the slaves if they were still enslaved. The impasse was solved in 1799, when Bonaparte seized power as First Consul. '*Je ferai ce que la majorité des habitants désire,*' he declared ('I shall do what the majority of inhabitants desire'). '*J'abolirai l'esclavage à Saint-Domingue, et je le rétablirai à l'Île de France.*' ('I shall abolish slavery on Santo Domingo, and restore it on the Isle of France.') The Consul's logic was dubious; he can only have been thinking of 'the majority' as meaning the majority of Frenchmen. But, much to the relief of the landowners, his will was enforced. 'Port Nord-Ouest' became 'Port Napoléon', Port Sud-Est became 'Port Impérial', and the Île de France became 'L'Île Bonaparte'.

Nonetheless, in the years after the Battle of Trafalgar in 1805, the French Empire had no answer to the Royal Navy, and in the War of the Third Coalition, colonial rivalry gained importance. The British landed on Rodriguez Island in 1809, turning it into the base for a general assault during the following year. The key naval battle, in the bay of Grand-Port (subsequently commemorated in the memorial on the Esplanade) contributed to a decisive British victory. General Abercrombie wrote to the governor-general of India on 3 December 1810, informing him of the island's submission. The name of the island reverted to its original Dutch form.

The British period of rule on Mauritius lasted for 158 years, from 1810 to 1968. It was formally regulated by the Treaty of Paris (1814), which confirmed British suzerainty over Mauritius, while restoring Réunion to France. It began with the new rulers stressing their intention of upholding local customs, and some said that nothing had changed except for the flying of the Union Flag. Yet, as the decades passed, numerous radical reforms were introduced. In 1835, by abolishing slavery, the British succeeded where revolutionary France had failed. The sugar industry was reorganized, and a major construction programme of roads, railways, and docks was instigated. Indian labourers were imported in increasing numbers to replace the liberated slaves and to meet the rising demands of the sugar trade. (Their working conditions were sometimes little better than slavery.) A small standing garrison was installed at the Abercrombie Barracks at Vacoas, and forts were built around the coast. A handful of civil servants ran the colony from the Hôtel du Gouvernement in Port-Louis; they were dominated by so-called 'white creoles', meaning assimilated people of creole origin, and answered to the Colonial Office in London. The legislative assembly remained in being, but fell completely under the control of the sugar barons. By 1894, when Queen Victoria's statue was erected in front of Government House, the island was considered a model colony.

In the British period, racial mixing proceeded apace. The colonial administrators in London were eager to avoid land seizures, and showed little interest in recruiting British settlers. The abolition of slavery, however, had far-reaching consequences. Former slaves fled the plantations en masse, leaving a vacuum that could only be filled by the steady flow of indentured labourers shipped in from British India. In the course of the nineteenth century the number of Indian immigrants overtook that of the host community, adding an important new element to the racial mix. What is more, being overwhelmingly male, the newcomers sought wives and partners among free black women, thereby creating the island's handsome and predominantly Afro-Dravidian race.[11] Many of the Indians belonged to lower castes who in India were traditionally barred from landowning. For them, the voyage to Mauritius opened up new opportunities. Some of them returned to the subcontinent after earning a modest financial nest egg. Others, having served out their contracted period of labour, were content to settle down in small-scale businesses as shopkeepers or traders. A few entered the big time as planters, industrialists, and refiners, and became the local Nalletamby, Arlanda, and Moutou dynasties. The Indian Hindus, many of them Tamils from southern India, were to reach the point of forming an absolute majority.

The present-day Chinese Mauritian community has similarly deep roots. Chinatown in Port-Louis dates from 1780, when a group of press-ganged sailors from Sumatra were brought ashore. After that, even though the Chinese were not allowed to buy land, their numbers increased and the later generations became highly assimilated. For the most part they speak creole, are converts to Roman Catholicism, and possess names that were mangled by colonial officials. 'Nearly all Sino-Mauritian families have funny or bizarre names,' writes Dr Edourd Leung Shing, a community leader: 'When we meet people from China, they just laugh.'[12] This did not prevent them succeeding, however. Although they represent less than 5 per cent of the population, the Chinese Mauritians exert considerable influence, controlling ten of the island's fifty biggest companies.

Mauritius has a special place in postal history. In 1840 Great Britain led the world by issuing the Penny Black. In the course of the next decade many countries followed suit – Brazil in 1843, the United States in 1847, France and Belgium in 1849, Austria, Prussia, and Switzerland in 1850. In the years that followed, letters and cards bearing postage stamps became a feature of everyday life, and philately or 'stamp collecting' a universal hobby, teaching generations about the world's make-up. More by accident than design, Mauritius had the distinction of issuing the very first postage stamps in the British Empire outside Great Britain. In 1847 a resident of Port-Louis, Joseph Osmond Barnard, who had recently arrived on the island as a stowaway, engraved two historic items. One was a 'One Penny' stamp in orange-red; the other a 'Two Pence' stamp in deep blue. Both bore a charmingly primitive profile of the young Queen Victoria with tiara and necklace, and both, in addition to their money value, were inscribed with the words: MAURITIUS, POSTAGE, and POST OFFICE. Only 500 of the stamps were printed from a single plate, and they were put into circulation on 21 September. Some twenty-seven are known to have survived, two of them in the National Postal Museum on the Waterfront at Port-Louis.[13]

Philatelists have always been excited by the rarity of Mauritius Nos. 1 and 2, but their enthusiasm was enhanced by their long-standing belief (only recently disproved) that the POST OFFICE inscription had been an error. The belief appeared to be supported by the fact that the second issue from Mauritius, in 1848, substituted the words POST PAID for POST OFFICE; and it was strengthened following publication of the definitive work on the island's postal history.[14]

Barnard, it was said, had been rushed into his mistake by the governor's wife, who was planning a grand ball and was desperate to see her

invitations sent out early. At all events, as leading collectors competed
for the dwindling pool of stamps on the market, prices soared. In
1904 the Prince of Wales, the future George V, Britain's most avid royal
philatelist, paid a record price at auction of £1,450 for a mint example
of the 'Post Office 2d Blue'. On opening a newspaper, one of his secre-
taries was reported to have exclaimed that 'some damn fool' had paid
'an astronomical sum' for one stamp. 'That damned fool,' the Prince
replied, 'is me.'[15]

By far the most famous item in the island's postal history, however,
is the so-called 'Bordeaux Cover'. Discovered in the 1860s by the
widow of the French merchant M. Borchard, to whom it had been
sent, the fading beige envelope displays two lines of address, a note on
the top left 'VIA ENGLAND', and in the opposite corner two beautiful,
franked, but undisfigured stamps side by side: the 1d Orange-Red and
the 2d Blue. It is regarded as the 'pièce de résistance' of all philately,
ahead of the Penny Black itself, the Swedish Treskilling Yellow, the
Hawaiian Missionary Stamps of 1851, and the triangulars from the
Cape of Good Hope. When last sold in public, in 1993, the 'Bordeaux
Cover' fetched a price of CHF 6,123,750, or 4 million euros.

But times move on, and the 'most expensive stamp' race continues.
In 2014 all previous record prices were topped by the sale of a British
Guiana 1-cent Magenta for $9.5 million.[16] The auctioneer, at Sotheby's
(New York), announced that he was selling the 'Holy Grail' of philately. And Holy Grails are more sensational than *pièces de résistance*.
Not long before, a Treskilling Yellow, which briefly topped the record
charts, was described as a philatelic 'Mona Lisa'. So that's the answer.
It's not the stamp alone that brings in the bidders – it's also the creative
hyperbole of the sellers. If the present owners of the 'Bordeaux Cover'
want to hit the auction heights again, all they have to do is to label it
'the Stamp Collectors' Dodo'.

For much of the British era, the jurisdiction of Mauritius extended far
beyond the home archipelago. In its original form it included both the
Seychelles (in a straight line 1,077 miles to the north) and the Chagos
Islands (1,339 miles to the north-east). Together, the associated territories formed an elongated triangle covering some 2,550 million square
miles of ocean. The Seychelles broke away to form a separate colony in
1895, but the Chagos remained attached to the end.

Even so, British rule proceeded relatively unruffled until fierce
struggles for self-government erupted. In its later stages, in the era of

decolonialization after 1945, it had to accommodate a surge of democratic movements, trade unions, and radical political parties. Negotiations with Britain began after the Lancaster House Conference of 1965. A new constitution was passed, and freedom was finally delivered by the Mauritian Independence Act of 12 March 1968, which also recognized the country as a sovereign member of the Commonwealth. Queen Elizabeth II remained head of state; the first non-British governor-general was Sir Abdool Raman Osman, and the first prime minister Dr Sir Seewoosagur Ramgoolam (1900–1985) – whose none-too-easy name inspired the sobriquet of 'SSR' that adorns the island's international airport.

SSR's road to fame is instructive. The son of an illiterate Indian immigrant, he was able to benefit both from improving conditions in the colony and from opportunities offered by the British Empire. As a young man, he studied at University College London, qualified as a medical doctor, and came under the influence both of the British Labour Party and of Mahatma Gandhi. Back in Mauritius, he joined the struggle to establish labour laws, pension rights, universal education, and a free health service, and, in the steps of India, to press for independence. In later life he was dubbed 'Father of the Nation'. His son, Dr Navinchandra Ramgoolam (b. 1947), educated in Ireland and at the London School of Economics, headed the Labour Party and twice served as premier of Mauritius, from 1995 to 2000 and from 2005 to 2014, before stepping down to face charges of conspiracy and money-laundering.

The political system as inherited from late colonial times is a British-style parliamentary democracy based on universal suffrage, a unicameral parliament, and the rule of law. All the main competing parties, including the Labour Party, the Militant Socialist Movement (MSM), the Mauritian Militant Movement (MMM), and the Parti Mauricien Social Démocrate (PMSD), possess a left-wing flavour. The dominant personality of the past forty years, six times prime minister and president for nearly ten years, has been RH Sir Anerood Jugnauth (b. 1930), leader of the MSM. Queen Elizabeth II remained head of state until 1992, when a republic was declared. According to the current Democracy Index, Mauritius is the only country on its African list to qualify as a 'full democracy'.[17] 'The island's democratic culture,' states the intellectual historian Sudhir Hazareesingh, born in Mauritius, 'is one of its most significant successes.'[18]

Sad to relate, however, the independence of Mauritius was attended by one of the most sordid deals of late imperial history. In 1965 the British government paid Mauritius £3 million for the cession of the Chagos Archipelago, and a further £650,000 to acquire the assets of the archipelago's main trading company. They then created a new legal entity called the British Indian Ocean Territory (BIOT), of which the archipelago's largest island, Diego Garcia, was the centre. In 1966 the BIOT was handed to the American Pentagon on a fifty-year lease, since extended, for the purpose of building an American military base. In 1971 the entire Chagossian population was forcibly deported, and further large sums were shelled out to Mauritius and the Seychelles for agreeing to take in the deportees. In 1973, on a now deserted Diego Garcia, the American military began construction of one of the world's largest bases, which includes a massive Naval Communication System, a huge Naval Supply Facility, and a five-runway airfield. At the time, the world was led to believe that the lease had been arranged without Britain receiving any special financial inducement. Decades later, it was revealed that in return for leasing Diego Garcia, the British government had been given a $14 million discount on the purchase of American Polaris submarines.[19] In 2016, a half-century after the scandal began, Britain's Supreme Court ruled that the Chagos islanders had no right of return.[20]

Nor did independent Mauritius itself enjoy unruffled stability. Soon after independence, the MMM emerged, claiming that all the old social and economic injustices had been preserved and promising endless disruption until its aims were met. A government formed by the MMM in 1982–3 fell apart through internal wrangling, but the militants' influence was not tamed until a 'Republic of Mauritius' was declared in 1992. Since then, politics has centred on the threefold rivalry of the Labour Party, the MSM, and the MMM, all of which have won elections and formed governments. Paul Bérenger (b. 1945), a graduate of the University of Wales and a co-founder of the MMM, has served six terms as leader of the opposition and once, in 2003–5, as prime minister.

Bérenger, who is a Christian of Franco-Mauritian descent, is the only non-Hindu to have reached the top of the political ladder. This fact underlines the wider reality, that since independence democracy has brought the island's Indian community to the fore. Nowadays, one hears talk of a 'Hindu Renaissance' or even a 'Hindu Miracle'. Articles on the subject stress both the revival of the Hindu religion, which had been falling into decline, and the sense of pride and confidence among members of a relatively prosperous community, whose forebears had been insecure, destitute immigrants.[21]

The physical remoteness of Mauritius has exercised a formative influence on its character and development. Despite the fact that neighbouring Madagascar was settled by ancient migrants from distant Melanesia, the first Europeans to see Mauritius – the Portuguese in 1507 – found no traces of earlier human settlement. As a result, all the island's modern population – Europeans, Africans, Indians, and Chinese – are relatively recent arrivals. Similarly, since the island was separated from the rest of the world for eons of time, the native fauna contained no mammals, no carnivores, and no predatory reptiles. Dogs, cats, pigs, mice, rats, and monkeys all landed from European ships. Just as Madagascar hosts ring-tailed lemurs, which have filled an evolutionary niche that pre-dates the African continent, so Mauritius hosted endemic plants and birds that have no known counterparts elsewhere. Among them are the black-spined flying fox, the Mauritius grey white-eye bird, the keel-scaled boa, the goby fish (*bichique*), and the giant tortoise (recently reintroduced from Réunion). Three hundred unique species of flowering trees have survived, although the national flower, the *Trochetia boutoniana* or 'boucle d'oreille', is now confined to a single mountainside. It is no accident that Mauritius was home to the dodo.[22]

The scientific name of zoology's most famous extinct species is *Raphus cucullatus*. (Thanks to its poor adaptation to the modern world, the founder of scientific classification, Carl Linnaeus, originally called it *Raphus ineptus*.) Its vernacular name is thought to derive from an old Dutch word, *dodars*, meaning, as does *cucullatus*, 'plump rump'. The flightless bird, which weighed up to 40–50 pounds, had no natural enemies and no sense of vulnerability, so it fell an easy victim to hungry sailors and herds of feral pigs. Several drawings and descriptions survive from the seventeenth century, and a few specimens were brought to Europe for expert examination. The last credible live sighting, on Amber Island off the north-east coast, dates from 1662.

Fortunately for the bird's later reputation, one of the stuffed specimens was deposited in the Natural History section of the Ashmolean Museum in Oxford. There it was seen by the Reverend Charles Dodgson or 'Lewis Carroll', who took it to his heart and immortalized it by a prominent role in *Alice in Wonderland*. Dodgson stammered badly, and was known to his friends, affectionately, as 'Do-Do-Dodgson'. The

French-born British author Hilaire Belloc sought to follow suit with a notorious piece of doggerel:

> The Dodo used to walk around
> And take the sun and air.
> The sun yet warms his native ground –
> The Dodo is not there.

> The voice which once did squawk and squeak
> Is now for ever dumb –
> Yet you may see his bones and beak
> All in the Mu-se-um.

Unlike the poor dodo, this verse *does* deserve to be extinct.

In the days of Louis XIV, the Roman Catholic Church enjoyed a monopoly in the Île de France. '*La religion du Roi*', it was said, '*est la religion du peuple.*' The *Code Noir* stated that all slaves had to be baptized, had to accept Christian names, and had to attend Holy Mass regularly:

Article I. All the slaves who can be found in the isles of Bourbon and France shall be instructed in the Catholic, Apostolic and Roman religion.[23]

In practice, owing to a shortage of priests, baptism did not always take place. But Christian names were routinely handed out at the point of purchase on the slave market, often being combined with a further name denoting the bearer's country of origin. Whatever their native names, therefore, Mauritian slaves were customarily known by forms such as 'Anna de Bengale', 'Simon de Malabar', 'Pierre de Bali', or 'Paul de Timor'.

By the same token, the Edict of Nantes (1685), which banned the Protestant religion from all the king's territories, excluded all Huguenots from Mauritius. (A small party of Huguenots who landed on the Île Rodrigues in the 1690s did not succeed in planting a permanent settlement.) In theory at least, all the islanders prayed to the same God in the same Gallic tradition. The cathedral of St Louis in Port-Louis was the seat of a Catholic bishop, who supposedly wielded undivided authority in the spiritual sphere. In reality, religious conformity was often only skin deep. Many of the imported Africans, for example, continued to observe traditional animist cults and rituals.

The British took over Mauritius at a moment when the Act of Uniformity, which ensured Anglican orthodoxy, was still in force in England. But the Treaty of Paris (1814), whereby the French surrendered the island, ensured that all existing 'customs and trad-itions' be upheld, and religious plurality was accepted from the outset, whereas at home it had to wait until 1829. An Anglican diocese was cre-ated, and the magnificent Anglican cathedral of St James was erected, but the bishop and his clergy ministered only to the tiny community of British officials and their families. The sway of Roman Catholicism was not significantly diminished. The Irish Catholics, Nonconformists, and Jews who landed on Mauritius suffered no discrimination, and the spectrum of Christian denominations resembled that which soon per-tained in Victorian Britain.

Religious diversity was dramatically expanded, however, by the influx of immigrants from India. Hindus and Muslims landed in num-bers, while smaller groups from Burma or Malaya introduced Buddhism. Within decades, every substantial township in the island sprouted mosques and assorted temples alongside Protestant and Cath-olic churches. Whether by accident or design – some would say by wise leadership – Mauritius cultivated a climate of tolerance and plurality. The lakeside Hindu Temple at Grand Bassin is a prime destination for sightseers. The principal Sunni mosque, Jammid Masjid, has stood on the Rue Royale in Port-Louis since 1853. The biggest concentration of Buddhist shrines can be found in Port-Louis' Chinatown. A handful of Sikh *gurdwaras* attest the presence of another religious minority. Among the many Christian churches, the most evocative undoubtedly stands on the tip of Cap Malheureux, on the island's northernmost extremity, peering out onto the boundless Indian Ocean as if onto the infinite life hereafter. (The 'Cape of Misfortune' was given its name by the French in 1810, because that was the point where the conquering British forces landed.)

No visitor, in fact, can fail to be impressed by the fervent devotions on display at the island's many religious festivals. Among Catholics, the biggest event is the Fête du Père Laval, which involves an annual pil-grimage and procession on the anniversary of the Blessed's death, 9 September. Jacques-Desiré Laval (1803–64), born in Normandy, was a medical doctor and missionary who devoted his life to the island's poor. He was known for extreme forms of self-denial, such as sleeping in a packing crate, while striving to improve agricultural methods, san-itation, and health services. After his death he was dubbed 'the Apostle of Mauritius' or 'l'Apôtre des Noirs', and was beatified in 1979 by Pope John Paul II.[24] During my visit Laval's tomb at the church of Sainte-Croix in Port-Louis was being renovated in preparation for the 150th anniversary of his death. When the *jour de fête* comes round, the pilgrims dance in celebration, and sing their song in a quaint mixture of French and Creole:

> A cause Père Laval combien miracle fine arrive
> A cause Père Laval combien la misère fine soulazer
> Tombeau Père Laval li pas difficile po nous aller
> A cause Père Laval li bien tranquille po nous prier.[25]

> (Thanks to Father Laval how many miracles have happened!
> Thanks to Father Laval how much misery has been assuaged.
> The tomb of Father Laval is not difficult for us to reach.
> Thanks to him, we can pray there in perfect peace.)

Since Hinduism commands the support of almost half the population, however, the nine-day festival of *Maha Shivaratri*, which is held in February, draws the biggest crowds. Thousands of devotees of the Goddess Shiva throng her temple at Grand Bassin, fasting and praying until an all-night vigil heralds 'The Day of Great Light'.

Yet traces also remain of still older belief systems. Voodoo or 'Black Witchcraft' can be found in many parts of the world affected by African migration, from Madagascar and Haiti to New Orleans, home of the renowned 'Voodoo Queen', Marie Laveau.[26] The particular variant of 'Fusion Voodoo', which evidently thrives on Mauritius despite being illegal, has been described both as 'an amalgam of Hinduism, Malagasque sorcery and Satanism' and as 'the *fleau*' or 'scourge' of the island. It is not the sort of thing that tourists are likely to meet, although they may come across fetish dolls or lighted candles left in coconut-shell holders under a roadside tree. Yet the *loganistes* or 'witch doctors' undoubtedly practise their profession, as do the more sinister *daines* or 'priestesses', who are said to gain their magic powers from the spirits of ritually murdered children. Their clients consult them to participate in esoteric rituals or obtain a wide variety of cures, curses, potions, and spells, which ward off disease, misfortune, or the Evil Eye. The prominent sorceress, Shan, formerly Catherine, who practises in the south, sees up to forty clients per day, charging between 25,000 and 50,000 Rs per session. 'Je ne fais que du bien,' she protests, 'jamais du mal.' To learn more, one can read the abundant works of a local author Pierre Manoury, or one can arrange for dispensations online, among others from the virtual sorceress 'Joséphine de l'Île Maurice', 'Grande Daine Mauricienne', who resides in Paris.[27]

Ancient superstitions, however, can hardly be regarded as the norm. Modern Mauritius is rightly famed for its generous and effective educational system. Since independence in 1968, universal education, free of charge, has been introduced for all boys and girls with impressive results, and a 95 per cent literacy rate has been achieved. Mauritian candidates regularly top the lists in the Cambridge-run exams at school-leaving and university entrance levels around the world.[28] The main campus of the University of Mauritius, inaugurated in 1972, is located in the Moka district, outside Port-Louis.[29]

By the same token, the Grande Daine in Paris cannot be seen as a central feature of the Mauritian diaspora. Substantial expat communities, made up of students, academics, business people, and professionals, have grown up in Britain, France, South Africa, and Australia. They make a significant contribution to the country's standing and economy.[30]

Whistle-stop tours of the island are touted by many agencies, and its compactness makes for easy outings. At 2,000 square kilometres it is three times the size of Singapore, but no one location is more than 50 miles from anywhere else. The traveller can choose from three types of destination: the City, the Highlands, or the Coast. Each has special attractions, and all can be savoured within a week.

Port-Louis is the only substantial city.[31] Dominated by the harbour, whose docks are publicized as the largest in the Indian Ocean, it is surrounded by a circle of high hills, offering fine panoramic views. The better suburbs are lined with elegant villas and tall trees, the less desirable districts with the overcrowded dwellings of dock workers. The city centre boasts numerous grand churches and public buildings, while keeping quiet about the traffic jams. The outstanding attraction – none-too-well advertised – has to be the Château de Labourdonnais: an enchanting combination of noble living, period garden, well-stocked museum, and first-class French restaurant.[32]

The Highlands of Mauritius are graded between foothills covered with dense tropical forest, a lofty central plateau, and a dramatic array of jagged volcanic peaks. One of the peaks, Le Pouce (812 m), overlooks Port-Louis; the tallest, Le Piton de la Petite Rivière Noire (828 m), lies in the south-west quarter. The Black River National Park is a treasure house of natural history. The crater of the Trou aux Cerfs, near Curepipe in the island's centre, belongs to a dormant volcano, whose appeal is heightened by the rumours that its dormancy may end at any moment.

Over two-thirds of the Mauritian coastline is covered with fine white coral sand, and lined by sea-green lagoons. Some locations have seen their beauty defaced by modern commercial tourism, but many have avoided the worst, and can still be enjoyed by lone walkers, swimmers, and beachcombers. Scores of uninhabited islets still await discovery by canoeists and boaters. A resort such as Grand Baie in the north – which the Dutch used to call *Die Bogt zonder Eynt*, 'the Beach Without End' – has been invaded by garish hotels, barbaric bazaars, concrete waterfronts, and intrusive tripper touts; but its western reaches, in the direction of the Pointe aux Canonniers, are largely untouched. A quieter village like Souillac in the south still contrives to preserve old-world charm with modern attractions such as surfing and deep-sea fishing.[33]

No description would be complete without mention of the black, volcanic headlands that protrude into the ocean and divide the coastline into self-contained bays and beaches. One of them hides a special cultural heritage. The promontory of Le Morne lies in the far southwest, and seen from the air looks like some giant lizard feeding in the lagoon. At close quarters, it becomes a huge, soaring, and precipitate jumble of rocks, rendered near-inaccessible by a maze of caves and chasms. In the days of slavery it was a favourite refuge for *maroons* or 'runaways'; in the early nineteenth century it was even the scene of a well-established Maroon Republic, whose inhabitants, having built a number of forts and hamlets, defended themselves successfully against the wrath of the authorities. It is, in fact, a classic example of permanent *Grand Marronage* or 'Haven for Fugitives', as it survived until slavery itself was abolished.[34] It has figured on the UNESCO list of World Heritage sites since 2005.

The linguistic landscape of Mauritius reflects its multi-ethnic society. But it does not resemble what might be expected from a country that has been a member of the British Empire and Commonwealth for more than two hundred years. English, though the main language of government, has never taken deep root beyond the public sphere, and French remains the preferred idiom of the old social elite. Hollywood films, for instance, are generally dubbed into French.[35] The main lingua franca is a French-based creole, which since independence has officially enjoyed co-equal status with English. In addition, a variety of Indian languages proliferate in particular communities. All in all, thirteen languages using nine alphabets are recognized: English, French, Creole,

Hindi, Tamil, Telugu, Marathi, Urdu, Gujarati, Bhojpuri, Sindi, Tarnoul, and (Chinese) Hakka.

French-based creoles are encountered in many parts of the world. One of them, Haitian, claims over 15 million speakers and is the first language of the state. Others, such as those from Guadeloupe or New Caledonia or the *Pale-Neg* of Louisiana, have fewer practitioners, and some, like *Tay-Boi* in Vietnam, are an endangered species. Despite their geographical closeness, the creoles of Mauritius and Réunion are not particularly similar.

The difference between creoles and pidgins is a sore point among linguists. Both derive from the efforts of non-native speakers to master a well-established tongue, and both produce far-reaching simplifications of vocabulary, grammar, morphology, and orthography. A creole language, however, is generally judged to be generated by the further evolution of a pidgin, and by the acquisition of more stable forms of speech.[36] All creoles, in other words, have grown out of an earlier pidgin, but not all pidgins evolve into a creole.

Mauritian *kreol* belongs to a linguistic sub-group whose members are known for historical reasons as 'Creoles Bourbonnais', and which include Agalega, Chagossian, *Réyoné* from Réunion, Rodriguan, and *Seselwa* from the Seychelles. It uses a straightforward phonetic alphabet – far more regular than the original French – and possesses a French-derived core lexicon; for anyone with a working knowledge of French, it can be readily understood after a couple of hours on the beach with a local guide or phrase book.[37] The word *napli*, for example, may cause consternation, until one twigs that it is just 'nonplus' written differently. The sentence *Dodo napli existe* is not a bad starting point. *Moris*, meaning 'Mauritius', is naturally an essential item of vocabulary.

Several basic features can be rapidly absorbed. Even though *kreol* has lost the use of articles, many nouns have been permanently fused with the articles that once attended them. Hence: *letan* = time, *lerat* = rat, *latet* = head, *lavi* = life, *later* = earth, *ler* = hour, *lide* = idea, and *loto* = motorcar. Equally, there are creole words that are beautifully fused with parts of speech other than articles. The word for 'God' is *Bondye*, for 'bread' *dipin*, and for 'wine' *diven*. Further, since gender agreement between nouns and adjectives no longer applies (to sighs of relief from the English), it is perfectly admissible to say *gros vas*, 'a large cow', or *zoli fam*, 'a pretty woman'. To augment an adjective, one simply adds on *byen-byen* ('very') to arrive at *byen-byen zoli fam*. And, since reversed word order has disappeared from interrogatives, one can easily turn a statement into a question by prefacing it with *eski* = 'est-ce que'. *Eski Dodo napli existe?* (Answer: *Pa existe, alas.*)

At first sight, *kreol* verbs do not look too forbidding; the infinitive forms are eminently recognizable: *fer* = faire, *dormi* = dormir, *alle* = aller, *vini* = venir, and *bwar* = boire. But then the going gets rougher. Since all declensions and inflections have been dropped, elements of tense, mood, and aspect have to be indicated either by functional adverbs, by verbal phrases or, most typically, by marker words placed immediately next to the root verb. Among the adverbs conveying indications of time, one meets *tulezur* (tous les jours) = 'continuously' or 'always'; *zordi* (aujourd'hui) = 'now' or 'in the present'; and *kitfwa* (quelquefois) = 'from time to time' or 'sporadically'. Among the verbal phrases, frequent use is made of *bizin* (besoin), which has the sense of 'one must', *devet* (from 'devoir'), which translates as 'one ought', and *dommage* ('pity'), which is employed to convey 'it's unfortunate that'. Of which, an unusual example caught my eye on a linguistic website: *Dommage Stalin fine alle fer marguerites pousse*: 'It's a shame that Stalin died' – literally 'that he went to push up the daisies'.[38]

Among the markers that pepper any French creole text, five are particularly important:

**ti** (derived from 'etait') indicating past action
**pu** (derived from 'pour') indicating definite future mood
**a** (derived from 'va') indicating the indefinite mood
**'n** (derived from 'finir') indicating the perfective aspect
**pe** (derived from 'après') indicating incomplete action

*Mo fer* means 'I do' while *Mo ti fer* means 'I did'. 'The Queen of England will visit Mauritius' comes out as *Larenn Langleter pu visit Moris*. (The monarch did make the journey once, in March 1972.)[39]

Creolistic typology, therefore, is not for the faint-hearted or for people in a rush. But Mauritian Creole (MC) features frequently in academic debates surrounding the subject. According to a recent study, MC's credentials for being regarded as a fully fledged archetypal creole language are 'impeccable'.[40] The standard exemplar for demonstrating the characteristics of any such language is the Pater Noster, 'Our Father', otherwise *Nou Papa*:

*Morisien:*
*Nou Papa ki dan lesiel*

*Fer rekonet ki to nom sin*
*Fer ki to regn vini*
*Fer to volonte akonpli*
*Lor later kouma dan lesiel.*
*Donn nou azordi*
*Dipin ki nou bizin.*
*Pardonn nou, nou bann ofans*
*Kouma nou osi*
*Pardonn lezot ki*
*Finn ofans nou.*
*Pa les nou tom*
*Dan tantation*
*Me tir nou depi lemal.*[41]

(Français:
Notre Père qui est aux cieux
Que ton nom soit sanctifié
Que ton règne vienne
Que ta volonté soit faite
Sur la terre comme au ciel.
Donne-nous aujourd'hui
Notre pain de ce jour.
Pardonne-nous nos offences
Comme nous pardonnons aussi
À ceux qui
Nous ont offensés.
Et ne nous soumets pas
À la tentation
Mais délivre-nous du mal.)

In the official view, 'Mauritius is a country of poets, writers and artists.'[42] It certainly exudes an ambiance of creativity. The Franco-Breton-Mauritian writer J. M. G. Le Clézio (b. 1940), winner of the Nobel Prize for Literature in 2008 and son of Mauritian-born parents, calls it his 'petite patrie'. 'Writing for me,' he once said, 'is like travelling. It's getting out of myself and living another life – perhaps a better life.'[43] Mainstream Mauritian literature is divided into the spheres of *Francophonie* and *Creolie*, and has generated much theorizing. The writer Camille de Rauville (1910–86) coined the term *Indo-océanisme*, in which he saw a distinct complex of human experiences. His younger compatriot, Khal Torabully (b. 1956), has invented the concept of transcultural 'coolitude'.

French, being the language of most educated Mauritians, long served as the preferred vehicle for poetic and fictional expression. Authors are legion, and one or two have entered the French canon. Robert Edward Hart (1891–1954), for example, whose home at Souillac has been turned into an intimate literary museum, was widely praised for the elegance and emotional precision of his pre-war verse. He has to be labelled a local patriot:

> *Terre des Morts et des Vivants*
>
> *Rien n'est doux à mon Coeur autant que cette terre*
> *Où j'ai vécu. Rien n'est plus haut que le ciel. Rien*
> *N'est plus sûr que la Mer Indienne où mes pères*
> *Ont arrêté l'élan de leur nef. Tout est bien*
> *Puisque, triste comme Jason en deuil des Toisons d'Or,*
> *J'ai retrouvé du moins le coeur de la patrie*
> *Où repose mon Coeur dont la fièvre s'endort*
> *Au rythme familier des choses tant chéries.*
> *Ici je puis encore évoquer mon enfance,*
> *Parmi le paysage où sommeillent mes morts,*
> *Et, penché sur le sol, écouter clairs et forts*
> *Les conseils maternels de mon Île de France.*
> *Ici je suis moi-même et tel que je me veux.*
> *Farouche et tendre, libre et doux, triste et joyeux*
> *Terroir qui m'a nourri, je te donne un poète,*
> *Et si je te dois mieux pour te payer ma dette*
> *Voici tout mon amour, mon bel amour d'hier:*
> *Un peu de cendre, hélas, dans le creux de ma main.*
> *Je mêle cette cendre à ton sol riche et fier.*
> *Puisse-t-elle fleurir une rose demain.*[44]

(Nothing is so gentle to my Heart as this land
From which I came. Nothing is so high as this sky. Nothing
Is more certain than the Indian Sea where my forefathers
Halted the surge of their prow. All is well
Since, sad like Jason mourning the Golden Fleeces,
I at least discovered the heart of a homeland
Where my own Heart can rest, and its fever subside
To the familiar rhythm of things so deeply loved.
Here, I can still evoke my childhood
Amidst the landscape where my ancestors sleep,

And where, fixed to the soil, I listen loud and clear
To the maternal counsels of my Isle of France.
Here I can be myself, just as I wish to be.
Oh land which nourished me – ferocious and gentle,
    wild and mild, sad and joyful – I give you a poet.
And, if I should do better to repay my debt
Here is all my love, my beautiful love from yesterday;
It is, alas, a mere snip of ashes in the hollow of my hand.
I mix this ash with your soil, so rich and proud.
May it flourish tomorrow as a rose.)

For the foreigner from Europe, the *Creolie* is less accessible. Its roots lie
in the oral traditions of slave-bound illiterates, and it has surfaced into
public view only recently. But it can be readily sampled like everything
else in the age of the internet: in other words: *kapav ekoute onnlainn.*
One of its chief advocates, once a Maoist, a student in Edinburgh, and a
militant politician, is Dev Virahsawmy (b. 1942), who is consciously
engaged in nation-building through language and literature. His view of
the homeland denies the role of Franco-Mauritians, whom he has classed
as 'Eurocreoles', but says much about contemporary developments:

> Mo pei li pa zis enn tapi karo kann
> Zis kristal fangourin ek parfin tamarin;
> Li pas zis enn choue pu sef roulman ravann
> Zis kadans saurian bann transink kas lerin.

Readers must wrestle with these lines as best they can.

In many ways, the most deeply rooted and thrilling branch of Mauritian
culture is *sega*, a unique combination of song and dance that developed
in the era of slavery, and a form of expression that was frowned upon by
the pre-independence authorities. The 'soul songs' are sung in creole.
The instruments used – the *bobre* (a stringed bow with a wooden reson-
ator), the *ravanna* (a tightly stretched goatskin drum), the *maravanne* (a
long wooden rattle), and the humble triangle – originated in Africa. The
beat is heavy and addictive. And the dancing, whose origins lie in pagan
ritual and magic, is both erotic and trancogenic. Among its many practitioners two names stand out. One, Ti Frère, was the *nom de guerre* of
Jean Alphonse Ravaton (1900–1992), the undisputed leader of the contemporary revival. In 1964, at a music festival held symbolically at Le
Morne, he was crowned 'King of Sega'. The other, Kaya, was the stage

name of Joseph Reginald Topize (1960–99). Kaya's lasting claim to fame, under the influence of Bob Marley, was to have married traditional *sega* with Jamaican *reggae*, thereby launching the new genre of *seggae*. In politics, he is remembered for the violent rioting that was provoked in February 1999 by his unexplained death in police custody. Together with others, he had been arrested during a police raid on illegal drug use, and was about to be released on bail. But on the morning of Sunday 21 February, through causes unknown, he was found dead in his cell, and Port-Louis erupted. His fate was strangely redolent of the dark legacy of oppression that *sega* was invented to soothe.

Yet the dance goes on, much as reported in the late eighteenth century by early French observers, who marvelled at the extraordinary vitality of the performances:

> The dancers take short lateral steps accompanied by a shaking of the hips. They dance in couples, the man facing the woman and the woman facing the man. Sometimes he turns around her, or moves off seeming to have lost her, before they come close again, brushing against each other but never touching. Sometimes another man moves between them; this is called 'cutting'. The woman then dances with him until it is her turn 'to be cut'. The couple periodically crouch down in front of each other with a constant 'shimmy of the pelvis' ... And they lean over each other, taking it in turn to dip over backwards until they touch the ground, only to come back up and lean over each other again. This step, which is called '*en bas en bas*' or '*ter a ter*', symbolises the sexual act: an act sublimated and transcended since the bodies never actually touch. Musicians and dancers constantly communicate. The intense excitement is heightened by the rhythm, by onomatopoeia [of the words], and by the short, snappy interjections [of the audience]: *alalaila! Mo vini! Bouze to le reins!* and *en bas en bas* ...[45]

Amen, Amen. *Bouze to le reins!*

Finally, food. 'Mauritius has many cuisines,' explained Nizam Peroo, a leading Mauritian chef. 'It's the only place in the world where Indian, Chinese and French cuisines exist side by side.'

He was acting as a guide to his visiting English counterpart, Henry Dimbleby, who both owns a chain of restaurants and writes a gastronomic press column. Nizam is a fifth-generation descendant of Indian plantation workers, and is proud of the heritage. He started by taking his visitors in the early morning to the Central Food Market in Port-Louis:

Stalls heave with . . . courgettes, garlic, and the small tomatoes known as *pommes d'amour*. Tamarind and fresh turmeric nestle alongside fresh fenugreek and curry leaves. Bouquet garni of pumpkin, carrot, cabbage, celery and turnip tied in a string are sold as the basis of broth. Specialist stalls congregate at the southern end . . . One sells *ticheviatta*: pungent dried fresh-water shrimps that are blended with chillies and garlic to create *mazaravou* paste, served as a condiment with rice. Another deals only in chillies; the island has eight types . . . [each] with a Creole name to describe its intensity, from the small green *petard* or 'firecracker' to the seriously explosive *roquette* . . .

The lesson continues as they stroll down Corderie Street to the Port Area and the Waterfront:

Mauritians have many cuisines, but at the same time only one . . . You might be served hot curries from South India or mild ones from the North, Chinese dim sum, a French *boeuf bourguignon*, and a spicy creole dish, all under one roof. If you are lucky enough to be invited to a traditional family Sunday lunch, to which every family member brings their own dish, you could be served all of them at the same meal.

As Henry told me later, he was in luck. He and his party had been invited for lunch to the beachside villa of a local MP. They were hoping to sample some of the delicacies that Nizam described: *Achard* (pickled vegetable salad), *Octopus Vindaloo*, and *Dholl Pourri* (lentil pancakes), or perhaps a curry made from unusual meats, such as *Carri Sauve-Souris* (bat curry) or *Carri Tangue* (curried Mauritian hedgehog served with rice):

Twenty of the family have turned up for lunch . . . and the full range of Mauritian food is on display. The mother-in-law [of the hostess], who has cooked a fine pickle from fat Mauritian olives, talks about the island prior to its independence in 1968 . . . 'How does the old Mauritius compare with the new?' [Henry] asks. 'I love them both,' she says, 'I love them both just the same.'[46]

Chatting to a Mauritian colleague about Henry's upbeat comments, I met a sceptical response. The key phrase in Nizam's quote is supposedly 'side by side'; one cannot assume that the fusion of the three cuisines is complete. Generally speaking, I was told, the Chinese don't like curries, and the Indians steer clear of Chinese dishes, for superstitious fear of

eating dog meat. And no self-respecting Hindu would dream of touching *boeuf bourguignon.*

Soon it was time to leave, to say 'Bye' and 'Orewar', and to remember
the words often attributed to Mark Twain. 'God created Mauritius first,
and Heaven second', he may or may not have said during his visit in 1896,
'so that Heaven was copied from Mauritius.' Literary experts hold this to
be a vulgar misquote. If it is, it is probably more inspiring than whatever
Twain did actually say. Mean-spirited pedantry would only sour the
memory of this island of heavenly colours and intense *métissage.*

Air Mauritius flies to Perth in Western Australia twice a week. MK
440 takes off on Tuesdays and Thursdays at 22.10, landing at 9.10 a.m.
five time zones ahead, and returning next day as MK 441. Unlike Abel
Tasman, the pilot knows exactly where he is going, and guides his vessel at more than one hundred times Tasman's speed.

When I flew over that part of the ocean, however, the world was
agog at the fate of another flight, Malaysian Airlines MH370. Scheduled to fly from Kuala Lumpur to Beijing on 8 March 2014, MH370 had
taken off shortly after midnight, heading north-north-east into the
night sky. It was carrying 239 people, including a crew of twelve. Its
captain, Zaharie Ahmad Shah, was one of Malaysia's most experienced
pilots, with over 18,000 hours of flying time in his log. The co-pilot,
Fariq Abdul Hamid, with nearly 3,000 hours, was also an experienced
pilot. Both, in terms of good health and competence, were beyond
reproach. One hour after take-off, the aircraft had reached its cruising
altitude of 11,000 metres and had crossed the coast into the Gulf of
Thailand. As it left Malaysian airspace, the cabin lights would have
been dimmed, and the passengers, mostly Chinese, would have been
dozing off, wrapped in their blankets. A pilot's voice from the cockpit
sent a routine farewell message to ground controllers: 'Goodnight.
Malaysian Three-Seven-Zero.' The voice was never heard again.

Then, in circumstances never ascertained, the plane's transponder
was turned off by hand in the cockpit, severing the main channel of
communication. At the same time, the on-board computer was accessed
to make a radical change in the plane's flightpath and to enter a new
waypoint; this manoeuvre could only have been made by someone,
whether on board or not, who had received specialist technical training. The huge Boeing 777-300ER, weighing some 260 tons, would
have entered a turning circle, its 200-foot wings angled between sea
and heaven as it headed back towards the Malaysian coast.

For a time, public reports misleadingly referred to the area where this manoeuvre took place as the 'disappearance point'. But, as was later admitted, the plane continued to be tracked by Malaysian military radar, which watched as it recrossed the peninsula, hugging the Thai frontier before turning north up the Malacca Strait. Some reports suggested that it was flying erratically, first very high, then very low, and that the plane's automated Satellite Data Unit (SDU) had attempted unsuccessfully to make a so-called electronic 'handshake'. Nonetheless, another automated on-board system called ACARS, which emits periodic bursts of non-locational data, having stopped for a time, later restarted. Most strangely, no distress call was received, and no fighter-interceptors were scrambled; the Malaysian military apparently decided that the wayward flight was not 'hostile'.

MH370 did not actually disappear, therefore, until it passed beyond radar range sometime in the early hours. Its last known position was 100 kilometres north of the Aceh coast of Sumatra and 1,000 kilometres east of Sri Lanka, heading west-north-west towards the Andaman Sea. At that juncture the Boeing 777 would still have had fuel for five to six hours' flying time, and this was where the ACARS transmissions restarted. Those transmissions would enable satellite technicians to calculate an arc of the flight's conjectured endpoints, stretching from Western Australia to Kazakhstan. The Malaysian government posted the plane as missing at 7.40 a.m., one hour after its original estimated arrival time at Beijing.[47]

For the first few days, rescue efforts were concentrated on the zone between Malaysia and Vietnam, in an area that some officials within Malaysian government agencies – if not necessarily government ministers – must have known to be pointless. They then moved to the Malacca Strait and the Andaman Sea, where islanders had reported seeing a large plane in distress. But once again no progress was made. There were no confirmed sightings, no wreckage, no oil slick, no message from potential kidnappers, terrorists, or suicide-bombers. The phrase 'total mystery' soon surfaced, together with vociferous denunciations of the Malaysian government's handling of information. A large group of friends and relatives of Chinese passengers raised money for an independent search fund, believing that the authorities were deliberately withholding what they knew.

In the second week after the disappearance, conspiracy theories began to multiply. MH370 had landed safely on one of India's Andaman Islands, and had been hidden. Or it had crossed the Himalayas, and had been spirited into western China by Uigur rebels. Or it had been kidnapped by Mossad. Or it had been 'stolen' by Russian special forces and flown to Kazakhstan. Or it had been taken over by CIA agents, and flown to the American air force base on Diego Garcia. (This last hypothesis was perhaps prompted by the plane's westerly course at the time of its disappearance.)

Speculation also arose following suggestions that gold bullion had been stored in the plane's hold, that the Chinese passengers included a group of advanced avionic specialists, and that two Iranians aboard possessed false passports. Friends and families reported that the mobile phones of their missing loved ones continued to emit ringing tones. BBC News posted a website listing these theories. The most intriguing contended that a transponderless aircraft could be positioned in the radar shadow of another passing plane and thereby fly undetected through the most heavily monitored airspace. And sure enough, a Singapore Airlines flight bound for Barcelona, SIA68 – another Boeing 777 – had overflown the revised 'disappearance zone' at exactly the right time.[48]

In the third week, information flooded in from satellite sources. The Chinese released images of presumed debris floating in the southern Indian Ocean, 2,500 kilometres to the south-west of Perth, Western Australia; the largest chunk was said to be a wing-shaped object 23 metres in length. A British commercial firm called Inmarsat, which produces satellite phone networks and which claimed to have read and analysed MH370's ACARS signals, confirmed a preliminary flight pattern that terminated in the same general area. The prime minister of Malaysia announced with trembling voice that the fateful flight had 'ended in the southern Indian Ocean'. The focus of the search shifted again, and the RAAF base at Pearce, Western Australia, hosted an international armada of search planes and search ships. But nothing except 'ocean rubbish' was recovered.

In the fourth week, the search shifted to a new sector of the ocean and the Chinese announced that one of their vessels had detected an underwater 'ping' that was compatible with the emissions of aviational flight recorders or 'black boxes'. The US 7th Fleet arrived with sensitive oceanic sonar microphones that can be towed along the seabed. HMS *Echo* steamed in carrying deep-sea salvage equipment. The Australians prepared to launch a mini-sub whose cameras can take pictures up to 4,500 metres beneath the surface. (The *Titanic* lies at 3,800 metres.) The Australian prime minister, Tony Abbott, opined that he was 'very confident' that the crucial breakthrough was imminent.

By now, the battery life of the MH370's black boxes was sure to be fading, and, though four separate 'acoustic incidents' were logged, none of them had led to a significant find. Time was running out, as oceanologists explained the staggering scale of operations. As one of them put it: 'We are looking for a needle in a haystack, and so far we haven't yet found the haystack.' Another one commented that the surface of the moon is much better mapped than the floor of the Indian Ocean. The reduced search area was roughly the size of Poland or New Mexico, and the available search instruments were only working at a snail's pace. One range of underwater mountains called Broken Ridge is not particularly precipitous, but the so-called Diamantina Deep, which lies at the foot of a huge escarpment, descends to 25,000 feet and more. Mont Blanc would fit inside it comfortably, and it was entirely possible that the wreckage was snagged on something as vast as an underwater Eiger or had been pulverized at the foot of a pitch-black sub-oceanic Grand Canyon. At 20,000 feet below, the water pressure of 8,900 pounds per square inch (approximately 4.5 tons for every square inch) renders work impossible for everything except the most sophisticated equipment.

My own brief view of the search area, from 12,176 feet, coincided with the day when MH370's black boxes were officially judged inoperable. I shielded my eyes against the sun's glare, peering downwards in the hope of glimpsing something other than clouds and rollers. There was absolutely nothing to be seen. The captain was making some soporific announcement; the stewardesses were walking the aisle handing out plastic cups of water; and most of the passengers, having closed the blinds, were dozing off, oblivious to the outside world. I had plenty of time to review the evidence in my head, such as I knew it, and concluded that the continuing search off the coast of Western Australia was driven largely by the lack of plausible alternatives. I remained, and remain, dubious about the assumption that the plane had crashed into that sector of the ocean. My bones told me that it must be somewhere else. I bet myself there and then that MH370's fate would not be resolved before the present book is published.

# 8

# Tassie

*The Down Under of Down Under*

By sending Abel Tasman in search of the 'Southland', the lords of the Dutch East India Company (VOC) were investigating a category of knowledge that the great epistemologist Donald Rumsfeld would have classified as 'a known unknown'. They were aware that they didn't know exactly where the Southland lay, or how big it was, but they knew that something was waiting to be found. Their confidence was based on two premises, one sound and the other false. The false premise was the existence of a land called Beach or Beoach, which earlier cartographers, such as Abraham Ortelius in 1570, had marked on maps of South-East Asia and which derived from a misreading of Marco Polo's *Travels*. (Tasman's orders mentioned Beoach as a suitable destination to be explored.) The sound premise was based on the verified existence of various stretches of coastland, far from Java, which had been seen and recorded by a string of Tasman's Dutch predecessors, notably Thijsz, van Colster, Hartog, and Janszoon. All these sailors belong collectively to the 'discoverers' of Australia.[1]

In 1627 Frans Thijsz (François Thijssen (d. 1638?)) had been sailing from the Cape of Good Hope to Batavia in the wonderfully named ship *'t Gulden Zeepaerdt (The Golden Seahorse)*. Blown far off course, he ran into an unexpected landmass entirely by chance. He then not only set foot on but carefully charted over 1,500 kilometres of a south-facing shoreline, naming it after a VOC colleague, Pieter Nuyts. But his achievements are largely forgotten. Few people have heard of Nuytsland, which now lies on the arid shore of South Australia, or of the nearby Nuyts Archipelago. But Jonathan Swift took note a century later: in *Gulliver's Travels* (1726–35), Nuytsland is where he imagined the land of Lilliput to lie.

In 1622 a Dutch ship named *Leeuwin (Lioness)* sighted land at the Southland's most south-westerly extremity, and charted a few miles of the surrounding coast. Little else is known about the voyage. But the name of Cape Leeuwin began appearing on Dutch maps before the end of the decade.

In 1623 another Dutch sea captain, Willem van Colster, had sailed south from the East Indies in his ship *Arnhem*, pursuing similar objectives to Tasman's. The VOC had recently established itself on Sulawesi Island, beyond Java, and had learned that traders from Makassar, like the Javanese fishermen further west, were accustomed to cross the southern sea – in their case in search of sea cucumbers, a valuable aphrodisiac. Losing contact with his sister ship, the *Pera*, van Colster followed the route of the Makassarian traders, and successfully found a north-facing coastline, which he named Arnhem Land. He believed he had reached a peninsula of Papua. In fact he was at the extremity of northern Australia.

Captain Dirk Hartog (1580–1621) of Amsterdam, diverted by westerly gales in the Indian Ocean, **had** steered his ship *Eendracht* (*Unity*) into the western coast of the Southland as far back as 1616. Going

ashore at what is now 'Shark Bay', the landing party nailed an inscribed pewter plate to a post and placed it on top of a cliff, hoping that it might be found by subsequent wanderers. The Hartog Plate was indeed found after some sixty years, and now resides in the Rijksmuseum. It reads:

*1616 den 25s Octoberis hier aengecomen het schip de EENDRACHT van Amsterdam de Opperkoopman Gillis Mibais van Luick. Schipper Dirck Hatichs van Amsterdam de 27 dito te seil geghn na Bantum, de Onderkopman Jan Stins, de Opperstivierman Pietr Dooke van Bill*

(Here, on the 25th of October in the year 1616, came the ship from Amsterdam called 'Eendracht': the first merchant [was] Gilles Mibais of Luyck. Skipper Dirk Hartog of Amsterdam set sail for Bantam on the 27th of the same month, the under-merchant [being] Jan Stoyn, and the chief steersman, Pieter Dockes of Bill.[2]

Yet even Hartog was not the first European to sight the elusive *Terra Australis*. Precedence probably goes to Willem Janszoon (*c.* 1570–1630), an old hand of the East Indies trade, who had left the Netherlands before the creation of the VOC and rose to serve as an admiral and colonial governor. On his third voyage, from 1603 to 1606, Janszoon skippered the pinnace *Duyfken* (*Little Dove*), which was sent to search for commercial opportunities among the many islands east of Java. Having crossed the Arafura Sea, he made landfall on 26 February 1606 at a river mouth on the west-facing coast of a long peninsula. (Like van Colster, he thought he was on Papua.) He mapped the coastline between 5 and 14 degrees south, founded a settlement, and named the territory *Nieuw Zeeland* (New Zealand). Losing ten of his men in a skirmish with natives, Janszoon then decided to beat a retreat. To the headland whence he started his return trip, he gave the name of *Kap Keerweer* ('Cape Turnabout').

At the time, Janszoon's achievement must have felt like failure. The territory he discovered had no commercial value. His name for it was not officially accepted and was stored away for future use. All he seemed to have done was to have made a minor addition to the maps of his day. Fortunately, Janszoon's log survived long enough for copies to be made. Janszoon's dismay was patent:

Vast regions were for the most part uncultivated, and certain parts inhabited by savage, cruel black barbarians, who slew some of our sailors, so that no information was obtained touching the exact situation of the country and regarding the commodities available and in demand.[3]

The deadly skirmish with the aborigines may have been sparked by his sailors' habit of chasing native women. Remarkably, memories of his short visit to what would become Queensland's Cape York Peninsula survived in the oral tradition of the Wik-Mungan People. The aborigines' recollections of the episode were written down by Australian anthropologists some four hundred years later:

> The Europeans sailed along from overseas and put up a building at Cape Keerweer. They said that they wanted to [build] a city. Well, the Keerweer people said it is alright. They allowed them to sink a well and to [erect] huts. To begin with, relations were good. The Europeans gave them tobacco [which] they kept. [They] gave them flour . . . and soap [which] they threw away. The Keerweer people kept to their own bush tucker.[4]

Such fleeting encounters emphasize the fact that geographic discovery, like most scientific research, is cumulative, not instantaneous.

Before leaving Batavia in August 1642, Abel Tasman would have been briefed on the state of existing knowledge, and would have familiarized himself with the latest charts and atlases. As he cruised eastwards from Mauritius, he would have peered expectantly over the rail of his ships, the *Heemskerk* (*Home Church*) and *Zeehaen* (*Gurnard*), racking his brain to form a coherent picture from many disconnected snippets of information. Tasman would have read reports about Arnhem Land, Cape Keerweer, and Cape Leeuwin, but he had no way of telling whether they were separated by open water or dry land. (As we know, but he didn't, they are connected by 3,000 miles of continuous continental earth.) And what filled the gap between Hartog's Shark Bay and Thijsz's Nuytsland? Tasman would probably have heard rumours about earlier Portuguese expeditions, and he may have pondered an old theory that the Earth's stability could only be explained by the existence of a large southern continent.[5]

When Tasman finally struck a west-facing coastline and named it Van Diemen's Land after the governor of Batavia of the day, he lay by his calculation at 43 degrees, 10 minutes below the equator. (He is now thought to have been at some point near modern Macquarie Harbour.) But he could not have known for sure whether or not he had encountered the continental mainland. Coasting south and east, he then rounded a couple of major promontories before entering the particularly complicated inlet of 'Storm Bay', with its scores of reefs and islands. Regaining the open ocean with difficulty, he headed east again, before turning at the headland of the magnificent peninsula that now bears his name. After weeks of buffeting by gales, he would have basked with delight in the calm waters that lie in the lee of the towering green and brown cliffs, and listened with wonder to the foaming surf that breaks onto the empty, cliff-foot beaches. Searching for a landing, he would first have seen the narrow strand of Eaglehawk Neck, across which one can look back into Storm Bay, and, after ten more miles, a second spit of low-lying land that divides the enclosed bay from the ocean. As he attempted to gain entry to what is now Blackman's Bay, the ship's carpenter dived overboard, swam through the surf, and planted a Dutch flag.

Nowadays, few visitors bother to stop at the tiny fishing pier of Dunalley on Blackman's Bay; their coaches rush past to the better-publicized sights of nearby Port Arthur. But the place is not unmarked. A simple, green-painted wooden board announces: ABEL TASMAN EXPEDITION 1642. And beside the hamlet's cabin-style restaurant a black metal plate, screwed into the concrete of a small monument, carries an outline map of Tasmania and a short inscription:

THIS MONUMENT
WAS ERECTED BY THE GOVERNMENT OF TASMANIA
IN 1942 TO COMMEMORATE THE TERCENTENARY
OF THE DISCOVERY OF THIS ISLAND IN 1642
BY HON. ABEL JANS TASMAN.

SHIPS BOATS COMMANDED BY
PILOT MAJOR VISSCHER
VISITED THIS BAY ON
DECEMBER 3$^{RD}$ 1642.

The Bass Strait, which separates mainland Australia from its offshore island, heaves into view through broken clouds. On the map, it looks like the English Channel, but it's almost ten times as wide, and its fast-running waters are notoriously rough. In ancient times it was all but impassable, ensuring that the future Tasmania was completely cut off for long periods of prehistory. In consequence, both the natural fauna and the native peoples show special peculiarities. The car ferry that runs from Melbourne to Devonport on the north coast of the island takes nine to ten hours, and tourists generally avoid it. But seen from 33,000 feet aboard a Qantas jet, the sea shines a perfect blue, with patches of green. No tell-tale ships' wakes are visible. The empty islands

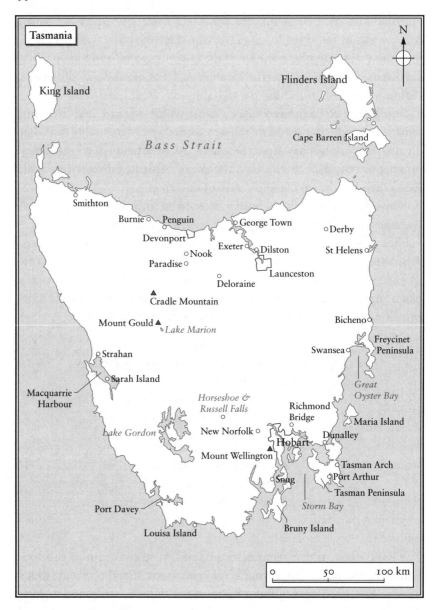

in the Strait – Flinders, King, and Cape Barren – pass by like floating
flotsam. It's Robinson Crusoe country. I could walk all the way around
them without meeting a soul, I think. Then the clouds close in.

Perusing the map before landing, I see that all the island's place
names are unswervingly British. LAUNCESTON is close to EXETER, and
DERBY to ST HELENS and SWANSEA. On the airport road, signposts
point to CAMBRIDGE and GLENORCHY and LINDISFARNE. One road

goes to SANDY BAY and the other to PORT ARTHUR. There are towns called PENGUIN and FLOWERPOT. A cute place called NOOK rivals SNUG, PARADISE, and the hamlet of NOWHERE ELSE. Nothing indicates that Tasmanians call their homeland TASSIE, and the Australian mainland NORTH ISLAND.

For this sector of the journey, my wife has joined me. We don't know what to expect, but Tasmania's reputation precedes it. 'We think of Tasmania as we think of Britain,' an Australian friend has told us: 'very remote, very wet, and full of old-fashioned folks.' But there is more. Australians tell tasteless jokes about 'Taswegians', just as the English do about the Irish, or the French about Belgians, or Americans about Poles. According to the historian Manning Clark, who wrote a six-volume history of Australia, Tasmania combines 'a gaiety in the very air' with the 'dark secrets of men's souls'.[6]

Modern art was not on our minds. A walk along one of those beaches, or a trip up Mount Wellington, were being contemplated. But the rain was lashing down, and our hosts were insistent. Our hostess gave us to understand that MONA, 'The Museum of Old and New Art', was the best thing in town.[7] So we rushed to the hotel to drop off our bags, and on through the rain to Berriedale.

Most people arrive at the museum by ferry. A fantastic complex of contemporary buildings – all glass, steel, and concrete in unusual shapes – rises beside a fine stretch of open water with cloud-topped, wooded hills beyond. 'It's the work of a local man, an on-line poker player,' we're told. 'He made a fortune and has opened his collection to the public.' Entry is free for Tasmanian residents, 20 dollars for non-residents. A woman hands us a set of earphones, and a radio-controlled guide device that looks like an iPhone.

'If you press the red beside an exhibit,' she explains, 'the screen lights up, and you get information about the artist and the concept.'

A middle-aged man with long straggly grey hair walks past.

'That's Mr Walsh – Walshie,' someone says, an exhibit in his own exhibition. 'He's being pursued by the tax man.' Then come the warnings. All the exhibits are housed in deep underground chambers. They are not labelled, nor laid out in any prescribed order. Disorientation is part of the exercise. Ancient artefacts, such as a Greek column or a Ming vase, are placed cheek by jowl next to up-to-date, pseudo-artistic contraptions – to see whether they resonate.

The lift takes us down into the darkness of Level –3. An Egyptian mummy-case, covered in hieroglyphics and surmounted by the face of a deceased physician from the 25th Dynasty, is wreathed in light from a spotlamp. You can have your picture taken with him if you want. Over the balcony wall, your peer into a murky abyss. Illuminated on the quarry wall opposite is a gigantic display of painted panels, perhaps a thousand of them, mounted in wave formation. The guide device announces *The Snake* (1972) by Sidney Nolan. This 'masterwork', which spent forty years in storage, is soon due to be returned whence it came. Nothing here must suggest permanence.

Further on, a wall case displays some magnificent Roman gold coins – Augustan *aurei*. Beside them, one confronts a metal-cased model of the human brain. We peer into the brain through portholes and see a dense network of electrical pathways illuminated by impulses of light. At each junction of the pathways, a small book opens and closes, as a tiny bird flits in and out.

The assault on the senses intensifies. An obsession with death, sex, and putrefaction creeps in. Coils of rope hang from massive meat hooks on a steel rack.

'Slabs of raw meat hung here,' our host tells us, 'until it started to reek.'

Around the corner, a whole wall is covered by a colossal graphic that pushes the enhanced genitals of a female torso right into your face; the vermillion lips are reminiscent of Andy Warhol's portrait of Marilyn Monroe. Raw meat, again. Then there's the 'euthanasia couch', where one fiddles with a computerized panel to simulate suicide. And, plumbing the depths, there's an arty machine that replicates human digestion and produces fake faeces.

'Art in the old sense is finished,' our hostess confides. 'This is all conceptual.'

We grimace as we poke our heads through a doorway into a long library where all the books are pure white and all the pages blank. 'You have to imagine what's in them.' Not good news for an author.

The assault continues relentlessly, until one longs for the lift and an escape to Tasmania's fresh air. The last stop is to press the button on the museum's visitor satisfaction device that offers a choice between 'Love' and 'Hate'. Pressing 'Love', you are shown a very large figure, such as 16,707,234; it's the number of visitors who have shared your satisfaction. If you press 'Hate' you are presented with a chilling announcement: '3 per cent of visitors share your negative feelings.' Visitors who may have preferred to think for themselves are being given a message:

anyone who dares to question the allure of rotting meat or vermillion vaginas officially belongs to a weird and marginal minority.

As soon as one escapes from MONA's publicists, however, opinions are more evenly divided. Online reviewers can say what they like. Some do say 'great and interesting museum' or 'eccentric, humorous and grotesque'. But the views of many can be summed up by 'What a disgrace!'

> 'Came here on many a recommendation. Searched for a deeper meaning, [but] left disgusted and somewhat traumatised ... I'm not a prude, I'd like to think I have an open mind, but this collection explores what the unattended human brain is capable of.'
>
> 'MONA is the result of telling a generation there is no wrong answer.'
>
> 'Go to Mount Wellington, go to Salamanca Place ... Hell, go to Cascade Brewery. But don't bother with MONA.'[8]

One soon sheds the misapprehension, therefore, that MONA is an art gallery: it's a post-modern fairground, a highbrow amusement park, which tries to make you scream like the old Ghost Train did. But it's also a temple of nihilist brainwashing where the mindless multitude can be persuaded to thrill to the concept of a book with blank pages. And it may be Art as Therapy, only Therapy for What? The pranks of a Joseph Beuys, one of the pioneers of performance art, who used to expound his theories about *Gesamtkunstwerk* to a dead hare, are intelligible in the context of a traumatized post-war Germany.[9] (The Ashmolean Museum in Oxford has examples of his work.) But why on earth does he have such a following in beautiful Tasmania? Perhaps 'beautiful Tasmania' has its own traumas, those 'dark secrets' which Manning Clark was hinting at.

That evening, our hosts serve us a plate of kangaroo; it feels like an extension of MONA.

'It's extremely nutritious,' we are informed, 'very low in fat.'

Oh dear! We were back at the childhood table: 'You horrible ungrateful child! There are millions of poor children in the world who are starving.' The chunks of dark-grilled meat sit on their bed of couscous; the green beans and beetroot add splashes of colour. But food is sometimes incredibly subjective. All I see are the darling furry creatures, hopping happily across the meadow.

The morning dawns bright. The rain has gone. A grant cactus spreads its spines across the window and the sun throws a broad sheet of light across the bay. A canoeist paddles across the sun-speckled waves, and yachts keel to the wind. All thoughts of mummies and dead meat dissolve.

The Salamanca Fair in Hobart offers a perfect antidote to the previous day's Chamber of Horrors. It matches the where and when of its surroundings. Stalls display all manner of local arts and crafts – in wood, wool, metal, and stone. Victorian trinkets are everywhere: beefeater mugs, willow-pattern plates, and Wedgwood boxes. Bush hats and folk-style blouses hang alongside landscape prints and amateur watercolours of herbs and flowers. Scottish pipers play Highland laments in competition with a jazz trumpet, a charity choir, and two guitarists. The amplified chords of Cary Lewincamp's seven-string guitar playing 'Salamanca Saturdays' work like a magnet.[10] The crowds stroll past, chatting, laughing, and buying: the antipodean version of Thomas Hardy's Madding Crowd, and Tasmania's positive face.

Tasmania has a human history of forty thousand years or more. The aboriginals who first populated the island remained in contact with those on the mainland until 10,000 years ago when the sea level rose and what is now the Bass Strait became, for practical purposes, uncrossable. For four thousand generations thereafter, they were on their own. The original party of non-indigenous settlers crossed from the mainland in September 1803. They came from the penal colony of Botany Bay in New South Wales, sailing under the command of the twenty-three-year-old Lieutenant John Bowen, RN, in the ship *Lady Nelson* and the whaler *Albion*. They were forty-two persons in all – three officials, eight soldiers, six freemen, and twenty-five convicts in chains; their orders were to found a subsidiary colony to relieve overcrowding. Their unwritten objective, since Britain was at war with France, was to forestall any possible French incursion. As recommended by the explorer George Bass, who had recently proved that Van Diemen's Land was an island,[11] they landed at Risdon Bay on the right bank of the river later christened Derwent. It was a bad choice; the soil was poor and fresh water scarce. For four years John Bowen lived with the convict woman Martha Hayes, who bore him two daughters.

In February 1804 a second party of settlers arrived, commanded by Colonel David Collins. It consisted of fifteen soldiers and forty-two convicts, who set up camp on the opposite bank of the Derwent. They had left Botany Bay at the same time as Bowen, but had spent five months vainly trying to establish a mainland foothold near the mouth of Phillip Bay. They now named their new settlement after Britain's Colonial Secretary, Lord Hobart, and liked the location. Before the year was out they were joined by Lieutenant Bowen's group from across the river. After the birth of Martha Hayes' first baby, the nascent colony's population rose to exactly one hundred. Colonel Collins was appointed governor. His tombstone still stands in Hobart's St David's Park, once the site of the town's first church, beside whose altar the memorial tablet was originally placed:

Sacred

To the Memory of

DAVID COLLINS, Esq.,

LIEUTENANT GOVERNOR OF THIS COLONY

And LT-COLONEL OF THE ROYAL MARINE FORCES.

On the first Establishment of the Colony of

New South Wales, he was employed as Deputy Judge Advocate

And in the year 1803

He was entrusted by His Majesty's Government

With the command of an expedition

Destined to form a settlement at Port Philip

On the South Coast of New Holland

But which was subsequently removed to

Van Diemen's Land.

Under his direction as Lt-Governor

The site of this town was chosen,

And the foundation of the first building

Laid, in 1804.

He died here on the 28th March 1810

Aged 56 years.

European settlement inevitably impinged on the customs and possessions of the native aborigines. Hobart was planted on the summer pastures of the Mouheneenner People, one of the constituent tribes of the Parlevar Nation,* who regularly migrated from the coast to the interior during the winter months. The ancestors of the Parlevar are thought to have drifted southwards from the mainland some 30,000–40,000 years ago, when their future homeland was still connected by a land bridge. From the time when sea levels rose and the land bridge was

---

* *Palawa* – or in English spelling, Parlevar – is the endonym for all Tasmanian aborigines. It is generally described as a 'Nation', and is subdivided into some fifty clans or 'tribes'.

submerged, they were totally cut off from the rest of humanity. They lived frozen in time and in Stone Age isolation; they were not warlike, did not possess ocean-sailing skills, and can never have seen a foreigner before the early European explorers and whalers. (Tasman did not report seeing any natives during his brief stay in 1642, but it is quite probable that he himself was being watched.) What the Europeans called 'Discovery', they regarded as 'Invasion'. Their unenviable fate, as described in the *Encyclopaedia Britannica* (1911), was explained exclusively in racial terms:

> The difficulties of the settlers were increased by the hostility of the blacks. The first collision took place a few days after the landing of Lt. Bowen's expedition, and for this the white settlers were entirely responsible. Hostilities between the races were incessant from 1802 to 1830. An attempt was made in the year 1830 to drive the natives to one corner of the island, but without success. In the following year, Mr. George Robinson induced the remnants of the blacks to leave the mainland and to take refuge, first in South Bruni [Island] and subsequently on Flinders Island, their numbers having then diminished from 5,000 – the original estimate of the aboriginal population – to 203. In 1842, there were only 44, in 1854 they had diminished to 16, and the last pure-blooded Tasmanian died in 1876, aged seventy-six.[12]

As we shall see, this account has since been proved false.

Antipodean distances and spaces are deceptive. Everything is bigger than Europeans think. To English eyes, Australia's second colony looks on the map like a small island, the same size as the Isle of Wight, or perhaps Malta. In reality, at 35,000 square miles, it is equal in size to Ireland or the state of Maine, and so the task facing the first, tiny group of settlers was immense. It took half a century for the principal districts to be colonized. And it was only achieved after suffering two great indignities – 'The Stain' and 'The Stigma'.

Tasmania's leading historian, however, does not open the story with the trials of the settlers, but with the 'utter astonishment' of the aborigines who saw them arrive. The aborigines had no vision of the wider Earth. They could not cross the Bass Strait. And the mainland lay well out of sight:

> They had lived in isolation from the rest of the world, since the time when Bass Strait flooded at least 8,000 years earlier. Some memory of migra-

tion from the distant mainland may have survived as legend, but for over 300 generations Tasmania was their all-embracing world, fellow island-ers the only known inhabitants of the universe, and their ways the time-honoured pattern for the whole of humankind.[13]

Between 1772 and 1803 eleven European expeditions called at 'Van Diemen's Land'; they were the first outsiders that the native population had ever seen. One of them, François Peron, reflected on the natives' mental confusion:

> We are seeing men at a time when all the faculties of their being are magni-fied. Our ships, the noise of our guns and their terrible effect, the colour of our skin, our clothing, our form, our gifts, everything we possess, every-thing that surrounds us, our gait, our actions, all are such marvels to them.[14]

Later, when some aborigines had learned English, they would recall those first sightings. One, known as Black Tom, who, as a boy, had watched the first European ship sail into Maria Island, told how 'his clan members were all frightened, and ran away from the coast. The ship looked like a small island, but they could not tell what it was ... [They] could not conceive how the white man came here.'[15] Modern writers try to capture that moment:

> The relatives with guns
> Have risen from the sea
> rinsed by death and stripped of skin.
> They stagger back along the valleys
> bent with their new possessions.
> The relatives with spears who greet them
> smile strangely at their pale forgetting.[16]

One historian has emphasized the natives' isolation among themselves. The basic social unit was the family or 'hearth-group', and several such families would consort with each other to form a band of some seventy or eighty persons who possessed a collective name and who lived, hunted, and fought together. Larger, looser groupings made up of allied bands have often been classed, somewhat dubiously, as 'tribes'. Each had their own territory, their own habitat – on coast, mountain, or river – their own customs, their own methods of food-gathering, and usually their own lan-guage. Their means of communication with other tribes was thus limited:

> Group A (whether called 'tribe' or not) could understand or come to grips
> with the language of its neighbouring Group B, members of which could

in turn communicate in a way with Group C – but Group A could not generally understand Group C. The only time that Groups A and C came into contact appears to have been on those occasions when ochre was being mined, or perhaps when gathering eggs . . .[17]

Being nomads, the aborigines shunned permanent dwellings, typically sleeping and cooking under a palm-leaf roof or behind a plaited wind-break. They ate half-cooked food, grilled over a campfire, and drank only water from shells. They moved around from day to day, carrying spears and firesticks, and frequently setting the bush alight to flush out animals and encourage the growth of succulent shoots. In winter they migrated to favourite coastland sites, and in summer to the uplands. They had no knowledge of metals, fashioning all they needed from wood, bone, stone, and plant materials:

> In appearance, the Aboriginal people were dark-skinned, with variations from very black to 'red'. Their stature was reported . . . to be 'average' in late 18th Century terms . . . They had few if any clothes. Women wore kangaroo skins arranged on the upper body and used for carrying children and a few pieces of equipment. The men as a rule went quite naked, though both sexes wore strips of skin and necklaces of shell. People over the age of puberty were frequently marked with cicatrices; the skin was cut then raised in patterned lines by inserting charcoal . . .
>
> The most striking feature of the Aborigines was their scalp hair, which was distinctively tight-curled. It was frequently chopped off short by the women, some of whom had tonsured hairstyles. Men tended to plaster their scalp hair with a mixture of red ochre and grease, so that it res-embled a mop (or as one observer noted wryly, the wig of a fashionable French lady of quality). Women also adorned themselves with charcoal and ochre, to the extent of using ochre on their pubic hair. Babies were sometimes marked with ochre on forehead and cheeks.[18]

The customary division of labour between the sexes in aboriginal soci-ety could have far-reaching consequences. Since time immemorial, aboriginal boys were taught to hunt, while aboriginal girls learned the arts of collecting seafood, and of diving for crabs, eels, and mussels off the seashore. As a result, aboriginal women were strong swimmers, whereas their menfolk were not. The first Europeans noticed it. If a band or tribe had to cross a river, the men would be ferried across on rafts, propelled by female swimmers. When sealers and whalers arrived, therefore, looking for assistance with tasks on boats or on the beach, they found that native women were more useful than the men. The practice soon developed whereby a tribe would lease out women as temporary labourers (and sexual partners) and would be paid in dogs – a previously unknown and especially desirable commodity.

For the British pioneers, 1807 was the hardest year. The anticipated supply ships did not arrive; fighting had broken out with the natives, and starvation loomed. Before that several 'firsts' had been recorded: the first mutiny by soldiers (1804); the first killing of aborigines (1804); the first divine service (1804); the first satellite settlement at George Town in the north (1804); the first Government House, a wooden cabin (1805); the first whaling station, at Ralph's Bay (1805); the first land grant, made to the Anglican chaplain, Reverend Robert Knopwood (1805); and the first island crossing on foot (1807), achieved in nine days by Lieutenant Thomas Laycock. The name of Tasmania, rather than Van Diemen's Land, first appeared on an atlas published in London in 1808.

The extraordinary lives, and deaths, of some of those earliest pioneers are recorded on the four sides of a single family tomb in St David's Park, Hobart:

SACRED

To the Memory of

ELIZABETH KELLY, wife of JAMES KELLY

PILOT OF THIS PORT

DEPARTED THIS LIFE, 2<sup>nd</sup> of July 1831, aged 33 years,

11 months, & 15 days

(also of their sons and daughters)

- ELIZABETH JANE KELLY, died 30<sup>th</sup> October 1828,

aged 14 years & 6 months

- HARRIET KELLY, died 9 June 1817, aged 2 days

- ELIZA KELLY, died 17<sup>th</sup> February 1823, aged 1 month & 11 days

- GEORGE KELLY, died 3<sup>rd</sup> February 1828, aged 5 months & 15 days

- JOHN KELLY, DIED 6<sup>TH</sup> JANUARY 1831, aged 1 day

In Memory of Thomas

THIRD SON OF JAMES AND ELIZABETH KELLY,

WHO WAS DROWNED BY THE UPSETTING OF A BOAT

IN THE RIVER DERWENT,

ON THE 18<sup>TH</sup> DAY OF OCTOBER 1842

AGED 16 YEARS AND 8 MONTHS

IN MEMORY OF JAMES BRUNI

ELDEST SON OF JAMES AND ELIZABETH KELLY

WHO WAS KILLED BY A BLOW FROM A WHALE,

ON 16<sup>TH</sup> AUGUST 1841

WHILE ON A WHALING VOYAGE FROM THIS PORT

ON BOARD THE BARQUE 'WILLIAM THE FOURTH',

CAPTAIN S. LINDSAY,

AGED 21 YEARS.

TO THE MEMORY OF JAMES KELLY

WHO DEPARTED THIS LIFE ON THE 20<sup>TH</sup> DAY OF APRIL 1859

In the 66<sup>th</sup> year of his age.

HE WAS BORN IN THE TOWN OF PARAMATTA, NEW SOUTH WALES,

On the 24<sup>th</sup> day of December 1791,

AND WHO HAS RESIDED THE PRINCIPAL PART OF HIS LIFE

IN VAN DIEMENS LAND,

NOW CALLED TASMANIA.

By this reckoning, James Kelly, one of the oldest Australian-born residents, outlived his wife and all his children, having lost two grown sons in accidents at sea, two sons and two daughters in infancy, and one teenage daughter. They belonged to a generation that believed implicitly in God's will.

Yet once the most perilous years were behind them, the surviving colonists pressed on. Large numbers of free settlers were brought in and given standard plots of 640 acres to clear and cultivate, and an allocation of convicts to tackle the back-breaking work. (Since the convict-prisoners were known as 'legitimates' – to distinguish them from runaways – the free settlers were given the odd title of 'illegitimates'.) New roads were cut through the forests. New towns and villages were founded. Launceston, the second city, sprang up in 1806. New Norfolk, 30 miles north-west of Hobart, was planted in 1808 by a group of 554 ex-convicts transferred from the lonely outpost of Norfolk Island, off New South Wales, which had been declared unviable. Many of these hardy farming folk were 'First Fleeters', who had sailed to Australia twenty years earlier and had already mastered their pioneering skills. In New Norfolk one can see the tombstone of Betty King (1767–1856), which reads 'the first white woman to set foot in Australia'; also Tasmania's oldest stone-built church, St Matthew's (1810), and Australia's oldest hotel, the Bush Inn (1814).

Fresh deliveries of convicts constantly swelled the labour pool. From

1817, transport ships arrived directly from Britain or Ireland, as Botany Bay wound down. Van Diemen's Land had been formally established by the British in the same decade that Ireland was joined to the United Kingdom, and Irish men and women formed an increasing proportion of the wretched cargoes of the transport ships. It is no accident that the emotions summoned up by early Van Diemen's Land have been best preserved in melancholy Irish ballads:

> Come all ye gallant poachers
> That ramble void of care,
> That walk you out on a moonlit night
> With your dog, your gun and snare.
> The harmless hare and pheasant
> You have at your command,
> Not thinking of your last career
> Upon Van Diemen's Land.
>
> The very day we landed
> Upon that fateful shore
> The planters came around us
> Some forty score or more.
> They yanked us off like horses
> And sold us out of hand
> And yoked us to the plough, brave boys,
> Upon Van Diemen's Land.
>
> God bless our wives and daughters
> Likewise that happy shore,
> That isle of sweet contentment
> That we shall see no more.
> As for the wretched females,
> We seldom take their hand,
> There are fourteen men to every girl
> Upon Van Diemen's Land.[19]

That last verse hints at where 'the dark secrets' may be hidden.

From 1807 to 1853 the transportation of convicts from Britain continued unabated. Up to two thousand were landed annually until the total passed 75,000. And the penal facilities expanded accordingly. In the early days, recalcitrants could be sentenced to fifty or a hundred lashes, or to 'water-boarding' in coffin-like 'dunking boxes', and in extreme cases to execution. In 1823 a remote punishment camp was opened on Sarah Island off the far west coast, and in 1830 the notorious Port Arthur prison was built on the Tasman Peninsula. These two hellholes had no equal in the whole of the British Empire. They were visited in the early 1830s by William Ullathorne, the vicar-general of New South Wales, who was outraged by what he saw:

> Fifty thousand souls are festering in bondage [in the British antipodes] . . . We have taken a vast portion of God's earth, and have made it a cess-pool; we have taken the oceans . . . which gird the globe and have made them the channels of a sink; we have poured down scum on scum, and dregs upon dregs of the offscourings of mankind, and, as they harden . . . we are building a nation of crime, to be, unless something be speedily done, a curse and a plague, and a by-word to all the people of the earth.[20]

Some 90 per cent of the convicts had been transported for various sorts of theft. George Smith had been convicted for stealing a handkerchief from a four-year-old child, Thomas Morgan for lifting a side of bacon from someone's larder, Eliza Bailey for receiving £2,000 of stolen money, and John Buck for embezzlement amounting to £1,900. John Adcock, a gamekeeper, had been prosecuted by his employer, Lord Stafford, for stealing three peacocks; it was his fifth offence. Other substantial categories included political agitators, especially from Ireland, and soldiers or sailors sentenced for mutiny, desertion, or disobeying orders. Thomas McBrain received a life sentence for absenting himself from duty for just one day. Only 5 per cent of convicts were transported for the most serious crimes such as abduction, arson, murder, rape, or treason; such offenders were usually executed without delay in Britain. Sexual crimes, including bigamy, incest, sodomy, and 'buggery with animals', were treated with special harshness. (Homosexuality remained a crime in Britain until 1967.) When the twenty-three-year-old John Demer was found guilty of 'buggery' in 1843, he received a vicious sentence reflecting the judge's abhorrence:

> To be transported for Life & to be sent to Port Arthur and be kept at hard labour, and not permitted to join any of the gangs & to take his meals separate & to sleep in a separate apartment . . . & and at all times to be kept under the immediate observation of the officers . . .[21]

Most convicts came from the working class or the destitute poor, though a few were ranked as 'ladies' or 'gentlemen'. Roughly one-fifth of the total were females, who were often released after arrival if they consented to marriage. And many were distressingly young. James Lynch, aged nine, was sentenced in 1844 to seven years for stealing toys. The oldest convict on record was eighty-six.[22]

The great majority of convicts, being illiterate, were incapable of writing diaries or memoirs. Henry Savery, a banker's son, was an exception. Sentenced in 1824 to transportation for life for forging a bill, he lived in officer's quarters on the outward voyage, was joined in exile by his wife, and was given work as a government clerk in Hobart. Falling into debt, however, Savery was cast into prison, where he wrote a collection of essays called *The Hermit in Van Diemen's Land* (1829) and a novel entitled *Quintus Servinton* (1831). He complained bitterly that he was shunned by the local gentry.[23]

During the voyage from Britain to Australia, the convicts endured life-threatening conditions and harsh military discipline. Kept under decks for much of the time, they had little exercise and fell easy prey to sickness, disease, and depression. And disasters were common. The ship *George III*, which sailed from England in 1834 with 220 male convicts aboard, lost 12 of its passengers to death from scurvy, with 60 seriously ill. On reaching the coast of Van Diemen's Land, it hit a reef and broke up. Soldiers fired shots from the top of the hatchways to stop the convicts escaping. In all, 133 persons perished.[24]

Convicts who behaved well during the voyage could earn a recommendation from the surgeon-superintendent, and on landing be assigned work on a farm or in domestic service in place of prison. William Booth, 'transported for unnatural crime with a mare', was one such beneficiary; the surgeon reported his conduct to have been 'uniformly good, useful as a Teacher'; he had 'turned to God by Faith in the Gospel'.[25]

The lucky ones, put out to work 'on assignment', had a reasonable chance of a tolerable existence. Some, of course, were treated abysmally, suffering all manner of abuse; minor misdemeanours or impertinences could lead to floggings or to further conviction by the magistrates. But others found a sympathetic master or mistress. A literate Irishman called John Martin, a political prisoner, wrote a valedictory letter in 1854, expressing gratitude:

> The forms of British law and opinion had concurred in pronouncing my comrades and myself 'felons' and 'traitors' . . . Yet I have received hospitable and friendly attentions from almost all the respectable families in whose neighbourhood I have been detained. My acquaintances and friends have been English, Scotch, Welsh and Irish in origin: Protestant

and Catholic by religion. From people of all races, sects, parties and classes . . . I have received kindness, or at least civility . . . I gratefully feel the soothing kindness of very many friends.[26]

Once they were caught up in the penal system, it was no easy matter for convicts to evade it. Since average life expectancy did not exceed forty years, many died in imprisonment. They could apply for a ticket of leave after serving half their sentence, subject to good behaviour and to regular reporting to a police station. They could also apply for a conditional pardon, providing that they never returned to Britain. 'Free Tickets' or absolute pardons were handed out quite generously to prisoners in good odour with the authorities. After that, they could usually find a job as a deckhand on an American whaler, or a cheap passage to New South Wales or New Zealand. Fewer than half, if they didn't die, stayed in Van Diemen's Land. Only a handful ever got back to Britain.

The escape of a convict always made headlines, but one in particular features in the island's annals. Alexander Pearce (1790–1826), transported from Armagh for stealing six pairs of shoes, escaped twice and was twice recaptured. On the first occasion, he boasted of eating his companions, but was not believed. On the second occasion, after the remains of his fellow escapee were found, there could be no doubt. He had killed the other man, he confessed, when they reached a river and his companion could not swim. At the Hobart Assizes of 1826, which sentenced him to hang, Pearce was defiant. 'Human flesh,' he told the magistrates, 'tastes better than beef or pork.'[27]

Three years later, the ship *Cyprus* was hijacked by convicts en route to detention at Macquarie Harbour on the rugged west coast. The hijackers first marooned those who refused to join them, then headed to China, where they posed as shipwrecked British sailors. Arriving back in Britain, they were dismayed to be greeted by one whom they had marooned, John Popjoy, who had built a coracle, flagged down a passing vessel, returned to Hobart, and earned himself a pardon. Popjoy's evidence secured the hijackers' execution at a court martial, except for one named William Swallow, who pleaded coercion, and became a famous ballad hero:

> Poor Tom Brown from Nottingham, Jack Williams and poor Joe,
> Three gallant poacher lads they were, their country that does know,
> And by the laws of the Game Act, that you may understand,
> They were fourteen years transported, unto Van Diemen's Land.

Down Hobart Town we gathered, on the *Cyprus Brig* conveyed.
Our topsails they were hoisted, boys, and our anchor it was weighed.
The wind it blew a nor' nor' west, and on we steered straightway
Till we brought her to an anchorage in a place called Recherche Bay.

Confined inside a dismal hole, those lads devised a plan
To take possession of that brig, or else die every man.
The plan it was agreed on, and we all retired to rest
And early in the morning, boys, we put them to the test.

Up steps bold Jack Muldemon, his comrades three or more,
We soon disarmed the sentry, and left him in his gore.
It's Liberty, Oh Liberty! It's Liberty that we crave.
Deliver up your arms, my boys, or the sea shall be your grave.

We landed first the soldiers, the captain and his crew.
We gave three cheers for Liberty, and bid them soon adieu.
William Swallow he was chosen, our captain for to be,
And we gave three cheers for Liberty, and boldly put to sea.

Play on your golden trumpets, boys, and sound a cheerful note.
The *Cyprus Brig*'s on the ocean, boys, by Justice does she float.[28]

In that same decade two groups of freemen started to plan a different
and legitimate sort of getaway. Both were based in Launceston, and
both aimed to mount an expedition to re-colonize Phillip Bay on the
mainland. One group, headed by John Batman (1801–39), a grazier and
bounty hunter, formed a syndicate, the Phillip Bay Association, which
pooled money for the purchase of land. The other, headed by John
Pascoe Fawkner (1792–1869), bought a couple of schooners and prepared to sail independently. Batman was first away. In May–June
1835 he surveyed the shores of Phillip Bay, identified a spot on the Yarra
River to serve as the site of 'a future village' (which he named 'Batma-
nia'), and signed a treaty with the local Kulin tribe. To his horror, the
governor of New South Wales promptly declared the treaty invalid on
the grounds that His Majesty's Government did not accept the natives'
title to land.

John Fawkner had his opportunity. He had sailed to Australia aged
ten more than thirty years earlier in the company of his convict father,
and had reached Hobart in 1804 in the party under Colonel Collins
that had abandoned the first attempt to found a colony at Port Phillip.
After his father's pardon, Fawkner worked on the land before being

apprenticed to a builder. In 1822 he married an ex-convict, Eliza Cobb, and the young couple loaded up a cart and travelled north to Launceston, where in the years that followed they started a series of thriving businesses. These included a bakery, bookshop, newspaper, timber store, and hotel. Yet Fawkner longed to develop the beautiful enclosed bay where he had briefly tarried as a boy, and he now had the means to do it. His schooner, the *Enterprize*, sailed from George Town with an advance party, and landed inside the as yet unnamed bay on the banks of the Yarra on 15 August 1835. This is now regarded as the founding act of Australia's first capital city. Two months later, the Fawkners joined forces with Batman, and jointly claimed their position as the city's founders. In 1837, the year of Queen Victoria's accession, the settlement was named after Victoria's prime minister, Lord Melbourne, and the bay after Governor Phillips.

Fawkner's success was a sign that his generation had passed beyond the stage of mere survival. The colonists were putting down roots in the land that they believed to be rightfully theirs. When Melbourne was founded, most of Tasmania was already divided into administrative Land districts, hundreds, and parishes, and the colony had gained its administrative authority from New South Wales. In 1825 it received an Executive Council, a fully fledged judicial system, and a Legislature. Boosted no doubt by news of the campaign for parliamentary reform in Britain, agitation began for representative government.

The Land Question, however, was crucial – the sine qua non of all other developments. As one historian has summarized:

> The single most important feature of the British expropriation of Aboriginal land was the belief that Australia in 1788 was a *terra nullius*, a land without owners. This enabled the settlers to convince themselves that they had a legal and moral right to the land because Australia had never actually become the property of the resident Aborigines. The idea had become the accepted legal doctrine in the first generation of settlement, and it has played a central role in the relations between black and white Australians ever since.[29]

Batman's treaty of 1835, though probably designed to swindle the natives, was a vital test case. The governor's ruling, that the aborigines held no title to the land, was repeatedly upheld until in 1889 it received the ultimate sanction of the empire's highest court of appeal, the Privy Council. The key phrase of their decision stated that Australia had been 'practically unoccupied, without settled inhabitants'. The

Councillors did not say that the aborigines had not been present, only that, as nomads, they had no firm claim of ownership.

Today, we would think differently. Nonetheless, one has to accept that many colonists often set out with good intentions. The instructions to Lieutenant-Governor Collins from 1804 ordered him to establish amicable relations with the natives: 'Endeavour by every means in your power to open an intercourse with the natives and to conciliate their goodwill, enjoining all persons under your Government to live in amity and kindness with them . . .'[30] Later, Lieutenant-Governor Arthur posted picture boards showing that the crimes of settlers and natives would be punished alike. At one point he tried to partition the island between colonial and aboriginal areas. And, in retirement, he was to regret the failure to sign a treaty similar to that achieved in New Zealand in 1840 (see Chapter 10). In practice, problems accumulated faster than they were solved: competition for resources, the disparity of numbers, and, above all, the inability to communicate.

The early contacts probably gave rise to an incipient and mutually intelligible form of pidgin speech. European seamen were familiar with so-called 'South Seas Jargon', and the hired women would have picked up enough to perform their tasks.[31] Even so, the linguistic barrier was never effectively surmounted. Examination of George Robinson's journal shows that his claim to speak the aborigines' language was a gross exaggeration. His notes for a sermon in a native hut on Bruny Island, 'preached to the aborigines in their own tongue', reveal a minimal vocabulary but no grasp of structure or syntax:

MOTTI (one) NYRAE (good) PALERDI (God) NOVILLY (bad) RAEGE-WROPPER (devil) PARLEDI (God) MAGGERER (stop) WARREN-GELLY (sky) RAEGEWROPPER (devil) MAGGERER (stop) TOOGENNER (below) UENEE (fire) . . . NOVILLY (bad) PARLEVAR (native) LOGGERNER (dead) TAGGERER (go) TEENY (road) TOOGENNER (below) RAEGEWROPPER (devil), UENEE (fire) MAGGERER (stop) UENEE (fire)[32]

To the congregation, the hell-fire message must have sounded like gibberish.

If some form of creole was emerging in the 1820s, there is no evidence that it progressed beyond the most elementary stages. The words of a dying man on Flinders Island were recorded by a missionary in 1837:

I said to Hector 'you are very sick'. *Hector, yes me plenty menaty* [sick].
You coethee God? Hector *'yes, me coethee plenty* . . . You very sick you
krakabuka by and bye? *Yes, me talbeete werthickathe[?] to God* . . .[33]

Hector had learned the rudiments of Christianity, but couldn't string a
sentence together without using an aboriginal word.

Those early days – the 1820s and 1830s – were the heyday of the bushrangers. Large tracts of virgin forest provided ideal cover for outlaw
gangs, ex-convicts, and army deserters who preyed on isolated
farms. The most celebrated of them was Matthew Brady (1799–1826),
a Mancunian known as the 'Gentleman Bushranger'. When Governor
Arthur issued a poster for his arrest, Brady circulated one for the governor's arrest. Wounded and captured, Brady was hanged in Hobart
during a year that witnessed a hundred other such hangings.

Martin Cash (1808–77) was one of the few bushrangers to die in his
own bed, despite being a double murderer and a multiple escapee. Born
in County Wexford, he arrived in Sydney on a convict ship aged nineteen, and promptly decamped to Van Diemen's Land, where he was
re-arrested for further offences. Incarcerated in Port Arthur, he twice
performed the feat of swimming to freedom, and in 1842–3 his gang
called 'Cash & Co' perpetrated numerous acts of robbery and violence.
He was sentenced to death for shooting one of the constables who
trapped him, but his sentence was commuted and he was eventually
granted conditional discharge. Thereafter, he variously earned a living
as a brothel-keeper in Wellington, New Zealand, and as guardian of
the Royal Botanical Gardens in Hobart.

The violence that prevailed among Europeans spilled over into relations with the aborigines. In a penal colony at the edge of the world,
death was omnipresent, and the raw instinct to survive was never far
below the surface. Unfortunately, historians do not agree on the exact
fate of Van Diemen's Land's natives, least of all on the narrative of
extinction. Some simply call it racial genocide, the source of an 'indelible stain'. Others are inclined to regard imported disease as the
principal culprit. One contrarian has suggested that the whole story is
just a fabrication.[34] But most would lean towards a combination of
massacres and epidemics. What is certain is that few full-blooded aborigines survived by the mid-century from an original population
variously estimated at between 5,000 and 15,000. There were three
phases. From 1804 to 1828 inter-racial relations deteriorated. Between

1828 and 1834 an all-out 'Black War' raged between colonists and aborigines. After 1835, when the largest group of survivors was removed for their safety, the colony put their fate out of sight and out of mind.

The confrontation of nineteenth-century Europeans with Palaeolithic tribesmen was never going to be a conflict between equals. Objectively, one might think, the side armed with muskets, pistols, and cannon had little to fear from neighbours armed only with spears. But disputes arose over the indiscriminate hunting of kangaroos, the destruction of ancient forests, and above all the stealing or raping of native women by sex-starved colonists and convicts. It's not that the natives were outraged by the treatment of their women – they practised theft and rape themselves. But the retaliation, required by custom, led not to low-level intertribal skirmishes but wholesale slaughter. So the frequency of massacres of aborigines grew. Yet the killings alone were not on a scale to cause catastrophic decline. Some other factor was at work. One possibility is that venereal diseases of European origin brought on widespread mortality, debilitation, infertility, and a dramatic drop in the aboriginal birth rate.

Towards the end of the 1820s a number of robberies and murders were perpetrated by aborigines on individuals in outlying farmsteads. In some sense, they were acts of desperation, but were seen by settlers as a declaration of war. The editor of a Hobart newspaper, *The Colonial Times*, called for official action:

> We make no pompous display of Philanthropy. We say this unequivocally: self-defense is the first law of Nature. The Government must remove the natives. If not, they will be hunted down and destroyed.[35]

In his view, the root problem lay in the aborigines' indolent and nomadic way of life:

> Let them be compelled to grow potatoes . . . and to catch seals and fish, and by degrees they will lose their roving disposition, and acquire some slight habits of industry, which is the first step of civilisation.[36]

The settlers' mood was turning ugly. Rightly or wrongly, they convinced themselves that they must kill the aborigines or be killed themselves.

With some delay, after consultation with London, Governor Arthur felt obliged in November 1828 to declare martial law. Armed patrols or 'roving parties' were authorized to defend all settlements, and in 1830 bounty payments of £5 per head (and £2 per child) were offered for every aborigine delivered to the authorities. Confusion ensued when the governor belatedly insisted that the captives were supposed to be alive. The largest operation was called the 'Black Line'. Thousands of soldiers and volunteers would form a human chain, like beaters in a pheasant hunt, and flush out aborigines hiding in the bush. For many months, they moved towards the Tasman Peninsula, where they hoped to corral the whole of the native population. To their dismay, they rounded up hundreds, not thousands.

In 1833 the Wybalena Aboriginal Reserve was created on Flinders Island to receive the native remnants. Officially, only 214 persons had survived to be sent there. What is more, instead of replenishing its num-bers in the Reserve, the community declined still further. Smallpox struck, and within four decades the aboriginal race was formally declared extinct. When Charles Darwin and his ship HMS *Beagle* passed by in February 1836, he expressed a view that would be widely accepted for the next century and more. 'The Aboriginal blacks are all removed,' he wrote, 'and are kept (in reality as prisoners) ... I believe that it was not possible to avoid this cruel step, although without doubt the misconduct of the Whites first led to the Necessity.'[37]

John Batman – the co-founder of Melbourne – was deeply involved in these events. Born in Parramatta, he is often seen as the archetypal, macho frontiersman. He was the bounty hunter who brought in Mat-thew Brady, receiving a large grant of land in reward; and, using 'Sydney Blacks' as trackers, he led one of the more aggressive 'roving parties' during the Black War. He was accompanied everywhere by an aboriginal boy, whose parents he had killed, and whom he took with him to Melbourne.[38]

George Augustus Robinson (1791–1866), known as 'the Conciliator', was Batman's rival and antithesis. He arrived in Hobart from England as a free settler in 1824 and came to prominence during the Black War, when he opposed the policy of coercion and instead advocated voluntary resettlement; he was one of those responsible for establishing the Flin-ders Island reserve. He would fearlessly enter aborigine camps unarmed, in the hope of persuading the natives to abandon their resistance, and boasted of speaking the natives' language. Moving to Melbourne, like Batman and Fawkner, he served in the 1840s as the government's Chief Protector of Aborigines, but in modern times he has, perhaps unfairly, been criticized for abandoning his charges on Flinders and for sending human remains to London's Natural History Museum.[39]

In more recent times, simmering controversy over the fate of Tasmania's natives broke into open conflict as the 'Aboriginal History

Wars'. A book published in 1981, *The Aboriginal Tasmanians*, launched a bold thesis which maintained that their extinction had never actually taken place; the 'myth of extinction' had been invented by colonial racists to justify the settlers' takeover. Lyndall Ryan argued that the dramatic exhibition of the skeleton of 'the Last Aboriginal', in Hobart's Natural History Museum was deliberately staged to divert attention from the fact of other aboriginal survivals. Colonial apologists had used supposedly modern statistical methods to demonstrate that the native population never exceeded 2,000 and hence that it was far down the road to extinction before the colony was founded. This sort of sophistry implied that the aborigines' fate was due to their own weaknesses, and by extension that the settlers could not be held responsible for it.[40]

As often happens in academic quarrels, Professor Ryan – once an assistant of the famous historian Manning Clark – was meanly assaulted by all manner of petty axe-grinders. In the usual style of critics lacking arguments of merit, she was accused of fabricating facts and of fiddling footnotes. But in the long run she overcame her detractors. Her expanded and revised account of the aboriginal story is now the standard.[41] In addition to numerous instances of violence, it contains ground-breaking chapters on episodes such as 'Creole Society, 1808–20' or the community of 'Oyster Cove, 1847–1905', and it triumphantly affirms that 'the extinction was a myth'. 'The account . . . is told with passion and eloquence,' wrote Henry Reynolds, 'and will inform and move anyone with an interest in Australian history.' In his own summary of the subject, Reynolds adds a question mark to the chapter's title – 'An Indelible Stain?'[42]

The 1840s were the last decade when convicts were landed in great numbers. The year 1842 saw the peak of 5,329 arrivals following the end of transportation to New South Wales. In the same year, the first census recorded the island's population to be 57,471. Two bishops came ashore, an Anglican and a Catholic; and a Jewish synagogue opened. The anti-transportation movement thrived. Van Diemen's Land was the empire's last penal colony.

The 1850s are often hailed as the time when the colony came of age. The transportation of convicts ended in 1853, but not before major shipments docked bringing in Irish politicals such as William Smith O'Brien. Medals were struck, and anthems were sung in jubilation:

> Sing, for the hour has come!
> Sing, for our happy home.

Our land is free.
Broken Tasmania's chain,
Wash'd out the hated stain;
Ended the strife and pain!
Blessed Jubilee![43]

Elections were held for non-appointed members of the Legislative Council, and the colony's first president, Thomas Horne, took office in 1856. The colony's name was officially changed to Tasmania that same year, but not before the ultimate status symbol of the era, a postage stamp, was issued. The 1d Blue of 1853, showing a right-facing profile of Queen Victoria's head surrounded by the circular inscription, VAN DIEMEN'S LAND ONE PENNY, is a prize item. The delivery of letters to England took up to eighteen months.

The 1850s were also the time of the Victorian Gold Rush, which shared many of the characteristics of its recent Californian predecessor in the United States. Indeed, it was a Californian prospector, Mr E. Hargraves, who made the first 'find' in February 1851 at Summerhill Creek near Bathurst in Victoria. Later that year further deposits were discovered at Benigo, at Anderson's Creek near Melbourne, and above all at Ballarat. Gold-fever erupted. Crowds of excited 'gold-diggers' arrived from Europe, North America, China, and New Zealand. Two thousand passengers were landing in Melbourne each week, and the population of Victoria doubled in twelve months.

In time Tasmania prospered, and in the last third of the nineteenth century it entered on a path of rapid modern development. In 1871 the railway age came to Tasmania with a line from Launceston to Deloraine. From 1872, an intercontinental undersea cable linked Hobart directly with London, putting an end to immemorial isolation. Valuable minerals such as tin, silver, and copper were discovered, stimulating industrial expansion. Agricultural exports boomed, especially in wool and wheat, and Tasmanian fruit-growers pioneered the long-distance apple trade to Europe. Universal schooling was introduced in 1885, and the streets of Hobart became the first in the southern hemisphere to be lit by electric lamps. Foundations were laid for sport, recreation, and tourism. And in 1895 Hobart hosted the opening conference of the Australian federal movement. In 1900 Tasmanians voted overwhelmingly for Federation. A year later, their elevation as a state of the united Australia marked an important milestone.

Nonetheless, the newborn state harboured deep psychological

complexes. Far from admitting to its past and moving on, Tasmanian society tried to deny all knowledge of its convict roots, as it concealed the truth about the fate of the aborigines by simply not mentioning these topics in public. The 'Great Stigma', more intense in isolated Tasmania than in New South Wales, was born of an awareness that the Mother Country looked down with contempt on its distant Australian colonies, a strong feeling of provincial inferiority, and the pain of prevailing stereotypes, which constantly hinted at criminality, homosexuality, and cannibalism. The figure of Magwitch, who appears in Charles Dickens's hugely popular novel *Great Expectations* (1861), and who was an escaped convict from Australia, did not help perceptions. The earnest Victorian novel *The Broad Arrow* (1859) by Caroline Leakey, which is set in convict-era Tasmania, could be published in London, but not in Hobart.[44] Habits of speech developed whereby family histories were discussed in code. An ex-convict was referred to as an 'Old Hand': 'what sent her here' meant her 'crime'. Social tensions, which originated in the mutual suspicions of convicts and freemen, were perpetuated in class relations. Landowners and prosperous middle-class families pretended that their forebears came exclusively from upright, irreproachable stock, while hinting that the workers were very largely descended from transportees. Everyone, irrespective of their station in life, craved respectability.

Not that a convict past barred people from social and economic advancement. There are myriad examples of 'Old Hands' who made good. Charles Davis (1824–1914), for example, convicted in London of stealing silk handkerchiefs, had been sent to Tasmania aged eighteen. He received his ticket of leave after five years, and set up business in Hobart as a tradesman and tinsmith, launching a firm called 'Davis & Semple', co-owned with fellow ex-con, John Semple. He married an ex-convict woman, Emma Hurst, attended the Congregational Church, and started a family. The business, known for employing ex-prisoners, took off in the 1850s and 1860s when it moved into gasfitting. In due course, it branched out into manufacturing, importing, and retailing in all the main towns. Its headquarters in Hobart formed part of the city's largest department store. In his later years Davis was one of the colony's prominent figures. He had married five times, fathered twelve children, and funded numerous municipal projects, notably the YMCA:

Charles Davis died in 1914, aged 90. Newspapers printed handsome obituaries . . . His funeral was enormous. The hearse, 'beautifully draped in purple and black', was followed by a long procession. At the cemetery, [scores] of sorrowing employees lined the path, and formed a circle . . . as the body was lowered . . . to its final resting place . . . Charles Davis's past was never mentioned, not by himself, and not publicly by his descendants for over a century.[45]

The First World War broke out in the year that Davis died. Tasmania threw itself into the war effort in what one historian has called a 'juggernaut of demented jingoism'. Some 12,000 men served from a total population of 200,000, that is, one man in eight, and 2,500 men, or 21 per cent of servicemen, died in the conflict. A White Feather League pursued 'scabs' and 'shirkers' with the same zeal that had once pursued bushrangers. A witch-hunt was mounted against settlers of the German 'race', and the inhabitants of Bismarck township, near Hobart, were interned. Effigies of the Kaiser were burned. Loyalty Leagues were formed after news arrived of the Easter Rising in Dublin in 1916, and Protestant patriots harassed Catholics. Unemployment soared, especially in the mines, as trade was severed with Germany, Tasmania's best pre-war customer. Pacifism and socialism gained adherents, thereby enraging the patriots further.

In anticipation of the looming centenary of the outbreak of the First World War, a joint academic/parliamentary seminar was held in Parliament House, Hobart, in the spring of 2014.[46] I provided a general introduction on the causes and consequences of the First World War, before half a dozen local historians presented papers on specific aspects. The analyses of wartime Tasmania were particularly insightful.

Henry Reynolds summed up the proceedings brilliantly. Forty men perished in 1914–18 from the tiny, picture-postcard village of Richmond, where he now lives: among them, three brothers from the house that is now his home. Two volunteers from the University of Tasmania won VCs. Great Britain invariably counted on the Dominions to supply loyal manpower, whose readiness to serve was taken for granted. Reynolds first asked a simple question: What were they fighting for? The answer was 'For King and Country'. His second question was more challenging: Which country did they regard as theirs – Britain or Australia?

As the travel brochures present it, Australia's southernmost island is a Garden of Eden. The superlatives trip off the page like the cascades of

Nelson Falls – 'gentle lifestyle', 'pristine wilderness', 'spectacular contrasts', 'heritage in abundance', 'ocean beaches', 'mountain fastness', and 'secret channels' galore. Unlike the mainland, much of Tasmania is green, and luxuriant; unlike Sydney or Melbourne, it is uncrowded and unhurried; and the oceanside climate is mild. The breeze blows; the sun shines; and the mist always clears.

Yet landscape in itself is no more than a lifeless picture unless linked in some way with human thoughts, emotions, and experiences. Exactly in the period when Van Diemen's Land was settled, Romantic poets were discovering the mechanisms whereby the sight of natural beauty can inspire us not merely to gasp in wonder but equally to reflect on deeper things. The appreciation of Nature opens the gates of the intangible but most profound realms that humans can penetrate. The classic texts of the genre are William Wordsworth's *The Prelude* (1805), Lamartine's 'Le Lac' (1820), and Leopardi's 'L'Infinito' (1819). Historians benefit like anyone else. They look at present reality, but they also see the past that no longer exists; and they compare the two to see what has changed:

> E come il vento
> Odo stormir tra queste piante, io quello
> Infinito silenzio a questa voce.
> Vo comparando: e mi sovvien l'eterno,
> E le morte stagioni, e la presente e viva.[47]

> (And when I hear the wind / Stir in these branches, I begin
> Comparing that endless stillness with this noise:
> And the eternal comes to mind,
> And the dead seasons, and the living present.)

In the case of Tasmania, one walks the beaches and climbs the peaks, but one is inspired by so doing to understand the people who went before: the aborigines, the colonists, the bushrangers, the convicts. One compares 'the dead seasons' with 'the living present'. It's a feeling that one encounters in the Highlands of Scotland. One looks at the empty grandeur of the lochs and the glens, then one remembers that not long ago this empty land was inhabited by Gaelic clans who were removed in the Clearances, so that sheep could replace humans. The purple heather and the pity are inseparable.

And there's something else. Anyone with a Romantic disposition is given to thinking that the works of Nature are sublime, while the works of mankind are deficient, deformed, and decadent. This contrast is particularly strong in Tasmania. The idyllic scenery, which flourished in isolation for eons of time, only heightens the sense of human frailty.[48] For anyone with access to a boat, the temptation of doing the rounds of Tasmania's sensational islands is irresistible. Some, like the Bruny Islands in Storm Bay, are favourite destinations for a day trip from Hobart. Mountainous Maria Island, once a convict station, lies off the east coast. Schouten Island is the final apostrophe at the end of the spectacular Freycinet Peninsula. King Island is far out in the Bass Strait. Macquarie Island seems halfway to Antarctica.

Landlubbers, in contrast, will probably explore Tasmania's unrivalled collection of protected National Parks, which occupy no less than 40 per cent of the land surface. There are seventeen to choose from. Rocky Cape Park overlooks the Bass Strait. Narawntapu specializes in wildlife and rare plants. The Tasmanian Wilderness Park includes Cradle Mountain, Lake St Clair, and the Walls of Jerusalem. Ben Lomond Park contains the island's leading ski resorts. And the long, white, crescent strands of Great Oyster Bay are incomparable.

Cradle Mountain is the most iconic site of all. A rugged, twin-peaked rock mass supported by sheer dolerite columns, it towers majestically over a glacial tarn, Dove Lake. As one walks warily round the lakeside path, the peaks alternately hide behind clouds or emerge to make dramatic reflections in the water; the colours change from hour to hour. In the morning, under a lowering sky, the mountain is black. At lunchtime, as the weather lifts, it is grey-brown. In the afternoon sunshine, its green slopes stand out against the blue sky, offering us a shimmering, four-peak reflection. Cradle is said to be rained on 360 days of the year. We hit on one of the five days when it wasn't.

The walk to Horseshoe Falls in the Mount Field National Park must come a close second. Open to moisture-laden winds, the steep slopes are clothed with dense, jungle-like undergrowth, and boast the biggest trees in the southern hemisphere. The *Eucalyptus regnans*, known prosaically as 'Tall Trees', rival California's sequoias, and with 100 metres of upright timber, make the stumbling hiker feel very small indeed.

A day in Penguin on the north coast offers welcome relief to tired legs. The penguin colony that provided the town's name still inhabits the headland. A curving, flower-lined promenade runs parallel to a vast beach. And a quaint memorial, accompanied by a giant Penguin, occupies a central position:

THIS MONUMENT IS ERECTED
BY THE PUBLIC IN MEMORY OF
TROOPERS THOMAS WILLIAM
BARKER AND GEOFFREY BROWN
OF PENGUIN
WHO DIED IN SOUTH AFRICA, 1900,
NOBLY DOING THEIR DUTY
FOR THEIR QUEEN AND EMPIRE.
TROOPER BARKER . . . DIED
AT BLOEMFONTEIN OF ENTERIC FEVER.
TROOPER BROWN OF THE
1ST IMPERIAL BUSHMEN
DIED OF WOUNDS RECEIVED AT WARMBATHS

The most pleasing sight is the Victorian railway station which, though long-closed, has been preserved. The weather boards have been repainted in beige and grey; plate-glass windows have been fitted to overlook the Strait; and the building now belongs to the Penguin History Group, Inc. The ticket hall is now a comfortable, dedicated History Room, 'Open Each Wednesday, 10 a.m.–Noon. Enquiries 6437 2582'. My enquiry would be: 'Please can I join?'

Port Arthur is the obvious place to start one's exploration of the convict legacy. Yet, on examination, the fearful penitentiary has lost most of its menace; it is the centre of a large open museum in a beautiful seaside setting surrounded by lush lawns, shady trees, and flowerbeds. There are exhibits to inspect and information boards to read. This was a place where men would kill in order to gain relief at the gallows. But its most striking aspect lies in the contrast between the horrific realities and the utopian ideals that seem to have inspired its creators. Much of the idealism stemmed from the utilitarian philosopher Jeremy Bentham (1748–1832), and his concept of a Panopticon: a corrective institution designed so that all inmates can, in theory, be watched by a single guard. He and his disciples wished to discard the lash and the cat-o'-nine-tails, by which prisoners had traditionally been restrained, and introduce a painless system that controlled prisoners' minds rather than their bodies. Convicts at Port Arthur were separated from each other and kept under constant observation; they were fed as a reward for good conduct, and starved as a punishment. Recalcitrants were hooded, and held in total silence. The devastating analysis of Michel Foucault has shown how misguided these methods were.[49] Many inmates were driven insane, and consigned to a mental asylum. Women and boys had their own blocks. And every day they all looked out onto the Isle of the Dead, whither the deceased were ferried for burial in unmarked, mass graves.[50] The Cascades 'Female Factory' in South Hobart, which functioned from 1828 to 1877, follows the same theme. Up to 1,000 women were held in a so-called 'reformatory'. The modern visitor cringes at the high stone walls that shut out the surrounding greenery, along with all hope of spiritual reform.

Tasmania's aboriginal legacy is harder to track down. In recent years, great strides have been made in recognizing the aboriginal past and in re-educating the public. Laws have been passed, apologies made, and welfare schemes launched to support aboriginal communities that are manifestly not extinct. Yet few sites are available for the interested visitor. There's a commercial aboriginal art gallery, ArtMob, on the Hobart waterfront. The Tasmanian Museum has one small room devoted to aboriginal matters; its grand title, 'Ningina Tunapri', means 'to give knowledge and understanding', and its one substantial exhibit is a replica bark canoe. The Tiagarra Museum on the distant north coast guards a prehistoric site adorned with rock carvings.

Most of the exhibits that once supported the extinction myth have been removed. The skeleton of Truganini (1812–76), the last full-blooded Tasmanian aborigine, which was shamefully displayed in the Tasmanian Museum from 1876 to 1947, has long since been buried at sea. The grave of her male counterpart, William Lanne (1835–69), which originally stood in St David's Cemetery, is also long gone. Nearby, one reads a pathetic, explanatory tablet:

> William Lanne, the last tribally-born Tasmanian Aboriginal Man, was buried here after he died of cholera contracted on a whaling voyage. His good nature had made him popular, and he was interred with great ceremony, attended by his shipmates. In the dead of night, two leading surgeons had his body dug up to secure the skeleton for scientific purposes. His body was never recovered, and fear of similar mutilation haunted Truganini's last years.

Yet the residue of past prejudices persists. Belief in the extinction myth has not been eradicated. History lessons still cause embarrassment:

> The last Tasmanian Aborigine
> died in 1876

hand goes up
but, teacher, I'm Aboriginal
how can you be
but teacher, I am, I am
Mum and Dad told me
No you are not
That's the end of it
Mouth turns down
Eyes glisten and slowly fill
Yes, teacher
Another lesson learnt
Of historical inaccuracies
Closed minds and white impassivity.[51]

Searchers not easily disheartened, therefore, are advised to scour the internet. Useful search words would be 'PARLEVAR', 'TRUGANINI', or 'ABORIGINALITY'. One finds that most of the existing organizations are directed toward the welfare of Tasmanians of aboriginal ancestry, and that their activities are hotly contested. Critics complain of do-gooders obsessed with political correctness who control government funds, and of self-interested activists who manipulate the all-important certificates of aboriginality.[52] An Aboriginal Land Council (ALCT) manages twelve reserved plots. The Tasmanian Aboriginal Land and Sea Council (TALSC) concentrates on cultural projects. The Aboriginal Heritage Office is run by the Department of Tourism. And the Tasmanian Aboriginal Corporation (TAC) strives to retrieve aboriginal remains and artefacts pillaged by Europeans.[53] All these bodies started up through the annulment of the doctrine of *terra nullius* in 1983, and the official Apology in the state House of Assembly reads:

RESOLVED nemine contradicente – That this house ... expresses its deep and sincere regret at the hurt and distress that was caused by past policies under which Aboriginal children were removed from their families and homes: apologises to the Aboriginal people for those past actions, and reaffirms its support for reconciliation between all Australians.[54]

The subterranean controversies surfaced unexpectedly in 2013 during an Australian middleweight boxing contest. The champion, Daniel Geale, presented himself as a Tasmanian aborigine. The contender, Anthony Mundine, a former rugby star, was a member of the Bundjalung people from New South Wales. Before the match, he made comments that only an aborigine would dare make. 'I thought they wiped all the Aborigines from Tasmania out,' he said blandly. 'He's got a white woman, and white kids.'[55] He then lost.

Aboriginal mythology provides an alternative route into the subject. The Parlevar people believed in sky spirits who determined mankind's destiny:

> Parlevar was the first Aborigine. To make him, Moihernee took some earth up to the sky, and fashioned a man who had a long tail like a kangaroo and legs without knee joints. This meant that Parlevar could not sit down, and had to sleep standing up. When Dromerdeener, the great star spirit, saw this, he decided to help. He cut off his tail, made [him] knee joints, and rubbed grease into the wounds. When Parlevar sat down for the first time, he said *Nyrarae* – 'it is good'.[56]

Anyone who wishes to dream the creation story for themselves must walk the South Coast Track for more than fifty miles in the shadow of the Ironbound Mountains, and continue beyond Louisa Island to a broad bay, now called Cox Bight. There on the shore sits a colossal boulder. It is all that was left of Moihernee, when he fell from the sky.

Regional accents are not a prominent feature of Australian English, and it needs a fine-tuned ear to catch the nuances. Tasmanians are said, like Melbournians, to speak slowly – 'Welcome to Malbourne'; they pronounce vowels in ways reminiscent of New Zealanders; and they typically say 'G'day, Cock' in place of 'G'day, Cobber'. For some reason, they eat 'eggs and bacon' rather than 'bacon and eggs'.

English-speaking outsiders, therefore, tend to notice things that could surprise them anywhere in Australia. They hear unfamiliar words and phrases such as *Sheila* for 'a woman', *dinkum* for 'very nice', or *Strine* for 'Australian speech'. They also become aware of individuals who speak 'Broad', using exaggerated diphthongs, like Barrie Humphries, and others who speak 'Cultivated', as if they worked for the BBC. Linguists typically divide Australian accents into the 'Broad', the 'Cultivated', and 'the General'.[57] The Welsh-born Julia Gillard was Australia's prime minister during our stay there, and her inimitable voice could not be classed as either 'cultivated' or 'general'. She would be a good candidate for a prize in the name of Winston Churchill, whose view of 'Strine' rated it 'the most brutal maltreatment that was ever inflicted on the mother-tongue of the great English-speaking nations'.[58]

Churchill's comment may or may not be *fair dinkum*, but one has to admire the Australian genius for characterful abbreviation:

| | |
|---|---|
| *arvo* | afternoon |
| *back o'bourke* | the back of beyond |
| *bludger* | lazy person |
| *bushbash* | outback trip |
| *chook* | chicken |
| *dilly* | handy bag |
| *drongo* | a no-hoper |
| *dunny* | latrine |
| *eskie* | ice-box or refrigerator |
| *garbo* | refuse collector |
| *journo* | journalist |
| *milko* | milkman |
| *mozzie* | mosquito |
| *postie* | postman |
| *salvo* | the Salvation Army |
| *strides* | trousers |
| *thingo* | thingamajig |
| *truckie* | lorry driver |
| *yobbo* | oaf |
| Oz | Australia.[59] |

Outsiders equally need time to adjust to the colourful demonyms which Australians use to identify the inhabitants of their country's different parts:

| | |
|---|---|
| *Bananabenders* | Queenslanders |
| *Croweaters* | South Australians |
| *Sandgropers* | 'Westralians' |
| *Mexicans* | Victorians (as seen from Sydney) |
| *Cockroaches* | the New South Welsh (as seen from Victoria) |
| *Top Enders* | inhabitants of the Northern Territories |
| *Apple Eaters* or *Taswegians* | Tasmanians |

And no one should leave Australia without hearing the Book of Genesis as translated into Strine:

There was this Sheila who came across a snake-in-the-grass with all the cunning of a con man. The snake asked her why she didn't just grab lunch off the tree in her garden. God, she said, had told her she'd be dead meat if her fruit salad came from that tree, but the snake told her she wouldn't die.

So she took a good squiz, and then a bite, and passed the fruit on to her bloke. Right then and there, they realised what they'd done, and felt starkers.[60]

The Strine version of the New Testament is not lacking in flavour either:

So Joe hiked up from Nazareth (in Galilee-shire) to Bethlehem (in Judea-shire), since that is the spot in the mulga where King David came from . . . He went there with his fiancée, Mary, who was pretty near nine months by this time. While they were there, she gave birth to a baby boy. She wrapped him in a bunny rug, and tucked him up in a feed trough in a back shed, because the pub was full to bursting.[61]

'Tasmanian cuisine' may sound to some like an oxymoron; it is not long since the ancient tradition of British fish and chips, and 'meat, gravy & two veg', reigned supreme. But Australia has progressed rapidly in recent decades. The arrival of Mediterranean and Asian immigrants made for richer diversity, and Tasmania has been well placed to supply many of the new food ingredients. Her crystal-clear waters are laden with superb crayfish and wild abalone, while domesticated Atlantic salmon supports a major industry. In addition to old staples like apples, dairy, and honey, her farms have moved into all branches of organic food. Black truffles have been found in abundance in her woods. And her best wines compete with those of New Zealand and Victoria. Tasmania's premier wine trail winds through the Tamar Valley, north of Launceston. Fruit of all sorts – apricots, raspberries, blueberries – are sold by the roadside on self-serve stalls armed with an honesty box. They are usually attended by a notice such as 'If you steal my fruit, I hope you choke!' A government ban on distilling, imposed in 1838, was not lifted until 1992. But in 2014 a Tassie whisky, Sullivans Cove, was voted 'the world's best single malt'.[62]

On the eve of our departure, with my wife busy elsewhere, I treated myself to a seafood lunch at Mures Upper Deck on the dockside of Hobart's Old Port. I sat by the first-floor window, watching fishermen mending nets below, listening to the cries of seagulls, and following the manoeuvres of a cruise liner out in the bay. I started with a chowder, packed with super-fresh prawns, mussels, sea trout, and garlic croustade, and served with sourdough bread. The main plate was line-caught wild-fish, accompanied by roasted baby beets, creamy risotto, grana padano, and crisp basil; the side dish combined marinated Tasmanian olives with spinach. Everything was washed down with a bottle of Bay of Fires Riesling 2011, and, as always, a single espresso. The meal was inexpensive, cheerfully served, and a far cry from fish and chips.

The theme of the 'dark secrets' begs to be solved before Tasmania is left behind. It is a delicate subject, where an oblique introduction may suit best. I recall a lecture presented by an unsuccessful candidate for a chair at London University; it was called 'Sex and Siberia' and I thought it rather good. Despite its provocative title, the lecture examined the appalling social and psychological consequences of exiling large numbers of maltreated males to a remote country where they had little chance of forming normal stable relationships. Male rape, criminal sex rings, untreated venereal disease, and unregulated prostitution headed a list of evils, which ran on into incest, inbreeding, congenital deformities, kidnapping of native women, child abuse, and insanity. This theme may not apply exclusively to Sakhalin or Kamchatka.

So the internet is called to the rescue. Combining the search words 'Tasmania' and 'Manning Clark', one discovers that the famous historian used to live at 1, Tasmania Circle, Canberra, where his former home is now a museum. This piece of trivia throws no light on the history of Tasmania.

The combination of 'Manning Clark' and 'Dark Secrets' throws up another item of interesting irrelevance. The much-lauded historian, it transpires, was not merely a Marxist and a pro-Communist fellow traveller – as was common in his generation – but he could well have been a Soviet agent, entrapped by clandestine sexual practices and employed by the Czechoslovak intelligence agency. A recent book, which characterizes him as 'The Tormented Myth-maker', contains some rich quotations. 'Maybe a victorious and purified Russia,' wrote Manning Clark, 'would light a cleansing fire in Australia.' Or again, 'Russia was filling with culture the vacuum where God had once been.'[63] Alas, the cleansing fire of Soviet Russia never reached Tasmania, and Clark would never have spotted the parallel with Siberia.

The next foray on the internet, combining 'Tasmania' and 'Supernatural', is slightly more illuminating. 'Of all the Australian states,

Tasmania is said to be the most haunted', offers one website, showing a photo of the haunted Addington Lodge in New Norfolk. 'Tasmania has more ghosts to the square mile than any other state in the Commonwealth', declares another. And ghost stories are soon revealed to be a strongpoint of Tasmanian literature.[64] The best-known legend centres on Richmond Bridge, in a charming old south-eastern town. Here, on misty nights, stalks the ghost of George Grover, a warder at Port Arthur and an ardent flogger, who was murdered, not surprisingly, by some of the men he had flogged.

When I type in 'Tasmania' and 'Image', it leads to the information that half of the world's opium poppies are grown on the island. 'GM poppies,' declares an outraged ecologist, 'are threatening Tasmania's image of green, clean agriculture.'[65]

'Tasmania' and 'Reputation' is more productive, not least because it subsumes Tasmania's 'bad reputation', which is attributed to 'hard core convicts, bad weather, and the Tasmanian Devil'. A historically minded website explores the campaign of the mid-nineteenth century to do away with the label of Van Diemen's Land.[66] 'The very name of Van Diemen's Land could send a shudder down the spine,' it states. It was connected not merely with the violent penal system but also with the horrendous series of serial murders that plagued the colony's earliest days. Alexander Pearce was far from unique. Thomas Jeffries – sadist, sexual predator, cannibal, and baby-killer, hanged in 1826 – was another; and Charles Routley, hanged in 1830, a third.[67] Routley, who had once escaped a death sentence in his native Devon, committed his worst crimes as an ex-prisoner released on a ticket of leave. He had lost both the left side of his jaw and half an arm, the stump of which was fitted with an iron hook. Yet his disabilities did not diminish his prowess as an expert gunman. Reporting his execution, the *Hobart Town Courier* described him as 'one of the most horrid and blood-thirsty monsters that have yet disgraced the annals of humanity'. At the end of a long run of robberies and killings, he was finally condemned for the calculated murder of a victim whom he roasted alive, presumably to be eaten. The event took place at Pitt Water, which today is a beautiful nature reserve close to Hobart Airport.

The breakthrough in my search was made when 'Reputation' was replaced by 'Insinuation'. An entry flashed up entitled 'Is Incest Legal in Tasmania?' It came from Yahoo's 'Question and Answer' service:

QUESTION: 'I heard that it is okay to hook up with your first cousin, as long as you don't get married. Is everyone really related in Tasmania?'

BEST ANSWER. 'Yawn. Here we go with the insane incest insinuation again. They may think that Tasmanians have two heads, but I swear that you couldn't find a single, creative thought among mainlanders.'

So the taboo was finally winkled into the open. The manifest Tasmanian resentment against mainlanders is fuelled by the sheer quantity and casual nature of the dastardly accusations. Any brief search under 'Incest', 'Two Heads', or 'Inbreeding' brings up a plethora of smears, jibes, tasteless jokes, crude drawings, and dubious stories, all at Tasmania's expense. The myths, which many Australians apparently believe, are that incestuous relationships form an established part of Tasmania's hidden culture, that 'sheep-shagging' is as prevalent as sheep-shearing, that the incidence of congenital deformities is exceptionally high, and that all manner of perversions can be credited to the island's convict past. An associated myth, usually graphically illustrated by pudenda, is that 'all Tasmanian women carry a map of the island on their body'.

The smears often resort to ambiguous slang, including 'mudbloods', 'Tasmaniacs', 'bogans', and 'underbelly baddies'. And they rarely miss the chance of referring to an extraordinary, real-life animal, the *echidna*, which is unique to Tasmania. Believe it or not, the *echidna* is a long-beaked, egg-laying, termite-eating, spiny-backed hedgehog – otherwise the porcupine anteater – which glories in 'the world's weirdest wedding-tackle' – that is, a four-headed penis.[68] To make things worse, some classically educated zoologist with a wicked sense of humour chose to name this totally innocent Tasmanian mammal after a mythological Greek 'She-Viper'; half-woman, half-serpent, the 'Mother of All Monsters'. And to cap it all, the Echidna of myth gave birth both to the two-headed dog Orthrus and the three-headed hound Cerberus, who guards the gates of Hades.[69]

After which, this passage from Manning Clark's autobiography must surely be presented in full:

> I visited Tasmania at the end of 1933. There, one golden day on the Derwent, near New Norfolk, under a gentler sky than I had known in Melbourne and Sydney, with Mount Wellington as a gaunt, majestic back-drop . . . I sensed that here was a society haunted by ghosts from the past – a society of people in which many things they had inherited from the mighty dead live on in them. I sensed then some contradiction between that gaiety in the very air, and [the] darkness in men's minds.[70]

At the time of Clark's visit, Australia had been shaken by sensational press reports about a raid by social workers on a farm at Black Bobs in Tasmania's Derwent Valley. The raid revealed that a variety of deformed children were kept tied to wooden posts in the farmyard. It was taken to be the 'smoking gun' supporting persistent rumours of incest. Further atrocities have surfaced. One from the 1940s revolved around rebellious young girls at a psychiatric hospital, another in the 1980s around a series of masochistic murders. The worst, in 1996, took place with horrible symbolism on the historic site of Port Arthur, where a crazed and rampaging Tasmanian-born gunman murdered thirty-five men, women, and children. The gunman, Martin Bryant, is still serving thirty-five full-life sentences plus 1,035 years of incarceration without the possibility of parole.[71]

Many thoughtful Tasmanians accept that the 'dark legacy' forms the backdrop, if not the direct cause, of the island's contemporary social and economic challenges. Tasmania is Australia's least prosperous and most crisis-stricken state. It struggles with low rates of educational attainment, high levels of illiteracy, teenage pregnancy, and unemployment, massive welfare dependence, and an overblown state sector. Most embarrassingly, as noted in 2010–11, the number of proven cases of child abuse was 56 per cent above the national average. Such statistics drive calls for outside intervention:

> Tasmania's underlying problem is simple but intractable. It has developed a way of life, a mode of doing things, a culture and associated economy, that reproduce under-achievement generation after generation.[72]

Politically, the 'underlying problem' explains why Tasmania's state parliament and government were held securely for sixteen years, from 1998 to 2014, by the socially sensitive Australian Labour Party. For the last three of those years the scene was dominated by the state's first woman premier, Larissa Tahireh Giddings, born in 1972 in Papua New Guinea and once Australia's youngest ever parliamentarian. Owing to a dead tie in the legislative elections between the ALP and the opposition Liberal Party, Prime Minister Giddings was obliged to govern through a coalition with the minority Green Party. During her premiership, Tasmania began to be depicted by the right-wing press as an economic basket case. 'Australia's Greece' was one of the jibes (with Western Australia given the role of Australia's Germany).[73] It was no surprise, therefore, when the election of March 2014 swept the Labour government from office. 'Lara' Giddings stepped down, both as prime minister and party leader.

Disappearances have long been a Tasmanian speciality. A mysterious disappearance lies at the heart of a Tasmanian eco-thriller film, *The Hunter*, whose premiere in 2011 was attended by Prime Minister Giddings.[74] The conflict between international corporations and local activists supplies the setting. The chief protagonist is a mercenary gunman hired by a shadowy bio-tech company to track down the DNA of the 'Tasmanian tiger'.

The Tasmanian tiger, the Thylacine, has indeed disappeared, hunted to extinction.[75] Moreover, starting in 1813 with the schooner *Unity*, which was stolen from Hobart harbour by armed convicts and never heard of again, presumed lost at sea, ships regularly disappeared from their moorings, hijacked in the night by convicts or bushrangers. Even George Bass, the island's original circumnavigator, disappeared. Having taken to smuggling, he sailed from Sydney harbour on the *Venus* in February 1803 bound for Tahiti, and vanished.[76]

A century later, the curious case of the son of a professor of biology at the University of Tasmania involved a different sort of disappearance. Twice expelled from school, the boy somehow contrived to complete his education in London, work as a tobacco-planter in New Guinea, and then return to England as an actor. Arriving in Hollywood in 1941, he described himself fancifully as an Irishman, and became the swashbuckling hero of *Captain Blood*, *The Adventures of Robin Hood*, and *The Sea Hawk*. He was the original male heartthrob of sound movies. Although few Tasmanians knew it, Errol Flynn (1909–59), the grandson of convicts, was one of them.[77]

The case of Frederick Valentich (1958–78) is still stranger. A young amateur aviator, Valentich took off from Melbourne's Moorabbin Airport on 21 October 1978, having filed a plan for a return flight across the Bass Strait. When the tiny Cessna 182-L was in mid-Channel, he radioed the Melbourne controller to report a 'large unknown aircraft', 'with four bright green landing lights', 'moving overhead at high speed'. Minutes later he said that the vehicle was 'not an aircraft', 'was hovering', and was giving him 'engine problems'. Then contact was lost. No trace of Valentich or his plane was ever found, and his name features prominently in UFO sagas.[78] All of which revives thoughts of MH370, and the strange reality that thousands of people around the world believe that it was captured by UFOs.

Similar irrational attitudes hide the 'dark secrets' of Tasmania. Many otherwise level-headed souls simply won't visit. 'It's a land of ghouls,' warned friends from Canberra. 'It's spooked; it's accursed.' Yet we had spent two happy months on 'Tassie' and had barely scratched the enchanting surface. We recrossed the Bass Strait at 12,000 feet, this time looking down on Flinders Island, where the Parlevar were wrongly said to have disappeared. We then disappeared ourselves, flying eastwards, high above the Tasman Sea.

# 9

# Kiwiland

*Flightless Birds and Long White Clouds*

Australians and New Zealanders will both try to tell you that they are entirely different.

'Oh, no, no, no,' protested one of our Tasmanian friends, 'those Kiwis are nothing like us.'

It's rather like arguing with a professional horticulturalist who wants to insist that no two peas in a pod are identical, but refuses to compare peas with beans. Outsiders tend to assume that 'Kiwis' and 'Ozzies', if not indistinguishable, are really rather similar. They both speak English with a similar twang; they both live in former British, antipodean colonies; they are each other's closest neighbours; and they often have relatives in Britain. But insiders won't have it; they shun the similarities and see only the contrasts.

In the arrivals hall at Wellington airport a flagstand displays the national flag. To the untutored eye, it could easily be mistaken for the flag that we last saw in the departure halls at Hobart and Sydney. It is the same dark Oxford blue: it has the same Union Flag in the top corner; and it carries a similar spangle of stars, which hide discreetly among the furls. There is something a trifle odd about those New Zealand stars: they are five-pointed, red in the middle, and outlined in silver. Where have I seen a star like that before? Perhaps Tito's Yugoslavia. At all events, this is what Tasmanians call 'completely different'.

Before gaining entry, one has to pass the boot test. For some reason, New Zealand officialdom is unusually suspicious not only of dangerous plants and seeds but also of hiking boots. Just as you think that you've passed passport control and are free to proceed, a funnel-shaped enclosure appears like the lanes and hurdles of a sheepdog trial. You are soon trapped like a bleating ewe in the Eco-Security channel from which there's no escape.

'Do you know what is in your case?' the officer asks pointedly. It's the local equivalent of the American question about past or present membership of the Communist Party.

'Well, yes,' I say feebly. 'I think so. More or less.'

He scents a kill.

'Examine this case,' he orders his smart, young underling. His taxpayers have invested large sums of money in X-ray machines that are calibrated to expose the size and shape of footwear.

'There are boots in this case,' the underling asserts, swinging my case onto an inspection table. He has already engineered a confrontation.

'No,' I say, 'there are no boots.'

'Can you describe the footwear, then?'

'One pair of sandals, one pair of trainers, and one pair of walking shoes.'

'So what do you use them for?'

'Walking, mainly,' I say.

The examination begins. The zip is yanked open and the lid thrown back. The underling rummages vigorously. His face lights up as his fingers make contact with a thick sole, but his crest falls as the offending item rises into view.

'Low-cut shoes with vibram soles!' he tells the woman at the X-ray machine, giving her a thunderous look. Deadly pause.

'Please could you repack the case?' I ask him.

He yanks the zip without straightening the rummaged clothing, and snags my new Indian suit.

'Actually, leave it to me,' I say.

He walks glumly away, and I move thankfully into the arrivals hall.

Back in the twelfth or thirteenth century, or perhaps earlier, when the legendary Polynesian explorer Kupe arrived here in his outrigger canoe, he faced no such indignities. He wasn't wearing boots or carrying a suitcase, and no inspectors were lying in wait to check his fruit and seeds. The two great, green islands in the southern ocean, which he discovered, were totally uninhabited. Not only were there no humans, there were no mammals: only wonderful birds and fishes, and a lush covering of exotic trees and flowering bushes that spread round the mountains, lakes, and fjords. Kupe's people, later known as Maoris, followed him to make the islands their home, sailing a thousand miles or more across the warm, fish-laden waters, and settling in undisputed possession of what they called *Ao-tea-roa*, 'The Land of the Long White Cloud'.

At the time, Zealand had no connection whatsoever with the antipodes. There were, in fact, two Zealands: one, the largest island in
Denmark, and the other, locally spelled Zeeland, a district in the north-
western parts of the Holy Roman Empire. In a straight line from
Aotearoa, they lay perhaps 5,000 leagues distant. Their ships, whether
from Denmark or the Netherlands, had never yet ventured outside Europe. They plied their wares of cloth and wool and wine along the
northern coasts; they crossed the North Sea to Scandinavia and to an
England ruled by the French Plantagenets, and they edged their way
round Iberia into the Mediterranean. But the Zealanders and Zeeland-
ers knew little of any continents that lay beyond the prows of their
luggers: and they knew no more about the Maoris than the Maoris
knew about them: that is, absolutely nothing.

Wellington, the pocket-sized capital, sits on the south-western corner
of North Island, overlooking the Cook Strait and the ferries that make
the three-hour crossing to South Island. On a clear day the snow-
capped peaks of the Kaikoura Range stand out on the horizon. Founded
in 1839, Wellington grew up round the magnificent sheltered harbour,
originally called Port Nicholson. It adopted the name of Wellington
when the victor of Waterloo was British prime minister in 1850, and it
became capital of the colony in 1865, when the government feared that
the North might split from the South. Its felicitous location commands
not only the Strait but also the sea lanes that spread out round the
islands' western and eastern coasts. Yet buffeted by the 'Roaring Forties', Wellington is extremely windy, and frequently deluged by rain. It
is popularly known as 'Wellywood', or just 'Welly', and to the Maoris
either as Poneke – a rendering of 'Port Nick' – or as Te Upoko-o-te
Ika – a reference to the 'Fish Hook' of the god Maui, who fished the
islands out of the ocean.[1]

We were welcomed in Wellington by the same sort of relentless
downpour that had filled our first day in Hobart. On such days the
obvious place to take refuge is the Museum of New Zealand, or the Te
Papa Tongarewa, 'Our Place of Treasures', which is housed in a brand-
new building on the Wellington waterfront.[2] The Te Papa project,
however, like the MONA in Hobart, has run into persistent controversy since the day of its opening in 1998. Outsiders cannot easily grasp
why the protests have been so vociferous and so sustained, and it is
hard to believe that issues such as overspending or earthquake protection really lie at the heart of the matter. The project leaders publicize

their commitment to 'unified collections', 'narratives of culture and place', 'the idea of forum', 'bi-cultural partnership', and 'an emphasis on diversity and multidisciplinary collaboration' – in other words to one particular view of the country's identity. The project's critics denounce it as a 'theme park' and 'the cultural equivalent to a fast-food outlet', evidently suspecting it of being a propaganda exercise for Aotearoa-New Zealand as opposed to New Zealand-Aotearoa. The slanging match conceals several conflicts rolled into one: the eternal conflict between cultural innovators and traditionalists, a political conflict between left-wingers and conservatives, and underneath everything an ill-defined unease about the place and proportions of the Maori presence. As things stand, the Maori element is far from overwhelming, and some of the initial irritants such as the statue of the *Virgin Mary with Condom* have been removed. (The statue would have suited MONA perfectly.) Almost three-quarters of the exhibits are devoted to Pakeha, that is, to non-Maori subjects. But to diehards, accustomed to the Maori legacy being consigned to a small back room in the old Colonial Museum, even a quarter or a third is considered 'the thin end of the wedge'.

A visit to Te Papa with an open mind quickly dispels many of the criticisms. In the entrance hall, the visitor sees a large, bilingual notice:

> *Haere Kupu Mihi* – Greeting
> *Haere mai, e te manuhiri tuarangi, haere mai ki tenei marae . . .*
> Welcome visitors, to this *marae*, this meeting place . . .

'These are the words,' the guidebook explains, '[that] you might hear at the gateway of Te Papa's *Marae*, at the start of a *powhiri*, a welcoming ceremony. They are part of a *karanga*, a call that invites you onto the host community's ground. So begins an encounter between a home people and their visitors.'[3] Alongside the notice a large photograph hangs of a mixed-race mother, with a partly tattooed face, rubbing noses with a young, European-looking girl. 'Two people *hangi* (press noses)', the subtitle reads: 'a common form of greeting in which they share "the breath of life"'. By this time, one realizes that no one can begin to explain Maori culture without using Maori words.

Contrary to the doomsayers' warnings, the exhibition is not overloaded with either political correctness, gender-speak, or superfluous Maori themes. It derives from a merger between the old National Museum and the National Art Gallery, and gives priority to the principle of 'something for everyone', attracting 1.4 million visitors each year, over 4,000 per working day. The English-language guide uses the simple term 'New Zealand' throughout, and lays emphasis on geology, the natural world, and maritime subjects. A section on 'The Settling of New Zealand' gives equal space to the 'Voyages to Aotearoa', the British 'Second Wave', and the 'Treaty'. A section on 'The Emergence of a Nation' stresses farming, trade, economic vicissitudes, and the 'Fair Go' tradition. The section on 'Art and Taonga Maori', though substantial, is balanced by one on 'New Communities' and another on 'Local and Global'. My own reaction was: why doesn't London have something similar?

Next day, still lashed by rain, we hung onto our umbrellas as we struggled up the hill to the Victoria University, where I was due to talk to a group of postgraduate historians. Founded in 1897, the university closely resembles its British red-brick counterparts. Both the name, the atmosphere, and the downpour reminded me of the Victoria University of Manchester.[4]

On 9 May, a Thursday, the rain finally clears and bright sun brings the city to life. It is 'Europe Day', and my main engagement is a luncheon at the residence of the French ambassador, where I have to present a small lunchtime talk to the assembled European Union diplomats. 'La Résidence' is a fine, white-painted, colonial-style suburban villa, surrounded by palm trees, a tropical garden, and a very high wall. I am greeted by the smiling ambassador, M. Francis Étienne, who is visibly delighted and amused by *un anglais* who insists on speaking French. Twenty years ago, few French diplomats would have wanted, or have been able, to speak English, and there were some awkward moments. Nowadays, all is resolved with smiles and extravagant gestures, and I am taken through to meet the British representative, who, since this is the Commonwealth, bears the title of High Commissioner. I am duly awed. The High Commissioner turns out to be a tall, sturdy woman with a large head of hair and oriental features. (Her website says that she was born in Malaysia, her mother being Singapore-Chinese and her French-Dutch father a member of the burgher community of Sri Lanka.)

'Hello,' she says, putting me at ease, 'I'm Vicki.'

If ever there was a right person in the right place, I think, this is it.

Diplomatic gatherings are hard to navigate for the unpractised. On the surface, everything is lubricated to perfection. The visitor is plied with a heady mixture of vintage claret, exquisite politeness, and absorbing questions, which reduce one's ability to catch the signals of the day's underlying business. I was introduced as the author of the Oxford History of Europe, and my short talk at the luncheon table on 'Trends in European History' served to keep the conversation flowing. But something else was in progress that I struggled to grasp. It was obviously connected with the arrival of the first representative of the European Union's new Foreign Service, whose office might have the potential to make the diplomats of member states redundant. The key person in question was self-effacing to the point of non-existence. The others were sizing him up, and he was deliberately making it difficult for them to do so. But what did his fellow diplomats in the room actually make of him? Was he welcome? Was he threatening? Was he an irrelevance? I had no idea.

In the evening, sticking with the diplomats, my wife and I went along to the private Wellington Club to attend a lecture and dinner for some 150 guests. The speaker was John Key, leader of the right-of-centre National Party and for the last five years prime minister, who was presenting something in the nature of a 'state of the union' speech. I watched a political ritual whose nuances I could not again decipher. The prime minister, who looked much younger than his fifty years, was slick, jokey, and, in terms of content, entirely bland. I could see that he was making a comprehensive *tour d'horizon*, first of domestic and then of international affairs, but I had few mental landmarks to orient myself with what he was really saying, or with what he omitted. As my neighbour pointed out, John Key had to be a very smooth operator. He entered politics after a successful career as a currency broker; like two previous premiers, he is of Jewish descent; and he headed a minority government that was kept afloat by a coalition of three minor groupings, including the Maori Party. He came to power in 2008 after an election victory over the Labour Party, which had served three full parliamentary terms under his predecessor, Helen Clark. But whether he was a leftist or a rightist was difficult to say. I found myself in the position that a Kiwi visitor to London might recognize. After Tony Blair abandoned socialism, David Cameron abandoned traditional Toryism and Theresa May abandoned the EU, all the basic political signposts have been uprooted. I shook the prime minister's hand with the confused feeling of being both far from home yet on familiar ground.

The history of Kiwiland has three clear segments. For the longest period it was exclusively concerned with the Maoris, who enjoyed undisputed ownership for 600 or 700 years. It took a radical new tack in the mid-nineteenth century with the arrival of the *Pakeha* – the 'strangers' – and the founding of a British colony, whose requirements were given absolute priority for over a century. From the late twentieth century onwards, however, it has focused on efforts to bring the Maori and Pakeha strands closer together and to create a unified, national community.[5]

The pre-colonial Maori, though illiterate, had a highly developed awareness of their origins. They did not produce the equivalent of an *Anglo-Saxon Chronicle*. But they possessed a language, an elaborate corpus of mythology, and a rich oral tradition of poetry and recital, within which their knowledge of former times, both mythological and historical, was incorporated.[6]

During the long centuries of their isolation, the Maori never progressed beyond the Neolithic. They arrived with a knowledge of fire-drilling, cloth-weaving, fishing, and agriculture, particularly the growing of *kumara*, a species of sweet potato. Owing to the lack of game in Aotearoa, they could not be hunters, but were highly skilled in the crafts of building, rope-making, carpentry, and carving. Thanks to their discovery of nephrite – a semi-precious, jade-like stone commonly known as *pounamu* or 'greenstone' – they produced high-quality tools, weapons, and ornaments.

Travellers who have crossed the Tasman Sea and learned a little history may reasonably ask themselves two questions. One is: 'Why have the Maoris survived, whilst the Tasmanian aborigines were decimated?' Another is: 'Where do the Maoris now stand in the global league table of indigenous peoples?'

The Maoris' survival presents no great puzzle. Firstly, being warlike, ocean-going, and resourceful Polynesians, they were much less vulnerable than their isolated, introverted, and technologically unsophisticated 'Australian' neighbours. Secondly, they had to contend with a markedly different breed of invader. The Europeans who landed on Aotearoa were free settlers, missionaries, traders, and miners, with views of the world that had little in common with those of the convicts, penal guards, and colonial officials who dominated Van Diemen's Land. And thirdly, by the Treaty of Waitangi, signed in 1840, a *modus vivendi* was achieved before the great mass of settlers arrived. One may argue that the Treaty was a swindle, and in many respects it was; but equally one can't deny that it did much to avert the possibility of a war to the death of the kind which took place in Tasmania.

The United Nations' List of Indigenous Peoples contains over eight thousand names of tribes, nations, and ethnic groups. Its contents vary from ancient European nations, like the Basques or the Welsh, whose life struggle has been observed for centuries, to obscure tribes of the Amazonian rainforest, who have been spotted from the air but not yet contacted directly. The Maoris belong to neither of these extremes. They can be classed in the biggest of all categories, those whose ancestral lands were overrun by European migrants in modern times, but who were not annihilated. They keep company with the 'Indians' of Peru or Mexico, the Native Americans, the indigenous peoples of Africa, the Palestinians, and the numerous minority nationalities of Russia.

The principal organization that campaigns for the rights of indigenous peoples, Survival International,[7] cites a wide gamut of vulnerability among them. 'Secure for the foreseeable future' is at one end of the scale, and 'Imminent Extinction' at the other. Once again, the Maoris would not find themselves at either extreme. Unlike the Tibetans, for instance, or most recently, the Rohingya of Burma, they are not under direct attack. At the same time, they are aware of ill-concealed hostility among sections of the majority population, and of confusion or indifference among sections of their own.

What is certain is that the game is still in play. The Maori cause has experienced something of a Renaissance. The Maori language now enjoys equal status with English. New Zealand's state authorities have introduced many more inclusive policies in education, history teaching, and museums. A handful of Maori celebrities, mainly opera singers or rugby players, have acquired worldwide fame. Yet it would be idle to suppose that the average Maori child can look forward to the same prospects as the average Pakeha child, or that Maori culture will ever carry the same clout as the global appeal of English and its culture. Inclusiveness is fine in theory. In practice it is hard to achieve.

Thinking of which, one wonders what Maoris make of their country's name; it is one of many things that have been thrust upon them, and few can have illusions that the majority will take 'Aotearoa' to their hearts. Yet the issue deserves consideration. If one thinks about it, 'New Zealand' is totally inappropriate not only for Maoris but equally for the great mass of citizens with family roots in the British Isles. Almost no one emigrated to Aotearoa from Zealand or Zeeland. So why not replace the name? The status quo, which prefers the clumsy 'New Zealand-Aotearoa' is something of a stop-gap, and alternatives do exist. 'Sealand', for example, as an intelligible translation, would be better, and the informal 'Kiwiland' is already in circulation.[8] It is part-Maori, part-English; it matches the well-established state emblem, and its tone is carefree and friendly. The main drawback is that it is widely used by Australians. Sceptics are bound to say that it will never fly. But to the more optimistic, it has a future, and would be a fitting partner to the Silver Fern or *Ponga* plant, which, after a lengthy campaign and a referendum, recently missed adoption as the national flag.[9] If 'the most beautiful country in the world' were to take on both the name of Kiwiland and the sign of the Silver Fern, it would cease to be regarded as a lesser version of Australia.

*

The Maori language is classed in comparative linguistics as a member of the Tahitic sub-group of Eastern Polynesian. Known to its native speakers as *Te Reo*, 'the Speech', it was imported by Polynesian migrants, and is itself one of the principal proofs of their geographic and ethnic origins. It is mutually intelligible with Tahitian and with Rarotongan from the Cook Islands, less so with Marquesan or Hawaiian. Tupaia, a Tahitian speaker who sailed aboard Captain Cook's *Endeavour*, had no difficulty communicating with the Maori when contact was first made in 1769–70. The word *Maori* means 'ordinary person'.[10]

Maori place names, long despised in colonial times, now enjoy equality, and add greatly to the flavour of life. *Aotearoa* was originally the name for North Island alone; South Island is called *Te Wai Pounamu*, 'the Waters of Greenstone'. Many names reflect incidents or discoveries connected to the Great Migration, or to Hawaiki, the Maoris' original and unidentified home. But most are simple geographic descriptions built on words such as *ao* (cloud), *ara* (road), *maunga* (mountain), *moana* (sea), *wai* (water), *whanga* (bay), or *roto* (lake). *Aoraki*, for example, stands for 'Sky Cloud' or 'Cloud Piercer', and is the older name for the country's highest peak, Mount Cook. *Aramoana* means 'Path beside the Sea', and *Moana-a-Toi*, the 'Sea of [the navigator] Toi', is the Maori name for the Bay of Plenty. The River *Waikato* comes from 'Flowing Water', *Whanganui* from 'Big Bay', and *Rotorua* from 'Two Lakes'. *Taumatawhakatangihangakoauauotamateapokaiwhenuakitanatahu*, meaning 'The Summit where Tamatea, the Land Traveller, played the flute to his beloved', is the Maori response to *Llanfairpwllgwyngyllgogerychwyrndrobwllllantysiliogogogoch* in Wales.

To this day, Maori society is organized around *waka*, 'canoes', *iwi*, 'tribes', *hapu*, 'clans', and *whanau*, 'extended families'. *Waka* is the standard word for canoe, but exists in many varieties, including *waka ama* or 'outrigger', *waka taua*, the fast, sleek 'war canoe', and *waka hourua*, the massive, double-hulled ocean-going vessels that most probably were used in the migration voyages. The last were up to 40 metres in length, and could carry between 100 and 200 passengers. According to the reigning consensus, they sailed from Hawaiki to Aotearoa not in one grand 'First Fleet', but in a series of separate voyages spread over decades or even centuries. When they landed, their passengers formed a distinct community that retained their canoe's name, and they claimed a particular piece of territory as their new homeland. They and their descendants have upheld a distinct identity ever since, and a score of them continue to function; they include the Tainui, the Mataatua, the Takitumu, the Horouta, the Kawhia, and the Aotea.

The Tainui *waka*, for example, landed around AD 1400 and settled in the Waikato region of North Island. Literally 'the Big Tide Canoe', they formed a dominant element in Maori society, and in the nineteenth century became the focus of the *Kingitanga* movement (see below). According to their historian, Pei Te Hurinui Jones, they spent their first fifty years on the island battling the indigenous people of the region, conquering them at the Battle of Atiamuri in 1450. This begs the question of who these 'indigenous people' might have been – most likely, though this is disputed, the offspring of a preceding Maori *waka* people. Today's Tainui form a confederation of four *iwi* or 'tribes': the Hauraki, the Ngati Maniapoto, the Ngati Raukawa, and the Waikato.[11]

Around AD 1500 a group of Maori tribes mounted an expedition to a small archipelago that lies some 420 miles to the south-east of North Island. Members of the expedition settled and created the community from which a new Polynesian nation, the Moriori, evolved. They called the archipelago *Rekohu* or 'Misty Sun', and lived there in isolation for three centuries. In 1791 a British naval squadron landed and gave the archipelago its English name of Chatham Islands. In 1835 a large party of Maori invaded, proceeding not only to seize the Moriori lands but also to massacre the people. 'It was our custom,' their leader explained. Only 10 per cent survived the genocide, a similar proportion to the Aborigines who survived in Tasmania.[12]

The usual definition of *iwi*, which literally means 'bone', is 'a set of people bound by common descent from one ancestor', and is usually translated as 'tribe'. Each of the great canoes carried a dozen men or more, who subsequently became the protoplast of a tribe and who acted as the leaders in establishing tribal territory. Today, more than a hundred such tribes continue to flourish, all but a dozen on North Island. The largest of them, the Ngapuhi, who are more than 100,000 strong, are a branch of the Mataatua *waka* people, and inhabit part of the Northland district. The smallest, the Patukirikiri, numbers just sixty persons. Roughly half of the *iwi* are registered and numbered from one to fifty-four in the organization of United Tribes (the Ngapuhi being No. 4). The other half are not registered. All of them maintain an administration that tracks members, holds tribal reunions and festivals, and promotes tribal identity.[13]

The *hapu* – literally 'pregnant' – is usually translated as 'subtribe' or 'clan', and is regarded as the basic unit of Maori society. Smaller than the *iwi* but larger than the *whanau*, it typically contains some three to five hundred genealogically connected members, who elect a chief, supply the clan's war party with warriors, and live in the vicinity of their stockaded *pa* or 'fort'. In early colonial times they were notorious for fighting each other rather than the invaders, and for selling off land without regard to the consequences. They raised flax, pigs, and potatoes in exchange for blankets, tools, and muskets.

The *whanau*, which means 'birth', are made up of the three or four generations of individuals who all possess the same grandparents or great-grandparents. They form a solid family unit, who typically live together in one house or compound. They are not the simple subdivision of a clan, however, since, through paternal and maternal lines, they are likely to be closely connected with two or more *hapu*. Their way of life is largely determined by traditional marriage customs. In former times, the union of infant boys and girls was arranged years in advance by their relatives, and often involved intricate, inter-clan land deals that could later cause disputes and conflicts.

Maori mythology combines cosmogenic stories, which explain the origins of the Earth and of mankind, national legends relating to the lost homeland of Hawaiki and the Great Migration, and tribal tales of 'great battles and great men' that justify the possession of territory and the authority of leaders.[14] It is thickly peopled with gods and demigods, and with god-procreated ancestors, and it makes no distinction between events that modern analysts might judge purely mythical and others that are plausibly semi-historical. Nonetheless, perhaps presaging the tripartite division of the history of Kiwiland, three time periods can be observed here too: the first from the beginning of the world to the departure from Hawaiki, the second linked to the discovery and settlement of Aotearoa, and the third from the landings on Aotearoa to the present.

Accounts of the creation of mankind centre on the divine union of the Sky-God, *Rangi*, and the Earth-Mother, *Papa*, and on the war of the gods that erupted among their offspring. The primordial couple, having produced a brood of boys, stayed locked in such a tight embrace that their sons, forced to live in the darkness between them, had no space to breathe. The elder brother, *Tu-matuenga*, 'Angry Face' and subsequently God of War, wanted to kill his parents. But the younger brother, *Tane*, God of the Forests, succeeded in separating them by lying on his back and pushing his father into the sky with his strong legs. He dressed his father with the sun, moon, and stars, and returning to Earth procreated the birds, fishes, and mammals. Some legends make Tu the progenitor of mankind, describing how he gained his predominance by eating his brothers. Others give the honour to Tane, who moulded a woman from the soil. No one master legend exists to present a coherent and universal narrative.

The separation of Rangi and Papa, however, caused lasting anguish. Rangi's tears fall as rain and snow, while Papa's writhing provokes earthquakes. Worst of all, their sons could not be reconciled. Havoc was raised by *Tawhirimatea*, the God of Storms, who joins his father in the sky, from where he attacks his brothers. Tane's forests are flattened. *Tangaroa*, the God of the Sea, is forced to flee. And *Rongo* and *Haumia*, the God of Cultivated Food and God of Wild Food respectively, are left desolate.

Another important figure is *Hine-nui-te-po*, 'the Great Goddess of Night'. She is the woman whom Tane moulded and with whom he then mated. She fled to the underworld in disgust, and became its ruler, where she discovered that her man-mate was also her father. Her vagina was said to be armed with obsidian teeth, which she used to kill the demigod, *Maui*, who had turned himself into a worm in order to penetrate her and to discover the source of life. Her would-be rapist thereby became the first person to die.

Maui features in a complex cycle of myths and legends, in which he performs supernatural feats marked by ingenuity and trickery. He had survived a trauma at birth; his mother, thinking the premature baby dead, had cast him into the sea wrapped in her topknot – hence his longer name, *Maui-tikitiki*, 'Maui the Topknot'. One of his many exploits was to restrain the sun, which he battered with the jawbone of an ancestress until it slowed down and made the days longer. Another was to rediscover the secret of fire, after mankind had lost it; he tricked the Goddess of Fire into giving him her flammable fingernails. And he created the two islands that became the Maoris' second home, hauling North Island from the ocean floor with his fishhook, and magically fashioning South Island from his canoe.

*Tawhaki* is another demigod, usually associated with thunder and lightning, who appears in multiple legends. The grandson of the cannibalistic goddess *Whaitiri*, he masters the secret of climbing into Heaven along the vine that forms the 'pathway to the sky'. Mounting to the highest of the ten heavens, he memorizes many of the spells that give the gods their hold over men. He possesses the power of destroying his foes with a mighty flood, and in the period when the Maori were exposed to Christianity, his father *Hema* was transformed into Shem, the son of Noah.

The *Maoritanga* or 'cultural heritage of the Maoris' has been preserved by the mechanisms of a complex oral tradition. Storytelling and mythology are just part of it. Poetry, song, dance, drama, rituals, customs, painting, sculpture, tattooing, and many other elements have played a role in perpetuating the beliefs of the ancestors and consolidate the identity of the growing generation. All the tribes and clans employ professional *tohunga* or 'shamans', bards and storytellers, who memorize the repertoire and lead the performances at regular gatherings. The recital of royal and tribal genealogies is especially important for the upkeep of a historical framework and demonstrates the essential link between men and the gods. Every community maintains its *marae* or 'ceremonial compound', in which the *wharenui* or 'meeting house' holds pride of place. As in all Polynesian cultures, mankind is seen as an integral part of Nature; men and women are cousins of animals and plants, and are imbued with a powerful sense of the sacred. Particular localities and individuals are declared to be *tapu* or 'divine' – hence the English 'taboo' – and are to be left severely alone on pain of retribution.

Singing is a particularly powerful Maori tradition, and a universally attractive part of ceremonial. Varying styles of song have been developed to meet every possible occasion:

> When there was direct assertion rather than complaint, a song was usually performed in recited style, without melodic organisation. Such songs were often associated with . . . strong social challenge. They included . . . paddlers' songs (*tuki waka*) dance songs (*haka*), women's songs against insults (*patere*) and watchmen's songs (*whakaaraara pa*) . . . There are also three kinds of song that were mainly concerned with the expression of love and sorrow . . . and sung rather than recited, with a melody repeated in each line. The kind known as *oriori* were sung to communicate to a boy or a girl the tribal circumstances they had inherited, [together with information about] the relatives who would offer their support. Those known as *pao* were epigrammatic couplets, most sung for entertainment, [expressing] love, greetings and comment on local events and scandals. The third kind, *waiata* . . . by far the most important, were laments and complaints, usually sung publicly . . . to express the poet's feelings, to convey a message, and [to] sway the listeners' emotions . . . They were sung very slowly, with melodies in which endlessly inventive use was made of a small range of notes.[15]

The *waiata* genre, moreover, can itself be divided into several sub-genres. The *waiata tangi* or 'weeping songs', for example, are sung at funerals or in the wake of disasters or lost battles. The *waiata aroha* or 'songs of love and longing' are sung by women, and are a vehicle for airing their complaints about lost lovers or neglectful husbands. The *waiata whaiaipo* or 'sweetheart songs' tell of flirtations, illicit affairs, or conflicted allegiances.

All these traditional song styles are now most frequently heard at public gatherings in the *marae*, often at night, by moonlight, and often interspersed by the oratorical performances, which are a speciality of Maori men. But in the nineteenth century, the subjects of the songs began to evolve significantly. For one thing, following the Treaty of Waitangi, tribal warfare decreased dramatically, as did the demand for songs of triumph and defeat. For another, with the advent of Christianity, biblical subjects appeared, often associated with themes of hope and reconciliation. Thirdly, the music itself was influenced by the Pakehas' own hymns and melodies. In the twentieth century, when the repertoire continued to expand, singing was harnessed to protest movements and all manner of contemporary issues.

Nonetheless, many of the old songs have been preserved. Some were written down by missionaries; others, by constant repetition, have become standards. The process of studying them, and recording them for posterity, is still in train. The melancholy melodies and words have perennial appeal:

*E pa to hau, he wini raro, he homai aroha*
*Kia tangi atu au i konei, he aroha ki te iwi . . .*

(The soft-blowing wind from the north brings longing
And I weep. My longing is for my people
Gone off to far Paerau. Who can find them there,
Where are my friends of those prosperous times?
It has come to this; we are separated, and I am desolate.)[16]

Songs with a Christian flavour often reflect the tension between old and new:

*E Hohepa e tangi, kati ra te tangi,*
*Me aha taua i te po inoi, i te po kauwhau? . . .*

(You are crying, Hohepa, but cry no more.
What must we do on the night of prayers, the night of preaching?

You must leap into the waters of Jordan
So that evil can be forgiven, and your sins removed, my son.
You must make your way to Turner's House*
And be taught the letters in the book –
The first chapter, the chapter of Genesis,
And the Gospel of Matthew, so you can learn,
So the eyes of your body can see, my son.)[17]

In the days of the *Kingitanga* movement, songs were composed in praise of the native monarchs. In 1894 an eyewitness reported the scene at Waikato, where the elevation of a new monarch was being celebrated. Mahuta's band marched into the *marae*, playing 'a modified version of an English popular air'. The people then stood and bowed, and a group of men and women sang the newly composed song:

*Ko Mahuta te kingi, hei kingi hou,*
*Hei kingi tuatoru mo te ao katoa . . .*

(Mahuta is king, the new king,
A third king for all the world.
His followers, the Fair Weather of Matariki,
His angels, will speed amongst our people.
We will carry you forth.
Go Mahuta, go out to all the world.)[18]

The world-famous *Haka* or 'War Chant' of the Maoris is but one example of a far wider genre, and its use by the multiracial All Blacks rugby team is condemned by purists. The warriors face their foe before battle, performing a routine of grunts, grimaces, and threatening gestures in unison. In the key central passage, the chant-leader shouts *Ke Mate! Ke Mate!* (I die! I die!), and the warriors reply *Ke Ora! Ke Ora!* (I live! I live!). In the Maori community itself, a variety of different *haka* are performed by men and women for ceremonial purposes or as a sign of welcome. In some versions, the men dance and the women sing. The particular 'Ke Mate' that everyone knows belongs to a category of war dances called *peruperu*.

As the 'Ke Mate' shows, however, violence was never far beneath the surface. It is all too easy for contemporary commentators to fall into the sentimental trap of hearing the dancing and mythology and

---

* In 1823 a Wesleyan mission was founded at Tokerau in the Northland; the minister was Reverend Nathaniel Turner.

regarding it as nothing more than colourful folklore. One has to realize that the ethos of traditional Maori life cannot be judged by modern Western standards, and that its cruel and brutal aspects must be taken as an integral part of the whole. One has also to accept that various gross forms of cruelty and brutality, from hanging, drawing and quartering to witch-hunts and slave-trading, were current in European, Christian society until quite recently. Among the Maori, slavery was rife, the tradition of *utu* or 'vendetta' was deeply embedded, and, as Captain Cook observed, cannibalism was practised without inhibition. Nor is it true, as some have argued, that cannibal feasts were confined to victory celebrations after battle. They took place, even within families, as established forms of retribution against any individual perceived as a transgressor. Human blood was drunk, hearts were cut out as prize morsels, brains were savoured, eyeballs were boiled as delicacies, and corpses roasted with relish. To the Maori, who saw humans as part of the undivided animal kingdom, eating human flesh was no different from eating the meat of fish or fowl.

Slavery could be either collective or individual. Entire clans could be subjugated following defeat in battle. Their warriors would be killed and eaten; their most nubile women would be seized to boost the reproductive potential of the victors; and the remainder would toil out the rest of their lives as tributaries. By the same token, all the *rangatira* or 'class of high-born families' within a clan or tribe would expect to be waited on by *mokai* or 'personal slaves', who would work to order as servants, labourers, or concubines. It is no accident that the worst insult that could be hurled at a Maori was *toenga kainga* or 'remnant of the feast', meaning someone who was not even good enough to be eaten.

For me, as a historian, the most fascinating realization was that the Maoris' traditional concept of time was completely different from our own. Europeans tend to imagine themselves standing in the present and peering forwards into a murky future, with the past behind them. But Maoris adopted the opposite mental posture. They stood, as it were, with their face to the past, observing the doings of gods and ancestors while turning a cold shoulder on what was still to come. Their vocabulary reflects this stance. The past is *ngaa raa o mue*, 'the days in front', while the future is *kei muri*, 'what is behind'. As one anthropologist has put it, the Maoris were 'walking backwards into the future'. Their gaze was firmly fixed on the past. And the idea of progress was absent.[19]

The question is posed, therefore: what was it that convinced Westerners to walk into the future looking forwards? It could have been the
ancient Greeks' sense of curiosity, or the Romans' aspirations to build
an empire. Most likely, it was the Christians' renunciation of the sins of
the past and their expectation of the Second Coming.

For 150 years the Maori were in contact with Europeans without either
side being seriously affected. After leaving Van Diemen's Land, Abel
Tasman made landfall in December 1642 near the northern tip of South
Island without knowing exactly where he was. He named it *Staten
Land*, after the United Provinces of the Netherlands. He departed after
some of his crew were killed in a skirmish at a place to which he
gave the Dutch equivalent of 'Murderers Bay'. He also discovered a
fine stretch of coast further north without realizing that he was on a
different island. Yet from then on, European navigators knew that
an attractive land lay to the east of Australia, and word would have
spread among the Maori that a race of white Pakeha possessed tall,
sail-driven canoes that could bring them over the ocean to Aotearoa.
Later accounts suggest that the Maori took the Pakeha captains to be
gods, and the sailors to be goblins, because they rowed their boats
backwards.

In the eighteenth century, Dutch, French, and eventually British
ships visited the islands more frequently, but without settling. A key
milestone was reached during Captain James Cook's First Voyage in
the *Endeavour* (1769–70), when he circumnavigated the islands and
made a detailed and accurate map of them. The French explorer Marc-
Joseph Marion du Fresne was killed and eaten by the Maori in the Bay
of Islands in 1772, anticipating Cook's only slightly less drastic fate on
Hawaii seven years later. A native of St Malo, du Fresne had earlier
made important discoveries, including the fact that Tasmania was not
*terra nullius*.[20] As from 1788, 'New Zealand' (as anglicized by Cook
from the Dutch) was included within the territories nominally assigned
to the British colony of New South Wales.

British activity gathered pace in the early decades of the nineteenth
century, bringing whalers, traders, missionaries, fugitives, and government officials to the islands. The first permanent Pakeha settler is said
to have been James Caddell, aged sixteen, and the only survivor of a
Maori attack on the crew of a British ship that landed on Stewart Island
in 1810. He married the daughter of a local chief, 'went native', became
a chief himself, and, as 'the tattooed man', could barely talk English to

the people who found him many years later. The first two European women to arrive, Charlotte Badger and Catherine Haggerty, were convict passengers on a ship from New South Wales, the *Venus*, whose crew mutinied in 1806 and sailed her to the Bay of Islands. Charlotte Bader lived as the concubine of a Maori chief from the Ngapuhi tribe. The first full-blooded Pakeha child, Thomas King, was born in 1815, the son of missionaries. Two towns vie for the title of the islands' oldest European settlement. The port of Bluff in South Island, established in 1823, claims to be the 'oldest permanently inhabited site'. More than fifty years after Captain Cook's expedition, the population of the islands was approximately 100,000, of which Europeans accounted for perhaps 0.01 per cent.

Three key events occurred during these years. Firstly, from 1807, the Maori obtained muskets, and plunged into a series of bloodthirsty tribal wars that lasted for more than thirty years. Hongi Hika (1772–1828), a Ngapuhi chief deeply involved in these Musket Wars, actively encouraged European settlement, and in 1820 visited England, where he was introduced to King George IV. Secondly, in December 1809, a horrific massacre took place when Maori warriors boarded a British ship, the *Boyd*, and killed virtually every person on board. The victims were ceremoniously eaten. The incident was an object lesson in the clash of cultures. The son of a Maori chief had joined the *Boyd* for a passage from Australia, and, suspected of theft, had been flogged. For the British, the flogging was a routine act of naval discipline. For the Maori, it broke taboo, and provoked an extreme response. Thirdly, in 1814, at the instigation of Hongi Hika, the Reverend Samuel Marsden (1765–1838), the senior Anglican chaplain in New South Wales, crossed the Tasman Sea, bought land at Kerikeri in the Northland for the price of forty-eight axes, planted vines, and introduced Christianity. The intended mission, owned by the London Missionary Society and originally called Gloucester Town, did not begin to operate until several years later. Marsden also undertook a series of expeditions that started the European exploration of North Island. The net result was that the opportunities for colonization and evangelization became much better known. So too, however, did opportunities for unconstrained mutual exploitation.

The British Colonial Office, which was technically in charge, was embarrassed by its impotence. New Zealand was one of the wildest of wild frontiers. Quite apart from the bloodshed and rampant cannibalism of the Musket Wars, an assortment of unsavoury Europeans were running riot. The crews of whalers and sealers, which frequented the South Pacific, were accustomed to living with native women. Now reports reached London that Maori chiefs were driving crowds of their girls to the nascent trading posts, and demanding that they be sexually serviced in exchange for guns and axes. Protestant and Catholic missionaries competed in no friendly manner, complaining that converts refused to abandon polygamy and infanticide. After a partial translation of the Bible was published in 1826, weird, pseudo-Christian practices appeared. A Maori chief called Papahurihia declared himself a prophet; his followers called themselves *Hurai* or 'Jews', and held services on Saturdays. Some thirty Maori chiefs petitioned London for protection, and self-appointed settler associations were demanding government intervention. Worst of all, French missionary and colonial societies were taking an interest.

So in 1832 the Colonial Office appointed an official British Resident, James Busby (1801–71). Busby's term of office, 1832–40, only illustrates the reigning chaos. He had spent time in Australia and was an enthusiast of viticulture. But on returning to New South Wales, he met the implacable opposition of the governor to his appointment, and had to pay for his passage from Sydney to Waitangi out of his own pocket. In theory, Busby was armed with full powers, but in practice he had no means of enforcement. He begged the Colonial Office in vain for a grant to support two constables – just one constable per island, in an area larger than Great Britain. He made one arrest – of a Maori for the murder of a settler – and in 1835, on hearing that Baron de Thierry, a French adventurer, was hatching a scheme of settlement, he persuaded a group of Maori chiefs to sign a Declaration of Independence that received royal approval but otherwise had no significance. Busby also designed a New Zealand flag.

At this point, in the late 1830s, two brothers from England provided the drive that resulted in the successful founding of a colony. Edward Gibbon Wakefield (1796–1862) and his younger brother, Colonel William Wakefield (1801–48), were enterprising to the point of being disreputable. They had spent three years in Newgate Prison for the abduction of an heiress. Edward then occupied himself with a variety of colonial ventures, mainly in Canada, while William went off to fight as a mercenary in the Carlist Wars in Spain. Edward's theoretical writings on colonialism were regarded as progressive by his contemporaries, but paid little regard to the interests of indigenous peoples. He condemned both slaveholding in America and the convict system in Australia, preferring a managed market for free labour and the creation of a model farming community. His watchword was: 'Possess yourself of the soil and you will be secure.'[21]

The New Zealand Company, which came into being at the Wakefields' inspiration, was defiantly independent of the Colonial Office. It had a faltering start and a chequered history, but was responsible for the organization, financing, and despatch of the first fleet of emigrant ships to leave Great Britain. Formed in 1837, the year of Queen Victoria's accession, it started its operations while the government and the House of Lords were still debating the islands' future. William Wakefield captained the *Tory*, which landed with the advance party at Port Nicholson on 20 September 1839,* closely followed by a team of surveyors on the *Cuba*. The *Aurora* joined them on 22 January 1840, carrying 150 colonists, who built the settlement of Britannia that was to grow into the city of Wellington. A dozen more ships sailed within a year.[22]

The Colonial Office, stung by the Company's initiative, sprang into action. It appointed Captain William Hobson (1792–1842) as lieutenant-governor, gave him instructions to negotiate a treaty with the native chiefs, and urged him to act swiftly. Hobson had visited New Zealand three years earlier, and, strongly lobbied by missionaries, had written a report on the influx of lawless fugitives from Australia. He now reached the Bay of Islands one week after the *Aurora* arrived in Port Nicholson. Loyally assisted by Busby but with no legal assistance, he drew up a document for presentation to the chiefs, and prepared for a grand gathering outside Busby's residence at Waitangi. The final version was ready within four days; a Maori translation by the missionary Henry Williams appeared on the fifth day. Hobson was in a hurry. News arrived from 'Britannia' that the New Zealand Company was planning to create a colony of its own. A gathering of natives was given a brief chance to discuss the proposal. Some chiefs, influenced by the French Catholic missionary Bishop Pompallier, opposed it. 'We don't need a Governor,' they said, 'we chiefs govern our ancestral lands.' But a majority were in favour. They appeared to be swayed by the argument that the strong rule of a British governor was needed to restrain the outlaws and the grog-sellers.

---

* What later became Wellington Harbour was named Port Nicholson in 1826 after the harbourmaster at Sydney.

The resultant Treaty of Waitangi was concluded on 6 February 1840 in a large tent erected on Busby's lawn. It contained a preamble and three articles:

1. that sovereignty was transferred to the 'Queen of England' (*sic*), under whom the Governor would serve;
2. that Maori ownership of the land, forests and fisheries was guaranteed; and
3. that Maoris would enjoy equal rights with all other British subjects.

Hobson was the first to sign. As over one hundred chiefs put their names or marks to the document, he repeatedly intoned the phrase *He iwi tahi tatou*, meaning 'We are now one people.' Eight copies of the original were then made and despatched to all inhabited areas. Some four hundred further Maori signatures were thereby obtained. This by no means brought in all the Maori leaders, but it was sufficient for Hobson to issue a proclamation on 21 May 1840 stating that the British Crown held sovereignty over the whole of New Zealand, 'the North Island by Treaty, and the South Island by discovery'. Six months later a second proclamation stated that New Zealand was to separate from New South Wales. The Treaty was then deposited in storage, and was not seriously discussed until the twentieth century.

Nonetheless, it does not require legal expertise to understand that the Treaty and its contents were questionable from the start. Quite apart from Victoria not being the 'Queen of England', it is self-evident that Hobson's Maori partners were never given a fair chance to study the proposal or prepare a reasoned response. The British representatives were united behind a document drawn up by them in English. The native signatories were just a collection of individuals who could not speak for the Maori nation as a whole, who had no sophisticated grasp of English and little experience of written Maori, and can only have been puzzled by a translation that had been knocked out in a rush by amateurs. According to modern scholars, all the key phrases signifying 'governorship', 'property', or 'chieftainship' were faulty, and the English version differed significantly from the Maori one. What is more, the Treaty was never officially ratified, and in the course of a legal case in 1877 a British judge dismissed it as a 'simple nullity'. Even so, British colonists were taught to regard it as an act of generosity. What is certain is that the Maori had no inkling that by signing the Treaty they were letting themselves in for a torrent of Pakeha migration, which would soon turn them into a minority in their own land.[23]

In the fifty years from 1831, the European population in New Zealand exploded to half a million. Roughly 400,000 sailed from Great Britain and Ireland, mainly young people, who reproduced rapidly. Over 100,000 of those had their passage paid by the Colonial Office. A similar number arrived during the Gold Rush after gold was discovered at Otago in 1861. Not all of them stayed, but the demographic increase was relentless. During that same period the Maori population halved. At least 100,000 at the time of the Treaty, it fell to 40,000 before the end of the century, mainly due to unfamiliar European diseases.

The history of the early pioneers is today a subject of major interest. Databases are being compiled to include the names and voyages of all the settler ships, together with their passengers and their origins. Early diaries are highly valued. The New Zealand Company's ship *London*, for example, sailed from Gravesend on 10 August 1840 and arrived at Port Nicholson on 12 December after a voyage of 121 days. A woman on board recorded her arrival:

> Rising at dawn, we crowded the ship's rails, anxious to get a first glimpse of the land which was to be our new home . . . The sea was calm as we sailed into Port Nicholson on that warm sunlit December morning in 1840 and soon shelters and shacks could be seen dotted along the waterfront . . . Presently, native canoes came paddling out from the shore . . . to greet us. Our long journey from England was coming to an end.[24]

Thanks to the Highland clearances, a major component of the settlers came from Scotland. A poster displayed in Glasgow in 1839–40 by the New Zealand Company announced sailings to THE FIRST SCOTCH COLONY. Many of the Scots settled on South Island, where they pioneered sheep farming, and where place names such as Dunedin and Invercargill attest their influence. The Irish were present in force as well. In order to attract them, the infant colony was divided in 1841 into three provinces – 'New Ulster' for North Island, 'New Munster' for South Island, and 'New Leinster' for the smaller Stewart Island. The provinces soon changed, but Irish emigrants kept coming. Most place names, however, are English, in line with the colony's official language. Auckland (1840) was named after Governor Hobson's patron, the Earl of Auckland, when it was chosen as the colony's capital. Greytown, Greymouth, and Grey River reflect the achievements of Sir George Grey (1812–98), the colony's longest-serving governor. Canterbury, South Island's largest region, was so named by the Canterbury Association, which was responsible for its settlement. Christchurch (1848) reflects the loyalties of an association member who was educated at Christ Church, Oxford. Whitby was Captain Cook's home town. In the early days, the incoming settlers ignored Maori names; but more recently many geographical landmarks have reverted to their original nomenclature.

From the very first day of the colony's existence, control of the land was 'Problem Number One'. The Treaty of Waitangi confirmed Maori ownership of the land, whilst also stating that all future land purchases must be made by the Crown. These provisions were an ill-concealed device for ensuring that the Crown could gain legal title to all purchases made, no matter what pressures were put on the Maori to sell. But they equally offended two important interested parties. They were resented by the New Zealand Company and other settler bodies that had already acquired land and that expected to have a free hand dealing with it. And the provisions were not accepted by the numerous Maori tribes, especially in North Island, whose chiefs had refused to sign the Treaty or those who, having signed, thought better of it. Conflict, therefore, was unavoidable. It broke out in the summer of 1843, and continued at intervals for thirty years in a series of campaigns that were once called 'the Maori Wars' and now tend to be called 'the Land Wars'.[25]

The opening shots were fired in the Wairau Valley in the north of South Island in April 1843. A group of New Zealand Company officials, who had prepared a forged claim to a block of territory, entered the valley intending to survey it and arrest a couple of uncooperative Maori chiefs. They were ambushed, and twenty-two people were killed. The settler press declared a 'massacre'. But when investigations were conducted by Hobson's successor as governor, Captain William Fitzroy, he ruled that the settlers were entirely to blame.

The next episode, known as the Flagstaff War, occurred in the Bay of Islands, in North Island, and lasted from July 1844 to January 1846. It was initiated by Hone Heke, a chief of the Ngapuhi, who was a Christian, a veteran of the Musket Wars, and a signatory of the Treaty, but who already felt deceived. He was apparently influenced by American whalers who told of the United States' successful rebellion against Britain. On three occasions he and his associates axed the flagstaff bearing the Union Jack at RRR (now Russell) and eventually laid waste to the settlement. Regular troops were brought in from Australia by Governor George Grey, and a number of indecisive engagements were fought. Hone Heke died of tuberculosis shortly afterwards. Yet he had gained great prestige from his defiance, and his warriors had shown that they could stand up to the Pakeha in battle. The design of his 'gunfighter pa', the standard Maori form of defensive fortification, proved particularly effective. Politically, however, the war showed that the Maori tribes were divided; some of them were prepared to take up arms in defence of the British, whereas others took to the field against them.[26]

Such was the state of affairs in the 1850s when a coalition of tribes in the rugged interior of North Island moved to turn their backs on the colony and govern themselves independently. The *Kingitanga* movement was inspired by a form of Maori nationalism, which pressed for the reinstatement of traditional customs, threatened to kill any Pakeha that set foot in its territory, and placed a total ban on the sale of Maori land. It centred on the Tainui *iwi* and its neighbours, and launched a Maori monarchy. At its height, it commanded the allegiance of perhaps 30 per cent of the Maori population, and formed a native state within the state. The first king was Potatau (r. 1858–60). The second, Tawhiao (r. 1860–94), had serious ambitions and petitioned Queen Victoria for recognition of a Maori assembly. The third, Tawhiao's son, was Mahuta (r. 1894–1912). His successors continue to reign to the present day, even though they have lost all but a ceremonial role.[27]

All the remaining campaigns of the Land Wars were aimed either directly against the *Kingitanga* or against their tribal allies. The largest operation, in 1863–5, in which 18,000 imperial troops were engaged, saw the invasion of the *Kingitanga* heartland in the Waikato region. It ended with a massive punitive programme of land confiscation that robbed the Maori tribes, rebel and loyalist alike, of more than three million acres. The injustice of the confiscation laws remained a bone of contention until redress was finally agreed in the 1990s.

The Land Wars encouraged the formation of colonial military units. One of them, the Forest Rangers, specialized in guerrilla tactics learned from the Maori, and one of their heroes was a mercenary, Colonel Leopold von Tempski (1828–68). A former officer of the Prussian Army and of Polish descent, von Tempski was eager for glory, charged a well-defended 'gunfighter pa', was felled by a hail of bullets, and was duly eaten. (There is a Polish proverb to match his fate: *Polak mądry po szkodzie*, 'A Pole gains wisdom from his injuries.')

After land, the second problem was religion. Victorian imperialism was intimately associated with Christian evangelization, and it is arguable that the Colonial Office was more closely aligned with the missionary lobby than with the settler movement. Indeed, the missionaries took to the field well ahead of the colonists. On Christmas Day 1814, when the first Christian service was held on the shore of the Bay of Islands, the Union Flag was raised. 'I saw the English flag flying,' wrote the Reverend Samuel Marsden, and 'I saw it as the dawn of civilisation, liberty and religion in this dark and benighted land.' All manner of troubles blighted the first decades. An account published by a visiting artist, Augustus Earle, *A Narrative of a Nine Months' Residence in New Zealand* (1832), strongly criticized the missionaries' lack of empathy for native customs. Nonetheless, forty-two missions were active by the time of the Treaty – Anglican, Wesleyan Methodist, and Roman Catholic.

The barriers to conversion of the natives were formidable. Although the Maoris possessed a clear concept of the afterlife, they lacked all sense of divine judgement and the need for redemption. Their traditional teaching held that men and women were rewarded or punished on Earth for their earthly conduct; when the spirits of the dead migrated to the mid-ocean island of paradise, they had no retribution to fear, and no reason to transfer their allegiance to the Christian God. Three factors acted in the missionaries' favour. Firstly, the large class of Maori slaves, and the substantial number of enslaved tribes, welcomed the Christian message as an escape route from their subjection. Secondly, in both the Musket Wars and the Land Wars, the missionaries were well viewed as peacemakers. In the campaigns against the *Kingitanga*, who had revitalized animist practices, it was tribes with Christian chiefs that most readily assisted the imperial forces. And thirdly, many Maori quickly recognized the value of literacy. They flocked to the missionary schools. The publication by the Church Missionary Society of a Maori New Testament in 1837 and a full Maori Bible in 1868 were important milestones. It has been estimated that by 1850 already 60 per cent of the Maori were at least nominally Christianized.[28]

Tensions, however, remained, sometimes in the least-expected quarters. In 1846, for example, in a letter known as the 'Blood and Treasure Despatch', Governor Grey wrote to the Colonial Secretary, W. E. Gladstone, complaining furiously about the missionaries' land-grabbing proclivities.[29] As a result, the Church Missionary Society relieved one of its most respected officers, Reverend Henry Williams, of his position. Friction between Protestants and Catholics continued, although social work by Catholic female orders such as the Sisters of Mercy was universally valued. Each of the main denominations tried to defend its territorial gains. In South Island, the Canterbury Association was an Anglican body, while Scottish Presbyterians built up Dunedin.

The third problem was government. The colony's extreme isolation in its formative years is hard to imagine. Prior to the arrival of the electric telegraph in the 1880s, governors could not expect a reply from London in much less than twelve months, and were forced to rely on their own unaided judgement. The British parliament's initial attempt to introduce a constitution in 1846 was sunk by Governor Grey's opposition to the proposal for separate Maori districts, but in 1852 the second constitution took root. The country was divided into six new provinces; an elected legislative assembly came into being; and from 1856 a prime minister headed the executive cabinet alongside the governor. In the 1890s, New Zealand politicians took part in negotiations for federation with Australia, but the concept was decisively defeated at home. New Zealand was established as a separate Dominion of the British Empire in 1907, equal in status to Australia and Canada.[30]

New Zealand's natural beauties and historical sites need weeks, indeed months, to explore. North Island is big and South Island even bigger. Day-trippers can be disappointed. There is a real danger of being bundled onto a 'Tiki Tour' and into a van that drives for hours and hours down narrow, winding lanes, with nothing to see but leafy hedges, and of then being dumped for a frustrating forty minutes on a World Heritage beach. The rule must be: do not even try to go if you don't have the time to take it all in at leisure. For the historically minded, two trips compete for pre-eminence. One, in North Island, is to the Waitangi Treaty Grounds, symbolic of the right-minded approach to the country's past that now prevails. The other, in South Island – for fans of alternative history – is to Akaroa, a small sleepy village that was once the site of Port Louis-Philippe, a French settlement established in August 1840, only six months after the signing of the Treaty of Waitangi.

To experience New Zealand to the full, however, one has to travel end to end – from the southernmost tip of South Island to the northernmost tip of North Island. The journey, by road, rail, and ferry, demands a minimum of a month and a thousand miles. Enchantment is the reward.[31]

The place to start is the harbour at Bluff – bluff by name and bluff by nature. Apart from those in southernmost South America, it is the most southerly settlement on Earth. (This is where Tasman might have landed if he had held to his intended course.) It's the terminal of

Highway 1, and of the ferry that sails to remote Stewart Island (Rakiura); beyond which there is nothing but the cold grey ocean and Antarctica. Bluff is the source of the country's best oysters. Life there can be hard, not to say tedious. Fred and Myrtle Flutey, who took up residence in Bluff before electricity or the telephone, beat the tedium by collecting paua shells, with which they lined every internal inch of their gale-blasted bungalow. Their 'Paua House' is now displayed in the Te Papa Museum.[32]

Driving north up Highway 1 via Invercargill and Balclutha, one senses the strong Scottish flavour of the Southland, which might easily be Sutherland. On the right-hand side, as one wends through the Catlins, Pacific breakers crash on lonely beaches. On the left-hand side extends an untamed wilderness of lakes, forests, and craggy hills. Beyond them is the Fiordland, New Zealand's Norway, almost as big and no less spectacular, home to the largest of National Parks and to glaciers, green glacial lakes, world-record waterfalls, and gloomy sea lochs.

Some 115 miles from Bluff lies Dunedin (the old Celtic name for Edinburgh), premier metropolis of South Island. Founded as 'New Edinburgh' by Scottish 'Wee Frees', who sought a sanctuary for their Presbyterian fundamentalism, and overtaken in the 1860s by the go-getters of the Gold Rush, it still exudes an air of indomitable Victorian endeavour. As if on purpose, many of its impossibly steep streets force its citizens to make an effort. The University of Otago, built in Scottish Gothic, is the country's oldest. The Settlers' Museum, where, in anticipation of the centenary of 1914, I presented a lecture on 'The Eastern Front in the First World War', is a model of its kind. The law courts, and above all the gorgeous railway station, attest to the taste as well as the willpower of the pioneers.[33]

The Highcliff Drive round the adjacent Otago Peninsula demands a full day's excursion. The brochures direct tourists to Larnarch Castle, a fine Victorian mansion, but no time should be lost in reaching the Royal Albatross Centre on Tairoa Head. The albatross exemplifies Nature's miraculous adaptability. Nine-week-old albatross chicks plunge instinctively off the cliffs before discovering the widest wings in the world and, circling the globe in celebration, inspiring the most reluctant traveller.[34]

North of Dunedin, at Moeraki, one passes moonscape boulders on the seashore, and stops for lunch in prim and pretty Oamaru, then turns off for a long diversion into the mountains, heading for Aoraki

(Mount Cook), the 'Cloud Piercer'. This is surrounded by seventy-two glaciers, and at 3,724 metres (12,217 feet) is higher than all but the highest of the European Alps. Not climbed until 1894, it was the training ground for Edmund Hillary and is now ringed by skiing and mountain-climbing resorts. Less mobile visitors must be content with pictures of the pure white pyramid reflected in the deep blue-green waters of Lake Pukaki.

Canterbury Province, in the centre of South Island, is as English as Otago is Scottish. Its rolling, agricultural countryside supports sheep in the hills and arable farms in the valleys. We go to Oxford, and find that it has its Woodstock Road. Two volunteers, man and wife, are staffing the local museum, which documents the changes in rural life. The town cemetery contains the graves of men killed at Gallipoli in 1915 and Montecassino in 1944.

Christchurch, the capital of Canterbury Province and 193 miles from Dunedin, is still recovering from the devastating earthquake of 2011. There are many ruins, a cardboard cathedral, a shopping street built of shipping containers, and endless repair zones, where sewers and water pipes are still being mended. The municipal accommodation office sells discounted 'rooms with a view', which turn out to overlook a vast parking lot for cranes and bulldozers. Fortunately, the magnificent Botanical Gardens and nearby provincial museum escaped damage.[35]

Christchurch, however, is the springboard for Akaroa/Port Louis-Philippe, and for a superb scenic drive around the Banks Peninsula. When the French captain Jean-François Langlois paid a deposit to the local Maori for the purchase of a piece of land at Akaroa in 1838, New Zealand was unclaimed territory in European eyes. By the time that he and his associates could return less than two years later, with an expedition of sixty-three emigrants, they found the Union Flag flying on the beach. Their ship, the *Comte de Paris*, landed on 18 August. The British ship *Britomart*, under Captain Owen Stanley RN, had landed two days earlier. The French had been pipped at the post, or, as they would have said, *'coiffés au poteau'*.[36] But they stayed on.

From Christchurch to Picton discerning travellers go by train, boarding the Coastal Pacific express on the southernmost section of KiwiRail and breaking the journey at one or two of the intermediate stations. This is not a Bullet Train or a TGV; it trundles along at a leisurely pace, stopping from time to time to catch breath. But the panoramic carriages, swaying gently, are comfortable, and at places the track runs astonishingly close to the ocean. Elsewhere, it passes through tunnels, round steep curves and across long bridges through forests and bare mountains. Passengers return in feeling to a past age.[37]

The oceanside resort of Kaikoura is the world capital of dolphin-dipping and whale-watching.[38] Speedboats power out for several miles into the bay, before heaving to and waiting for the marvellous sea mammals to appear. Within a few minutes the more intrepid holiday-makers, dressed in wetsuits, are swimming in the water with the dusky dolphins, who nuzzle up close from curiosity but always behave. Great humpbacks and sperm whales generally keep their distance, but habit-ually surface and salute their admirers with a mighty blow-out. Seals lie thick on the inshore islets, and a basket of bait thrown overboard brings in a squabbling flock of seabirds which fight for the food. Where else can one watch an albatross circling overhead at close quarters before landing on the water like a seaplane? This is a rare place, where, for a day, cosseted specimens of modern humankind can retake their due position among God's creatures. Afterwards, the head spins in wonder as one walks up the headland or along the giant beach, looking forward to a fine supper at the Green Dolphin and to blissful dreams in a studio at the waterfront Anchor Inn.

Further up the line, the accent jumps from whales to wines, from trundling trains to fast-moving industry. The train stops at Blenheim, chief town of the Marlborough District, and one needs to pause for at least a week. There are 167 wineries to sample, and a striking history to imbibe:

> In past centuries, Maori hunted Moa here, and cultivated vast kumara crops . . . In 1873, pioneering Scottish farmer and grape-grower, David Herd, planted the first vineyard . . . And today, Marlborough is recog-nized as one of the world's premier wine regions.[39]

The region's rise has been dramatic. It was only in 1973 that the first commercial vineyard opened for business at Brancott Estate. In 1986 Hunter's Fumé Blanc won the gold medal at London's prestigious Vintage Festival – a mere thirteen years of frantic planting, harvesting, and refining had sufficed to reach the summit of the wine trade. The key to success, apart from hard work and brave initial investment, lay in matchless sunshine, the lack of frosts, low rainfall, a high range between diurnal and nocturnal temperatures, and variable soil con-ditions. Vineyards spread rapidly from Blenheim Township to the Richmond Ranges, the Wairau Valley, and Cape Campbell. By 2012, the export trade had passed the $1 billion mark, and accounted for 72 per cent of New Zealand's overall exports. The names to remember are Cloudy Bay Sauvignon Blanc, Oyster Bay Sauvignon Blanc and Pinot Noir, Terravin Pinot Noir, Stoneleigh Latitude Chardonnay, Te Whare Ra Gewürztraminer, Cabbage Tree Merlot, and Cellier le Brun sparkling.[40] They bear responsibility for our many missings of the train.

Picton, 462 miles from Bluff, sees the end of the line and the ferry to the Cook Strait. It is the opposite of Bluff in all senses – a wind-free, sun-drenched cove with palm trees on the shore. It is the focal point of South Island's northern extremity, standing between the exquisite wooded ridges of Queen Charlotte Sound and the equally delightful inlets of the Marlborough Sounds. It has an excellent museum devoted to the history of early pioneers and whaling. Further west is a mass of delectable coastal paths, the tiny city of Nelson, founded in 1842, and, surprisingly, the peaks and lakes of the northern reaches of the southern Alps. The Gateway Motel at Picton is the presumed last resting-place of my favourite, velvet plush black cap.

The Cook Strait, only 17 miles in width at its narrowest point, is for visitors who wish to feel the force of Nature. According to Maori legend, it was discovered by Kupe, who was following a giant octopus, which he killed in the Tory Channel in the Marlborough Sounds. The Cook Strait was seen in 1642 by Abel Tasman, who wrongly thought it a cul-de-sac and watered in nearby Murderers' Bay (now Golden Bay), but it was properly charted by Captain Cook in 1770. To begin with, the ferry from Picton glides serenely along the protected Tory Channel. But emerging into open water, it is roughly buffeted by the fierce west wind and rocked by the contending currents: one wind-driven from the Tasman Sea, the other surging from the Pacific swell. 'The Cook Strait', says the guidebook, 'is one of the most dangerous sea passages on earth.'[41] It gave immigrant ships their last heart-in-mouth experience before entering Wellington Bay.

Wellington is not just the capital and linchpin of the two main islands; it is also a major transport junction, at which North Island's three main roads converge. Highway 1, last seen at Picton, resumes its route heading north towards Auckland through the tangled and mountainous centre. Highway 2 wends its way around the well-developed east coast, and Highway 3 around the lonely west coast.

As in South Island, the windward, west coast north of Wellington is overloaded with beautiful scenery but undersupplied with people. New Plymouth possesses the one and only deep-water port on the Tasman

Sea, and houses the country's main petroleum industry. The perfect volcanic cone of Mount Egmont (Taranaki) dominates the more southerly region, and the Coromandel Peninsula, once the scene of a gold rush, the more northerly one. The leeward east coast, in contrast, is adorned by a string of towns, resorts, and recreation areas. Hawke's Bay, which used to be the premier wine district, is separated from the Bay of Plenty by the massive promontory of East Cape. Towns of note include Napier, Gisborne, Opotiki, Whakatane, Te Puke, Tauranga, Katikati, Waihi, and Whangamata: an etymologist's delight. Mount Ruapehu, which last erupted in 1905, reaches 9,176 feet and, despite the latitude, is permanently capped with snow.

Central North Island is sometime called 'the real New Zealand'. It is blessed with natural wonders in abundance, and is Maori Country par excellence. Lakeside Rotorua is its iconic heart. This is where the insurgent tribes held out during the Maori Wars, and Tamaki Maori Village is where contemporary trippers receive a taste of indigenous culture and customs. The geysers of Rotorua, the 'magical' Waitomo Caves, the Emerald Lakes of Tongariro, and the Bridal Veil Falls at Raglan all amazed the early pioneers. Hamilton, New Zealand's only inland city, grew up around a military settlement beside the mighty Waikato River. Thirty miles east of Hamilton, the Hobbiton Movie Set, where the *Lord of the Rings* and the *Hobbit* were filmed, attracts hordes of visitors.[42] The films' director, Peter Jackson – a Kiwi himself – picked Central North Island as the ideal location to portray Tolkien's Middle-earth.

Auckland, the largest metropolis, the 'City of Sails', 306 miles from Wellington, spans a narrow spit of land that links the main part of North Island with the volcanic expanses of the Northland beyond. An inlet of the Tasman Sea laps the city on one side, and an arm of the Pacific on the other. It is New Zealand's gateway to Melanesia and Polynesia.[43]

The lookout on Mount Eden is the best place to start any visit to Auckland. Although close to the city centre, its volcanic cone rises high above the highest skyscraper and Sky Tower, presenting a panoramic overview of the city's spectacular location. We pass signs saying PLEASE MIND THE CRATER before reaching the circular bronze orientation table listing the distances to the most important places on the planet. London is 18,339 kilometres to the north-west, New York a mere 14,197 kilometres to the north-east. Reference points across the Pacific include Vancouver at 11,362 kilometres, Los Angeles at 10,478, and Santiago de Chile at 9,861. Auckland itself is a labyrinth of inlets and islands. To the left is Manukau Harbour, which lies on the Tasman Sea: to the right the Rangitoto Channel, which leads into the Pacific. In between, one can easily identify the narrow isthmus separating the two and on which the nascent city was born. Before the volcanic eruption that created the isthmus from molten lava, the land to the north would have formed a separate island. Stumps and cones left by ancient volcanic activity litter the landscape. The most recent explosions, some 300 or 400 years ago, occurred during Maori times and left their traces in legends. They would have been watched with alarm from the fortified Maori encampment atop Mount Eden (which they call Maungawhau).

The Northland beyond Auckland has been dubbed 'the birthplace of the nation'. It was at Rangihoua that the first European mission was settled in 1814, at Waitangi that the Anglo-Maori Treaty was signed in 1840, and at Russell, formerly Kororareka, that the original so-called capital was created. For a time, Russell was a lawless outpost of civilization, known to whalers as 'the Hell-Hole of the Pacific'. Appropriately, it now boasts the country's oldest surviving Christian church. The sheltered Bay of Islands, which contains 150 of them and attracted the first settlers, is now given over to deep-sea marlin fishing, kayaking, and paragliding.

At the Waitangi Treaty Grounds, the old Busby 'Residency' was restored for the centenary celebrations of 1940, and a fine Maori meeting place, *Te Whare Runanga*, was erected beside it. Visitors learn not only of the circumstances that led to the Treaty but also of the contemporary campaign to construct a more balanced historical narrative. The hour-long 'Maori Culture Show', which features energetic singing and dancing, and the full-size replica of an ocean-going *waka*, are highly praised in the visitors' book. Every year, on the anniversary of the Treaty, the signing ceremony is ritually re-enacted.[44]

North of Waitangi, the sort of fanatics who cycle for fun from Land's End to John o'Groats will love pressing on up the Aupouri Peninsula and the Ninety-Mile Beach until they reach the end of the road at Cape Reinga, where Highway 1 runs up to the lighthouse and the desolate cliff edge. *Reinga* means 'Underworld', and Maori myths tell how the spirits of the dead leap off the cliff at the start of their journey into the afterlife. The seashore below is called 'Spirits Beach'. At 34 degrees south, visitors still alive will be on the same latitude as Sydney, Australia, or in the opposite direction of Buenos Aires, Argentina. They will be some 1,000 kilometres south from New Caledonia, and 870 miles, as the crow flies, north from Bluff. But no one flies with the

crows from Bluff to Reinga. By road, rail, and ferry they will have covered 1,128 exhilarating miles.

I gave my lecture on European history for non-Europeans at Auckland
University. But it was obvious as we entered the university's central campus on Princes Street that there was a perspective here that was less
European than in the country's other cities. The university's website aims to recruit students by publicizing its own top ranking, crowing
about the city's high quality of life, and stressing the country's diversity:

> Kiwis are very proud of their diverse heritage, strongly influenced by
> indigenous Maori culture, by the past British colony, and by more recent
> migrants mainly from the Pacific Islands and Asia. New Zealand people
> are well travelled and outward looking with a reputation for being warm,
> welcoming and friendly to visitors.[45]

Auckland's special interests are underlined by the extensive range of
non-European courses on offer at the university's Arts Faculty. One
should not exaggerate. All the mainline subjects, typical of an English-
speaking university, are present. At the same time, the Maori Studies
Department, which offers twenty-eight undergraduate courses, is larger
than the French, German, and Spanish departments, and Asian Studies
is even larger. Each of the Social Sciences contains segments relevant to
Asia or the Pacific, and the languages taught include Chinese, Japanese,
Korean, New Zealand Maori, Cook Island Maori, Tongan, and
Samoan.[46] None of these were present twenty years ago.

Lunchtime at the Jin Hai Wan Seafood Restaurant on Wakefield
Street gives us a glimpse of present realities. A multicoloured aquarium
fills the entrance. Beyond it, a long low room is filled with perhaps
150 tables, few of them empty. Teams of black-clad waiters scurry
around, interspersed by diminutive waitresses in red dresses, white
aprons, and bandana-style kerchiefs. None of them speaks a word of
intelligible English (or Maori); they are from mainland China. We are
given a menu covered in Chinese characters with only occasional English names. We cannot find any prices, but gather that the dishes are
listed 'Small', 'Medium', or 'Large'. Before we can order, however, a
waitress dumps a round bamboo box of pork and rice in the middle of
our table:

'If you wan',' she says.

'Yes,' I respond, pointing to the menu, 'we do want to order – one
portion of prawn dumplings, and one beef ribs with black bean sauce.'

'If you wan'.'

'Yes, I do want.'

'If you wan'.'

The manager comes over, looking worried.

'How does it work?' I begin. 'Do we order our food, or do you bring us a selection of dishes?'

His answer, mixed with grins and bows, contains no identifiable vocabulary except for 'spoon', and ends with 'If you wan'.' A young waiter jumps to his aid. We point to prawn dumplings on the card, and the spare ribs.

'If you wan',' he says, running off to the kitchen.

We tackle the pork, now cold, and the rice envelopes. Two portions of dumplings arrive, one prawn, the other spinach.

'Ah, here are your spinach dumplings,' I tell my wife, 'if you wan'.'

Then a bowl of gristled beef appears, but no sauce.

'Rice?' I ask a passing waiter. 'Steamed rice?'

Fried rice soon appears. The bustle is constant, the non-comprehension near complete. This part of Auckland, it seems, presents a city of recent immigrants, run by and for immigrants.

The city's demographics confirm our impression. In a total population of 1,415,000 (2013), those of European descent still hold a slight majority of 55 per cent, but their share has dropped, and is still dropping, from 68 per cent only a dozen years ago. The Asian numbers, in contrast, have more than doubled in the same period to 307,000 (22 per cent). The number of Pacific Islanders (14 per cent) and Maoris (10 per cent) has also been rising. The city houses more Polynesians than anywhere else in the world. The laconic motto on the municipal coat of arms is 'Advance'.[47]

Eating out in Auckland, however, does not have to be Asian and can be a real adventure. 'Meet at the harbour at 5.30', were the instructions. We envisage a harbour-side bistro, or perhaps a restaurant across the river. Instead, a catamaran is waiting, and a journey of fifty minutes out to Waiheke Island on the edge of the Pacific. We sit on the upper back deck, sprinkled by spray from the churning wake but riveted by the view of Auckland's fast-receding lights and the huge black clouds forming in the twilight sky. 'See that eagle with outspread wings?' I say.

At Waiheke landing, a car is waiting and we are driven at high speed round narrow lanes, up hill and down dale. The driver, in his haste, loses his way. But eventually the rustic sign of TE WHAU LODGE is spotted. Meanwhile, night has fallen. As we clamber out of the vehicle, the stars of the southern sky demand attention. They are brilliant, twinkling and mostly unfamiliar. We've learned to recognize the Southern Cross, but Orion is lying forlornly on his side, scabbard pointing upwards.

Our host is waiting on the verandah. Gene only cooks for dinner parties of six or eight, and his speciality is local island produce and local wines. We are taken onto the darkened balcony to peer across the water at the city lights, and realize how far we've come.

'Seventeen kilometres in a straight line,' he says, 'except that you can't travel in a straight line.'

Then, we're taken in to sit on a sofa in front of a low table covered in goodies.

'The canapés this evening,' Gene explains, 'are Burgundian-style cheese balls, spoons of fresh smoked salmon on black noodles, and caviar on roundlets baked in one of the island's two craft bakeries. I recommend either a Chardonnay from over the hill or a Waiheke Pinot Noir.'

After some small talk about vineyards, Gene introduces the main meal.

'Today, I am roasting lamb, which is fast approaching perfection. It will be served on a bed of onions supplemented by green peas and green beans – not very original, but a wonderful textural contrast. Please give me half-an-hour.'

For the wines, obviously the Pinot Noir again, or perhaps a Shiraz. The meal is exquisite. The dessert is pure Kiwi. But the evening flies past. Suddenly, Gene declares:

'If you want to catch the catamaran, there's no time for coffee.'

Before we know it, we're climbing back onto the quay in Auckland, wondering where we've been.

New Zealand, like Australia, enjoys an outdoors lifestyle; and it is tempting to assume that culture is confined, if not exclusively to All Black rugby and all-white sheep-shearing, then at the most to what are called in England 'country pursuits': that is, hunting, shooting, fishing of many sorts, golfing, bowling, cricketing, rambling, camping, sailing, rowing, orienteering, surfing, horse-riding, dog-racing, pigeon-fancying, deer-stalking, hare-coursing, tree-felling, log-chopping, birdwatching, flower-pressing, butterfly-netting, river-rafting, salt- and sweet-water swimming, sunbathing, potholing, rock-climbing, cross-country walking, star-gazing, beach-running, and beachcombing – not to forget, in

New Zealand's special case, extreme-ironing, canyon-cruising, base-jumping, waterfall-quaffing, whirlpool-diving, and volcano-vaulting. As a result, it is said, rather unkindly, that Kiwis, like 'Ozzies', go indoors only to visit the toilet – and that's quite recent. Unfortunately, they have no Barry Humphries to take the strain. 'New Zealand has thirty thousand million sheep,' declared Humphries in the guise of his leering cultural attaché Sir Les Patterson, 'and three million of them think they're humans.' For Kiwis, such jibes are cruel, especially coming from Melbourne.

In the English-speaking world nowhere is more geographically peripheral than New Zealand. Kiwis live as far as one can get from Stratford-upon-Avon or the Royal Albert Hall; and it is tempting to assume that the arts, as performed in the antipodes, are no more than imitative or bucolic. Yet the assumption is misplaced. As may be readily ascertained on the spot, the Australians and New Zealanders who follow high culture are often more dedicated, more passionate, and sometimes more skilled than their counterparts in Europe. The explanation lies partly in those none-too-distant times, without radio and television, when friends and families had to make their own entertainment; and partly in feelings of isolation and vulnerability, created by distance and the pangs of emigration. The early pioneers had to fight not only for their own survival, but for the survival and growth of the culture that they brought with them.

In music, for example, strong traditions of brass bands and church choirs flourished from the start. They, in turn, fostered the founding of town orchestras, choral societies, and eventually of opera houses. Wellington's Opera House was founded in 1911. NZOpera stages regular performances in Wellington, Auckland, and Christchurch. In 2014 its energies focused on Verdi's *La Traviata*, Puccini's *La Bohème*, and Mozart's *Don Giovanni*. It is no accident that New Zealand has produced operatic stars such as Dame Joan Hammond (1912–96) and Dame Kiri Te Kanawa (b. 1944).[48]

Painters lack no source of inspiration in New Zealand – not least from the quality of light. Landscapes, portraits, and the depiction of Maori life were the dominant early genres, some of a high standard. Charles Heaphy's watercolour of *Mt Egmont from the Southward* (1840) and William Allsworth's *The Emigrants* (1844) are iconic works. In the twentieth century, Rita Angus (1908–70) and Colin McCahon (1919–87) applied the principles of impressionism and expressionism to create a distinctive local style.[49]

Drama, too, has its acolytes. The Theatre Royal opened in Wellington in 1843, and a counterpart in Auckland in 1844, within a few years of the colony's foundation. The 'List of New Zealand Playwrights and Dramatists' contains over forty names. Those frequently mentioned include Bruce Mason (1921–82), playwright, actor, and critic, who interwove Maori and Pakeha themes; Mervyn Thompson (1936–92), a radical playwright and theatre director; and Makerita Urale, one of the best-known Polynesian playwrights.

New Zealand literature spans all aspects of fiction and non-fiction. It was launched to a wider audience by Samuel Butler's *Erewhon* (1872); life on a remote sheep farm clearly stimulated the author's imagination. Kiwi novelists include Ngaio Marsh (1895–1982), one of the founding 'Queens of Crime', Ruth Park (1917–2010), and David Ballantyne (1924–86), journalist, novelist, and social critic. Two New Zealanders, Keri Hulme and Eleanor Catton, have won the Booker Prize for Fiction (1985 and 2013 respectively). Kiwi poetry kicked off with some mawkish but officially encouraged gems of patriotic verse, such as Thomas Bracken's 'God Defend New Zealand' (1870s) and Robert Pope's 'New Zealand, My Homeland' (1910):

There's a land far across the ocean
And I hear it calling me home.
It's my homeland, my own land, New Zealand,
And I miss her wherever I roam.

And the songs that I love remind me
Of the people and places I know.
Til the day I return to my homeland
You'll hear me singing, wherever I go.
        Me He Manu Rere
        E Whitu Nga Waka
        Hoke Mai, and Pokarekare Ana.
        And I'll sing
        Haere Ra e Hine
        Waikaremoana
        That's home sweet home to me.[50]

Arthur Henry Adams (1872–1936), however, author of *Maoriland and Other Verses* (1899), struck a sweeter note. And the eccentric Count Geoffrey Potocki de Montalk (1903–97), born in Auckland and *soi-disant* Pretender to the long-defunct Polish throne, earned an

international career. More recently, great attention has homed in on
Hone Tuwhare (1922–2008), an English-language poet of Maori descent:

> I can hear you making
> small holes in the silence
> rain
>
> If I were deaf
> the pores of my skin
> would open to you
> and shut
>
> And I should know you
> by the lick of you
> if I were blind;
>
> the steady drum-roll
> sound you make
> when the wind drops
>
> the something
> special smell of you
> when the sun cakes
> the ground
>
> But I should not
> hear,
> smell or feel or see you
>
> You would still
> define me
> disperse me
> wash over me
> rain.[51]

Efforts to reconcile Pakeha and Maori were long delayed. Over the
decades, the Pakeha community had established a position of overwhelming numerical, political, economic, and cultural supremacy,
which they were reluctant to relinquish. The Maori, for their part, were
slow to challenge the subordinate status to which they had been consigned. Yet eventually the two sides came to realize that closer
co-operation lay in everyone's interests. In the course of the twentieth
century, increasing numbers of Maori migrated to the towns from their
rural *marae*, gained an education, entered professional and business

circles, and formed an active lobby. One of the archetypical figures was Sir Hugh Kawharu (1927–2006), a son of the Ngati Whatua tribe, who attended Auckland Grammar School, studied at Auckland University, gained higher degrees at both Oxford and Cambridge, and returned home to a distinguished academic career in anthropology. He and people like him breathed life into the moribund Maori Council and pressurized the government to abandon its complacency.[52]

The long process, which began in the 1970s, of putting New Zealand's two main peoples and cultures onto a more equal footing, is very far from complete. But its aims have gained wide acceptance. The key moment, both legal and symbolic, came in 1975 with the passing of the Treaty of Waitangi Act and the creation of the Waitangi Tribunal. The Act formally acknowledged that many promises made to the Maori in 1840 and afterwards had not been honoured, and that numerous forms of injustice, perpetrated by governments, companies, and individuals, had escaped scrutiny. The workings of the Tribunal are painfully slow. The Ngai Tahu Claim, for example, which was brought by one of the *iwi* from South Island, lasted twelve years from 1986 to 1998. But it ended in success. The title of ownership of Mount Cook-Aoraki was returned to the Maori; an official apology was issued; and compensation of $170 million was paid. Once the Tribunal's decision was made, the Ngai Tahu presented Aoraki as a gift to the nation.[53]

Throughout colonial and imperial times, New Zealanders accepted Britain's national anthem as their own. But a home-grown counterpart, 'God Defend New Zealand', was steadily growing in popularity. Composed in 1876, it was finally adopted as a co-equal anthem during the centennial celebrations of 1940. Critics would say that the melody by J. J. Woods is more effective than Thomas Bracken's words. But few would deny that the simple phonology of the Maori language is well matched to metrical Protestant hymns. And no one seems to mind that the splendid Maori lyrics, composed in 1878, do not follow the original too exactly:

| | | |
|---|---|---|
| God of Nations at Thy feet, | *I Ihowa Atua* | (O Lord God |
| In the bonds of love we meet. | *O nga iwi matou ra* | Of all the tribes |
| Hear our voices, we entreat. | *Ata whakarongona* | Listen to our voices. |
| God defend our own free land. | *Me aroha noa.* | Cherish us your people. |
| Guard Pacific's triple star | *Kia hua ko te pai* | May the rightful Good prevail. |
| From the shafts of strife and war. | *Kia tau to atawhai* | May your blessings flow |

| Make her praises heard afar. | *Manaakitia mai* | May your mighty hand defend |
| God defend New Zea-ea-land. | *Ao-tea-ro-o-a.* | Ao-tea-ro-o-a.)[54] |

The mystery remains, however, how the language of the majority of the inhabitants of Kiwiland has acquired its inimitable peculiarities. Australians, in particular, who eat 'Feesh and Cheeps', can be highly amused when Kiwis order 'Fush and Chups' and then ask for the 'Bull'. For some reason, the climate to the east of the Tasman Sea has proved uncongenial to the short vowels 'a', 'e', and 'i', and to the ability of Kiwi speakers to distinguish between them. The internet is awash with websites that offer assistance to visitors, especially from Australia, who 'can't believe their ears'. The recommended rules can be reduced to four:

1. End every sentence as if you are asking a question, especially if you're not.
2. Make sure to change the 'a' sound to 'e', 'e' to 'ee', and 'i' to 'u'.
3. Beware of words that sound familiar, but have different meanings.
4. If in doubt, abbreviate. Kiwi speakers (like Australians, who are loath to admit it) are addicted to ingenious abbreviations.

Many websites are not content with stating the rules, however; they offer their users glossaries to guide them through the labyrinth.[55] The main categories are Maori loan words, abbreviations, and 'false friends':

### Lees'n Suxty-Sux

**Maori Loan Words**

| | | |
|---|---|---|
| *aroha* (love) | *kai* (food) | *whanau* (family) |
| *drongo* (idiot) | *Kia Ora* (Hello, | *whanga* (harbour) |
| *Haere mai* (Come | Good Day!) | *wopwops* (back of |
| here!) | *kumara* (potatoes) | beyond) |
| *hamu* (meal) | *waka* (motor car) | |

**Abbreviations**

| | | |
|---|---|---|
| *arvie* (afternoon) | *chippies* (crisps) | NZ (New Zealand) |
| *beanie* (wool hat) | *cuzzies* (relatives) | *pressie* (present) |
| *brekkie* (breakfast) | *dairy* (corner shop) | *rej* (reject) |
| *bro* (friend, mate) | *hottie* (bed warmer) | |

**'False Friends'**

*arm* as in English 'hm' or 'er'

*beer* wild animal, black or brown

*bid* another place to sleep

*chuck* offspring of poultry

*cud* child, a young goat

*Den* Daniel's nickname

*dutch* excavated depression

*fen* an enthusiastic supporter

*fest* quick

*grup* a tight hold

*guess* vapour

*jug* an Irish dance

*leather* soap and water foam

*led* a young boy

*lift* departed

*mckennock* a repairer of cars

*men* a human male

*min* human males (plural)

*nut* a nit or gnat

*pig* for hanging clothes on a line

*pit* a domesticated animal

*punk* a colour between red and white

*rug* for extracting oil from the sea

*six* copulation, otherwise *seex*

*sucks* one more than five

*teen* one more than nine

*volley* space between two hills: a *velley*

*win* interrogative like what/where/who?

*wit* the opposite of dry

*wreck* as in *wrecking* one's brains

*zid* as in *In Zid*, the country's name

The geographical vocabulary of Kiwispeak has its charms, too.[56] The popular name for the Tasman Sea, very appropriately, is 'the Dutch', in other words 'the Ditch', so going to Australia is, rather appropriately, 'Across the Dutch'. South Island is commonly called 'the Mainland'. And 'the Islands' do not refer to 'In-Zid' itself but to the Pacific Islands as a whole. They were to be my next destination.

# 10

# Otaheiti

*The Hunt for Paradise in a Distant Land*

Flying out of Auckland into the South Pacific, I knew that I was heading for one of the vastiest regions of the globe. At 64 million square miles the Pacific Ocean covers an area greater than that of all the continents put together, and hosts up to 30,000 islands. And yet, gazing down for hours at the unending blue-green water, I was conscious of glaring gaps in my knowledge. Like most westerners, I could summon up a few trite images of coral reefs, coconut palms, and bronze-breasted beauties, but in essence I knew little more than the early European explorers who had passed this way some 300 to 500 years ago. I had read *Robinson Crusoe* as a boy, as Captain Cook might have done, and knew that one of the world's first novels was based on the true-life story of a shipwrecked Scottish sailor. But I could not have placed Crusoe's island on a map for love nor money.* I had also read R. L. Stevenson's *Treasure Island*, many times, but without pausing to think where the action took place. Above all, I had thrilled to Thor Heyerdahl's adventure story *The Kon Tiki Expedition*, had gasped at the life-and-death struggles of his crew on a storm-tossed balsa-wood raft, and was completely convinced by his hypothesis about Polynesia having been populated from South America. But that was sixty years ago. I had no idea where the Polynesian debate had gone in the meantime.

Then came the films. In the late fifties, like almost everyone else, I enjoyed the film version of the musical *South Pacific*. I was not aware of its controversial overtones, but was mainly impressed by the sybaritic life lived by American GIs who were supposedly fighting a terrible war against Japan. Like the rest of the audience in the Bolton Odeon, I warmed to the seductive tones of 'Bali Ha'i':

* In 1704–9 Alexander Selkirk, a crewman serving under the buccaneer William Dampier, spent nearly five years marooned on Más a Tierra (now Isla Róbinson Crusoe), in the Juan Fernández Archipelago off Chile.

Bali Ha'i may call you,
Any night, any day.
In your heart you'll hear it call you:
'Come away, Come away.'
Bali Ha'i will whisper
On the wind of the sea:
'Here am I, your special island!
Come to me, Come to me!'

But was Bali Ha'i just a piece of make-believe?

Next came *Mutiny on the Bounty* (1962), with Marlon Brando strutting the deck as Fletcher Christian and Trevor Howard as the dastardly Captain Bligh. The story is crammed with hatred, crime, cruelty, sex, treachery, and endurance. The mutineers, led by Christian, set Bligh adrift in a tiny boat before sailing off with a bevy of native women for Pitcairn Island. Where exactly does Pitcairn lie? And what happened to Fletcher Christian, not to mention the women?

The flight to Tahiti, I was told, would last for five to six hours and cover 2,545 miles. I had plenty of time to contemplate the complications of crossing the International Date Line. I left Auckland on a Monday morning and was due to arrive at Papeete on the preceding Sunday evening. This information was totally bewildering. I lived through two consecutive Sunday evenings and two back-to-back Mondays. My pocket diary couldn't cope. The week was filled to overflowing with eight days, and I had to insert an additional box so as to accommodate the additional twenty-four hours.

To increase my confusion, a website seems to tell me that there is no such thing as an official International Date Line.[1] There is the theoretical line of longitude, 180 degrees both east and west of Greenwich, which divides the Earth into Western and Eastern Hemispheres. And there is another line produced in 1884 by an agreement among commercial steamship companies, which deviates in several places from the simple line of longitude. This agreement, apparently, has not been ratified by any international authority. Nor is the so-called IDL recognized, for example, by the world's leading rabbinical bodies, which claim the dividing line lies 180 degrees east not of Greenwich but of Jerusalem.[2] By their reckoning, Tahiti lies in the Eastern Hemisphere. Umberto Eco has written a novel about it.[3]

At Tahiti's international airport, arrangements are still made to give arriving passengers a special welcome. As they walk across the tarmac,

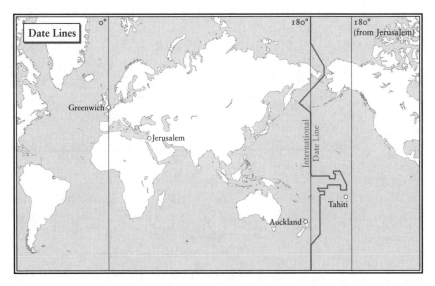

a Polynesian band breaks into song. Ukuleles strum under a palm-leaf roof, voices soar in harmonious thirds, and a 'dusky maiden' gyrates, clad only in a garland of flowers and a strategic handful of bright yellow petals. She is flanked by two gendarmes, replete with kepis, smart uniforms, and immaculate white gloves. Her skin, like theirs, is a warm shade of brown. Arrows point PASSEPORTS EUROPÉENS to the left, AUTRES PASSEPORTS to the right. The French signs are written in black on white, or white on black, to make them visible from afar: POLICE – IMMIGRATION ET DOUANES - RIEN À DÉCLARER. Alternative English signs are small and unreadable, painted in a faint beige colour. The customs form requires you to *cocher les cases,* 'to cross the boxes'. Except for the heat and the flowering hibiscus, this could be Calais in the 1950s. For me, it's nostalgic. Citizens of the European Union need no visa for a temporary stay.

'Bonsoir,' the lady taxi driver begins.

'Bonsoir Madame, Hotel Manava, s'il vous plaît.'

'Très bien, c'est un joli hôtel, tout nouveau.'

Outside the airport, the English signs dry up completely. VOUS N'AVEZ PAS LA PRIORITÉ appears before the first roundabout, still warning Polynesians against the old PRIORITÉ À DROITE. Every property that we pass is called a SERVITUDE. The taxi fare is paid in francs, not euros: 2,200 francs. The change comes in heavy silver coins like Maria Theresa dollars, marked with 'Marianne' and RÉPUBLIQUE FRANÇAISE on one side, and with a jagged island peak surrounded by POLYNÉSIE FRANÇAISE on the reverse. At the hotel reception, the row

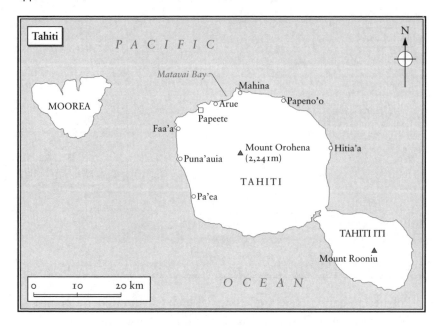

of clocks show it to be 6 o'clock in both Tahiti and Paris: 6 p.m. today in Papeete, and 6 a.m. tomorrow in Paris.

In the hotel room one has a choice of a dozen French-speaking television channels, and one Tahitian-language channel, but none in English. I put my feet up and read the travel brochures. In the drawer of the bedside table, apart from a copy of the *Nouveau Testament,* a superb government publication awaits – the *Annuaire Polynésien 2011.*[4] Divided into chapters, sections, sub-sections, and sub-sub-sections, it's a chunky, glossy, multi-coloured compendium containing more information than anyone could possibly absorb. Each of its 362 pages bears a miniature tricolour in the top corner, together with 'Liberté – Égalité – Fraternité'. Nothing is missing. If you are looking for the big boss, the Haut-Commissaire de la République, it's M. Richard Didier, born 23 February 1961 at Châtou-Yvelines and a graduate of the École Nationale d'Administration (ENA). His address is Avenue Pouvana'a a O'opa, BP 115, 98713 Papeete: his telephone 689 46 86 86: his e-mail standard@polynesie-francaise.pref.gouv.fr.

A magnificently coloured map fills the *Annuaire*'s centre spread. The expanses of the ocean are shown in a deep *bleu de travail* and divided into twenty rectangular sections by fine white lines. The top is at 5 degrees south, the bottom at 25 degrees south, the Tropic of Capricorn. Each of French Polynesia's five archipelagos is surrounded by an area in a mid-blue, and each of the main islands by smaller areas of light blue. A few, such as Tahiti or Bora Bora, are large enough to be marked in yellow, but most appear as tiny dots. Tiny red aeroplane symbols mark scores of local airports. No single island has a French name.

Tahiti, to the west of centre, lies in a small grouping called *Les Îles du Vent* (The Windwards). Its nearest neighbours, between 100 and 300 miles further west, including Raiatea, Tahaa, and Bora Bora, form *Les Îles du Sous-Vent* (The Leewards). Together, they constitute the *Archipel de la Société* (the Society Islands).

A much larger archipelago, that of Tuamotu, is strung out between 15 and 25 degrees south far to the east of Tahiti. It covers 20,000 square kilometres, and many of its myriad atolls are uninhabited. Its principal island, Rangiroa, meaning 'Immense Sky', forms the centre of 240 atolls linked to a vast underwater coral reef, where black pearls abound.

The *Archipel des Gambier* (the Gambier Islands) forms an appendix at the far eastern end of the Tuamotus, 1,600 kilometres from Tahiti. Its main island, Mangareva, is known as the 'cradle of Pacific Catholicism'.

The equatorial *Archipel des Marquises*, originally *Las Marquesas* (the Marchioness Islands), is over 1,000 miles to the north of Tahiti. Like the Societies, it consists of two insular groupings, one centred on the mountainous Nuku Hiva and the other on Hiva Oa. According to the *Annuaire*, it is *'le premier foyer de peuplement dans le Triangle Polynésien'*.[5]

Finally, far to the south of Tahiti, the *Archipel des Australes* (the Austral Islands) bestrides the Tropic of Capricorn. Its cool climate favours agriculture. Its furthest outlier, the isle of Rapa, lies halfway to Easter Island, with whose mysterious, lost civilization it has some distant connection. Its full Tahitian name, *Rapa Iti*, or 'Little Rapa', contrasts with Easter Island's *Rapa Nui*, or 'Rapa le Grand'.

Peering at a map of the Pacific is akin to looking into the night sky. It starts with wonderment, and moves swiftly into disorientation. There are far too many islands and too many archipelagos and sub-groups to remember, and far too few recognizable shapes, patterns, and points of mental reference. Like the stars of the Milky Way, the isles and atolls of Polynesia are overwhelming. It is only with time that one's eyes become accustomed, and one's mind can begin to comprehend the immensity of the galaxies and the constellations. An American writer tried to solve the problem by urging readers to compare Polynesia with better-known entities:

French Polynesia embraces a vast ocean area strewn with faraway islands, each with a mystique of its own. The 118 islands and atolls are scattered over an expanse of water eighteen times the size of California, though . . . the dry land . . . is only slightly bigger than Rhode Island. Every oceanic type is represented in these sprawling archipelagos . . . The coral atolls of the Tuamotus are so low they are threatened by rising sea levels, while volcanic Tahiti soars to 2,241 metres.[6]

Here, water is king and land a marginal extra. Europeans and Americans are used to the opposite, where land provides the base and seas the surrounding frame. Yet seen at close quarters Tahiti, too, is largely made from water; the main island nestles inside a lagoon in the centre of 'a clutch of lagoon-lapped islands within a larger clutch of islands'. It's a big mistake to have come here without a boat. And the travel literature talks rather insistently of 'paradise'.[7]

A Tahitian sunset concludes the day of arrival. A giant golden orb plummets towards the horizon between a high-flying cloud and the sensationally jagged peaks of an offshore island. That must be Bali Ha'i. For a moment or two the intervening waters of the lagoon are bathed in luminous orange light, while the mountain peaks stand out black, and the high arch of the sky remains silver and silvery-blue. Then night falls suddenly, like a coconut dropping with a thud from the bunch at the top of the palm.

'Polynesia' is not a Polynesian term. It is not even the calque of a Polynesian original. It was coined in the mid-eighteenth century by the French *philosophe* Charles de Brosses, who was writing a book on the history of European voyages to the 'South Seas', and who, being trained in the classics, created a new geographical name by combining two Greek words – *poly* meaning 'many' and *nesos* meaning 'island'. Although Europeans had long known of the world's largest ocean, and had widely accepted Ferdinand Magellan's characterization of it as the *Pacifico* or 'Calm One', their knowledge had never been systematized. De Brosses, it seems, used his new term ambiguously: sometimes as a collective name for 'all the Pacific islands', but mainly for those enclosed by one of the three seas into which he arbitrarily divided the ocean – namely, the seas of *Australasie*, *Magellanique*, and *Polynésie*.[8]

Charles de Brosses (1709–77), Comte de Tournay, long-time president of the parliament of Dijon, an outspoken critic of royal absolutism and a correspondent with all the leading *philosophes*, set himself

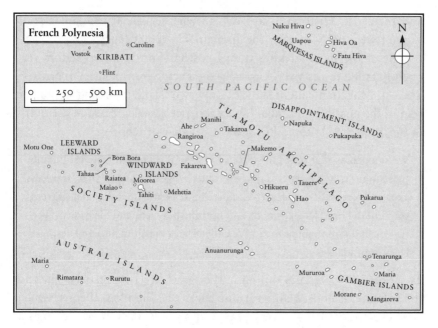

the task of collating all existing information about the Pacific into one volume. He was a man of short stature but great intellectual range. Published twelve years before Captain Cook set sail on his First Voyage in the *Endeavour*, his *Histoire des Navigations aux Terres Australes* (1756) strongly influenced the explorers of the following decades.[9] He must be regarded as the pioneer *par excellence* of Pacific studies.

De Brosses, alas, endured a particularly quarrelsome relationship with Voltaire, who had bought a life-tenancy for the use of the count's ancestral Château de Tournay. Both men indulged in prolonged exchanges of threats and accusations. When the Académie Française nominated the count as a candidate for membership, Voltaire blocked the appointment by threatening to resign.[10]

Nonetheless, given the constraints under which he laboured, the magnitude of de Brosses's achievement cannot be doubted. None of the navigators whose exploits he relates was equipped to pass on accurate accounts of their discoveries. All of them named islands in any language they saw fit, and few left accurate records of where they had been. Most were contracted to governments wedded to the monopolistic concept of *mare clausum* or 'closed sea', treating all information as confidential. Their navigational measurements were often rudimentary. In consequence, numerous Pacific islands had been discovered, and then lost. Historians still debate whether the Hawaiian Islands were or were not visited by the Spaniards in the 1540s.[11]

One of the most striking things is what European navigators frequently failed to discover. Crossing the Pacific from South America in 1520–1, Magellan caught sight of only two islands, missing 99.99 per cent of the possible landfalls. His experience was described in the diary of his shipmate, Antonio Pigafetta, Chevalier de Rhodes:

> We ran across that vast gulf of sea for several thousand leagues, during three months and twenty days, without seeing any land in that limitless expanse except for two desert islands, one at 15 and the other at 9 degrees south of the line. Those islands had nothing but trees and birds: no quadrupeds and no inhabitants . . . We called them the Unfortunate Isles, Las Desventuradas.[12]

Two Spanish successors sailing in the same direction reached Fiji and the Solomon Islands, before turning back. The Manila Galleons, which criss-crossed the Pacific every year from 1565 to 1815, used Guam as a staging-post. But they rarely thought of searching for other islands. Above all, no one followed up on Tasman's pioneering investigations into the *Terra Australis Incognita*. As late as 1770, an English author published a fantastical description which related that the Southland had a coastline of 5,323 miles in length and was inhabited by 50 million people.[13] Antarctica remained out of range until 1820.

The earliest European navigators in the Pacific, Spaniards out of Mexico, suffered from a major impediment: not having mastered the prevailing winds and currents, they knew how to sail from east to west in the Pacific, but not from west to east. Magellan, who blazed the trail, hugged the coast of South America until he met the easterly winds that accompany the South Equatorial Current. But neither he nor his immediate successors could return along the route by which they came. The solution was only found by trial and error. In 1565 Friar Andrés de Urdaneta, the second circumnavigator of the globe (Enrique de Malacca being the first), adopted the Portuguese technique of the *Volta do Mar*, or 'ocean gyre', from which Tasman also benefited. Steering from the Philippines beyond Japan, he reached latitude 38 degrees north before hitting westerly winds and the east-flowing North Pacific Current. A hunger-struck voyage of 130 days and 12,000 miles eventually brought him to his original starting point at Acapulco in Mexico. Meanwhile, his old commander, Miguel López de Legazpi, conquered the Philippines and founded

Manila. From then on, the annual fleet of Manila Galleons used 'Urdaneta's Route' to return to America. But, by regarding the whole of the Pacific as a Spanish domain, they prevented others from sharing their knowledge.

It is not surprising, therefore, that de Brosses was unable to present the dimensions or divisions of the Pacific with any great certainty. He invented the term 'Polynesia' because no previous commentator had seen the need for it. Two other terms that he used were no less imprecise. *Australasie*, meaning 'south of Asia', referred to a large but undefined maritime region, lying below the so-called 'East Indies'. The *Magellanique* or 'Sea of Magellan' and its associated region, *Magellanie*, referred to the oceanic expanses that westbound navigators entered after passing through the eponymous Straits.

The 'Table of Voyages' drawn up by de Brosses listed sixty-three voyages in all. Thirty of them were included under the heading *En Magellanie*, starting with 'Americ Vespucce' in 1501 and ending with 'Le Hen-Brignon' in 1747. Eleven more, starting in 1503 with Jean Binot Paulmier de Gonneville, who mistook Brazil for the *Terra Australis*, were placed under the heading of *Australasie*, and twenty-two under *En Polynésie*. Magellan's pioneering voyage was classified as *En Magellanique et en Polynésie*.

Among the Polynesian voyages, de Brosses paid special tribute to the English buccaneer 'François Drake', not only for his navigational skills, but also for his temerity in challenging Spanish supremacy. De Brosses recounted *in extenso* Queen Elizabeth's admonition of the Spanish ambassador to England who had protested at Drake's activities:

> The Queen responded [to the ambassador by saying] that the Southern Sea, like the rest of the ocean, was the common property of everyone . . . that the donation made by the Bishop of Rome of a country that did not belong to him was a *chimera*, a fanciful conception: that the Spaniards had no more rights than anyone else to something that they had usurped from its original owners: and that one did not become the proprietor of a country by building a few cabins there or by giving the name of a saint to a headland or river . . .[14]

Yet the Dutch were no less proprietorial than the Spaniards. In 1699, when the English captain William Dampier put into East Timor on his second voyage, he told the governor 'we are Englishmen in the King's ship':

But the Governor replied that he had orders not to supply any ships but their own East India Company, nor must they allow any Europeans to come the way that we did . . . I will have you therefore be gone, with all speed.[15]

It sounds as though the governor did not know that William of Orange was both King of England and Stadtholder of the Netherlands.

De Brosses had several imitators and continuators, especially in Great Britain, which he had accused of establishing a *monarchie universelle de la mer*, 'a universal maritime monarchy'. John Callander published the first volume of his *Terra Australis Cognita* in 1766, in Edinburgh; he shamelessly pirated the work of de Brosses, failing to mention its author and regularly substituting the name of 'England' for 'France' for patriotic effect.[16]

The first European to discover what would later become Tahiti, Captain Samuel Wallis RN (1728–95), a Cornishman and the world's thirteenth circumnavigator, edged towards the shore of Taiapuru on 18 June 1767. Soon after arriving, he ordered a broadside of grapeshot to be fired when his ship, HMS *Dolphin*, was mobbed by stone-throwing warriors in over two thousand canoes. The islanders, who had no previous familiarity with Europeans, duly granted him semi-divine status, willingly entered into trade, and offered no further resistance. He moved to Matavai Bay on the north coast:

The Lieutenant was now despatched with boats manned and armed, and with orders to land . . . This being effected, he hoisted a pendant on a staff, and took possession of the place for his sovereign in the name of King George III's Island. He then mixed some rum with river water, and every person drank the King's health.[17]

Most remarkable, however, was the reaction of native women to the British sailors. They behaved as if they had been waiting since time immemorial for these exotic foreign males. The sailors had been cooped up on a tiny ship for months. Together they greeted the onset of a new Iron Age:

The women were particularly urgent for the sailors to land, pulling off their cloathes and [giving] hints of the most indelicate nature how acceptable their company would be . . .

A traffic of a singular kind was now established between the Indian women and the sailors. The price of a lady's favour was one nail or two. But since the tars could not always get nails, they drew them out from several parts of the ship . . . The damage done could not easily be repaired, and the sailors, in consequence of their connection with the women, became so impatient of control that the captain ordered the articles of war to be read, to awe them into obedience.[18]

This Euro-Polynesian sexual concourse was to turn into a plague.

Less than a year after Wallis left Matavai, a French ship landed on the opposite side of the island, unaware of the Briton's earlier visit. Its captain, Louis-Antoine de Bougainville (1729–1811), had taken part in the project for settling displaced Acadians in the Malvine Islands (soon to be renamed as the Falklands). He was now inspired by de Brosses. His two ships, the frigate *L'Étoile* and its supply vessel, *La Boudeuse*, were carrying over 300 men and a fully equipped scientific expedition led by the botanist Philibert de Commerçon. Unbeknown to the captain, they were also carrying the first woman to circumnavigate the world, Jeanne Baret, Commerçon's concubine, who had been smuggled aboard disguised as a manservant.[19] The youthful Comte de La Pérouse, who was heading for fame in his own right, was serving as a volunteer seaman. The seeds of the Brazilian plant that Commerçon had already named *Bougainvillea* were in the hold. The Frenchmen dropped anchor in the bay of Hitia'a on 6 April 1768, naming the island 'La Nouvelle Cythère'.[20]

Bougainville stayed for only two weeks, but he left with two sensational items of cargo. One of them, in his own head, was the idea that he had discovered a Garden of Eden, where the 'Children of Nature' could indulge their needs and desires uncorrupted by the evils of modern civilization. The other was a young, tall, and very handsome man called Aoutouro, whom he took with him to France to prove his theory. Bougainville's account of his *Voyage autour du monde* (1771) proved one of the best-sellers of the age. It cemented the legend of the 'noble savage', which Jean-Jacques Rousseau had floated earlier, and provided much of the material whereby Denis Diderot, in his *Supplément au voyage de Bougainville* (1772), launched a frontal attack on prevailing views about religion and morality.[21]

Captain James Cook, therefore, was the third European captain to set foot on what he called, as Wallis had also done, 'King George's Island'. Cook was the greatest of the early Pacific navigators, a peerless master mariner, meticulous cartographer, and marvellous man-manager. His ship, the *Endeavour*, dropped anchor in January 1778 in Matavai Bay, where the *Dolphin* had anchored before her:

This island is called by the natives OTAHEITE, and was first discovered by Captain Wallis in His Majesty's ship, *Dolphin* ... and, to the
Credit of him and his officers, the Longitude of the Royal Bay was settled
to within half a degree of the Truth ... It is situated between the Latitude
of 17 degrees 29 minutes and 17 degrees 53 minutes South, and between
149 degrees 10 minutes and 149 degrees 39 minutes West of the Meridian
of Greenwich. The Shores of the island are mostly guarded from the sea
by reefs of coral rocks, and these form several excellent Bays and Harbours, wherein are room and depth of Water sufficient for the largest
ships.[22]

Otaheiti, Cook learned, meant 'Distant Land'. He continued with
lengthy accounts of the island's produce, animals, cooking, people,
clothes, customs, music, housing, canoes, tools, arms, religion, priests,
rituals, computing of time, climate, and magnetic fields. On the matters that had most interested Bougainville and the *Dolphin*'s lusty tars,
Cook was decidedly cool:

One amusement ... I must mention, is founded upon a Custom so
inhuman and contrary to human nature. It is this: that one half of the
better sort of the inhabitants have enter'd into a resolution of injoying
free liberty in Love, without being Troubled by the consequences. They
mix and Co-habit with the greatest freedom, and the children so unfortunate to be thus begot are smother'd at the Moment of their Birth ...

The sexes express the most indecent ideas in conversation without the
least emotion ... Chastity is little valued; if a Wife is found guilty ... her
only punishment is a beating from her husband. The Men very often offer
Young Women to Strangers, even their own Daughters, and think it very
strange if you refuse them ...[23]

On the widespread custom of tattooing, Cook sounds more neutral:

Both sexes paint their Bodys, Tattow as it is in their language. This is done
by inlaying the Colour of Black under their skins, in such a manner as is
indelible. Some have ill-design'd figures of men, birds or dogs ... [or]
Circles and Crescents, which they have on their Arms and Legs ... All
agree in having their buttocks covered in a Deep Black. Over this most
have Arches drawn one over another ... [which] men and women show
with great pleasure.[24]

Cook had originally been sent to the central Pacific, on what turned out
to be his First Voyage (1768–71), to make astronomical observations of

the transit of Venus, after which his sealed orders told him to search for signs of the *Terra Australis* – almost as if Tasman's discoveries had never taken place. They show how uncertain the Admiralty still was about the geography of the South Seas. Cook first made a very exact chart of New Zealand, proving that it was not connected to a more southerly landmass, and then charted the east coast of Australia from end to end. He landed at Botany Bay in April 1770 and named it, and refitted the *Endeavour* on a Queensland beach before returning home via Batavia and the Cape of Good Hope.

The object of Cook's Second Voyage (1772–5) was once again *Terra Australis*. The Admiralty now knew that both New Holland (Australia) and New Zealand were discrete islands, but were (rightly) convinced that major discoveries remained to be made. Their orders despatched Cook's new ship, HMS *Resolution*, to record-breaking southerly latitudes. He crossed the Antarctic Circle in mid-ocean, retraced his steps to Otaheiti for recreation, before logging a latitude of 71 degrees 10 minutes south. If he had kept going for a further 75 miles – or for one more day – he would have found Antarctica. But he didn't, and instead returned to England with no inkling of the existence of the Earth's most southern continent. So the assumption that the South Pacific stretched across the South Pole to merge with the Atlantic was not challenged.

Cook's Third Voyage (1776–80) turned to the exploration of the North Pacific and of the North-West Passage. To this end, he made meticulous surveys both of Hawaii and North America's north-west coast. He was killed on Hawaii on 14 February 1779 following an altercation with the islanders.[25] Charles Clerke took over command of the expedition, but he was to die of tuberculosis. The crews returned to England in October 1780 under Captain John Gore.

All these voyages and discoveries – those of Wallis, Bougainville, Cook – came in a cluster thanks to the end of the Seven Years War in 1763, and to recent technical advances. Cook had departed on his First Voyage without the aid of a modern chronometer, relying instead on the tiresome 'lunar distance method' and on the moon tables of the *Nautical Almanac* to calculate longitude. In this he was assisted by a professional astronomer, Charles Green, who had served as a judge in the scandalously incompetent trials of John Harrison's H4 chronometer. Harrison, the genial London clockmaker, did not receive his prize for solving the longitude problem until 1773.[26] Henceforth, chronometers were in regular use, and navigators could begin the long task of correcting their predecessors' charts.

Some regard Cook's voyages as the end of a chapter and the harbinger of a new scientific era. 'After Cook', states the most widely consulted source, 'nothing remained [to be found] but detail.' The novelist Joseph Conrad, a seaman in his own right, is often quoted as an authority:

> The voyages of the early explorers were prompted by ... the desire for loot disguised more or less in fine words. But Cook's three voyages ... belong [with] the single-minded fathers of militant geography, whose object was to search for truth.[27]

This interpretation is manifestly incorrect. Despite his accomplishments, Cook was not alone in seeking the truth in a scientific manner, and he left many problems unsolved. In his lifetime, the parameters of only three sides of the Pacific – the West, the North, and the East – had been determined; the South remained a mystery. No one could yet calculate the Pacific's true size.

To cap it all, the standards of disseminating information were extremely unreliable. Denis Diderot completed publication of his great seventeen-volume *Encyclopédie* in 1772. It contained some 72,000 articles on all conceivable branches of knowledge, and was followed up with a lavish collection of world maps. Cook would have been appalled to learn that this, the most prestigious atlas of the age, was packed with errors, fantasies, and outdated information.[28]

In 1785, not to be outdone by the British, France's royal government despatched a major scientific expedition to the Pacific in emulation of Cook. The commander was a professional naval officer, the Comte de La Pérouse (1741–88), who had accompanied Bougainville and now sailed from Brest with 220 men and two substantial ships, the *Astrolabe* and the *Boussole*. Over the next three years he sailed up and down the Pacific Ocean, mapping, recording, and collecting specimens at Hawaii, Alaska, California, Macao, Manila, Japan, Sakhalin, Samoa, and finally Australia. He coincided at Botany Bay with the First Fleet and made the acquaintance of the colony's first governor, Captain Arthur Phillip. For six weeks the two expeditions stayed in close proximity; the French celebrated Australia's first Catholic mass, set up the first observatory, and planted the first garden. They accepted an offer to send their journals and specimens back to Europe on a British ship, thereby (as it happened) ensuring their survival.[29]

At the end of the summer, in March 1788, La Pérouse and his ships weighed anchor in what was later called Sydney Bay and sailed for France on an eastbound course. He left word of his intended route, which was due to take him through the Central Pacific and round Cape Horn. His estimated time of arrival in France was June 1789, which would have brought him home in time for the storming of the Bastille a month later. Instead, he, his crews, and his ships simply vanished.

Landing in Otaheiti in the 1760s, the Europeans had discovered a political order that was strictly local and tribal. There was nothing resembling a Polynesian federation or empire with which to co-operate. Tahiti had a senior chief, Teu Tunuieaiteatua, whom some outsiders called 'king'; he was the head of an old hereditary dynasty, but his influence over other chieftains was limited and over distant islands minimal. Moreover, the chieftains engaged in endless petty wars. Tiny bands of warriors, armed only with spears and arrows, did not have the strength either to subdue their adversaries or garrison captured islands. Raids and ambushes could never ensure victory.

In the two decades following Wallis's arrival, however, two notable developments disturbed this state of equipoise. Firstly, the Polynesians were hit by deadly epidemics brought on by imported diseases. The epithet of *Pōmare*, which 'King' Teu took for himself and his descendants, derives from a prime symptom of tuberculosis; it means 'Night-cougher'. Secondly, the captains of visiting ships upset the primeval state of military impotence by selling guns. Warriors armed with muskets could achieve feats unimaginable to their ancestors, and chieftains commanding an armed guard could dream of imposing permanent control on their neighbours. The Royal House of Otaheiti did not miss its chance. In the 1780s Prince Pōmare, 'King' Teu's son, took over the whole of Tahiti along with the neighbouring islands of Moorea, Mehetia, and Tetiaroa; he was the ruler who in 1788 received Captain William Bligh (1754–1817), who had been Captain Cook's sailing master on the Third Voyage aboard *Resolution* and who returned eleven years later in command of his own expedition aboard HMS *Bounty*.

Bligh had set sail from Spithead in December 1787, before La Pérouse had reached Australia, and rounded the Cape of Good Hope in the wake of the First Fleet. One of his aims was to collect Polynesian breadfruit plants and transport them to the West Indies. British planters in Jamaica and Barbados were chafing at the cost of feeding their slaves, and the breadfruit, as described by Cook, offered a cheap, nutritious diet. For five months the *Bounty* rode at anchor off Otaheiti. Breadfruit plants were carefully selected, replanted in trays, and stacked into the *Bounty*'s stern area. Bligh had to vacate his cabin, and many of the crew, including the master's mate, Fletcher Christian, established liaisons with local women. One crewman called Churchill was murdered by a fellow sailor, who was then killed in revenge by Churchill's local relatives. The famous mutiny broke out soon after the start of the return voyage in April 1789. Somewhere at sea, close to Tonga, the mutineers seized the ship, cast Bligh adrift in an open sloop with a handful of loyal crewmen, and doubled back to Otaheiti to recover their womenfolk. Then, taking once more to the sea, they vanished – just like La Pérouse.[30]

The Spaniards, too, were determined to stay in the game. King Charles III had strongly advocated scientific endeavour; Spain's budget for science was second to none; and the Malaspina Expedition of 1789–94 under Charles IV was more lavishly supported than that of either Cook or La Pérouse. Alessandro Malaspina's two corvettes, the *Descubierta* and the *Atrevida*, sailed from Cadiz on 30 July 1789. Their extensive itinerary was similar to that of La Pérouse but concentrated on a search for the North-West Passage, spending many months at Nootka Sound on Vancouver Island.

Both the British and the French, meanwhile, launched expeditions to investigate the fate of their vanished ships. In 1790–91 HMS *Pandora* sailed from the Solent in search of the *Bounty*. Her captain, Edward Edwards, carried with him a couple of sailors who had managed to return to England with Bligh, after miraculously steering an open boat over 6,000 miles to Timor. The *Pandora* duly docked in Papeete, but failed to find any trace of Bligh's ship. Her crew captured a dozen mutineers and imprisoned them on deck, in a cage known as 'Pandora's Box'. Returning home, Edwards saw smoke rising from the island of Vanikoro in the Solomons but disregarded it, believing that deserters would not seek to attract attention. Shortly afterwards, the *Pandora* ran aground on the Great Barrier Reef, where many crewmen and captives perished.[31]

Within a month of the *Pandora*'s loss, Antoine Bruni d'Entrecasteaux left Brest with the *Recherche* and the *Espérance*; his orders were to look diligently for La Pérouse and to conduct scientific explorations en route. Despite some valuable work in Van Diemen's Land, his voyage ended tragically. He himself died of scurvy; his crew were bitterly divided between royalists and revolutionaries; and his vessels were surrendered to the Dutch in Batavia.[32]

Malaspina fared little better. Continuing his voyage, he spent 1792–3 in Australia before sailing east across the Pacific as La Pérouse had intended to do. Arriving in Spain, he was arrested, allegedly for political reasons, and his journals were seized, never to be published in his lifetime. He had made the best Pacific measurements to date, but his findings were lost to his generation.

During the Napoleonic Wars scientific exploration was largely shelved, but the Englishman Matthew Flinders (1774–1814) was one of the few to pursue earlier investigations. Starting in 1791, he made three voyages, through which, having circumnavigated New Holland, New South Wales, and Tasmania, he finally confirmed that they all belonged to one self-contained continent. Held prisoner for six years by the French on the Île de France (Mauritius), he wrote up his journals, composing a reasoned account, which made the novel suggestion that the old term of *Terra Australis* should be reserved for the newly defined continent. Only then was the modern concept of Australia born.[33]

In 1820 no fewer than three expeditions – Russian, American, and British – sighted what looked like land at 74 degrees south. Yet none could be sure whether the surface ice lay above land or water. Many still suspected that the South Pole, like the North Pole, lay beneath a frozen ocean.

The twin mysteries of the vanished ships from the 1780s were only solved – separately and by accident – after several decades. On 6 February 1808 an American whaler out of Boston, the *Topaz* under Captain Mayhew Folger, ran up against Pitcairn, an isolated island in the South Pacific, which had been discovered by the Royal Navy in 1767, but subsequently lost. (Cook had tried in vain to relocate it on his Second Voyage.) Folger stayed there for only ten hours, but learned an astonishing story. As usual, a clutch of native canoes put out to meet him. But the subsequent conversation was far from usual:

> He was met by a double canoe made in the manner of Otahaite and carrying several young men who hailed him in English. He answered them and told them that he was an American from Boston. 'You are an American?,' they repeated quizzically. 'Where is America? Is it in Ireland?'[34]

The boys had good English and brown skins, but no sense of geography:

> Captain Folger enquired . . . 'Who are you?' – 'We are Englishmen.' – 'Where were you born? – 'On the island that you can see.' – 'How then are you Englishmen?' – 'We are English because our father is English.' – 'Who is your father?' – 'Aleck' – 'Who is Aleck?' – 'Don't you know Aleck?' – 'How should I know Aleck?' – 'Well then, did you know Captain Bligh of the *Bounty*?' . . .[35]

Eighteen years after the mutiny, these were the teenage sons of the last surviving mutineer, John Adams (1767–1829), who used the pseudo-nym of Alexander Smith. 'Aleck' made his visitor welcome, shouted 'Olde England forever', impressed Folger with his religiosity, and entrusted him with the *Bounty*'s chronometer. The *Bounty* had been burned; Fletcher Christian was dead, and all his comrades had been killed either by each other or by their Tahitian 'wives'. Aleck reigned alone as patriarch of a Polynesian harem.[36]

Nearly twenty years later, a South Seas trader from Martinique named Peter Dillon called at Tokapia in the middle of the Coral Sea, and was invited to buy some old French naval swords. Asking after their origin, he learned that two ships had been wrecked on the neigh-bouring island of Vanikoro late in the previous century. Returning in 1827, he discovered cannonballs, chains, and anchors from La Pérouse's *Astrolabe* and *Boussole*. It transpired that a group of sailors had sur-vived the shipwreck, including a 'chief', and had continued to live on the island. The 'chief' may or may not have been La Pérouse himself, but the smoke signals that the *Pandora* had ignored in 1791 were very probably made by his men.[37]

In this same post-Napoleonic period, a key role in the advancement of geographical knowledge, both practical and theoretical, was played by the Frenchman Jules Dumont d'Urville (1790–1842), the successor to La Pérouse. He undertook two major voyages, one in 1826–9 and the other in 1837–40. During the first, he made important additions to the cartography of New Zealand and recovered the wreck of La Pérouse's *Astrolabe*. During the second, aboard *Astrolabe II*, he was searching for the magnetic South Pole.[38]

Even before d'Urville sailed, geographers of the French school had tackled the crucial task of global nomenclature, that is, of dividing the globe into recognized regions; and the Pacific was an important part of the exercise. The concept of Oceania, for example, was first floated by the French-Danish geographer Conrad Malte-Brun (1775–1826), in his highly influential, six-volume work, *Géographie mathématique, physique et politique*.[39] Initially, Oceania had covered the whole area between the Asian mainland and the Americas. Nowadays it appears in a number of variants.

Back in France, d'Urville addressed the task of defining the sub-divisions of Oceania. He simplified preceding studies, and produced a reasoned threefold structure based on wide cultural and linguistic criteria. In a lecture at the *Société de Géographie* in Paris, he presented three terms that have since passed into general usage – Micronesia, Melanesia, and a modified Polynesia.

Micronesia, as defined by d'Urville, is a region of 'small islands' separated from the neighbouring larger islands – Borneo, Papua-New Guinea, the Celebes, and the Philippines. It forms an oblong block of the South-West Pacific containing four principal archipelagos – the Carolines, the Gilberts, the Marianas, and the Marshalls, together with Nauru and Wake. Historically, it was dominated by a constellation of Spanish-ruled territories centred on Guam, and collectively known as 'the Spanish East Indies'. Most of Micronesia's inhabitants speak languages from the Oceanic sub-group, although Chamorro (the language of Guam) and Kapingamarangi are classed as Polynesian outliers.

Melanesia, which means 'Black Islands', received its name from the presence of dark-skinned people whom French researchers had dubbed *mélaniens*. It is roughly the same size as Micronesia, and comprises a wide arc of archipelagos lying to the north of New Guinea and often New Guinea itself. Its present-day constituents are Fiji, the Solomon Islands, Vanuatu, New Caledonia, and Papua-New Guinea. The inhabitants speak an astonishing array of 1,319 recorded languages, which together make up the Melanesian branch of the Austronesian family and represent the densest concentration of linguistic varieties on Earth.

Polynesia, therefore – in d'Urville's definition rather than that of de Brosses – constitutes the third and largest sub-division of Oceania. It forms a huge triangle, whose northern tip rests on Hawaii and whose bottom end runs from New Zealand to Easter Island (Rapa Nui). The central belt of the triangle takes in Tuvalu, Tokelau, Wallis and Futuna, Samoa, Tonga, and French Polynesia. The total area of 10 million square miles is equivalent to nearly twice Russia's land surface, though the ratio of land to water is infinitesimal. All the islands were formed either by sub-oceanic volcanoes or coral reefs.

Significantly, d'Urville's work left vast stretches of the Pacific unallocated. The higher latitudes of the Northern Pacific, between Japan and North America, or the vast expanses of the Southern Pacific below Polynesia, or between Polynesia and Latin America, do not possess a regional name. Individual islands or groups of islands that exist amidst these empty seas, such as the Île de Passion (now Clipperton Island) or the Galapagos, are regarded as 'isolates'.

D'Urville's second voyage, of 1837–40, together with the parallel

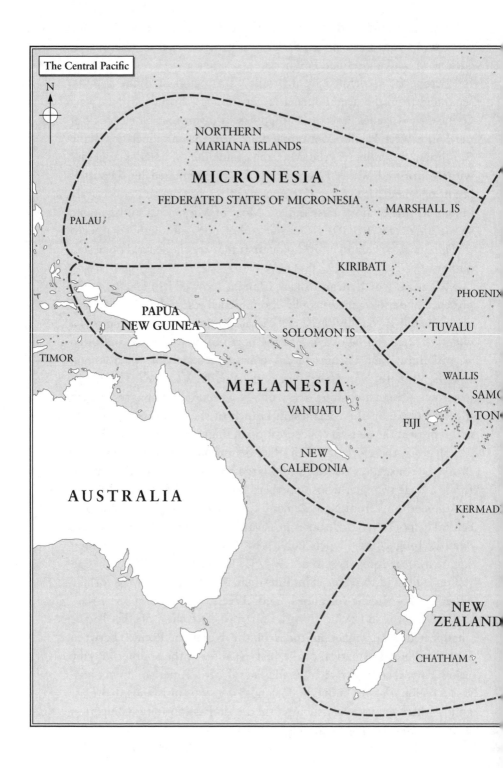

The Central Pacific

N

NORTHERN MARIANA ISLANDS

MICRONESIA

FEDERATED STATES OF MICRONESIA

PALAU

MARSHALL IS

KIRIBATI

PHOENIX

PAPUA NEW GUINEA

SOLOMON IS

TUVALU

TIMOR

WALLIS

MELANESIA

SAMO

VANUATU

FIJI

TON

NEW CALEDONIA

AUSTRALIA

KERMAD

NEW ZEALAND

CHATHAM

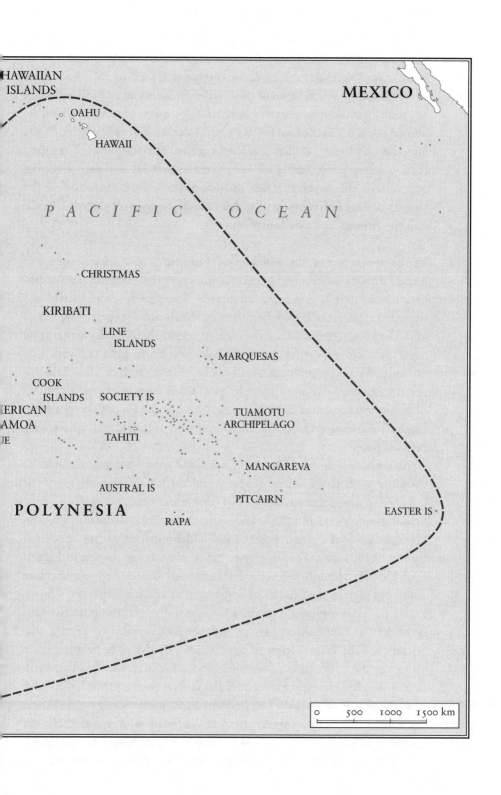

HAWAIIAN
ISLANDS

MEXICO

OAHU

HAWAII

*P A C I F I C    O C E A N*

CHRISTMAS

KIRIBATI

LINE
ISLANDS

MARQUESAS

COOK
ISLANDS    SOCIETY IS

ERICAN
AMOA                    TUAMOTU
JE                        ARCHIPELAGO
            TAHITI

                        MANGAREVA

AUSTRAL IS
                    PITCAIRN
**POLYNESIA**                        EASTER IS
            RAPA

| 0 | 500 | 1000 | 1500 km |

expeditions of the American Charles Wilkes and the Briton James Ross, sealed the great age of naval exploration. Sailing south from Hobart in Tasmania, d'Urville was initially forced to turn back. But leaving Hobart for the second time in the midsummer of January 1840, he finally landed three weeks later on an ice-bound shore, which he named Adelie Land after his wife, and declared it to be part of yet another 'continent'. Wilkes and Ross confirmed his findings. They gave their discovery the name of Antarctica – that is, a polar continent opposite to the Arctic.[40] They thus completed the delineation of the world's seven continents, whilst demonstrating the fact that the Pacific and the Atlantic are not contiguous.

In the modern era the number of European states with sufficient naval capacity to reach the mid-Pacific could be counted on the fingers of one hand. After the Spaniards, Portuguese, and Dutch had departed, the French and British were left unchallenged. Americans and Germans joined in as the age of exploration and colonization drew to a close. Yet for many decades the Europeans showed little inclination to exert political control. The islands produced few valuable resources; they were not linked by vital trade routes; and no expanses of virgin territory awaited settlement. None of the great powers sought urgently to annex Oceania. Their uninterest opened the gate to the missionaries.

As we have seen, the Church Militant had often marched shoulder to shoulder with the soldiers, traders, and settlers of imperialism. The conversion of indigenous peoples to Christianity was viewed in Europe as a natural good, and the role of Roman Catholic orders in Spanish, Portuguese, and French possessions had long formed an important thread of the story. The missionary urge was no less strong in Protestant Europe, though religious authority was more fragmented. State Churches such as the Church of England or the Dutch Reformed Church rarely put the emphasis on saving foreign souls; and the initiative was often left to non-conformists or independent bodies. In Britain, the Society for the Propagation of the Gospel (SPG) had been founded in 1701 for 'the conversion of heathens and infidels' in the American colonies; but after the establishment of the United States, it was looking for new spheres of operation. The London Missionary Society (LMS) was launched in 1795 by a mixed group of Anglicans and non-conformists seeking to evangelize foreign parts, and the British and Foreign Bible Society, founded in 1804, was also ecumenical and non-denominational.

All these societies took Polynesia to their heart, and, as a bonus, played a leading role in establishing monarchical forms of governance.

In the late eighteenth century, thanks to the reports and romantic descriptions of explorers such as Bougainville, the 'noble savages' of Polynesia were considered especially receptive to the Word of God. Christian missionaries turned eagerly to the South Seas, therefore, undeterred by the lack of governmental support. Two expeditions had far-reaching consequences. In 1796 the London Missionary Society dispatched a mission to Otaheiti hoping to establish a permanent presence. And in 1801 a French captain called Marquand landed in the Marquesas Islands, 832 miles to the north, renamed them Les Marquises, and claimed them for France.

After surviving numerous death-defying perils, the LMS mission took root. Its tiny ship the *Duff* arrived in Tahiti on 5 March 1797 carrying eighteen crew and thirty missionaries; its volunteer captain, having landed his cargo, journeyed home aiming to return with a second shipload. Tragically, the ship was captured by privateers, and the struggling mission was never resupplied. Even worse, few of the natives proved to be 'noble savages':

> The Tahitians murdered at the slightest provocation . . . Wars and venereal diseases decimated their populations. [Warriors] wore the skins of their enemies as trophies. When a temple was built, its roof-stakes were driven through living human sacrifices. Tahitians sacrificed children to volcano gods, water gods, and sharks. The old and the infirm were buried alive in holes dug to receive them. No girl over twelve remained a virgin. King Pomare I killed an estimated 2,000 men himself.[41]

Several missionaries died, were killed, or fled. Only a handful remained under the brave and determined leadership of a former bricklayer from Bristol called Henry Nott (1774–1844), who showed missionary mettle of the highest order. Losing his newly wedded wife, he shepherded his flock through many travails, befriended Prince Pōmare, and won him over as his first convert after twenty-two years of endeavour. Nott planted the seed that changed the islands for ever:[42]

> Thirty persons [were] brought in by the missionary ship *Duff*. Though befriended by Pomare I (who lived to 1805), they [suffered] from the constant wars, and at length they fled with Pomare to Eimeo, and ultimately to New South Wales, only returning in 1812, when Pomare renounced heathenism.[43]

Henceforth, the fate of the growing mission and that of the nascent monarchy became irretrievably entwined; both aroused the hostility of Polynesian traditionalists, who intended to submit neither to Christianity nor to a central government. Yet the missionaries were pacifists; they had instructions to befriend the natives, and to win their trust by upright and practical living. Hence, while they busied themselves with agriculture, industry, and education, it was the new monarch, Pōmare II (r. 1805–24), who battled the resisters. He emerged triumphant after two pitched battles, one in 1808 at Te Feipi, and the other at Feii in November 1815. Furthermore, in defiance of traditional practice, he followed the missionaries' advice to pardon the defeated. His timely action ensured lasting reconciliation.

Political, economic, social, and cultural affairs could now be reordered. Under Nott's guidance, Pōmare II promulgated a constitution, guaranteeing the right to life and property, established a judiciary, and sanctified marriage and the observation of the Sabbath. On 16 May 1819 he was formally baptized at the Royal Chapel in Papeete; three LMS missionaries – Henry Bicknell, William Henry, and Charles Wilson – preached at the service.

Thereafter, the missionaries launched an educational campaign to teach the Polynesians to read, introduced European dress, encouraged the rudiments of medical care, and demonstrated the link between economic progress and science. Within a couple of years, they had opened a sugar refinery, textile factory, and printing press. 'For a time they made good progress ... but soon there came a relapse into heathen practices and immorality.'[44] Christianity was certainly the agent of modernity, but belief in its superior magic faltered.

The dynasty of Pōmare also faltered. Over the next sixty years its authority ceased to be contested by rival tribes, but it was constantly beset by afflictions, and it soon collided with the European powers. Pōmare II, like his father, died of alcohol-related causes in 1824; and his infant grandson Pōmare III (r. 1824–7) lived only to the age of seven. The dynasty's burdens, therefore, descended on Pōmare III's half-sister, Aimata, who was a spirited woman of exceptionally sound health. Her name, which Europeans wrongly took to mean 'Beloved', actually signified 'Eyeball-eater' and derived from one ancient habit of eating defeated enemies. Adopting the title of Pōmare IV and the pose of national matriarch, she introduced all the trappings of royalty – a royal palace at Papeete, the royal cemetery and mausoleum at Arue, a coat of arms, a national flag, and two coronations.

Nonetheless, the queen was bombarded with crises throughout the fifty years of her reign. 'In 1828, a new sect, the "Mamaia", arose; its leader proclaimed that he was Jesus Christ, and promised his followers a sensual paradise.'[45] In 1829 the queen invited the Pitcairners, descendants of the *Bounty* mutineers, to return. They immediately died in droves from disease, and begged to be sent back. In November 1835 she paid a visit to the newly arrived captain and crew of HMS *Beagle*, including Chailes Darwin, who was incubating his theory of evolution and who had a wonderfully positive view of what he was encountering:

> The luxuriant vegetation of the lower part was not discernible, [but] as the clouds rolled past, the wildest and most precipitous peaks showed themselves . . . In Matavai Bay, we were surrounded by canoes. This was our Sunday, but the Monday of Tahiti; if the case had been reversed, we should not have received a single visit, for the injunction not to launch a canoe on the Sabbath is rigidly obeyed. After dinner, we landed to enjoy all the delights produced . . . by the charming [Tahitians]. A crowd of men, women and children had collected . . . to receive us with merry, laughing faces. They [led] us to the house of Mr. Wilson, the missionary of the district, who met us on the road and gave us a very friendly reception.[46]

Yet animosity between Catholic and Protestant missions was spreading throughout the Pacific, and the European powers were being dragged into their quarrels. In Hawaii, Catholics were being persecuted by a ruler advised by American Protestants, and in 1841 the French Admiral Abel Dupetit-Thouars, commander of France's Pacific Fleet, was ordered to sail for the Marquesas Islands to protect their tiny Catholic mission. His action in turn provoked a protest from George Pritchard, who combined missionary work with the post of Britain's acting consul on Tahiti. A bigoted anti-Catholic, Pritchard was acting as Queen Pōmare's adviser; he had already expelled two uninvited French priests, and had begged Lord Palmerston to install a British protectorate, but it was too late. A French warship, the *Reine Blanche*, sailed into Papeete harbour in November 1843. Dupetit-Thouars descended the gangway, demanded an audience with the queen, and summarily announced that her kingdom had been transformed into a French protectorate. The British acting consul was soon arrested and then deported.

Later accounts show how risky the episode had been. According to Pritchard's nephew, Admiral Dupetit-Thouars had burst into the royal palace, where the queen was lying in childbirth. The admiral then issued an ultimatum: 'Sign this paper, or pay ten thousand dollars within twenty-four hours ... [or] I fire on Papeete without further notice.'[47]

By a curious coincidence, the admiral's flagship had reached Papeete in the company of an American whaler, the *Lucy Ann*, among whose crew was none other than Herman Melville, the future author of *Moby Dick*. Melville's biographers relate how the captain of the *Lucy Ann* was so stricken with venereal disease that he had steered for port in search of medical assistance. After he went ashore, the crew went on strike. The French admiral then sent a party of marines to collar the strikers and restore order.[48]

The ensuing 'War of Tahitian Independence' could easily have led to a violent confrontation between Britain and France on the far side of the world. Anglo-French relations were already at a low ebb, and Lord Palmerston was quite capable of treating the manhandling of a British consul as a *cause de guerre*. Tribal chiefs hostile to Queen Pōmare gained French aid, and she was forced into exile. Fortunately, Lord Aberdeen, who took charge in London, was friendly with France's new first minister, François Guizot, and made no objection to the queen's rapprochement with the French, insisting only that Tahiti be declared an independent kingdom (at least nominally). It is in the correspondence between Aberdeen and Guizot that the phrase *entente cordiale* first appears.

So although the kingdom and its monarchy survived, French officialdom tightened its grip on every aspect of the administration. The French navy guarded access to the Polynesian Triangle. French soldiers garrisoned the island. French Catholic orders moved in to boost a Catholic community that would soon challenge the Protestant ascendancy. And the French version of Otaheiti's name – Tahiti – became standard.

Queen Pōmare IV died in 1877 from natural causes, leaving numerous children. Her son and heir, Teri'i Tari'a Te-ra-tane, succeeded on 17 September and was duly crowned as Pōmare V. This last king was newly married to a second wife, Joanna Marau Salmon, who benefited from her husband's feebleness to dominate the court. But all the levers of power remained firmly in French hands.

After only three years the French authorities called a halt to the puppet-show. On 29 June 1880 they presented the king with an ultimatum; he signed away the kingdom's nominal sovereignty in return for the Legion d'Honneur and a handsome pension. He then proceeded, like his forebears, to drink himself slowly to death. The end came in

1891. His blackstone obelisk stands in the open in Arue's cemetery, and the royal line of 'Night-coughers' reached its term. Judged by the austere missionary ideals that had once raised it to the throne, the dynasty's pathetic demise represented a miserable failure.

In that second half of the nineteenth century, the formal annexation of the Pacific islands by the major maritime powers was proceeding steadily by stealth. The French established a penal colony in New Caledonia (in Melanesia) in 1853, and, following the last king's demise, downgraded Tahiti to a colony.

In Paris the administrators of the Third Republic set about devising political arrangements. In addition to Tahiti they had other island groups such as the Marquises, the Gambiers, and the Tuamotus to consider. A governor and ruling council had been appointed in 1885, providing a centralized colonial framework to replace the ramshackle organs of the defunct kingdom. The appellation of *Établissements de l'Océanie* (Oceanic Settlements) was adopted, until it was modified in 1903 as *Établissements Français de l'Océanie* – an integral unit of *France d'Outre Mer* (France Overseas). Its name lasted until it was replaced in 1958 by 'Polynésie Française'.

The British, in contrast, were generally satisfied by their strongholds in Australia and New Zealand, though this did not prevent them from annexing Fiji and Tokelau in 1877, Tuvalu in 1892, the Solomon Islands and Cook Islands in 1893, and the Gilbert and Ellice Islands in 1916. The Germans, who had long-standing commercial interests in New Guinea, took it over as a colony in 1884. They bought the Carolines and Mariannas from Spain in 1889, and ceded the North Solomons to Britain in 1899, in return for Samoa. Not to be outdone, the Americans forced Hawaii into submission by stages. Decimated by disease, and ruled like Tahiti by an enfeebled native monarchy, the Hawaiians were in no state to resist. They watched helplessly until the American-run Hawaiian Republic was incorporated into the United States in 1898. Following victory in the Spanish-American War, the United States acquired the Philippines and Guam the same year. Britain, Germany, and the United States partitioned the Samoan islands between them in 1900.

Uniquely, the only Pacific island to escape the clutches of foreign imperialists was Tonga, which successfully signed a 'Friendship Treaty' with Britain instead of accepting 'protection'. The tiny Polynesian kingdom thereby remained a sovereign state, its government stayed under local control, and, as from 1900, the British installed a consul instead

of a colonial governor. Queen Sālote Tupou III (1900–1965) was a star
at the coronation of Queen Elizabeth II in 1953.

Whenever the late colonial era is mentioned, Uncle Norman's stamp
album inevitably comes to mind. At first sight it is hard to believe that
it might have included items from Polynesia. On inspection of the
French Colonies section, however, a small, battered, and smudged
stamp catches my eye, squeezed between pictorials from Guadeloupe
and Martinique. Frail and forlorn, it is clearly a '1 cent black on blue'
of France's 'Peace and Commerce' type (1877+), which circulated in all
the colonies. It is overprinted in red capitals with a word whose two
leading letters could be identified under the magnifying glass as 'T' and
'A'. Since the name of only one French colony started with those letters,
there is good reason to suppose that the missing letters are -HITI.
Under 'French Polynesia' Scott's American *Standard Postage Stamp
Catalogue* reveals that the issue current from 1892 to 1907 bore the
colony's overprinted name 'either in blue or in carmine'.[49] That clinches
it. By some inexplicable means, one lonely, low-value stamp had wended
its way across the world from Tahiti to Bolton. And it had done so at
the very juncture when the Kingdom of Tahiti was vanishing. Behind
this humble stamp there hangs a tortured tale of missionaries, misfit
monarchs, and manifold misfortunes.

Polynesia did not escape the two world wars completely; all the impe-
rial powers milked their colonies for the war effort. A battalion of
Tahitian troops was sent to the Western Front in 1914, and a German
ship shelled Papeete in September of that year. In 1918 the defeated
Germans were stripped of their colonies, reducing the number of active
Pacific imperialists to three.

    During the Second World War, the Japanese occupied a large part of
the Western Pacific, but not Polynesia. The French authorities of the
Oceanic Settlements stayed loyal to the Vichy regime for a time, and
issued postage stamps to demonstrate it. But those authorities were
overthrown in September 1940 by a referendum, which gave a crushing
majority to de Gaulle's Free French forces. Pro-Vichy officials were
interned in New Caledonia as de Gaulle's governor-general arrived in
Papeete. A local military unit, *le Bataillon du Pacifique*, joined Free
French units in North Africa, and served in the Italian campaign. From
1943 to 1945 an American naval refuelling base operated at Bora Bora –
which some claim was the inspiration for Bali Ha'i.

*

The painter Paul Gauguin (1848–1903) landed in Tahiti in 1891, the same year that the last king died. He went 'to escape European civilization and everything that is artificial and conventional', and was starting an important phase in his artistic career. In other respects, preoccupied with the eroticism of local women, treatment for syphilis, persistent litigation, and abandonment of his family, he was living out a delusion. He had to die for his art – sensuous, visionary and arguably exploitative depictions of the islands and people – to be appreciated. Unlike many artists, he also knew how to use words. 'In order to see,' he once said, 'I shut my eyes', and 'Civilization makes you sick'. Best of all, 'We never know what stupidity is until we have experimented with it on ourselves.'[50]

Robert Louis Stevenson (1850–94), author of *Kidnapped* and *Treasure Island*, was another European who fled to the South Seas to escape civilization and improve his failing health. From 1888 to 1891, when Pōmare V was sliding from the throne, Stevenson was sailing round the Pacific on a three-year voyage to Hawaii, Tahiti, and his last resting place in Samoa. It is ironic that a man who suffered all his life from diseased lungs should have sought refuge on islands that had themselves been ravished by tuberculosis. The opening scene of his novel *The Ebb-Tide* (1894), written during his final voyage, unfolds at Papeete:

> Throughout the island world of The Pacific, scattered men of many European races . . . disseminate disease. Some prosper; some vegetate. Some have mounted the steps of thrones . . . Others again must marry for a livelihood . . . They sprawl in palm-leaf verandahs and entertain an island audience with memoirs of the music hall. And there are still others . . . less capable, less fortunate . . . who continue, even in these isles of plenty, to lack bread.
>
> At the far end of the town of Papeete, three such men were seated on the beach under a *purao* tree. It was late, the band had broken up long ago . . . Darkness and silence had gone from house to house in the tiny pagan city. Only the street lights shone on, making a glow-worm halo in the umbrageous alleys [and] a tremulous image on the waters of the port.
>
> But the men under the *purao* had no thought of sleep . . . It was bitter cold for the South Seas . . . They wore flimsy cotton clothes, the same they had sweated in by day . . . and to complete their evil case, they had no breakfast to mention, less dinner and no supper at all. In the telling South Sea phrase, these men were 'on the beach'.

Not long before, a ship form Peru had brought an influenza and it
now raged . . . in Papeete. From all around the *purao,* a dismal sound rose
and fell, of men coughing and strangling as they coughed. The sick
natives . . . had crawled from their houses to be cool, squatting on the
shore or on the beached-canoes, painfully expecting the new day . . .
Excesses of coughing arose and spread and died in the distance, and
sprang up again. Each miserable shiverer caught the suggestion of his
neighbour, was caught for some minutes by that cruel ecstasy and left
spent without voice or courage. If a man had pity to spend, Papeete
Beach on that cold night and in that infected season was a place to
spend it in.[51]

The scene may have been imagined, but it was indeed telling. Tahiti, in
those days, like Stevenson's own health, was 'on the beach'. Before the
novel was published, Stevenson's superb 'Requiem' was being carved
onto his Samoan gravestone:

> Under the wide and starry sky,
> Dig the grave and let me lie.
> Glad did I live, and gladly die,
>     And I laid me down with a will.
>
> This be the verse you grave for me:
> *Here he lies where he longed to be;*
> *Home is the sailor, home from the sea,*
>     *And the hunter home from the hill.*[52]

My boyhood hero Thor Heyerdahl, an academic from the University
of Oslo, landed in Polynesia in January 1937, together with his new bride,
Liv. After a brief stop in Tahiti, they sailed for Fatu Hiva, the southernmost of the Marquesas Islands. The official purpose of their expedition
was to collect specimens of insects and to address the question of entomo-
logical migration. Their real aim was to 'return to Nature' and to live in
total seclusion, relying entirely on a prehistoric diet of fish, berries, and
wild fruit. They built a cabin in the wilderness near the island's eastern
shore, and survived there for almost eighteen months. They gambolled
naked in the woods and bathed in the mountain streams. Their contact
with local people was minimal. One of their few friends was a middle-
aged Marquesan man called Tei Tua, who claimed to be the island's last
cannibal. Tei Tua showed them caves where human sacrifices were once
performed and where piles of skulls still littered the ground. He told them
legends of the Marquesan gods and of the mythical Marquesan chieftain

Tiki. Heyerdahl's account of the adventure was published in English as *Hunt for Paradise.*[53] It was an inducement for a return visit.

In the 1950s and early 1960s, Polynesia remained extremely remote. But the isolation which had attracted Heyerdahl was about to change for ever. The American actor Marlon Brando landed on Tahiti in 1960. The iconic star of *The Wild One* and *On the Waterfront* was Hollywood's top-earning name, and came to film the second version of *The Mutiny on the Bounty* on location. Yet the effects of his stay lingered long after the film-making. Brando had undoubtedly earned his reputation as a titan among actors, but equally displayed less savoury traits. Despite being the father of a newborn son by a first wife and being newly married to a second, he relentlessly pursued his eighteen-year-old Polynesian co-star Tarita Teriipaia until she succumbed and married him as his third wife in 1962. As part of his infatuation, he bought an idyllic group of islets thirty miles off Tahiti, where he established a luxurious tropical residence. Brando's spectacular philandering, which produced a dozen known children from assorted wives and concubines, is usually shrugged off as par for the course in Hollywood. Yet it is peculiarly emblematic not only of the abuse of Polynesia by Europeans but also of Tahiti's lasting image as a paradise filled with pain and remorse. Brando's long-abandoned widow, Tarita, was left to write her tortured memoirs, *Marlon: My Love and My Torment.*[54]

Throughout the twentieth century, Tahiti and the neighbouring archipelagos continued to act as a magnet for Europe's misfits, escapees, and invalids. The island's palpable melancholy suited them even more than the tropical climate. In 1975 the latest of a long line of civilizational fugitives, the Belgian singer-songwriter Jacques Brel (1929–78), heir to the *Rois-Chansonniers*, settled with his wife on Hiva Oa in the Marquises. He was nursing lung cancer. Like Stevenson, he adored ocean sailing, and like him, planned a three-year voyage. He learned to fly a light plane, so that he could shuttle back and forth to Tahiti. The collection of heart-breaking songs that he wrote in Polynesia includes 'Vieillir' ('Growing Old'), 'Le Bon Dieu' ('The Good Lord'), 'L'Amour est Mort' ('Love is Dead'), and 'Les Marquises':

> *Le rire est dans le coeur, le mot dans le regard.*
> *Le coeur est voyageur, l'avenir est au hasard.*
> *Et passent des cocotiers qui écrivent des chants d'amour,*
> *Que les soeurs d'alentours ignorent d'ignorer.*
> *Les pirogues s'en vont, les pirogues s'en viennent,*

*Et mes souvenirs deviennent ce que les vieux en font.*
*Veux-tu que je te dise: gémir n'est pas de mise*
*Aux Marquises.*[55]

(Laughter is in the heart, the word is in the glance.
The heart is a traveller, and the future a game of chance.
Passing coconut-palms write love songs
Which the nuns of the neighbourhood don't notice having missed.
The canoes come, and the canoes go.
And my memories become whatever old men make of them.
Surely, you don't want me to say: whining is not in order
In the Marquises.)

After completing his geographical inquiries, Charles de Brosses moved on to new fields of study that greatly expanded public awareness of the Pacific. He was fascinated by the distant origins of human behaviour, fearlessly plunging into areas of knowledge that had rarely or never been explored before. In 1760, for example, he published *Les Dieux Fétiches* (*Fetish Gods*), basing his reflections on the religious practices of Ancient Greece, Ancient Egypt, and Black Africa.[56] By suggesting that religion arose from basic human needs and impulses he risked serious confrontation with the Church. But he was opening up a topic that would soon be very relevant to the motivations of Christian missionaries. Then, in 1765, he published his *Traité de la formation mécanique des langues* (*Treatise on the Mechanical Formation of Languages*). It expounded a theory that would now be called Sound Symbolism, and is considered a founding work of the science of linguistics. Exploring links between verbal sounds and writing systems, including Chinese pictograms, it boldly postulated the existence of a single ancestral form of human speech from which all modern languages were descended. De Brosses ruminated on the origin of the Celtic languages and Sanskrit, though not on those of the Far East. Nonetheless, he helped put in motion a process that would eventually lead to research on the Pacific languages first encountered by his doughty navigators.

Captain Cook himself found that the native man whom he took aboard *Endeavour* in Tahiti had few problems conversing with the distant Maoris in New Zealand (see Chapter 9). He pointed to the probability that the Polynesians shared a common origin and had been dispersed around the Pacific at a relatively late stage. 'How shall we account,' Cook had asked in his *Journal*, 'for this nation spreading itself so far over this vast ocean?' In the second edition of Bougainville's *Voyage* (1772) he made some crucial philological reflections: his chapter discussing the island's 'Vocabulaire' benefited from a conversation in Paris with Joseph Banks, who had sailed with Cook, and it includes the ground-breaking sentence: 'Cependant, les Anglois . . . ont constaté que le language des habitants de la Nouvelle Zélande est a peu-près le même que celui des Tahitiens.'[57] Comparative Pacific philology was on the move.

The second half of the eighteenth century, the 'Age of Dr Johnson', was a period when earlier inquiries into philology and etymology were systematized and new theories launched. Johnson's famous *Dictionary of the English Language* (1755) contained entries on *Linguist*, 'one skilful in languages'; on *Philologer/Philologist*, 'a grammarian'; and, hilariously, on *Lexicographer*, 'a writer of dictionaries, a harmless drudge'. Both Cook and Bougainville compiled simple Polynesian vocabularies.[58] Further advances were associated with the Scot Lord Monboddo (1714–99), the Welshman William Jones (1746–94), and the German Wilhelm von Humboldt (1767–1835). But a long time passed before scholars broke free of the discipline's Eurocentric roots. Monboddo, a leading light of the Scottish Enlightenment, observed the capacity of languages to change and evolve, and is remembered as the 'father of historical linguistics'. 'Orientalist' Jones, who was a judge employed by the East India Company in Calcutta, identified the common Indo-European roots of Greek, Latin, and Sanskrit, as also of Welsh, English, and Bengali. Humboldt, the brother of the naturalist and explorer Alexander von Humboldt, and co-founder of the University of Berlin, greatly expanded language theory, establishing the principle that languages were rule-based systems, not random compilations of words and sounds. He started by studying Basque, but was eager to link Sanskrit with the oriental languages beyond India. His culminating work, *Über die Kawi-Sprache* (1839), addressed the origins of Java's Kavi language. He was the first to hypothesize about a linguistic family stretching from Madagascar to the Pacific islands.[59]

Nonetheless, the puzzle of Polynesian origins turned into one of the longest-running scientific sagas of modern times. Theories can be divided into those proposing origins in the West, in Asia, and others rooting for origins in the East, in America. The 'westernists' relied heavily on racial considerations, in particular on the supposed similarities between Polynesians and Malays, and on the fact that 'island-hopping' was available for primitive navigators coming from Asia. The 'easternists' were inspired by supposed similarities between Polynesians and Native Americans, and by the presence of the sweet potato in both Polynesia and Peru. Scholars also debated the rhythms and patterns of Polynesian dispersal. Did it occur at one go, or in a series of protracted movements? Three hypotheses contended: the 'Express Train Model', the 'Entangled Bank Model', and the 'Slow Boat Model'.[60]

Knowledge of Pacific cultures remained meagre throughout the nineteenth century. Linguistic studies, in particular, stalled, lacking any coherent theoretical framework. A certain amount of practical work was undertaken in Tahiti or Hawaii by Protestant missionaries, who strove to translate the Bible into local languages. But wild speculation was in fashion, and would-be researchers were confused by prevailing theories of race. In New Zealand, for example, the earliest attempt to place Maori culture into a wider setting, Edward Tregear's *The Aryan Maori* (1885), falsely assumed that Polynesians were of Indo-European origin.[61] It was a good example of what the philosopher Gottfried Leibniz once called '*gropismo*', after meeting a Dutchman of his day, Jan van Gorp, who held that Hebrew was derived from Dutch. Similar delusions overshadowed work on Polynesia.[62]

D'Urville had excluded the East Indies from Oceania, but it was from there that a model appeared to indicate how studies of the Pacific might proceed. The key figure was a British naturalist, Alfred Russel Wallace (1823–1913), who devised a theory of evolution independent of Darwin, and who is often known as 'the father of biogeography'. Wallace's *Malay Archipelago* (1869) was a phenomenal scientific achievement, with implications for anthropology and linguistics as well as botany, zoology, and ecology.[63] In the sphere of regional nomenclature, it was Wallace who determined that the 'East Indies' should henceforth be classed as Maritime South-East Asia. A British missionary, Robert Henry Codrington (1830–1922), pursued similar research in Melanesia, publishing *The Melanesian Languages* in 1885 and *The Melanesians: Studies in Anthropology and Folklore* in 1891.[64]

Despite Wallace, Pacific Studies lingered in the doldrums until Germany's acquisition of colonies in Papua and Samoa during the 1880s provided the spur to a substantial contingent of philologists. The scholar who set the field of Pacific linguistics and ethnography onto a more rational path was the Catholic missionary Father Wilhelm

Schmidt (1868–1954), founder of the journal *Anthropos* (1906), who is credited with the key concept of Austronesian languages.[65] His compatriot Professor Otto Dempwolff (1871–1938) consolidated the subject, in works published during the First World War.[66] In that same era, the Polish-born anthropologist Bronisław Malinowski (1884–1942), a graduate of the LST, undertook a scientific expedition to the Trobriand Islands in Melanesia, where he honed the ideas that were published in his famous *Argonauts of the Western Pacific* (1922) and *The Sexual Life of Savages in North-West Melanesia* (1929). Malinowski's method of 'participatory observation' required intensive study in language and culture, and is a foundation stone of modern anthropology.[67]

Unlike Micronesia, Melanesia or Polynesia, Austronesia – which means 'Southern Islands' – does not refer to a particular island grouping, still less to all the islands in a particular area. Rather, it is a term of convenience for all the places in the world where the Austronesian languages are spoken, and as Wilhelm von Humboldt correctly foresaw, it stretches all the way from Madagascar to Polynesia, overlying multiple geographic regions in between.

The Mormon contribution to these debates is interesting, if only because it illustrates their penchant for unverified speculation. The Latter-Day Saints arrived at an early stage, establishing a mission on Hawaii in 1850 that grew into a permanent community. The Brigham Young University, at Laie on Oahu, together with the adjoining Polynesian Cultural Center, are the products of a century-long effort and attest to the dedication of the Latter-Day Saints to their supposed Polynesian origins. 'For Mormons,' writes one of their scholars, 'the relationship of the Polynesian peoples with the House of Israel is an unquestioned fact. It is, however, based on faith.'

Throughout the twentieth century, scholarly work proceeded on the knotty problems of Pacific culture, especially on linguistics. The elaboration of the Austronesian linguistic family tree, first mooted by Wilhelm Schmidt and Otto Dempwolff, has yet to be completed, but scholars now generally agree that the best evidence for the earliest Austronesian-speaking language groups comes from aboriginal, pre-Chinese Taiwan. (The Han Chinese did not invade Taiwan until the seventeenth century AD.) No fewer than fifteen tiny Austronesian communities have survived on Taiwan, and together they are now taken to be the linguistic ancestors of all later sub-branches of the family.[68] From Taiwan, Austronesian speakers migrated in ancient times to the Malay Archipelago, and from there their offshoots moved both westward across the Indian Ocean and eastward into the Pacific. At each stage, the descendant languages evolved and multiplied, interacting with the speech of existing populations. The net result is a linguistic super-family encompassing up to three thousand languages.[69]

The Polynesian component within Austronesian is made up of a score of related languages that are today spoken by up to a million people. The largest of them is Samoan with over 300,000 speakers, followed by Tahitian (c. 125,000), Tongan (c. 110,000), Maori (c. 100,000), Rarotongan or 'Cook Islands Maori' (14,000), Marquesan (8,700), and Hawaiian (24,000). The Tahitian language, which describes itself as *Reo Mao'hi* or 'Tahitian Speech', is the leader of the Tahitic grouping, which is descended from the original Austronesian linguistic family via the Malayo-Polynesian, Oceanic, Fijio-Polynesian, and Nuclear Polynesian branches. A few Polynesian dialects, such as Moriori on the Chatham Islands, have become extinct within living memory.

The anthropologists redoubled their efforts in the wake of Malinowski. In Hawaii, traditional family structure was taken to be a template for Polynesia as a whole; Tahiti provided the raw material for work on the concept of taboo. The classic work on this subject was published in London by Franz Steiner in 1956.[70]

Heyerdahl's famous post-war expedition came about through the coincidence of pre-war information garnered on Fatu Hiva and the fruits of later research in Peru. Heyerdahl was fascinated by stories of a white-skinned people who had inhabited the Andes before the Incas, and who had left strange, unexplained monuments on the shores of Lake Titicaca. To his enormous excitement, he found that the leader of this mysterious people was called Kon Tiki, and that he had been driven out, sailing into the sunset from South America's western coast. Heyerdahl's deductions are summarized in the introduction to his thrilling book, *The Kon Tiki Expedition* (1948). He organized his operation to prove his hunch that Stone Age navigators were capable of crossing the Pacific from east to west, and that a rough-hewn balsa-wood raft could survive all the ocean's perils. When the *Kon Tiki* reached its goal in the islands of the central Pacific, the 'easternists' were greatly encouraged.[71]

Archaeology also played its part. In the 1950s a large find of prehistoric pottery came to light at a site called Lapita on the Melanesian island of Grande Terre in New Caledonia. Sophisticated geometric designs on red and black clay announced an established culture. Lapita ware was also present on numerous sites spread over several thousand

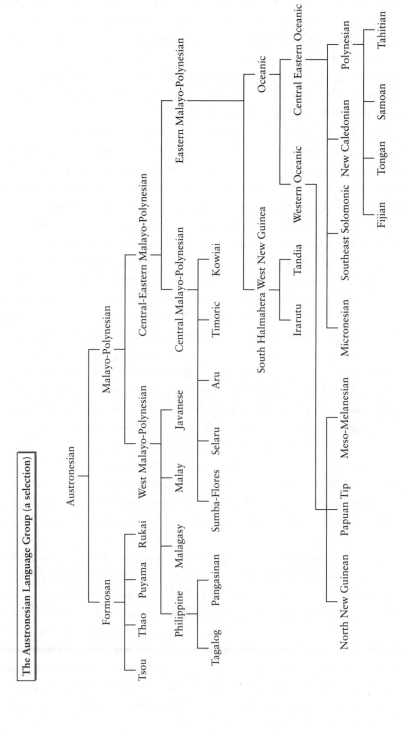

The Austronesian Language Group (a selection)

miles, including the 'Bird's Head' peninsula of New Guinea to Samoa. Analysts then decided that the 'Lapita Trail' marked the pathway of Polynesian peoples as they migrated eastwards in the second and first millennia BC. Their findings greatly strengthened the case for a western origin of the Polynesians, and in some circles were taken as decisive. Yet they left key questions unanswered. If the 'Lapita Peoples' were indeed the Polynesians' ancestors, why did their trademark pottery trail not reach into the Polynesian heartland?

In the 1960s another academic furore broke out over the question of Polynesian navigation. In his book *Ancient Voyagers in the Pacific*, Andrew Sharp, a New Zealander, made the obvious point that it is not logically possible to steer with skill and precision to an unknown destination. Discovery must precede purposeful expeditions. Sharp concluded that the Polynesians must have mounted two separate sorts of operation. Organized migrations could only take place once a new destination had been located, and a route tried and tested.[72]

As the twentieth century wore on, the 'westernists' in the debate on Polynesian origins grew in confidence, as the consensus tipped steadily in their direction. Heyerdahl's findings were repeatedly slammed. 'The Kon-Tiki Theory,' wrote one critic, 'is about as plausible as the tales of Atlantis.' 'Heyerdahl,' wrote another, 'ignored the overwhelming body of linguistic, ethnographic, and ethnobotanical evidence' and was 'patently wrong'.[73] But the knock-out blow had to await the arrival of DNA testing. In the 1990s, the pioneer of the subject, Professor Bryan Sykes of Wolfson College, Oxford, examined mitochondrial DNA from natives of the Cook Islands, and declared that the nearest match for their genes was located in the Molucca Islands of Indonesia.[74] Modern technology confirmed the earlier linguistic hypotheses. The origin of the Polynesians had been nailed not only to the West but to a particular location in maritime South-East Asia.

Another surprising genetic discovery linked the Melanesians to pre-human hominids from the Denisova Cave in southern Siberia. Between 10 and 25 per cent of Melanesian DNA is said to derive from the Denisovan gene pool, indicating substantial interbreeding at a very early point in evolutionary history. Where and when the proto-Melanesians encountered the Denisovans is not yet clear.[75] Anyone who peers into the growing field of Pacific genetic studies, therefore, gets a strong feeling of déjà vu. The field of study is vast. The researches of historical geneticists resemble nothing more than the voyages of the early

navigators who ventured into the South Seas in ages past, and the pin-
pricks of verified knowledge form tiny isolated atolls in a boundless
ocean of uncertainty. The pitfalls are glaring. The early studies based
on maternal lines of descent, mitochondrial DNA, produced markedly
different results from studies based on Y-chromosome DNA and paternal ancestry. As one researcher from New Zealand put it, we were
being told that Maori men came from Indonesia and Maori women
from Taiwan.[76] For another thing, it was manifestly absurd to expect
that the whole proto-Polynesian nation climbed into its boats and
sailed into the central Pacific in one great convoy. It is far more likely
that Polynesia's present-day population shares a number of ancestral
strands, and that successive waves of migrants mingled with other populations at various points on the route.[77] This supposition permits one
to believe that the founding wave started to expand perhaps 10,000 years
ago,[78] and that the Austronesian languages were carried to Polynesia in
the mouths of later and separate waves of migrants who reached
Hawaii c. AD 200, Otaheiti c. 1000, and Aotearoa c. 1200.

Nor is it necessary to abandon all hope of finding a historic link
between Polynesia and the Americas. If it is discovered, it will likely be
one of several minor ancestral strands, part of the overall genetic mix.
Recent findings point in that direction. One study from 2008 provides
'unequivocal evidence' for the pre-Columbian introduction of chickens
to South America and 'an indication' of 'the likely source' being Polynesia.[79] Chickens can't swim across the sea for 5,000 miles. Another
study, from 2013, found genetic material from Polynesia in the bones of
dead Botocudo tribesmen from south-eastern Brazil.[80] A third relies on
the information that both Polynesians and Malagasques were sent to
Brazil as part of the nineteenth-century slave trade. So the Mormons
need not despair.

Many people, in fact, continue to question assumptions that others
take to be proven fact. For instance, they question the widespread conviction that the ancestors of Native Americans could only have left Asia
via a land bridge at the present-day Bering Strait. Believing instead in
the prowess of prehistoric navigators – as the Polynesian Voyaging Society does[81] – they maintain that the proto-Americans could have reached
their future homeland by boat. The puzzle of the Polynesian Pathways is
certainly not finally solved.[82] One thing is certain: the good Count
Charles de Brosses, sitting in his armchair in Dijon in the days of Louis
XV, could not possibly have imagined what he was starting.

*

French nuclear testing in Polynesia began after Algerian independence had closed down previous test sites in the Sahara. In 1962, 1,250 kilometres to the south-east of Tahiti, President de Gaulle personally watched an early test at Mururoa atoll. The tests were initially staged in the atmosphere, then from 1974 to 1995 underground. Almost 200 in number, they provoked a chorus of international protests, notably from New Zealand, and in 1985, in *Opération Satanique*, French special forces notoriously sank a protest ship, the *Rainbow Warrior*, in Auckland harbour. The final explosion in 1996, shortly before France signed the Comprehensive Test Ban Treaty, caused particular outrage.

Nuclear testing had several important consequences. It raised the value of Polynesia in the eyes of Paris; and the presence in Polynesia of tens of thousands of military, scientific, and support staff gave a huge boost both to the local economy and to demographic growth. It justified the building in 1962 of the international airport at Faa'a on Tahiti, which in turn provided the *sine qua non* of a modern tourist industry. The influx of foreign protesters encouraged the rise of local political movements and demands for autonomy.

That same era also saw the creation of a semi-democratic political system, which, in line with the constitution of 1958, reduced the colonial prerogatives of the French government and established a Polynesian parliament and executive. The President of France remained head of state of this 'Territoire d'Outre Mer' (TOM),* and Paris continued to control foreign affairs, defence, and overall finance, but important powers were devolved to a regional government elected by the unicameral and multi-party assembly.

Since that time, Polynesian politics has been dominated by two main party groupings and two veteran leaders. One of them, Gaston Flosse (b. 1931), is the conservative, who sees autonomy as the limit of Tahitian aspirations. The other, Oscar Temaru (b. 1944), advocates full independence. Their support is nicely balanced, and in the first decade of the twenty-first century the two rivals were still taking turns at holding the presidency in an unbroken impasse.

Full-blooded nationalists, however, risk severe treatment. One such firebrand, Pouvanaa a Oopa (1895–1977), who campaigned in the 1950s under the slogan 'Tahiti for the Tahitians, and Frenchmen for the sea', was arrested and sentenced to twenty-three years' exile. Visiting French presidents, most recently François Hollande, now place wreaths on his grave.[83]

* Since upgraded to a 'Collectivité d'Outre Mer' (COM).

Unexpectedly, pretenders to the supposedly defunct Kingdom of Tahiti persistently resurface. The principal claimant, M. Tauatomo Mairau, Pōmare V's great-grandson, who died in 2013, based his claim to the non-existent throne on the terms of the 1880 agreement, which, in his lawyers' view, the French government had failed to implement. A rival relative, M. Joinville Pōmare (b. 1953), declared himself to be King Pōmare XI in 2009; his démarche was however contested by M. Leopold Pōmare (b. 1935), who appears to be the same person as 'King Taginuihoe'. The latter ingeniously declared himself to be head of 'a republican monarchy' and regards the island of Moorea as the independent 'Republic of Paku-motu'. Having annulled all debts and bank loans, he was imprisoned for distributing illegal identity cards and driving licences. Undeterred, his loyal subjects appear to have put the Royal Republic's illegal currency, the *Patu*, into circulation, inviting further criminal prosecution.[84]

Notwithstanding these tergiversations, population growth in Tahiti has soared. According to the census of 1907, the number of French Polynesians had dropped to 30,600 – less than a quarter of an average Parisian *arrondissement*. In 1939 it had barely reached 50,000, and in 1962, at the time of the Mururoa Test, 84,551. Yet twenty years later it had doubled, and by 2002 tripled. In 2016, at 285,735, it represented a very healthy recovery.

Tourism is pitched at affluent vacationers from Australia, Japan, or the USA, and particularly from France and French-speaking Quebec, who are not deterred by lengthy and expensive flights. (Air France flies daily and direct from Paris-Charles de Gaulle to Papeete.) These are not the sort of tourists who are easily satisfied with a mere beach shade and nightly disco. They demand top-class golf courses, deep-sea fishing, snorkelling around coral reefs, exciting 4×4 volcano rides, starlit pony treks, bathyscope-diving, underwater caving, and helicopter rides. And, as one overhears at the reception desk of the Hotel Manava, they're not slow to complain.

'Goddamit,' one resident whines, 'we spent six hundred dollars on this hotel.' He meant per night.

Very few stay on in Tahiti for long; they briefly rest from their exhausting flight, then depart for their bijoux residences on secluded private islands, where they see little of local life, and are not seen themselves. They are imitation Marlon Brandos.

Tahiti is a bilingual country, and it is a poor sort of tourist who ignores it. Some 98 per cent of the population either speak French fluently or understand it readily. Yet a majority still speak the Tahitian language at home, and participate in its public revival. For me, French is familiar and pleasantly reassuring. Tahitian is totally unfamiliar, and difficult to absorb. Its syllables seem so simple and repetitive, they are forgotten as fast as they are learned. You learn the numbers from 1 to 100 in ten minutes before going to bed, but by the morning they have evaporated:

| | | | |
|---|---|---|---|
| 1 | *ho'e* | 9 | *iva* |
| 2 | *piti* | 10 | *'ahuru* |
| 3 | *toru* | 11 | *'ahuru ma ho'e* |
| 4 | *maha* | 20 | *piti 'ahuru* |
| 5 | *pae* | 100 | *hanere* |
| 6 | *ono* | 200 | *piti hanere* |
| 7 | *hitu* | 1,000 | *tautini* |
| 8 | *va'u* | | |

The Tahitian Revival began in the 1970s in tandem with the country's political awakening. A group of activists, headed by the poet Henri Hiro (1944–90), took to protesting against both the nuclear tests and the neglect of the language. They rescued it from near oblivion by compulsory inclusion in the school curriculum, published anthologies of songs and poems, founded a Tahitian Academy, and helped to create an educated, bilingual class who no longer regard French as the sole medium for higher forms of expression.

No one masters a foreign language in the space of days or weeks, but words emanate spirit as well as literal meaning, Tahitian words for the wonders of Nature are specially rich and evocative:

| | | |
|---|---|---|
| *anuanua* (rainbow) | *marama* (moon) | *poe* (pearl) |
| *eiya* (fish) | *mata'i* (wind) | *pupu* (seashell) |
| *fetia* (star) | *miti* (sea, river) | *ra'au* (tree) |
| *hiona* (snow) | *moana* (ocean) | *reva* (sky) |
| *ma'a* (fruit) | *motu* (island) | *tane* (man) |
| *mahana* (sun) | *mou'a* (mountain) | *tiare* (flower) |
| *manu* (bird) | *one* (sand) | *ua* (rain) |
| *ma'o* (shark) | *pape* (water) | *vahine* (woman) |

Many of these common words recur in place names and personal names. Although contemporary Tahitians are mostly Christians, they never took willingly to Christian names. The old pagan first names still flourish and inevitably flavour their owners' sense of identity:

| For men | For women | For men or women |
|---|---|---|
| *Aitu* (Priest) | *Eeva* (Rising Star) | *Afa* (Hurricane) |
| *Amana* (Sovereign) | *Hereata* (Love Cloud) | *Afi* (Fire) |
| *Anapa* (Sunlit Sea) | *Herenui* (Big Love) | *Akoheho* (Storm) |
| *Anui* (Big Canoe) | *Matahina* (Goddess Eye) | *Ahomena* (Thunder) |
| *Areiti* (Little Wave) | *Meherio* (Mermaid) | *Aisea* (God Saves) |
| *Ari'i* (Prince) | *Miri* (Caress) | *Alipate* (Bright) |
| *Hoanui* (Big Friend) | *Orama* (Flame) | *Amanaki* (Hope) |
| *Mana* (Power) | *Poenui* (Big Pearl) | *Aata* (Moon Child) |
| *Manuari'i* (Royal Bird) | *Puaiti* (Little Flower) | *Manutea* (White Bird) |
| *Rahiti* (Rising Sun) | *Puaura* (Red Flower) | *Purotu* (Fair Child) |
| *Tahitoa* (First Warrior) | *Ra'imere* (Sky Angel) | *Temaru* (King's Dawn) |
| *Tamahere* (Loved Child) | *Ranitea* (Clear Sky) | *Temoe* (Sunset) |
| *Teiki* (King Child) | *Teora* (Life) | *Tita* (Sun Fruit) |
| *Toanui* (Great Warrior) | *Vaea* (Peace) | *Uira* (Lightning) |

As so often, songs provide the best route into a language. In the Tahitian case, they were central to traditional oral culture, and to the preservation of the language during decades of official persecution. Love songs, laments, children's rhymes, and canoeing chants are popular: bilingual people love bilingual lyrics; but it's the rhythm that drives the words:

| A Hoe, A Hoe, | Rame, Rame | (Paddle, paddle |
| --- | --- | --- |
| A Hoe i te Va'a | Rame la pirogue | Paddle your canoe. |
| A Rave'a a Mau i te Hoe | Ramer, seule solution. | Paddling's the only way. |
| A Hoe I te Va'a | Rame la piroque | Paddle your canoe |
| Na ni'a I te moana | Rame-la sur l'océan | Paddle it over the sea |
| A Hoe i te Va'a. | Rame la pirogue. | Paddle your canoe.)[85] |

The best place to see traditional Polynesian culture on display is at the annual *Heiva* or 'Celebration of Life' that takes place in Papeete every July. The *Heiva* has been tied to Bastille Day ever since 1895, when French officialdom cunningly decided to link loyalty to France with long-neglected traditional events, even though they risked the ire of killjoy Protestant missionaries, who disdained such 'heathen practices'. The week of festivities starts on 14 July with a parade and the singing of *La Marseillaise*, before moving on to competitions of Tahitian song and oratory, to demonstrations of local crafts such as fire-walking or coconut palm-climbing, and above all to long-distance canoe races. The most prestigious race takes ten-man canoes around a 50-mile course that crosses the strait between Tahiti and Moorea, and circumnavigates Moorea before returning to the finish in Papeete.

Tattoos are a Polynesian speciality. *Tatu*, like *tabu*, is a Polynesian word, recorded by Captain Cook. But the missionaries banned tattooing, and the fashion only returned as part of the cultural revival. Nowadays, both Tahitians and tourists love it, and tattoo parlours have sprung up on every other street corner. It is Tahiti's contribution to globalization. Sporting a dashing design on face, back, or limbs is the way for young people the world over to display their personality.[86] Not everyone knows, however, that tattoos can be applied to the body's less public parts. Strictly for men only, a specialized line exists in so-called 'Mobiles', which have inspired one of the island's racier jokes. Two young ladies, so it goes, shared the same boyfriend. One says:

'Have you seen Pepe's mobile?'

'Of course,' the other replies, 'it just shows his name, "PEPE".'

'That's odd,' the other muses. 'When I saw it last, it read PEPE-PAPUA-PAPEETE.'

Papeete, the capital of Tahiti, is the sole city in the whole of Polynesia, and even there the 'city' title is somewhat flattering. An American couple on the bus into town sounded cheated, calling it 'shabby' and 'run-down'. If they were looking for some dinky, sanitized pseudo-colonial toytown, they had been misinformed. For, like many French towns, Papeete displays an inimitable mixture of the imposing and the nondescript. A handful of fine public buildings are miniatures of their prototypes in France. Away from the waterfront, the streets are narrow and crowded. Dense tropical vegetation and giant trees dominate the open spaces. In the oppressive heat of the day, people seek out every inch of shade – sitting, squatting, or gasping for air. The commonest phrase, the guidebook says, is *Haere maru* – a bit like Spanish *mañana* – translating as 'Slow down' or 'Relax'.

The bus drops us off near *Les Halles*, the market hall, the *Mapuru a Paraita*. Stalls piled high with local food fill one end with yams, taro, and sweet potatoes, and a textile section occupies the other. Joseph would have had no problem here finding his coat of many colours. It's a photographer's delight, but only for those used to working in a sauna.

Papeete means 'Water basket', and in such heat drinking-fountains are indeed essential. Air-conditioning is absent, and the humid air chokes the throat. With her permission, I snap a stall-keeper dressed from head to foot in a tiara of flowers and a shocking shade of yellow, and flee.

The Catholic cathedral of Nôtre-Dame lies beyond the Pearl Market – a modest white-and-beige building with a red spire and small, iron-railed garden. All the doors are flung open in the hope of catching a *soupçon* of breeze. Shady pews promise respite. Roman Catholicism, once favoured by the authorities, attracts the allegiance of 35 per cent of the population, but a higher percentage remain stubbornly Protestant. Religious devotion is strong, and hymns figure prominently in the repertoire of local folksong. In 1992 a Tahitian choir from Rapa Iti became a worldwide hit. Their singing style, called *himene tarava* or 'polyphonic hymnody', mixing rich melodic cadences with sudden drops of pitch and staccato grunting, evokes echoes of long-lost times.[87]

Papeete's town centre contains three notable public buildings. The elegant town hall or *Mairie*, with its multiple verandahs, is a replica of the demolished royal palace. The ultra-modern residence of the Haut-Commissaire is concealed behind high steel fencing and still higher tropical shrubbery. But the 'National Assembly', the parliament, stands in a central position, surrounded by soaring palms and flowering ferns, and open for all to see. The notice on the red-painted gates reads:

– ASSEMBLÉE DE LA POLYNÉSIE FRANÇAISE –
APOR'ORA'A RAHINO TE FENUA

When I called in, the Assembly was not in session. There was no information office and no sign of a security guard. As in the cathedral, all the doors of the high-gabled, pseudo-primitive style building were wide open to catch the breeze. So anyone could wander into the semi-circular, wood-panelled chamber, and take pictures of themselves sitting in the Speaker's Chair. Most striking, though, was an outline map of French Polynesia hanging in the lobby and superimposed on the map of Europe. The Society Islands overlap with Paris and southern England, the Marquises with Sweden and Denmark, the Australs with Sardinia and Sicily, the Tuamotus with Poland, and the Gambiers with Romania.

At first sight, the people on the street can be divided into Polynesians and Europeans, whom the locals call *popoa*, the equivalent of the Maori *pakeha*. But an important mixed-race class of so-called *Demi* has evolved, and oriental, Chinese faces are also common. Everyone dresses with extreme casualness – usually in T-shirts, baggy beach shorts and flip-flops. In the evening, young people often wear a flower in their hair. A flower behind the left ear means 'engaged' or 'unavailable'; a bloom behind the right ear signals 'Come hither'.

There is no shortage of French and oriental restaurants with mouthwatering menus posted outside. On the first day, while finding my feet, I plump instead for a meal in the open beside one of the ubiquitous *roulottes* or 'food vans'. I sit at a wooden table by the roadside. A plate of *saucisses* with a buttered maize cob, washed down with a glass of coconut water, appears in a flash, and is delicious. The van staff could not be friendlier.

'Tu es français?' the cook asks.

'Non, je m'excuse,' I reply. 'Britannique.'

'Sans blague,' he says. 'C'est un Anglo!' he whispers to his wife.

Next day, my island guide turns up in his battered Peugeot. He's a smiling young man called Arnaud Dardet – the e-mail friend of a friend of a friend in Paris. He enjoys meeting foreigners and showing them round.

'Heureux de faire ta connaissance,' he says using the familiar second-person 'tu' form, as the *roulottier* had done.

'Ah, c'est comme à Québec,' I say. (In Quebec you say 'tu' to everyone.)

'Oui, naturellement,' he confirms, adding untranslatably, 'Mais je peux te vouvoyer, si tu le veux.' ('But I can address you as *vous*, if you wish.')

'Non, ça va, ça va.'

Within minutes, Arnaud is happily telling me all about himself. His French father, who had fought in the Resistance, came out after the war and set up a building business. His mother was part-Polynesian, part-Chinese. His paternal grandma Anna was Polish. His elder brother, in whose apartment he lives, is prospering in real estate and helping his *benjamin* to start a firm installing solar panels.

'Pas mal de soleil par ici,' Arnaud says. 'Les panneaux solaires se vendent bien.' ('Quite a lot of sun here. Solar panels sell well.') 'Mes copains tahitiens,' he then announces, 'disent que je suis blanc.' ('My Tahitian friends tell me I'm white.')

'But in France, they say the opposite,' I venture.

'Je m'en fous.' ('I couldn't care less.')

In an empty street behind the Assembly, we suddenly come across the disturbing sight of a drink-sodden man shamelessly beating his screaming wife. I set off to help her. Arnaud restrains me.

'Pas la peine,' he says. ('It's not worth it.') 'If you intervene, he will beat her even harder when they get home.'

Wife-beating, alcoholism, obesity, and *pakalolu*, the local brand of marijuana, are perennial problems.

'If you're interested,' Arnaud adds, 'you can read about it in a novel that everyone here knows; it's called *Breadfruit*.'[88]

We head to the Université de la Polynésie Française (UPF), where I had been expecting to meet the dean. It stands amidst dense tropical vegetation on the top of a cliff overlooking the airport at Faa'a.[89] The white-painted colonial-style buildings fill a tiny fenced-off campus. At the back a small structure with a corrugated-iron roof bears the inscription BIBLIOTHÈQUE UNIVERSITAIRE. It's Wednesday afternoon. There's not a student or a teacher in sight; the car park is totally empty.

'Ce sont les vacances?' I ask. ('Is this holiday time?')

'Non, pas de tout.'

We knock on a door. Springing to life, a secretary sitting sleepily beneath a cooling fan offers us some unwanted brochures on extra-curricular evening classes.

'Would it be possible to meet the dean?' I ask. Apparently not.

'Qu'est-ce qu'elle a, cette UPF?' I enquire of Arnaud. ('So what's the matter with the UPF?')

The story is that it was founded in 1980 as one campus of the French University of Oceania, the other campus being in Nouvelle Calédonie, three thousand miles away. The experiment didn't work; the two halves split up, and the 'Phantom of Faa'a' has been left waiting for a rescue ever since.

'Tu as fais tes études ici?' I ask Arnaud. ('Were you a student here?')

He gives me a funny look. 'Mon père m'a envoyé en France.'

His father had sent him to study in France, which is ten thousand miles away.

There's only one road on Tahiti; it's about a hundred kilometres long, a narrow metalled track, and runs around the island's circumference. (There are no roads or villages in the island's wild, volcanic interior.)

'On va faire la tour de l'île,' Arnaud announces. ('We'll make a tour of the island.') 'With stops, it takes three to four hours.'

He drives off in an anti-clockwise direction, ensuring that the windows on the passenger side look directly onto a spectacular succession of emerald lagoons, seaside coconut groves, and surf-rinsed beaches. From time to time, on the left, we get equally dramatic views up steep clefts and valleys towards the black volcanic heart of Mount Orohena.

The first stop, somewhere beyond Puna'auia, is at a small lagoon-side cemetery, an unfailing repository of history. The ancestors lie in shallow earth that trembles to the rumble of the breakers. Most of the dazzling white graves are wreathed with tropical flowers. Headstones bear bilingual inscriptions:

A MON ÉPOUX
NOTRE PAPA BIEN AIMÉ
POUR TOUJOURS
TERII 'TEMATAHIAPO' ROY
23.3.1944–4.10.1989
O IEHOVA TOU TIAIA

The second stop is at the Musée Gauguin, near Pa'ea. The gate is firmly shut despite a notice on the door – OUVERT TOUS LES JOURS DE 9 À 17 H.

'Tant pis, mais il était dégueulasse, ce Gauguin,' says Arnaud. ('Too bad, but Gauguin was pretty disgusting, you know.')

Further on, the Musée des Îles overlooks the western coast, at one of Tahiti's most idyllic spots. Two Polynesian-style buildings surround a shady courtyard; one still hears the shush of the waves, glimpses the turquoise lagoon between the palms, watches the rainbow sparrows hopping around the exotic shrubs, and counts the centuries. The permanent exhibition is static and old-fashioned but visually attractive and, with the help of numerous wall maps, tableaux, and dioramas, admirably clear. One progresses from the creation of volcanoes and atolls to the arrival of Europeans, missionaries, and photography. 'Bougainville,' a placard proclaims, 'fut plus culturel que Cook.'

After a delicious break in a courtyard filled with birdsong, the 'Temporary Exhibition' beckons. It's entitled 'Nos Ancêtres de Taiwan'. What a wonderful shock! The 'westernists' appear to have finally won. Supported no doubt by the government of Taipei, the exhibition promotes the hypothesis that the Polynesians are genetically related to the indigenous, pre-Chinese peoples of Taiwan – such as the Ami, Atakai, Bunun, Tsou, and Kim[90] – who set off on long voyages of migration thousands of years ago. The gallery of coloured photographs is breathtaking. The strongest message for me is that migration is a universal human experience. Wherever we think that our homeland lies, at some distance or another our ancestors were invariably migrants from somewhere else.

Beyond the turning for Tahiti Iti or 'Tahiti Minor', which but for a narrow neck of land would be a separate island, the road opens out through fields and cow pastures. The east coast is unprotected by lagoons, and the surf rolls in unhampered. On the wide coastal strip low, modest homesteads cluster around simple churches, each of a different denomination. Wild cocks and mangy dogs clutter the roadway. At the *Trou du Souffle* we stop for a snack of coconuts and braised chestnuts, before examining the blast of seawater that shoots every few minutes from a natural pipeway at the foot of the cliffs. At Papeno'o, where the coast forms a funnel in front of a river mouth, we pass a prime surfing beach; the posted forecast predicts breakers of 6 to 9 metres.

Eventually the eastern suburbs of Papeete approach with their petrol stations, apartment blocks, and flyovers. Arue contains the site of the royal mausoleum. It doesn't prompt a visit. The circuit ends as we pull into the hotel courtyard.

'Moi, je vais à la mer,' Arnaud reports. ('I'm off for a swim.') 'Here in Tahiti, we go to bed early, to catch the best morning hours between six and nine; it's too hot at midday. So we swim in the early morning or afternoon.'

This is the equator, dark from six to six.

'See you later for supper.'

Eating out in Tahiti is an evening activity, and best done within reach of the sea breeze. Later, we go down to the Marina Taina with Arnaud's friend, to an eating-place surrounded by yachts, and sit under the stars.

'Mon frère vient d'acheter un voilier,' Arnaud tells us. ('My brother has just bought a sailing boat.') '*Magnifique* – We just sail away whenever we want and stay out for as long as we like. We don't talk; I do my reading.'

The waitress enquires about aperitifs.

'Ricard,' I say.

'Tiens, tu connais le Ricard?'

'Are there local wines?' I ask.

'De Rurataoa, oui, mais très mauvais.'

So Tahitians stick to Burgundy and Bordeaux. The waitress brings the drinks but forgets to take the food order. Arnaud sorts it out.

'Voilà Tahiti,' he sighs, 'That's Tahiti for you; they won't serve you if they can avoid it. *Haere maru!* Qu'est-ce qu'on mange?' ('What are we eating?')

As we wait for supper, late evening flights are still landing at nearby

Faa'a Airport, which connects Tahiti with fifty Polynesian islands. The planes seem to hang in the air before making the final descent. Five years earlier, one of them didn't make it. Flight 1121 of Air Moorea, a DHC-6 Twin Otter on the shuttle service between Papeete and Tema'e on Moorea, plunged mysteriously into the sea.[91] Calamity in Paradise is unsettling for round-the-globe fliers.

Tahitian cuisine is famed for its super-fresh local products. Coconuts are served in a hundred ways, and the *ahima'a* or 'underground oven' is used to bake anything to hand. 'Pit-roasted pork' is a speciality. But I go for the *poisson cru* or *ia ota* (marinated raw tuna), followed by a plate of prawns in coconut vanilla sauce. The dessert is pit-roasted mango. And *Eau Royale, pétillante*. Then Arnaud brusquely announces:

'Au lit! Tu dois te reposer.' ('Bedtime! You need some sleep.')

Check-in for tomorrow's flight is at 6 a.m. – 'Air France direct'.

There's something infinitely and insistently sad about Tahiti. It's a melancholy born of a polluted paradise – the legacy of killer epidemics and all those heartless foreign crewmen who loved and left, of political failures, and, not too long ago, of bone-headed colonialism symbolized by nuclear radiation. They sing a song, 'Te Vahine Tahiti' – 'Woman of Tahiti'. The guitars strum, a *to'ere* drum taps out the pulse, and a girl's simpering voice floats along the beach:

| | |
|---|---|
| *Iorana, Iorana, Iorana e* | Bonjour! Bonjour! Et Bonjour! |
| *Te Vahine Tahiti* | Oui, Madame de Tahiti. |
| *Aue, Aue, te nehe nehe.* | Hélas, Hélas. Mais quelle beauté.[92] |

'*Aue, Aue*' means 'Alas, Alas'. To the English ear it sounds like 'Away, Away', 'I'm bound away.'

# 11

# Tejas

*Comanche, Chicanos, Frontiersmen:*
*Friends and Enemies*

The United States of America is a big country, comprehending half a continent, fifty-one states, and four major coastlines – east, west, south, and Alaskan. The latter, by one method of measurement 49,000 miles in length, is longer than all the others put together. For some reason, however, Americans pretend that they have only two coasts; they talk about a nation stretching 'from coast to coast', and in their national anthem sing 'from sea to shining sea'. But as well as the Alaskan littoral, America's southern coast on the Gulf of Mexico is also considerably longer than that in the west, from California to Canada, and it fronts the largest of the Union's contiguous states.

Houston's George Bush Intercontinental Airport, dedicated to the elder of the two Bush presidents, is spacious, efficient, and itself entirely forgettable.[1] But the souvenir stalls selling Stetsons, cowboy boots, and sheriff's badges remind everyone that this is the gateway to the Lone Star State. Outside the arrivals hall, the air is sultry and oppressive. The road downtown leads through the smog along 37 miles of monotonous concrete. My hotel, like the airport, is also spacious, efficient, and entirely forgettable. The ambience, to put it mildly, is not promising.

Houston, today, is a megalopolis: one of those ultra-large cities whose proportions defy the understanding even when you're there. You can't locate a centre from amidst the overlapping urban sprawls; you can't see the city limits when you're standing atop the tallest skyscraper; and you can't read the minuscule print of the street names even though the city map is six feet square. Off the cuff, I classed it as antipathetic. I disagree with a journalist who, despite being mugged at gunpoint, rates Houston 'the next great American city'. 'Everyone here,' he remarked, 'has a gun.'[2]

The people of Texas are famed for possessing a unique sense of size, and its largest city – though not its capital – is no exception. The Houston area is dominated by a monstrous network of raised concrete motorways – thruways, freeways, beltways, and expressways – that circle, plunge, and thrust in every direction. One of the main thorough-fares, the east-west Interstate 10, is twenty lanes wide, its two ten-lane carriageways separated by a further multi-lane toll road that runs down the middle. The traffic on this diabolical network, largely SUVs, pick-up trucks, and spacious saloons, trundles sedately along from jam to jam, fearful of missing the exit – a lapse that could cost one 20 or 30 miles. The drivers have nothing to see beyond the concrete parapet, except for the roofs of houses, garages, and petrol stations, or the occa-sional mall or tower block. They sit at the wheel like zombies, relieved to have escaped from somewhere, but condemned to sensory purgatory before they reach somewhere else. They curse and edge from lane to lane, hoping for a miniscule advantage to result in ten or fifteen min-utes' time, and peer bemused at the colossal green sign boards, designed on the false assumption that every exit must be leading exactly North, East, South or West. As a result, most of them rely entirely on their GPS navigation devices. Hence the most inimitable of all Houston roadway admonitions: OBEY ALL ROAD SIGNS – STATE LAW. Despite this agony, the drivers are visibly proud of their homeland. The bumper stickers read: I'M FROM TEXAS. WHAT COUNTRY ARE YOU FROM?

At first sight, therefore, General Sam Houston (1793–1863) is far more interesting than the city that bears his name. One of the great figures of American legend and history, he was born in Virginia, the fifth son of a Scots-Irish family, which subsequently moved west with the expanding frontier. As a teenager, he ran away from home to live for years with the Cherokee, and, after returning to 'civilization', rose to serve as governor of the newly formed state of Tennessee. Then, moving on again with the moving frontier, he sought his fortune in a vast, lawless territory, into which American settlers were driving their wagons towards looming conflict both with Mexico and with the Native Americans of the Plains. He lived long enough not only to help transform that territory into a republic, serving both as military gen-eral and president, but also to see the republic transformed into a state of the Union. Yet he was no American chauvinist. 'I liked the wild liberty of the Red Men,' he said, 'better than the tyranny of my brothers.'[3]

History and geography are crucial to any understanding of Sam Hous-ton's creation. The coast of the Gulf of Mexico runs in a great arc for nearly two thousand miles from Central America to the tip of Florida.

The delta of the Mississippi lies in the centre of the arc, providing easy access to the continental interior and carrying waters from the farthest reaches of its colossal river basin: from the Rocky Mountains, the vicinity of the Great Lakes, and the slopes of the Appalachians. Early European settlement concentrated on the arc's two extremities and the delta in the middle. Already in the sixteenth century, Spaniards claimed 'New Spain' in the west and Florida in the east. The French founded New Orleans in the delta in the seventeenth century, giving them an unbroken line of communication with their distant possessions in Canada. Yet neither Spain nor France showed much interest in the swamp-ridden coastlands on either side of the delta, or in the hinterland, where 'Indians' ruled supreme. England's thirteen colonies were far, far away. The French successfully extended their Louisiana colony to the east when they founded Fort Louis (now Mobile, Alabama) in 1702. But the near-impassable terrain blocked their attempts to expand westwards. The Spaniards, too, though worried by French ambitions, failed to tame the coastland beyond 'New Spain' or the more open land behind it. So a vast swathe of the continent remained in its primeval state, untouched by the plough or the hooves of cattle. The plains of the interior were peopled by buffalo herds and buffalo-hunters. Native tribes lived by their immemorial customs, communing with Nature and fighting internecine wars. Before 1800 the fertile hills and valleys to the west of the Mississippi rarely saw a white man, apart from the occasional trader or trapper. Half a dozen fine rivers without European names flowed into the Gulf. And ships ranging the coast sailed by river mouths, anchorages, and landings with indifference. Centuries passed before the regional power of European states waned, before the infant United States became involved, before relations between Indians and Europeans reached a tipping point, and before the pristine Eden disappeared for ever.[4] In the year that Sam Houston was born, there was no such place as Texas.

The opening item on my agenda in Houston was, for me, a new departure. Like the visit to the MONA museum in Tasmania, it possessed a somewhat whacky dimension, but, as it proved, supplied an original introduction to some of the prominent features of American life: a dream career from rags to riches, astronomically expensive medical services, strident controversy, and unending litigation.

Thanks to the city's affluence, and also to the Texan spirit of enterprise, Houston possesses the largest concentration of private medical

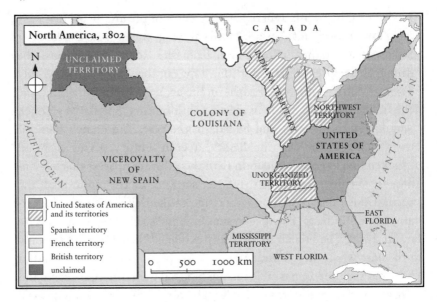

institutions in the world; medical research centres, private hospitals, and pharmaceutical corporations abound. The owners of one of the city's most newsworthy clinics happened to be long-standing readers of my books. We had been corresponding, and I was invited to visit them and to learn their remarkable story.

Forty-five years ago, Dr Stanislaw Burzynski arrived in the United States with $14 in his pocket – a $20 banknote less the taxi fare from the airport to his uncle's home in the Bronx. Today, he is a multi-multi-millionaire. His biography is an object lesson not only in the American dream, but also in the vituperative dogfights that can beset its realization. Burzynski specialized in oncology, and especially in bio-chemical therapies designed to target virulent cancer cells without destroying adjacent healthy tissue. Armed with the necessary patents and licences, he enjoyed success in treating inoperable brain tumours, before building up a complex business combining cancer care, medical research, drug production, and seductive publicity:

> The Burzynski Clinic does not believe in 'one size fits all' in treatments for cancer patients ... For over 35 years, [it] has been inspired by the philosophy of the physician Hippocrates – First, do no harm. True to this philosophy, our approach to treatments is based on the natural bio-chemical defence system of our body, capable of combating cancer with minimal impact on healthy cells ...[5]

Predictably, Dr Burzynski has had his critics from the outset. Prominent among them is Professor David Gorski, founder of the Institute of Scientific Medicine, whose supporters appear to have composed a deeply sceptical entry in Wikipedia: 'The Burzynski Clinic is a clinic in Texas, USA . . . offering unproven cancer treatment', it begins. 'The clinic is best known for the controversial "anti-neoplaston" therapy . . . Although [the] therapy is marketed as a non-toxic alternative to chemotherapy, it is . . . a form of chemotherapy with known side effects . . .'[6] The critics also complain bitterly about the clinic's marketing techniques. Yet what the layman sees under the heading of 'Tomorrow's Cancer Treatment Today', is a series of unobjectionable offers: 'innovative and cutting-edge personalized cancer therapy', 'customized treatment for over 50 types of malignancies', and 'medical expertise based on over 40 years' experience'.

'Criticism', however, is an understatement. Terms such as 'quack', 'cheat', 'fraud', and 'suckers' proliferate. And the bile has been attended by public accusations, journalistic denunciations, and a succession of lawsuits brought by rival firms, by disgruntled clients or their families, and most recently by federal and state agencies. At the time of my visit, however, as they told me, the Burzyńskis were claiming victory after fifteen years of litigation, and were looking forward to a payment of $63 million in damages.

The black stretch limousine glided up to my hotel lobby, blocking the entire roadway. Dr Burzynski Jnr bounded out, inviting me and my local guide first to his family's laboratories, and then to their private clinic. Behind the limo's tinted windows, we sit in luxurious leather armchairs distributed in conference mode. (It is the best way to travel on the Houston freeway, because one can't see it.) Crystal decanters glint on the interior bar; the TV screen flickers into life, and the journey passes pleasantly to the patter of company promo talk. Burzynski's R&D institute is filled with automated state-of-the-art drug-production units: each is accompanied by vast electronic control panels reminiscent of the computerized signal boxes that run the London Underground. Not a cent of federal or state aid has been used to finance this space-age complex, but we are shown some of the old-fashioned switches and fuse boxes that had to be assembled by hand in the company's early days. To reduce the possibility of industrial espionage, practically every single employee, from bio-engineers to lab technicians, has been brought over from the owner's native Poland. The clinic is housed at

9432 Katy Freeway in a stunning, rectangular, four-storey building clad in huge panels of jet-black glass. The motto 'First Do No Harm' gleams on the facade. The reception area is dominated by an encased tropical garden filled with luxuriant foliage, orchids, and tiger lilies; beside it is a discreet Attorney's Office, 'manned 24/7'.

We are greeted by Dr Barbara Burzynska, the owner's wife. She is a short, blonde, bubbly woman, exuding warmth and confidence.

'These are some of my children,' she says pointing to photographs of former patients; 'the oldest of them, who came to us as an infant condemned to die, is now aged thirty-six.'

The first floor is devoted to small, discreet consulting rooms.

'The celebrities,' Dr Burzyńska explains, 'require privacy.'

The corridors are hung with oversize pictures in gilded frames. One, in a conference room, is a copy of Jacques-Louis David's heroic *Napoleon Crossing the St Bernard Pass*. The second floor is given over to treatment and recovery rooms. The clinic has no wards, and provides few overnight stays. Patients are referred instead to a series of nearby guest houses. A young girl is wheeled past, her little face bloated, her eyes closed, and her nose attached to breathing tubes. A weary young intern is introduced.

'This is our daughter, Helena,' explains Dr Burzynska. 'It's been a tough day here, as it sometimes is.'

Finally we meet a smiling accountant, who promptly disappears into the lift. The top floor, one assumes, is reserved for the administration and the owners' penthouse.

Dr Burzynski himself appears, dressed in a long white coat. Short, brown-haired, moustachioed, with twinkling eyes set in a face like a cherubic apple, he smiles and chuckles non-stop. He turns out to be a well-read history buff. He invites us to join his family in a rapid lunch of 'surf and turf', reliving with us the origins of the Black Death. His wife insists that he shed his white coat.

'The next big epidemic will be liver cancer,' he announces in a matter-of-fact tone. 'It will carry off 30 or even 50 million, especially in China.'[7]

Then, the limo is re-summoned. As the revolving door delivers us outside, we catch a glance of the clinic's other motto 'Where There is Hope' – a reference to the old saying, 'Where there is life there is hope.'

Months after my departure, press releases announced that Dr Burzynski was still embroiled in the courts. Actions had been brought against him both by the US Food and Drug Administration and by the

Texas Medical Board.[8] A documentary film produced by the BBC's investigative *Panorama* team carried the heading 'Curing Cancer or "Selling Hope" to the Vulnerable?'[9] Most pointedly, as the critics resharpened their knives Dr Burzynski won the none too prestigious Pigasus Award that is announced annually on April Fools' Day:

> The Burzynski Clinic is a highly profitable miracle cancer cure fraud . . . run by . . . the Polish-born 'Dr' Stanislaw Burzynski – at least, he says that he is a doctor, but his alma mater are rather equivocal on the matter . . . It is notable for the invention . . . of 'neoplaston therapy' (ANP), a name coined by Burzynski for a mix of various peptides extracted from urine. Yes, in a very literal sense he's taking the piss.[10]

One shakes one's head in disbelief. I think, 'Only in America.' And yet, as someone who has walked through the tunnel of cancer myself, I hesitate to join the siren chorus. Cancer treatments cannot guarantee cures; but, by giving solace to at least some of those who stumble in the tunnel's darkness, they are not pointless.

Next on the schedule, as a complete change of tone, is a lecture billed as a fund-raising event for one of the departments of the University of Texas and held in the prestigious Petroleum Club.[11] At short notice, I have been asked to be a co-speaker on 'Poland and Russia: Players in the Geopolitics of Energy in Eastern Europe'.

The Petroleum Club is one of Houston's most elite, exclusive, and well-heeled institutions, the haunt of CEOs, bankers, and socialites. It is located on the 43rd and 44th floors of the ExxonMobil Building, a mid-town, pagoda-style high-rise. One ascends by a super-swift, dedicated, non-stop elevator, furnished in chintz. The entrance hall and ante-chambers are lined with highly conventional canvases of highly conventional past presidents: all in the same seated pose, all dressed in the same suits and ties, all sporting the same immaculately combed hair, and all wearing the same grin. The bars and smoking rooms are furnished with giant-sized leather armchairs. The plate-glass windows of the dining room look down onto the flagpoles of lesser establishments. Dinner accompanies the lecture. The beefsteak is superb, if impossibly thick. And the introductions are endless. A club member introduces the chairman, who introduces the chief organizer, who introduces Speaker No. 1, who is billed as an expert on shale gas. He is followed by another club member and another chairman, who is due to introduce Speaker No. 2, that is, me. The diners are uncertain whether to concentrate on their steak, on the speakers, or on the sunset outside. The wine, words, and sparkling water flow for nearly three hours before an emergency comfort break has to be called. As yet, the advertised discussion on geopolitics has not been broached. It must be like this when a drilling rig runs out of control and the motor can't be switched off. A blow-out is imminent. Speaker No. 2 decides to smother the audience in a heavy blanket of dubious points about Vladimir Putin being a paper tiger and that the EU's Eastern Partnership could yet be a brilliant success. Anxieties subside. Geopolitics is forgotten. Energy flags, and, as the brandy circulates, getaway looms. The legendary blow-controller Red Adair always said: 'Keep the back door open.' Funds have been raised, but few issues resolved. The elevator whisks us down forty-four floors to fresh air and an escape along the now slightly more free-flowing freeway.

In times not too distant, the Petroleum Club was frequented by a coterie of America's richest men. The so-called 'Big Four' included the most iconic figures – H. Roy Cullen (1881–1957), H. L. Hunt (1889–1974), Sid W. Richardson (1891–1959), and Clint Murchison Snr (1895–1969). Collectively known as 'the Big Rich', all had been swept by the oil tide, and by their ability to swim in it from humble beginnings to positions of great wealth, influence, and sometimes scandal.[12] Cullen became a philanthropist, the driving force behind the University of Houston. Hunt, a poker-player who used his winnings to buy his first oilfield, was reputedly the prototype for the character of J. R. Ewing in the *Dallas* TV series.[13] Richardson, an art collector, was a major contributor to the Republican Party and, in particular, to the post-war career of General Eisenhower. Murchison, an associate of J. Edgar Hoover, supported the Democratic Party, funding the rise of another Texan, Lyndon B. Johnson, who as a young man once worked as a schoolteacher in Houston.[14] More sinisterly, his name, together with that of H. L. Hunt, features prominently in one of the many conspiracy theories surrounding the assassination of President Kennedy.[15]

Such biographies underline the fact that oilmen were no less significant than earlier generations of cowboys to the growth of Texas. Houston, in particular, owes its prominence to the state's first gusher at nearby Spindletop in 1901 and to the resultant oil boom. The city's population multiplied fivefold in the first three decades of the twentieth century, when the world's biggest concentration of refineries and petrochemical factories was assembled there.[16]

Several worldwide businesses trace their origins to the Texas Oil

45. (*above*) The Dutch in
Mauritius, 1598: a scene
following the landing of
sailors who called the
island Prins Maurits
van Nassaueiland.

46. (*left*) A dodo (1638):
a picture painted from the life
in the first year of permanent
settlement on Mauritius.

47. (*above*) Transport by a
slave-carried *palanquin* on the
Île de France (as Mauritius
was renamed in 1715). French
settlement was accompanied
by the introduction of slavery.

48. (*right*) Bertrand-François
Mahé, Comte de la
Bourbonnais, Governor of
the Île de France, 1735–46.

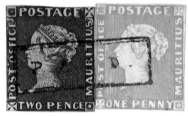

49. (*top*) Hindus at prayer, 1858. Indentured Indian labourers imported by the British came to form the largest ethnic community on Mauritius.

50. (*above*) Mauritius No. 1 and No. 2: a one penny orange-red and a two pence blue (1847). Postage stamps from the Bordeaux Cover, the 'pièce de résistance' of all philately.

51. (*left*) Sir Seewoosagur Ramgoolam (1900–1985), the first Prime Minister of independent Mauritius.

52. (*above*) Heart of Tasmania: Cradle Mountain National Park.

53. (*right*) Van Diemen's Land: illustrated proclamation, showing that all people – regardless of race – would face the same retributive justice, by Governor George Arthur, 1830. It didn't quite work out that way.

54. (*top*) A hell-hole inspired by utopian ideals: the notorious penitentiary at Port Arthur in southern Tasmania.

55. (*above left*) Captain Abel Tasman (1603–59): circumnavigator of Australia, discoverer of Tasmania and New Zealand.

56. (*above right*) A native of Van Diemen's Land (1777). Sketch by John Webber, artist of James Cook's Third Voyage.

57. (*top*) Maori war canoe (1770), a sketch by Sidney Parkinson, artist on Cook's First Voyage.

58. (*above left*) Maori man (1769), also by Parkinson. Unlike Tasmania's Aborigines, the Maoris were relatively recent Polynesian migrants.

59. (*above right*) King Tukaroto Matutaera Tawhiao (r. 1860–94), leader of the Waikato tribes.

60. (*above*) William Allsworth, *The Emigrants* (1844), painted soon after the Treaty of Waitangi and the start of British settlement in New Zealand.

61. (*below*) *The New Zealand Wars*, 1845–72, by Orlando Norie. The British attack a Maori stockade.

62. (*left*) Charles de Brosses, Comte de Tournai (1709–77): *philosophe extraordinaire*, pioneer of Pacific Studies.

63. (*below*) Breadfruit, harvest of Tahiti and the Royal Navy's answer to scurvy. Engraving, 1773.

64. Captain de Bougainville lands at Otaheite, April 1767. His *Voyage autour du monde* (1771) popularized the European concept of the 'noble savage'.

65. (*top*) *Oaitepeha Bay, Tahiti; palms and volcanoes*, by William Hodges, *c.* 1775.

66. (*above*) *Tahitian Dance*, copper engraving (1784) after J. Webber.

67. (*left*) Queen Pömare IV (r. 1828–77), aka Aimata, 'the Eyeball-eater'.

68. (*below*) Établissements de l'Océanie, 1 cent grey (1934).

69. Comanche horsemen, 1834–5. The Comanches' phenomenal horsemanship was unusual among Native Americans.

70. (*above*) Texas broadside: an advertisement for recruiting American settlers, 1836.

71. (*right*) Quanah Parker (1845–1911), Comanche chief and son of the kidnapped American woman Cynthia Ann Parker.

72. (*top left*) Antonio López de Santa Anna (1794–1876), 'Man of Destiny',
Mexican general and eleven times president.

73. (*top right*) Sam Houston (1793–1863), frontiersman, US Senator, Tennessee Governor
and President of the Texian Republic.

74. (*above*) Texas gusher, Port Arthur, east of Galveston, 1901. The wealth of Texas
was built on oil and cattle.

*t' Fort nieüw Amsterdam op de Manhatans*

75. (*top*) *The Landing in 1608 at Ver Planck Point,* by Robert Walter Weir (1842): the Lenape greet Henry Hudson's expedition.

76. (*above*) The fort of New Amsterdam, 1614: an early view of the city prior to permanent settlement.

77. (*above*) *The Toppling of King George III's Gilded Statue* at Bowling Green, New York, July 1776. The black slaves who actually pulled the statue down are absent.

78. (*below left*) Lappawinsoe, Lenape Delaware Chief, 1737. The Lenape nation was cleared from its homeland in stages; remnants remain in the Mid-West and Canada.

79. (*below right*) Israel Zangwill (1864–1926), British immigrant, writer, playwright, and inventor of the term 'The Melting Pot'.

80. (*top*) Porto do Cruz, Madeira – Portugal's Atlantic staging-post.

81. (*above*) Peterhouse, Cambridge's oldest college, founded 1284: the Combination Room, *c.* 1900.

82. (*right*) Diogo Cão, the first European navigator to enter the southern hemisphere and to see the southern sky at night.

83. (*top*) Winston Churchill painting at Camara do Lobos, Madeira, 1953. Churchill reached Madeira by flying-boat.

84. (*above left*) The ascent to the Basilica of Senhora Do Monte, Funchal: shrine of the Blessed Karl von Habsburg.

85. (*above right*) Imperial Exiles: Empress Zita and Emperor Charles in Madeira, 1921.

86. (*right*) Journey of No Return: 'The Flying Dutchman', KLM poster, 1938.

87. (*below*) Malaysian Airways Flight MH 370: to date an unsolved mystery.

88. (*bottom*) *Unterschweinstiege*, the 'Lower Wild Boar Ascent', Frankfurt *Stadtwald*.

Boom. Gulf Oil, for example, was created in 1901 by a group of investors, headed by William Mellon of Pittsburgh, who first came together
to finance the refining of oil from Spindletop.[17] Texaco, trading originally as the Texas Fuel Company, was founded in the same year. Its
Lone-Star logo still adorns filling stations on many a continent.[18] 'The
formula for success in life,' said Paul Getty (who wasn't a Texan), 'is
"Rise Early, Work Hard, and Strike Oil".'

In order to get one's bearings in Houston, one needs to find a spot
where one can see with one's own eyes what the outspread map displays. One such spot is the San Jacinto Monument, which stands on the
edge of Trinity Bay two or three miles to the east of Downtown. Apart
from the monument itself – a tall obelisk commemorating a key battle
of the so-called 'Texan Revolution' (see below) – one sees that Houston
started to grow on the banks of a transverse creek, the Buffalo Bayou,
whose waters empty into the Bay. Looking out across the Bay, the city
is at one's back, the interior of the state is on the left-hand side, and the
Gulf Coast is almost fifty miles distant on the right. Out of sight, at the
southern entrance to the Bay, lies Galveston Island, which shelters the
inland waters from Gulf storms, and on which the region's main port
is based. In the old days, ocean-going ships would dock at Galveston,
and barges would carry their cargoes up the Bay and into the creek.
The first European settlement within the present urban area, Harrisburg, was founded in 1823 on the banks of the Buffalo Bayou. A dozen
years later, after Harrisburg had burned down in the revolutionary
wars, the city was refounded a couple of miles further up the creek, and
renamed Houston. Since then, the urban sprawl has grown constantly;
the creek has been turned into a regulated ship canal, and a small port
constructed to form the focus for the original city centre.

On the landward side, Houston's layout, which baffles people driving around the freeways for the first time, can best be comprehended by
locating Highway 10, running west to east a couple of miles north of
Downtown. Highway 10 follows the route of the old track that ran
parallel to the Gulf Coast from San Antonio, 190 miles to the west, to
the Mississippi crossing at Baton Rouge, 256 miles to the east. The
city's north–south axis is supplied by Main Street, which runs from
Downtown to Highway 10, crossing the upper part of the creek on the
way. An inner ring road circles Downtown, and the other principal
thoroughfares spread out like the spokes of a wheel – north towards
Dallas-Fort Worth, south to Angleton on the Gulf Coast, north-west to

Austin, the state capital, north-east to Nacogdoches, south-west towards Corpus Christi, and south-east to Galveston. 'Spindletop' – 'the place where the Texan oil industry was born' – is situated in the town of Beaumont, eighty miles eastwards along Highway 10.

When I visited, Houston's bicentenary was still twenty years ahead, but the local press was already taking pride in the story, which saw a clutch of log cabins, huddled beside the Buffalo Bayou, swell to the present-day megalopolis.[19] A population of more than 6 million leaves it well short of New York or Chicago; but, in a state where space is no object, its acreage is rivalled only by Los Angeles.[20]

My next engagement was an evening lecture at Rice University, Houston's principal private seat of learning.[21] Three facts about Rice excite interest. Firstly, its grandiose buildings were opened in 1912 following the murder of its founder. William Marsh Rice (1816–1900) was a businessman who had made a fortune building railways, selling real estate, and trading cotton. He was poisoned by his butler in a vain attempt to divert his fortune to the pockets of a New York lawyer. Secondly, the new university was reserved for white males only. Thirdly, it was at Rice Stadium in September 1962 that President J. F. Kennedy announced 'We choose to go to the moon', and that the United States aimed to be 'the world's leading space-faring nation'.

All these meetings drew my attention to the inimitable sounds of the ubiquitous Texas drawl. According to linguists, Texan English is an outgrowth of the language of the neighbouring Southern states, from which most English-speaking immigrants came. But it has evolved further than the idioms of Louisiana, Alabama, and Mississippi, and possesses many striking characteristics. One of these is the use of 'y'all' for the main form of the second-person plural address. Another is what grammarians call 'multiple modals': the practice of using two or more auxiliaries in verbal phrases: hence, 'I may should go', or 'we might supposed to', or 'they might oughta do it'. A third is the habit of elongating vowels, sometimes to the point of parody. 'America' comes out rather like *Amur-kha*. Furthermore, Texan vocabulary as popularized by Western films is peppered with a striking mix of folksy terms and Spanish words, both of which reflect the state's origins:

| | |
|---|---|
| *alrighty* – very well then | *jalapeño* – chilli pepper |
| *howdy!* – how do you do | *lariat* (*la reata*) – lasso |

*fixin' to* – getting ready to

*ah' mo* – I am going to

*blue norther* – cold north wind

*gully-flusher* – heavy rain

*maverick* – stray, unbranded calf

*arroyo* – gulch or ravine

*chaparral* – brushwood, dry terrain

*frijoles* – kidney beans

*vaquero* – cowboy

*chaparejos* – chaps/cowboy trousers[22]

The best-known put-down of a Texan is that he is 'all hat and no cattle'. 'Texas is a state of mind,' wrote the novelist John Steinbeck. 'But more than that, it is a mystique closely approximating a religion.'[23]

As always, you can find out a lot about a place from what it eats, and eating out in Houston demands submission to ritual. 'A Taste of Texas' is somewhere out on the beltway.[24] Diners paying $100 a head are crammed into a cavernous barn where singing and shouting, and the enacting of a sanitized version of *The Cowboy's Homecoming*, form part of the entertainment. The menu, which surprisingly is in Russian as well as English and Spanish, offers steak, steak, steak, or steak: 10 oz, 14 oz, 18 oz, or 24 oz. – Rib-eye, Centre Cut, Porterhouse, or T-Bone. The bumper 'Cowboy Steak', which weighs in at 24 oz or 680 grammes, can, as a concession, be ordered for two diners. Baked potatoes, green beans, or salad make for marginal variety, and anyone still suffering from pangs of hunger afterwards can relish a dessert such as 'Texas Pecan Pie' or 'Texas Tower Chocolate Cake'. The plates are almost as wide as the table.

Eating is preceded by an initiation ceremony.

'If y'all are nu te Texus,' the waiter drawls, 'we've sompt'n for yer.'

Newcomers fear being obliged to drain beer from a Stetson or sing 'The Yellow Rose' solo without a tuning fork. But panic is misplaced. Having pumped up the tension, all they do is tie a red-patterned cowboy kerchief around your neck and ask you to enjoy your meal.

The musical accompaniment of 'singing cowboys', whose repertoire is filled with all the old standards of the genre, is as uncomplicated as the menu. But the quality of simple melody lines matches the exquisite quality of the meat, and the lyrics' unmistakable melancholy adds a touch of mustard:

> Then come sit by my side if you love me
> Do not hasten to bid me adieu
> Just remember the Red River Valley
> And the cowboy who loved you so true.

...
As I walked out in the streets of Laredo
As I walked out in Laredo one day
I spied a young cowboy, wrapped all in white linen
Wrapped in white linen as cold as the clay.[25]

The alternative to steak is 'Tex-Mex' cuisine. Contrary to common belief, 'Tex-Mex' is not just Mexican food as served in Texas. It is the product of cultural integration whereby American ingredients and American cooking styles intermingle in the original Spanish-Mexican dishes.[26] The name came from the Texas-Mexican Railway, opened in 1875 between Corpus Christi and Rancho Banquete, which used the abbreviation in its timetables. Its archetypal dish is *chilli con carne*, which, starting with a base of spiced beans on a bed of tortillas, adds minced beef or pork and lashings of grated yellow cheese. Some restaurants in Houston advertise themselves as 'Mex-Mex', meaning genuine Mexican, and others as 'Mix-Mex', meaning that both Mexican and 'Tex-Mex' cuisines are available. The oldest Tex-Mex establishment in town is one of a chain called Molina's Cantina.[27]

Tex-Mex music has the same characteristics as the cuisine. It is not just Mexican, but a mix of Latino lyrics and melodies adapted to rhythms, harmonies, and instruments imported by Central European immigrants in the mid-nineteenth century. The Czech *polka* and German *oom-pa-pa* waltz time supply very recognizable elements, as does the ubiquitous accordion. Aficionados, who decry later accretions of rock and big-beat styles, insist on the label of *Conjunto* – meaning 'Fusion' – and the purists on *Conjunto Puro*. These are the songs popularized by the singer Selena, known as 'The Queen of Tejano', brutally murdered in 1995, which are played non-stop on the numberless Tex-Mex radio stations and help kill the boredom of the freeway:

> *Este dolor que yo tengo muy dentro di me*
> *Es debido a mi terco corazón.*
> *Mi terco corazón que nunca aprendio*
> *El precio que tienes que pagar*
> *Cuando cae en las redes del amor.*
> *Terco corazón, terco corazón!*[28]

*Dolor* means 'pain', *terco* 'stubborn', *corazón* 'heart', and *las redes del amor* 'the nets (or entanglements) of love'.

The strong presence of Mexican Americans, variously described as

*Chicanos, Tejanos,* or *Latinos,*\* points to the fact that Texas in general
and Houston in particular started life in Mexico. Local historians talk
of a period that they call 'Mexican Texas' and which, in their view,
lasted from 1821 to 1836. However, to understand the origins of state
and city, one has to retreat still further, back to the early eighteenth
century in fact, and examine the circumstances that determined the
development of the huge tract of no man's land lying between the
northern reaches of New Spain (the future Mexico) and the French
colony of Louisiana. The three parties most interested in the fate of
that no man's land were the indigenous 'Indian' tribes; the authorities
of New Spain and their successors; and the American frontiersmen,
who were pushing westwards from the Deep South into the near-empty
lands of the 'frontier'. For the time being, the last were largely held
back by the intervening French-held territories. But their time would
come.

At the turn of the seventeenth and eighteenth centuries, the vast swathe
of sparsely inhabited territory between the Rio Grande and the Mississippi had no fixed name, and no firm international status. Its earliest,
short-lived name – Amichel – invented by the earliest Spanish explorers
for the Gulf Coast and its hinterland – did not take root; and in the
eighteenth century the Spaniards were used to talking either of *Comancheria*, namely the 'Land of the Comanche', for the northern and
western districts, or of *Los Tejas* for the eastern region only. Each of
these terms had similar derivations. The Comanche, the fiercest nation
among the Native Americans, were in many respects 'the new kids on
the block'. They had recently migrated from their original homeland
far to the north, and were feared and disliked as much by other tribes
as by the Spaniards. *Comantsi*, meaning 'Enemy', was not the name
that they called themselves, but an epithet bestowed on them by their
traditional foes, notably by the Utes. (The Comanche called themselves
*Numunu*, meaning 'the People'.) *Tejas*, in contrast, which sounded to
the Spanish ear like a plural noun, was the nearest the conquistadors

---

\* *Chicano* – an abbreviated form of the Spanish word *Mexicano* – is a term that embraces
all Mexican-Americans. Overlapping in meaning with other terms such as *Latino* or *Hispanic*, it used to have a derogatory flavour, but lost it thanks to the Chicano Movement
of the 1960s, which celebrated all the positive aspects of *chicanismo*. *Tejano*, in contrast,
and its feminine counterpart, *Tejana*, relate exclusively to the Mexican-American community in Texas. First coined in New Spain for people migrating to the new northern
province, it later became the standard term for all Texans of Hispanic descent.

could get to the Caddo-Indian word *Taysha*, meaning 'Friend'. *Taysha* was the usual form of greeting that Caddo braves would utter when meeting a stranger in a spirit of peace. One might say that the contested no man's land was the 'Land of Friends and Enemies'.

The astonishing diversity of Native American cultures is a fact that passes many people by.[29] The indigenous tribes or 'nations', of which there were several thousand, had no common language, no common way of life, and no sense of solidarity. They varied from the Inuit in the far Arctic to nomadic Plains Indians, settled agriculturalists, and primitive hunter-gatherers. Scholars classify them by ethno-linguistic, regional, and anthropological criteria, which give rise to complex, overlapping groupings. In 'the Land of Friends and Enemies' alone, no fewer than twenty-eight nations resided:

| | | |
|---|---|---|
| Alabama-Coushatta | Coahuiltecan | Pakana |
| Anadarko | Comanche | Potawatomi |
| Apache | Delaware | Shawnee |
| Arapaho | Hasinai | Tawakoni |
| Bidai | Jumano | Tigua |
| Biloxi | Karankawa | Tonkawa |
| Caddo | Kichai | Waco |
| Cherokee | Kickapoo | Wichita[30] |
| Cheyenne | Kiowa | |
| Chickasaw | Muscogee | |

It is a simple fact, therefore, that the Native Americans were even more divided among themselves than the Europeans were. The group that the British called the 'Five Civilized Nations', led by the Cherokee, and which originally lived to the east of the Mississippi, had adopted a semi-European way of life, living in wooden cabins and fixed villages. The Caddo, Wichita, and Waco tribes, on the other hand, who occupied lands deep in the interior, were semi-itinerant farmers. The Jumano were a 'Pueblo People', akin to the Hopi and Navajo further west: the Coahuiltecans were still at the hunter-gathering stage; the coastal Karankawa people lived from fishing. Few had reason to join the war-like, buffalo-hunting Apache or Comanche, whose incessant raiding and feuding threatened all their neighbours. A kaleidoscope of constantly shifting tribal alliances was the norm.[31]

Of the twenty-two language groups then current among Native

Americans, three were represented in 'the Land of Friends and Enemies'. The Caddoan languages were spoken on the Great Plains. The language of the Caddo nation was related to that of the Wichita, and further afield to Pawnee. The Nadene language group was spoken by a far-flung constellation of tribes, whose self-appellation is a variant of *Na-Dene*, meaning 'the People'. Its main concentration is in the far north-west, in Alaska, and is thought to have links to the Yakutian language of eastern Siberia. Its southernmost sub-group consists of the Navajo and Apache languages. The Uto-Aztecan group originated in the Sierra Nevada and consists of some thirty languages in eight sub-groups. Its northern concentration includes Utean and Shoshonian; its southern concentration, Hopi and Aztec. The Numic sub-group of Uto-Aztecan embraces the languages of half a dozen nations, whose self-appellation is a variant of *Nu*, meaning 'Person'. Its principal members are Shoshonian and Comanchean. The Shoshoni and the Comanche, though geographically distant in modern times, are linguistically very close.[32]

Before the twentieth century, no European was in a position to comprehend the overall patterns or complexities of Native American culture. Individual explorers, missionaries, or traders could learn the language and customs of particular tribes with whom they made contact, but they could not see the wider picture. In any case, Europeans were mainly interested in the way that the natives reacted to their own presence. In Texas they soon learned that some, like the Hasinai

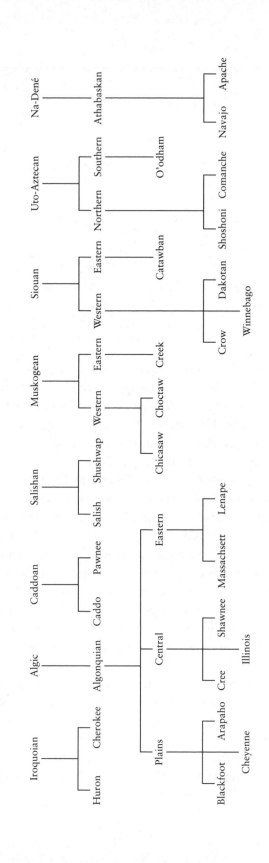

North American Native Languages (a selection)

Confederacy, were relatively friendly, whereas the Comanche were distinctly – some would have said congenitally – hostile.

The Hasinai Confederacy was a political grouping of Caddo-speaking tribes, based in the area between the Sabine and Trinity rivers in the eastern part of the 'Land of Friends and Enemies'. When first encountered in the 1680s, the Hasinai did not attack their French and Spanish visitors, who saw that they possessed an elaborate system of government. A Supreme Chief, 'the Grand Xinesi', both a political and religious leader, lived in a secluded palace and presided over a council of elders from each of the confederated 'cantonments'. The Hasinai were, above all, traders, middlemen between the 'Civilized Nations' of the east and the isolated nations of the interior. Their early contact with Europeans was rewarded by early epidemics of deadly European diseases.[33]

The Comanche were not known in the 'Land of Friends and Enemies' until 1743. In that year a band of Comanche warriors rode up to the gates of the Spanish mission at San Antonio seeking a rival band of Lipan Apaches, whom they regarded as enemies and suspected of being Spanish collaborators. Fifteen years later, a much bigger war party arrived before the mission of Santa Cruz de San Sabá, which had been built by Jesuits for the Apache, and sacked it. They then decisively repulsed a Spanish punitive expedition sent out to pursue the perpetrators. This was the turning point. It was not for nothing that the Comanche boasted of being 'the Lords of the Plains'. In the half-century since they had acquired horses and guns, they had transformed their lifestyle, riding down into the Plains from the north-western mountains as irresistible conquerors. Also, by refining the techniques of hunting buffalo on horseback, they greatly increased their food supply, their numbers, and their territorial reach. As the Spaniards discovered to their cost, the Comanche had reached the stage when they did not fear to challenge white men in battle.

Several eyewitness accounts of Comanche life have survived from this early period. Observers were impressed, above all, by their horsemanship; braves and squaws were taught equestrian skills from infancy. The Comanche were dressed in buffalo-hide and buckskin; they lived in tepees or 'wigwams', which were easily packed up and moved; and their success as traders embraced special lines in horses, stolen cattle, and human captives. It was also noted that Comanche bands were governed by principles that permitted a high degree of individualism. Each band was subject to a duo of chieftains, one for peacetime, who presided over councils of elders, and the other for wartime. But no decision of the chieftains was binding unless supported by general consent. As a result, negotiating with the Comanche was especially tricky; one group might agree to a deal, only for the next one to repudiate it.

Militarily, the Comanche were known for the ability of their constituent bands to coalesce or disperse as circumstances required. The northern Comanche, who roamed the interior furthest from the Gulf Coast, included the *Kotsoteka* or 'Buffalo-eaters', the *Yamparika* or 'Root-eaters', the *Quahadi* or 'Antelopes', and others. The 'Middle Comanche' were made up of the *Nokoni* or 'Back-turners', the *Tanima* or 'Liver-eaters', and the *Tenawa* or 'Downstreamers'. The southern Comanche were dominated by the largest of all the bands, the *Penateka* or 'Honey-eaters'. Due to their location, it was the Penateka who had the closest relations with Europeans.[34]

European settlement in the region had started in the sixteenth century, but had never progressed very far. When the first Spanish explorers arrived in 1527, they found the area unattractive: hot, steamy, or parched by turns, vulnerable to attack by Indians, and blighted by tornadoes. So for many long decades little attempt was made to extend the settled territory of New Spain northwards. In 1685 the French tried to establish a fort on the north-west corner of the Gulf Coast at Matagorda Bay, but it was wiped out by an Indian attack. Five years later, Spanish friars set up the mission of San Francisco de los Tejas, at a site some hundred miles inland from present-day Houston; it was struck by floods, smallpox, and supply problems, and the missionaries withdrew.

As from 1718, however, the establishment of the French colony of *Louisianie* on the lower Mississippi – named after King Louis XV – cut off Spanish possessions at the western end of the Gulf Coast from those at the opposite end, in Florida. Thereafter, the French city and port of *La Nouvelle-Orléans* (New Orleans) grew rapidly into the major commercial and communication centre of the region. In response, the Spanish authorities felt obliged to strengthen New Spain's northern borders. The fort of San Antonio de Béxar was founded on a river of the same name in the year that Louisiana was established.[35] It was surrounded by a ring of six Catholic missions charged with converting the Indians and turning them into loyal Spanish subjects. These were *Misión Concepción*, *Misión San José*, *Misión San Juan*, *Misión San Miguel*, *Misión Espada*, and *Misión San Antonio de Valero*, popularly known as 'the Alamo', the Spanish name for the aspen tree. A dozen more missions were spread out further east. The policy proved ineffective. The French made no move to cross the Mississippi to the west; their strategic aim was to strengthen the northern route to Canada. Very few European would-be settlers presented themselves. The Spaniards could not protect the sedentary Native American tribes from the Apache and the Comanche; and the Native Americans showed little interest in Catholicism. All of the missions in the east were closed, and in 1793 the mission at the Alamo was turned into a military outpost.

The year of Sam Houston's birth, 1793, happened to come shortly after the dark days when Europe was cast into the turmoil of the French Revolutionary Wars. For more than two decades, the 'Old Continent' was enveloped in crisis that destroyed the peace not only of many European states but equally of their colonies. France, under the revolutionary regime and then under Napoleon, was the central actor. Spain, which Napoleon invaded and occupied, and its colonies, were among the principal victims. An exhausted Britain, together with the newly independent United States, found itself eventually among the leading beneficiaries. Their rivalries brought three fundamental changes in quick succession to the slumbering lands on the Gulf of Mexico.

Firstly, in 1800, by the Treaty of Ildefonso, Napoleon forced the Spaniards to hand over a substantial slice of their North American possessions. The following year, Spain's American Empire began to crumble further. San Domingo was the first to go, followed by Bolivia, Venezuela, Uruguay, Chile, Peru, Argentina, and Colombia.[36] Finally, in 1803, fearing the dominance of Britain's Royal Navy, Napoleon decided to dispose of all of France's American possessions by selling them off to the United States in the so-called Louisiana Purchase, which from the French perspective was the 'Great Louisiana Sell-off'. This extraordinary deal doubled the size of the United States overnight, incorporating 828,000 square miles at the cost of 3 cents per acre and bringing the south-western border of the USA to the line of the Mississippi. It also inspired the expedition of Lewis and Clark, who, starting from St Louis in May 1804, explored and charted the lands between the Mississippi and the Pacific for the first time.[37]

In 1812–13 'New Spain' declared itself to be the independent 'Empire of Mexico'. The break from Spain was an untidy business.[38] It caused a long drawn-out civil war, and, thanks to the resurgence of loyalist forces, was not complete until 1821. It also encouraged the almost total neglect of New Spain's northern reaches, which in the opening decades of the nineteenth century became a no man's land contested by all and sundry: by predatory 'Indians', especially the Comanche, by the incoming Mexicans, and increasingly by English-speaking Americans, invited and uninvited, who were beginning to drift across the Mississippi.

Between 1813 and 1815, as a premonition of things to come, a large gang of filibusters – piratical adventurers – rode into the contested area from the east, menacing isolated settlements such as Nacogdoches and La Bahía. Led by a supporter of the anti-Spanish Mexican rebels, José Bernardo Gutiérrez, and a disgruntled American army officer, August Magee, the rag-tag army reached San Antonio, where its defeat preceded brutal repression and mass executions. They were but the latest of numerous brigands who plagued the region in the early decades of the nineteenth century.[39]

In 1820, as a last desperate attempt to stem the anarchy, Spanish administrators adopted a policy of regulated immigration into the border districts. Designated plots of land were offered to settlers, irrespective of their nationality or religion. Several thousand Mexicans availed themselves of the offer – the original Tejanos – as did a handful of Americans. The best known of the Americans was Moses Austin (1761–1821), a pioneer of lead mining from West Virginia, who purchased the right to bring in colonists in 1821, but died before the project was realized. In 1824 John Richardson Harris (1790–1829), one of Austin's former associates, purchased 4,428 acres at the junction of Bray's and Buffalo bayous, and proceeded to lay the foundations of Harrisburg. (The county, of which Houston is the centre, still bears Harris's name.)

As the human population rose, so, too, did the animal one. Thanks to the political chaos and the abandonment of isolated Spanish missions and ranches, numerous herds of cattle strayed onto the open plains. Mainly longhorns – a hardy, multicoloured breed with Iberian ancestry – they spread out, multiplied mightily in the well-watered valleys, and, in their feral state, quickly became a recognized feature of the landscape. Initially a nuisance, they were destined to provide the staple of the local economy.[40]

Among the earliest of those who moved from US territory to the Spanish-Mexican no-man's land, three names stand out. Jesse Chisholm (1805–68), a mixed-race scout, trader, and interpreter, was born in Tennessee, the son of a Scottish loyalist father and a Cherokee mother. Thanks to the hostility to Indians in the Southern states, he was taken as a child by his mother to an area long known simply as 'the Indian

Territory' (now Oklahoma), where he honed his skills as a go-between, welcomed by both Europeans and Indians. He was to play an important role in a number of key developments.[41] Stephen Austin (1793–1836), sometimes labelled 'the Father of Texas', was another reluctant migrant. Born in Virginia, the son of Moses Austin, he inherited his father's land grant and heard confirmation of Mexico's declaration of independence in 1821 in New Orleans where he was recruiting colonists. Travelling to Mexico City, his official status as an *empresario* or 'land agent' was confirmed, and, after many tribulations, he succeeded in 1825 in guiding the first substantial group of American settlers – the 'Old Three Hundred' – to a district bounded by the Brazos River.[42] At the time, Sam Houston was serving as a congressman in Washington, and still had two years to complete as governor of Tennessee. But in 1830, having embroiled himself in a troublesome lawsuit, he fled to Mexico. In this way, and with no inkling of the unintended consequences, Houston found himself in the part of the world where his name would be written in gold.[43]

The 'Texan Revolution' is something of a misnomer. Like the American Revolution, whose lexicon it borrowed, it did not involve a thoroughgoing overthrow of the social, economic, and political order. It was, in essence, a successful revolt, an independence movement that replaced one set of rulers with another. The regime expelled was that of newly independent Mexico; the new political systems introduced by the 'Revolution' were, from 1836, the Republic of Texas, and from 1845, the United States of America.[44] Apart from that, historians have curiously adopted one adjective, 'Texian', for matters relating to Texas before 1845, and another, 'Texan', for the period after 1845. For the sake of consistency, therefore, about 1836 one ought to be writing about the 'Texian Revolution'.

The origins of the eruptions in Texas lay in the earlier 'Revolution' in Mexico, which was completed in August 1821 by the Treaty of Córdoba and the subsequent entry of General Agustín de Iturbide's rebel army into Mexico City. Having ensured the withdrawal of the former Spanish authorities, Iturbide's followers declared him 'Emperor of Mexico' and proceeded to install a repressive, ultra-religious government.[45] One of their measures was to decree that all immigrants had to be Catholic. Most of the settlers and would-be immigrants from the United States were Protestant, and it was now unclear whether they would be free to reside in Mexico legally.

The Mexican 'Empire' did not last long. It was overturned after only two years in favour of a secular republic, which attempted to introduce a modern centralized administration, but which remained extremely fragile and fractious. Inspiring the epithet of 'the Republic of Coups', it could not provide stable government, and was typified by its central figure, General Antonio López de Santa Anna (1794–1876), the eight-time president, who was a masterly political trimmer. Having repulsed Spain's last feeble attempt to recover Mexico, Santa Anna declared himself 'The Saviour of the Motherland' and 'the Napoleon of the West', but did little to provide the republic with unity and cohesion.[46]

The Mexican Constitution of 1824 divided the republic's territory into a score of autonomous states and border regions. The northern 'Land of Friends and Enemies', centred on San Antonio, was designated as the District of Bexar within the state of the 'Coahuila y Tejas'. In this way, it was treated differently from the republic's other northern border regions such as the *Territorio de Alta California* and the *Territorio de Nuevo México*, and appeared to be facing a greater degree of central control. Not without reason, its inhabitants feared that military conscription and general taxation would soon be imposed.

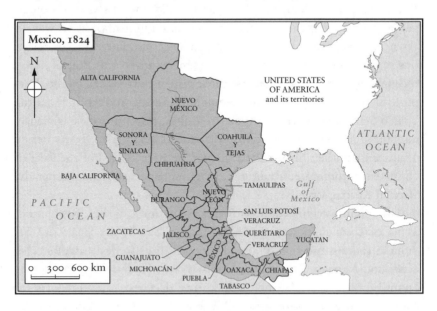

In 1825 the state of Coahuila y Tejas introduced its own colonization law (from which Stephen Austin was one of the earlier beneficiaries). Colonists were needed to act as a buffer against Apache and Comanche raids. They were freed from previous religious restrictions, and given the right to form their own militias. Over three thousand applications for land grants were made, the great majority on behalf of Anglo-Americans. Within the next decade, the number of 'Anglo' settlers passed the 30,000 mark – a minority within the state as a whole, but 80 per cent in the District of Bexar. The 'Anglos' of the district began to call themselves 'Texians' as distinct from the Spanish-speaking Tejanos.

The immigrants from the United States included a substantial number of blacks and mixed-race people, for whom it was easier to cross into Mexico than to head north on the underground 'railroad', which took slaves to safety in anti-slavery states. They were a mixture of slaves, fugitives, and free persons, who could find work as farm labourers or domestics. One of them, Emily West, a free woman from New York, arrived as the indentured servant of a land agent, and passed into the lyrics of a popular song:

> There's a yellow rose of Texas that I am going to see
> No other darky knows her, no darky only me.
> She cried so when I left her, it liked to broke my heart,
> And if I ever find her, we nevermore will part.
> (chorus)     She's the sweetest rose of color this darky ever knew.
> Her eyes are bright as diamonds, they sparkle like the dew.
> You may talk about your Dearest May or sing of Rosie Lee,
> But the yellow rose of Texas is the only girl for me.

Of course, by the time that the song became a hit in the twentieth century, linguistic sensitivities had changed. The word 'darky' became 'soldier', and the 'sweetest rose of color' became 'the sweetest little rosebud'. 'Yellow' was originally a slang term used by African-Americans to describe mixed-race mulattos.[47]

Different *empresarios* instilled different attitudes in their colonies. Stephen Austin, for example, was a law-abiding man who encouraged the inhabitants of his colony to respect the laws of Mexico and the terms of their land grants. Haden Edwards was the opposite. He thought that he and his settlers in the district of Nacogdoches in east Texas could behave as they liked. His colony's name, 'Fredonia', was a Latinized form of 'Freedom', but it invited licence. On arrival in 1825, Haden proceeded to expel both the Indians and the Tejanos of the area. When his grant was revoked, he tried to make a stand in the Old Stone Fort at Nacogdoches, but he and his charges fled as the Mexican military and the Comanche both arrived to see them off.

'Austin's Colony', in contrast, put down strong roots. This was the place that had welcomed the 'Old Three Hundred' – the very first substantial group of American settlers in the 1820s. Centred on the Brazos River to the west of Trinity Bay, its main town was built in a central position at San Felipe. The colony's northern boundary lay on the old San Antonio Road, and the southern boundary stopped short of the Gulf Coast. Plantations were created at the best agricultural sites, and named after their owners – Hunter's, Foster, Cunningham, Cartwright, and Jones. Settlements sprang up such as 'Holland', 'New Kentucky', 'Pine Point', and 'Fort Settlement', often at fords and ferry points on the Lavaca, Navidad, Brazos, Colorado, and St Bernardo rivers. Tracks were blazed and roads constructed linking villages and homesteads, and three strongpoints were fortified against Indian attacks at Moore's Fort, Wood's Fort, and Fort Bend. As from 1830, the steamboat *Yellowstone*, pride of the colony, plied the Brazos River, carrying passengers, cattle, and cotton bales. Ready access was available to the sea at Velasco, at the mouth of the Brazos, and to Trinity Bay via the Buffalo Bayou and Harrisburg.[48] Many of the founding settlements formed the core of later counties, including Austin, Colorado, Fort Bend, Harris, Fayette, and Washington.

In 1827 the legislature of Coahuila y Tejas, which sat in Saltillo, two hundred miles south. San Antonio, addressed the sensitive issue of slavery. Mexican public opinion at large supported emancipation, and some progress had already been made. The slave trade had been abolished, and the children of slaves had been given their freedom from the age of fourteen. But a new law now demanded that all slaves imported from the United States should be freed within six months. This dealt a serious blow to a large group of American settlers in eastern parts of the District of Bexar, who were setting up cotton plantations worked by slave labour. The state's governor applied for temporary exemption.

The republic's attempts to provide the District of Bexar with military defences, against both Mexico's central government and illegal interlopers, were inadequate. A command post was established at Laredo, and two small garrisons at the Alamo and the Presidio La Bahía at Goliad. Three militias were raised: one at Bexar, another at Goliad, and a third in Austin's Colony. The last of these tiny formations formed the core of the nascent Texas Rangers.

Nonetheless, despite the dangers and uncertainties of frontier life, the District of Brexar's economy thrived. By the early 1830s, thousands of tons of cotton and thousands of head of cattle were being exported, mainly to the United States; and cattle ranching gained a new lease of life. Large feral herds of longhorn and mustangs awaited concerted drives to round them up, to brand them, and to appropriate them. The old Spanish *vaqueros* became the new cowboys, who adopted their vocabulary of *lariat*, *chaparejos*, and *bandana*. And the *rancho* became a ranch. But settlers resented customs posts, and smuggling was rife.

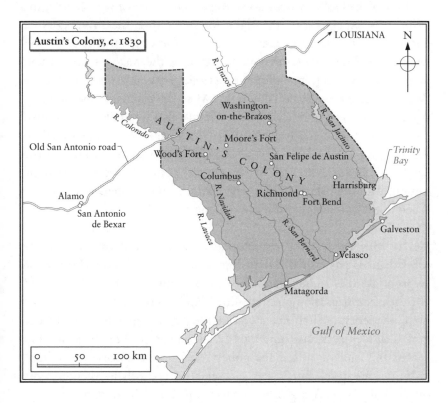

Between 1827 and 1835 discussions intensified over the District of Bexar's future. The American government twice offered to buy the District from Mexico for $1 million, and was twice rejected. The Mexican authorities despaired at their inability to enforce legislation; in 1830 they rescinded the colonization law, only to find that illegal immigration increased. Violent disturbances occurred at Anahuac on the eastern shore of Trinity Bay over attempts to establish a state customs post. Some of the Anglos adopted a truculent stance, though their leaders repeatedly sought a modus vivendi. In 1832 a convention at San Felipe de los Brazos, attended by both Stephen Austin and Sam Houston, made proposals for organizing the state of Coahuila y Tejas more efficiently, and in 1834 they obtained an important concession over the use of English as the second official language. As late as January 1835,

Stephen Austin published his treatise *An Explanation to the Public Concerning the Affairs of Texas*, in which the District's loyalty to Mexico was not questioned.[49]

Meanwhile, to the east of the Mississippi, the states of the Deep South were adopting drastic policies that would affect all the lands bordering the Gulf. Two issues were paramount. One was slavery; the other was expressed as 'the rights of states over the sovereignty of Indian nations'. In 1818 Georgia, one of the original Thirteen Colonies, prohibited manumission. In 1819, in the teeth of opposition, Alabama was admitted to the Union as a slave-owning state. In 1820 the Missouri Compromise laid down that Missouri could join the Union as a slave state on condition that Maine joined as a free state. It also ruled that slavery would not be permitted to the north of the 36th Parallel. In Louisiana, an American state since 1812 and a close neighbour of the District of Bexar, New Orleans operated the largest slave market in the Union. Although slave-trading was banned on the open seas, it flourished in the Mississippi Valley and along the Gulf Coast.[50]

On 28 May 1830, at the instigation of President Andrew Jackson, the US Congress passed the Indian Removal Act, which provided for the expropriation of Indian nations living on lands within the Union and for their compensation with unsettled lands to the west of the Mississippi. In theory, the implementation of the Act was voluntary; in practice it was ruthless, coercive, and bloody. In the view of President Jackson, it was the fruit of 'a humane policy', which would 'save the Indians from annihilation'. But it was a reversal of the policies of presidents Washington and Jefferson, who had planned for the Indians to retain their lands and be gradually assimilated; and it changed the American South for ever.[51]

The deportations principally affected the five 'Civilized Nations' – the Chickasaw, the Choctaw, the Creek, the Seminoles, and the Cherokee – and were pushed through in stages in the 1830s. Over 25 million acres of land in the Southern states were opened for white settlement, and up to 100,000 Indians were displaced. The year 1831 saw the first mass removal of Choctaw from central Mississippi to an area now officially designated as 'Indian Territory' (the future Oklahoma); the brutality was such that the episode was given the name of 'The Trail of Tears'. In the same year the US Supreme Court heard a case brought by the Cherokee nation against the state of Georgia; it ruled that the Cherokee did not constitute a sovereign body and were not entitled to appear before the Court. The Seminoles of Florida, who engaged in active wars against the US Army, were removed in 1832. The Creek from northern Alabama followed in 1834, and the Chickasaw from Missouri in 1837. When the Cherokee were driven out of eastern Tennessee and western Georgia in 1838, a quarter of the deportees died. Individual Indians were allowed to remain on condition that they renounced all title to their lands.[52] It was a very effective example of what would now be called 'ethnic cleansing'.

The formal establishment of the Indian Territory, and the arrival of tribes accustomed to a settled way of life, had important consequences for the adjacent District of Bexar. It reduced the free rein of the Comanche. It opened a new market for traded goods, and new commercial opportunities on the Territory's southern border. Jesse Chisholm, who had helped blaze a trail from Fort Gibson to Fort Towson in 1830, married a trader's daughter in 1836, and built his home beside his father-in-law's station at the confluence of the Little and Canadian rivers. He was to be the principal linkman between South and North.

The growing disaffection of the inhabitants of the District of Bexar was no greater and no less than that of many other Mexican subjects. They felt that their government was at once too demanding, too distant, and too unresponsive. Yet, as elsewhere, they had shown patience, and their disaffection only turned to open defiance in 1835–6 when General Santa Anna took measures to dismantle the republic's existing constitution, to install a military dictatorship, and to suppress all opposition by force.

Santa Anna, who was undoubtedly inspired by the recent 'July Revolution' in France, where Louis Philippe had overthrown the reactionary Bourbon monarchy, regarded himself as a liberal and a modernizer. But he was exasperated by the inertia of successive republican governments and their inability to assert their authority against reactionary landowners and clerics. In May 1835 he ordered the disbandment of all local militias, and, in the 'Seven Laws' of December that year, inserted a drastic provision for abolishing Mexico's constituent states, which were to be replaced by centralized departments on the French model. Not surprisingly, the leaders of nearly all Mexico's states, facing abolition, declared their intention to secede. The state of Coahuila y Tejas followed exactly the same line as Yucatán, Zacatecas, and a dozen others. Santa Anna, however, showed determination by marching his army into central Mexico and defeating the Zacatecan rebels in battle.

In the winter of 1835–6 confusion reigned in the District of Bexar. On the one hand, a political Consultation held at San Felipe in November, in which Sam Houston participated, affirmed the District's desire to remain in Mexico. At the same time, following a skirmish at Gonzales in October, when Mexican soldiers had tried to seize the militia's cannon, the District began organizing a self-defence force. Existing Mexican garrisons were driven out. A division of regular paid troops was put under the command of Sam Houston, and a grouping of local militias chose John Henry Moore as their colonel. Irregular American units, such as the New Orleans Greys, the Mississippi Marauders, and the Kentucky Mustangs, prepared to give assistance. A showdown was looming.

Santa Anna's decision to mete out the same treatment to the District of Bexar as to Zacatecas was mainly motivated by fears of American intervention. He suspected, though could not prove, that the Texians were acting as tools of the American government, and was provoked by news of the so-called Matamoros Expedition, whereby a group of hotheaded Texians had planned to seize a Mexican port. At all events, the Mexican army marched north. After laying siege to the Presidio San Antonio de Béxar in late February, it moved on further and surrounded the isolated outpost of the Alamo.

As the military situation became critical, a Congress of elected representatives met at Washington-on-the-Brazos. Some of the representatives wanted to express solidarity with the state of Coahuila y Tejas, which was itself on the point of seceding from Mexico. Others favoured outright independence. Under the pressure of Santa Anna's advance, the voices for independence won the day. On 1 March 1836 the sovereign Republic of Texas was declared.[53]

The defenders of the Alamo were already dying, therefore, when the declaration of independence was issued. Some 189 men under the command of Colonel William Travis had sworn to fight to the death, spurning the chance to flee or to surrender. On 6 March, after a thirteen-day siege, Santa Anna's men stormed the inner compound, and killed the few remaining resisters, including the famous frontiersman, Davy Crockett. Shortly afterwards, at the Presidio La Bahía at Goliad, a large group of Texian prisoners were slaughtered in cold blood. These events cemented irreconcilable enmity on both sides. They gave the infant republic the will to fight on. Its battle cry was 'Remember the Alamo'.[54]

*

On the day of its inception, the Republic of Texas had no agreed leadership, no laws, no fixed territory, and no clear plans for the future. Its supporters were passionately opposed to 'tyranny', as personified by General Santa Anna, and they wanted to break from the Mexican government. But they were cheering for an undefined 'freedom'. Their relationship with the state of Coahuila y Tejas, whose leadership in the town of Santiago de Monclova had also broken away from Mexico on 2 March, was uncertain. Their attitudes to the United States were ambiguous. And no one had consulted the Tejanos or the 'Indians'.

Much depended on the outcome of the war, which the fight at the Alamo had started. Given the small numbers of soldiers, and the vast spaces for manoeuvre, one might have expected it to drag on for months or even years. It actually lasted for six weeks, and ended in a battle that lasted only eighteen minutes. Santa Anna progressed slowly from west to east, passing through Austin's Colony on the way. His men, who greatly outnumbered the Texian army that was tracking them, carried out lootings, burnings, arrests, and executions. Many colonists, both Texian and Tejano, fled in what was known as the 'Runaway Scrape'. In mid-April, Santa Anna reached the environs of Galveston, burned Harrisburg, then set up camp on a headland at the point where the San Jacinto River enters Trinity Bay. Failing to post lookouts, his army was taken by surprise on the afternoon of 21 April. Sam Houston led the infantry in person, Mirabeau Lamar the cavalry. At the cost of eight dead, and several wounded (including Houston, who was hit in the ankle), they killed hundreds of trapped Mexicans, and forced the rest to surrender. Santa Anna, who had fled in disguise, was captured the next day. (According to legend, his fatal complacency had been caused by a none too gallant rendezvous with Emily Morgan, the 'Yellow Rose', who had successfully distracted him.) What the Texians called 'the Battle of San Jacinto', the Mexicans called *La Siesta di San Jacinto*.[55] At the subsequent Treaty of Velasco and its secret protocol, Santa Anna agreed, in exchange for his army's safe withdrawal, to press for the republic's recognition in Mexico City, and for fixing its southern boundary on the Rio Grande.[56]

Contrary to common belief, therefore, the Republic of Texas did not emerge instantly in 1836 as a fully fledged 'sovereign nation'. It was recognized by the United States in March 1837 and France in 1841, but not yet by Mexico or any other powers. It was in a similar uneasy position to other breakaway Mexican districts, such as Yucatán, Tabasco,

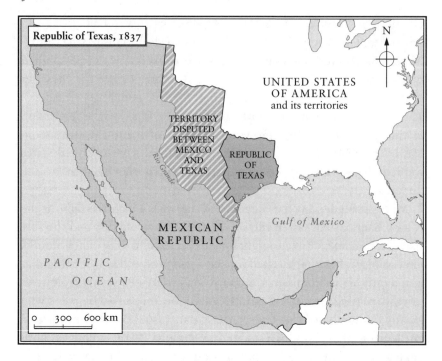

and 'the Republic of the Rio Grande', which briefly emerged in those years.

In that same spring of 1836 the Comanche made their presence felt. An American family from Illinois, the Parkers, had set up a settlement in the deep interior near the headwaters of the Navasota river. In May a Comanche band razed Fort Parker, killed several of its inhabitants, and carried off the rest into captivity. Among them was Cynthia Ann Parker (c. 1825–71), then aged ten, who stayed with the Comanche for most of her life, married a native warrior, and became the mother of a famous Comanche chief, Quanah Parker.[57]

In September 1836 the Second Congress of the Republic of Texas assembled at the settlement of Columbia (now West Columbia). A US-style constitution was adopted, setting up a Republic, a Presidency, a Senate and House of Representatives, a Supreme Court, a flag, and a capital city.[58] Sam Houston was elected president. The flag bore a single silver star on an azure field. The capital, initially at Washington-on-the-Brazos, was moved in 1837 to the new town of Houston, and in 1839 to the settlement of Waterloo, which was renamed 'Austin' in honour of Stephen Austin, who had recently died. All residents except 'Africans and Indians' were admitted to citizenship.

No agreement could be reached, however, on the republic's

boundaries. One faction headed by President Houston favoured the retention of the limits of the District of Bexar. Another, headed by Mirabeau Lamar, talked of extending Texas to the Pacific. Their minimum demands claimed lands beyond the Rio Grande and the Territory of Nuevo México.

The rivalry between Houston and Lamar soon became the central feature of Texian politics. Houston advised conciliation towards Mexico; Lamar wanted to fight. Houston proposed a series of treaties with the Indians; Lamar advocated their total removal as in 'The Trail of Tears'. As the tides of argument flowed back and forth, Houston and Lamar occupied the presidency in turns.

The issue of slavery came to the fore. The black population was sympathetic to Mexico, where slavery had been abolished. At the Alamo, Colonel Travis kept a black slave, who was released by the Mexicans and survived. In contrast, republic's legislature took a hard line. In 1836 free blacks were required to petition the courts for residential status. In 1837 a system of apartheid was introduced. Every person of African heritage, defined as possessing one or more black grandparents, was forbidden to vote, testify in court, own property, or intermarry with whites. The importation of black slaves into eastern Texas proceeded apace.

Relations with the Indians also deteriorated. In 1839 President Lamar claimed to have signed an agreement with the Cherokee providing for their removal from east Texas to the Arkansas Territory. When the Cherokee prevaricated, they were attacked at the Battle of the Neches, and two of their chiefs were killed. After the battle, Chief Bowl was found to have been carrying a sword presented to him by Sam Houston.

The Comanche, who numbered 30,000–40,000, posed a bigger problem, and only one of their tribes, the Penateka, were prepared to pow-pow. In March 1840 a party of forty Penateka elders arrived for talks at the Council House at San Antonio. But, when they surrendered fewer hostages than expected, a fracas ensued and all the visitors were gunned down or taken captive. In revenge, the Penateka chief Potsunkurahipu, 'Buffalo Hump', launched a 'Great Raid' later in the year. A war band of 500 braves rode all the way to the coast, and sacked the little port of Linnville. On their way back, laden with loot, they were confronted by Texas Rangers at Plum Creek, where cannon were fired at the slow-moving column, with predictably bloody results. President Lamar's spending on the military reached a level equivalent to the republic's annual income.

To boost the republic's finances, and to strengthen the embattled American community, the first steps were also taken to encourage systematic immigration from Europe. The creation of the Republic of Texas had coincided with the establishment in Germany of several societies dedicated to sending migrants to North America. So a natural alliance arose whereby the republic's authorities sold land grants to German entrepreneurs and the societies organized the transport of immigrants.[59] The principal entrepreneur was Prince Karl von Solms-Braunfels (1812–75), a stepson of the King of Hanover and a distant relative of the British royal family.[60] The leading society was the Mainzer *Adelsverein* from the Rhineland, which signed the first contract in 1842. The chosen port of entry was Indianola, soon to be renamed Karlshafen, in Matagorda Bay west of Houston. And the earliest settlements, established in 1844–5, were at Bettina, Castell, and Leiningen in Llano County, and elsewhere at Fredericksburg, Nassau,[61] New Braunfels, Sisterdale, Tusculum, and New Ulm.[62] The settlers of Fredericksburg, named after Prince Frederick of Prussia, now in Gillespie County, headed for a site in the Comancheria, whose occupation required protracted negotiations with the Penateka tribe.[63]

In his second term, President Houston turned to more even-handed policies. He ordered the Rangers to punish intrusions by unauthorized settlers as well as Indian raiders; he put much energy into negotiating with all tribes willing to talk; and he sought to delineate a clear frontier between Texian and Indian territory. In 1842 he talked with the Caddo, in 1843 with the Delaware and Wichita, and finally in 1844 with the Comanche. Jesse Chisholm acted as middleman and interpreter at these meetings. In essence, the Indians were offered permanent security in exchange for an end to raiding and hostage-taking. The Frontier was quietening down.

Events beyond Texas, however, were taking control. The US government had stored up a long list of complaints against Mexico, and in February 1845 a Bill was introduced in Congress to annex Texas with or without Texian approval. Washington did not hide its appetite for grabbing large swathes of Mexico's far-flung lands, and the Texians were in a weak position to temper American cupidity. Washington won them over with an offer to repay all of the republic's considerable debts. A Texian convention then accepted US proposals with only one dissenting vote, and a popular referendum confirmed the terms on which the Republic of Texas would be transformed into the twenty-eighth state of the United States. The principle of slave-holding was to be upheld, and all obstacles to the slave trade were to be removed. The USA was to be given title to all territories claimed, but not controlled, by Texas. The official transition took place on 29 December 1845. International legalities and the views of the Mexican government were effectively ignored.

With Texas secured, the US Army attacked and invaded Mexico with deliberation and aforethought.[64] A pretext for war was found in the so-called 'Thornton Affair', in which an American patrol on the Rio Grande had been dispersed by Mexican troops. By the end of 1846, both New Mexico and California were in American hands, and in 1847 the US Army mounted an expedition to Mexico City. (The Battle of Chapultepec in September 1847 inspired the opening line about 'The Halls of Montezuma' in the hymn of the US Marines.) In February 1848, by the Treaty of Guadalupe Hidalgo, a helpless Mexico was forced to cede vast territories that would become the states of California, New Mexico, and Texas.[65] The treaty legalized the fruits of a series of predatory raids which the Comanche themselves could not have bettered.

Political arrangements between Texas and the United States were finalized by the so-called 'Compromise' of 1850. The Texians were no more able to haggle over terms than the Mexicans had been. The US government repaid $10 million of the late republic's debt, fixed the state's boundaries as preserved to the present day, pocketed various territories that would duly form parts of New Mexico, Colorado, Kansas, Oklahoma, and Wyoming, and fully incorporated the twenty-eighth state of the Union. The Texian Revolution was complete.

After annexation, the influx of European immigrants redoubled. One notable development occurred in 1854, when a German ship docked at Galveston bringing an immigrant group from Silesia – a province of Prussia, whose population was part German-Protestant and part Polish-Catholic. The Polish element in the group, led by a Franciscan friar, Brother Leopold Moczygęba, then trekked across country to their destination in Karnes County near San Antonio, where they founded the settlement of Panna Maria, literally of 'the 'Virgin Mary'. They were the vanguard of the USA's Polish American community, which in time would number millions.[66] In that same year, another group of Slavic Central Europeans, Wends from Lusatia, followed in the steps of the Polish Silesians to enrich the growing diversity of the Texan population.[67]

Numerous personalities who had graced the pages of the late

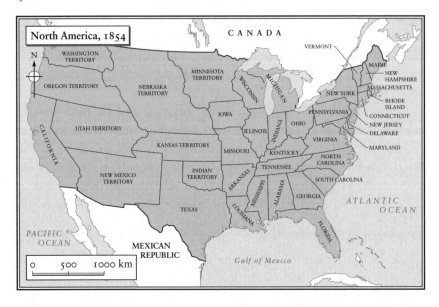

republic's history reappeared in new roles. In the 1850s Jesse Chisholm blazed the great 'Texas Cattle Trail' that bears his name and which transformed the economy of the Midwest. In 1858 Chief 'Buffalo Hump' reluctantly led the surviving members of his harassed Comanche tribe to the 'Indian Territory'. In 1860 a Ranger patrol picked up a blue-eyed Comanche woman, part of an Indian band stopped for 'illegal fishing'. It was the former Cynthia Ann Parker, who could no longer speak English, and who, after being forcibly returned to her American relatives, made repeated attempts to escape.

In 1861, at the outbreak of the Civil War, Texas seceded from the United States and joined the Confederate states. Throughout that decade an oil prospector named Lyne Barret was drilling at Oil Springs near Nacogdoches. He was in no hurry; after eleven years, his well was producing only ten barrels a day, and he gave up, thinking that prospecting had no future in those parts.

Sam Houston, meanwhile, had married for a third time, fathered eight children, and, having once converted to Roman Catholicism to qualify for Mexican residence, reconverted to Methodism on the insistence of his new wife. Residing in his mansion on the banks of Trinity Bay, he re-entered politics, returned to the US Senate, and was serving as governor of Texas when the Civil War intervened. As a slave-owner, he was not an abolitionist, but his sympathies lay with the Union, so he was relieved of his post by the Confederate authorities, retiring to his home at Huntsville in central Texas, where he died in 1863. His gravestone listed his virtues:

A Brave Soldier – A Fearless Statesman
A Great Orator – a Pure Patriot
A Faithful Friend – a Loyal Citizen
A devoted Husband and Father
A Consistent Christian – an Honest Man[68]

His legacy was to include the saying: 'Texas has yet to learn submission to any form of suppression.'

By that time, the Confederate states had adopted not only the Lone-Star Flag, but also the anthem 'The Bonnie Blue Flag', which had been inspired by it. The anthem's exact words and the flag's origins are hotly disputed, and Texans are not the only claimants. Yet a particular version, popular in modern Texas, was composed by one of Sam Houston's daughters, 'Nettie' – Antoinette Power Bringhurst (1852–1932) – and the spirit of 'the band of brothers' certainly fitted well with the legacy of the late Texian Republic. Many other versions followed:

We are a band of brothers
And native to the soil
Fighting for the property
We gained by honest toil.
And when our rights were threatened
The cry rose near and far:
Hoorah – Hoorah – a thousand times Hoorah,
Hoorah for the bonnie blue flag that bears a single star.[69]

Despite the monotony of the freeways and the bleakness of the surrounding countryside, the Houston area has much to offer tourists. Anyone with a historical bent is spoilt for choice. There is a multitude of museums and monuments, a profusion of cultural festivals, and a surfeit of suggestions for tours of historical interest. The 'Independence Trail', for example, as recommended by the Texas Highways Department, follows a circular 450-mile route from Houston to San Antonio and back; one can either rush around a small number of important sites such as the Alamo and Washington-on-the-Brazos (where the declaration of independence was made in 1836) or dawdle leisurely from stop to stop, starting at the Gonzales Memorial Site (where the first shots were fired in 1836), the Houston Oak on Route 361 (under which Sam Houston rested), and the Presidio La Bahía (where 300 Texian prisoners were massacred).[70] The longer 'Chisholm Trail' is for vacationers with more time on their hands. Starting at the Stillman Mansion in Brownsville, the home of a cattle baron who had started life as a steamboat captain on the Rio Grande, it follows the 897-mile route to Abilene, Kansas, with over fifty stops on the way. Highlights en route include the town of Goliad (where the earliest of all the great cattle ranches was situated, at the Spanish Mission of Nuestra Señora del Espíritu Santo), the Suspension Bridge at Waco (across which millions of cattle were driven), and the Stock Yards at Fort Worth.[71]

The Alamo itself arouses mixed feelings. For Britishers, it is the American equivalent of Rourke's Drift as portrayed in the film *Zulu*, and witnessed a heroic last stand to the death. The heroes are Colonel William Travis, Jim Bowie, and Davy Crockett. It is a shrine to unabashed American patriotism, and the subject of many a ballad:

> In the southern part of Texas, in the town of San Antone,
> There's a fortress all in ruins, that the weeds have overgrown.
> You may look in vain for crosses, and you'll never see a-one.
> But sometimes between the setting and the rising of the sun,
> You can hear a ghostly bugle, as the men go marching by;
> You can hear them as they answer to the roll-call in the sky.[72]

'Hey-up, Santa Anna, they're killing your soldiers below,
So the rest of Texas will know
And remember the Alamo!'[73]

It's rousing stuff, sanctified by sacrifice. The one thing missing is any pause for reflection on Mexican motives. The unwary could be forgiven for thinking that Santa Anna had invaded the United States. It's similar to patriotic British attitudes to the Zulu Wars in South Africa. Why would those dastardly, savage Zulus attack us? One of the failings of patriotism is its blindness to the patriotism of others.

Attendance at a Latino festival could act as a suitable antidote to the Alamo, and these days there are plenty of them. All the main towns and cities in Texas celebrate the *Cinco de Mayo*, on 5 May, and the *Día de Muertos* on All Souls' Day, 1 November.[74] A trip to an Indian Reservation would also bring rewards. After all, the history of Native Americans in this territory is longer than anyone else's. There's an Alabama-Coushatta Reservation in Polk County, a Tigua Reservation near El Paso, and a Kickapoo Reservation at Eagle Pass in Maverick County on the Rio Grande. Unfortunately, visits are only permitted in conjunction with an expensive entrance ticket to the reservations' casinos.[75] There is a small town called Comanche in central Texas, which is a centre for deer-hunting, and a Comanche County Historical Museum. Alas, a brief inspection of the museum's website reveals that it contains nothing about the Comanche.[76]

Some would say that visiting Texas without seeing a rodeo is like visiting Rome and missing the Colosseum. Both Houston and Fort Worth hold annual stock shows and rodeos, and scores of smaller venues put on lesser events. But cowboys lived in the outback, and it is small country towns that often cultivate their ranching heritage. Stamford, near Fort Worth, has its Cowboy Country Museum.[77] Both Gatesville and Bandera are advertised as 'cowboy capitals', where you can 'Embrace Your Inner Cowboy'.

Like every other visitor, I wish to have my outing, but a choice must be made. Mary, an academic from the University of Texas, has offered her services as guide and chauffeur. And we are joined by Yarek, a British expat, who now resides in Texas but used to teach at Eton. (His late father, whom I knew, had survived Auschwitz.)

'What do you want to see?' they enquire politely.

'Anything,' I reply, 'so long as it's out of Houston and off the freeway.' Then a thought strikes.

'Are there any traces of the "Old Three Hundred" or of Fort Bend?'
I ask.

Mary opens a large-scale map that shows Fort Bend County only
thirty miles distant, to the south-west of Houston. And a quick scan of
Yarek's tablet shows that the county has a museum. So off we go in
Mary's air-conditioned limousine – in search of the very 'First Texians'.

Richmond, it transpires, is the county seat of Fort Bend County. It lies
beyond Sugar Land, where the state's first sugar mill was built, and it can
be approached from West Houston on the '762 Loopway (North)'. After
nearly two hours, we are totally lost, having circled Richmond from all
directions. Repeated enquiries at assorted churches and gas stations only
increase the confusion. But then a stray road sign points to RICHMOND
CITY CENTRE – three miles. It's state law that signs are to be obeyed.
Better still, another stray sign on Jackson Street points to FORT BEND
MUSEUM. Left. Right. Left again, YIELD, ONE WAY STREET, past the
New Courthouse, LEFT, RIGHT, past the Old Courthouse, LEFT,
RIGHT, FIRE HYDRANT. And there it is; a long low building opposite
the First Baptist Church (or possibly the Second Baptist Church).

'Given all these churches,' Mary exclaims, 'this country should be a
saintly place.'

We race to the front door. But catastrophe strikes.

'Of course,' says Yarek, adding an unsaintly word, 'it's Monday; all
Texas museums are shut!'

The humiliation of the moment gives Mary the courage to persist. Reading a telephone number on the museum door, she rings the
Richmond City Council from her cell phone.

'This is Mary,' she announces importantly, 'I have some visitors
with me, and the museum is shut. Is there anyone there who could
spare a few minutes for a quick historical tour?'

Glen Gilmour, the city manager of Richmond, is a real period gentleman. He strolls out of the Council Offices in his open pink shirt and
elastic braces, his hair as white as milk, his face as tanned and wrinkled
as a walnut.

'I'm trying to retire,' he opens, 'but my son shows no sign of completing his studies at UT. So I'm stuck; I have time on my hands. This
is a bedroom town, only 11,000 people.'

We climb into the cab of his monster eight-seater pick-up truck, and
rumble off for an unforgettable half hour. Richmond's grid of perhaps
twenty streets is an extraordinary mixture of old, new, and empty blocks.
Heritage buildings stand side by side with supermarkets and apartments.

'Jane Long,* the Mother of Texas, ran a guest house over there,' Mr Gilmour says, pointing to an expanse of baked mud. 'You know, a sort of guest house.'

'Santa Anna stopped here on the way to San Jacinto,' he continues. 'Sam Houston ferried his troops across the river on the *Yellowstone* steamboat . . . And that's the original station house; we've renovated it a bit.'

We wait for a Union Pacific freight train to pass, pulling a hundred wagons of gravel.

'President Lamar, the first head of our republic [he wasn't quite right about that] is buried in the cemetery here,' Mr Gilmour goes on.

A quick tour of Morton Cemetery contains several such pioneer graves, each marked by a Texan flag and a biographical signboard.

'This was the home town of Kerry Nation, y'all know,' he adds, moving forward in time. 'Y'all know, our Kerry was the woman who took an axe to the anti-prohibitionists.'

Steven Spielberg made his first film here. 'It was called *Sugar Land Express*,' Mr Gilmour informs us.

Finally, we go to a small square to see a statue erected to the town's mayor, Hilmar G. Moore, born in 1920 and still in office.

'Y'alls from England,' he goes on. 'We had the BBC here recently, talking to our mayor: he's the longest-serving mayor in the USA, longer on the throne than your Queen. Would y'all like to talk to him?'

The mayoral residence is a long, low house on the edge of town, surrounded by gardens and shady trees. Mr Hilmar and Mrs Evelyn Moore were waiting by the open door.

'Howdy, come in,' they chime in chorus. 'The office rang to tell us. We love having guests. Y'alls in time for tea.'[78]

The entrance hall has the feel of an art gallery. Oil paintings line the walls – landscapes, portraits, pictures of favourite dogs, horses, and bulls. Pride of place is taken by a painting of Hilmar Moore mounted on a superb, rearing chestnut.

'I'm a cattleman,' the mayor says, drawling out the 'me-a-an'. 'They was fixin' me to be a lawyer. But I thank the Lord I didn't make it. I earned enough money playing poker to buy a decent herd of cattle.'

As we learn, people around here are classed by the size of their herds.

---

* Jane Long (1798–1880), who accompanied the filibusters across the Mississippi, was reputedly the first English-speaking woman to give birth in Texas, and donated the land on which Richmond was built.

The living room can be measured in acres. It has a spacious dais at the near end, a sitting section in the middle furnished with giant sofas and fronds of overhanging plants, and another open area in the distance. The mayor's rocking-chair is placed centre stage, beside the tea-trolley. Mrs Moore pours the tea. She is younger than her husband by forty years at least.

'Mr Moore is 91,' she begins, 'I'm just a local girl.'

The mayor rocks approvingly in his chair. He is short, stocky, and restless, his face and forearms tanned to a deep shade of mahogany.

'Working cattle on horseback has kept me going. I still go out every day. But what do y'all wanna know?'

I have a question ready.

'Does the old Fort Bend still exist? Can one go and see it?'

'No, the Fort has gone,' he replies. 'It's probably in the river. But the bend is still there. This is the Brazos,' pointing through the window, 'which runs down into the Gulf.'

As I had read, Stephen Austin's original land grant formed an enormous rectangle between the Brazos and Colorado rivers. The grantees received a minimum of 177 acres each for arable farming or 4,428 acres for livestock ranching. They bought the land for 12.50 cents an acre, which was one-tenth the going rate in the United States at the time, and they were promised ten years free of taxation.

'We've hit the jackpot,' I whisper to Mary during a lull. We were talking to a direct descendant of the 'Old Three Hundred'. 'The mayor must be the great-grandson, or possibly the great-great-grandson.'

The name of Colonel John Henry Moore (1800–1880) figures on the list of 297 grantees in the original colony. Born in Tennessee, he reputedly ran away in order to avoid learning Latin. He built Moore's Fort (1828) in Fayette County to hold off the Comanche, and was made a colonel in the army of the republic.

'I am interested,' I say to the mayor, 'in those early days.'

Mayor Moore shows little admiration for any of the people concerned.

'The Mexicans came across the river to steal cattle,' he says. 'They were rustlers. The Indians, too, were pretty wild; they were into hostage-taking and raiding farms ... The Comanche,' in particular, 'were really mean and aggressive.'

But in conclusion he adds: 'They were later more abused than anybody. We took away everything they had.'

'I'm a historian, I write history books,' I say in response to the mayor's query as to my occupation.

'Hmm,' he muses. 'History is mostly people's opinions.' He speaks as if from hard experience. But he goes on to reminisce willingly about his family.

'My grandpa was a doctor during the Civil War; he had 7,000 acres and 12,000 cattle. But after the war, he started buying up larger tracts of land, and put his holdings up to 60,000 acres.'

The key moment of his grandfather's career came at the Cattleman's Convention in San Antonio. '[Grandpa] saw a demonstration of barbed wire, and he bought miles and miles and miles of it.'

That must have been somewhere around 1875–80. Barbed wire, as everyone here knows, changed the American West for ever.

'But, like me, he never wore cowboy boots or a Stetson.'

The mayor's grandfather, John Moore Snr, became a US Congressman and owner of the mansion in which the Fort Bend Museum is now housed. His father John Moore Jnr was a judge: his mother was a Guenther, and heiress to the Pioneer Flour Mills in San Antonio.

'My aunt used to run the business.'

Yarek, meanwhile, has strolled to the far end of the room, and is gesticulating wildly.

'He's found my trophies,' the mayor chuckled.

The young Hilmar Moore went on several hunting expeditions to Africa in the 1930s. The massive horned head of an African buffalo is hanging on the wall. A stuffed rhino stands in the corner, and in front of it a magnificently maned lion. We all have our photographs snapped standing with the mayor and the lion.

'I am a hunter, not a killer,' the mayor insists. 'I've never shot an elephant, and I wouldn't eat zebra; it reminds me of my horse.'

'Mr Moore still hunts a bit,' his wife adds, 'but only for quail.'

We ask about his friends and neighbours.

'My best friend was Milton Rabinowitz,' he says. 'His parents came from Minsk, and set up a kosher butcher's shop in this town . . . He was very devout, and attended rabbinical school.'

Their family business grew into a chain of twenty-eight retail stores.

'There was prejudice against Jews in those days; in each of his stores he had to use a Gentile frontman,' the mayor continues. Milt's partners wanted him to change his name to 'Robin', but he refused.

'Milt would say, "We've all got faces like the map of Jerusalem, so what's the point?"' said the mayor.

I tell the mayor I had written a book about the Second World War.

'Yes, I was in the service,' he says.

He had taught navigation for the US Air Force in the Pacific, and served in air-sea rescue. Then he flew on escort duties over Japan, and witnessed both the firestorm at Yokohama and the bombing of Hiroshima. He was flying alongside the *Enola Gay* in a B17, 120 miles beyond Hiroshima, when the A-Bomb exploded.

'One strike and the city had gone,' he says. 'But I was a very bad soldier; I like giving orders, not obeying them.'

Which leads the conversation painlessly to the sixty-two years of our host's mayoralty.

'What's the secret?' we ask.

'No secret,' he insists, 'no secret – only don't lie and don't promise anything you can't deliver. The worst thing is to procrastinate. And you can't please everyone all the time.'

Mayor Moore is a believer in small government, and in municipal non-interventionism.

'It's wrong for us to look after other people's children,' he proclaims, and tells us an anecdote. One day, after heavy rains, a woman showed up, announcing that her 'yard was flooded'. She clearly expected the mayor to sort it out.

'Next mornin',' he says grinning, 'I rode over with a large placard, and stuck it in her yard. It read: NO FISHING.'

He then returns to our earlier question.

'Yeah, there *is* a secret: I can't do everything. I just get good people and let them manage what I can't do.'

Mrs Moore signals gently that time is up; left to himself, her husband would talk all day. The entrance hall becomes the departure gate. The mayor glances again at his mounted portrait.

'Please remember that you've met the last cowboy in Texas', is his parting shot.[79] And we leave, repeating the jingle that he has taught us with relish:

> Other states were carved or born
> But Texas grew from hide and horn.

# 12

## Mannahatta

*Delawares, Dutchmen, and Many Slaves*

JFK Airport is the gateway to New York, just as New York is the traditional gateway to the United States from Europe. Founded in 1948 to relieve the pressure on North Beach Field (now LaGuardia), it was built twelve miles from City Hall on the southern shores of Long Island, adjacent to Jamaica Bay and on the site of a golf course at Idlewild Beach. Separated from the Atlantic breakers by the narrow Rockaway Peninsula, it swallowed up 5,000 acres of pristine wetland, once the preserve of eel-fishers, duck-hunters, and crab-trappers. From the outset, it handled long-haul transatlantic traffic, mainly leaving domestic airline traffic to its older partner. Flying from Houston to New York, for example, one usually lands at LaGuardia; flying from New York to Europe or vice versa, one would normally use JFK. For its first fifteen years, prior to the assassination of the thirty-fifth president, New York International Airport was officially called Anderson Field, but was universally and popularly known as 'Idlewild'.[1]

I remember the magical name of Idlewild from my boyhood. My elder cousin Sylvia, who worked as a teacher in New York, used to come home to England for summer vacations, and for many years would 'cross the pond' in style on the *Queen Mary* or the *Queen Elizabeth*. But the day came, in 1959 or 1960, when she arrived to announce 'I've just flown in from Idlewild.' What a romantic ring that name had! It conjured up images of lazy days in America's great open spaces, and it didn't sound authentically English. It was probably invented by the novelist Lucy Montgomery, for the children's secret forest hideaway in *Anne of Green Gables*. Rockaway is a much older name of Native American derivation, meaning 'Place of Sands'.[2]

After 250 years of mass immigration, New York still is the paramount city for arrivals. In the era before air travel, JFK had several predecessors. Clinton Castle, near Battery Point, acted as the main reception area for much of the nineteenth century. But it was Ellis

Island in New York harbour that housed the USA's most important immigration station. Between 1892 and 1954 over 11 million passed through it on the way to new lives in North America. Since their closure, the buildings on Ellis Island have been turned into a museum where visitors can relive the immigrant experience. The Great Hall, where lines of anxious arrivals awaited the all-important interview with an inspector, has been restored to its original condition. The interview is the subject of many legends and stories. Few of the fierce inspectors spoke a foreign language. Apart from the Irish, few immigrants spoke English; interpreters were scarce, and misunderstandings common. Many of those handed the vital piece of paper recording 'Permission to Land' found their names garbled, and lived with the misspelled surnames for ever after. The archives of the US Immigration Service from that period can be consulted online.[3]

Nowadays, the trip to Ellis Island by ferry from Battery Point makes for an excellent half-day outing. The Statue of Liberty stands on its own little island on one side. The cranes of Brooklyn Naval Yard rise on the other, behind Governors Island. In front, the broad waters of the Bay stretch out towards the graceful suspension bridge at the Verrazano Narrows in the distance.[4]

The return trip from Ellis Island is especially redolent of the immigrant experience. The white-painted ferryboat chugs across the same half mile that brought the exhausted travellers to their journey's end. You see the Statue of Liberty as they saw it, on the port bow, her right arm raised aloft in welcome, her hand holding the Torch of Freedom. The perils of the Arrivals Hall were behind them. In front, the final landing stage of a new continent awaited amidst a cluster of super-sized buildings. When I first made the trip in the 1970s, the skyline was dominated by the twin towers of the World Trade Center. I cherish a picture holding my young son on the topmost deck. As from 2015, after a long gap, the single, bevelled tower of '1WTC' soars in the same place to a symbolic 1,776 feet.

One of the millions who passed through Ellis Island was Israel Zangwill (1864–1926), the British-born writer of Polish-Jewish descent. Zangwill has been credited with inventing two extremely influential phrases – the first, 'The Melting Pot', about the USA, the other, more questionably, 'A country without people for a people without a country', about Palestine. The former took off thanks to his play The

*Melting Pot*, which was staged in New York in 1909. President Theodore Roosevelt, who attended the opening night, leaned from his box during the interval and shouted to the author sitting below: 'This is a very great play, Mr Zangwill!' And the central concept has stood the test of time:

> America is God's Crucible, the great Melting Pot, where all the races of Europe are melting and re-forming! . . . Germans and Frenchmen, Irishmen and Englishmen, Jews and Russians – into the Crucible with you all! God is making the American.[5]

Zangwill's use of the word 'races' was referring to 'ethnic groups' or 'nationalities'. He said of himself that he 'was a Jew who no longer wanted to be a Jew'.

Of course, the extent to which the Melting Pot has continued to function is an open question. 'Americanization' has not erased all signs of its constituent elements, and the diversity within America's unity is very evident in New York. All the signs at JFK these days are bilingual. The tape that keeps de-boarding passengers in line reads NO EXIT/NO PASAR. One has arrived at a GATE/PUERTA. And the toilet signs show a little male or female figure together with the words CABALLEROS and DAMAS. The Spanish-speaking Latinos are the first major wave of immigrants who often have little intention of learning English.

Almost one half of New Yorkers speak a language other than English at home, and distinct 'ethnic ghettos' are one of the city's most obvious features. Years ago, when I worked at Columbia University and lived on the East Side, on E78th, my apartment was in a small area known as 'Little Hungary'; Magyar was spoken in the shops, and restaurants feeding their customers with goulash and Egri Bikavér were everywhere. A few streets uptown was 'Little Germany', a few streets further south 'Little Italy'. Harlem, above 125th Street, was almost solidly a black area. Several neighbourhoods across the bridge in Brooklyn were almost exclusively Jewish. The Pot appeared to be losing its power to melt.

I first landed at JFK in 1973 or 1974, benefiting from the super-economy fares offered by the now defunct Laker Airways and heading for my first American book tour. The details of that landing have long since disappeared into the mists of fading memory. But two moments were imprinted for ever. One was the encounter with the question on the immigration form: 'Are you, or have you ever been, a member of the Nazi party?'* The other was the very first, and sadly unsuccessful, exchange that I ever had with an American citizen. When I finally emerged from the endurance tests of immigration control and baggage hall, I was looking for an exit from which I could take a taxi to my cousin's apartment in Forest Hills. I surged with the crowd through the corridors and the final set of automatic doors to face the rainbow sea of eager faces waiting to greet their passengers, and made a beeline for a woman behind the crush barrier.

'Excuse me,' I said, 'is there an information desk round here?' (I should have asked for the 'info counter'.)

I was met by a stare of total incomprehension, followed by a grimace of annoyance and a grin of embarrassment. After ten or twenty agonizing seconds, the woman geared herself up to utter something, clearing her throat and eventually producing the remark 'What a strange accent!' The sound of 'strange' was strangely elongated, and the word 'accent' was doubly accented to sound like an exotic combination of 'ache' and 'scent'. Thoroughly confused, I set out to find the taxi rank (or rather the cab stand) under my own steam.

The experience taught me two things. One was the truth of what George Bernard Shaw did not quite say, namely that 'England and America are two nations divided by a common language.' The other concerned sensitivity to the experiences of others. Travellers arriving in a new country are eager to record their own impressions, and observe things from their own viewpoint. They should be equally alert to the effect that their arrival has on the locals.

The Lenape People had lived on the shores of the Great Bay for ten thousand winters. Like their neighbours, the Susquehannock and the Mohawks, who both belonged to the Five Nations of the Iroquois, they had no recollection of their earlier migrations, and were still fixed in the Stone Age, knowing neither metal nor horses nor writing. Lacking

---

* The US Immigration's infamous catch-all questions have varied over time, sometimes referring to the 'Nazi Party' sometimes to the 'Communist Party', sometimes to the protection of the American Constitution, and most recently to terrorism. A short-sighted German friend of mine, now a distinguished professor emeritus, was once denied entry to the USA after ticking the box about Nazi membership, having mistaken it for the immediately adjacent box about 'the importation of seeds, fruit and other farm produce'. During the early stages of the Cold War, the irascible but much-loved BBC commentator Gilbert Harding (1907–60), a hero of my youth, was excluded from the USA for a similar offence. In answer to the question, 'Do you intend to subvert the Constitution of the United States?', he reportedly wrote 'Sole purpose of visit'.

seagoing vessels, their range of movement was limited, as was their knowledge of the world beyond the Narrows. They had no concept of what lay across the ocean; for most of those ten thousand winters they never even heard of the 'men-in-ships', the 'Salt-water People', who would soon be sailing into their world. (Their eponym means 'Real Men' or 'Genuine Humans', but in English they acquired the misleading appellation 'Delawares' after encountering settlers from Virginia in the Delaware Valley.)[6] On the coast, the *Lenapehoking* or 'Lenape territory' stretched some 150 miles from the midpoint of the *Sewanhacky*, the Long Island, which formed one shore of the Bay, to the estuary of the *Lenape Seepu* (the Delaware). In the interior, it took in the whole basin of the Delaware and all but the most distant streams in the Great Bay's catchment area.

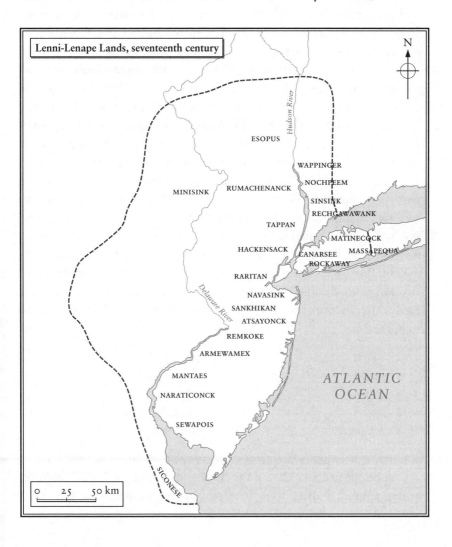

Lenni-Lenape Lands, seventeenth century

Unlike the nomadic tribes of the Great Plains, the Lenape followed a semi-sedentary, localized way of life. They were familiar with prim-itive agriculture, which was largely practised by their women; the men, trained as warriors and hunters, drew on the produce of the rivers and the abundant game of the seaside forests. All manner of fish were caught both in freshwater and in the brine of the Bay; clams and shell-fish were collected on the shore; berries, herbs, and mushrooms were gathered in the woods. Their settlements crowded round the clearings in the forest, where they would 'slash and burn', raise crops of maize and beans, and move on after a few seasons. In the winter, they lived in log-built longhouses; in the summer, they moved to encampments of dome-shaped wigwams. As a result, they had no sense of permanent land ownership. The tribal elders might make temporary allocations to particular clans or families to avoid collisions. But no one thought that men could claim outright possession of the Great Creator's Earth.

The Lenapes' language belonged to the much larger Algonquian lin-guistic family, more precisely to the Delawaran sub-branch of Eastern Algonquian, which was not written down until the nineteenth century. Not being readily intelligible to the neighbouring Iroquois, it heightened their sense both of identity and of isolation. According to philologists, it can be characterized among other things by 'polysynthetic morphology'; its nouns follow the rules of animate and inanimate gender, but not of masculine, feminine, or neuter; and its vocabulary is hermetic. There were two main dialects, one called *Munsee* in the district of the Great Bay, and another called *Unami* in districts further south. (Modern phil-ologists classify these dialects as separate languages.) According to William Penn, who first met the Lenape in 1682, their word for 'mother' was *anna*, for 'brother' *issimus*, and for 'friend' *netap*. The numbers from 1 to 10 bore no resemblance to anything he had previously encountered:

| 1 | *kweti* | 6 | *kwetash* |
|---|---------|----|-----------|
| 2 | *nisha* | 7 | *nishash* |
| 3 | *naxa* | 8 | *xash* |
| 4 | *newa* | 9 | *peshkunk* |
| 5 | *palenaxk* | 10 | *telen* |

Communication with Europeans was problematical, to say the least.[7]

Lenape culture, like that of the Algonquins in general, was based on strong animist beliefs that stressed the commonality of mankind and animals. They believed in the *Manitou* or 'Great Creator Spirit', and were followers of the *Midewiwin*, 'the Right Path', which was perpetuated by a rich repertoire of rites, rituals, symbols, and stories. The shaman or 'medicine man' was guardian of the tribal lore, preparing herbal potions for the sick, casting spells and blessings in turn, painting the sacred petroglyphs on the rocks, and teaching the children to learn his rhymes and tales by heart. One of his key functions was to keep the tribe in harmony with the spirits that had been left behind both by their ancestors and by the animals that they killed for food. Maintaining the balance between humankind and Nature was paramount.[8]

The Lenape sense of time was finely calibrated. Based on observation of the skies and the seasons, they counted the number of 'nights' that made up each lunar cycle, and the twelve or thirteen cycles that made up each year or 'winter'. These numbers were notched on calendar sticks, or knotted on ropes or strings of beads. The Lenape cultivated an awareness of the passage of generations, and within each 'winter', the progression of natural events – the first buds of spring, the spawning of the salmon, the ripening of the corn, and the rutting of the deer. Of the longer term, the Lenape talked of 'the Ancient Time', when human life was no different from that of animals; of the 'Golden Age', when humans developed their special skills, and of the 'Here and Now', when wars and conflicts arose.

The organization of Lenape society was based on two separate and overlapping systems, whose interactions render conventional terms such as 'tribes' and 'clans' both inappropriate and confusing. One system was made up of kinship groups, of which there may once have been as many as fifty, but which had now been reduced to three – those of the Wolf, the Turtle, and the Turkey. These groups existed to enforce strict marriage customs and prevent inbreeding, and consisted of several sub-groups or 'clans'. Each was headed by a matriarch, who inherited her position through the female line, and all identified themselves as *omamiwinni* or 'kinsfolk'. Young brides were required to stay with their own clan, while taking husbands from outside it. The Turkey grouping, for example, the *Pul-la'-ook*, whose chief was often regarded as supreme leader of the Lenape, was divided into twelve clans:

Big Bird (*Mor-har-a-la*)

Bird's Cry (*Le-le-wa'-you*)

Eye Pain (*Moo-kwung-wa-ho'ki*)

Scratch the Path (*Moo-har-mo-wi-kar'-nu*)

Opossum Ground (*O-ping-ho'-ki*)

Old Shin (*Muh-ho-we-ka'-ken*)

Drift Log (*Tong-o-na-o-to*)

Living in Water (*Nool-a-mar-lar'-mo*)

Root Digger (*Muh-krent-har'-ne*)

Red Face (*Mur-karm-huk-se*)

Pine Region (*Koo-wa-ho'ke*)

Ground Scratcher (*Oo-ckuk'-ham*)[9]

At the same time, the kinship clans were distributed among a larger number of territorial communities, often called 'bands' by later settlers, each bearing a name that derived either from the local terrain or from exonyms. In the vicinity of the Great Bay, more than a score of such Lenape communities seem to have managed their economic and agricultural activities collectively. They are usually listed according to their dialect and their location:

**Munsee**

(West of the 'North River')

*Esopus* ('High Banks')

*Minisink* ('Islanders')

*Rumachenanck*\*

*Ramapo* ('Mountain People')

*Tappan* ('Cold Water')

*Ack-kinkas-hacky/Hackensack* ('Stony Ground')

*Navasink* ('Red Bank')

*Raritan* ('Forked River')

(East of the 'North River')

*Wappinger* ('Easterners')

*Nochpeem* ('Misty Place')

*Housatonic* ('Beyond the Mountain')

*Kichtawanks*

*Sinsink*

*Rechgawawanks* ('Manhattans')

*Nayack* ('Fishing Place')

---

\* Later called the *Haverstroo* or 'Oat-Straw People' by the Dutch.

| (On the Long Island) | *Canarsee* |
| | *Rockaway* ('Place of Sands') |
| | *Massapequa* |
| | *Matinecock* |
| **Unami** | |
| (Lower 'South River' Valley) | *Atsayonck* |
| | *Remkoke* |
| | *Armewamex* |
| | *Mantaes* |
| | *Naraticonck* |
| **Unalachtigo** | |
| (Coastal Tideways) | *Sankhikan* |
| | *Siconese* |
| | *Sewapois* |
| | *Nanticoke* ('Tideway')[10] |

All these designations are tentative. The Nochpeem, for example, are sometimes presented as an autonomous band, sometimes as a sub-band of the Wappingers. Unalachtigo may or may not have been a sub-dialect of Unami.

Echoes of the former inhabitants can sometimes be found in modern place names – like Minisink, Haverstraw, Tappan Zee, Oscawana, Nyack, or Rockaway. But the names by which the Lenape themselves described locations within their homeland have mainly been lost. Only a few have survived, invariably in garbled form, having been adopted by the foreign settlers of a later age. Almost uniquely, one of them – *Manna-hatta*, meaning 'island of hills' – was written down by a crewman of a European ship.[11] Others have been the subject of orthographic nightmares and wishful etymological inventions:

*Manna-hatta* = 'Hilly Isle'/ Manhattan

*Mohicanituk* = 'Two Way River'/ Hudson

*Kapsee* = 'Rocky Point'/Battery Point

*Muhealcantute ?* also the Hudson

*Pagganck* = 'Isle of Nuts'/ Governors Island

*Mespeatches* = 'Bad Swamp'/ Maspeth, NY

*Rechtank* = 'Sandy Spit'/ Corlear's Hook

*Meghgectecock* = 'May Apple Orchard'/Newark Bay, NJ

*Lapinikan* = 'Ploughed Fields'/ Greenwich

*Sicomac* = 'Burial Site'/Wyckoff, NJ

*Kintecoying* = 'Assembly
      Field'/Astor Place
*Paumanok* = 'Land of Tribute'/
      Long Island
*Sewanhacky* = 'Place of Shells'/
      Long Island
*Muscooten* = 'Blind Water'/
      Harlem River

*Rechawegh* = 'Place of Sands'/
      Rockaway
*Canarsee* (a tribal name)/
      Canarsie, NY
*Manhasset* (a tribal name)/
      Manhasset, NY
*Mericoke* (a tribal name)/
      Merrick, NY
*Lenape Seepu* = 'Lenape River'/
      Delaware[12]

Relations with the non-Lenape peoples were extremely unstable. They included the Iroquoian *Susquehannok* and *Mohawks* to the west and north-west; the Algonquin *Mohicans*, *Pocomtuc*, and *Mattabesic* to the north and north-east; and the *Metoac* group of tribes, including the *Shinnekok* on Long Island. Skirmishes could quickly develop into wars, and the more warlike nations such as the Mohawks showed no compunction in attacking or subordinating their less powerful neighbours. Yet intertribal co-operation can also be observed in the shared maintenance of the 'Great Trail' that was used for the fur trade, for seasonal migrations, and for access to the cultivated 'deerfield' meadows. Thanks to their role as intertribal mediators, the Lenape were widely known as 'Grandfathers'.

No memory or record has survived among the Lenape from the day when the 'men-in-ships' arrived from across the ocean. The event may well have inspired a story about 'The Winter of the Big Canoe' or 'The Morning of the Ship with Sails'. If so, the story was forgotten. The encounter is known exclusively from the perspective of the 'men-in-ships', who recorded it, according to their own time system, in the Year of Our Lord, 1524. Giovanni da Verrazzano (1485–1528) was a Florentine captain sailing in the French service; on his second voyage to the West, he had been commissioned to find a sea route to the Pacific. He left Dieppe a full thirty years after the 'discovery' of 'the Indies' by Christopher Columbus, twenty after Vespucci's confirmation of the existence of the two American continents, and two following the circumnavigation of the globe by Magellan's expedition. Hence, when Verrazzano set course for the Terra Nova in January 1524, he was not heading, like Columbus, for the totally unknown. He made a landfall at what is now Cape Fear, North Carolina, and sailed north. Somewhere along that coast, a landing party recorded a historic encounter:

We found a man who came to the shore to see what people we were, who stood hesitating and ready for flight. Watching us, he did not permit himself to be approached. He was handsome, nude, of olive colour, and with his hair fastened back in a knot. We were about twenty ashore, and coaxing him, he approached to about two fathoms, showing us a burning stick as if to offer us fire. And we made fire with powder and flint-and-steel, and he trembled all over as we fired the shot. He stopped as if astonished, and prayed, worshipping like a monk, lifting his finger to the sky, and pointing to the sea and the ship he appeared to bless us.[13]

Circumventing the estuaries of what would later be called the Chesapeake and the Delaware, Verrazzano then approached the Narrows which now bear his name:

After a hundred leagues, we found a very agreeable place between two small but prominent hills, and between them a very wide river, deep at its mouth, [which] flowed into the sea. And with the help of the tide, which rises eight feet, any laden ship could have passed safely into the river estuary. Yet, [not wanting to run] risks, we took the small boat up the river to land, which we found [to be] densely populated.

The people were almost the same as the others [we had seen], dressed in birds' feathers of various colours; and they came towards us joyfully, uttering loud cries of wonderment and showing us where to land the boat ... We went up the river about half a league, where we saw that it formed a beautiful lake ... About thirty of their boats ran to and fro across the lake with innumerable people aboard, who were crossing from one side to the other to see us ...[14]

He had mistaken the Great Bay for a lake, and named the country 'Angoulême'. He twice made further contact with Native Americans, before sailing up to Newfoundland and returning to France in July.[15]

In the following year, a Portuguese captain in the Castilian service, Estêvão Gomes (c. 1483–1538), led another expedition to North America and probably entered the Great Bay. He was the likeliest source of the information that enabled Diego Ribeiro, in his world map of 1529, to draw the outline of the North American coast with great precision. Ribeiro marked the area on both sides of the Great Bay as the 'Tierra de Estevan Gomez'.[16]

The extent of Native Americans' awareness of the growing European presence on their continent is hard to determine. Yet the Lenape could hardly have seen the full picture. They would probably have

heard of the French settlements in a country twenty days' march to the
north. They may possibly have caught echoes of the Spaniards' takeover of the Land of the Mayas far to the south. They would have had
no difficulty in understanding the fact that the 'men-in-ships' belonged,
like themselves, to different tribes that spoke different languages and
frequently quarrelled.

Since the lifespan of Native Americans did not exceed thirty-five to
forty years, three or four generations must have passed between the first
sighting by the Lenape of the 'men-in-ships' and the second. No fewer
than eighty-five annual notches would have been cut into the calendar
sticks. The Great Bay remained hidden to the 'men-in-ships' just as
knowledge of their provenance remained hidden from the Lenape. In the
meantime, the natives of the region learned to use copper for ornamental
purposes. In this, they lagged far behind many of the pre-Columbian
peoples, especially in South America. Copper had been mined for centuries at several sites on the shores of the Great Lakes, but familiarity with
its uses spread very slowly. It was fashioned into bracelets, necklaces,
headdresses, breastplates, and funerary regalia. But on the Atlantic coast
it was not mixed with tin or zinc to produce hardened alloys such as
bronze, leaving the Lenape essentially stranded in the Stone Age.

Nonetheless, the day duly dawned when the foreigners returned. It was
a day in the season of ripening corn, in the eighty-fifth or eighty-sixth
winter since their predecessors had left. Heavy mist had covered the Narrows in the morning, but in the afternoon, when visibility improved, a
small boat appeared carrying six or eight passengers; it was smoothly
propelled not by paddles but by straight wooden spars protruding from
the sides and moving back and forth in regular movements controlled by
men sitting at the sides. The commander stood in the prow with a spy-
glass to his eye; another sailor in the stern was measuring the depth of the
water with a weighted line; and a guard sat with him carrying a fire-stick
at the ready. After a while this first canoe turned on its tracks, and sped
back beyond the Narrows. Then it was that the huge white canvas sheets
of a Great Canoe heaved into sight, marvellously driven forward by the
sea breeze. The vessel was perhaps forty paces in length; its body rose ten
or fifteen feet above the water; and the three strong trunks that carried
the canvas stretched as high as the tallest trees. A war standard made up
of three horizontal stripes, red, white, and blue, flew from the highest
mast, and the high stern was adorned with the carving of a crescent
moon. Edging towards the shallows amidst much barking of orders, the
vessel slowed; a heavy iron claw was lowered on a rope to fix it to the

seabed, until the vessel juddered to a halt. Overcome with curiosity, the first native canoes paddled out cautiously to meet the shipmen.

These same events, however, were recorded in detail from the shipboard perspective. An English sea captain in the Dutch service, Henry Hudson, was exploring the North American coast and taking his ship, the *Half Moon*, into all the coastal estuaries, hoping to find a channel joining the Atlantic to the Pacific – the so-called 'North-West Passage'. As written down by the ship's mate, Robert Juet, the *Half Moon*'s log fixed the day as 3 September, AD 1609:

> The Third, the morning mystie untill ten of the clocke, then it cleered, and the wind came to the South South-east. So wee weighed and stood to the Northward. The Land is very pleasant and high, and bold to fall withhall. At three of the clocke in the after-noone, wee came to three great Rivers. So we stood along to the Northernmost, thinking to haue gone into it, but we found it to have a very shoald barre before it, for we had but ten foot water. Then wee cast about to the Southward, and found two fathoms, three fathoms, and three and a quarter, till we came to the Southern side of them, then we had five and sixe fathoms, and Anchored. So wee sent in our Boate, and they found no lesse water then five, sixe, and seven fathoms, and returned in an houre and a halfe. So wee weighed and went in, and rode in five fathoms . . . and saw many Salmons, and Mullets, and Rayes very great. The height is 40 degrees 30 minutes.[17]

For a whole week Hudson tarried in the Bay, whose position he had calculated with reasonable accuracy,* judging it 'a very good Harbour'. His men spent the time fishing, exploring the woods, and trading with the natives:

> Then our Boate went on Land with our Net to Fish, and caught ten great Mullets, of a foot and a halfe long a peace, and a Ray as great as foure men could haul into the ship. So wee trimmed our Boate and rode still all day. At night the wind blew hard at the North-west, and our Anchor came home, and wee drove on shoare, but tooke no hurt, thanked bee God . . . This day the people of the Countrey came aboard of us, seeming very glad of our comming, and brought greene Tabacco, and gave us of it for Knives and Beads. They goe in Deere skins loose, well dressed. They have yellow Copper. They desire Clothes, and are very civil. They have great store of Maiz or *Indian* Wheate, whereof they make good Bread. The Countrey is full of great and tall Oakes.'

---

* The *Half Moon*'s exact position was at 40 degrees, 42 minutes, and 51 seconds north.

The fifth, in the morning as soone as the day was light, the wind ceased and the Flood came. So we heaved off our ship againe into five fathoms water, and sent our Boate to sound the Bay, and we found that there was three fathoms hard by the Souther shoare. Our men went on Land there, and saw great Store of Men, Women and Children, who gave them Tabacco at their coming on Land. So they went up into the Woods, and saw great store of very goodly Oakes, and some Currants. For one of them came aboord and brought some dryed, and gave me some, which were sweet and good. This day many of the people came aboord, some in Mantles of Feathers, and some in Skinnes of divers sorts of good Furres. Some women also came to us with Hempe. They had red Copper Tabacco pipes, and other things of Copper they did weare about their neckes.

A day later, on 6 September, a sailor called Colman was shot by an arrow through the throat, and was buried at a place they named 'Colmans Point'. On 11 September Hudson's party sailed up the river that enters the Bay, to explore it, travelling up to twenty leagues (60 miles) per day. The river, which was tidal, was called *Muhheakantuck*\* by the Lenape, the 'River That Flows in Two Directions':

The fourteenth, in the morning being very faire weather, the wind Southeast, we sayled up the River twelve leagues, and had five fathoms, and five fathoms and a quarter lesse; and came to a Streight betweene two Points, and had eight, nine, and ten fathoms; and it trended North-east by North, one league: and wee had twelve, thirteene and fourteene fathomes. The River is a mile broad: there is very high Land on both sides. Then wee went up North-west, a league and a halfe deepe water. Then North-east by North five miles; then North-west by North two leagues, and anchored. The Land grew very high and Mountainous. The River is full of fish.[18]

Finally, since the season was late and the river had narrowed, they realized that their chance of finding the elusive 'Passage to China' had passed. They were into October. The only option was to return and make for Europe:

The fourth, was faire weather, and the wind at North North-west, wee weighed and came out of the River, into which we had runne so farre. Within a while after, wee came out also of the great mouth of the great River, that runneth up to the North-west, borrowing upon the Norther side

\* In its upper reaches the river was known in the Mohican language as *Muh-he-kun-ne-tuk*, and in the language of the Iroquois as *Ca-ho-ha-ta-te-a*.

of the same, thinking to have deepe water: for wee had founded a great way with our Boat at our first going in, and found seven, six, and five fathomes. So we came out that way, two fathomes and an halfe . . . And by twelve of the clocke we were cleere of all the Inlet. Then we tooke in our Boat, and set our mayne-sayle and sprit-sayle, and our top-sayles, and steered away . . . into the mayne sea; and the Land on the Souther-side of the Bay or Inlet, did beare at noone West and by South foure leagues from us.

The fifth, was faire weather, and the wind variable . . . Wee held on our course South-east by East. At noone I . . . found our height to bee 39 degrees 30 minutes. Our Compasse varied sixe degrees to the West. We continued our course toward *England*, without seeing any Land . . . all the rest . . . of October; And on the seventh day of November . . . being Saturday; by the Grace of God we safely arrived in the Range of *Dartmouth* in *Devonshire*, in the yeere 1609.[19]

What exactly the Lenape made of the *Half Moon*'s brief visit can only be conjectured. Once again, the 'men-in-ships' had come and gone, leaving no indication of their ultimate intentions. There was no telling whether, or when, they might come back. Yet the natives of the Great Bay must surely have got wind by now of developments along 'The Big River of Canada'. They certainly knew that the 'men-in-ships' were eager to barter for fur, and could turn their trading-posts into more permanent, self-supporting settlements. They may not have known the name of the merchant François Du Pont Gravé (or of the navigator, Pierre de Chauvin Tonnetuit); but they were very likely to have gleaned something on the 'Indian Grapevine' about their fur-station at Totouskak (Tadoussac), which, nine winters before the *Half Moon*'s visit to the Great Bay, had been transformed into a fortified colony inhabited by men, women, and children. Nearer home, the Lenape would have been aware of another French colony at Port-Royal less than a moontime's journey by canoe up the coast. Sometime later, they would have received news that another Frenchman, Samuel de Champlain, had created a colony at Stadacona on the 'Big River'. The Lenape would have understood the Algonquin name of *Kebec*, meaning 'River Narrows', by which the Stadacona colony was later known. And they would certainly have taken notice on hearing that the Big River settlers had helped local tribes to fight the Iroquois. Holding off the Iroquois was an existential problem for the Lenapes, and the prospect of the 'men-in-ships' not only buying furs but helping to defend their tribe must have been more than welcome.

Hudson's log says nothing about interpreters or extended conversations with the Lenape. It is virtually impossible that he had anyone to hand who could have translated his Jacobean English into Munsee. So if he had tried to convey that he was from England and a subject of James VI and I, or that his ship had sailed from the 'Dutch Republic', it is doubtful whether he could have made much progress. At the same time, it is well known that people born into complicated multilingual societies are adept at picking up foreign languages, and it is probable that some of the natives would have quickly acquired a smattering of English, if only for the purposes of barter. The Lenape would also have responded to pictorial symbols, and would have pondered the significance of the Dutch tricolour. At some point, they would have worked out that the 'Tribe of the Tricolour' was different from the 'Tribe of the Lilies' whose standard flew above the forts on the Big River or at Port-Royal.

Back in Europe, a comparison of the accounts of Verrazzano and Hudson revealed a curious discrepancy. The former noted that the population round the Great Bay had been 'dense', the latter that it was 'sparse'. Historians now think that the Lenape may have been decimated after 1524 by imported diseases.

Hudson's career would end tragically. On his Fourth Voyage in 1610–11 he entered the greatest of North America's great bays (which, like the river he had explored, is named after him), but, trapped in the ice, decided to wait in the far north for the spring. When it came, however, a mutinous crew set him adrift in an open boat, never to be seen again.[20]

The United Provinces of the Netherlands were the richest and most successful country in early modern Europe. They were small – less than a quarter the size of England. Yet the great ports of Amsterdam and Rotterdam commanded both the sea trade of northern Europe and the river trade of the Rhine. The fabulous East Indies spice trade had recently been wrested from the Portuguese. The taxes raised on all this commercial activity supported a powerful navy. The Dutch led the field in maritime technology, mercantile institutions, municipal organization, and artistic patronage. They had, to borrow a phrase from a celebrated study of the period, 'an embarrassment of riches'.[21]

The international connections of the United Provinces were not simple. In the fifteenth century they had formed part of the precocious Duchy of Burgundy; in the sixteenth century they had passed to the Burgundian Circle of the Holy Roman Empire, and after 1555 under the rule of Spain. Yet they were strongly affected by the Protestant Reformation, and in 1579, under William of Orange, seven northern provinces formed an anti-Spanish league to claim their independence. From then until 1648, a period of almost seventy years, they remained at war with Spain, the greatest power of the age. Yet the King of Spain could neither crush them by land nor cut off their trade, and was eventually forced to relent. No wonder that the 'Father of International Law', Hugo Grotius (1583–1645), was a Dutchman.

The political culture of the United Provinces in their Golden Age was characterized by democratic structures, provincial autonomy, and religious tolerance. At a time when England was struggling to put down the first roots of constitutional monarchy, and was bound by enforced religious uniformity, the Dutch Republic set a shining example of resistance to oppressive Absolutism which many Europeans then admired. Commercial expertise went hand in hand with constitutionalism, artistic brilliance, and religious pluralism. The Bank of Amsterdam and the Dutch Stock Exchange were financial pioneers. The painters Vermeer and Rembrandt were contemporaries of the philosopher Benedict Spinoza (1632–77), a free-thinking Sephardic Jew who was excommunicated by his own community but protected by society at large. Spinoza was working on the idea of a social contract a century before Rousseau. Despite the prominence of Protestant burghers, the republic had a large Catholic population, and a lot of Jewish refugees from Spain. By seventeenth-century standards, they all lived together in surprising harmony. Their founding document, the Union of Utrecht, contained a guarantee that 'Everyone shall remain free in religion, and no one shall be persecuted or investigated because of religion.'

The Dutch East India Company (*Verenigde Oost-Indische Compagnie* or VOC, founded in 1602) has been described as the world's first multinational corporation. It was formed to manage the spice trade with the distant Moluccas (in today's Indonesia) and its shares were floated on the stock market. Its main problem was the sheer length of its lines of communication. Less than a century after the initial circumnavigation of the globe, the voyage to the East Indies, which could only be effected round the Cape of Good Hope, was four times longer than the Atlantic crossing to North America. So the search for an alternative route to Asia was urgent. It was to this end that the VOC employed Hudson, about whom little is known beyond his voyages. In 1607 Hudson had sailed north to the Arctic to test the theory that the sunshine of the polar summer would melt the ice and open a seasonal route to the East. In 1608 he sailed north-east in a vain attempt to find a seaway along Russia's Arctic coast. And in 1609, after some hesitation, he sailed in the tiny *Halve Maen* to America. The day-by-day diary of Hudson's Third Voyage tells how the *Half Moon* had first sailed around Norway's North Cape, before its captain changed his mind, and crossed the Atlantic to the New World.[22]

The Estates-General of Holland encouraged exploration, but did not regard colonization as a priority. On the other hand, the Dutch possessed excellent naval and commercial organizations that would benefit from foreign colonies; and, when so many other countries started planting colonies in North America, they did not intend to be left out.[23] The French had been in Canada for nearly a century. The Spaniards had been in Florida and Mexico even longer. The English, at the third attempt, had established themselves in Virginia. Even the Swedes were making plans. Hundreds of islands in the Antilles were waiting to be claimed, and the long stretch of Atlantic coastline north of Virginia was there for the taking. So after Hudson's disappearance, there was no shortage of sea captains and fur traders to take his place. They knew the contents of his last *Report*, and understood the benefits to be gained. Several of them had successfully completed the longer but well-tried run to the East Indies, and were not deterred by the Atlantic. Their complicated affairs can be glimpsed through the court records of their legal disputes. They usually described their new destination in America either as 'Terra Nova' or as 'New Virginia'. They included Symen Lambertsz Mau, Cornelis Rijser, Thijs Volkertsz Mossel, Hendrik Christiansen, and the best-known of them, Adriaen Block (1567–1627). Mau was reported as having perished on the American coast in 1610, the year after Hudson's visit there. Rijser returned safely in 1611 in his ship *St Pieter*. Christiansen and Block sailed together in 1612, taking two ships and returning next spring not only with furs but with the two sons of a native Sachem. In 1613 Block and Mossel tangled in a dispute over the price paid to natives for a beaver fur; Mossel had paid three times the going rate, thereby beggaring his competitors. In his fourth and final voyage Block lost his ship, the *Tyger*, which caught fire at its moorings in the Great Bay. With aid from the Lenape he built a replacement vessel, the 16-ton *Onrust* (Restless) in which he navigated the *Hellegat* (Hell Gate), the Long Island Sound, and the Connecticut River. His fine map published in Amsterdam in 1614 identified the whole region between English Virginia and French Canada as 'Nieuw Nederland'.[24]

The dispute between Block and Mossel revealed another bone of contention. One of Mossel's crewmen, 'a mulatto from San Domingo', who had shown himself very adept in dealings with the natives, had been left behind on the island of Mannahatta to spend the winter there alone and continue trading. Block complained in court that the crewman, Jan Rodrigues, a Spanish subject and therefore an enemy, had exceeded his duties. Mossel responded by saying that Rodrigues had jumped ship of his own accord, receiving '80 hatchets, some knives, a musket and a sword' in lieu of wages. At all events, Rodrigues is now widely touted as the first permanent resident of the nascent colony.[25]

The year 1613 is equally the presumed date of the so-called 'Two Row Wampum Treaty' – an agreement supposedly reached somewhere on the upper Hudson River between Dutch representatives and leaders of the Iroquois Federation. The terms of the treaty, in which the parties agreed to be brothers and 'not to steer each other's vessel', were reflected in the pattern of white and purple wampum beads sewn into a long belt, which shows an Indian canoe alongside a European sailing ship. Descendants of the Iroquois claim that the treaty is still valid in the twenty-first century. Questions for the historian include: who could those Dutch representatives have been? And was the treaty confused with a later event?[26]

The ground seemed to have been well prepared, therefore, when, in October 1614, the Estates-General issued a charter of incorporation to the company of the *Nieuw Nederland*. Block and Christiansen were among twelve burghers who had earlier signed a petition to this effect. The concession was granted to settle land on the American seaboard between 45 and 40 degrees latitude. A small trading-post called Fort Nassau was planted in 1615 on an island in the upper reaches of the *Muhheakantuck*, which the Dutch now christened the *Noortrivier*, the 'North River'. But the Spanish War flared; regular supplies were interrupted; trading ceased; and the Dutch East India Company's rights inevitably lapsed.

Finally, in 1621, the Dutch West India Company was chartered to replace its failed predecessor. Capital was again raised, ships were bought, and recruits were found among Protestant refugees. This time the focus was to be on the lower reaches of the 'North River', and this time the venture would not fail.

A curious footnote relates to the English 'Pilgrim Fathers', who had been living in Leiden in the years when the *Nieuw Nederland* project was gestating. These English exiles also knew of Hudson's *Report*, and when their decision was taken to sail from Holland, they, too, intended to make for the Great Bay and the island of Mannahatta. Indeed, having sighted Cape Cod on 9 November 1620, the crew of the *Mayflower* actually attempted to sail down the coast towards the Narrows. It was only because they then ran into fierce currents and dangerous shoals that they changed course and made their permanent landing further north at what became the Plymouth Colony. Had they succeeded in reaching their intended destination, one may presume that a knot of grim-faced English Puritans would have been waiting on the shore when the Dutch arrived.[27]

As it was, the first shipload of Dutch pioneers were landed from the good ship *Nieuw Nederland* in May 1624 without an English reception. They consisted of thirty families, mainly French-speaking Walloon refugees from the southern Netherlands, and they called their initial foothold *Noten Eylant*, 'The Isle of Nuts'. Before the summer was out, some of them were sent upriver to found Fort Orange on the site of Fort Nassau, while others sailed down the coast to found the settlement of *Swaanendael*, 'Swan Valley', on the *Zuidrivier* or 'South River' (which the English Virginians were already calling the Delaware).

The new colony was named 'Nieuw Nederland', like their ship. Its governor was the ship's captain, Cornelis May, and its Council consisted of seven members, whose names in the Burgundian tradition had dual French and Dutch Forms. Franchoys Fezard (Francis Veersaert) built a Dutch-style windmill on Noten Eylant. The settlers' instructions contained a clause from the ordinances of Holland enjoining religious tolerance and protecting freedom of conscience. Their ethos stood in stark contrast to that of the neighbouring, theocratic Plymouth Colony, not to mention the French and Spanish colonies of the era.

In June 1625 more ships reached Nieuw Nederland. The *Oranjeboom* was sent to Swan Valley. But the *Makreel* and three cargo vessels transported forty-five more colonists to the Great Bay together with a substantial delivery of livestock. They also brought a military engineer, Crijn Frederiksz van Lobbrecht, whose task was to lay foundations for a citadel at the tip of the large island overlooking the North River estuary. Fort Amsterdam had to be erected strongly and quickly. The Dutch could only operate freely in periods of truce during the ongoing war with Spain, and a Spanish punishment raid had to be expected at any time.

The first group of blacks, probably from Africa, was brought ashore from a Portuguese ship in the colony's second year. Manpower was in

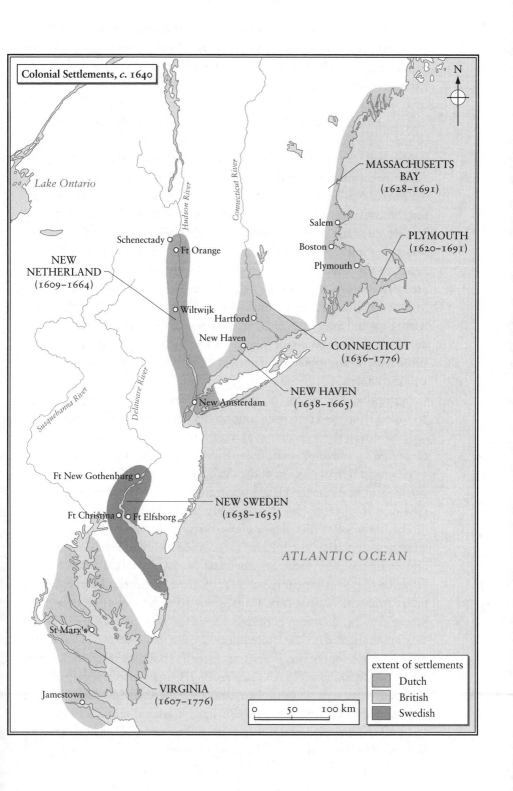

Colonial Settlements, *c.* 1640

N

*Lake Ontario*

MASSACHUSETTS
BAY
(1628–1691)

Salem ○

Schenectady ○
○ Ft Orange

*Hudson River*

*Connecticut River*

Boston ○

PLYMOUTH
(1620–1691)

NEW
NETHERLAND
(1609–1664)

Plymouth ○

○ Wiltwijk

Hartford ○

New Haven ○

CONNECTICUT
(1636–1776)

*Susquehanna River*

*Delaware River*

○ New Amsterdam

NEW HAVEN
(1638–1665)

Ft New Gothenburg ○

Ft Christina ○ ○ Ft Elfsborg

NEW SWEDEN
(1638–1655)

ATLANTIC OCEAN

St Mary's ○

Jamestown ○

VIRGINIA
(1607–1776)

○        50        100 km

extent of settlements
Dutch
British
Swedish

short supply and slavery became an accepted practice, as in other European colonies. The sixteen males, who had been obtained either by sale or kidnap, were classed as the property of the Dutch West India Company, worked under an 'Overseer of Negroes', and lived in separate quarters. The location of the Slave Quarter has been identified as a site on the bank of the East River (very close, appropriately enough, to that of the United Nations Building). Their children remained slaves until adulthood. Over two thousand slaves were imported in the next decade.

Yet in terms of future development the most significant event of the era probably seemed fairly trivial. In 1626, as an afterthought to starting the construction of Fort Amsterdam, the Dutch director of Nieuw Nederland, Peter Minuit, formally bought the island on which the fort was being built. According to later legend, he paid 24 dollars in glass beads to the Lenape who lived there. But the legend is not substantiated. The figure of 24 dollars should be 60 guilders; and the 'beads' included blankets, kettles, and trinkets. Yet the transaction's dubious nature should be self-evident. It was not a valid agreement between equal partners. It no doubt lubricated European consciences, but it was principally a sop to keep the natives quiet while Fort Amsterdam was still incomplete.

Naturally, the views of the Lenape on such matters were not recorded. But the consensus among historians holds that they could only have seen the transaction as a form of lease or allocation. The payment of 60 guilders was not regarded as a sale price but rather as a gift or easement in recognition of the deal. Similar transactions occurred in subsequent years: at the Hell Gate Strait (1637), on western Long Island (1639), at Rockaway (1643), and at Brooklyn (1652).[28]

For forty years the new colony thrived. At its greatest extent it stretched along the North River from Schenectady to Fort Amsterdam, and along the coast from Swaanendael on the Delaware to Fort Good Hope on the Connecticut River (near modern Hartford). Its population, apart from the Native Americans, grew from 270 in 1628 to around 9,000 in 1644, of whom perhaps 10 per cent were black. Close contact was maintained with the United Provinces' larger colony in Dutch Brazil, on whose supply line it became a staging-post. Its inhabitants were highly cosmopolitan. In 1643 a visiting Dutch pastor reported that eighteen languages were spoken, and that the Calvinist majority had been joined by Catholics, English Puritans, Lutherans, and Anabaptists.

In all, Nieuw Nederland was managed by seven governors, the five later ones being known as directors-general:

| 1624–5   | Cornelius May              |
|----------|----------------------------|
| 1625–6   | Willem Verhulst            |
| 1626–32  | Peter Minuit/Pieter Minuyt |
| 1632–3   | Sebastien Crol             |
| 1633–7   | Wouter van Twiller         |
| 1638–47  | Willem Kieft               |
| 1647–64  | Pieter Stuyvesant          |

In 1633 the governor's authority was strengthened by the arrival of a 104-man military detachment, which was stationed in Fort Amsterdam. The soldiers' duties were to guard against the unpredictable conduct both of Indian tribes and of neighbouring colonies. During 1643–5 in 'Kieft's War', bloody engagements were fought against the Wesquae-geek Indians in the southern coastland.

To encourage agriculture, the Dutch West India Company issued a Charter of Privileges and Exemptions (1629). Any settler was entitled to gain possession of any unoccupied tract of land measuring 16 miles on the coast, or 8 miles on either side of a river, on condition, first, of purchasing the land from the Indians, and second, of bringing in fifty adult settlers within four years. On this basis, Michael Pauw established the settlement of Pavonia opposite the 'Isle of Nuts'; and Kilian van Rensselaer established Rensselaerwyck, 145 miles up the North River next to Fort Orange. The entrepreneurs who took advantage of the Charter were called *patroons*. In 1638 the hard-pressed Company abandoned its monopoly on foreign trade. Henceforth, all settlers could engage in commerce so long as their goods were carried in the Company's ships, and taxes were paid. In 1642 a man by the name of Anthony van Corlaer was drowned while attempting to swim the North River at *Spuyten Duyvil*, the 'Devil's Spout'.

The Company also found itself in difficulties around the principle of religious toleration. In the early decades, the authorities could not have afforded to be choosy. But in the 1640s a hard-line Calvinist element surfaced. Attempts were made to exclude both Lutherans and Quakers, and the admission of as well as Catholics, Sephardi Jewish refugees from Dutch Brazil was contested. The Company pointed out that it had Jewish shareholders to consider, and in 1655 full rights were extended to all Jews, both Sephardi and Ashkenazi, cementing a lasting bond. Permission was given to erect a synagogue and open a Jewish burial ground. The Quakers had a harder time. Some were expelled, imprisoned, fined, or even tortured. Others met secretly in John Bowne's house on Long Island. Yet in 1657, after the Flushing Remonstrance had been made public in the Netherlands, the governor was ordered to desist. The Remonstrance had urged 'not to judge lest wee be judged, neither to condemn lest we bee condemned, but rather let every man stand on his own'.

In those same decades, colonists congregated in the shadow of Fort Amsterdam, building houses and laying out streets as far as the boundary wall. All the usual amenities duly followed – a school, post office, poor house, jail, and several windmills and inns. In 1640 a regular ferry to Long Island began to operate, resulting in the growth of a village called Breucklyn beside the eastern landing place. Under Governor Stuyvesant, the harbour wall was strengthened, a pier was built, market squares were defined, and some streets were paved. But Stuyvesant was also a stickler for regulations. He banished Sunday working, introduced harsh punishments for brawling, adultery, and sodomy, enforced a 9 p.m. curfew, and tried to make church attendance compulsory. One of his opponents, Adriaen van der Donck, returned to Holland and complained directly to the Company. The outcome, in 1653, was the grant of a municipal charter, foreseeing an advisory Board of Nine in addition to the executive Council of Seven. The municipality, New Amsterdam, was building self-government.

As the colony expanded, so, too, did the importation of slaves. In the early years they belonged exclusively to the Company. Slave gangs cleared forests, dug roads, and built Fort Amsterdam. In time, however, private citizens were permitted to buy slaves, and use them as domestics or as labourers on their estates. By all accounts, conditions were more benign than in later times. Slaves were accepted as members of the Dutch Reformed Church, and could be formally baptised. They could apply for manumission, which was regularly conceded, and could work for payment. Their numbers increased to around 10,000.

Even so, the Company planned to make New Amsterdam a hub of the international slave trade. The first slave auction was held in 1655, when a large slave-ship, the *Witte Paert*, entered port and offered its cargo for sale at 1,200 silver florins per head. In 1660 a hospital for sick slaves was opened.[29]

The colony's open land borders demanded constant vigilance. There was no fixed frontier, and relations with the native tribes, who moved back and forth, were in constant flux. The tribes themselves were frequently at war. In the north, for example, round the headwaters of the North River, the Iroquois Mohawk Nation was dominant, especially after subjugating their Mohican neighbours. In 1628 the Dutch granted the Mohawk a monopoly on the sale of beaver pelts, selling them guns in return. This arrangement brought temporary peace, while planting the seeds of future disturbance. By arming the Mohawks, the Dutch gave the Iroquois Federation the means to expand their power all the way to the Great Lakes, and in the next generation to launch the murderous Beaver Wars.

As from the 1630s, tensions increased along the growing colony's north-eastern and south-western borders. The English were expanding fast down the coast from New England, and in 1634 they founded New Haven on land that was hitherto considered part of Nieuw Nederland. In 1635 they doubled the threat by founding Fort Saybrook (in honour of Lords Saye and Brook) in a commanding position at the mouth of the Connecticut River, on which stood the Dutch Fort Good Hope (now Hartford). To aggravate matters, the English engineer hired to build Fort Saybrook, Captain Lion Gardiner, a former employee of the Dutch East India Company, had a Dutch wife. In 1639 he obtained a private charter from King Charles I, sealing his purchase of a small strategic island – now called Great Island – facing Saybrook; the 'sale price' paid to the Montaukett tribe, like that for Manhattan, was ludicrous: 'a large black dog, a barrel of powder and shot, and a pile of Dutch blankets'. Outflanked, Governor Stuyvesant felt obliged to retreat and to redraw the frontier west of New Haven. The Dutch-English border on Long Island remained undefined.

Disturbances at the southern end of the colony arose from a multi-sided conflict in the lands around the South River Estuary. There the Dutch were competing both with the English, who were moving up from Virginia and Maryland, and with the Swedes, who in 1638 had set up their short-lived colony of New Sweden around Fort Christina (the modern Wilmington). The Swedes were initially led by none other than Peter Minuit, the former governor of New Amsterdam, whom they had hired; and they skilfully drove a wedge between the English and Dutch. They supported the warlike Susquehannock in trade disputes with the English, and created two up-country strongpoints – one Fort Nya Elfsborg on the South River's left bank, the other Fort Nya Gothenburg on the right bank near modern Philadelphia. Yet in 1654 they overstepped the mark. By capturing the Dutch Fort Casimir (now New Castle, Delaware), they invited retaliation. The next summer, Governor Stuyvesant landed a strong force, crushed resistance, and annexed New Sweden whole.[30]

Over the years, the Dutch grew more familiar with Nieuw Nederland's natives. One prominent tribe, generally known as the 'Wappinger', meaning 'Easterners', were based on the Hudson's eastern bank. Their name exists in dozens of forms including Wappans, Wappinx, and Wabinga, and a score of associated sub-bands have been identified among the Kichtawank, Sinsink, and Wecquaesgeek. Each grouping would have had its own *sachem* or 'chieftain'.

The larger story, however, is that the Native American population continued to decline drastically in the first half of the seventeenth century. Contact with Europeans was proving near-fatal. Commercial collapse played its part. By exchanging fur for Dutch manufactures, the Lenape exhausted local resources. Intertribal wars broke out. The Lenape were seriously harassed by the Iroquois, and in 1632, a large band of Lenape were driven across Delaware Bay into the coastal marshlands of what is now southern New Jersey; ever since, they have been known as the *Unalachtigo* or 'Tidewater Indians'. The Lenape began talking of the Iroquois as their 'uncles', implying tributary status.

Yet the real killer was smallpox. Everywhere that Europeans went in the New World, they brought diseases against which the natives possessed no natural bio-immunity. Infantile contagions such as measles, mumps, or chickenpox could wipe out entire families, and smallpox in the Americas can only be compared to the Black Death. Alcohol, also introduced by the Dutch, caused mass debilitation. Famed for their folk medicine, but not conversant with bacteriology, the Lenape could not explain their vulnerability; their one recourse was to head for the empty but healthy hills. The demography of Lenapehoking was in steep decline long before compulsory deportations were thought of.

Wars with the Dutch only made matters worse. Major conflicts had initially been avoided. But in February 1643, Governor Kieft determined to punish a Lenape tribe, the Weckquaesgeek, who had been driven out of their northern homes by Mohicans and Mohawks, and had set up an illegal refugee camp at *Communipaw* (now Jersey City). A large company of the governor's soldiers descended on the refugees, slaughtering 120:

> Infants were torn from their mother's breasts, and hacked to pieces in the presence of their parents, and pieces thrown into the fire and the water . . . in a manner to move a heart of stone. Some were thrown in the river, and when fathers and mothers endeavoured to save them . . . the soldiers made both parents and children drown . . .[31]

This 'Pavonia Massacre' provoked a general Indian rising. In the autumn of 1643 some 1,500 native warriors spread out over New Netherland, burning farmhouses, pillaging settlements, and killing settlers. This time it was New Amsterdam's turn to be packed with destitute and frightened refugees. The mayhem continued for two years. Eleven tribes participated. A militia was raised to retaliate, and their guns slew thousands. A truce was signed from mutual exhaustion in August 1645, but by then large numbers of colonists had opted to go home.

The 'Peach Tree War' of 1655 involved a similar concerted Indian attack. An army of 500 to 600 warriors assembled by the Susquehannock, and were transported directly by canoe to Manhattan. Bands of painted and feathered braves ran through the streets of New Amsterdam, shouting their war cries, raising havoc, and taking hostages. The attack was said to be in revenge for the murder of a Wappinger girl, who had been caught stealing a peach. In reality, it was the natives' response to Stuyvesant's conquest of New Sweden. The conflict ended after the governor agreed to re-purchase the right of the Dutch to settle land between the North River and the Hackensack River.

Indian wars notwithstanding, the Dutch settlements on Manhattan continued to expand. In 1658 Mynheer Hendrik de Forest established an agricultural village called *Nieuw Haarlem* five miles north of the colony's defensive wall. It probably replaced a farm owned by De Forest, destroyed in the recent war, and known only by its Lenape name of *Muscoota*, meaning 'Flat Place'. The nearby hill (now Mount Morris) was named *Slang Berg*, or 'Snake Hill'. A Dutch Reformed Church was opened on Elmendorf's waterside in 1660. An early engraving of the church clearly depicts an adjacent group of headstones, thought to be part of an African Burial Ground made necessary by casualties among the imported work gangs.[32]

The two Esopus Wars of 1659–60 and 1663 were triggered by the founding of a Dutch outpost at Wiltwijk (now Kingston, New York), sixty miles upriver from New Amsterdam. The local *Esopus* clan of Lenape had repeatedly reacted violently to encroachments in the area, and in September 1659 edgy Dutch settlers attacked a group of exuberant natives who had fired off a musket. Raids and counter-raids persisted for eight months. Four years later a larger explosion was ignited by continuing native discontents. On 7 June 1663 hundreds of Esopus crowded through the open gates of Fort Wiltwijk posing as peaceful traders. Having thus distracted the garrison, they passed the signal to a larger force of warriors who proceeded to demolish the nearby village of Nieu Dorp (now Hurley, New York). Humiliated, the Dutch methodically prepared a punitive expedition under Captain Martin Kriegerand with the aid of Mohawk allies. In August they moved off into the hills, burning native encampments on their way to besieging the main Esopus stronghold. In a pitched battle the Esopus *sachem*, Papequanaehen, perished. Then the tribe dispersed; their stronghold was razed; and the Dutch tramped back to base.

More serious disturbances involved the Iroquois, who had long been warring against the French-backed Indian Nations of the Great Lakes region such as the Huron, and had provoked the so-called 'Beaver Wars'. In 1660, as the Iroquois besieged distant Montreal, the English-backed Susquehanna attacked the Dutch-backed Iroquois-Mohawk, turning tribal quarrels into a far-flung conflagration.

Cultural life in a remote colony was necessarily limited by primitive material conditions and the constant struggle against the elements. Music was restricted to the churches and private houses. Books had to be imported. Yet in three fields – painting, poetry, and prose – New Netherland proved surprisingly creative.[33]

Portrait painting, of course, was a well-established Dutch tradition, and the colonists brought the skills with them. The so-called Patroon School went into business in the 1630s. It was America's first indigenous school. The portrait of the *Rev. Lazare Bayard*, now in the possession of the New-York Historical Society, dates from 1636. Portraits of Governor Stuyvesant and his relatives date from the late 1640s and 1650s. The finest pictures of female subjects, such as *Mrs. David Verplenck* (1718) or *Elsie Rutgers Schuyler* (1723), were painted in the early 1700s. 'Dutch art in all its forms was the first to come to New York.'[34]

New Nederland's select company of poets wrote both in Dutch and Latin. They seem to have had a penchant for lengthy epics. Henryk Selyns (1636–1701) was a pastor. His *Bruydloft Toorts* or *Bridal Torch* (1663) celebrated the marriage of Aegidius Luyck, dean of New Amsterdam's Latin school, to Judith van Isendoorn. It starts with a highly inappropriate line:

> *Hoe ras wordt 't minnevyer door 't oorlogsvyer geblust!*[35]
> (How soon the flame of war the flame of love destroys!)

It goes on to postulate a war between Cupid and Mars, mentioning earthquakes, Indian massacres, and the roasting of captives alive.

It is Jacob Steendam (*c.* 1616–72), however, who is generally accepted as the colony's first poet. He lived in New Amsterdam between 1649 and 1662, and published an anthology of poems there entitled *Der Distelvink* (1650), or *The Goldfinch.* Yet he also appears to have written verse to order. His first substantial work, *Klagt van Nieuw Amsterdam* (1660), or *The Lament of New Amsterdam,* elaborates a litany of discontent provoked by the English conquest. His second, *t'Lof van Nuw Nederland* (1661), reads like a nostalgic company plug for the lost colony:

> *O vrucht-rijk Land, vol zeegens, opgehoopt . . .*

> (O fruitful land! Heaped up with blessings kind
> Who'er your several virtues bring to mind –
> Its proper value to each gift assigned
> Will soon discover.)

And thus for stanza after stanza:

> *Dit is het LAND, daar Melk en Honig vloeyd:*
> *Dit is't geweest, daar't Kruyd (als dist'len) groeyd:*
> *Dit is de Plaats, daar Arons-Roode bloeyd:*
> *Dit is het EDEN.*

> (This is the Land where milk and honey flow,
> Where plants distilling perfumes grow,
> Where Aaron's rod with budding blossoms blow,
> A very Eden.)[36]

It is notable that the poem is dedicated to '*Cornelis van Ruyven, raad en geheymschrijver van de E. West-Indische Maatschap*' ('To Cornelius van Ruyven, counsellor and secretary to the Distinguished West-India Company').[37]

Adriaen van der Donck (*c.* 1618–55), in contrast, was an intellectual of the highest order. Born in Breda and educated at Leiden, he went to America out of a spirit of adventure, working for three years as a *schout* or 'legal officer' for Kiliaen von Rensselaer on his estate in the colony's far north. There, Van der Donck observed the customs of the Mohawks and Mohicans, and learned their language. Fired by Rensselaer, he made himself invaluable to Governor Kieft, who rewarded Van der Donck with 24,000 acres on the mainland north of Manhattan, where he set out his farm at Colen Donck. Under Governor Stuyvesant, he was elected to the advisory 'Board of Nine', then in 1648 to be

President of the Commonality. Constantly agitating for the colony's greater self-government, Van der Donck sailed to remonstrate with the Estates-General in person. He was away for four years; to pass his time during the First Anglo-Dutch War, he composed his beautiful *Beschry-vinge van Nieuw-Nederlant* (*A Description of New Netherland*).[38]

No summary of Van der Donck's *Description*, a masterpiece of topographical prose, can do justice to its elegant style, sustained tone of wonderment, and superb observation of detail. It consists of two main parts, one on 'The Country' divided into thirty-two short chapters, and the other on 'The Original Natives' divided into twenty-six chapters. There follows a longer essay on 'The nature, amazing ways and properties of Beavers', and 'a Conversation between a Dutch Patriot and a New Netherlander'. A fine engraved map shows that Nova Belgica functioned as the alternative Latin name for Nieuw Nederland.[39]

Many sections of the *Description* are based on the earlier *Vertoogh* or 'Remonstrance', which was taken to Amsterdam by the delegation of which Van der Donck was a member. Both documents argue that the colony is a land of wonderful potential that mismanagement by the Verenigde Oost-Indische Compagnie is failing to achieve. Both underline Van der Donck's fascination with the people whom the Dutch called the *Wilder*, 'the Wild Ones':

> The natives are generally well limbed, slender about the waist, broad shouldered, all having black hair and brown eyes; they are very nimble and swift of pace, well adapted to travel on foot and carry heavy burdens. They make light of all hardships, being from youth upward accustomed thereto. They resemble Brazilians in color and are as tawny as those people who sometimes ramble through the Netherlands and are called Gipsies. Generally, the men have little or no beard . . . They use very few words . . . Naturally they are quite modest and without guile . . . [But] as soldiers they are perfidious and accomplish their designs by treachery . . . The thirst for revenge seems innate in them; they are very pertinacious in self-defence . . . and they make little of death, when it is inevitable, and despise all tortures that can be inflicted on them at the stake, exhibiting no faintheartedness, but generally singing until they are dead . . .[40]

Torture, of course, was universal in the seventeenth century, inflicted by Europeans on Europeans and by Indians on Indians. Ironically, it may not be irrelevant to Van der Donck's own untimely death. He disappeared in 1655 during the 'Peach Tree War', aged only 37, presumed killed.

\*

Wars between the European powers posed a different scale of threat. Seventeenth-century practice permitted belligerents to seize their enemy's colonies, and to exploit them pending peace negotiations. Maritime rivalry between England and the United Provinces, therefore, spelled danger for Nieuw Nederland. Three Anglo-Dutch Wars were fought during 1652–4, 1664–7, and 1672–4. New Netherland escaped the First War. But on 27 August 1664 four English frigates commanded by Colonel Richard Nicolls, agent for the Lord High Admiral, the Duke of York (the future James II), sailed into the harbour of New Amsterdam. Between them the *Guinea*, *Elias*, *Martin*, and *William and Nicholas* carried ninety-two guns and 450 soldiers. Volunteers from New England were camped in Breucklyn. Officers from the fleet demanded the surrender of 'the town on the island commonly known by the name of Manhatoes with all the forts thereunto belonging'. Governor Stuyvesant did not possess the means to resist. In the Articles of Transfer he inserted a clause about freedom of religion aimed to preserve Calvinists from the fate of English non-conformists. In the climate of England's Restoration, when Cromwell's corpse had been exhumed and publicly hanged, he was pushing his luck. But Nicholls sensibly sought to win over the burgesses of New Amsterdam. Dutch citizens were free to stay or leave. Equal rights were proclaimed. Nieuw Nederland was renamed New York; Fort Amsterdam became Fort James; Fort Orange – Albany and the North River – became the Hudson. The Treaty of Breda (1667) left these local arrangements intact. Yet this first English occupation would not last for long.[41]

One change of lasting importance, however, was totally unexpected. Shortly after the English conquest, it transpired that the Duke of York had promised to gift the southern section of Nieuw Nederland to his supporter, Vice-Admiral Sir George Carteret (1610–80), a Jerseyman, who thereby proceeded to take possession of 'New Jersey' as a separate, proprietary colony. The administrators on Manhattan, who had earlier named the territory south of the Bay 'Albania', weren't even informed. Initial relations between New York and New Jersey were rocky. The *Lenapehoking* was divided in two. And the former New Sweden, now renamed West Jersey, was cut off from New England. The Duke of York's royalist entourage, of course, had no sympathy for the 'Roundheads' of New England: New York was to administer the southern sector of Massachusetts.

As it happened, the English were given barely six years to consolidate. A post road was opened to Boston, thereby linking New York to

New England. A mayor was appointed by the governor, and the city limits were extended to the whole of Manhattan, incorporating the hamlet of New Harlem, now renamed Lancaster. An improved *Breede Weg* or 'Broadway' linked one end of the island to the other. Outlying districts on Long Island and Staten Island formed a new county called, predictably, 'Yorkshire'.

The Dutch took their revenge in the summer of 1673. On the outbreak of the Third Anglo-Dutch War, the Zeeland Chamber of the West Indies Company fitted out a huge fleet consisting of twenty-one ships and 1,600 troops under Vice-Admiral Cornelis Evertsen. Having raided English possessions in the Caribbean and Virginia, Evertsen's flagship, the *Swaenenburgh*, sailed into New York harbour on 30 July, training its guns on Fort James. English cannon were spiked by Dutch saboteurs; 600 Dutch marines marched down Broadway; and the English commander was called on 'to restore the country's obedience to their High Mightinesses, the Lords States General'. This time, 'with the enemy in our Bowells', it was the turn of the English governor to surrender. The colony returned to the status quo ante. New York was renamed New Orange.[42]

Once again, however, the switch in fortunes did not last. Although their naval campaigns were prospering, the Dutch were heavily defeated on land, and their government was forced to reset its alliances. The Anglo-Dutch Treaty of Westminster (1674) was dictated by the preceding 'years of disaster', and the abandonment of New Netherland was part of the agreed price. The United Provinces, attacked simultaneously by Louis XIV and by England, had come close to calamity. The Stadtholder, William of Orange, realizing his mistakes, prepared for a rapprochement with England and a political marriage with Charles II's daughter, Mary. When news broke of King Charles's secret contacts with the Catholic French, England's House of Commons demanded a parallel realignment of foreign policy. The English and the Dutch would now confront Louis XIV in unison. And though none of them could have foreseen it, the Stadtholder would soon be King of England.

Assessing their colonial empire, the Dutch now decided that their North American venture had harmed their principal interests. The Dutch East Indies were the first priority. The Royal Navy was building bigger and stronger ships; and its Atlantic dominance could no longer be contested. England's American colonies were multiplying – Carolina, Virginia, Maryland, Rhode Island, New Jersey, New York, Connecticut, Massachusetts, and Maine – and one isolated Dutch colony could not hold its own among them. In essence, therefore, 'New Orange' had to be traded in against the Celebes. The English could keep New Netherland if they stopped disputing Dutch possessions elsewhere. Manhattan could be swapped for the island of Rhun.* At the time, back in The Hague, the deal seemed a fair one. To New York's Dutch it was a dirty sell-out.[43]

The deal, however, presented the returning English with many headaches. During the brief existence of New Orange, several frontier disputes had flared up; the Beaver Wars continued unresolved; and the French were challenging control of Nova Scotia. Immediately after the surrender of New Orange, one of the bloodiest of all the Indian Wars broke out in Massachusetts against the Grand Sachem of the Wampanoag Tribe, Metacomet. In 1675, after six men from Metacomet's tribe had been tried and hanged for the murder of a Christian convert, a general native rising erupted. Metacomet, whom the colonists called 'King Philip', was hunted down and killed, but peace was not quickly restored.

Such was the setting for the far-sighted vision towards the Indians of Sir Edmund Andros, governor of restored New York from 1674 to 1681, and later of Virginia, Maryland, and the united Dominium of New England. Andros later gained a reputation among the colonists for high-handiness, but in regard to native affairs he was the architect of a scheme that brought relative calm and stability for many decades, and which came to be known as the Covenant Chain. In 1676, having created a Department of Indian Affairs, he signed a treaty with the Mohawks, which ended 'King Philip's War'. Henceforth a Council of chiefs and colonial representatives was to meet regularly at Albany. In 1677 a second treaty brought in the whole Iroquois Confederation and the Lenape.[44]

A further link to the Covenant Chain was added by William Penn's establishment of his new Quaker colony, which started life in the Delaware Valley on a section of the *Lenapehoking* originally developed by New Sweden. Exceptionally, Penn had written to the native chiefs prior to his arrival, and in November 1682 at the Lenape village of Shackamaxon he met with Chief Tamanend, head of the Lenape Turtles, to express his goodwill but also to secure what he regarded as a purchase

---

* Rhun or Pulau Run, the focal point of the Banda Islands, now in Indonesia, was the prime source of nutmeg and mace, and it remained in Dutch hands until 1945.

of land. 'When the purchase was agreed,' he wrote, 'great promises passed between us of kindness and good neighbourhood, and that the Indians and the English must live in love as long as the sun gave light.' This unminuted meeting became legendary. Voltaire praised it as 'the only treaty that was never sworn to and never broken'. And long after his death, 'King Tammany' became an icon of early American patriotism.[45]

Records of New Netherland are in plentiful supply for those who can read Old Dutch. Extensive archival collections exist both in Amsterdam and in New York. In the 1960s a cache of a further 12,000 original documents was discovered in the New York Public Library and is still being researched.[46]

Yet the pictorial and cartographic records are equally impressive. The progress of the colony can be followed through the maps and prints that were very much in fashion. The earliest item of interest is Adrian Block's Map of 1614, which presents the Atlantic coast from 'Virginia' to 'Nova Franciae, Pars' (Nova Scotia). The central area, on the coast and in the interior, is shaded blue almost as far as the future Cape Cod, implying some form of claim, and the name NIEUW NEDERLANDT spreads right across the map to Canada.[47]

The work of Joan Vingboon, the colony's map-maker, is both attractive and informative. His map of Manhattan entitled *MANATUS* (1639) was discovered in a private collection in 1892; in addition to the layout of New Amsterdam, it features an inset containing a numbered list of the main *bouveries* or 'farms' and plantations, together with the names of their owners. It proved an invaluable aid to researchers who were able to reconstruct a comprehensive survey both of the exact identity and provenance of the settlers and of their colonial properties. Vingboon's watercolour *Gezicht op Nieuw Amsterdam* (1664), was painted in the very last weeks prior to the English conquest.[48]

The so-called Castello Plan (1660) was drawn by the surveyor of New Amsterdam, Jacques Cortelyou, at the very end of the Dutch period. It is remarkably similar to a modern satellite image, showing individual houses, trees, and gardens; and it is known in two versions, one in monotone sepia, the other colour-painted. The area covered, at the tip of Manhattan, stretches from the South Pier to the open country immediately beyond the Wall. The harbour, and inner harbour, are clearly visible. Fort Amsterdam, star-shaped with four massive bastions at the corners, stands at the bottom of the West Side, overlooking the cannons of its artillery park, or 'battery'. The Broad Way starts immediately north of the Fort as a wide, open space surrounding the bowling green, then gradually narrows until it is only three or four times larger than the average street. Two hundred yards or so to the east ran another Dutch-style Broad Street, with carriageways on either side of a canal. The Great Wall itself had seven bastions evenly spaced over half a mile from West Side to East Side, where it was extended along the riverfront towards the Battery. Almost all the houses back onto gardens; and orchards grace the unoccupied blocks. North of the Wall, a few buildings are marked on Broad Way, and on the East Side riverfront, where the Stuyvesant farm once stood. But the cityscape mostly gives immediate way to green fields.

The Plan was engraved in Holland. One copy, bound into a volume sold to Italy, came to light in the library of the Villa Castello in Florence around the turn of the twentieth century. Its details agree very closely with the much simpler, English 'Duke's Plan', dated 1664, otherwise A DESCRIPTION OF THE TOWNE OF MANNADOS OR NEW AMSTERDAM, which purports to show the city as it had been three years earlier.[49]

In contrast, as its name suggests, the 'Restitutio' map appears to date from the period 1673–8 when New Netherland was reclaimed by the Dutch. The author was Hugo Allard, and the full title TOTIUS NEOBELGII NOVA ET ACCURATISSIMA TABULA (A New and Precise Representation of the Whole of New Netherland). It covers the area from the Atlantic Seaboard to 'Quebeqc', and from Delaware to the Connecticut River. Some of the place names such as Lange Eylandt are in Dutch, others like Nieu Jarsey are in semi-English. The details in the Hudson Valley are too crowded to be read even with a magnifying glass. But Fort Orange stands out, as do many of the Indian tribal names.

Allard had produced the original copperplate as early as 1656; and the view in the bottom right-hand corner shows the city's appearance sometime before that. Seventeen years later, however, the map was reissued with a completely new graphic, etched by Romeyn de Hooghe, who reconstructed the scene of 24 August. Dutch warships ride at anchor in the harbour. A cannon is firing a salute from the battery. A large body of troops is marching along the waterfront. And the Dutch flag flies on a high mast. The caption reads: 'New Amsterdam previously called New York, and recaptured by the Netherlands on 24 August 1673.' Copies were reissued in Holland through the eighteenth century.[50]

The cartography of New Netherland exudes an authentic period appeal. Peering at the map by Gerritsz and De Leat, *Nova Anglia, Novum Belgium et Virginia* (1630), which first publicized the names of New Netherland and New Amsterdam, one feels the wonder of contemporaries struggling to imagine the new continent. Examining the fine sailing chart by Pieter Goos, *Nieu Nederlandt en de Engelsche Virginies* (1666), one realizes the breathtaking skill of the ship's captains. And admiring Peter Schenk's engraving *Nieu Amsterdam* (1702), lovingly copied from Romeyn de Hooghe and others, one feels the nostalgia for the lost colony, which long pained Dutch hearts.[51]

The population of New Netherlands had consisted of three main groups: firstly, the Native Americans, above all the Lenape; secondly, the Dutch settlers; and thirdly, the black slaves, whose numbers were greater than their meagre records suggest. Each group continued in place after England's takeover, until all were gradually overtaken by the new immigrants.

The eighteenth century saw the terminal decline of the Lenape in their original homeland. In 1737 the heirs and successors of William Penn perpetrated the so-called 'Walking Purchase', which is widely regarded as a blatantly fraudulent land grab: over 1 million acres of land acquired in Pennsylvania, which the Lenape were then forced to vacate. The portrait of Chief Lapowinsa, who signed the agreement, was painted at the time by Gustavus Hesselius.[52] Twenty year later, at the time of the French and Indian Wars, the Lenape figured among several native nations who were cajoled and bribed to accept the Treaty of Easton (1757), whereby they were either transferred into reservations, like that at Brotherton, New Jersey, or pushed across the Frontier into the Ohio Territory. They were starting a tortuous odyssey that would take their scattered descendants to Oklahoma, Kansas, Wisconsin, Ontario, and even Texas. Some were led by missionaries of the Moravian Church, who had started to evangelize earlier and who launched the so-called 'Christian Munsee'.[53]

The Dutch community of Nieuw Nederland stayed on to act as leaven to the immigrant masses that followed. As the original trend-setters in many fields, they had no small impact on the final outcome. Their gradual assimilation took place in the century that followed the Treaty of Westminster. In the first stage, during the fourth quarter of the seventeenth century, when the Dutch were still in a majority, they played the central role in negotiating the city's new system of self-government, culminating in the New York Assembly and the City Charter (1686). They also sympathized with the rebellion of Jakob Leisler, a German merchant who had withheld his taxes from 'a Papist', namely James II, and who in 1689–90, aided by the municipal militia, overran the entire city. Leisler's supporters were driven by the feeling that the king had reneged on agreements. Order was restored by the accession of 'William and Mary', that is, of joint Dutch and English monarchs.

The Dutch long remained influential among the mercantile classes; and they are clearly visible in the struggles against successive English and British governors, striving for press freedom and the independence of the judiciary. In 1733–5, for example, during a dispute between Governor Cosby and the president of the Council, Rip van Dam, a newspaper editor John Zenger was imprisoned for refusing to obey the governor's orders, and the chief justice was dismissed for refusing to condemn the editor. Zenger's acquittal at a jury trial is seen as a milestone in the rule of law.[54]

Several prominent families held on to their status right into the era of American Independence and beyond. The Schuylers, the van Burens, and the van Cortlandts retained their property and original identity for many generations. Others, such as the Roosevelts, Rutgers, or Rockefellers, cherished their Dutch descent, and supported the Dutch Reformed Church. In the 1880s William H. Vanderbilt (1821–85) was reputed to be America's richest man, and Mrs Vanderbilt's annual 'Fancy Dress Ball' provided the occasion where the 'List of 400' of the city's elite families was drawn up.

Many Dutch place names were retained, but in anglicized form. Breucklyn became Brooklyn, Haarlem – Harlem, Vlissingen – Flushing, and *Konynen Eylant* – Coney Island. Block Island was named for Adriaen Block, the Bronx for Jonas Bronck, and Staten Island for the Dutch Estates-General. Noten Island, the original landing place, was renamed Governors Island.

New York's black slave community, like the Dutch, did not migrate or disappear, but neither, for the most part, did it assimilate. The slaves stayed on, largely unnoticed, living apart from genteel society and suffering under English laws of intensifying severity. Charles II ruled that no Christians could be enslaved. As a result, blacks were excluded from the Churches, and in 1687 were barred from burial in the churchyards, thereby requiring the establishment of a separate 'Negro Burial Ground'. Bans were introduced against entertaining blacks in houses, against serving them alcohol, against buying goods from them, against their right of assembly, against their acting as witnesses in court, and against their walking in the street at night without a lantern. The city employed a 'Chief Whipper' to inflict punishment on offenders; runaways were to be put to death. In 1703, 42 per cent of all New York households were slave-owners.

In the course of that century, the desperate lot of the black slaves barely improved. In 1712 and again in 1741 panic spread amidst rumours of a slave revolt; executions and burnings-at-the-stake ensued.[55] Slave-trading multiplied. As from 1711, a permanent slave-market operated on Wall Street, and New York harbour acted as the base to a fleet of fast slave-ships that could make the return trip to Africa in forty days. Almost 5,000 slaves were imported up to 1769; merchants' profits soared, and the city's coffers filled with taxes. By 1771, 20,000 slaves lived in New York within a total population of 168,000, making it second only to Charleston as a slave-city. Opposition, however, grew. During the War of Independence, when the British Army occupied New York, freedom was promised to all blacks who joined the British ranks. As from 1785, when New York started its brief shift as the new nation's capital, the Manumission Society was active; and one-third of the city's blacks were freed. Yet full abolition only took place in 1827. Anyone who imagines that American slavery was confined to the Deep South is mistaken.

Contemporary records, however, rarely convey the full reality. In July 1776, when American Independence was declared, crowds gathered on the Bowling Green in Lower Manhattan to witness a patriotic ceremony. The centrepiece of the action was to be the toppling of an equestrian statue of King George III, which had been erected there in the previous decade. A surviving print from the era shows how the demolition was done. A number of ropes were fastened around the monarch's head and that of his horse, and a gang of black slaves, stripped to the waist, were brought in to heave on the ropes in rhythmic unison and to pull the monument crashing down. Yet half a century later, when the scene was painted for posterity by the German-American clergyman and artist Johannes Oertel (1823–1909), the details were incomplete. The picture now hangs in the museum of the New-York Historical Society, and one can see the sleight of hand for oneself.[56] The statue and a crowd of pale-faced onlookers are depicted. A family of feathered Native Americans is prominently displayed on the left-hand side. But the Afro-American slave gang that actually did the work is nowhere to be seen. Such was the self-image that the newly liberated citizens wished to portray.

*

Interest in the historical origins of New York gathered pace in the early nineteenth century, and has never eased. The first academic survey was published in 1829.[57] But it had been preceded twenty years earlier by an extraordinary work of long-lasting influence. Washington Irvine's *History of New York* (1809)[58] did not pretend to accuracy or to scientific method; it was a brilliant satire purporting to be authored by an imaginary Dutch scholar, Dr Diedrich Knickerbocker. Becoming extremely popular, it contrived to raise public awareness of numerous basic issues. Book I, Chapter V, for instance, deals with Europeans' supposed entitlement to seize other people's land. 'The first source of right, by which property is acquired in a country,' Irvine wrote, 'is DISCOVERY ... nothing being necessary ... but simply to prove that [America] was totally uninhabited':

> This would at first appear to be a point of some difficulty, for it is well known that this quarter of the world abounded with certain animals that walked erect on two feet, had something of the human countenance, uttered certain unintelligible sounds very like language, in short had a marvellous resemblance to human beings. But the zealous and enlightened fathers, who accompanied the discoverers for the purpose of promoting the kingdom of heaven ... soon cleared up this point ... They plainly proved ... that the two-legged race of animals before mentioned were mere cannibals, detestable monsters ... giants ... and outlaws.[59]

The next significant volume was published anonymously in 1853, describing itself as a 'Historical Sketch'. It was, in fact, a substantial text covering more than two centuries between the arrival of Henry Hudson and the introduction of gaslight. It presents an uncritical account of the transition of New Netherland to the 'just and liberal rule' of the English. Yet despite a fondness for purple passages, it has some striking moments. The opening page begins not with the 'Discovery' but with 'A Strange Sight':

> On the 3rd day of September, in the year 1609, a strange and unaccountable phenomenon was witnessed by the wandering savages who happened to be in ... the place where the waters of the Lower Bay unite with the ocean. A creature of a size and proportions that quite surpassed their conceptions, came moving as if self-impelled across the face of the water, apparently ascending from the clouds or coming from the dim and mysterious regions of the great deep. Passing through the entrance that leads from the untamed wastes of the wide ocean into the sleeping or sporting ripples of the inland bay, the wonderful stranger advanced to a

considerable distance onward, and then stopped suddenly, and remained unmoved.[60]

A Native American perspective is not what everyone expected in 1853.

In that mid-century, efforts were made to introduce professional standards to New York's history-making. The city appointed a young historian who was instructed to copy documents from archives in Britain, France, and the Netherlands.[61] The outcome was the first document-based history of the city[62] and the launch of two vast collections of printed documents.[63] In 1895 the State of New York appointed the first of its long line of official historians.

On several occasions, leaders of New York's Dutch community expressed dissatisfaction at historians' disparagement of Nieuw Nederland. Their feelings no doubt underlay the decision of their circle's most prominent man to try his hand himself. Still in his thirties, the young historian was a man of uncommon energy, a big-game hunter, a rancher in the Dakota Territory, and a rising politician.[64] He would soon be governor of New York State, whence his aphorism of 'Speak softly and carry a big stick' would travel round the world. His view of the city's history avoided the Native Americans almost completely:

> Early in September 1609, the ship *Half-Moon* restlessly skirting the American coast, in a vain quest for . . . a water route to India, came to the mouth of a great lonely river, flowing silently from the heart of the unknown continent . . .[65]

It also takes pains to underplay the English element of the story. 'The bulk of the population,' one reads, 'has never been English.' Judgement of the transformation of New Amsterdamers into New Yorkers was very positive:

> The comparative rapidity of the fusion of [Dutch and English] in New York . . . stands in sharp contrast to the slowness of intermingling where the English and their successors have moved into communities of Catholic French or Spaniards.[66]

When the book was reprinted in 1906, its author, Theodore Roosevelt, was already in the fifth year of the USA's twenty-sixth presidency.

Advocates of the Native Americans have often complained that the first inhabitants were forgotten. One writes eloquently of the city's amnesia:

> [New York] is a city of displaced people in a displaced world . . . [It] doesn't know its past. It steams blindly towards the future like a ship

without a rudder. It is a city of amnesia; [and], like a person so afflicted, it doesn't know what is missing.

Nowhere is the displacement of a great people by another great people so complete . . . Nowhere is the contrast more dramatic between what was lost and what replaced it. Over the last five hundred years, the great metropolis of the nature-loving Lenape . . . has been completely eradi-cated and replaced by a culture in denial of the natural world. The long history, geography [and wisdom] of the previous culture were cast aside in a frenzied rush to the future; their humble pathways were buried deep beneath the dust of progress, their ochred bones crushed and crusted over with miles of concrete and asphalt . . .[67]

The pessimism, however, is somewhat misplaced. One of the best-loved American historical novels, James Fenimore Cooper's *The Last of the Mohicans* (1826), put the lost heritage of the local tribes into the fore-front of attention. Set in 1757, it recounts the fictional adventures of a group of frontiersmen in the midst of the Indian Wars, and skilfully reconstructs the mentalities of both Europeans and Indians. The chief hero, Natty Bumppo, known as Hawk-eye and based on the real-life Daniel Boone, is a white man raised by Indians; his companion, Chin-gachgook, is a Lenape warrior. One day they are discussing the origins of their respective peoples:

'Your fathers came from the setting sun,' said Hawk-eye, 'crossed the big river, fought the people of the country, and took the land; and mine came from the red sky of the morning, over the salt lake, and did their work much after the fashion that had been set by yours. Then let God judge the matter between us, and friends spare their words.'

'My fathers fought with the naked red-man,' returned the Indian sternly, in the same language. 'Is there no difference, Hawk-eye, between the stone-headed arrow of the warriors, and the leaden bullet with which you kill?'[68]

On the last page, Chief Tamenund delivers the heart-breaking judgement:

'It is enough', he said. 'Go, children of the Lenape . . . The pale-faces are masters of the earth, and the time of the red-men has not yet come again. My day has been too long. In the morning, I saw the sons of Unamis happy and strong; and yet, before the night, have I lived to see the last warrior of the wise race of the Mohicans.'[69]

The huge popularity of Fenimore Cooper's novel helped boost growing interest in Native American culture. Other impulses came from

Christian missionaries, philologists, and ethnographers. David Zeisberger (1721–1808), a Moravian from Germany, ministered to the
Lenape in their Ohio exile and composed the first ever grammar of
their language.[70] Daniel G. Brinton (1837–99), a pioneer of Amerindian
studies, published works on ethnography, comparative religion, mythology, and philology, including a Lenape-English Dictionary. The
dictionary's introduction opens magnificently: 'Whoever will speak in
Indian,' one reads, 'must learn to think in Indian.'[71]

In 1855 Americans were treated to, and often shocked by, the publication of Walt Whitman's first volume of uninhibited, unmetred free
verse. It contained a poetic invocation of New York inspired by its
'upsprung aboriginal name':

> Now I see what there is in a name, a word, liquid, sane, unruly,
>     musical, self-sufficient;
> I see the word nested in nests of water-bays, superb with tall and
>     wonderful spires,
> Rich, hemm'd thick with sailships and steamships – an island
>     sixteen miles long, solid-founded;
> Numberless crowded streets – high growths of iron, slender,
>     strong, light, splendidly uprising towards clear skies; . . .
> The down-town streets, the jobbers' houses of business – the
>     houses of business of the ship-merchants and money-brokers –
>     the river-streets;
> Immigrants arriving, fifty or twenty thousand in a week . . .
> Trottoirs throng'd – vehicles – Broadway – the women, the shops
>     and the shows,
> The parades, the processions, bugles blowing, flags waving, drums
>     beating;
> A million people – manners free and superb – open voices –
>     hospitality;
> The free city, the beautiful city, the city of hurried and sparkling
>     waters,
> The city of spires and masts, the city nested in bays! My city![72]

More than a century on from Walt Whitman and 'Teddy' Roosevelt,
people still wonder how much New York's formative decades may have
determined its contemporary character. Contrary to expectations, some
descendants of the Lenape survived, and the Museum of the American
Indian has occupied a fine building in the heart of Lower Manhattan
since 1922. The brainchild of the anthropologist George Gustav Heye

(1874–1957), it seeks to illustrate the broad spectrum of pre-Columbian societies rather than regional nations.[73]

Anyone intent on tracking down present-day traces of the Lenape has to drive westwards two or three hours out of New York into the hills bordering New Jersey and Pennsylvania. They first see signposts to Lenape Valley, New Jersey. In Allentown, they find a Lenape Museum of Indian Culture in an old farmhouse.[74] The cultural centre of the Lenape Nation of Pennsylvania functions at Easton.

Small groups of Lenape survivors are alive and well even within the historic *Lenapehoking*. They go under a variety of names – Lenape, Delaware, Lenni-Lenape, Nanticoke, and Unalachtigo; and they frequently seem to be at cross purposes. The Nanticoke Lenni-Lenape Tribe, for example, which has been a registered body since 1978 claiming 3,000 enrolled members, is fiercely opposed to the gaming concessions that support many Native American communities. The rival 'Unalachtigo Band of the Nanticoke Lenni-Lenape Nation' takes the opposite view. Their leader, James Brent Thomas Jnr, is said to be intent on setting up a casino close to New York City.[75] To see more substantial groups one needs to travel either to Oklahoma or to Ontario.

The move to preserve Lenape culture was long overdue. The overwhelming majority of modern 'Delawares' speak English. The Unami language is extinct, and only a handful of Munsee speakers are holding out. Nonetheless, since the 1970s, the rise of the Native American Movement or 'Red Power' has strengthened consciousness. Thanks to the internet, genealogy and local history are enhanced. No fewer than 87,241 registered New Yorkers claim Native American descent, and an American Indian Community House, representing seventy-two nations, operates off Broadway.[76]

Academic study of the Lenape is now firmly established. The pioneer was Clinton A. Weslager (1909–94), a local historian, whose book *The Delaware Indians* (1972) proved both influential and readable.[77] The archaeologist Herbert Kraft (1927–2000), of Seton Hall University, pushed the topic further with *The Lenape or Delaware Indians* (1996) and *The Lenape-Delaware Indian Heritage* (2001).[78] Jack D. Forbes (1934–2011), partly of Lenape descent, was a founding member of the Native American Movement and used his exploration of Lenape culture to pursue its aims.[79]

Since myths and songs have always formed a central part of Lenape culture, it is not surprising that some of the present-day enthusiasts employ fiction and poetry as vehicles for the revival. Jake George, for instance, has authored two Lenape novels;[80] Jack Forbes has published Lenape poems, which he calls *Lenaapay Aasheem-Aaptonakaana* or 'Dream Words':

HOO PAY-YOK

| | |
|---|---|
| *Aasheem aaptonakaana* | Dream words |
| *hoo pay-yok* | they will come |
| *nai-yoo topeenay-yo* | they are here |
| *sheekee aaptonakaana* | pretty words |
| *kaashee aaptonakaana* | strong words |
| *chipee aaptonakaana* | dangerous words |
| *xengwee aaptonakaana* | big words |
| *tokay aaptonakaana* | soft words |
| *aasheem aaptonakaana* | dream words |
| *hoo pay-yok* | they will come.[81] |

Children's fiction, tribal stories, and language aids all thrive, not least online.[82]

The Dutch legacy, in contrast, has never been an endangered species. New York acquired some of its outstanding present-day characteristics from the Dutch. Its entrepreneurial spirit was nurtured in Dutch soil. New York's religious tolerance was exceptional among the founding colonies. Its republicanism, its desire for self-government, and its cosmopolitanism were always present. It is no accident that Europe's religious minority par excellence, the Jews, flocked to New York during the nineteenth and twentieth centuries, making it the largest Jewish metropolis on Earth, just as their forebears once flocked to Amsterdam.[83] New York was no foundling; it had a pedigree, a purposeful upbringing, and a vigorous start to life. America's greatest port city was the child of one of Europe's prime ports. Amsterdam's legacy was much more significant than the superficial link with English York.

Dutch Americans, who now number some 5 million, enjoy established esteem. Apart from the two Roosevelt presidents, they include the early tycoon Cornelius Vanderbilt, who started his career on Hudson River steamboats, Humphrey Bogart, the film actor and star of *Casablanca*, and the celebrated painter Willem de Kooning. More recent celebrities include Bruce Springsteen, Dick Van Dyke, and Jane Fonda.[84]

At 3.5 million, New York's black population represents a quarter of

the total. In the shadow of the 'Great Migration' from the South after the Civil War, memories of its earlier history were passed over. Historians charted the rise of black neighbourhoods in Brooklyn in the nineteenth century, or of Harlem in the 1920s and 1930s, but not, for much of the time, the community's origins.[85] And the demographics constantly change. A quarter of today's New York blacks are foreign-born – mainly from Jamaica, Haiti, or Puerto Rico.

The recent discovery of large-scale human remains during building work at Foley Square in Lower Manhattan, therefore, made headline news. The site of the 'Negro Burial Ground' had been completely forgotten and built over. Excavations showed that the cemetery contained the burial sites of up to 20,000 people from the colonial period. They inspired the groundbreaking exhibition on 'Slavery in New York', mounted by the New-York Historical Society in 2005. The 'African Burial Ground National Monument' was consecrated in 2009.[86]

*

The foundation of New Amsterdam was the result of a protracted process that lasted for sixteen years from Hudson's 'discovery' in 1609 to the landing of the first colonists in 1624. One may assume that celebrations of the city's quatercentenary will be equally protracted.

Anniversaries are memory prompts. People remember birthdays; states remember their independence days; cities remember the dates of their foundation. Unfortunately, there are far too many anniversaries to mark with any significance, and everyone is left with painful choices.

Memorial sites are produced by the same problem. Amidst the clamour of competing claims, they come into being in order to ensure that some particular person, place, or event is publicly remembered, whereas others are not. They inevitably reflect the preferences of the choosers. The selection of the memory-selectors is key. In 1909, for the tercentenary, monuments were erected to Verrazzano in Battery Park and to Hudson at Spuyten Duyvil in the Bronx.

The beginning of the most recent round of celebrations passed off in style in 2009 during the 'NYC400' Festival. On 8 September a full-scale replica of Hudson's *Half Moon* sailed into New York Harbour escorted by a Dutch flotilla. Next day, Prince Willem Alexander of the Netherlands opened the Pavilion in Battery Park, a gift from the Dutch government. A glittering display of 50,000 Dutch lilies and tulips adorned the city's Botanical Garden; a procession of flat-bottomed Dutch barges sailed up the Hudson; and a reconstruction of the village of New Amsterdam could be visited in Bowling Green Park. The Museum of the City of New York staged an exhibition called 'Amsterdam – New Amsterdam: The Worlds of Henry Hudson'; and the South Street Seaport Museum followed suit with an exhibition entitled 'Island at the Center of the World'; the prize exhibit was the letter of 5 November 1626 reporting 'the purchase of Manhattan'. An art colony, 'Boulevard of Broken Dreams', was installed on Governors Island, the springboard for New York's entire history, where proposals also exist to open a 'Park of Tolerance'.[87]

Good intentions, however, are easily knocked off course. In the first decade of the twenty-first century, for example, preliminary preparations for the quatercentenary were overtaken by a rush for the remembrance of '9/11'. And plans to redevelop Ground Zero were beset by public objections, flaming rows, ballooning costs, and massive delays. Vitriol of unprecedented proportions erupted in 2010, when an application for planning permission was lodged for an Islamic Cultural Center (ICC) in nearby Park Place. Headlines denounced the 'Ground

Zero Mosque'. Protesters gathered with placards announcing ISLAM
BUILDS MONUMENTS AT THE SITE OF ITS CONQUEST. President Obama
intervened.

'We in New York are Jews, Christians and Muslims, and always
have been,' declared the city's mayor, Michael Bloomberg, in support.
'There is nowhere in the five boroughs that is off limits to religion.'

But the protests redoubled. Ex-mayor Rudy Giuliani condemned the
'desecration'. Rabbi Meyer May labelled the ICC's organizers 'idiots'.
And Mark Williams of the Tea Party railed against 'a mosque for the
worship of the terrorists' Monkey God'.

'There should be no mosque at Ground Zero,' huffed Republican
leader Newt Gingrich, 'so long as there are no churches or synagogues
in Saudi Arabia.'

Despite the invective, planning permission was granted, and the
ICC started to function at 'Park51' in 2011. And the much-modified
memorial skyscraper '1WTC' finally emerged in November 2014, the
city's most expensive and tallest building.

One fact may help ease another looming collision. Both Fort Amsterdam and the World Trade Center stood close to the point to which
those millions of immigrants, the 'wretched refuse of your teeming
shore', were brought in from Ellis Island. If Fort Amsterdam had not
been demolished, the first thing seen by those immigrants would have
been the Dutch-designed and slave-built fortress. Here is the spot where
the memories of New Amsterdam and of '9/11' could be best reconciled. The act of American history most worthy of remembrance has
always been that first step into the 'Melting Pot', 'The Land of the Free'.

All of which reminds us that migration is a central feature of human
history. It brought the Anglo-Saxons into post-Roman Britain, including Cornwall. It propelled the Turkic tribes into Azerbaijan, the Moguls
into India, the Chinese into Malaya and Singapore, the Africans and
Indians into Mauritius, the British into Tasmania and New Zealand,
the Polynesians into the Pacific, and the Americans into Texas. The
Pilgrim Fathers were refugees. The teeming mass of steerage passengers
arriving at Ellis Island were economic migrants. Migration built the
world's most powerful state, and its 'biggest Apple'.

# 13

# Transatlantic

*Sunwise and Withershins*

One of the Earth's permanent characteristics is that it moves by laevorotation – in other words, it spins on its axis in a direction that the modern English language calls 'anticlockwise' and American usage 'counterclockwise'. For anyone preparing to cross the Atlantic, this fact has a considerable bearing. It determines the movement of prevailing winds and weather systems, and hence influences the speed of ships on the sea and planes in the air. In the jet age, a non-stop eastbound flight between New York and Frankfurt will be scheduled to take on average seven hours and thirty-five minutes; westbound between Frankfurt and New York it takes about nine hours. Historically, the Earth's rotation meant that sailing from Europe to North America was harder and slower than sailing from North America to Europe. If only the Lenape had invented seagoing ships, they might have landed in Portugal or Spain before Leif Erikson reached Newfoundland or Columbus hit the Bahamas.

Like everything else, all these scientific matters have a history. The Earth's rotation belongs to geoscience,[1] which, though presaged by the ancient Chinese, Hindus, and Greeks, began its modern career in the works of Copernicus.[2] Winds and weather systems belong to the science of meteorology, on which Aristotle himself wrote a treatise.[3] Aristotle's successor in Athens, Theophrastus, who is often labelled 'the father of botany', dabbled equally in geoscience and meteorology; his reflections on 'Time, Space and Motion' are of special interest not only to physicists but also to historians.[4] Aerology, in contrast – the study of the skies or the atmosphere – is a relative newcomer. It was long held back by man's inability either to enter or access the atmosphere. Its founder was the Frenchman Dr Léon-Philippe Teisserenc de Bort (1855–1913), who investigated atmospheric conditions by means of helium balloons. He established the distinction between the lower-level 'troposphere' and the high-level 'stratosphere'.[5]

For the purposes of understanding air travel, the jet stream has capital importance.[6] The existence of fast-moving air currents at high
altitude was noted by scientists watching the worldwide dispersion of
volcanic dust from the eruption of Krakatoa after 1883.[7] But the man
who wrote the first scientific description of the phenomenon was Dr
Wasaburo Oishi (1874–1950), who, in the steps of De Bort, was des-
patching stratospheric balloons into the sky in the 1920s from his
observatory on the slopes of Mount Fuji. His findings would have been
better known had he not published them exclusively in Esperanto.[8] The
scientist who in 1939 coined the technical German term for 'jet
stream' – *Strahlströmmung** – was Dr Heinrich Seilkopf (1895–1968),
an employee of the Third Reich's *Kriegsmarine* and a specialist in
marine aerology.[9]

Thanks to the Earth's laevorotation, transatlantic jet streams invariably move from west to east – that is, dextrorotationally – and usually
at an altitude of 23,000 to 39,000 feet. Their typical position coincides
almost exactly with the optimum cruising altitude of modern jetliners.
They tend to be narrow, between 10 and 15 miles wide, and relatively
shallow, around 2,000 to 3,000 feet deep; the air inside them is stable
in the centre but turbulent at the margins. Above all, they travel fast,
and exert great pressure on other objects in the sky. If encountered,
they can often reduce the speed of a westbound aeroplane, or increase
that of an eastbound one, by 100 mph. The all-time record for the jetstream effect was made on 10 January 2015, when a British Airways
Boeing 777-200 – identical to the missing MH370 – flew from JFK to
London Heathrow in 5 hours, 16 minutes, cutting over two and a half
hours off its scheduled time. The record-breaker habitually cruised at
560 mph; on that day, flying at 745 mph, it very nearly broke the sound
barrier.[10] On leaving JFK, it would have overflown the site of a much
older airfield with a record-breaking connection of its own.

The US Naval Air Station, Rockaway, long since demolished, is
largely forgotten. From 1917 to 1930 it occupied the western end of the
Rockaway Peninsula, adjacent to the seaward perimeter of JFK Airport, and has been replaced by one of New York's recreational parks.
But it, too, had its moment in history. It provided the starting point for
the world's first-ever transatlantic flight.

To be certain of this, one first needs to define what a transatlantic
flight entails, because the honours for the feat are widely and

---

* *Der Strahlstrom* in present-day German, or more usually *der Jetstream*.

mistakenly awarded either to the British fliers, John Alcock and Arthur Brown, or to America's 'Lone Eagle', Charles Lindbergh. To be precise, it only requires that an aeroplane be flown from one side of the Atlantic to the other, and from one continental mainland to the other. And it does not require the flight to be fast or slow, or to be undertaken in one continuous motion. By these criteria, the honours go to the US Naval Air Force's pioneering flying boat the Curtiss NC4.

Glenn Curtiss (1878–1930), who in 1907 was billed 'the fastest man in the world' for riding a motorcycle at 136 mph, soon left land-based speeding to become a leading aircraft designer. In 1909 he beat Louis Blériot to win the first Gordon Bennett Trophy at Reims, and in 1911 he was given Pilot's Licence No. 1 by the US Aero Club. Curtiss was subsequently credited with creating the first American seaplane, the first hard-hulled flying boat, the famous JN-4 'Jenny' trainer, and the H-12, the only US plane to see combat during the First World War. Between 1917 and 1919 a contract between his company and the US Navy led to the design and production of a group of four flying boats – the NC1, NC2, NC3, and NC4 – whose prowess they hoped to demonstrate during a transatlantic test flight.[11]

In the preparations for that test flight in the spring of 1919, no fewer than fifty-three naval destroyers were stationed 50 miles apart in two chains: one joining Halifax, Nova Scotia, with the Azores, and the other between the Azores and mainland Portugal. Their role was to guide the planes overhead by radio links, advise on weather and visibility, and, if necessary, act as rescue vessels. Each aeroplane had a crew of six, made up of a navigator, a radio operator, two flight engineers, and two pilots. Before any of them could reach the starting blocks, NC2 had to be cannibalized to provide spare parts for the others, and one of the flight engineers from NC4 had to be replaced, his hand having been amputated by a whirling propeller.

The three remaining aircraft mustered at Rockaway, which they left on 8 May 1919, flying to Halifax in two days via Chatham, Massachusetts. The flotilla then took off from Halifax Harbour on 16 May, not expecting to reach the Azores before nightfall. On the way, both NC1 and NC3 were forced to ditch in the sea, and their crews were rescued. But NC4, piloted by Walter Hinton and Elmer Stone, flew on overnight, touching down safely on 17 May near Horta on Faial Island after 1,200 miles and 15 hours, 18 minutes in the air. The crew then took three days' rest, while the second line of destroyers took up position. On 20 May NC4 left Faial, but interrupted its flight after only

150 miles for repairs at Ponta Delgada on Saõ Miguel. It stayed there for a whole week, before taking off again on 27 May for the final leg to Lisbon over 900 miles and 9 hours, 43 minutes. The successful ocean crossing took place over 2,250 miles with a total flying time of 26 hours, 46 minutes, at an average speed of 84 mph.[12]

The achievement of NC4 was duly noted in the world press, and has remained in the record books. But in terms of publicity it was massively eclipsed only two weeks later, when Alcock and Brown landed in a bog in County Galway, each earning a knighthood from King George V, the huge *Daily Mail* prize of £10,000, and a bonus payment of 2,000 guineas. The *Daily Mail*'s rules had specified that the winning aviator must cross the Atlantic 'in a flight from any point in the USA, Canada or Newfoundland to any point in Great Britain or Ireland in 72 continuous hours'. The Vickers Vimy IV bomber of the two British pilots had covered the 1,890 miles from St John's, Newfoundland, in 15 hours, 57 minutes, at an average speed of 115 mph.[13] As I later realized, though their route hopped from one offshore island to another, it was not dissimilar to my own.

In geographical terms, the stories of NC4 and Alcock and Brown underline the fact that transatlantic crossings can always be assisted by the presence of mid-ocean islands. The North Atlantic is not quite as empty as some of the world's other oceans. Europe-bound sailors and aviators have long made use of convenient staging-posts – Newfoundland, Greenland, Iceland, Ireland, and Great Britain, or further south the archipelago of the Azores and the beautiful isle of Madeira.

Peterhouse, founded in 1284, is the oldest college in Cambridge, and one that keeps up the old traditions.[14] For the last forty years, it has been hoping to live down the distinctly ridiculous reputation – entirely undeserved – that it acquired from Tom Sharpe's satirical novel *Porterhouse Blue* (1974), and the hilarious TV mini-series that followed. In the novel, the college song is *Dives in Omnia* ('Excess in Everything'); there is only one active scholar; the students and fellows dine on roast swan *flambé*; and the college porter, Skullion, leads the underground resistance against the designs of a new reformist Master.[15]

Nonetheless, in real life, the dons of Peterhouse still put on their black gowns for High Table at 'Formal Hall', follow the Master in silence into the tiny, oak-beamed dining hall, and sit down by candlelight on hard wooden benches on either side of the single oaken table.

Gazing at an extract from the Pater Noster inscribed on the opposing wall, they stand for several minutes while a scholar reads out two lengthy Latin graces:

> Benedic nos Domine, et dona Tua, quae de Tua largitate sumus sumpturi, et concede, ut illis salubriter nutriti, Tibi debitum obsequium praestare valeamus, per Christum Nostrum, Amen.
>
> Deus est caritas, et qui manet in caritate in Deo manet, et Deus in eo; sit Deus in nobis, et nos maneamus in ipso. Amen.

The second grace comes from the First Epistle of St John. On special occasions, the choir sings in the gallery. All then say 'Amen' in chorus and take their seats again in strict order of seniority. (It is said that they can only move up a place at the table when one of their number dies.) In recent times, since the college agreed to admit female fellows and female students, women dons (but not wives) can dine alongside the men. The centre of the table is adorned with a shining selection of the college silver, a grand array of wine glasses, and bouquets of flowers. Four courses are served – hors d'oeuvres, soup, meat, and dessert – accompanied by a couple of fine wines from the college's cellar. Then, to the surprise of unforewarned guests, comes the Peterhouse special – a so-called 'savoury' more suited to breakfast: sometimes a bacon roll, or sometimes mushrooms on toast. It is a blow struck in deliberate and ineffable bad taste *pour épater les bourgeois*, instituted by a long-forgotten Master and never repealed.

For Dessert, as opposed to dessert, the Fellows file from the Hall into the adjacent oak-panelled Combination Room. There, in winter, a blazing open fire provides both heat and light, and a second dining table awaits at which free seating applies. The fare includes a Dairy Plate loaded with a dozen cheeses and a Fruit Plate filled with grapes, mandarins, apricots, kiwis, and figs. Two cut-glass decanters circulate; the port is passed round to the left, clockwise, the madeira to the right, anticlockwise. (That, at least, is what I remember.)

In the days when etiquette mattered, to pass the port or madeira in the wrong direction, or to obstruct the circulation of the decanters, were gaffes of such magnitude that the conversational hum would momentarily drop and the Senior Fellow would politely clear his throat in reprimand. It was considered bad form if one of the diners failed to pass a decanter on, but not so bad as the faux pas caused by someone asking for the decanter directly. In many of the older Oxbridge colleges,

the next person to the man who failed to pass the decanter was expected
to drop a hint by asking:

'Do you know the Bishop of Norwich?'

If the hint was still not taken, the accepted thing was to announce:

'The Bishop is very absent-minded and often forgets to pass the
decanters round the table.'

In Peterhouse, the question to ask was: 'Do you know the Bishop of
Ely?' (As Hugo de Balsham, he was the college's founder.)

Both port and madeira are wines from Portugal. Being fortified,
they travel well, and they have been making their stormy way across
the Bay of Biscay for over 600 years. The Anglo-Portuguese wine trade
is a major by-product of the Anglo-Portuguese Alliance, which is the
oldest unbroken diplomatic treaty in the world, and almost as old as
Peterhouse itself. Negotiations for the Alliance were formally initiated
in 1384, on the centenary of Peterhouse's foundation, although earlier
contacts dated from the preceding century.

The Treaty of Windsor between Portugal and England was concluded in 1386, and was cemented in February 1387 in the cathedral of
Porto by the proxy marriage of King John I with 'Filipa de Lencastre',
otherwise Philippa of Lancaster, daughter of John of Gaunt and sister
of the future Henry IV. The bride was unusually well educated for her
day, having close family relations with Geoffrey Chaucer, Jean Frois-
sart, and John Wycliffe.

In those distant days, no one talked of 'clockwise' because no one
was wise about clocks. Mechanical clocks had been invented; one of
the earliest in England was installed in the Abbey of St Albans around
1337. But they indicated the time by striking the hours on a bell, not by
propelling fingers around a dial.[16] The term that preceded 'clockwise',
therefore, was 'sunwise'. It derived from an everyday observation in
Europe that the sun appears to move across the sky from left to right.
Its opposite was the extraordinary *widdershins* or *withershins*, which
indicated movement that circled from right to left. In a superstitious
age, it gained the connotation of moving 'in the wrong direction', or
'contrary to Nature', or even 'in the Devil's Path'.

It is not that dials were unknown. They had been an integral part of
shadow-clocks and sundials since ancient times, and there is no shortage of them in Cambridge. The university's six-sided and most
publicized sundial, which surmounts the Gate of Honour at Gonville
and Caius College, dates from 1565.[17] Another particularly fine, wall-
mounted example, dating from 1642, can be found in the Old Court of

Queen's College.[18] In 1996 Peterhouse was donated an ultramodern armillary sphere sundial, which stands in the Herb Garden and is similar to one in the Rose Garden at Downing College. The latest impressive addition, showing both Babylonian and Italian hours, was installed in Selwyn College in 2010.[19] The city's sundial trail is well worth taking.[20]

Sundials frequently carry apposite quotes, aphorisms, and inscriptions, usually in Latin. TEMPUS FUGIT and CARPE DIEM are commonplace, but one also finds TEMPUS EDAX RERUM (TIME THE DEVOURER OF THINGS), TEMPUS NEMINEM MANET (TIME WAITS FOR NO ONE), UT HORA SIC FUGIT VITA (LIFE FLEES LIKE THE HOUR), and TRANSIT UMBRA, LUX PERMANET (THE SHADOW PASSES, THE LIGHT REMAINS). In English there are LIVE THE HOUR, TIME HAS ASKED ME NOT TO ASK FOR MORE, and GROW OLD WITH ME – THE BEST IS STILL TO BE.

Sundial design is highly complex, and beyond the comprehension of mere historians. But even a casual observer can see that some dials put the noonday marker at the top and others at the bottom. In the former case, the hours are numbered from left to right, and in the latter (as with the dial in Queen's College) from right to left. This fact throws my brain into lockdown. Depending on the dial's positioning and the gnomon's angle, I am tempted to conclude that the sun's shadow sometimes moves around the dial sunwise, and sometimes withershins. Surely not?

The *Oxford English Dictionary* offers two definitions of *withershins*:

1. in a direction opposite to the usual; the wrong way.
2. in a direction contrary to the apparent course of the sun (considered as unlucky or causing disaster).[21]

The etymology is clearly Germanic – from *wider* meaning 'contrary' or 'against' and *sinn* meaning 'direction'. It is less common in standard English than in Scots, where it is often associated with witches: 'Withershins is the way of witch and trow.' In all good productions of Shakespeare's *Macbeth*, the witches open the play by stirring their cauldron left-handed, 'in the wrong direction'.

The French language has its own conventions. My old *Dictionnaire Quillet* defines *le sens direct* as 'contraire au déplacement des aiguilles d'un montre' ('opposite to the movement of the hands of a watch'), while its antonym is *le sens rétrograde*. This seems to suggest that the French mind regards 'clockwise' or 'sunwise' to be retrograde, and 'anticlockwise' to be direct.[22]

It is all very odd. There doesn't even seem to be a consensus about the movement of madeira around the table. Several sources connected to regimental traditions in the British Army indicate that the decanters of port and madeira should circulate in the officers' mess in tandem or even – perish the thought – clockwise.[23]

At any rate, madeira probably reached Peterhouse College before clocks did, and probably before port, which only attained the peak of its popularity after the Peninsular War (1808–14). In mediaeval times, England's favourite tipple was malmsey, a sweet wine made from Greek Malvasia grapes, which became one of Madeira's staple products at an early date. One can't know for certain. But it is a plausible assumption that the port would pass *sunwise*, and the malmsey *withershins*.

Madeira – *la perola do mar*, 'the pearl of the sea' – is a small, lonely, mountainous and volcanic island in the middle of the Gulf Stream. It is larger than Malta or Elba, but smaller than Rhode Island. It is surrounded by a stormy Atlantic Ocean, and constantly buffeted by winds that vacillate between fresh and hurricane. Gentle breezes are rare. It suffers from numerous handicaps to human habitation, but also enjoys numerous advantages, including its fine sea air, mild climate, abundance of flowers, and prime value as a naval staging-post.[24]

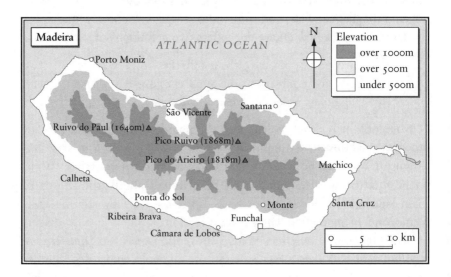

Traditionally, Madeira was said to have been discovered by accident in the summer of AD 1418. João Gonçalves, known as *Zarco*, 'the Squinter', was a sea captain sailing in the service of Prince Henry of Portugal, 'the Navigator', son of Philippa of Lancaster. Zarco was intending to explore the western coast of North Africa, but, blown off course, beached his ships on the sandy shore of an unknown island that he called Porto Santo. He spied a larger island through the mist. Portuguese sailors had mastered the art of tacking against the wind, and with the use of stars and a compass were able to make reasonable estimates of their location. Zarco returned the following year, crossed from Porto Santo to the larger island, which he called Madeira, the 'Isle of Timber', and laid formal claim to them in the name of the King of Portugal. He found that his new discovery, unlike the adjacent Canary Islands, which were claimed by Castile, was completely uninhabited. So, in an act of ecological barbarity, he torched the forests to clear the land, and caused a fire that burned for seven years. Settlers were duly sent out, and Madeira was added to the list of Portuguese provinces in 1425.

The only sign of previous life that Zarco found was two graves by the seashore of the bay where he landed. They belonged to a couple of star-crossed and shipwrecked lovers. According to Madeiran legend, 'Roberto Machim' was an English knight from the court of Edward III (r. 1327–77), and 'Ana d'Arfet' was his high-born compatriot. In real life, Richard Machin or Machyn was a Bristol merchant engaged in the Bordeaux trade, and Anne of Hertford a married noblewoman. Having fallen in love, the two decided to elope and make a new life in the king's French possessions. Instead, running into a storm in the Bay of Biscay, their ship was washed up on the shore of an empty, wooded island. Anne was killed in the shipwreck. Richard allegedly died of a broken heart. And the crew, having buried the lovers, sailed away on a raft made from the ship's timbers and survived to tell the tale. The legend is the source of the name of Madeira's second town – Machico.[25]

None of which explains why the Medici Atlas of 1351, and several other fourteenth-century maps, mark an island in the exact spot where the future Madeira lies.[26] Common sense suggests that neither Zarco nor 'Roberto and Ana' were the first people to set foot there.

As soon as the island began to be settled, the long list of natural obstacles made itself felt. There was no level ground on which to clear fields. At no point along the island's precipitous coastline was there the possibility of making a cart track, let alone roads. And there was no deep, protected harbour. Ingenious solutions had to be found on all fronts. In place of fields, the Madeirans built thousands of terraces, on which they could plant vines and construct their cabins. Mountainside ropeways pulled people and goods from lower to higher locations. Downhill journeys were undertaken (and still are) by dry-run toboggans.

Mules and packhorses provided the only means of heavy transport. At Funchal, lighters ferried cargoes and passengers from ships anchored in the bay and deposited them on the beach. A protective harbour wall and port basin were not built there until the 1960s.

The shrine of *Nossa Senhora do Monte* was founded in 1470 by a man claiming to have been the first baby born on Madeira. Dedicated to the Virgin Mary, it perches on a rocky outcrop 598 metres above Funchal, halfway up the coastal ridge, commanding a superb view across the Bay. It quickly became a place of pilgrimage, and a focus for Madeira's particular brand of intense Catholic piety. The original late-mediaeval building was brought down by the earthquakes of 1740 and replaced by an imposing Baroque edifice, which is characterized by a facade in black volcanic stone and bright white plaster. It is approached by a colossal stone stairway on which pilgrims edge their way upward on bleeding knees.[27]

Madeira's first commercial sensation came not from wine but from sugar, and one of its pioneers was none other than Christopher Columbus. Sent from Genoa to Madeira in 1478 to conclude contracts for the delivery of sugar, Columbus married a local woman, Filipa Moniz, and lived on Porto Santo for four years. It is inconceivable that he left Madeira without dreaming about the lands that might lie beyond the western horizon By the time he reached the Americas, in 1492, 3,000 Moorish slaves were already working Madeira's plantations.

After Portugal's colonization of Brazil in 1500 and Angola in 1575, Madeira established its strategic role as a re-victualling station and the first port of call on the kingdom's two main imperial routes. Even today, the great cruise liners edge inshore for a brief stop on their way to more distant climes. Over the centuries, most of the great westbound navigators and explorers stopped here, including Captain Cook, and Charles Darwin aboard HMS *Beagle*.

Throughout the Age of Discovery, therefore, Madeira provided the first stop for ships sailing southwards from Europe either to the Caribbean or the west coast of Africa. Positioned at 32 degrees north of latitude, some 440 miles off Africa and 700 miles from Gibraltar, the island enabled Portuguese explorers to work their way steadily towards the equator, which before Lopes Gonçalves in 1473–4, no European had yet crossed.

Madeira's wine industry evolved over the centuries. It began using techniques brought from the Minho region of Portugal, where vines for the *vinho verde* harvest were tended on raised trellises. The Negro Mole grape was the standard base for reds and the imported Malvasia for whites. After the mediaeval fashion for over-sweet malmsey faded, the modern fortified version took hold, not least because it travelled well in the rolling holds of sailing ships. English colonists took a taste for it to America, where it became the preferred drink of the educated and landed classes:

> Madeira became the best-known and most popular wine in colonial America by quirks of geography and politics. First, the Gulf Stream and the trade winds, which pass Madeira, carried sailing ships naturally towards our ports. In 1664, King Charles II put heavy taxes on to French wines going to the [English] colonies, and later it was requited that European goods travel only in British ships. Since Madeira was technically in Africa, its wines were exempt from such requirements, and soon swept the colonies. By the late 18th century, it was considered patriotic to drink Madeira and thereby to avoid paying taxes to the Crown, and Madeira became the mother's milk of the American Revolution. Madeira also suited the colonials' taste for sweet wines.[28]

Thomas Jefferson, the 'Father of the Constitution', was a dedicated connoisseur, who kept detailed notes and accounts of his purchases and consumption of wine. Madeira filled the largest number of casks in his cellar at Monticello. In 1981 archaeological excavations there threw up a fine, cut-glass, English-made Madeira decanter from the 1760s, complete with wheel-engraved cartouche and grapevine motifs.[29]

The tradition of 'wintering' in Madeira has a long pedigree. It attracted the wealthy, the intrepid, the sick, and the desperate, especially Britishers. In the mid-nineteenth century it became a flood, greatly assisted by the illustrated journal of an Englishwoman, Isabella da França, who had married a Madeiran.[30] The journal's pictures show 'Madam' being driven up to the *Monte* on a bullock-drawn sled, 'Madam' being carried in a hammock up the tortuous path to Curral, and 'Madam' being brought ashore from a rowing boat at Calheta by a combined team of sailors and swimmers. Many VIPs and celebrities followed in her wake. The Empress of Austria, 'Sissi', the wife of Francis-Joseph, was one of the best remembered. She arrived on Queen Victoria's private yacht in 1859, and stayed for several months at the newly opened Reid's Palace Hotel. Edward VII came, too, as did everyone from George Bernard Shaw to the exiled Cuban dictator, General Fulgencio Batista, and Winston Churchill. (He went to Madeira to paint, first visiting in 1899.)

One of the early 'winterers' was John Davis Blandy (1783–1855) of

Piddletrenthide in Dorset, who was sent to Madeira in 1808 for the sake of his health. The change of air clearly had the desired effect. He recovered to found both a family wine business, Blandy and Blandy, and a dynasty of heirs and successors who have stayed at the head of the family firm to the present day. He married Jennet Burden in 1811, the same year that the firm was founded, and their son, Charles Ridpath Blandy (1812–79), was born on Madeira the following year. In 1826 he bought the family villa, the Quinta de Santa Luzia, which overlooks the bay from the slopes of the *Monte*. Blandy senior launched himself into the international wine trade with his two brothers, while his son, having established the Blandy Wine Lodge on Avenida Arriaga in the centre of Funchal, made a fortune by buying up all the stocks of vintage madeira on the island. Seven generations on, the firm is run by Chris Blandy. Their current list of vintage Madeiran wines is topped by the 'Blandy's Malmsey 1994 Harvest'.[31]

The most famous bottle of Blandy madeira, however, was the one offered to Napoleon Bonaparte in July 1815 when HMS *Bellerophon* dropped anchor in the bay on its way to St Helena. The imprisoned former emperor declined the offer as a form of protest for not being allowed ashore, even though John Blandy had presented the gift in person. (The *Bellerophon*'s British officers left the ship to carouse at the Royal Navy station built during the Napoleonic Wars to keep the French out.) Yet the rejected bottle had a future.

In 1873 one of Britain's most celebrated scientists, Lord Kelvin (1824–1907), visited Madeira. Born William Thomson in Belfast, Kelvin had been both a student and a Fellow at Peterhouse, where the decanter of madeira would undoubtedly have passed through his hands. But in the 1870s he was engaged as chief adviser to the laying of transatlantic cables. When his cable-laying ship developed problems on its way to Brazil, he was forced to make an unscheduled stop at Funchal, where Charles Blandy entertained him. More importantly, as a fifty-year-old widower, he made the acquaintance of Charles's thirty-seven-year-old daughter, Frances Anna, known as 'Fanny'. It became a famous love match.

In the scientific world, Kelvin is best known for the Kelvin Scale of temperature and for the Kelvin Conundrum: 'Is it possible to believe in God and Science?' But on Madeira he is remembered for the spectacular events of 2 May 1874. On that day his 126-ton yacht the *Lalla Rookh*, sailed into Funchal Bay flying a semaphore signal that could be clearly read from Quinta Santa Luzia through the watching telescopes.

The signal read 'Will you marry me?' And Fanny's reply was run up on the Blandy villa's own signal mast. It read 'Yes.' The wedding took place within the month, and the pair lived happily ever after at Kelvin's Netherhall mansion at Largs on the Clyde.

As the rich and famous landed, thousands of native Madeirans departed. Local society had long been divided by extremes of wealth and poverty. The land-owning *grandes* lived in style in their cliff-top *quintas*, controlling the courts, the forces of order, the Church, and economic life. Their tenant farmers handed over half their income as rent, rarely received an education, and toiled from cradle to grave. For them, an outward ticket on the ships always waited. By the twentieth century, there were more Madeirans living abroad – in Brazil, Venezuela, and South Africa – than at home.

In 1893 Funchal's funicular railway was opened to take visitors up the *Monte* as far as the Levada of Santa Luzia, near the Blandy's villa. In 1912 it was extended to the higher Terreiro da Luta, near the shrine of Nossa Senhora. Nowadays one goes by cable car, and takes lunch at one of the local restaurants. On the way down, one can choose between the hair-raising, bone-shaking sledge ride, steered from the back by boatered guides, or a more sedate walk via the glorious Botanical Gardens. 'Faith and Flowers' would make a good motto for the outing.

In November 1921, conveyed by a British cruiser, the exiled former Emperor of Austria and once King of Hungary, Karl von Habsburg (1887–1922), landed on Madeira with his wife, Zita, and seven children. Also known as Charles I of Austria and Charles IV of Hungary, the successor to Francis-Joseph, he was a political casualty of the First World War, and had reigned for only two years. He never formally abdicated, having renounced 'participation in the affairs of state'. But he was brutally excluded, first in 1918 by the Republic of Austria and then in 1919–20 by the post-war regimes in Hungary. Frail and fragile, he accepted permanent exile with stoicism. He died from pneumonia on 1 April 1922, and was buried in the church of Nossa Senhora do Monte.[32]

Since his death, the reputation of 'Charles of Austria' has steadily grown as a man of humility and peace. His tragic plight appealed to Madeiran sensibilities, which had been sorely offended only a dozen years earlier by the dethronement of Portugal's own 'Patriot and Catholic King', Manuel II. Charles's cult attracted both local and international support. It was strengthened in 2003 by his elevation to the ranks of the 'Venerable' and crowned in 2004 by beatification. In his homily during the ceremony of beatification in Rome, Pope John Paul II stressed the Christian virtues of the late emperor:

> The decisive task of Christians consists of seeking, recognising and follow-ing God's will in all things. The Christian statesman, [the Blessed] Charles Austria, confronted this challenge every day. To his eyes, war appeared as 'something appalling'. Amid the tumult of the First World War, he strove to promote the peace initiative of my Predecessor, Benedict XV.[33]

Some think of the beatifier of 'Santo Carlos' as the Polish pope; others know him to have been Karol Wojtyła, the son of one of the last emperor's faithful sergeants, who named the boy after his former commander-in-chief.

One of the handicaps that long constrained the growth of modern tour-ism on Madeira was the absence of a coastal plain and hence of a suitable airport site. The problem was partially solved in 1960, when landing facilities were made available at Santa Cruz by extending an existing airstrip onto a stretch of artificial land built over the sea on piles.[34] Even so, the landing experience can still be taxing both for pilots and passengers. As the plane descends, one feels that the wing-tips are brushing the cliff faces into which the airport has been carved. It's an old feeling in Madeira. When passengers finally set foot on terra firma, they do so with a strong sense of relief.

Madeira's lack of a regular airport gave rise to one of the most excit-ing episodes of commercial aviation. Aquila Airways flew flying boats between Southampton and Funchal, and sometimes to the Canaries, between 1948 and 1958. The flights of their Short Sunderlands resem-bled that of a fun fair or space capsule – not to mention passengers on the Curtiss NC4 surviving the nine-hour ordeal with the assistance of lavish servings of champagne. They would take their seats in the pas-senger cabin, sitting below sea level in the murky waters of the Solent. From there, they were catapulted into the air with a roar, and were kept plied with every conceivable form of luxury food and drink until they splashed down in the bay off Funchal, whence they were taken ashore by a lighter. A single ticket cost £87 – the equivalent of per-haps £1,000 today. The service ended after one of the flying boats, G-AKNU, was damaged during take-off and crashed into cliffs on the Isle of Wight, killing forty-five people.[35]

Inevitably, one of the many colourful stories about Madeira's flying-boat service features Winston Churchill. In the winter of 1950–51, during his last stay, he was alerted by news that a general election had been called in Britain, and that he, as leader of the opposition, had a good chance of returning to Downing Street. So he left in a hurry by flying boat, but not, apparently, without a Winstonian flourish. The story goes that, before leaving the island for ever, he was offered the bottle of madeira that Napoleon had refused, whereupon he drank it up on the spot, and returned to London to win his second term of office as prime minister.[36]

Madeira is memorable, above all, for its flowers. Hibiscus, bougain-villea, mimosa, oleander, passion flowers, heliotropic sunflowers, angel's trumpets, arum lilies, poinsettias, and wild orchids grow in profusion, often in the unlikeliest of nooks and crannies on the cliffs – not forget-ting the bright blue *Echium candicans* or 'Pride of Madeira'.[37] A stroll along the flower-strewn clifftop path from Funchal to Câmara de Lobos (where the Churchills loved to stay), accompanied by the music of the breakers, is guaranteed to restore the weariest of souls. The mere memory of it is enough to revive a tiring author, who is now approach-ing the end both of his voyage and of this book.

Renaissance navigators were familiar with the fact that the Earth is a sphere, and that the equator divides it into northern and southern hem-ispheres. The work of the third-century BCE Greek geographer and mathematician Eratosthenes, who calculated the Earth's circumference fairly accurately, had been preserved by Arab scholars and was avail-able in retranslated form.[38] Ptolemy's World Map from the second century AD, which was reproduced in the fifteenth century, bears both latitudinal and longitudinal lines.[39] Already in the fourteenth century, Dante Alighieri had imagined that Mount Purgatory was an island in the southern ocean, beyond the equator. He even realized, when describing his fictional journey and his climb from the bowels of the Earth into the southern hemisphere, that the noonday sun would be shining in the north.[40]

Armed with this basic knowledge, the Portuguese pressed ever fur-ther south from Madeira. In 1443 they reached the island of Arguin off Mauretania, at 20 degrees north, and built a trading-post there. In 1456 they reached the Cape Verde Islands at 15 degrees north, estab-lishing a major hub for their future slave trade. In the 1460s interest waned after Prince Henry the Navigator died, and several years passed before a consortium of merchants formed a Guinea Company to pick

up the earlier threads. Finally, in 1473–4 one of the Company's captains, Lopes Gonçalves, sailed to the Cape named after him (now in
Gabon) and on to Cape Catherine (in present-day Angola) at 2 degrees
south, thereby becoming the very first European to make a recorded
voyage beyond the equator.[41]

At the time, no one in Europe knew what lay on the western side of
the Atlantic; no one had visited the Caribbean islands, rounded the
southern tip of Africa, or taken ship from Europe to India or China.
Misconceptions about the length of the equator, propagated, among
others, by Cardinal D'Ailly's *Imago Mundi* (1410), strengthened the
false belief that China and 'the Indies' lay somewhere not too far from
Europe's Atlantic seaboard.[42]

During that fifteenth century, with the Renaissance coming into bloom,
stargazing was still an essential aspect of maritime navigation. Although
limited to what could be seen by the naked eye, sailors stood on the
heaving decks of their tiny ships and, in the interests of self-preservation,
eagerly tracked the movements of sun, moon, and stars. They were
conversant with the five visible planets – Mercury, Venus, Mars, Jupi-
ter, and Saturn – with the major northern constellations, and the
brightest stars, such as Sirius, the 'Dog Star', Canopus, 'the Spartan
Pilot' (after Homer), and Polaris, the 'North Star'. European scholars,
though trailing their Islamic counterparts, were deeply involved in
astronomy, 'the oldest of the natural sciences'. For the time being, their
focus was on rediscovering the discoveries of the ancients. On the central question of the structural dynamics of the universe, the consensus
still upheld the geocentrism of Aristotle, though the heliocentrism of
Aristarchus of Samos (*c.* 310–230 BCE) was known, and would fascinate
the young Nicholas Copernicus (1473–1543). Over two thousand miles
from Madeira, in the Polish city of Toruń, Copernicus had been born
in the same year that Lopes Gonçalves weighed anchor.

Such was the state of play when Diogo Cão (*c.* 1452–86) embarked
on the two voyages that took him still further south. Born at Vila Real
in the Douro Valley, in the heart of the port wine country, and patronized by the young king, John II, the 'Perfect Prince', he set off in 1482 to
sail beyond the Congo River, where he first put into practice his habit of
erecting a *padrão* or 'marker stone' at the farthest point of his exploration. In 1484, on his second voyage, Cão outran his previous farthest
point, left a marker stone near present-day Matadi in Angola, and sailed
on to Cape Cross. He was then at 22 degrees south, close to the Tropic
of Capricorn, at the most southerly point ever reached by Europeans.

The constellation of the Southern Cross, after which the headland took its name, could not have been previously seen by Europeans. The godly Portuguese took its sighting as an affirmation of their Christian faith. Yet Sirius and Canopus were both shining brightly, and even stranger things were on show. For one, the bright crescent of the young moon was placed on its left-hand side, not on its right as seen from Madeira. For another, the full moon appeared upside down. Strangest of all, Orion the Hunter was standing on his head; his belt and sword had assumed the shape of a saucepan.

Orion, which sits in the sky immediately over the equator, is one of the celestial constellations that can be observed from both hemispheres. Its familiar posture over Portugal between 42 and 32 degrees north was probably thought to be fixed. But for every degree of latitude that Diogo Cão covered on his southbound voyage, the 'Hunter' would have appeared to swing slowly on his axis in a slow-motion cartwheel. Every night the sailors would have observed him in a slightly different position, until at Cape Cross he was literally head over heels. The two bright stars Alpha Orionis (Betelgeuse) and Beta Orionis (Rigel), which in the north form Orion's shoulders, here in the south appeared beneath him.[43] There must have been much scratching of heads.

All four *padrãos* placed by Diogo Cão have survived. The one at Cape Cross (now in northern Namibia) was removed in 1893 by a German sea captain and deposited in a Berlin museum. It has since been replaced by a replica:

In the year 6685 after the Creation of the world and 1485 after the birth of Christ, the brilliant, far-sighted King John of Portugal, ordered Diogo Cão, Knight of his court, to discover this land and to erect this marker here.[44]

The marker's message is echoed in the opening stanza of one of the best-known Portuguese poems of the twentieth century, 'Padrão' by Fernando Pessoa:

O esforço é grande, e o homem é pequeno.
Eu, Diogo Cão, navegador, deixei
Este padrão ao pé do areal moreno.
E para diante naveguei.[45]

(The effort is great, and man is puny.
I, Diogo Cão, navigator, placed
This stone on the golden sands.
And ahead we sail.)

What was not recorded, alas, were the reactions of Cão and his crew to the apparently changed movements of the sun. At the equator, they would have seen the sun directly overhead; days and nights would have been of exactly the same length, and subtle changes hard to detect. But, on approaching the Tropic of Capricorn, the typical arrangements of the southern hemisphere would have been become fully visible. The sun would have risen each day in the east and set in the west, but at midday, surprisingly, it would have been in the north. It moved across the sky not from left to right, but from right to left. For the first time in history, Europeans watched a sunwise movement that was no longer the traditional sunwise. In the view of Diogo Cão and his men, *no sentido do sol* would have been changed into *no sentido contrario ao sol*. Sunwise had gone withershins.

One may assume that this phenomenon, when first noticed, caused a degree of consternation. It may have been almost as disconcerting as my most recent visit to Cambridge. As a lifetime Petrean, who once swore by candlelight to uphold the college statutes, repeating the Latin words after the Master, I was pleased to take my place again at High Table. The shocks were considerable. Not only had the Fellows just concluded the grammatically discordant election of a woman Master, but at dessert they had dropped the age-old custom of serving madeira. *O Tempora! O Mores!* Skullion must be turning in his grave – *withershins*.

# 14

# FRA

*Boarding, Flying, Crashing, Vanishing, and Landing*

Flug
Flight
nach
to
über
via
US 781 PHILADELPHIA 11 15
OA 166 ATHEN-THESSALONIKI 11 20
AZ 403 ROM 11 20
LH 754 BANGALORE 11 20
DE 2066 ANCHORAGE-WHITEHORSE 11 20
OS 122 WIEN 11 20
DL 015 ATLANTA 11 20
CO 051 NEW YORK-NEWARK 11 20
BA 903 LONDON-HEATHROW 11 30
LH 6790 STUTTGART HBF. 11 30
GF 016 MUSCAT-BAHRAIN 11 30
IY 741 SANAA-ROM 11 30
OS 290 KLAGENFURT 11 30
LH 178 BERLIN-TEGEL 11 30
AB 8702 ZUERICH 11 30
LH 968 MUENCHEN 11 35
LH 758 MADRAS 11 40
DL 107 NEW YORK 11 40
4412 MADRID 11 45
4940 EDINBURGH 11 45
193 CHARLOTTE 11 45
126 HYDERABAD-MUMBAI 11 45
8733 LONDON-CITY 11 50
ISTANBUL

If flying around the world is the intention, Frankfurt am Main is a better starting point than most. The *Rhein-Main-Flughafen* at Frankfurt lists more destinations in the world than any other airport, though in terms of passenger numbers it is slightly less busy than some of its world rivals. It is the home base of Lufthansa, one of the mainstays of the worldwide Star Alliance, whose round-the-world ticket I had purchased. At the risk of a terrible pun, one can say that 'flying is in the air' here: the entire ambience is determined by aviation, aircraft, air-crews, and airlines.[1]

The state of Hesse – of which Frankfurt is the largest city – is as thoroughly German as any other part of the country. It takes its name and historic identity from the Germanic tribe of the *Chatti*, who occupied the region in the first century BCE. Over the millennium that followed, the Hessians were squeezed between the Franks and the Saxons, while building an ethnically homogeneous society; there were no more significant waves of immigration until the arrival of Turkish *gastarbeiter* in the 1960s. In the second millennium, the Landgraves of Hesse gradually strengthened their position within the Holy Roman Empire until in 1803, on the eve of the empire's demise, they were declared Electors. In the nineteenth century, after the Napoleonic interlude, one clutch of Hessian provinces formed an independent Grand Duchy ruled from Darmstadt, and another clutch were annexed by Prussia. The Grand Duchy's full name was the *Grossherzogtum Hessen und bei Rhein* – a fine example of the German predilection for ostentatiously long names.[2]

Through much of its history, the city of Frankfurt am Main strove to uphold a semi-detached status in relation to the surrounding Hessian lands. The town at 'The Ford of the Franks' was first mentioned in 794, in the heyday of the Frankish emperor Charlemagne. It was granted the valuable right to hold an annual *Messe* or 'international Fair' from 1190. It became a *Reichstadt* or 'Free Imperial City' of the

Holy Roman Empire from 1372, and from 1558 to 1792 the scene of imperial coronations. The birthplace of Goethe, it grew into a leading centre of Enlightenment and liberalism, which in turn gave rise to a distinguished university. In 1848 the city lay at the heart of the abortive 'German Revolution', hosting the first German parliament, but in 1866 it was taken over by Prussia and turned into the capital of the Prussian province of Hesse-Nassau. Thereafter, it took a leading place in the affairs of the successive states of a united Germany – the German Empire, the Weimar Republic, the Third Reich, and the Federal Republic.[3]

The dense and impenetrable forest within which the Frankfurt airport was built can be clearly seen from windows on either side of landing planes, and had lain untouched since time immemorial. Originally an imperial hunting ground, it was granted by Emperor Heinrich VII to the Teutonic Knights in 1291, who sold it in 1484 to the city of Frankfurt, thereby becoming the Frankfurter *Stadtwald*. It once stretched all the way to the southern bank of the River Main opposite the Old City. Today, the forest still occupies an impressive 48 square miles, engulfing the airport on all sides.

The Frankfurt airport was built between 1933 and 1936, an early showpiece project of the newly founded Third Reich. It replaced the city's previous airport, which from 1909 to 1924 had housed the world's first airline, the *Deutsche Luftschiffahrts-Aktiengesellschaft* (DELAG). Its construction, including two lengths of concrete motorway, the A3 and the A5, which intersect near the south-eastern perimeter at the massive *Frankfurter Autobahn Kreuz*, was planned in 1930 but not undertaken until the Nazis' seizure of power swept away all bureaucratic and financial obstacles. The sod-cutting ceremony on 23 September 1933 was attended by Adolf Hitler, who personally shovelled away the first load of earth. The first stretch of autobahn to be finished, in May 1935, ran the 23 kilometres from Frankfurt to Darmstadt. The Rhein-Main-Flughafen was then formally opened on 8 July 1936.[4] Until the Hindenburg disaster of the following year, it served as the base both for Lufthansa and the world's largest airships – the *Graf Zeppelin*, the *LZ-130*, and the *Hindenburg*.[5]

Lufthansa – originally *Deutsche Luft Hansa A.G.* – had started life in 1926 as the state-owned airline of the Weimar Republic, changing its name to *Deutsche Lufthansa* after the advent of the Third Reich.[6]

Little was more important to the Nazi regime than the rapid extension of Germany's communication networks. The autobahns, known in Nazi propaganda as the *Strassen Adolf Hitlers* (Adolf Hitler roads), grew to nearly 9,000 kilometres in length between 1933 and 1939. In 1941 plans were laid to extend them as far as Kiev and Athens. The German Railways, the *Reichsbahn*, absorbed numerous foreign state-owned companies throughout occupied Europe, from Austria and Czechoslovakia to Poland, Yugoslavia, Greece, and parts of the USSR. Lufthansa, the Third Reich's flagship civilian carrier, extended both its intercontinental routes and its key role within Germany's expanding *Lebensraum*. As the era of airships and seaplanes receded, a regular postal service by aeroplane was established from 1934 to 1939 between Germany and Brazil, via Spain, the Canary Islands, and Gambia. In 1938 a DLH Focke-Wulf Condor completed the first non-stop flight between Germany and New York.

After the Second World War, when international air travel was reorganized and post-war administrators were preparing for Frankfurt Airport's second great expansion, the International Air Transport Association (IATA) gave it the three-letter code of FRA. Local planners were also looking for a site on which to build a flagship airport hotel. They were drawn to the site of the Wald Restaurant, situated in a dilapidated eighteenth-century building that had been left standing only a couple of hundred yards from the northern perimeter, and the decision was taken to incorporate the old restaurant within a new hotel complex. The contract was awarded to the Steigenberger Hotel Group, a local family-run business started by Albert Steigenberger (d. 1958), who had created a chain of prestigious international hotels from the ashes of war. This company was the natural choice to rescue the Wald Restaurant and then launch the Steigenberger Airport Hotel in 1969.[7]

The outcome was an extraordinarily eclectic architectural cluster. On one side, the double wings of the modernist Steigenberger Airport Hotel rise to a dozen storeys. On the other, a tall multilevel car park is disguised by horizontal aluminium slats and, to exploit the forest theme, by long vertical sheets of black plastic covered with images of deep green foliage. Right in the middle, surrounded by a clump of ancient oaks, the elderly Wald Restaurant survives to the present day.

Airport hotels rarely provide thrills and frills. Their purpose is to supply the no-nonsense comforts required by short-stay visitors. They also cater, through meeting rooms and conference facilities, for the special category of business people who meet only at airports. To these ends, an efficient shuttle-bus service between hotel and terminals is essential. The Steigenberger runs two spacious shuttle buses that operate constantly between the first landing at 5 a.m. and the last take-off at 11 p.m.

At the start of my global journey, the search for the shuttle bus at FRA gave me more hassle than almost anything else at a score of international airports. Arriving in Frankfurt from our home in Cracow on the eve of the first big flight of my journey, I entered the airport's main building and stepped into a torture chamber of sensory bombardment. The 'rendezvous point' in the arrivals hall is a place of pandemonium. Hundreds of people scurry around, pushing others aside and tripping over trailing cases. Further hundreds peer deep into my face, looking to determine whether I am the awaited guest or loved one. Bright lights flash and shine in all directions. Dozens of multilingual signs dangle in deep confusion. Incomprehensible messages in multiple languages constantly blare from loudspeakers, drowning out the feeble voice-recordings on wall-mounted, automated devices that aim to tell passengers where the shuttle buses stop.

Outside, in the vast, cavernous, and bewildering underground pick-up zone, a new array of olfactory, visual, and audio tests awaits. The stench of diesel oil mixes with the triumphant, smoky roar of vehicles that have found their clients. At the kerbside, an endless line of coaches, taxis, and private cars defy one to ask yet again for the 'Steigenberger'. Meaningless blue signs marked 'A', 'B', and 'C' hang from the ceiling. Minibuses from every known hotel chain trundle past, driven by robots staring straight ahead. Another half-audible voice in another information device is drowned out by yet another loudspeaker announcement. A youth sprints down the roadway, vaults the barrier, and gives chase to a fast-disappearing minibus. Was that for the Steigenberger? One passer-by says, 'Go to "A"!' The next one says, 'Go to "C"!'

Staggering towards the taxi rank, I step off the pavement to flag down a driver, who otherwise had no intention of stopping. He hurls my cases into the boot. I throw myself into the back seat:

'Wohin?' he asks, already changing into second gear.

'The Steigenberger,' I say.

He stamps on the brake, brings the car to a shuddering halt, and throws his arms in the air.

'Not again,' he curses, amidst a string of Turkish expletives. 'Everyone wants the Steigenberger, and it's not worth my while to go there. The Steigenberger is just round the corner,' he laments. 'You could walk there. Don't you know there's a shuttle bus?'

'Yes, I do, but I couldn't find it,' I plead. 'Here's a twenty-dollar bill just to get me out of here.' With which, I was driven just round the corner.

The Steigenberger calmed me down. The online Turez booking worked faultlessly. Registration was swift, the room spacious, the air-conditioning unintrusive, the sound-proofing efficient, the shower powerful, the room-service meal still warm, the Pilsner palatable, the bed comfortable, and the flow of jetliners past the window constant. There was time for a swim in the ninth-floor pool, and for a moment on the glass-fronted terrace overlooking the runway. Then the blessed silence of the *Naechtliche Stille* descended.

LH 630 was scheduled to depart next day at 09.15 hours. Working backwards, this meant a 7.15 check-in, a 6.30 shuttle to make sure of finding the right terminal, a 5.30 breakfast, and a wake-up call at 4.45. So the curtains were left open and all possible alarms were set. I need not have bothered. Exactly 30 seconds past five o'clock, the bedroom window darkened as the morning's first Jumbo passed silently over-head, heading for landing. I felt I could have poked it with a decent-sized umbrella. Thereafter, the procession of monster flying machines was relentless. As soon as one was above the hotel, the next was already skimming the treetops of the forest, and the lights of the next but one were piercing the distant morning clouds.

Watching the undersides of giant jets from close quarters feels like a reversion to childhood under the family dining table, from where one once examined the shoes, shoelaces, socks, stockings, skirts, and trou-ser legs of the eating adults. I could now examine all the underparts of aeroplanes that usually escape notice. With nose up and tail down, the great birds floated overhead, displaying a vast expanse of flat metal, and exuding sulky resentment at being observed in such an ungainly pose. The engines looked improbably small, hanging apologetically beneath the wings. The flaps on wings and tail were extended, increas-ing the dark underside area. The long struts of the landing-gear ended in huge pods of six or eight tightly packed wheels, protruding like the outstretched feet of a goose about to hit the water. The cockpit win-dows appeared tiny and ill-placed, giving the pilots a fine view of the heavens but only an awkward squint at the approaching ground. The beam of powerful nose-mounted searchlights went before the planes as they gently pitched and yawed, fighting the breeze to hold position. Having committed themselves to landing, some wobbled their wings in a shrug of resignation; others, alarmingly, lowered their undercarriage at the very last moment. Each of them must have weighed anything from 100 to 300 tons. But seen from in front or below, all seemed to be moving so very slowly that they were certain to stall. This terrifying vision concentrates the mind of a would-be aerial globe-trotter, bringing him face to face with the mysteries of flight, and the strange, invisible force that holds these monsters aloft. The German word for 'co-efficient of lift' must be impossibly long.

Checking out at Reception, I noticed the hotel's address on the bill. 'What does *Unterschweinstiege* mean?' I asked.

'*Oje*,' sighed the receptionist, 'it's untranslatable.'

So, waiting for the shuttle, I tried to translate it myself. What I came up with (wrongly) was 'Under the Pigsty': an odd location for a high-class airport hotel.

The history of aviation is not quite so short or straightforward as the modern term suggests, and certainly does not start in 1903 with the Wright Brothers.[8] According to the dictionary, *aviation* means 'flying in an aeroplane' or 'the activity of flying aircraft', and it entered the English language in 1887.[9] (It originated in French as a form of *locomotion aériennne*, and can be traced to 1863.)[10] Yet its literal meaning is 'flying like a bird', after the Latin *avis*, so the activity possesses much greater antiquity than that of aircraft. Flying like a bird began, in fact, with *Archaeopteryx*, the winged dinosaur, or possibly its relative, the *Aurornis*, which took to the skies in the late Jurassic period around 160–150 million years ago; these are the evolutionary predecessors of all birds.

The history of human flight is a different category, and begins, theoretically, with the myth of Daedalus and Icarus from the second millennium BC, and, in the case of human-controlled flight, with the Chinese invention of kites *circa* 500 BCE. In Europe, the mediaeval philosopher Roger Bacon designed an *ornithopter*, three hundred years before Leonardo da Vinci; the Brothers Montgolfier, the French balloonists, and their partners pioneered the first viable aircraft in 1782, and the first manned flight in 1783. Leading British contributors included the Oxford pastry chef, James Sadler (1753–1828), whose balloon successfully took off from Christ Church Meadow in Oxford on 4 October 1784,[11] and Sir George Cayley (1773–1857), the 'Father of Aerodynamics', who first formulated the four vector forces of weight, lift, drag, and thrust, which determine whether something flies or not. Cayley's unmanned glider took to the air in 1804. Nearly half a century later, his loyal coachman is reputed to have piloted a manned glider across Brompton Dale in Yorkshire.[12]

The history of air crashes must have begun almost as soon as aviation itself. One has to assume that *Archaeopteryx* came to grief more than once. More recently, in May 1785, an unmanned balloon crashed into the town of Tullamore, County Offaly, in Ireland, setting one hundred houses alight and qualifying as the world's first aeronautical disaster. Only one month later, at Wimereux near Boulogne, Pilâtre de Rozier and his companion crashed their balloon on take-off while attempting to fly across the English Channel, thereby becoming the world's first aviationary fatalities. In May 1908, while testing the Wright Flyer III at Kitty Hawk in North Carolina, Orville Wright (1871–1948) pulled one of the control levers in the wrong direction and propelled his machine into the sand at over 60 mph. He emerged with a few bruises and a broken nose, later claiming to have been both 'the first aviator and the first to survive an air crash'. He was the author of two memorable remarks: 'The airplane stays up because it doesn't have the time to fall' and 'No flying machine will ever fly from New York to Paris.' He lived long enough to see transcontinental flying, but not space flight.[13]

As enthusiasts of the popular TV series 'Air Crash Investigation' can confirm,[14] the causes of aeronautical disasters are manifold. They include pilot error, technical faults, metal fatigue, fuel leaks, fires, engine failure, collapse of cabin pressure, wake turbulence, bird-strikes, foreign objects, storms, ice accumulation, volcanic ash, mid-air and runway collisions, air-piracy or 'skyjacking', bombs, suicidal passengers or crew members, and military action. The deadliest incident on record occurred at Tenerife in 1977, when two Boeing 747s collided on a runway killing 583 people. Mistakes by pilots provide the most frequent cause. The worst year for accident rates measured in fatalities per miles flown remains 1929.

In the First World War era, military pilots were sent up in open cockpits with no form of safety equipment. Reports on casualties were coldly factual:

## ROYAL FLYING CORPS
## REPORT ON CASUALTIES TO PERSONNEL
## AND MACHINES (WHEN FLYING)

| | |
|---|---|
| Type & No. of Machine | Bristol Fighter, F2B D7900 |
| Engine | Rolls Royce 3/Fal/39 WD 18519 |
| Pilot | 2/Lt N. DAVIES. RAF |
| Duty | Practice |

| | |
|---|---|
| Locality | Aerodrome |
| Camera | No |
| Wireless | No |
| Other equipment | 1.2 inch Aldis Sight, 1.112 Bomb Carrier (all damaged) |
| Where brought down | Adjoining aerodrome |
| (date) | 5 September 1918 |
| Time of Leaving | 11.35 am |
| Time of Casualty | 11.45 am |
| Fate of Personnel | Killed |
| Cause | Got into a spin when turning and crashed |
| Damage | Machine, Engine and Gun totally wrecked |
| Recommended | Wreckage to Salvage No 1, ASB |
| (Signed) | Major K. P. Park, Commanding 48 Squadron |
| Remarks: | MACHINE, ENGINE, AND GUN – STRUCK OFF STRENGTH of No. 48 Squadron and of RAF in the Field. Remains to be returned Wing-Commander S. H. Bowman, Major, 11 Wing Brigade-Commander, Write-Off T. T. Debb-Bowen, Brigadier-General OC 2nd Brigade, RFC.[15] |

The aerodrome in this case was at St Omer, Pas-de-Calais, France, some 20 miles behind the nearest trenches of the Western Front at Hazebrouck. The 'Remains', presumably, were all that was left of Uncle Norman, the stamp-collecting pilot. He wasn't shot down; he crashed. His grave lies in the British War Cemetery at nearby Longuenesse. A brief reminder of his loss flits across my mind every time I board an aeroplane.

Sometime later, a box from the Ministry of War was delivered to Norman's parents in Bolton. It contained his few remaining papers and possessions, a couple of cheap be-ribboned campaign medals, a larger bronze medal depicting Britannia and the British lion, inscribed with his name, and a mass-produced scroll headed by the royal coat of arms:

He whom this scroll commemorates was numbered among those who, at the call of King and Country, left all that was dear to them, endured hardness, faced danger, and finally passed out of the sight of men by the path of duty and self-sacrifice, giving up their own lives that others may live in freedom.

Let those who come after see to it
that his name be not forgotten.

2<sup>nd</sup> Lieut. Norman Davies, 48<sup>th</sup> Sqdn. Royal Air Force[16]

He was one of millions. The key phrase, I always think, was draped around the royal coat of arms: 'Honi soit qui mal y pense.'

Since then, both air safety and air security have steadily improved. Safety refers to the prevention of accidents, security to the prevention of attacks. National and international organizations investigate the causes of disasters and near misses, and initiate the compulsory installation of counter-measures. These have included navigational aids, altometers, ejector seats, instrument landing systems, ground-controlled approach (GPA), flight recorders, surveillance radar, air-traffic control, and most recently augmented geo-positioning systems (SBAS). Nonetheless, loopholes persist. The International Civil Aviation Organization called for an urgent meeting in Montreal in 2016 to discuss two pressing issues: one was 'global plane-tracking', the other was 'overflight of conflict zones'. Both were prompted by the loss of two near-identical Malaysian airliners: MH370 and MH17.[17]

The airline industry is always telling us dubiously that air travel is safer than all other modes of transport. Everything depends on the mode of measurement. Air travel only comes out top if one measures the number of fatalities against the number of miles travelled; by that reckoning it is indeed sixty times safer than travel by motorcar. However, if one counts the ratio of fatalities per journey, car travel wins over air travel with 40 per billion as opposed to 117 per billion for air travel. Neither car nor plane nor train is nearly as dangerous as travel by motorcycle.

In the first fourteen years of the twenty-first century, commercial aviation witnessed a steady drop in the worldwide incidence of fatalities. In 2001 a total of 4,140 deaths occurred from 200 accidents.* In 2013 the number of deaths dropped to 265, and of accidents to 138.[18] Due to MH370 and MH17, however, the accidental death toll rose in

---

* The events of 9/11 were not classed as accidents.

2014 to 969 – provided, of course, that the two Malaysian losses are definitively rated 'accidental'.

The history of maritime disasters provides many precedents for their aeronautical counterparts. It contains a similar list of human errors, navigational blunders, foul weather, technical and structural failures, as well as piracy and hostile action. But it also introduces the doom-laden issues of barratry, of disappearances and unsolved mysteries. The worst disaster at sea in European history seems to have occurred during the First Punic War, when a major Roman transport fleet sank off Carthage with the loss of 90,000 soldiers.[19] In world history, the largest such catastrophe is taken to have been caused in 1274, when the so-called *Kamikaze* or 'Divine Wind' destroyed the fleet of the Mongol Empire and, by drowning over 100,000 would-be invaders, saved Japan.[20] By comparison, the loss in 1912 of the *Titanic* and 1,500 of its passengers fades into insignificance.

Barratry, in maritime law, is the ancient term for gross, pre-planned fraud, which deprives ships' owners of their property; introduced into English in 1622, the offence was punishable by death. The barrators were usually the ship's captain or crew, who might divert their vessel's cargo for profit, stage a deliberate disaster, or otherwise present a fraudulent insurance claim. In 1885 a classic case was tried in court in Boston to test a claim prompted by the shipwreck of the *Amazon* off the coast of Haiti. Both the captain and the mate were found dead and the description of the cargo was found to be fraudulent. Bottles of fine wine were filled with water, and 'silver cutlery' turned out to be tin dog collars. The claim was dismissed, and the wreck remained stranded.[21]

A hundred years later, an elaborate fictional case was developed in Tom Clancy's novel *The Hunt for Red October* (1984), where the captain of a Soviet submarine diverts his vessel for the purpose of defecting to the West. From the perspective of Soviet law, he was guilty both of mutiny and of barratry.[22]

The disappearance of vessels is an age-old phenomenon. In the days before radio communication and modern salvage techniques, it was commonplace for a ship to founder in the open sea, not only without trace but also without anyone suspecting its loss for months or years. In February 1881, for example, the training ship HMS *Atalanta* left Bermuda with 281 men aboard, and was never seen again. Even in the twentieth century the list is not short. On 26 July 1910 the 16,000-ton SS *Waratah* of the Blue Anchor Line, serving the emigrant trade, sailed from Durban for Cape Town and vanished.[23]

Yet 'unsolved maritime mysteries' covers a wide spectrum of mis-haps. Most famous is the case of the *Mary Celeste*, a small, 236-ton British brigantine, which was found on 14 December 1872 drifting on a calm sea in mid-Atlantic, undamaged but unmanned. There were signs that the captain, passengers, and crew had taken hastily to the ship's yawl or 'row boat', which had been axed from its moorings; that nine days had passed since the ship's abandonment; and that the trag-edy was in some way connected to the cargo of alcoholic spirit. At the inquest in Gibraltar, the magistrate deduced that the thirsty crew had drunk the raw spirit, murdered the captain and passengers, and then debunked taking the evidence with them. He was not widely believed.

The *Mary Celeste* provoked a tidal wave of speculation, a host of conspiracy theories, and several works of literature. Speculation started after the inquest at the court of inquiry in Gibraltar, where the drifting ship's salvagers had claimed it as a prize. The theories ranged from an underwater 'seaquake' to Barbary pirates, who had taken their cap-tives to a slave market in North Africa. The literary works included a brilliant short story called 'J. Habakuk Jephson's Statement', which subtly changed the ship's name to 'Marie Celeste' and launched the career of Arthur Conan Doyle.[24] Public interest intensified dramati-cally, however, when it emerged that the drifting 'ghost ship' was one and the same as the vessel at the centre of a Boston barratry trial a dozen years earlier. In the time between the trial and the inquiry the *Mary Celeste* had changed owners seventeen times, had been repeat-edly renamed and left in a state of disrepair, and (it seems) bought by its last, disreputable owner in order to perpetrate another insurance fraud.[25]

As that complicated case indicates, many maritime mysteries have been solved, but only after extreme delays. Several such 'postponed solutions' involve ships trapped in Arctic or Antarctic ice. An early example – perhaps not fully substantiated – is that of the *Octavius*, a British merchantman that left China bound for England in 1762. It was supposedly found drifting and derelict off the coast of Greenland in 1775 with the crew still frozen in their hammocks and the captain still fixed to his desk. The assumption was that the captain had failed in an attempt to run the North-West Passage.[26] A later example concerns the schooner *Jenny*, which sailed from the Isle of Wight in 1822 and called at the Peruvian port of Callao before disappearing. She was found by a whaler in 1840, trapped in the ice of the Drake Passage, south of Tierra del Fuego. Her immaculate captain, like that of the *Octavius*, was frozen to his desk. The last entry in his log, dated 4 May 1823, read: 'No food for 71 days. I'm the only one left.'[27]

Nothing, however, beats the story of the 'Flying Dutchman', which gave rise to one of Richard Wagner's operas. The story, it seems, may have a basis in fact. A seventeenth-century sailing captain, Bernard Fokke (Barend Fockesz), employed by the Verenigde Oost-Indische Compagnie or VOC, was renowned for the amazing speed of his voyages between Amsterdam and Batavia. In 1678 he completed the voyage of 12,000 miles in the record time of three months and four days. (If true, his feat would have matched Tasman's time sailing between Batavia and Mauritius.)[28] After his death, a statue was erected to Fokke close to the harbour of Batavia. Subsequently, the story developed in a variety of directions. Firstly, the Flying Dutchman was said to have achieved his supernatural powers through a pact with the Devil. Secondly, he was no longer steering a real vessel but a ghost-ship, a 'spectre-bark', a phantom. Thirdly, the ship was the bearer of misfortune to all who came across it. Its sailors would hand out letters to be delivered to addressees who always turned out to be dead. In the early nineteenth century, the story was used or echoed by a number of Romantic writers, including Thomas Moore, Walter Scott, Edgar Allan Poe, and, most famously, Samuel Taylor Coleridge in *The Rime of the Ancient Mariner*. In 1821 it appeared in fully fledged form in an article published in Edinburgh by *Blackwood's Magazine*. By this time, the captain had the new name of Hendrich Vanderdecken, and was condemned to sail on in league with the Devil until the Day of Judgement.[29] In Paris, the story was turned into a popular opera,[30] and in Germany it formed the central theme of a satirical novel by Heinrich Heine from 1833, *Aus den Memoiren des Herren von Schnabelewopski*.[31]

Ghost-ships were the equivalent of UFOs in the folklore of the Romantic period; many people claimed to have seen them. They were explained away by more rational minds as some sort of optical illusion or mirage or Fata Morgana. Nevertheless, none other than the heir to the British throne, Prince George, the future George V, was among those who were convinced that they had seen the apparition for themselves. In 1881, in the company of his brother, Prince Albert Victor, he was serving as a midshipman aboard the Royal Navy corvette, HMS *Bacchante*, which was cruising off the southern coast of Australia:

> At 4 am, the *Flying Dutchman* crossed our bow. A strange red light as of a phantom ship all aglow, in the middle of which light the mast, spars and

sails of a brig some 200 yards distant stood out in strong relief as she came up on the port bow, where also the officer of the watch from the bridge clearly saw her, as did the quarterdeck midshipman ... Thirteen persons altogether saw her ... At 10.45 the ordinary seaman, who had this morning reported the *Flying Dutchman*, fell from the foretopmast crosstrees on to the topgallant forecastle, and was smashed to atoms.[32]

In writing the libretto for *Der fliegende Holländer* in 1840–41, Richard Wagner relied heavily on Heine's novel, emphasizing the idea that the ghost-ship's captain and crew could only be saved by the love of a faithful woman. For the opening scene, the stage directions state dramatically: 'the sea occupies the greater part of the stage'. In the final scene, the bass-baritone hero reveals to the heroine, Senta, that he is the accursed 'Flying Dutchman' and that he is condemned to depart on his eternal voyage. Senta flings herself into the sea in despair, vowing faithfulness till death and breaking the spell. The ghost-ship disappears. The happy sailors rejoice in chorus, and the reunited couple ascend to Heaven:

> *Preis Deinen Engel und sein Gebot*
> *Hier steh'ich treu Dir bis zum Tod!*
>
> (Be cheerful Thy mind, be joyous Thy heart,
> Thine will I be till death do us part!)
> *The sea rises high and sinks back in a whirlpool. In the glow of the sunset, over the wreck of the ship, the forms of Senta and the Dutchman are clearly seen, embracing, rising from the sea and floating upwards.*[33]

Transposing the features and folklore of maritime tradition into aviation history, one discovers remarkable similarities. The old crime of barratry, for example, has now been supplemented by the new crime of 'air barratry', which entered the frame in discussions over MH370.[34] Present-day practice in the insurance of commercial airliners makes clear distinctions between the claims of the owners and those of the passengers. As soon as a disaster is classified 'accidental', the owners can expect a rapid and full compensation payment; the passengers can expect nothing more from the insurers than a token or interim payment.[35]

Disappearing aircraft, if not very frequent, are an established part of the record. The female American aviator Amelia Earhart, who had already emulated Charles Lindbergh in a solo crossing of the Atlantic, set off in June 1937 to cross the Pacific on the first stage of her planned circumnavigation of the equator. She, her navigator, and their Lockheed Electra never reached the intended stopover point on Howland Island in the Phoenix Group, and were presumed lost.[36] In 1945 a group of USAAF trainee pilots disappeared in the so-called Bermuda Triangle. Although the wreckage of their planes was eventually found, the search party sent out from Miami was not.[37] In 1956 an American B47 Stratojet, reputedly carrying a nuclear bomb or bombs, disappeared over the Mediterranean.[38] In March 1962 a chartered American military plane, a Lockheed L-1049 Super Constellation propliner, operated as Flight 739 by the Flying Tiger company, disappeared without trace after refuelling at Guam on its way to Saigon, with 107 people aboard. Investigations were complicated by a simultaneous disaster on the Aleutian Islands, where another of Flying Tiger's Super Constellations crashed. Sabotage was suspected.[39]

Unsolved air mysteries, therefore, are not lacking. A particularly intriguing incident in November 1971 over the American north-west has defied every attempt by the FBI to identify the culprit or determine his fate. A passenger who had checked in at Portland, Oregon, under the false name of 'Dan Cooper' boarded Northwest Orient Airlines Flight 305; midway to Seattle he entered the cockpit and drew a gun. Communicating by scribbled notes (to avoid his voice being caught on the flight recorder), he ordered the pilot of the Boeing 727 to land, release all forty-three passengers, obtain four parachutes* together with $200,000 in banknotes, and then restart the engines and take off. In the second stage of the operation, he gave the pilot precise instructions written on a placard about the required flight path, speed, and altitude; he locked the three flight attendants into the cockpit with the pilot, and proceeded to the hold, where, by pressing the appropriate buttons, he opened the aircraft's fuselage hatch and lowered the rear air stairs. His meticulous planning was obviously informed by expert knowledge of the Boeing 727's equipment. Strapping on a parachute and a rucksack filled with the money but wearing no helmet, he then walked down the air stairs and jumped into the ice-cold, rain-lashed, and pitch-black night. The crew felt the plane judder as he left. They landed safely at Reno in Nevada. The FBI were convinced that the bold

---

* By demanding four parachutes instead of one, he cleverly led the authorities to believe he might force one or more hostages to jump from the aircraft with him. This guaranteed he wouldn't deliberately be supplied with a sabotaged parachute.

skyjacker could not have survived the extreme conditions that pertained both in the air and on the ground. But no body, no parachute, no clothing, and no money were ever retrieved. The serial numbers of the missing banknotes can still be found online.[40]

Few such events resist an explanation indefinitely, but the solution is sometimes very slow in coming. Fifty-one years, for example, separated the disappearance in August 1947 of a British South American Airways Avro Lancastrian 3 called *Stardust* and the start of the wreck's recovery in 1998. The plane had been flying from Buenos Aires in Argentina to Santiago in Chile, and in the final phase was routed across the high ridge of the Andes. Encountering heavy snowstorms and a powerful head wind, the crew miscalculated, and started their descent too soon. *Stardust* ploughed into the near vertical ice-wall of a glacier on Mount Tupungato (6,570 metres) bordering the two countries, and penetrated deep under the glacier's surface. More than half a century later, when the requisite section of the glacier had moved down the mountain and was beginning to melt, a group of climbers noticed a Rolls-Royce Merlin engine protruding from the ice. Bit by bit, over the next four years, the glacier released its secrets.[41]

Over that half-century great strides were taken in aviation technology, but some things do not change. Foremost among the unchangeables is human fallibility, the capacity to blunder. Having been legally classed an 'injured party' in the wake of the Smolensk disaster of 10 April 2010 – even though my wife and I were on the preceding flight to Smolensk, which landed safely – I follow developments keenly; and I confirm without equivocation that multiple human errors – in planning, training, and, above all, in navigational decisions which broke all manner of established rules – were the prime cause of the fatal crash of the Polish Airlines Tupolev plane Tu-154 101 that killed President Lech Kaczyński, his wife Maria, and nearly a hundred senior officials.[42]

International rivalries constantly breed mistrust, and, if a disaster occurs, hamper investigative procedures. At Smolensk, the none-too-happy relations between Poland and Russia led first to misunderstandings between the pilot and ground control, and later to disputes between Polish and Russian investigators. The Russian Commission into Tu-154 101 decided not only that an unauthorized Polish general had been present in the cockpit, but also that the general had been drinking.[43] Rather like the Gibraltarian magistrate in the case of *Mary Celeste*, the conclusions of this investigation were not widely believed. Yet Poland and Russia are by no means the only offenders. Air disasters frequently involve the authorities of more than one country, protracted inquiries, and the participation of international teams. In the case of MH370, the mistrust between the Malaysians, the plane's owners and operators, and Chinese officials, representing the majority of the victims, was palpable. Worst of all, in a world where conflicts abound and intelligence agencies compete, secrecy continues to cloak many aspects of key information. Military agencies are reluctant to share knowledge, and government spokespersons feed doctored news to the press and public alike. Every country gives priority to its own perceptions of security and only releases selective information, even to its allies. Everyone knows that the Earth is ringed with satellites, and that satellites in space can reputedly read the cards of poker players sitting around a table at ground level. Over ten thousand satellites are operating around the Earth night and day. One of them took a snapshot of MH17 under attack from a surface-to-air missile. Is it conceivable that none of them could catch sight of another 300-ton airliner, MH370, that kept flying for hours after it left its intended route? The official answer is 'Yes'. There are apparently parts of the globe that are not covered by round-the-clock surveillance.

One of the main differences between maritime and aerial disappearances is that stricken or abandoned ships can stay afloat. Stricken aeroplanes, in contrast, obviously cannot stay in the air indefinitely; they are condemned either to land safely or, within a short time, to crash.

As I write, almost four years have passed since Flight MH370, a Boeing 777-200ER,* soared out of Kuala Lumpur towards a fate as yet unascertained. The international search has been suspended.[44] The only definite clues centre on a handful of items of debris that have been officially identified with the missing aircraft. The first of these, a solitary barnacled flaperon, was washed up on a beach on Réunion Island in August 2015, immediately eliminating all the lingering hopes of a safe landing.[45] Yet the baffled investigators are still examining an unresolved mystery. Reason dictates that the Boeing 777-200ER is lying somewhere, either intact or in pieces. It cannot have embarked, like the Flying Dutchman, on a perpetual voyage.

Historians do not usually contribute to such mysteries. Few are

---

* The Boeing 777-200ER (Extended Range) is the second of eight current variants of the basic 777 model.

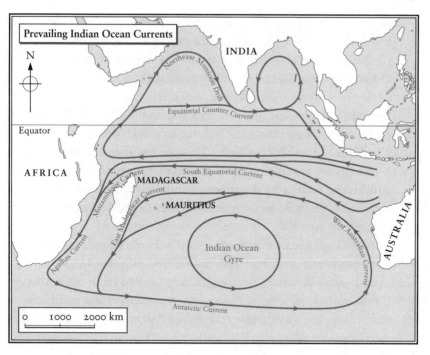

Prevailing Indian Ocean Currents

familiar with the complexities of aviation. On the other hand, they do operate in a branch of detective work. The best of them are trained to sift verified facts from suppositions and hypotheses, weigh motives, establish sequential chronologies, and observe the chains of cause and effect. In reconstructing their narratives of the past, they are practised in imaginative puzzle-solving and separating wild explanations from sober ones. Since they probe causation, they habitually weigh a hierarchy of possibilities and impossibilities, listing implausibles, plausibles, likelihoods, strong probabilities, and near-certainties. In the age of 'fake news', 'alternative facts', and 'data overload', their pennyworth may not be entirely useless.

So, to start with the small pool of facts:

* The abnormal phase of MH370's flight began roughly one hour after take-off, when the plane's communication transponder was deliberately switched off, and the coordinates of a new waypoint were entered into the on-board computer. By general consent, these operations could only have been effected by someone with expert knowledge of advanced aviation equipment.

* MH370 was diverted over an area adjacent to islands in the South China Sea, which is the subject of growing international tensions.[46] Joint US-Thai military manoeuvres codenamed Operation Cope Tiger were in progress nearby.[47]

* Malaysia has made many foreign enemies in recent years. It hosts an independent War Crimes Commission (KLWCT) set up in 2007 in opposition to the International Criminal Court at The Hague. A tribunal at Kuala Lumpur has found Western leaders guilty *in absentia* of crimes against peace in Iraq, condemned torture by the American administration at Guantanamo Bay, and held Israel responsible for genocide against the Palestinian people.[48]

* There is strong reason to suspect that MH370's cargo manifest was inaccurate, and hence that undeclared cargo 'of special interest' was aboard.[49] Since all its cargo would have fallen into Chinese hands in Beijing, Chinese agencies attract less suspicion than others for seeking to interrupt the flight.

* Non-stop surveillance of the Earth's surface by space-stationed spy satellites has long since left the realm of science fiction. America's National Reconnaissance Office, whose emblem is the 'World Octopus' and its motto 'Nothing Beyond Our Reach', is the major player.[50] Yet a marked discrepancy exists between the NRO's reaction to the downing of MH17, when satellite images were swiftly produced, and its silence over the fate of MH370.[51]

* Advanced avionics is one of the specialities of the Texas-based Freescale Superconductors Corporation, which issued an early statement that twenty of its employees, mainly Malaysians of Chinese descent, were on the missing plane. No further public information about them has surfaced.[52]

* MH370's initial disappearance took place within range of two or three separate military radar systems with enhanced capacity for tracking aircraft. After much delay, Malaysia admitted that its own military radar had tracked MH370 for several hours. At least in public, the countries in the area with similar facilities have maintained their silence.[53]

* MH370's 'black boxes', though often said to carry the best clues to the disaster, are unlikely, even if found, to have preserved data on the plane's initial diversion. The recorders use tapes on a two-hour loop. All data from the flight's early phase would have been erased during the many hours of continued flying.

* After the initial diversion, which set MH370 on an east–west
flight path over the Malay Peninsula, the plane performed
several unexplained manoeuvres. In one, it apparently ascended
to 45,000 feet before plunging to near-ground level. Next, on
reaching the Malacca Strait, it followed a smooth, anticlockwise course around the northern tip of Sumatra. And
thirdly, after protracted hesitations over the Andaman Sea, it
embarked on a longer and more consistent course, which was
later identified from the second series of the plane's ACARS
transmissions. Analysed by technicians from the British Inmarsat company, these transmissions triggered the inconclusive
search off Western Australia.[54]
* The flaperon washed up on Réunion adds little to ruminations
about the disaster's ultimate causes and does nothing to indicate
how this one small section became detached from the wing.
Floating in seawater for many months, it had been transported by
the great Indian Ocean Gyre, whose currents move in an anticlockwise circle over thousands of miles of the ocean's outer rim.[55]
* During the investigations, a consensus emerged among international experts that MH370 must have flown for hours on
autopilot, and that all passengers and crew would have been
either dead or unconscious from absence of oxygen long before
the catastrophic climax.[56] A clear precedent exists for this from
August 2005, when Flight 522 of Helios Airways, whose pilots
were disabled by a faulty air supply, flew for hours on autopilot
before diving into a Greek hillside.[57]
* Thanks to the numerous dead ends of inquiry, much curiosity
has been drawn to the workings of the particular autopilot with
which the Boeing 777-200ER was fitted: the Boeing Honeywell
Uninterruptible Auto Pilot (BHUAP).[58] Developed after 9/11,
this sophisticated device was designed to prevent skyjackings.
Using established drone technology, it gives access to cyber
signals from remote controllers, who, through radio or satellite
links, can override commands generated in the cockpit. (Hence
the adjective 'Uninterruptible', not yet listed in the OED.)
Authorized remote controllers would have had little difficulty in
wresting control of the plane from a rogue pilot, or in landing it
safely on a pre-prepared ground strip. Furthermore, since
intelligence agencies such as the NRO can now take over
unsuspecting planes remotely, one can be sure that rival

agencies, hackers, and cyber foes will have been trying hard to
develop the same capacity.[59]
* Three years on, the largest organized group of relatives and friends
  of the missing passengers resolutely refuse to accept official reports
  about MH370, convinced that the biggest cover-up in aviation
  history is in progress. Many of them have filed lawsuits.[60]
* All the official reports, and most media comments, are characterized by extreme caution. They are clearly inhibited by the
  wilder speculations that proliferate in the 'blogosphere', and are
  reluctant to discuss hypotheses unsupported by hard evidence or
  precedent. More thought obviously needs to be directed towards
  the possibility of unprecedented circumstances.

One swallow doesn't make a summer, and a heap of assorted facts does
not amount to a credible argument. The truth is that the ratio of
knowns to unknowns in the case of MH370 is very low. There are no
indications of technical failure, no hints about motives, no leads concerning possible perpetrators. It is a fine teaser. For the time being, the
best that can be done is to make a list of alternative solutions and order
them in degrees of probability.

The sequence of events is always significant. The fact that MH370
was deliberately diverted early on over the South China Sea suggests
that the aim of the diversion could have been to stop the aircraft reaching China. That it navigated its way around the Malacca Strait with
great precision suggests the plane was still in the hands of competent
and unflustered pilots or controllers. Yet the fact that it then wandered
aimlessly over the open ocean before making a further radical change
of direction has serious implications. Added to the report that the
ACARS system had restarted only after a substantial pause, it strengthens the suspicion that the controlling agents of the preceding phase had
somehow lost their grip, and that a second external diversion might
have occurred. The plane's patterns of behaviour were markedly dissimilar in each stage of the flight.

The hierarchy of possibilities, therefore, demands exposition:

* Despite the weight of opinion in the 'blogosphere', it is *not
  possible* that MH370 was abducted by UFOs or aliens from
  outer space. After the discovery of the flaperon, and of other
  fragments in Mozambique and Madagascar,[61] it is also impossible to accept theories that MH370 was flown intact to
  Kazakhstan, Tel Aviv, Diego Garcia, or anywhere else.

* It is *improbable* that MH370 was taken over by old-fashioned, gun-toting 'skyjackers.' Strict countermeasures have been enforced since 9/11. The cockpit door would have been locked; the crew were trained; and a 'Mayday' call could easily have been made. These circumstances reduce the gallery of plausible culprits to the pilots, the senior steward (who held the code to the cockpit's door lock), or some external agency.

* It is *reasonably likely*, therefore, that MH370 was the object of the first-ever instance of cyber skyjacking. Such an action is well within the scope of twenty-first-century technology, even though a limited group of countries possess the necessary know-how. The USA would top the list, followed by major NATO countries, Russia, China, and Israel. Yet two other likelihoods inhabit the scenario. One supposes that the original game plan of the remote controllers went horribly wrong. The other suggests that the first remote strike provoked a second, retaliatory strike. Each of these scenarios helps to lift the fog surrounding the kidnappers' motives. If MH370 was indeed captured by remote controllers, the prime motive for their action must have been to prevent the plane and its cargo from reaching China. If a second set of remote controllers became involved, their motive can only have been to thwart the designs of the plane's original captors and stop them from flying their prize to a safe destination.

* It is *very probable* that Flight MH370 ended in catastrophic disaster, whether by design or mischance. So the mystery comes full circle: What caused the disaster? Where is the wreck? What happened to the passengers? And who was responsible?

* In the last reckoning, it must be a *near-certainty* that someone in the world knows more about Flight MH370 than they have chosen to reveal. Their reticence might be explained by either the secretive rules of a state intelligence agency or the simple fear of being held to blame.

* It can also be rated *all but certain* that the mystery will eventually be solved, either by persistent sleuthing or by accident. The fate of the *Octavius* was revealed after thirteen years, of the *Jenny* after seventeen years, of the *Bounty* after eighteen years, of the ships of La Pérouse after thirty-eight years, and of British South American Airways *Stardust* after fifty-one years.

I naturally wonder, too, what may be wrong in that chain of reasoning.

Mysterious events and inexplicable happenings are a frequent feature of the historical record, as are the flights of fancy that they inspire. And one does not need to resort to the supernatural to speculate in a positive spirit. The location of MH370's last resting place, for example, continues to defy all the sophisticated methods deployed to identify it. It does so either because all the available devices for scouring the seabed at 7,000 metres are inadequate to the task, or, more convincingly, because the searchers have not been scouring the appropriate section of the ocean.

One investigative weak link stands out. The rectangle of sea 1,500 miles off the coast of Western Australia, where the search was concentrated (see p. 342 above), was chosen as the result of two calculations, one about the plane's line of flight and the other about the distance that the Boeing 777-200ER would have flown on its residual fuel supply. If either of those calculations or the assumptions underlying them were faulty, the searchers must have been sent on a mission that was pointless from the start. It was universally assumed, for example, that the 777-200ER, which has a maximum range of 13,084 kilometres and is capable of flying for fourteen hours, was carrying fuel for only seven hours (as required by the intended flight to Beijing); and in the final phase that the autopilot necessarily set the engines to the optimal cruising speed of 554 mph. Any change in these assumptions would push the search in the Indian Ocean to a new location.

Many historians fear speculation, and condemn it as no better than unwarranted conjecture, surmise, or gossip. The genre of 'speculative history' is often equated with 'pseudo-history'. Yet the original meaning of speculation was 'intelligent observation', and it should not be confused with ignorant guesswork. Wherever one is faced with a perplexing conundrum, informed speculation has its place. It is the chosen tool of philosophers. 'In speculative thought,' wrote Spinoza, 'we are compelled to follow truth.'

Please imagine an eccentric scenario, therefore, just for a moment, and ignore the risk of its being proved wrong. Put your mind for a moment into unfettered mode. Try to imagine what the unseen controllers of MH370 (or a crazed pilot) might have done if their aim was to cover their tracks and despatch the plane to a destination that would never be found: in other words, a cold-blooded, premeditated vanishing act. The seabed of the Diamantina Deep, an ocean trench off Western Australia whose lowest point lies at −8,042 metres

(−26,401 feet), would not have been a bad choice. But a hiding place under the Antarctic pack ice, secure from the prying eyes of sonar probes and space satellites, could be even better.

In that case, the 'controllers' would have been obliged to extend the plane's range beyond that which official investigators have taken for granted. If their plotting had preceded take-off, for example, they might have arranged for more fuel to be loaded at Kuala Lumpur than was accounted for. They could have falsified the fuel record as well as the cargo manifest. Alternatively, if the action was forced on them in mid-flight, perhaps to repel a retaliatory takeover, they would have had various options to hand. They would have known not only that modern airliners can glide for long intervals without engine power, but also that they lose speed and height quite slowly in the first stage of a free-fall descent. (A Boeing 777 losing power at 30,000 feet can descend to the ground gracefully over 92 miles.)[62] They could even have resorted to a combination of cruising and gliding. Hence, if MH370's autopilot were programmed to switch the engines to idling mode for 10 minutes every half hour, the 7-hour flying time could be stretched to 9 hours 20 minutes without the addition of extra fuel. Most critically, the mileage covered (based on an estimated 3,439 miles of jet-propelled flight and 1,500 miles of gliding) would increase dramatically from 3,800 to 4,939 miles. Assisted by favourable side and tail winds above the 'Roaring Forties', the plane would be driven a little to the east but could comfortably have crossed the 5,000-mile mark. This extraordinary distance is equivalent to 72 degrees of latitude. It would have taken MH370 from the Andaman Sea (at 10 degrees north) to a point below 62 degrees south, not far from the Magnetic South Pole and well within the limits of Antarctic pack ice.

What a thought! Instead of nose-diving into the designated rectangle of the Indian Ocean, MH370 could have floated gently to the sea's surface far to the south like an albatross or an *Archaeopteryx*, passing stately icebergs as it touched down somewhere between Cape Adare and the Dumont D'Urville Sea. It would have sunk largely intact through the lightly scattered ice floes of an antipodean autumn – losing perhaps two or three flaps, fairings, or tailfins, but not the deceased, oxygen-starved passengers and crew, still strapped in their seats; and it would have come to rest on the seabed of the Antarctic Shelf. In the following days and weeks, the southern winter would have set in, the pack ice would have hardened and consolidated. The Indian Ocean Gyre would have removed bits of wreckage from the scene, and any more debris that rose from the depths would have been trapped beneath the ice. The crime was perfect. And the unseen controllers could breathe a secret sigh of relief.

This sort of scenario may be fanciful but is not ludicrous. Where facts fail, fancy invariably steps in:

> Time is a thief at the end of the road, a river;
> Time is a dream, a life contained in a moment –
> Well, have it your own way . . .
> But the miracle passes simply, amazement is wordless,
> Discovery silent, stumbling suddenly into
> Truth in a landless sea . . .
>
> This was the story of a ship caught in a bottle,
> And that bottle was Time – I confuse it with another image –
> Becalmed in Time, and sealed with a cork of ice;
> Frozen and still in the bottle, ice on the rigging,
> Over masts and yards, the drops suspended
> Frozen for forty years . . .
> Quiet on the decks, so wordless that one would say
> 'This is a vessel of drowned men' . . .
> Or else one might say – 'This was a ship of disaster.'
> Think of the bodies, splintered and broken, the cabin
> With blood on the walls, dried now to a faint inscription,
> The thundering fist to the jaw, the lamp left swinging,
> The glasses tumbled – wine dripping over the tables.
> And all of them killed, you say? What a tale of fury!
> But the truth of it is that this is a ship of the living
> Locked in a wall of ice, suspended in Time.
> And, listen,
> If we could stand on the deck with them we might hear voices.
> That was the story. Question the manner of telling,
> But be sure at least of pain and ice and silence.
> Of Time? Well, there one can never be certain –
> For you a thing to be measured perhaps – for me, a searching:
> And for [those] alone on a frozen ship? I wonder.
> However, it is beyond our chance of knowing.[63]

Speculation remains speculation, and fancy is fancy; and poetry is licensed to stray. But such were the mind games with which the globe-trotter passed his time on the long last stages of his global wanderings. The flier became obsessed with flying. Thoughts about indigenous peoples, human migrations, and other historical matters were temporarily shelved.

Many months and a score of countries after my departure from Frankfurt, Air Canada 874 touched down on time at 6.30 a.m. on a Saturday morning at the same airport. I had wound my way back from North America by a roundabout route. A contented passenger was closing the circle after a journey of some 30,000 miles, as Eratosthenes and Al Masudi foresaw. This time, the whereabouts of the shuttle stop posed no nightmares. The Steigenberger Hotel showed a familiar face. My wife was sleeping sweetly in Room 218. A quick dip in the ninth-floor pool served as a final relaxation before the sheets opened, and sleep descended with a rush like a Tahitian sunset.

Jet lag is often accompanied by pangs of hunger. Waking in mid-afternoon, I set off with my wife in search of sustenance; the ladies at reception recommend the Wald Restaurant.

'Just turn right and follow the signs into the courtyard,' they say. 'It opens at 5.30.'

A Forest Restaurant in the middle of an airport hotel was a novelty, completely missed during the earlier stay. And how romantic! My favourite German poet, Joseph von Eichendorff, would have been impressed by this brave attempt to summon the forest spirits to such unpromising surroundings:

> O Taeler weit, o Hoehen,
> O schoener, gruener Wald,
> Du meiner Lust und Wehen
> Andaecht'ger Aufenthalt!
>
> (O valleys broad! O soaring crags!
> And fair green woods below!
> My refuge for reflecting
> On all life's joy and sorrow.)[64]

On the way to eat, we pick up a brochure that promises us GENIESSEN AUS TRADITION, 'The Flavours of Tradition', and HERRLICH IDYLL-ISCH, 'Moments of Bliss'. 'The historical ambience of the 230-year-old "Forester's Lodge" offers traditional Frankfurter congeniality at its best.'[65] This place was here long before aeroplanes and airports, even before Eichendorff's time. When it was built in 1782 the Holy Roman Empire was still intact.

The guidebook had forewarned us about Hesse's modest culinary specialities. They included *apfelwein* (applewine), *Grüne Sosse*, or 'cold green sauce', made from herbs, sour cream and boiled eggs, and, of course, *Frankfurter* sausages, the global standard for 'hot dogs'. *Frankfurter Rippchen* are straightforward pork cutlets with sauerkraut, whilst the *Handkäse mit Musik*, literally 'hand-made cheese with music', is famed for its flatulent counterpoint.[66]

Even so, it had been spring when I left Frankfurt, and it was high summer when I returned. So a meal *al fresco* and the promise of 'typical German cuisine' sounded attractive. The restaurant is laid out round the four sides of a rectangular courtyard. The central serving area, arranged under the branches of an ancient oak, is open to the sky. Dining tables are placed in deep alcoves protected by the beams of the black-timbered roof that runs around the periphery. Diners sit under the canopy at wooden tables on comfortable chairs upholstered in green and yellow. The tables are set so far back that there is no chance of being rained on. One can see the trunk of the oak tree in the middle, but not the open sky above it.

The waiter, Kevin, came to take our order. I had seen *Wildschweinkotelette* on the menu, but not liking game, neither ordered it nor thought to connect it with the restaurant's origins. Instead, we chose fish; my wife went for *Schollenfilet* (plaice) and I for *Forelle Muelleri* (trout). The main course was preceded for me by *Selleriesuppe*, for my wife by a *Romana salat*. Shouldn't that be either *Insalata Romana* or *Römisch Zalat*? No matter. Even if the salad had the wrong gender, it turned out to be a memorable gastronomic item. The Romans' custom is to mix both fruit and vegetables with the lettuce and olive oil. 'Pears and Cucumber' is one combination. 'Strawberries, prawns, and asparagus' is another, and my wife was enthusing about it long after I had drained my glass of *Paulaner*.

The one thing not mentioned was the meal's unprecedented tintinnabulous accompaniment: the *essen mit Musik*. There was, almost literally, an invisible Jumbo in the room. The waiters seemed oblivious. The management was in a state of deep, deep denial. Everyone pretended that it wasn't there. No one reacted. Yet every other minute, in between each mouthful, the timbers of the roof began to vibrate. After ten or fifteen seconds, the crockery struck up. And thirty seconds in, the cutlery was jumping merrily off the tablecloth. For a short time, as the Pratt and Whitneys and Rolls-Royce Brents were skimming the restaurant's roof, the decibels rose to such a pitch, straining to preserve the coefficient of lift, that all conversations were drowned, all swallowing was interrupted, and all thinking stifled. I was reminded of the peculiar state of mental paralysis that affected many Germans about their recent history after 1945. A ghoulish uncle of mine once travelled to Berchtesgaden in Bavaria to peer at the site of Hitler's *Berghof*. Asking a passer-by for the whereabouts of 'Adolf Hitler's House', he received the polite reply: 'I'm sorry, who is Adolf Hitler?' I am absolutely sure that Kevin, on instructions from the management, would have replied in similar vein had I enquired about the noise.

'I'm sorry,' he would have said. 'What noise?'

Instead, I decided to ask him about the history of the Wald Restaurant. He had been well trained. As soon as the city gained possession of its forest, it transpired, measures were enacted to control the many sounders of wild boar that lived on the profusion of acorns and beech nuts, but which, if left to multiply unhindered, could become a nuisance. Hence, it was decreed in 1491 that the boars be rounded up once a year, counted, and culled. At the end of the operation, the city fathers would proclaim a great feast during which boars were roasted whole and hungry citizens could gorge themselves on the succulent *Wildschweinkotelettes*. To aid the proceedings, two stockaded compounds were created where counting and culling could take place. One of them, on the edge of a lake and closer to the city, became known as the *Ober-* or 'Upper Compound'; the other, deeper in the forest, was named the *Unter-* or 'Lower Compound'. Municipal records show that in 1779 no fewer than 1,470 boars were counted. As a result, a permanent, stone-built and red-roofed building was constructed on this site two years later. Finally, sometime after 1866, when Frankfurt was joined to the Kingdom of Prussia, the royal tax collectors imposed a tax of 1.5 gulden on every animal counted. One assumes that the tax killed off the feasts and mediaeval boar culls. Kevin handed us a leaflet where all the information had come from.

'So if *Stiege* means "compound",' I asked, having paid the bill for 97.80 euros and thanked him for the meal, '*Unterschweinstiege* stands for "Lower Wild Boar Compound". Right?'

Kevin thought for a minute. He was Irish, but his German was clearly proficient.

'Actually, no,' he said with a grin. 'As far as I know, *Die Stiege* is the ordinary German word for a "staircase". But it can also mean "twenty" or "a score", as in *eine Stiege Eier*, "a score of eggs". I'm sorry, I can't help you.'

'That's very odd,' I muttered. Lower wild boars in Germany either run up and down staircases or munch on oversize boxes of eggs.

Well fed and well content, my wife and I left for an evening stroll. Our destination was the forest, the *Stadtwald*, whose dense stands of oaks could be glimpsed in full leaf from Reception. Dodging the traffic on the autobahn slip road, we slipped through a gap in the fence and entered a different world, like Alice falling down the rabbit hole. Shafts of sunlight shone through the branches. Neat stacks of timber awaited collection and a long clearing wound invitingly through the trees. Surely, we had found Eichendorff's 'refuge for recollecting life's joys and sorrows'. A couple of hikers strode past purposefully. A cyclist pedalled by, bent over the handlebars. And a city jogger, huffing and puffing, rounded the bend. Something stirred in the undergrowth. I froze to see whether it was a deer, or even a wild boar.

And then, in the space of a minute, we were shaken from our reveries by a pair of bolts from the blue. Firstly, our eardrums were assaulted by the thunderous roar of a 777-200 directly overhead. Looking up, I again experienced the thrill produced by a close view of the underside of a giant plane. There was no 'quiet telling truth' to be found here. Secondly, nailed to an oak, I spied an old metal sign, which bore an inscription written in white Gothic letters on a background of Prussian blue. It read *Unterschweinstiegschneisse*. How old was that? As I snapped the sign with my camera, the branches around it were quivering, and the sign itself was rattling like the cutlery in the restaurant.

Frankfurt, of course, was no more than a stopover. After more than 30,000 miles, a period of home recovery was needed, to re-adapt to the idea of standing still, of stepping off the fairground carousel and letting the Earth spin of its own accord. Memories of continents crowded in, and the long task of reducing the mass of those memories into a coherent narrative beckoned.

Two things could not be lightly put aside. One was the realization that I had come safely home, whereas some travellers don't. When MH370 disappeared, it was discovered that two young Iranians had boarded the plane carrying false passports. Press reports targeted them as potential terrorists. In reality, they were illegal migrants planning to make a new life in Europe. The younger man, Pouria Nour Mehrdad, eighteen, had hoped to start afresh in Germany. His mother was waiting for him at Flughafen FRA, but he never arrived.[67]

The other worry was the niggling puzzle of the sign outside the airport hotel and its translation-defying inscription. Its old-fashioned Gothic-printed script, known as *Fraktur*, and its handwriting counterpart called *Suetterlin*, had been used in Germany from the sixteenth century until 1941, when the Nazis had banned them without warning as 'Jewish letters'. They were reinstated in 1945–6, but soon dropped again in the post-war wave of modernization.[68] This means that the road sign could have been nailed to its oak at any time before 1941 or after the war, in 1945–6. The latter is the more probable. Frankfurt had repeatedly been attacked by Allied bombers, which completely demolished the mediaeval city centre and killed over 5,000 citizens.[69] The airport was also a target; and the area around the Wald Restaurant must have needed a massive post-war clean-up. I had been mightily impressed by watching the undersides of Boeings and Airbuses; Frankfurters of the wartime generation must have been even more impressed by looking up at the undersides of Lancasters and Flying Fortresses, or terrified at the prospect that their bomb bays might open.

The exact significance of *Unterschweinstiegschneisse*, however, continued to escape me. By this time, *Unter-* (meaning 'Under' or 'Lower'), *Schwein* ('Pig' or 'Wild Boar'), and *Schneise* ('Path') were offering no real resistance. But the twin near-homophones of *der Stieg* and *die Stiege* were defying all decoding. Although apparently derived from the same verb *steigen*, 'to rise or climb', both figured in various dictionaries in a baffling array of English meanings – from 'rose' and 'increase' to 'staircase', 'score', 'crate', and 'climb'. Online translation aids were particularly dubious. *Schweinstieg*, for example, produced 'Pig Rose'. (The German footballer Bastian Schweinsteiger, the 'Pig Climber', was born close to the Bavarian village of Schweinstieg.)[70]

Defeated and dismayed, I sought assistance in vain from three distinguished colleagues, all Germans or Germanists. So, as with the mystery of MH370, I had to risk my own speculative explanation. After much pondering of the fifteenth-century German, I decided that the concept of the 'Wild Boars' Staircase' fits fairly well if one doesn't insist on too literal a rendering. All one has to do is imagine the boars being driven from the low-lying parts of the forest onto an 'uphill track' or 'steep ascent'. Further, since the map shows two such tracks, one higher and the other lower, it is a simple matter to arrive at a 'Lower Track' and a 'Higher Track'. Sometime later – orthography notwithstanding – footpaths for walkers were laid out along the old mediaeval pig tracks, thereby producing, among others, the *Unterschweinstiegschneisse* – 'the

footpath that follows the Lower Wild Boars' Uphill Ascent'. I searched
the map in vain for the *Überschweinstiegschneisse*.

Which reminded me of the shuttle bus. Would I have had more success if I had asked someone for the *Pendelverkehrbushaltestelle*? 'It is
beyond our chance of knowing.'

Homer of course never landed at FRA, but his books were on sale in
the airport bookshop. And I, like Odysseus, had 'wandered wondrous
farre', returning home to my European Ithaca, my little Liré. I had cir-
cumvented the world's conflict zones and bypassed many important
countries. Even so, I had seen a fair selection of foreign lands, and a
great variety of peoples. Travelling had allowed me to think freely
about the subject I have spent most of my life studying, history. I would
like to think, at least in some modest respects, that 'I saw and knew'.

All journeys end on a particular note. The *Pilgrim's Progress* ends
with an exhortation – 'to throw away the dross and yet preserve the
gold'. The *Odyssey* ends with the goddess Athena bringing reconciliation, the *Aeneid* with yet another killing, and the incomparable *Divina
Commedia* on a note of ecstatic wonderment:

> *All'alta fantasia qui manca possa:*
> *Ma già volgeva, il mio disio e 'l velle,*
> *Sì come rota ch'igualmente è mossa,*
> *L'Amor che move il sole e l'altre stelle.*

> (Here vigour fail'd the towering fantasy:
> But yet the will roll'd onward, like a wheel
> In even motion, by the love impell'd,
> That moves the sun in heaven and all the stars.)[71]

# 15

# Imperium

*European History for Export*[1]

Hardened historians who set off on lengthy tours invariably carry a set of lecture notes in their back pocket – just in case. Since I was visiting a string of countries that had served time in the British Empire, and was looking forward to presenting a few talks, I chose to carry the outlines of a lecture on the general topic of 'Empires'. I assumed that a wandering British lecturer would be expected to say something about the interaction between the ex-imperialists and the ex-imperialized.

At the same time, being alerted to the emotions that surround the topic, I looked for an unfamiliar line of argument to keep my audiences interested and avoid any possible turbulence. The Indian writer Arundhati Roy has given fair warning of the ferocity of feeling. 'Our strategy should not only be to confront empire,' she wrote, 'but to lay siege to it, to deprive it of oxygen, to shame it . . . and to tell our own stories.'[2] I decided, therefore – after relating some of my recent encounters with the imperial theme – to draw on my experience as a historian of Europe and to deconstruct the stereotype which equates all Europeans with imperialists. It might be news to some, I hoped, that some Europeans have frequently been the victims of imperialism, and not just its perpetrators.

Before he became a celebrated novelist, William Golding, the centenary of whose birth was marked in 2011, had been a schoolmaster and history teacher, as I had been; by sheer coincidence we both taught the same subjects at the same school in Maidstone, though at different times. As a boy, I had once started to read his famous novel, *Lord of the Flies*, first published in 1954, but had been too scared to finish it. So, before leaving on my global journey, I began to read it once again; it was my companion on the early flights of my circumnavigation.

As the blurb on the jacket promises, *Lord of the Flies* is 'terrifying' and 'horrifying'; it tells the tale of a group of English schoolboys stranded on a desert island who, in their search for survival, gradually lose their veneer of civilization and descend into a tribalistic state of hostility, fear, violence, and eventually murder. Golding describes how a tropical Garden of Eden was turned into a war zone by the arrival of these Europeans, and how they are themselves transformed from youthful innocents into monsters. 'What are we?' one of the characters asks. 'Humans? Or animals? Or savages?' Or later, when the boys have been led to believe that a ravenous Beast is loose on the island: 'Maybe there is no beast . . maybe it's only us.'[3]

Some commentators have taken this disturbing novel to be an allegory of the Second World War, in which Golding served as a naval officer; he is said to have observed the sinking of the *Bismarck*. Others take it to be a thinly disguised exposé of the British in their imperial heyday, uprooted from their native environment and drawn by the darker side of human nature into a mentality of savagery. Many of the study guides to the novel contain a section on 'Britain and Imperialism' or 'Britain's Colonial Past'. The key point about Golding's fictional youngsters is that they behave on their tropical island in ways that they would never have entertained at home; unrestrained by family or by familiar surroundings, the primitive aspects of human nature reassert themselves – the urge to dominate, the 'cruel desire for mastery', and the instinct for creating fear. 'We've got to have rules and obey them,' says one of the boys desperately. 'After all, we're not savages. We're English, and the English are best at everything.' The reader senses that the ground is sinking beneath the speaker's feet, even as the words are spoken. And true enough, everything starts to go wrong, and the descent begins towards strife and killing.

At the novel's conclusion, Golding avoids anything resembling a happy ending. The protagonist, Ralph, is lying on the beach exhausted, torched from his hiding place, expecting to be found any minute by the rival gang and be torn to pieces:

> Suddenly, Ralph looks up to see a naval officer standing over him. The officer tells the boy that his ship has come to the island after seeing the blazing fire in the jungle . . . When he finds what has happened . . . [he] is reproachful: how could this group of boys – and English boys at that – have lost all reverence for the rules of civilisation in so short a time? For his part, Ralph is overwhelmed by the knowledge that he has been rescued, and that he will escape . . . Ralph wept for the end of innocence [and] the darkness of men's hearts.[4]

More recently, I have been reading another sort of book, a travelogue called *Empire of the Mind: A Journey through Great Britain* (2007) by Iqbal Ahmed. Here, the scenario is the opposite to that of Golding's novel; it is written by a traveller from the Indian subcontinent who found himself stranded on another desert island, Great Britain, and discovered that the country was radically different from the land of his imagination. The author, a Kashmiri from Srinagar, an educated bibliophile and keen cyclist, had heard many things about the heart of the British Empire; nearly all of them on inspection proved to be wrong. The book opens, for example, with visits to Oxford and Cambridge, the two universities with which these days I am most associated:

> Our first port of call [in Oxford] was Jesus College. We followed the guide into the quad where the grass was as velvety as a bowling green. He led us into a corner . . . for an introductory talk on notable former pupils of the college. The first name he mentioned was Richard Burton – not the actor but the 19th-century explorer. [Burton, it transpired] was rusticated [i.e. expelled] after only a brief stay, he felt that he had 'fallen among grocers' in Oxford. [He] joined the East India Company as a lieutenant, translated the *Kama Sutra* and the *Arabian Nights* into English, and it is said, learned to speak Arabic like a native.

On reaching London after leaving Oxford, Ahmed wrote, 'I felt a profound sense of relief.'[5] Further surprises awaited him in Cambridge, not least in the hallowed halls of Trinity College:

> The [Christopher Wren] library was located on the east side of the court. To enter it, I climbed up a staircase . . . Marble busts of Trinity men were arranged in a row on either side of the floor, presided over by a full-length statue of Lord Byron. [Yet] when Vladimir Nabokov was a student at Trinity in the 1920s, he never went near its library, and his name was not mentioned among the college notables . . . I asked an elderly [librarian] the reason for this omission. She replied that the college had Milton, Tennyson and [Isaac] Newton among its alumni, [implying that it didn't need any more]; she seemed oblivious of 20th-century names . . . [Pandit] Nehru, the first Prime Minister of independent India, had been a student at Trinity . . . According to his memoirs, he spent his time there riding, [playing] tennis and gambling.[6]

And so it goes on. Iqbal Ahmed records a large measure of disharmony between his considerable knowledge of Britain and that of the British themselves.

In this regard, I was reminded of a startling sentence in *Lord of the Flies*. Describing the conflicting attitudes that had developed among the boys on the island, Golding wrote of 'two continents of experience and feeling, unable to communicate'. 'A continent of experience and feeling' is a wonderful phrase. A similar divide, mental, intellectual, and emotional, can be perceived, I believe, not only between European History as understood by Europeans and non-Europeans, but also as understood by different sorts of Europeans and different sorts of non-Europeans.

A third book on my mind was *Ghosts of Empire*[7] by the British-Ghanaian writer, old Etonian, and Westminster MP Kwasi Kwarteng.[8] The book consists of six separate studies each relating to a different country, and argues that the British Empire was unique in terms of its heterogeneity.

I was particularly drawn to Kwarteng's chapter on Iraq, partly because its ongoing tragedy has been headline news for the last decade and partly because in February 2003, for the only time in our lives, my wife and I were inspired to attend a massive demonstration in London against the looming Iraq War. Reading Kwarteng, I was soon convinced that the British government's conduct when creating Iraq in 1918–22 was no less unscrupulous than in 2002–3, when, in blind support for the policy of the United States, it used phoney intelligence reports to justify the invasion and destruction of Saddam Hussein's republic.

Iraq, it transpired, was an artificial construct from the start. It was assembled from three contrasting provinces of the Ottoman Empire – those of Mosul, Baghdad, and Basra – and was claimed for Britain by right of conquest. Its acquisition was legitimized by a post-dated League of Nations Mandate, and its political system was organized around a British-controlled client monarchy. Its very existence was dominated, as Kwarteng puts it, 'by the smell of oil'.

His book starts with a scene in Lancaster House, London, on 21 November 1918, only ten days after the Armistice. Lord Curzon, Foreign Secretary, former Viceroy of India, and 'arch-imperialist', was telling the Inter-Allied Petroleum Dinner that 'the Allied Cause had floated to victory on a wave of oil'. His pride was inspired by the Royal Navy's oil-fired battleships, the British Army's dependence on diesel-engined lorries, and the RAF's petrol-driven airplanes. Curzon's remarks also reflected a recent report by a senior civil servant, Sir

Edmund Slade, 'On the Petroleum Situation in the British Empire', which had stressed Britain's unwelcome reliance on American oil, and, in the interests of self-sufficiency, the urgent need for exploration, especially in Mesopotamia. The Cabinet Secretary, Sir Maurice Hankey, declared that 'the retention of the oil-bearing regions of Mesopotamia and Persia [was] a first-class British war aim'.[9]

Shortly afterwards, on 1 December, the prime minister, David Lloyd George, met his French counterpart, Georges Clemenceau. Mesopotamian oil was one of the topics discussed. According to the secret Sykes–Picot Agreement of 1916, which had paved the way for the partition of Ottoman territories, the British had inadvertently left the province of Mosul on the French side of the line. This oversight was now rectified. The French ceded their claim to Mosul on condition that they receive one-quarter of all its future oil revenues.

British imperial administrators could then set to work. Sir Percy Cox, nicknamed 'Coccus', the highly experienced High Commissioner for the Persian Gulf, was the man in charge of the region; he was said 'to keep his silence in a dozen languages'. His deputy for civilian affairs, Lieutenant-Colonel Arnold Wilson, ex-Indian Army, nicknamed 'the Despot of the Mess-pot', had supervised the first discovery of oil in the Gulf in 1908, and at the Peace Conference in Paris in 1919 was responsible for replacing the classical Greek name of Mesopotamia with the Arabic name of Iraq. Sir Percy's 'oriental secretary' was the redoubtable Gertrude Bell (1868–1927), then aged fifty, who had once been the very first woman to be awarded a first-class degree at Oxford. Athlete, linguist, traveller, archaeologist, and a lifelong spinster, she has been called 'Daughter of the Desert' and 'the Desert Queen' by her biographers. She was a fluent speaker of both Arabic and Farsi, had spent twenty years exploring and studying the Middle East, enjoyed the support of Britain's secret services, and wielded an authority far in excess of her nominal position. Echoing problems that would arise nearly a century later, she was reported to have said: 'We cannot leave the country in the state of chaos that we have created.'[10] Lord Curzon would never have uttered such words in public. 'The British have done more for Iraq in two years,' he said loftily, 'than the Turks in two centuries.'[11]

Iraq's new rulers faced two challenges: one to devise an effective form of government, the other to retain control of the oil industry. In the sphere of governance, three steps were required. The first was to cement Britain's presence in Iraq through a Class-A Mandate from the League of Nations; this was arranged at the Inter-Allied Conference at

The Middle East in the 1920s

N

Black Sea

SOVIET
UNION

Caspian Sea

Istanbul

Ankara

TURKEY

CYPRUS

Tehran

SYRIA

IRAQ

LEBANON

Mediterranean Sea

Damascus

Baghdad

PERSIA

PALESTINE

Amman

TRANSJORDAN

Cairo

KUWAIT

Persian Gulf

Gulf of Oman

EGYPT

ARABIA

Red Sea

Riyadh

TRUCIAL STATES

MUSCAT and
OMAN

ANGLO-
EGYPTIAN
SUDAN

YEMEN

ADEN PROTECTORATES

Arabian
Sea

Gulf of Aden

ITALIAN
SOMALILAND

FRENCH
SOMALILAND

BRITISH
SOMALILAND

ETHIOPIA

0        50        100 km

under British suzerainty
or protection

British mandates

French mandates

French colonies

Italian colonies

San Remo in April 1920. The second was to establish an Iraqi monarchy in line with the British Empire's usual principle of indirect control. This was done by promoting Prince Faisal, son of the Hashemite Sheriff of Mecca, brother of the soon-to-be-installed Emir of Transjordan, and a failed candidate to be King of Syria. The third was to dress up arrangements with a public facade of pious declarations about Iraq's future independence. From Lord Curzon's private terminology, which talked of 'imperial tutelage', 'a perpetual lease', and 'a veil of constitutional fictions', it is clear that the British did not intend to relinquish control anytime soon. The truest words on this subject were spoken between Gertrude Bell and a prominent Iraqi official. 'Britain aims to give Iraq complete independence,' said Gertrude. 'My lady,' replied Jafar Pasha Al-Askari, 'complete independence is never given; it is always taken.'[12]

In the sphere of oil, the key operation lay in gaining full control of the pre-existing Turkish Petroleum Company (TPC), which possessed all outstanding rights to production and exploration. Matters were taken in hand by the brilliant Armenian financier Calouste Gulbenkian (1869–1955), 'Mr Five Percent', who thereby made himself a multi-million fortune. Ottoman and German shares were sequestrated. A dominant holding was granted to Anglo-Iranian Oil (now BP), and lesser holdings were handed to Royal Dutch Shell, the French, King Faisal, and, of course, Gulbenkian. In 1927, after the discovery of oil, the company name changed to Iraq Petroleum Company (IPC). This exploitative set-up earned the wrath of Lawrence of Arabia, whose letter to *The Times* in July 1920 fumed with indignation. 'The Arabs did not rebel against the Turks,' it said, 'just to change masters.' But that is exactly what happened, and indirect imperial rule in Iraq outlasted all of its architects. It survived two revolts, the declaration of independence in 1932, the premature deaths of both Faisal and his son, and the Second World War.

The showdown did not occur until 14 July 1958, when an Army coup seized power and ended the pre-existing order. The young king, Faisal II, was murdered and mutilated. A British consul was axed to death, and a republic was declared. In the 1960s, however, when the USSR was trying to establish hegemonic power in the Arab world, the Iraqi Army turned to Ba'athist politics to support its anti-Western turn, and a Soviet-style one-party state was introduced. General Saddam Hussein then emerged as the new strong man. In 1972 the oil industry was nationalized, and rich revenues were poured into social welfare. It is easy to understand, therefore, why, in the early phase of his reign, before his military adventures, Saddam Hussein was a popular leader.

During the four decades of British domination, not just the common people but the Americans, too, had been denied their slice of the pie. Washington habitually denounced British and French policy while, on the issue of oil, demanding what it called 'an open door'. What the American government wanted was both the luxury of anti-imperialist rhetoric and, as a victorious Allied power, a share of the loot. The Americans were imperialists alright, but not of the traditional sort. Oddly enough, the man who helped them most was a typical member of the British establishment, who 'went native'.

Although less well known than his wayward son Kim, Harry St John Philby (1885–1960) lived a still more extraordinary life. At first sight, he was an archetypal, upper-crust Englishman of his day – formed at public school, Oxford, and the Army. Bernard Montgomery, the future field marshal, was best man at his wedding. Yet under the surface, Philby was a rebel and a maverick: an early socialist, a lover of exotic languages such as Punjabi and Baluchi, a bold explorer, a double-crosser, and a man who dabbled with extreme political views. From 1915 to 1925, schooled in the arts of intelligence by Percy Cox and Gertrude Bell, he was based in Iraq and employed by His Majesty's Secret Service. Between 1918 and 1920 he served as the first Minister of the Interior of the Iraqi Kingdom. Yet, like Lawrence, he became convinced that the Arabs had been given a raw deal, whilst also har-bouring a deep dislike of the Hashemites. As a result, he gradually attached himself to the cause of Sheikh Ibn Saud, the Hashemites' chief rival for control of the Arabian Peninsula.

In 1925, the year when Ibn Saud ousted their rivals from Mecca, Harry Philby moved permanently to Riyadh, where he duly embraced Islam, married a slave-girl bought in the market, and, under the name of Sheikh Abdullah, installed himself in the Saudis' innermost counsels. All the while, he was befriending American oilmen, urging them to invest in exploration and create a competitor for the IPC. In 1932 he organized Ibn Saud's coronation, which initiated the Kingdom of Saudi Arabia, and in 1933 he was deeply involved in negotiations for the basic American Oil Concession that gave rise in due course to Aramco. As if this were not enough, Philby returned to Britain in 1939 to stand in the Hythe by-election as the candidate of the fascist British People's Party, after which, having opposed the war with Nazi Germany, he was duly interned. By the time he returned to Saudi Arabia in 1943 or 1944,

Aramco had eclipsed the IPC, and the United States had gained a permanent foothold, which would enable them to outpace British influence in the Middle East. Today, Saudi Arabia is the world's largest oil producer, and American power, though faltering, is still dominant.[13]

Such were the empire-builders who stamped their priorities on international relations a century ago. In 1878, in the aftermath of the Congress of Berlin, Queen Victoria's prime minister, Benjamin Disraeli, declared that 'Our Empire is an empire of liberty, truth and justice.' As Kwasi Kwarteng observes, Disraeli's shortlist of imperial virtues left much to be desired. The empire brought liberty for the few and subordination for the many; it only spoke truth when convenient; and, though legal institutions often brought order out of chaos, social justice and human equality were not high on the agenda. Democracy, which edged its way into the 'Mother Country' in the early twentieth century, did not find its way to most of the colonies. Hierarchy, class privilege, and snobbery were always in the ascendant. Even so, Kwarteng argues that the British Empire was neither wholly good nor wholly bad, and must be understood in its own terms. 'In its scale and ethos, [it was] completely unlike any system of government that the world has ever known.'[14]

People living in other continents may be forgiven for thinking that empires and imperialism form the main if not the only feature of European history worth discussing; yet there is much else besides. It would take up far too much time, however, to list here all the numerous perceptions of European history that currently circulate; for that, you will have to read the introduction to my *Europe: A History*.[15] Suffice it to say that the list would include both the American-sponsored and self-congratulatory concept of Western Civilization, and the very common idea that European History is nothing more than a rag-bag collection of national stories – British, French, German, Polish, et cetera. Here, I shall draw your attention to only a couple of the most influential approaches to the topic in recent years. One of them, 'the Great Divergence', first coined by Samuel Huntington, has been developed and promoted by Niall Ferguson, who once studied at Magdalen College, Oxford, as I did, and taught history at Jesus College, which Iqbal Ahmed visited. (Indeed, if my calculations are correct, Ferguson would probably have been in residence at Jesus when the visitor from Kashmir was walking round the quad.) 'The Great Divergence' is a shorthand term for the lengthy period from the late fifteenth to the mid-twentieth century during which Europe surged ahead of the other continents and came to dominate them. This idea, in its general outline, is incontrovertible, although there are many debates about why the divergence happened, when it started, and what ended it. Ferguson rejects the old ideas of geographical advantage and national character. And he insists: 'You can't just blame imperialism.' Instead, he presents a list of main causes, which he modishly calls 'apps', including naval power and intercontinental trade, science and medicine, property rights and the rule of law, consumerism and the work ethic, and, of special importance, fierce competition among European powers. Economic, political, and military rivalry between the Spanish, Portuguese, French, British, and Dutch was, he says, crucial. 'Western decline isn't inevitable,' he concludes, 'but the Divergence is over, folks.'[16]

A different approach to the same topic is offered by Jared Diamond, an unusually broad-minded professor of geography and physiology from California, who has been described as a 'trans-disciplinary polymath'. He came to history via the study of human evolution and indigenous peoples, especially in New Guinea. His books teem with startling theories, starting with *The Third Chimpanzee* (1991) on 'the human animal' and leading most recently to *The World Until Yesterday* (2012) on the wisdom of traditional societies.[17] Diamond believes that the sources of Europe's precocious development lie in its ecology. 'History followed different courses for different peoples because of differences in peoples' environments,' he wrote in his best-selling *Guns, Germs and Steel* (1997), 'not because of biological differences among the peoples themselves.' He is especially hostile to the notion that Europeans or European culture possessed any sort of innate superiority:

> In short, Europe's colonization of Africa had nothing to do with the differences between European and African peoples themselves, as white racists assume. Rather, it was due to accidents of geography and biogeography – in particular to the continent's different areas, axes, and suites of wild plant and animal species. That is, the different historical trajectories of Africa and Europe stem ultimately from differences in real estate.[18]

As Diamond says and we all know, the Great Divergence has reached its term, together with Europe's former domination of the globe. But the varied ways in which different people view that important period of history continue to colour our lives. Unsurprisingly basing their knowledge on their own experience, non-Europeans judge European history by the effects it has had *on them*. Hence, those of them who are not of

European descent often see nothing but a long catalogue of negative effects (including diseases, missionaries, economic exploitation, and imperial rule). What is more, each non-European community tends to know only one European partner or oppressor. In many places, it was the British who once held sway; in Indochina or North Africa, it was the French; in Indonesia, the Dutch; in Latin America, the Spaniards and Portuguese. Inevitably, this limited contact tends to afford a limited view that requires correction.

Both Ferguson's and Diamond's presentations have a characteristic shared by many otherwise contrasting points of view – their common reliance on a binary, or, as the Marxists would say, a dialectic view of the world. On the one hand, we are presented with Europeans, together with their typical European values and modes of conduct. On the other, we are shown the non-Europeans with their own set of attitudes and reactions. The scenario reminds me of a sort of global football match, in which a highly trained team of professionals, wearing a pristine, all-white strip, takes on a scratch team of amateurs playing in a motley collection of red, brown, yellow, or black jerseys: in other words, two unequal teams, one equipped with its 'killer apps' or 'guns, germs and steel' and the other with markedly inferior kit and training, all engaged in a match that produces a predictable result.

This is a scenario that I wish to contest, and which I hope my travelogue in this book has contested. I don't believe that the world can be divided into two clear-cut teams, or that Europeans themselves can be reasonably depicted as possessing uniform aims or traditions. In addition to being British, I have had much to do with Eastern Europe – which undoubtedly informs my perspective. I shall marshal my remarks under ten headings.

1. **Imperial powers.** However much one might like to equate Europe with imperialism, it has to be said from the outset that most European countries were never engaged in transcontinental, imperialist projects. Of the forty-five present-day member states of the Council of Europe, only a dozen, or roughly one-quarter, have ever possessed overseas territories. Portugal, Spain, France, Britain, and Russia were the imperialists par excellence. Belgium, the Netherlands, Italy, Germany, Sweden, and Denmark were involved, but on a more modest scale. And Austria, despite its extensive holdings in Europe, only gained one overseas territory – the Nicobar Islands – and for just five years, between 1778 and 1783. Apart from that, the rest of Europe never experienced imperialism unless it was

on the receiving end. The typical European country should not be likened to Britain, France, or Russia; it would be small or middling in size, and played little or no part in the imperial game.

I put to you the case of Poland, a country that I know well but which does not figure prominently in European history books. Yet Poland can boast a history of more than a thousand years. It has lived through extreme swings of fortune; for a brief spell in the sixteenth century it commanded the largest state in Europe, and at the end of the eighteenth century it was totally destroyed, only to rise again at the beginning of the twentieth century. At the height of its power, Poland dominated and colonized large expanses of what are now Lithuania, Belarus, and Ukraine. But it was never engaged in lands beyond Europe.[19]

Actually, historians should never say 'never'. At one point, in 1639, the wealthy Duke of Courland, a vassal of the King of Poland, briefly established a foothold on Tobago in the West Indies, and in 1651 built a trading-post on an island in the Gambia River in West Africa. Before ceding his overseas possessions to England, he could briefly claim to be a colonial ruler. In later times, when the Poles could not compete with their powerful German and Russian neighbours, they could at least point to the glorious past when they ruled, indirectly, over a small piece of Africa.

Germany is another interesting case. At the zenith of the 'Imperial Age', it undoubtedly headed the league of Europe's richest and strongest nations. Yet its participation in imperial and colonial enterprises was modest, if not minimal, bearing little relation to its comparative power and wealth on the European continent. The united German Empire was not formed until 1871, and of the empire's six main colonies, all were remote, relatively small, and acquired very late: German West Africa (Togoland and North-East Cameroon), German South-West Africa (Namibia) and German New Guinea in 1884, German East Africa (Tanganyika, Burundi, and Rwanda) in 1885, the Kiautschou Concession in China in 1898, and Samoa in 1899. As a result, political circles in Germany swelled with resentment; they felt they had been cheated of their due 'place in the sun'. Their high sense of denied entitlement played no small part in the gathering storm that led to the cataclysm of the First World War.[20]

2. **Europe as a victim of imperialism.** Many regions and countries of Europe have been poor and weak over the centuries, and have often been dominated and exploited by their neighbours, in ways very similar to those suffered by overseas colonies. In this respect, the classic

case has to be Ireland. Conquered by the kings of England in the twelfth century, it was ruled from London for nearly eight hundred years, experiencing all manner of political, cultural, and economic oppression. It was the object of numerous 'plantations' of foreign settlers, most notably in Ulster and in the Pale of Settlement around Dublin; it was blighted by Land Laws, which favoured English landowners, and Penal Laws, which discriminated against the predominantly Catholic population; and it was the scene of repeated wars, uprisings, and punitive expeditions. After the Act of Union in 1801, it formed an integral part of the United Kingdom, at the heart of the greatest empire on Earth. Yet throughout that imperial nineteenth century, Ireland was battered and bleeding. It lost the system of self-government that it had enjoyed in the preceding period; it struggled to realize a minimum of religious toleration as guaranteed by the Act of Union; and in 1846 it was devastated by a famine as severe as any that occurred in any of Britain's overseas possessions. Yes, prolonged famine in the midst of the world's richest state. As it was, over a million Irish people died, and millions more were forced to emigrate either to Great Britain or to the United States. Ireland's population was halved, and has never since recovered.[21]

One must also spare a thought for the Dual Monarchy of Austro-Hungary, one of the largest empires of modern Europe. Although many parts of the Habsburg dominions were acquired by dynastic dealings, some were hauled in by more predatory means. Austria's acquisition of Galicia in the late eighteenth century, for example, an episode of the Partitions of Poland, was engineered in conjunction with the Prussians and Russians as an act of international banditry. Vienna's demand at the Congress of Berlin in 1878 to be granted Bosnia-Herzegovina had no basis in international law.[22]

3. **European imperialism** in reality, therefore, targeted fellow Europeans almost as frequently as it targeted Africans, Asians, or Native Americans. British imperialism began as English expansion directed against the non-English nations of the Isles – the Irish, the Welsh, the Cornish, and the Scots. The plantation of Ulster was launched in 1606, in the same year that the first English colony in America was established in Virginia.[23] French imperialism began likewise at home, as the royal Crown lands were expanded far and wide from their original base around Paris in the Île-de-France.[24]

Similarly in Eastern Europe, Russian, that is Muscovite, imperialism started up by absorbing the lands and peoples of neighbouring states, such as the Republic of Novgorod or the Grand Duchy of Lithuania, before moving on to conquests further and further afield. In the late sixteenth century, Muscovite adventurers crossed the Urals into Asian Siberia and took Astrakhan at the mouth of the Volga. Russian Cossacks rode up to the shores of the Pacific, 4,000 miles from Moscow, in 1648; they took Kiev from Poland in 1662. In the eighteenth century the Russians opened their 'window on the West' in the Baltic, descended the Caspian Sea to the confines of Persia, and crossed the Bering Strait to Alaska. In the nineteenth century they sailed from Alaska to California, swallowed the rump Congress Kingdom of Poland and Finland in the west, digested the Black Sea coastland in the south, turning Ukraine into so-called 'New Russia', and spread from the Caucasus and Siberia into Central Asia. Key moments came in 1801, when Odessa was founded on the Black Sea and the conquest of Georgia was completed; in 1842, when Fort Ross in California was inexplicably abandoned; and in 1873, when the Khanate of Khiva became a Russian protectorate. During this long process of unprecedented proportions, scores of foreign peoples and territories were overrun, so that Lenin, in the early twentieth century, could declare the Russian Empire to be 'the Jailhouse of Nations'. Apart from the sale of Alaska to the United States in 1865, no major setback to the empire occurred until 1905–6, when the Japanese put an end to Russian expansion in the Far East.[25]

In the Balkans, the Muslim Ottomans ruled for centuries from their capital at Constantinople. Their empire stretched from the Danube to the Tigris and Euphrates, ruling over Slavs, Turks, Arabs, Armenians, Georgians, and Kurds. On its western frontiers, it was bounded by the Holy Roman Empire, Poland, and Russia; in the east by Persia. In the nineteenth century, however, as 'the Sick Man of Europe', the Ottoman Empire was in steep decline. Its provinces crumbled under the pressure of national revolts and international enemies. Russia supported independence movements among fellow Orthodox Christians, who reached their goal first in Greece (1828), later in Romania (1856), Montenegro (1878), and Bulgaria (1908). Then France and Britain attacked Russia during the Crimean War of 1853–6 to curb its ambitions, but ended up during the First World War by carving out large parts of the Ottoman-ruled Middle East for themselves.[26]

Indigenous peoples are notoriously some of the principal casualties of imperial expansion. The miserable fate of Native Americans or of Australian aborigines is now widely recognized as a stain on civilized values. The low point may have been reached in British-ruled Van

Diemen's Land (Tasmania), where no single native was once thought to have survived (see Chapter 9). Similar horrors were noted during the Herero and Namaqua Genocide in South-West Africa, where German troops suppressed native uprisings in 1905–7.

The disappearance of indigenous peoples, however, can rarely be attributed solely to deliberate mass killings; it usually happens through a mixture of violence, imported disease, and 'cultural genocide'. Here, European history provides many precedents for what was to happen abroad. An early example would be that of the Etruscans, who were overrun by the Romans and absorbed into Latin culture.[27] A mediaeval example comes from ancient Prussia, where the Teutonic Knights forcibly Germanized the native Balts, promising them death or Christian conversion, and turning their homeland into a bastion of *Germantum*.[28] In the British Isles, all the Celtic peoples have been struggling for centuries to preserve themselves from the onward march of the English. In Cornwall, as we saw in Chapter 1, the struggle appeared to have been lost in 1799, when the last native speaker of Cornish passed away. The Welsh have been more successful, but the Gaelic speakers of Ireland and Scotland are facing extinction.

Not that the Celts can really be counted as indigenous to Cornwall, Wales, Ireland, or any other part of the so-called British Isles. 'Britain' itself – or 'Prydain' in Welsh – is a Celtic name imposed at some point in prehistory on the Celts' unidentified predecessors. The group of peoples speaking related Celtic languages moved into Central Europe in the late Bronze Age, displacing or absorbing predecessors known only from archaeological cultures. Their homeland in the early part of the first millennium BC was centred on an area stretching from the Austrian Alps to the Jura, and marked by the sites at Hallstatt near Salzburg and La Tène on Lake Neuchâtel. From there, they spread out westwards to Gaul, Iberia, and the British Isles, and southwards into Italy. The earliest Celtic chariot burials in Britain are dated to *c.* 500 BCE. Rome was sacked in 390 BCE by the Celtic tribe of Senones. Yet there were many earlier Europeans whose existence has been blotted out. The Basques are the last remnant of the population that inhabited northern Iberia before the Celts arrived.

4. **Chronology** is important, because colonial expansion impacted parts of Europe long before it was directed against distant continents. Ancient Greek cities, for example, launched hundreds of 'daughter cities' all around the Mediterranean and Black Sea.[29] The Roman Empire,

Europe's greatest, was built on the systematic spread of agricultural colonies. Indeed, the very word 'colony' is a direct descendant of the Latin *colonia*, and of its root in the verb *colere* – 'to till, tend or cultivate'. The Romans first colonized Italy, before moving on to Gaul, Iberia, North Africa, Britannia, and most of Europe south of the Danube. Every colony was linked to fortified towns and a magnificent network of paved roads that acted as the arteries of military, political, and economic integration.[30]

The Roman example was followed in mediaeval times by numerous European rulers, who strove to extend their power and wealth. In Spain, from the ninth century, the Christian monarchs of Castile, Portugal, and Aragon patiently pursued the long-running *Reconquista*, until, after half a millennium, the whole of the Iberian Peninsula had been won back from Moorish domination.[31] In the same era, another parallel campaign was starting up at the other end of Europe. The *Drang nach Osten*, the 'Drive to the East', saw columns of German colonists heading into Central and Eastern Europe; their destinations ranged from the Baltic countries in the north, to Silesia or Slovakia in the centre, or to Transylvania in the south-east.[32]

Later, it was the turn of the Poles. The prowess of Polish arms had long shown its mettle in the wars against Turks, Tartars, and Cossacks; and in the mid-sixteenth century, when the southern reaches of the Grand Duchy of Lithuania were joined to the Kingdom of Poland, vast expanses of Ukraine were opened up to colonization. (*Ukraina*, meaning literally 'On the Edge', carries much of the same connotation that the 'Frontier' had in North America.) With the king's permission, numerous Polish lords moved into the open steppe, bringing armies and peasant settlers with them. They also introduced Jews as traders and administrators, Poland being the only country in Europe at the time where a large Jewish population flourished. The Polish lords' exploits are recorded and embellished in a celebrated novel by Henryk Sienkiewicz, *With Fire and Sword* (1884).[33] And if Poles started the colonization of Ukraine, it was the Russians who completed it. In the decades following the capture of Crimea from the Sublime Porte in 1783, Catherine the Great created a new province called 'New Russia' and peopled it with immigrants from all over the empire.[34] These are the lands that top Vladimir Putin's list for re-annexation.

5. **Violence**, many would say, is inherent to the imperialist and colonialist story. It moves in cycles. Imperial regimes employ violent methods

to conquer and then control the subject peoples. Their subjects revolt and rebel, directing random or terrorist violence against their oppressors. The regimes then launch new waves of punitive violence to bring the rebels to heel.

Nonetheless, the fact remains that by far the largest and most horrific campaigns of violence have been perpetrated by Europeans at home rather than abroad. In England, we had the Wars of the Roses in the fifteenth century and the brutal Civil War of the seventeenth century. After that, in the eighteenth century, Scotland twice rebelled against the Union introduced in 1707, and the Jacobite Risings provoked an all-out assault on the language, culture, and livelihood of the Highlands. The terrible Clearances that ensued were an affront to humanity, and it is no accident that to this day, as a result, there are more Gaelic speakers in Canada than in their Scottish homeland.[35] On the Continent, the Wars of Religion in France during the sixteenth century, the Thirty Years War of 1618–48 in Central Europe, and the Swedish and Cossack Wars in Poland (1648–68) involved frightful atrocities and catastrophic demographic traumas. The Revolutionary and Napoleonic Wars of 1792–1815, which ranged from Portugal in the west to Russia in the east, brought unparalleled levels of slaughter in their wake. And in the twentieth century, Europe's global supremacy was lost through its addiction to internecine conflict as demonstrated in two successive world wars. In the Gospel according to St Matthew, Jesus Christ says 'those who take up the sword shall perish by the sword'. This is one of many warnings that nominally Christian Europeans have frequently chosen to ignore.

It should be no surprise, therefore, that a link exists between European violence in the colonies and European violence at home. It seems that some Europeans used their foreign possessions as laboratories of experimental violence. The first genocide of the twentieth century, for example, is generally taken to be that perpetrated by German colonists in South-West Africa, where the Herero and Nama peoples were all but wiped out between 1904 and 1907 (although at that time the term 'genocide' had not been invented). And then one finds that among the Nazi leaders there were men, like Hermann Göring, whose family had lived in South-West Africa and whose level of sensitivity to mass violence turned out to be notoriously low.[36]

Another example might be that of so-called 'area bombing', which was employed by British and American air forces over Germany during the Second World War with enormous, deliberate, and appalling loss of life. The main exponent of the technique, Air Chief Marshal Sir Arthur 'Bomber' Harris (1892–1984), won the argument with his opponents in 1941–2, after the earlier policy of precision bombing against exclusively military or industrial targets had proved ineffective. Yet from the historical point of view, the interesting question is where the idea of 'strategic' or 'blanket' bombing came from. The answer is that it originated in British-ruled Palestine and Iraq, where in the 1930s the RAF maintained internal security, and where rebel villages were routinely bombed from the air. Harris, who had been in South-West Africa during the First World War and worked from 1936 to 1939 in the Middle East Air Command, is reported to have said that 'one 500 lb bomb on each village that speaks out of turn will solve the problem'.[37]

6. **Imperialism** has always involved an important cultural aspect, and the imposition of cultural norms by imperial powers give rise to some of the most durable consequences. The full list of those norms would include artistic, ethical, institutional, behavioural, and linguistic elements. In the British case, the introduction of the English language into many countries of Asia and Africa has long outlasted other impositions. Yet one must never imagine that the enforcement of linguistic uniformity is somehow peculiar to colonial or overseas administrations. On the contrary, almost all governments in the modern period have sought to promote a single language of state in opposition to all the other vernacular tongues that happen to be spoken; and to this end they introduced and financed state-backed schooling. In France, francophone education was a key instrument in turning 'peasants into Frenchmen'. In Prussia, the government in Berlin had to shoulder the heavy task of turning the king's Polish or Danish subjects into loyal Germans. In the late nineteenth century, conscription into the army served this purpose; at the end of their period of service, conscripts were not released until they had mastered the rudiments of German speech. And in the realms of the Tsar, where a hundred languages were spoken, it was Russian and Russian alone that received official approval.

In the British Isles, the enforcement of English went hand in hand with rule from London since Tudor times, just as it did later on in the British Empire overseas. Apart from numerous regional dialects, standard English faced four major Celtic rivals – Cornish, Welsh, Irish Gaelic, and Scottish Gaelic. Cornish was eliminated during the Reformation by the policy of excluding it from the churches and from religious practice in general. In Wales, in contrast, the Bible and the

Book of Common Prayer were translated into Welsh, churches and chapels became the bastions of the non-English community, and the Welsh language has survived. In Ireland, where the majority of the population were Roman Catholics, the language of the Church was Latin, and religious practice thereby unwittingly assisted the aims of the state. Gaelic had been all but eliminated by the time that Irish independence was won, and it was decreed to be the official language of the Irish Free State (and later of the Republic) as a symbolic gesture of defiance. In Scotland, the Gaelic of the Highlands and Islands underwent almost two centuries of proscription before it entered the present era of toleration in a greatly weakened condition; it is unlikely to recover. If there are people in the former British Empire who resent the imperial assault on their culture and identity, they should know that many people in the British Isles feel exactly the same way.

7. **Social oppression** was another near-universal element of imperial rule. No one needs to be reminded how incoming European colonists, having gained control of a territory, would habitually introduce exploitative socio-economic systems ranging from formal slavery to various types of apartheid. Whatever the local arrangements, the Europeans would expect to enjoy a privileged status whilst leaving the non-Europeans in varying degrees of subordination.

The mistake is to assume that these oppressive social systems were somehow the exclusive preserve of overseas empires. In reality, there were large parts of Europe where the natives were dominated and held in bondage in similar fashion to their counterparts in Asia or Africa, and where the oppression lasted every bit as long. Serfdom provides a vivid illustration. In theory, serfdom was distinct from slavery; it permitted human beings to be bought and sold but only in conjunction with the sale of the land to which the serfs were bound; and it required serfs to work for their lord without payment, but usually for only a set part of their time. In Russia, for example, slavery was abolished in 1723, whereas rural serfdom was retained until 1861. In practice, though, serfs often lived in conditions that were indistinguishable from those of slaves. Without their lord's express permission, they could not move freely; they could not accept outside work; and they could not educate themselves or their children. As a result, they remained a static, totally dependent, and illiterate workforce well into the second half of the nineteenth century. Serfdom was still going strong in Prussia, Austria, and Russia when the British parliament passed Acts for the abolition of the slave trade (1807) and slave-owning (1833). Prussia abandoned serfdom in stages after 1815, Austria in 1848, and the Russian Empire between 1861 and 1866. The United States abolished slavery in 1863 with the Emancipation Proclamation.[38]

Yet one should not rush to celebrate an early end to the story. Many analysts would now contend that Stalin's introduction of forcible collectivization into the Soviet Union in 1931 was essentially a return to serfdom. For the next four or five decades, millions of Soviet collective farmers were tied to the land; they were not allowed to visit the local market without permission. They were subject to brutal discipline enforced by Communist managers; and, exactly like serfs, they were not allowed to possess anything but their tiny family plots – often not even that. By the time that the Soviet system collapsed in 1991, much of the rest of the world had been free from such extreme forms of oppression for more than a century.[39]

8. Capitalism. There can be no disputing the fact that the great overseas empires of Western Europe were developed and sustained through trade, and that trade in its turn was dependent on the financial mechanisms of capitalism. As a result, 'capitalist' and 'imperialist' have become complementary and overlapping terms of abuse. I have no intention here of trying to defend capitalism's record – it has many very able defenders – but I do need to point out that its origins lie not in extra-European ventures but in domestic economic operations.[40] The very first banks, founded in Florence and Genoa in the early fourteenth century, grew up to service the Italian wool trade; and it was England's increasing capacity for wool exports that attracted the 'Lombards' to medieval London. Merchant bankers, who established themselves slightly later in the Low Countries, notably at Bruges, Ghent, and Amsterdam, were operating in local continental markets long before they fixed their sights further afield. In the sixteenth century, when 'the Great Divergence' began to diverge, the Baltic Grain Trade or trade within the Mediterranean was every bit as important in commercial terms as the multiplying contacts with the New World, Africa, and the Far East. Indeed, more so. The Castilians and Portuguese could not have sent their sailors and colonists across the Atlantic without lessons learned from their previous missions to West Africa and the islands off the African coast. After all, Christopher Columbus started his career as a sugar merchant in Madeira. Similarly, the Dutch were only able to finance and organize their extraordinary expeditions to the 'Spice Islands' (in

modern Indonesia) because of their long experience and expertise built up much nearer home; and the English could not have thought of colonizing New England without their earlier mediaeval links with Aquitaine and Ireland. Seen in this light, the usual division between European and extra-European history starts to look distinctly artificial.

9. **Race.** It has often been pointed out that the Europeans who set out to conquer the world in the early modern period were not aware of being Europeans; they thought of themselves in the first place as Christians and secondly as subjects of their respective monarchs. If they knew of a precedent for their activities, they would have identified above all with the mediaeval crusaders of *Outre Mer*, who had sailed across the seas to win over lands and peoples to the banner of Christ.[41] As soon as they landed on other continents, however, they soon realized that they belonged to a specific branch of humanity whose racial characteristics were different from those of non-European peoples. The temptation arose, therefore, to regard the pagan natives as subhuman, not least because it had become normal practice in mediaeval times to force non-Christians into slavery. With some delay, the Vatican reacted to this issue decisively, and in the bull *Sublimis Deus* of 1537 Pope Paul III stated unequivocally that 'the Indians of South and West' were human beings, strongly rejecting 'recent knowledge' that held them to be 'dumb brutes created for our service'. The bull continued:

> We consider that the Indians are truly men, not only capable of understanding the Catholic Faith but eager to receive it. By these our letters, therefore, we define and declare that the said Indians are by no means to be deprived of their liberty or their property, nor should they in any way be enslaved . . .[42]

Some historians have chosen to regard *Sublimis Deus* as a milestone in the history of human rights; others take it as evidence of the more compassionate approach of Catholics as compared to the harsh, predestinarian tendencies of Protestant imperialists. It is certainly true that some Europeans, notably the Portuguese, were more flexible on race issues than were others. Yet all have to accept that the fine rhetoric of Pope Paul III was largely observed in the breach; once the conquistadors took control of subject peoples they rarely showed much restraint. In North America, many of the laws that banned racial mixing dated from colonial times.

Nonetheless, one cannot be too careful. The history of miscegenation and of laws surrounding it is not simple. The most extreme instance of systematic racial discrimination comes not from overseas empires or from South African apartheid but from Nazi Germany, in the heart of twentieth-century Europe.[43]

10. **Historiography.** Much of the misunderstanding and confusion surrounding the above issues derives from the fact that standard narratives of 'Europe Overseas' are largely disconnected from narratives of Europe's internal affairs.[44] In particular, it is rarely the case that a historian sees a link between the conduct of (mainly West) European imperialists abroad and (mainly Central and East) European imperialists at home. And it is unusual for scholars seeking the roots of imperialism to jump beyond their favoured period and to delve into the mentality and praxis of earlier ages. To which, one can only say 'Alas'. One suspects that there are far more continuities than meet the eye.

And so?

Firstly, Europeans' long record of inhumanity to each other disqualifies them from any pretensions of superiority over the peoples of other continents. One cannot overlook the stern fact that the worst pages of European history, whether in the Wars of Religion, the Holocaust, or the mass crimes of Joseph Stalin, were written at home.

Secondly, European imperialism and colonialism can only be understood as systems that were started at home and then exported.

Thirdly, the customary divide between domestic European history and the history of the interaction of Europeans and non-Europeans quickly fades under scrutiny. Global history or the history of humanity is all that there really is.

Certainly, we must recognize that the context is changing rapidly. In my own lifetime, we have moved from an era when a substantial proportion of Europeans were engaged in imperial and colonial enterprises to a new one today, in which those activities have ceased. As a result, Europeans tend to look on their past with a mixture of bewilderment, anxiety, nostalgia, or guilt. The old imperial assumptions of God-given superiority are no longer credible. The best scenario that can be envisaged for the future Europe shows the old continent clinging to its present status as one among several equals. The worst – from the European perspective – sees the start of another 'Great Divergence', where Europe falls steadily behind and the rest pull steadily ahead.

*

Such were the thoughts that I presented on successive occasions to a variety of audiences on my round-the-world lecture tour. As a historian of Europe, who was turning up in a series of non-European countries that had previously eluded me, I guessed that my listeners would want to hear some general reflections about European history. But I could not foresee how they would react. In the event, I think that they were slightly bemused. They listened to me politely, and always asked questions on particular episodes. But I can't say that I succeeded in convincing them of anything. All of which left me in something of a quandary. The whole of my intellectual baggage was European, and, as I crossed successive lines of longitude, I became increasingly conscious of my shortcomings. Long before the end, I realized that the main effect of my journey had been not so much to impart information as to learn and discover.

At some point, the realization dawned that I, as a European, by taking an interest in the histories and cultures of non-European peoples, and daring to write about them, might be running the risk of arousing suspicion. Accusations of 'cultural appropriation' are rife among the younger generation of academics at present. The belief seems to be that the culture, artefacts, and image of vulnerable groups need to be protected from the inroads of outsiders, no matter how well intentioned, and 'insiders' are alone entitled to determine how their private intellectual property is to be used. Be they embattled nations, feminists, homosexuals, ethnic communities, or indigenous people, they increasingly claim to be the 'owners' of what they regard as their private 'intellectual property'.

I had forgotten. I encountered very similar attitudes forty or fifty years ago after publishing a book on the history of Poland. The very first review that I ever received began with the priceless sentence: 'As the work of a non-Pole, this book is not as bad as might have been expected.' The reviewer was a patriarch of Poland's nationalist camp, and his governing principles were twofold: firstly, that Polish history can only be properly understood by Poles, and secondly that Polish scholars are the only legitimate arbiters of how the history of the Polish nation should be interpreted. In the nationalist view, the nation is the collective proprietor of its past. Sad to relate, the latest Polish government, elected in 2015, is driven by similar ideas and is pursuing a brand of 'historical politics' that aims to overturn all contradictory views.

Come to think of it, I had come across the proprietorial approach to history much earlier. One of the few history lessons that I clearly

remember from my schooldays took place on the day that the sixth-
form history set was summoned to the headmaster's study for a special
pep talk. The headmaster, F. R. Poskitt, was a Cambridge-educated
historian himself, and was an imposing figure endowed with a huge
head of pure white hair and a booming voice. He was supposed to be
asking each of us about our own interests in History, but instead, as
was his habit, he launched into a booming monologue addressed to the
ceiling. His chosen topic was 'Why should English history only be written by English historians?' In half an hour he ranged over all sorts of
topics from objectivity and sources, to historiography, historians as
intellectual authorities, and History as a vehicle for patriotic education.
His punch line was 'The best history of nineteenth-century England
was written by Élie Halévy, who was a Frenchman.'[45] It was sufficiently
shocking to have stuck in my mind for sixty years.

Not that narrow nationalism, and nationalistic views of history, are
confined to one or two countries; they derive from a way of thinking
that has its advocates in all nations. At present, it is strongly cultivated
in Putin's Russia, and it constitutes one prominent aspect of the insurgent movements that are challenging political establishments around
the world. It is certainly not absent in Britain, where the idea of 'Britain
First' triumphed amidst the uproar surrounding the EU Referendum of
June 2016.

On the academic front, another of my belated realizations relates to
the fact that many of the modish concepts such as 'cultural appropriation', or 'cultural imperialism', 'governmentality', and 'identity politics',
are not nearly as innovatory as their contemporary propagators imply.
'Cultural imperialism', for example, which features prominently in
today's lexicon of social-science jargon, is said to have originated in the
1960s and 1970s in the thinking of Michel Foucault, Edward Said, and
George Lipsitz. This may or may not be correct in the literal sense. Yet
the ideas and practices that underlie the phraseology are as old as the
hills; they are the by-products of every empire that has ever existed.
Ancient Rome's policy of imposing Roman law and the Latin language,
and of suppressing many local customs and religions, is a classical case
of Foucault's 'governmentality' without the ugly name. The French
Empire of Napoleonic vintage, though short lived, was another great
normalizer. By introducing the Code Napoléon (1804) to numerous
French-occupied countries, it laid the foundations of modern legal systems not only in many parts of Europe from Spain to Poland but also,
by emulation, in places as disparate as Egypt or Chile. What is more, by

the sheer weight of its impositions, it prompted resistance movements such as that of the *carbonari* of Italy, which became the harbingers of national consciousness and ultimately national liberation.

In which regard, the definition of *'impérialisme'* in my old French *Dictionnaire Encyclopédique* (1935) can only be described as *piquante*:

> Impérialisme, n.m. (de *impérial*). Doctrine de l'Angleterre au XIXe siècle tendant à grouper fortement ces colonies autour de la métropole, et donner à la puissance britannique la plus grande expansion possible.[46]
>
> (Imperialism, n.m. (from *imperial*). A doctrine of nineteenth-century England, which aims to bind its colonies strongly around the metropolis, and to expand British power to the maximum possible extent.)

*Sacré bleu!* The French, who built the world's third-largest empire in modern times, with centralizing tendencies surpassed only by those of Russia, did not apparently regard themselves as imperialists. Illustrating the phrasal use of the I-word, the *Dictionnaire* offers the phrase: 'L'impérialisme des États-Unis'.

In that same imperial era, the 11th edition of the *Encyclopaedia Britannica* contains no entry on 'imperialism', but has plenty to say about 'Empire':

> EMPIRE, a term now used to denote a state of large size and also (as a rule) of composite character, often, but not necessarily, ruled by an emperor – a state which may be a federation, like the German Empire, a unitary state, like the Russian, or even, like the British empire, a loose commonwealth of free states united to a number of subordinate dependencies. For many centuries, the writers of the Church ... conceived of a cycle of four empires – the Assyrian, the Persian, the Macedonian and the Roman. But in reality the conception of Empire, like the term itself (Lat. *imperium*), is of Roman origin.[47]

Fifteen thousand words follow on the evolution of the Roman, Holy Roman, and Byzantine empires. When modern times are finally reached, the discussion moves to comparisons between the main ruling empires of the day. The Russian Emperor, the 'Tsar', for example, was 'in theory and very largely in fact, the successor of the old East Roman emperor, the head of the Orthodox Church with the mission of vengeance on Islam for the fall of Constantinople'. The 'Empire of Austria' is dismissed rather casually as 'a convenient designation for the sum of the territories ruled by a single sovereign under various titles'. Its Habsburg emperors, 'though the lineal descendants of the old Holy Roman emperors', had been sidelined by the rise of the 'modern German Empire' and replaced by the Prussian Hohenzollerns as the true successors of the former *Kaiserzeit*. The declining Ottoman Empire did not even rate a mention. To the Victorian mind, the French concept of empire provided the main point of contrast:

> In France, [the word 'empire'] has been the apanage of the Bonapartes, and has meant a centralised system of government by an efficient Caesar, resting immediately on the people and eliminating the powers of the people's representatives. Under Napoleon I, this conception had a Carolingian colour: under Napoleon III, there is . . . more of Caesarism, more of a popular dictatorship. Whereas in the modern period France has meant autocracy . . . in Germany it has meant greater national unity and federal government.[48]

The *Encyclopaedia Britannica* lavishes a further 16,000 words on a separate entry on the 'British Empire', where care is taken to avoid invidious comparisons:

> BRITISH EMPIRE, the name now loosely given to the whole aggregate of territory, the inhabitants of which, under various forms of government, ultimately look to the British crown as the supreme head. The term 'empire' in this connexion is obviously used rather for convenience than in any sense equivalent to that of the older or despotic empires of history.[49]

Obviously. British imperialism had nothing whatsoever to do with despotism. Amazingly, in the eyes of its promoters, it had everything to do with freedom, federalism, and self-government:

> This imperialism, which is federalism viewed as making for a single whole, is very different from that of Bonapartist imperialism, which means autocracy; for its essence is free co-ordination, and the self-government of each co-ordinated part.

And then, more honestly:

> The British Empire is, in a sense, an aspiration rather than a reality, a thought rather than a fact; but, just for that reason, it is like the old Empire of which we have spoken; and though it be neither Roman nor Holy, yet it has like its prototype, one law, if not the law of Rome, and one faith, if not in matters of religion, at any rate in the field of political and social ideals.[50]

At the height of empire, British views on imperialism were evidently not only complacent but also incoherent. One is forced to ask, therefore, if the loss of empire has made the British more self-critical and humble and a little less smug. I fear not. Britain is not one of the countries that has undertaken a reassessment of its past as modern Germany has. At present, it has no single museum dedicated to the history of the British Empire, though several years ago such an institution functioned briefly in Bristol.[51] 'Britain has a lazy tradition of taking a rosy view of its past', a thoughtful, end-of-the-year leader article in *The Guardian* declared. 'National crimes play no part . . . and there is no lesson except British greatness.'[52]

Nowadays, of course, wholehearted and unashamed champions of benign imperialism are few and far between. A eulogistic biography of Cecil Rhodes or King Leopold II of Belgium cannot be expected any time soon. Yet there are plenty of prominent historians who resist the tide of blanket condemnation and seek a balanced view, listing the positive aspects of imperialism alongside the negatives.[53] They write, for example, about the unifying effects of empire, which supposedly broke down the tribalism of many traditional societies and halted age-old internecine tribal wars. They write with approval about the introduction of the rule of law, a precondition for later democratization. They stress the benefits of economic modernization, which brought industries, railways, and increased productivity to the colonies. And they probe the ambiguous interactions of liberalism and imperialism in the Victorian Age.[54] Above all, they point to the undeniable link between intercontinental imperial trade and the origins of globalization.[55]

Anti-imperialist critics understandably pounce on these attempts at fair-mindedness. The principle of 'Divide et Impera', they say, was far more central than policies of unification. Imperial legal systems were used to harass, arrest, and silence political opponents. And the profits of colonial economic development were sent straight back to the imperial 'Homeland'. Nonetheless, one contention is hard to substantiate, namely that all forms of imperialism were identical and were identically evil. In the league table of modern empires, there were significant variations in both theory and practice. Every empire had its own ethos, traditions, and methods. Russian imperial rule was not the same as its French or British counterparts. And Dutch, Belgian, German, Italian, Japanese, and American variants must also be considered. On first hearing of these comparisons, the idea was definitely planted in my mind as an Oxford student that, for all its faults, the British Empire was less oppressive than all the others. The reasons given centred on the fact that the British built their empire on naval power, while possessing only tiny military forces to impose their will. As a result, they were invariably obliged to rely in large measure on alliances with local rulers, who made up for the scarcity of direct imperial oppression. But that was sixty years ago. I am sure to be completely out of date.

Oh dear! This is getting interesting. I now wish I had talked less during my peregrinations on the panorama of imperialism and more on modern attitudes and the language, both ancient and modern, in which imperialism is debated.

Unfortunately, I was already safely back home before hearing of a speech that would have provided excellent material for discussion on my tour. The event was a recent debate at the Oxford Union featuring an Indian politician who was opposing the motion that 'Britain Owes Reparations to her Former Colonies'. The brilliant performance by Dr Shashi Tharoor was not an even-handed assessment, but a finely controlled rant, a pithy polemic, packed with relevant facts, quotations, and jokes. Loot, he said, was a Hindi word. 'We paid for our own oppression.' India had been 'a cash cow'. 'The moral debt is there', and 'reparations are a tool to atone'. Then he demolished his adversaries one by one. My friend Professor Roger Louis, a Texan, who is Oxford's leading historian of the British Empire, took a blow on the chin. He was, said Dr Tharoor, using a Texan proverb, 'all hat and no cattle'.

'You say,' he continued, 'that [the British] gave [their colonies] democracy. It's a bit rich to oppress, enslave, torture and kill people for two hundred years, and then to celebrate democracy at the end of it . . . You say that they gave us railways; the Indian railways were built to suit British interests. And you say that they built our economy; India's share of the global economy stood in 1750 at 23 per cent and in 1947 at 4 per cent.'

And so it went on. Dr Tharoor spoke of famines, of war dead, and of Churchill's notorious question: 'If food is scarce, why isn't Gandhi dead yet?' Yet the biggest howl of laughter was raised by his closing punch line:

'No wonder that the sun never set on the Empire,' he quipped. 'Even God would never trust the English in the dark.'[56]

# Afterword

Having reached the end of the trail, both of journeying and of describing the journey, I feel that a small number of clarifications are called for. Authors are advised not to let too much daylight in on the magic, but some observant readers may have noticed discrepancies which deserve some explanation.

It is a matter of historical record, confirmed by my diary, that I travelled around the world, from Frankfurt to Frankfurt, in the first half of 2012. The initial flight left FRA for Dubai on Tuesday, 10 April 2012, over five years ago; and from the Gulf, I made my way in easy stages, as described, to India, South-East Asia, 'Anzac', Polynesia, the United States, and back to Europe. In the twenty-first century such peregrinations are commonplace, and I don't think that the book contains any inaccurate statements relating to them. The itinerary was not dictated by any principle other than that of keeping on the move in the general direction of the sunrise.

In the following period, however, several additions and adjustments were made to the basic chronicle, inevitably prompting textual elisions. Firstly, I added a couple of chapters, one about Cornwall and the other about New York, which fitted neatly into the overall scheme but were originally intended for inclusion in my earlier book, *Vanished Kingdoms*. Secondly, I travelled to three destinations – Baku, Mauritius, and Madeira – on separate trips that did not form part of the main, global expedition. And thirdly, my wife and I travelled to Singapore, Tasmania, and New Zealand twice: once in 2012, when our movements in 'Kiwiland' were confined to North Island, and then again in 2014, when we returned to tour South Island. I should also explain that my stay in Mauritius formed part of that second extended journey, whose antipodean sector followed the route from Christchurch to Johannesburg via Sydney, Hobart, Melbourne, Perth, and Mauritius. During my flight across the Indian Ocean, therefore, which took me directly over the search area for MH370, I was actually travelling westwards and not, as was perhaps implied, eastwards.

My travels in the years when this book was in the making were further increased by the demands of a completely different project. This parallel undertaking centred on the wartime saga of the Army of General Anders – the victor of Monte Cassino - and involved yet another series of strenuous trips that took me to Russia, Iran, Jerusalem, and the Gaza Strip, and eventually to Italy. It all ended happily with the publication in 2015 of *Trail of Hope: The Anders Army, an Odyssey across Three Continents.*[1] But it also contributed to the state of exhaustion that prompted my less memorable travels by ambulance to the Stroke Department of the John Radcliffe Hospital, to the operating theatre of the Churchill Hospital, and eventually to the Oncology Unit of the Manor Hospital. The journey through cancer, which lasted much longer than my circumnavigation of the world, gave occasion for encounters with many wonderful people, both carers and fellow patients. Memories of the many colourful, complex, and endlessly stimulating countries that I had recently visited played a major part in my recovery.

Profuse expressions of gratitude are due to more people than could possibly be mentioned. My long-suffering wife, Maria-Myszka, accompanied me not only to the tropics and antipodes but also through successive consulting rooms, medical procedures and hospital wards. My debt to her is incalculable. A long line of ambassadors and consuls, principally from Poland's excellent Diplomatic Service, eased my passage through many a frontier, lecture room, and airport. A literary prize funded by the Kronenberg Foundation covered the cost of air tickets. Our good friend, Magda Rabiega, organized the transformation of my handwritten manuscript into digital text. Roger Moorhouse drafted the maps and selected the pictures. A number of readers, some anonymous and some more enthusiastic than others, helped improve the contents of particular chapters. And my unflagging editor at Penguin Books, Stuart Proffitt, was responsible both for a wealth of notes and comments and for frequent words of generous encouragement, which kept my mind active and eventually brought me over the finishing line. The final text was copy-edited by Richard Mason, who clearly enjoyed the task, fed me with poetic contributions of his own, and gave encouraging early signals of the book's acceptability. It was then skilfully steered through the press by the managing editor of Allen Lane, Richard Duguid. Other individuals to whom a special word of thanks is due include David Godwin, Katarzyna Pisarska, Ranjit Majumdar, Andrzej and Barbara Pikulski, Eugene Rogan, Don Baker, Jan Nitecki,

Brian Holmes, Panstwo Sobczyńscy, Paul Flather, Rajeev Bhargava, John Martin, Karolina Marchocka, Christopher Tremewan, Sudhir Hazareesingh, Henry Dimbleby, Jan and Zosia Pachulski, Ian and Margaret Willis, Val and Roger Roberts, Beata Stoczyńska, Wojciech and Cecilia Klobukowski, Arnaud Dardel, Joanna Frybes, Mary Neuburger, Mary Gawron, Jarek Garlinski, Brendan Simms, Ben Sinyor, Fraser Harley, Ian Lindsey, and the late and much missed Andrzej Findeisen.

Thanks to an invitation to be the Visiting scholar at Pembroke College, Cambridge, the proofs were corrected in great calm and comfort in Pembroke College Library.

Summertown, 28 August 2017

# Notes

## INTRODUCTION

1. John Bunyan, *The Pilgrim's Progress* (1678) (Oxford, 1926), illustrated. 2. Alexandre Dumas, *The Count of Monte Cristo* (1846) (London, 1924), 2 vols. 3. 'The Pilgrim's Hymn', *The English Hymnal* (Oxford, 1906), no. 402. 4. *Cwm Rhondda*, 'Prayer for strength for the journey through the world's wilderness', original Welsh words (1762) by William Williams 'Pantycelyn' (1717–91), English translation (1771) by Peter Williams, melody (1907) by John Hughes. www. en.wikipedia.org/wiki/Cwm_Rhondda. 5. Ibid. Numerous versions and translations exist, but it is not true that the original was composed in English. 6. 'There's a long, long trail' (1914), American: lyrics by S. King, music by 'Zo' Elliot. 7. William Hazlitt, 'On Going a Journey' (1822), in *Selected Essays* (London, 1930). 8. William Blake, 'Ah! Sun-flower', from *Songs of Experience* (1794). 9. William Cobbett, *Rural Rides* (London, 1912), vol. 1, pp. 34–5. Entry for 18 November 1821. 10. Fictional travel: Jules Verne, *Twenty Thousand Leagues under the Sea* (1870), Arthur Conan Doyle, *The Lost World* (1912), H. Rider Haggard, *King Solomon's Mines* (1885), H. G. Wells, *The Time Machine* (1895). 11. Best travel books, www.telegraph.co.uk/travel/artsandculture/ travelbooks/4932008/The-20-best-travel-books-of-all-time.html (16 February 2015). 12. J. W. von Goethe, *Italienische Reise* (1816–17), published in translation as *Italian Journey*, ed. W. H. Auden (Harmondsworth, 1970). 13. J. W. von Goethe, from *Wilhelm Meister*, vol. III, part I. 14. Gilbert Highet, *Poets in a Landscape* (Oxford, 1957). 15. Gilbert Highet, *The Classical Tradition* (Oxford, 1949). 16. Gilbert Highet, from *People, Places and Books* (New York, 1953). 17. Joachim du Bellay, *Les Regrets*, Sonnet XXXI (1558). 18. Homer, *The Odyssey*, trans. E. V. Rieu, Penguin Classics (Harmondsworth, 1954), p. 25. 19. John Keats, 'On First Looking into Chapman's Homer' (1816), lines 1–4. 20. George Chapman, *The Odyssey* (1616), 'The Invocation'. 21. Virgil, *The Aeneid*, book I, lines 1–7. 22. Virgil, *The Aeneid*, trans. W. F. Jackson Knight, Penguin Classics (Harmondsworth, 1956), p. 27. 23. Mark Twain, from *The Innocents Abroad* (1869). 24. Stewart Green, 'The Story of the World's First Alpinist', *Thought.Co* (2015), https://thoughtco.com/francesco-petrarch-ascent-of-mont-ventoux-755828 (2015). 25. Petrarch, 'The Ascent of Mont Ventoux' (1336), in *Epistolae Familiares*, Book IV, 1. 26. William Cobbett,

*Rural Rides* (London, 1912), vol. II, p. 156; Arthur Young (1741–1820) was Cobbett's contemporary, vying with him for published accounts of his extensive travels through the British Isles. His famous tour of France took place in 1787. **27.** Ribchester Museum, see www.ribchesterromanmuseum.org. **28.** Norman Davies, *Vanished Kingdoms* (London, 2012), ch. 2, 'Alt Clud: The Kingdom of the Rock'. **29.** Evelyn Waugh, *Edmund Campion* (London, 1947). **30.** Cobbett, from *Rural Rides*, op. cit. **31.** Edward Gibbon, from *Decline and Fall of the Roman Empire* (London, 1776), ch. 50. **32.** William Shakespeare, Sonnet no. 27. **33.** Rainer Maria Rilke, 'A Walk', translated by Robert Bly. **34.** Robert Louis Stevenson, 'Travel', in *Great Poems*, compiled by Kate Miles (Great Bardfield, 2005), pp. 100–102. **35.** Charles Baudelaire, 'Le Voyage', http:/fleursdu-mal.org/poem/231 (16 February 2015). **36.** Dante Alighieri, *Inferno*, Canto XXVI, lines 94–102 trans. Robert Pinsky. **37.** Ibid., lines 112–23. **38.** O. Sobolev and R. Milner-Gulland, 'Winter Road: An Analysis', in R. Reid, ed., *Two Hundred Years of Pushkin* (Amsterdam, 2004), vol. 3, pp. 125–40. **39.** An earlier version of this translation was published in Norman Davies, 'Adam Mickiewicz and His Times', in *Telling Lives*, ed. Alistair Horne (London, 2000), pp. 250–51. **40.** Jean Potocki, *Voyage dans l'Empire de Maroc* (1792), *Histoire Primitive des Peuples de la Russie* (1802), *Voyage au Caucase et en Chine* (Paris, 1980), *Manuscrit Trouvé à Saragosse* (1815). See also *The Manuscript Found in Saragossa*, trans. Ian Maclean (London, 1996), Nina Terlecka-Taylor, *Jan Potocki and his Polish Milieu* (Cambridge, 2002). **41.** Ryszard Przybylski, *Podróż Juliusza Słowackiego na Wschód* (Kraków, 1982). **42.** Ibid., stanza 50. **43.** Jack Cox, *Don Davies: 'An Old International'* (London, 1962). **44.** James Elroy Flecker (1884–1915), from *The Golden Journey to Samarkand* (London, 1913). **45.** Alfred, Lord Tennyson, from *Ulysses* (1842), lines 51–70.

## CHAPTER I. KERNO

**1.** www.english-heritage.org.uk (2008). **2.** BBC News (18 January 2002), 'Historic Signs Case Trio Bound Over', http://news.bbc.co.uk/1/hi/england/1768853.stm (2008). **3.** See www.timelessmyths.com/arthurian/cornwall.html (2008). **4.** See Norman Davies, *Europe: A History* (London, 1996), pp. 223–4. **5.** Lewis Spence, *Legends and Romances of Brittany* (London, 1917); 'Comorre, le Barbe-bleue breton', www.bretagne.com/fr/culture_bretonne/contes_et_legendes/barbe_bleue; Mike Dash, 'The Breton Bluebeard – a Blast from the Past', www.mikedashhistory.com/2015/12/28/the-breton-bluebeard (14 September 2016). **6.** Camors (Kamorzh), Morbihan: www.camors56.fr/tourisme-activites/97-chateau-de-barbe-bleue (15 September 2016). **7.** Gregory of Tours, *Historia Francorum*, Book IV, trans. E. Brehaut (1916). See also Gregory of Tours, *The History of the Franks* (Harmondsworth, 1974). **8.** G. H. Doble, *Lives of the Welsh Saints* (Cardiff, 1971). **9.** Léon Fleuriot, *Les Origines de la Bretagne* (Paris, 1980). **10.** www.babelstone.blogspot.co.uk/2009/11/ogham-stones-of-cornwall-and-devon.html, (31 October 2015). **11.** Alistair Moffat, *Arthur and* *the Lost Kingdoms* (London, 1999).   12. The Arthurian Centre, Camelford, www.visitcornwall.com/things-to-do/north-cornwall/tintagel/arthurian-centre#. VjsYyjZOflu (2015).   13. en.wikipedia.org/wiki/List_of_legendary_rulers_of_ Cornwall, also 'Cornish Kings' under en.wikipedia.org/wiki/List_of_kings_of_ Dumnonia (30 October 2015). Sheila Brynjulfson, 'The Quest for the Historical Arthur', www.vortigernstudies.org/artgue/guestsheila2.htm (2016).   14. Alistair Moffat, *The Sea Kingdoms* (London, 2001).   15. Procopius, *Bellum Gothicum*, IV. 20.6–9, quoted by E. A. Thompson, 'Procopius on Brittia and Britannia', *Classical Quarterly* (1980).   16. See M. Jones and P. Galliou, *The Bretons* (Oxford, 1991); Jean Delumeau, *Histoire de la Bretagne* (Paris, 2000).   17. Gilbert Hunter Doble, *The Saints of Cornwall* (Chatham, 1960); id., *Saints Perran, Keverne and Kerrian* (Shipston-on-Stour, 1931).   18. G. H. Doble, *Saint Petrock, Abbot and Confessor* (Shipston-on-Stour, 1938).   19. Tim Severin, *The Brendan Voyage* (London, 1996).   20. Brendan Lehane, *Early Celtic Christianity* (London, 1993).   21. Daphne du Maurier, *Vanishing Cornwall: The Spirit and History of Cornwall* (London, 1972), p. 25.   22. Alfred, Lord Tennyson, 'Merlin and Vivion', lines 6–13, from *The Idylls of the King* (London, 1859–85).   23. Norman Davies, 'Borussia: Watery Land of the Prusai', *Vanished Kingdoms* (London, 2012), Chapter 7.   24. See www.culturalgenocide.org; 'Dalai Lama Condemns China's "cultural genocide" of Tibet', *Daily Telegraph* (16 March 2008). 25. 'The Song of the Western Men', composed by Robert Stephen Hawker, 1825; for a dissident view of the 'Prayer Book Rebellion', see www.cornwallinformation. co.uk/news/the-anglo-cornish-war-of-june-august-1549. 26. 'Trelawny', trans. Henry Jenner, in *Cornish Notes and Queries* (London, 1906); www.califcornishcousins.com/Trelawny/Trelawny_cornish.php (2014); 27. Jon Mills, 'Genocide and Ethnocide: The Suppression of the Cornish Language', in J. Partridge (ed.), *Interfaces in Language* (Newcastle, 2010), pp. 189– 206.   28. Bridget Kendall, 'Re-awakening Language', The Forum, BBC Radio 4, (3 September 2016).   29. See Norman Davies, 'The Midnight Isles', *The Isles: A History* (London, 1999), pp. 3–27.   30. A. L. Rowse, *Quiller-Couch: A Portrait of 'Q'* (London, 1988).   31. www.izquotes.com/quote/159257 (18 September 2016).   32. A. L. Rowse, *Tudor Cornwall: Portrait of a Society* (London, 1941), *The West in English History* (London, 1949), *A Cornish Childhood* (London, 1944), *The Contribution of Cornwall and the Cornish to Britain* (Newton Abbot, 1969), and *The Spirit of English History* (London, 1943).   33. 'Poldark' TV series, www.imdb.com/title/tt3636060 (2016).   34. See Margaret Forster, *Daphne du Maurier* (London, 1993).   35. Daphne Du Maurier, *Rule Britannia* (London, 1972); 'Rule Britannia – published 1972', <dumaurier.org/menu_page. php?id=123>. See also Robert Stiby, letter to *The Times* (1 July 2016). 36. www.cornishchoughs.org/choughs (31 October 2015).   37. www.chough. org (November 2015).   38. See http://en.wikipedia.org/wiki/Stolen_Generations (2009); 'Sorry Day and the Stolen Generations', <australia.gov.au/about-Australia/Australian-story/sorry-day-stolen-generations> (2015).   39. P. Fontaine and B. Farber, 'What Canada Committed Against First Nations was Genocide',

*Globe and Mail* (14 October 2013).  40. 'Warlinenn: The Cornish Language Fellowship Online', at www.cornish-language.org/english> or www.cornish-language.org/cornish.asp (2008).  41. Henry Jenner, *A Handbook of the Cornish Language* (London, 1904); also *History in Cornish Place-Names* (Penryn, 1912).  42. 'Gorsedh Kernow – The Celtic Spirit in Cornwall', http://gorsedhker now.org (2015).  43. Maga: The Cornish Language Partnership, Cornwall Council, Truro TR1 3AY, at www.magakernow.org.uk (2008).  44. Cornish Stannary Parliament (CSP), at http://cornishstannaryparliament.co.uk (2008).  45. Marjorie Filbee, *Celtic Cornwall* (London, 1996); Mark Stoyle, *West Britons: Cornish Identities and the Early British State* (Exeter, 2002); H. Jenner, *The Celts in Cornwall* (Penzance, 2001).  46. See <thisisnotengland.co.uk/history/cornwall-background.html>, <thisisnotcornwall.co.uk/index-english.html>, and 'Tyr-Gwyr-Gweryn' (Land, Truth, People), www.kernowtgg.co.uk (2015).  47. Norman Berdichevsky, *Modern Hebrew: The Past and Future of a Revitalized Language* (Jefferson, NC, 2014).  48. www.omniglot.com/writing/hawaian.htm (12 September 2016).  49. Mark Turin, *Linguistic Diversity and the Preservation of Endangered Languages: A Case Study from Nepal* (Kathmandu, 2007).  50. www.gov.uk/news/cornish-granted-minority-status (25 April 2014).  51. Quoted by Philip Payton, *A. L. Rowse and Cornwall: A Paradoxical Patriot* (Exeter, 2005), p. 6.  52. Severin Carrell, 'Cornish Chuffed at the Return of the Chough', *Independent* (17 September 2011); 'The Return of the Chough', <nationaltrust.org.uk/article-1355816537870> (4 November 2015).  53. Du Maurier, *Vanishing Cornwall*, pp. 12–13.  54. Norman Davies, *West Cornwall Poems: Impressions* (St Ives, 1995), pp. 35, 66, 68.

## CHAPTER 2. BAKI-BAKU

1. Norman Davies, *Europe: A History* (Oxford, 1996), p. 8.  2. Azerbaijan Ministry of Foreign Affairs Visa Requirements, quoted by Wikipedia (2013).  3. Ibid.  4. Thomas de Waal, *Black Garden: Armenia and Azerbaijan through Peace and War* (New York, 2003); Vahe Gabreliyan, *Artsakh: The Land and People of Karabakh* (Yerevan, 2011).  5. S. Adamczak et al., *Gruzja, Armenia I Azerbaijan* (Bielsko Biala, 2013), pp. 14–15.  6. 'Sex in Azerbaijan', www.azerb.com/az-sex.html?i=1 (2013); www.naughtynomad.com/2012/12/16/ city-guide-baku-azerbaijan (2016).  7. *Azernews*, no. 72 (875) (September 2013). Price 49 gapiks.  8. 'Stabilising the Pipedreams of Europe', *Azerbaijan: A Phoenix Rising, The Report Company* (2013), pp. 5–6.  9. See Robert Conquest, *Stalin and the Kirov Murder* (London, 1989); M. Lenoe, *The Kirov Murder and Soviet History* (New Haven, 2010).  10. <en.wikipedia.org/wiki/National_Museum_of_History_of_Azerbaijan> (2013).  11. <en.wikipedia.org/wiki/Nizami_Museum_of_Azerbaijani_Literature> (2013).  12. V. I. Lenin, open letter, 'To the Comrades Communists of Azerbaijan, Georgia, Armenia, Daghestan and the Mountaineer Republics' (14 April 1921), *Collected Works*, vol. 32 (Moscow,

1965), pp. 316–18.13. See Jamil Hasanli, *At the Dawn of the Cold War: The Soviet-American Crisis over Iranian Azerbaijan, 1941–46* (Lanham, 2006). 14. 'Freedom in the World 2014', www.freedomhouse.org/report/freedom-world-2014 (2015). 15. www.transparency.org/cp/2014 (2015). 16. Committee to Protect Journalists (CPJ), www.cpj.org/awards/2009/eynulla-fatullayev-editor-realny-azeerbaijan.pth (2015). 17. 'Comment is Free', *The Guardian* (27 September 2013). 18. 'The Axeman Goeth', *The Economist* (8 September 2012). 19. Caucasus Election Watch (19 September 2013). 20. I. Aliyev, ed., *Istoriya Azerbaidzhana: s drevneishykh vryemyen do nachala XX vyeka* (Baku, 1995), p. 430. 21. L. Sadigova, 'Gobustan's Mysterious Inscriptions Made by Romans', *Azernews* (13 October 2016), www.azernews.az/culture/91386.html (2016). 22. Paul Kriwaczek, *In Search of Zarathustra: The First Prophet and the Ideas that Changed the World* (London, 2003). 23. <religion.wiki.com/wiki/Church_of_Caucasian_Albania> (2015). 24. C. J. F. Dowsett, *The History of the Caucasian Albanians* (Oxford, 1961). 25. The 'Panorama of Baccu' by Engelbert Kaempfer, from the atlas of Johan Baptist Homan (1683). 26. L. A. Hanafew, *The Historical Monuments of Isfahan* (Teheran, 1969–). 27. See Steve LeVine, *The Oil and the Glory: The Pursuit of Empire and Fortune on the Caspian Sen* (New York, 2007). 28. R. W. Tolf, *The Russian Rockefellers: The Saga of the Nobel Family and the Russian Oil Industry* (Stanford, 1976). 29. M. Suleymanov, 'Stories of Taghiyev: Baku's Most Renowned Oil Baron', *Azerbaijan International*, vol. 10, no. 2 (Summer 2002), pp. 42–9. 30. 'Quotable Quotes', *Azerbaijan International*, www.azer.com/aiweb/categories/53_folder/53_quotablequotes.html (2014). 31. Ibid. 32. 'Baku Commune of 1918', <encyclopedia2.thefreedictionary.com/Baku+Commune+of+1918> (from the former *Great Soviet Encyclopedia*) (2016). 33. Kaya T. Çağlayan, *British Policy towards Transcaucasia, 1917–21* (Istanbul, 2004). 34. R. G. Suny, *The Baku Commune, 1917–18* (Princeton, 1972). 35. Ludwell Denny, *We Fight for Oil* (New York and London, 1928). 36. L. C. Dunsterville, *The Adventures of Dunsterforce* (London, 1920, reprinted Uckfield, 2007). 37. J. Stalin, 'The Shooting of the Twenty-Six Comrades by the Agents of British Imperialism', *Izvestia* (23 April 1919), www.marxists.org/reference/archive/stalin/works/1919/04/23.htm (2016). 38. Ohannes Geukjian, *Ethnicity, Nationalism and Conflict in the South Caucasus* (Farnham, 2012). 39. Tadeusz Swietochowski, *Russian Azerbaijan, 1905–1920: The Shaping of National Identity in a Muslim Community* (Cambridge, 1985), pp. 129–78. 40. Jamil Hasanli, *The Foreign Policy of the Republic of Azerbaijan, 1918–20* (New York, 2014). 41. Swietochowski, op. cit., p. 193. 42. 'Biography: William Montgomery Thomson (1877–1964), <en.wikipedia.org/wiki/William_Montgomery_Thomson> (2016). 43. See Norman Davies, *White Eagle, Red Star: The Polish-Soviet War of 1919–20* (London, 1972). 44. Swietochowski, op. cit., pp. 177–8, 182, 198. 45. Z. Asadullayeva, 'When the Bolsheviks Came: An Oil Baron's Daughter Revisits Baku', *Azerbaijan International*, vol. 7, no. 3 (Autumn 1999), pp. 24–5. 46. Levon Chorbajian, *The Making of Nagorno-Karabagh: From Secession to Republic* (Basingstoke, 2001). 47. K. Popov, 'Yesenin in Baku', *Vestnik Kavkaza* (15 October 2012);

S. Kinzer, 'The Fallen Commissars of 1918: Now Fallen Idols', *The New York Times* (9 September 1997). **48.** 'Brothers Nobel', www.branobelhistory.com (2015). **49.** Soviet Russia had been recognized two years earlier by the provisional government of the first Irish Republic. **50.** Philip Gillette, 'American Capital in the Contest for Soviet Oil, 1920–23', *Soviet Studies*, vol. 24, no. 4 (1973), pp. 477–90. **51.** B. Czaplicki, *Ks. Konstanty Budkiewicz, 1867–1923* (Katowice, 2004). **52.** H. Flory, 'The Arcos Raid and the Rupture of Anglo-Soviet Relations, 1927', *Journal of Contemporary History*, vol. 12, no. 4 (1977), pp. 707–27. **53.** *House of Commons Debates* (Hansard) (5 December 1932), vol. 272, cc 1218–19: hansard.millbanksystems.com/commons/1932/dec/05/baku (2015). **54.** Hasanli, *At the Dawn of the Cold War.* **55.** See V. Andriyanov and G. Miramalov, *Geidar Aliev* (Baku, 2005). **56.** S. V. Utechin, *Everyman's Concise Encyclopaedia of Russia* (London, 1961), pp. 43–4. **57.** A. Mikoyan, *The Memoirs of Anastas Mikoyan: The Path of Struggle* (Madison, 1988); Simon Sebag Montefiore, *Stalin: The Court of the Red Tsar* (London, 2003). **58.** Michael Croissant, *The Armenia-Azerbaijan Conflict: Causes and Implications* (London, 1998). **59.** 'Sumgait Massacres', *Budapest Case,* http://budapest.sumgait.info (2015). **60.** <en.wikipedia.org/wiki/Kirovabad_pogrom> (2015); Caroline Cox, *Ethnic Cleansing in Progress: War in Nagorno-Karabakh* (Zurich, 1993). **61.** Human Rights Watch, Azerbaijan: *Seven Years of Conflict in Nagorno-Karabakh* (London, 1994). **62.** Samad Velikov (Vurgun, 1906–56): quoted by Andriyanov and Miramalov, op. cit., p. 386. **63.** S. Rayment, 'SAS Hired Out to Woo Tyrant of Azerbaijan', *The Sunday Times* (20 October 2013). **64.** www.insidespanishfootball.com/99619/atletico (2014). **65.** <en.wikipedia.org/wiki/List_of_renamed_cities_in_Azerbaijan> (2015). **66.** G. Lomsadze, 'Azerbaijan Moves to Dump Russian Last-Name Endings', Eurasianet.org (10 January 2011). **67.** G. Lomsadze, 'Will Azerbaijan Change its Name?', Eurasianet.org (2 February 2012). **68.** Roy Allison, *Challenges for the Former Soviet South* (Washington, 1996); Shirin Akiner, *The Caspian: Politics, Energy and Security* (London, 2004); Lutz Kleveman, *The New Great Game: Blood and Oil in Central Asia* (London, 2004). **69.** Edmund Herzig, *The New Caucasus: Armenia, Azerbaijan, and Georgia* (London, 1999); Firuz Kazemzadah, *The Struggle for Transcaucasia (1917–1921)* (London, 2008). **70.** 'Ambassadors', www.bbc.co.uk/programmes/p01jd3vx (2015). **71.** www.good-country.org/overall (11 August 2014). **72.** I. Nechepurenko, 'Putin's Visit to Baku Highlights Russia's "Clout"', *The Moscow Times* (13 August 2013). **73.** Max Fisher, 'Oops! Azerbaijan Released Results before Voting had Started', *Washington Post* (9 October 2013); BBC News, 'Azerbaijan's Ilham Aliyev Claims Victory' (9 October 2013). **74.** 'Putin, Aliyev Meet in Baku', *The Armenian Weekly* (8 August 2016). **75.** W. Kolarz, *Russia and her Colonies* (London, 1952).

## CHAPTER 3. AL-IMARAT

1. Sarah Riches, 'International Curriculum', *Time Out Abu Dhabi* (23–29 April 2014), pp. 16–19.   2. www.ehow.com/list_uae_universities.html (2012-07-15). 3. Higher Colleges of Technology, www.hct.ac.ae/en (2016).   4. <guinnessworld-records.com/news/2014/9/8-burj-khalifa-records-for-skyscraper-59996> (2014). 5. 'Burj Al-Arab Hotel', www.Jumeirah.com/Burj-Al-Arab-Dubai (2015). 6. 'Palm Island', www.thepalmdubai.com/palm-island-dubai/about-dubai/facts. html (2015).   7. 'Jumeirah Mosque: Key Feature of Old Dubai', *Gulf News* (26 August 2014).   8. Michael Deakin, *Ras-al-Khaimah: Flame in the Desert* (London, 1976). See also *The Times*, Supplement on Ras al-Khaimah (25 May 2017).   9. 'Prayer Timings', *Khaleej Times* (Dubai), www.khaleejtimes. com/prayer-time-uae (2014).   10. *The Gulf Today*, vol. 18, no. 277 (19 January 2014).   11. *Gulf News* (19 January 2014).   12. Karen Young, 'Gulf States are Torn between Economic Sense and Military Ambition', *The Conversation* (19 September 2016), www.theconversation.com/-/65509 (September 2016). 13. www.udayalaraji.com (September 2016).   14. 'Profile: Gulf Co-operation Council', www.news.bbc.uk/1/hi/world/middle_east/country_profiles/4155001. stm (2016).   15. 'Emirates on the Road to Recovery', *World Business Times* (7 June 2012).   16. 'Dubai Plan 2021', www.dubai.ae/en/Lists/Articles/Disp Form.aspx?ID=108£category (2014).   17. Tom Arnold, 'Vision 2030: Abu Dhabi Focusing on Growth Strategy', *The National* (11 March 2013). 18. 'Khalifa Port', www.adpc.ae/en/article/ports/khalifa-port.html (2014).   19. 'Kizad', www.adpc.ae/en/article/industrial-zone/kizad-1.html (2014).   20. 'Saadiyat Island', www.saadiyat.ae (2014).   21. See Paolo Soleri, *Arcology: Cities in the Image of Man* (Cambridge, MA, 1969).   22. 'Masdar City', www. masdar.ae/en (2014); Tom Heap, 'Masdar: Abu Dhabi's Carbon-Neutral City', BBC News (28 March 2010).   23. Tim Kruger, 'The UAE Wants to Build a "Rain-Making Mountain"', *The Conversation* (9 May 2016), www.theconversation. com/-/59024; Saleem H. Ali, 'Power and Peace: How Nations can go Nuclear without Weapons', ibid. (17 May 2015), no. 41462; Jill Stuart, 'The Emirates Paves the Way for a Middle East Space Programme with its Mission to Mars', ibid. (22 July 2014), no. 29489 (September 2016).   24. A. Wheatcroft, *With United Strength: H.H. Shaikh Zayid Bin Sultan Al Nahyan* (Abu Dhabi, 2004).   25. N. Ouroussoff, 'Building Museums: A Fresh Arab Identity', *The New York Times* (26 November 2010).   26. 'Anti-Slavery International', www.antislavery.org/ homepage/resources/cameljockeygallery.htm (2015).   27. www.digplanet.com/wiki/ Crime_in_the_United_Arab_Emirates (2015).   28. W. Al Marzouqi, 'Fatal Traditions: Female Circumcision in the UAE', *The National* (23 July 2011).   29. Yvonne Randall, *Al-Wathba: The Hell Hole*, www.foreignprisoners.com/news-saudi02. htm.   30. 'Bushire', www.britishempire.co.uk/maproom/bushire.htm (2016). 31. See H. Moyse-Bartlett, *The Pirates of Trucial Oman* (London, 1956); Donald Hawley, *The Trucial States* (London, 1970); P. Tuson and E. Quick, eds., *Arabian Treaties, 1600–1960* (Slough, 1992), 4 vols.   32. 'Arabia', *Encyclopaedia Britannica*, 11th edn. (1910–11), vol. II, pp. 254–76.   33. 'Oman', ibid., vol. 20,

pp. 99–100.   34. Frauke Heard-Bey, 'The Beginning of the Post-Imperial Era for the Trucial States from World War One to the 1960s', www.uaeinteract.com/ueaint_misc/pdf/perspectives/05.pdf (2016).   35. 'Memories 2', Ahmed from Ajman (20 February 2015), www.glimpsesofuae.com/category/memories (2016).   36. Afshan Ahmed, 'The UAE's History Lesson', *The National* (8 November 2011). 37. James Doran, 'The Alchemist who Turned Fields of Scrap into a Factory of Gold', *The National* (7 April 2013).   38. Jim Atkinson, <http://www.air-despatch.co.uk/pages/opendoor/o2goats/goats.htm> (2012.07.18).   39. Wilfred Thesiger, *Arabian Sands* (London, 2007), Introduction by Rory Stewart; from Chapter 3, 'The Sands of Ghanim'.   40. Robert Aldrich, *Colonialism and Homo-sexuality* (London, 2003), pp. 48–50.   41. Gerald Butt, 'Oil and Gas in the UAE', www.uaeinteract.com/uaeint_misc/pdf/perspectives/11.pdf (2014).   42. Frauke Heard-Bey, *From Trucial States to United Arab Emirates* (London, 1982); Malcolm Peck, *The United Arab Emirates: A Venture in Unity* (Boulder, CO, 1986); 'Withdrawal from Empire', www.britishempire.co.uk/maproom/trucialoman.htm (2015).   43. A. Blaustein et al. (eds.), *Independence Documents of the World* (New York, 1977), pp. 722–3.   44. Index Mundi, 'UAE Crude Oil Production by Year', http://www.indexmundi.com/energy/aspx? (24.08.2014). 45. http://www.swfinstitute.org/swfs/abu-dhabi-invest-authority (24.08.2014). 46. http://worldpopulationreview.com/countries/UAE (24.08.2014).   47. Hossein Askari, *Conflicts in the Persian Gulf* (Basingstoke, 2013), pp. 92–4. 48. 'Emirates Act to End Coup Crisis', *Chicago Tribune* (19 and 23 June 1987). 49. Simon Bowers, 'Files Close on BCCI Scandal', *The Guardian* (17 May 2012). 50. 'Britain's Biggest Banking Scandal', BBC News (13 December 2004); <news.bbc.co.uk/1/hi/business/3383461.stm> (2014).   51. Stella Dawson, 'Corrupt Money Hides in Dubai', *Thomson Reuters Foundation News* (13 December 2013), <news.trust.org/item/20131213143038-zrhib/?source=hptop> (2014).   52. Eva Joly, https://en.wikipedia.org/wiki/Eva_Joly (2014).   53. Sandra Laville, 'India Arrests Hawala Money Laundering Suspect, Naresh Jain', *The Guardian* (8 December 2009).   54. A. Torchia, 'Gold Industry Shifts East', *Reuters Middle East* (5 May 2014).   55. UAE Constitution, www.refworld.org/pdfid/48eca8132.pdf (2014).   56. Andrea Rugh, *The Political Culture of the UAE* (Basingstoke, 2010).   57. 'Human Rights Watch – UAE', https://www.hrw.org/middle-east/n-africa/united-arab-emirates (2014).   58. B. O'Malley, 'Labour Guidelines 'violated' on NYU-Abu Dhabi Campus', *University World/News* (14 October 2016).   59. Malcolm O'Neill, 'Stopover in Dubai – Kingdom of Bling', *Hiking New Zealand* (8 December 2015).   60. Annabel Kantaria, 'Living in Dubai: Why Don't Expats Integrate with Emiratis?', *The Telegraph* (26 March 2016).   61. Aoil Tabbara, 'Emiratis Get Tetchy with Expats', *The Telegraph* (7 October 2016).   62. Ibid.   63. 'Thousands of Shia Coercively Deported from UAE', *Shiite News* (9 February 2013).   64. https://en.wikipedia.org/wiki/Zayed_Center_for_Coordination_and_Follow-up (2014).   65. S. Marks, 'Harvard Returns Gift to Arab President', *The Harvard Crimson* (2 July 2004).   66. http://www.uoj.ac.ae (23/8/2014).   67. E. Akpan-Inwang, 'LSE's Libya Connection is only the Iceberg's Tip', *Guardian* (4 March 2011).   68. www.uaeinteract.com/society/

education (27.08.2014). 69. Y. Bahoumy, 'UAE Court Jails Scores of Emiratis in Coup Plot Trial', *Reuters* (2 July 2013). 70. www.uctsucks.org (2012). 71. 'Ranking Web of World Universities: Top Arab World', http://www.webometrics. info/top100_continent.asp?cont=aw (2012-07-15). 72. www.islamawareness.net/ Education/importance.html (2015), www.al-islam.org/articles/education-in-islam-sayyed-muhammed-rizui (2015); Safa Faisal, 'Muslim Girls Struggle for Education', BBC News (24 September 2003). 73. 'Memory 3', Khor Fakkan of Sharjah (27 February 2015), www.glimpsesofuae.com/category/memories (2016).

## CHAPTER 4. DILLI – DELHI

1. Colin Masica, *The Indo-Aryan Languages* (Cambridge, 1991); Sanford Steever, *The Dravidian Languages* (London, 1993). 2. Rosie Llewellyn-Jones, 'Delhi: Short-lived Capital of the Raj', *History Today* (December 2011), pp. 23–7; Mary Lutyens, *Edwin Lutyens* (London, 1991); Tristram Hunt, 'New Delhi', in *Ten Cities that Made an Empire* (London, 2014). 3. *The Coronation Durbar, Delhi 1911: Official Directory with Maps* (Calcutta, 1911). 4. <metrolyrics.com/jana-gana-mana-lyrics-national-anthem.html> (2015). 5. 'Indian Flag', www.mapsofindia. com/maps/india/national-flag.htm (2016). 6. Charles Allen, *Ashoka: The Search for India's Lost Emperor* (London, 2012). 7. See B. R. Ambedkar, *Annihilation of Caste* (1935), republished in an annotated critical edition by S. Anand and Arundhati Roy (eds.) (London, 2014); also his *Who Were the Shudras?* (Bombay, 1949). 8. Susan Bayly, *Caste, Society and Politics in India from the 18th Century to the Modern Age* (Cambridge, 2001); K. S. Singh, *The Scheduled Castes* (Calcutta, 1993). 9. Symptomatically, Wikipedia's entry on the 'List of Indian Castes' is undergoing reconstruction, although a mind-boggling outline can be found at www.speedydeletion.wikia.com/wiki/List_of_Indian_castes (17 December 2016). 10. R. Deliège and Nora Scott, *The Untouchables of India* (Oxford, 1999); S. M. Michael, *Dalits in Modern India: Vision and Values* (Los Angeles, 2007). 11. Alexander Robertson, *The Mahar Folk: A Study of Untouchables in Maharastra* (Calcutta, 1938); T. Pillai-Vetschera, *The Mahars* (New Delhi, 1994). 12. Rupa Viswanath, *The Pariah Problem: Caste, Religion, and the Social in Modern India* (New York, 2014). 13. Shiva Swamy, *Depressed Classes and Backward Classes of India* (Jaipur, 2009). 14. C. R. Bijoy, 'The Adivasis of India: A History of Discrimination, Conflict and Resistance' (2003), www.pucl.org/topics/dalit-tribal/2003/adivasi.htm (2015). 15. Sipra Sen, *The Tribes of Nagaland* (Delhi, 1987). 16. Michael Bergunder, *Ritual, Caste, and Religion in Colonial South India* (Halle, 2010). 17. Arundhati Roy, 'India's Shame', *Prospect* (December 2014), pp. 26–34. 18. BBC News, 'India's Lost Girls' (4 February 2003). 19. Mary Grey, *The Unheard Scream: The Struggle of Dali women* (New Delhi, 2004). 20. World Council of Churches and World YWCA, 'Dalit Fact Sheet' (2015). <overcomingviolence.org/en/resources/campaigns/women-against-violence/dalit-fact-sheet.html>. 21. 'Atrocities against Bhotmange Family in Khairlanji' (sentences rearranged), www.vakindia.org/pdf/khairlanji.pdf (17 December 2016);

Roy, op. cit., pp. 26–9. **22.** 'Death Sentence Dropped for Mob Murder of Dalits', BBC News (14 July 2012). **23.** 'Jogini System Still Prevalent in City', *The Hindu* (3 November 2012); 'Women in Ritual Slavery: Devadasi, Jogin and Mathamma', *Anti-Slavery International*, Document no. 1930 (2007). **24.** Moni Basu, 'The Girl whose Rape Changed a Country', <edition.cnn.com/interactive/2013/11/world/india-rape> (2013). **25.** Suzanne Moore, 'Delhi Gang-Rape: In India, Anger is Overtaking Fear', *The Guardian* (31 December 2012); Helen Pidd, 'A Bad Place to be a Woman', *The Guardian Weekly* (10 August 2012). **26.** J. Drèze and Amartya Sen, *An Uncertain Glory: India and its Contradictions* (London, 2013). **27.** Geeta Gupta, 'Delhi's Unending Search for Water', *Indian Express* (17 February 2013). **28.** Victor Mallet, 'The Polarising Outsider Set to Revolutionise Indian Politics', *The Financial Times* (17 May 2014); Jason Burke, 'Landslide for Modi Shatters Congress's Grip on Power', *The Guardian* (17 May 2014). **29.** Adam Taylor, 'Why Did Narendra Modi Keep his Wife Secret for Almost Fifty Years?', *Washington Post* (10 April 2014). **30.** M. Tewari, 'Delhi's Unknown Nirbhaya', and 'Around Seventy Delhi Police Officers Face "Rape" Charges', *MailOnlineIndia* (7 February 2014). **31.** 'India: Gang Rape', CNN Edition (31 May 2014). **32.** Gavin D. Flood, *An Introduction to Hinduism* (Cambridge, 2003); K. M. Sen, *Hinduism* (London, 2005). **33.** http://en.wikipedia.org/wiki/Akshardham_Delhi (2013). **34.** M. Tobias, *Life Force: The World of Jainism* (Berkeley, 1991); L. A. Babb, *Understanding Jainism* (Edinburgh, 2015). **35.** Brian White, 'A Five-Minute Introduction', http://www.buddhanet.net/e-learning/5minbud.htm (2013). **36.** http://en.wikipedia.org/wiki/Muhammad_of_Ghor (2013-03-16). **37.** W. O. Cole, *Sikhism* (London, 2013). **38.** From http://en.wikipedia.org/wiki/Mul_Mantar (2013). **39.** Roy, op. cit., p. 26. **40.** Stephen Neill, *A History of Christianity in India* (Cambridge, 2004). **41.** John Ferraby, *All Things Made New: A Comprehensive Outline of the Bahá'í faith* (London, 1987). **42.** Baha'i website, www.bahia.orgfaqfactsbahaifaith (2013). **43.** N. Sanyal, *The Development of Indian Railways* (Calcutta, 1930). **44.** Ibid., pp. 2, 8. **45.** 'National Rail Museum', <delhitourism.gov.in/delhitourism/entertainment/national_rail_museum.jsp> (2013). **46.** 'History of Indian Stamps', www.hamiltonphilatelic.org/presentations/indian states.pdf. (2016); www.sandafayre.com/rarestamps/rareindianstatesstamps.html (2016). **47.** Sir William Lee-Warner, *The Native States of India* (London, 1910, reprinted 2012). **48.** *Encyclopaedia Britannica*, 11th edition (1910–11), vol. 5, p. 813. **49.** 'Chamba', <en.wikipedia.org/wiki/Chamba_Himachal_Pradesh> (2015). **50.** 'Chamba', www.hpchamba.nic.in/tourism.htm (2015). **51.** 'The History and Register of the Princely States of India', *Nobility of the World*, vol. 8 – India, www.almanachdegota.org/id242.html (2015). **52.** 'National Identity Elements of India', <www.knowindia.gov.inknowindianational-symbols.php> (2016). **53.** B. R. Nanda, *Jawaharlal Nehru: Rebel and Statesman* (Oxford, 1998); Jawaharlal Nehru, *The Discovery of India* (London, 1946). **54.** 'Vande Mataram: The National Song of India', composed in 1875, www.hindujagruti.org/activities/campaigns/national/vandemataram (2016). **55.** Sam Chacko, 'Defining Indianness', About. com, nd. www.geography.about.com/od/indiamaps/a/Defining-Indianness.htm (2016). **56.** Pankaj Mishra, 'The Many Strands of Indian Identity', *The Wall Street Journal*

(13 February 2015).    57. Wendy Doniger, *Hindu Myths: A Sourcebook* (London, 1975); *The Rig Veda: An Anthology* (London, 1981); *The Hindus: An Alternative History* (London, 2009); *Love's Subtle Magic: An Indian Islamic Literary Tradition, 1379–1545* (New York, 2013); *Pluralism and Democracy in India: Debating the Hindu Right* (New York, 2015); *The Mare's Trap: Nature and Culture in the Kamasutra* (New Delhi, 2015).    58. Itty Abraham, *The Making of the Indian Atomic Bomb* (London, 1998).    59. S. Ganguli and S. P. Kapur, *India, Pakistan and the Bomb* (New York, 2010).    60. 'India's Daughter of Fire', *The Straits Times* (Singapore) (21 April 2012).    61. Mohan Malik, *China and India: Great Power Rivals* (Boulder, 2011).    62. Andrew Cooper, *The BRICS: A Very Short Introduction* (Oxford, 2016).    63. R. E. Vickery, *The Eagle and the Elephant* (Washington, DC, 2011).    64. www.nd6.com/insightwithVickramBahl.html (2012).    65. Original text at www.youtube.com/playlist.list19April2012 (2012).

## CHAPTER 5. MELAYU

1. Kuala Lumpur International Airport, www.klia.com.my (2014).    2. Malaysia Airlines, www.malaysiaairlines.com (2014).    3. *Sin Chew Daily* (*Petaling Jaya*) (10 June 2013). The banner was also in Mandarin and Tamil.    4. *Utusan Malaysia* (*The Malaysian Courier*) (24 April 2012), www.utusan.com.my (2014).    5. Victor T. King, *Malaysia* (London, 2008), pp. 45–50; see also Meredith Weiss, *The Routledge Handbook of Contemporary Malaysia* (London, 2015).    6. Kuala Lumpur, Selangor, www.geografia.com/malaysiaselangor.html (2014).    7. Petronas Towers, www.petronastwintowers.com.my (2014).    8. Thean Hou Buddhist Shrine, www.malaysian-explorer.com/theanHouTemple.html (2014).    9. National Mosque, <kuala-lumpur.attractionsinmalaysia.com/National.Mosque.php> (2014).    10. Hindu Shrine, www.wonderfulmalaysia.com/attractions/sri-mahamariamman-temple.htm (2014).    11. 'Rivers Deep or Mountains High? The Origins of the Word "Melayu"', www.sabrizain.org/malayamalays4.htm (2016).    12. 'Manglish', https://en.wikipedia.org/wiki/Manglish (2014).    13. 'No Can Do', *Malaysia Today* (online) (13 February 2014).    14. Tugu Negara, www.malysia-explorer.com/tuguNegara.html (2014).    15. Muzium Negara, www.jmm.gov.my/en/museum.muzium-negara (2014).    16. M. C. Ricklefs, *A History of Modern Indonesia since c. 1300* (Basingstoke, 1993); R. E. Elson, *The Idea of Indonesia: A History* (Cambridge, 2008).    17. Iskandar Carey, *Orang Asli: The Aboriginal Tribes of Peninsular Malaysia* (London, 1976); Roy Jumper, *Power and Politics: The Story of Malaysia's Orang Asli* (Lanham, 1997).    18. 'Malaysia's Indigenous Peoples', <malaysiasite.nl/orangeng.htm> (2014).    19. 'Ethnic Malays', <en.wikipedia.org/wiki/Ethnic_Malays> (2014).    20. George Coedès, *The Indianized States of South-East Asia* (1964; Honolulu, 1968); *Sriwijaya: History, Religion and Language of an Early Malay Polity* (Kuala Lumpur, 1992).    21. John Guy et al., *Lost Kingdoms: Hindu-Buddhist Sculpture of Early South-East Asia* (New York, 2014).    22. I-Tsin, *A Record of the Buddhist Religion as Practised in India and the Malay Archipelago (AD 671–95)*

(Oxford, 1896), p. xxxix. **23.** Ibid., pp. xl–xli. **24.** http://www.lonelyplanet. com/madagascar/history (2014). **25.** J. Dumarçay, *Borobudur* (Oxford, 1991). **26.** 'Majapahit Empire', http://en.wikipedia.org/wiki/Majapahit (2014). **27.** 'Ritual Networks and Royal Power in Majapahit Java', p. 100: http:// www.persee.fr/web/revues/home/prescriptarticle/arch_0044-8613_1996_num_52_1_ 3357. **28.** Theodore Pigeaud, *Java in the Fourteenth Century: A Study in Cultural History* (The Hague, 1960–63), 5 vols. **29.** Barbara Watson Andaya, 'Malacca', in C. Edmund Bosworth, ed., *Historic Cities of the Islamic World* (Leiden, 2007), pp. 309ff. **30.** Tomé Pires: see his *Suma Oriental: An Account of the East from the Red Sea to Japan, written in Malacca and India 1512–15* (Google Books). **31.** Rosemary Robson, *The Epic of Hang Tuah* (Kuala Lumpur, 2010). **32.** Fei Hsin, *Hsing-ch'a-sheng-lan: The Overall Survey of the Star Raft*, Roderich Ptak, ed., J. V. G. Mills, trans. (Wiesbaden, 1996); Edward Dreyer, *Zheng He: China and the Oceans in the Early Ming Dynasty, 1405–33* (London, 2007). **33.** M. A. Khan, *Islamic Jihad: A Legacy of Forced Conversion, Imperialism, and Slavery* (Bloomington, IN, 2009), pp. 140–41. **34.** Nicholas Tarling, *Anglo-Dutch Rivalry in the Malay World* (Cambridge, 1962). **35.** L. A. Mills, *British Malaya, 1824–67*, PhD thesis (Oxford, 1924, Singapore, 1961); C. D. Cowan, *Nineteenth-Century Malaya: The Origins of British Control* (London, 1961); J. G. Butcher, *The British in Malaya, 1880–1941* (Oxford, 1979). **36.** H. S. Barlow, *Swettenham* (Kuala Lumpur, 1995); F. S. Clark, *Men of Malaya* (London, 1942). **37.** F. W. Swettenham, *A Vocabulary of the English and Malay Languages*, 2 vols. (London, 1883–7); *About Perak* (Singapore, 1893); *Malay Sketches* (London, 1895); *The Real Malay: Pen Pictures* (London, 1900); *British Malaya: An Account of the Origins and Progress of British Influence in Malaya* (London, 1948); *Sir Frank Swettenham's Malayan Journals, 1874–76* (Kuala Lumpur, 1973). **38.** Swettenham, *The Real Malay*, pp. ix–x. **39.** Ibid., pp. 2–3. **40.** Ibid., pp. 7–8. **41.** S. H. Alatas, *The Myth of the Lazy Native: A Study in the Image of Malays, Filipinos, and Javanese . . . and its Function in the Ideology of Colonial Capitalism* (London, 1977). **42.** *SOED*, vol. I, p. 63. **43.** Frank Swettenham, from 'Amok', *Malay Sketches*, pp. 38–42. **44.** P. J. Drake, 'The Economic Development of British Malaya to 1914', *Journal of South-Eastern Asian Studies*, vol. 10, no. 2 (1979), pp. 262–90. **45.** J. Hagan and A. Wells, 'The British and Rubber in Malaya, c. 1860–1940', University of Wollongong Research Online, http://ro.uow.edu.au/cgi/viewcontent. cgi?arti (22 September 2014). **46.** Owen Rutter, *British North Borneo: An Account of its History, Resources and Native Tribes* (London, 1922); D. J. M. Tate, *Rajah Brooke's Borneo* (Hong Kong, 1998); Margaret Brooke, *My Life in Sarawak* (London, 1913, Singapore, 1986). **47.** S. R. Evans, *The History of Labuan Island* (Singapore, 1998). **48.** *Stanley Gibbons' Simplified Stamp Catalogue* (London, 1948), p. 1,218. **49.** *Encyclopaedia Britannica*, 11th edition (London, 1910–11), vol. 17, pp. 453–4. **50.** P. Kratoska, *Malaya and Singapore during the Japanese Occupation* (Singapore, 1995). **51.** Albert Lau, *The Malayan Union Controversy* (Oxford, 1991). **52.** Robert Jackson, *Malayan Emergency: The Commonwealth Wars, 1948–66* (London, 1991). **53.** John

Cloake, *Templer, Tiger of Malaya: The Life of Field Marshal Sir Gerald Templer* (London, 1985). **54.** Harry Miller, *Prince and Premier: A Biography of Tunku Abdul Rahman* (London, 1959). **55.** Roger Lewis, *Anthony Burgess* (London, 2002): Paul Phillips, *A Clockwork Counterpoint: The Music and Literature of Anthony Burgess* (Manchester, 2010). **56.** Anthony Burgess, 'The Enemy in the Blanket', *The Malayan Trilogy* (London, 2000), pp. 191-2. **57.** Will Fowler, *Britain's Secret War: The Indonesian Confrontation, 1962-66* (Oxford, 2006). **58.** J. J. Raj, *The Struggle for Malaysian Independence* (Petaling Jaya, 2007). **59.** Rukunegara, http://www.jpnin.gov.my/isytihar_km (16 September 2014). **60.** BBC News, '1MDB: The Case that has Riveted Malaysia' (27 July 2016). **61.** South-East Asia Regional Center for Counter Terrorism, www.searcct.gov.my (2015). **62.** *Sydney Morning Herald* (30 March 2014). **63.** Association of Southeast Asian Nations, www.asean.org (2015). **64.** *The Star* (24 April 2012), www.thestar.com.my (2014). **65.** BFM Radio, www.liveonlineradio.net/malaysia/bfm-radio.htm (2014). **66.** J. Pak, 'Malaysia Focuses on a High-Tech Future', BBC News – Business (1 September 2011). **67.** 'Freescale Malaysia was Acquired by NXP Semiconductors in December 2015', <Bloomberg.com/research-stocksprivatesnapshot.asp?privcapld=5475809> (2015). **68.** GDP (PPP), https://en.wikipedia.org/wiki/List_of_countries_by_GDP_(PPP) (2014). **69.** Freedom House, https://en.wikipedia.org/wiki/List_of_freedom_indices (2014).

## CHAPTER 6. SINGAPURA

**1.** Singapore's Population, www.worldometers.info/world-population/singapore-population (4 November 2016). **2.** Insight Guide, *Singapore*, 14th edition (Singapore, 2014). **3.** GDP 2015, www.tradeconomics.com/singapore/gdp-per-capita (2016). **4.** *Vadavaka* in the original Tamil, or *le pompoir* (French), *der Kegel* (German), *kabazza* (Arabic), the 'Shanghai Squeeze', 'the Snapping Turtle', or 'the Quivering Butterfly'. See Carrie Weisman, 'The Ancient but Largely Forgotten Technique', www.alternet.org (2015). **5.** 'Tigers in Singapore', www.eresources.nlb.gov.sg/infopedia/articles/SIP_1081_2007_01_17.html (23 April 2013). **6.** B. Yeoh and W. Lin, 'Rapid Growth in Singapore's Immigrant Population Brings Policy Challenges', Migration Policy Institute (Washington) (3 April 2012), www.migrationpolicy.org/article (2016). **7.** Carl Trocki, *Opium and Empire: Chinese Society in Colonial Singapore, 1800-1910* (London 1990). **8.** See O. S. Song, *One Hundred Years' History of the Chinese in Singapore* (Singapore, 1967). **9.** Tessa Wong, 'The Rise of Singlish', BBC News (6 August 2015). **10.** 'Singapore MRT Map', <subway.umka.org/map-singapore.html> (2013); Brenda Yeoh, *Portraits of Places: History, Community and Identity in Singapore* (Singapore, 1995). **11.** 'Singapore Brothels', www.mademan.com/mm/singapores-10-best-brothels.html (2013). **12.** 'The Best Singapore Jokes', www.askmelah.com, My Favourites (2013). **13.** https://en.wikipedia.org/wiki/President_of_Singapore (2013). **14.** Yao Souchou, 'Oral Sex, Natural Sex and National Enjoyment', in *Singapore: The State and the Culture of Excess* (London, 2007). **15.** https://www.

indexoncensorship.org/2009/11/singapore-censorship-city (2013). **16.** Palash Gosh, 'Singapore: Drug Laws and the Death Penalty', *International Business Times* (22 June 2011). **17.** Amnesty International, 'Singapore: The Death Penalty – A Hidden Toll of Executions' (2003), www.amnesty.org/en/countries/asia-and-the-pacific/singapore (2013). **18.** Alan Shadrake, *Once a Jolly Hangman: Singapore Justice in the Dock* (Millers Point, 2010); P. Barkham, 'Jailed for Writing a Book They Didn't Like', *The Guardian* (27 July 2011). **19.** International Crime Rates, www.numbeo.com/crime/rankings_by_country.jsp (4 January 2016); Germany is 99th, the UK 68th, the USA 45th, and Venezuela at no. 1, bottom of the league. **20.** Lee Kuan Yew, *From Third World to the First: Singapore 1965–2000* (Singapore, 2000). **21.** Expedia.co.uk, Currency Converter (30 December 2015). **22.** 'Our Healthcare System', www.moh.gov.sg/content/moh_web/home our_healthcare_system.html (2013). **23.** OECD online, *Handbook for Internationally Comparative Education Statistics* (2013). **24.** P. Waring and V. Drewe, 'Singapore's Global Schoolhouse Strategy: The First Ten Years', *The Observatory on Borderless Higher Education* (2012; 2013). **25.** www.topuniversities.com/university-rankings/world-university-rankings.2015; Singapore's Nanyang Technological University stood at no. 13. **26.** National University of Singapore, www.nus.edu.sg (2013). **27.** See P. J. Thum, 'History of Singapore' podcast, <itunes.apple.com/gb/podcast/the-history-of-singapore/id1024071280?mt=2> (2016). **28.** Lee Kuan Yew, *The Singapore Story: Memoirs of Lee Kuan Yew* (Singapore, 1998). **29.** See Chris Tremewan, *The Political Economy of Social Control in Singapore* (Basingstoke, 1994); Han Fook Kwang et al., *Lee Kuan Yew: The Man and his Ideas* (Singapore, 1998); 'Days of Reflection for the Man who Defined Singapore', transcript from *New York Times* (Singapore) 13.9.2010; Lee Kuan Yew, *One Man's View of the World* (Singapore, 2013). **30.** Majulah Anthem, http:en.wikipedia.orgwikiMajulah_Singapura (2013). **31.** Noel Barber, *The Singapore Story: From Raffles to Lee Kwan Yew* (London, 1978); C. M. Turnbull, *A History of Singapore 1819–1988* (Singapore, 1989); E. Chew and E. Lee, *A History of Singapore* (Singapore, 1990); Carl Trocki, *Singapore: Wealth, Power and Control* (London, 2006). **32.** Charles Wurtzburg, *Raffles of the Eastern Isles* (Oxford, 1986); Maurice Collis, *Raffles* (London, 1988); V. Glendinning, *Raffles and the Golden Opportunity* (London, 2012). **33.** Letter from Penang (19 February 1819), quoted by Sophia, Lady Raffles, *Memoir of the Life and Public Services of Sir Thomas Stamford Raffles FRS* (1830) (Singapore, 1991), p. 377. **34.** Raffles to the Duchess of Somerset (22 February 1819), in ibid., p. 378. **35.** Philip Ziegler, *Diana Cooper: The Biography of Lady Diana Cooper* (London, 1982). **36.** Noel Barber, *A Sinister Twilight: The Fall of Singapore* (Boston, 1968); Frank Owen, *The Fall of Singapore* (1960) (London, 2001); Cecil Lee, *Sunset of the Raj* (Edinburgh, 1994); Timothy Hall, *The Fall of Singapore* (Melbourne, 1990); Peter Elphick, *Singapore: The Pregnable Fortress* (London, 1995). **37.** Alan Warren, *Singapore 1942: Britain's Greatest Defeat* (London, 2002); Richard Hughes, 'End of an Edifice', *The New York Times* (30 June 1968): a review of Barber, op. cit. **38.** Benjamin Schwarz, 'Their Lousiest Hour', *The New York Times* (17 August 2005): a review of C. Bayly and

T. Harper, *Forgotten Armies: The Fall of British Asia, 1941–45* (Harvard, 2005). **39.** Quoted by Hughes, op. cit. **40.** From F. Spencer-Chapman, *The Jungle is Neutral* (London, 1949). **41.** Lt. Gen. A. E. Percival, *The War in Malaya* (London, 1949), 'The Battle for Singapore I', pp. 281ff. **42.** S. E. Morison, *Rising Sun in the Pacific* (Oxford, 1948), pp. 188–90. **43.** Martin Middlebrook, *Battleship: The Loss of the Prince of Wales and the Repulse* (London, 1979). **44.** V. Semenov, *The Battle of Tsu-shima between the Japanese and Russian Fleets, 1905* (London, 1906). **45.** Owen, op. cit., pp. 131–2. **46.** Lionel Wigmore, *The Japanese Thrust* (Canberra, 1957), quoted by Owen, op. cit., p. 134. **47.** Owen, op. cit., p. 139. **48.** <www.en.wikipedia.org/wiki/Malaya_Campaign> (2014). **49.** From W. S. Churchill, *The Second World War*, vol. III (London, 1950). **50.** Hughes, op. cit. **51.** Percival, op. cit., p. 293. **52.** Ibid., p. 294. **53.** *The New York Times* (17 February 1942). **54.** See Edward Russell, *The Knights of Bushido: A Short History of Japanese War Crimes* (London, 1960). **55.** Changi POW Camp, www.historylearningsite.co.uk/world-war-two/prisoners-of-war-in-ww2/changi-pow-camp (2014). **56.** Quoted by Hughes, op. cit. **57.** 'End of Occupation', <en.wikipedia.org/Japanese_occupation_of_Singapore> (2015). **58.** Hughes, op. cit. **59.** D. Black, *In His Own Words: John Curtin's Speeches and Writings* (Perth, 1995). **60.** *The New York Times* (16 February 1942). **61.** Quoted by H. E. Wilson, *Social Engineering in Singapore, 1819–1972* (Singapore, 1978). **62.** Tim Huxley, *Defending the Lion City: The Armed Forces of Singapore* (St. Leonard's, 2000). **63.** Marina Bay, www.marina-bay.sg (2014); https://www.marinabaysands.com (2014). **64.** J. G. Farrell, *The Singapore Grip* (London, 1978), p. 1. **65.** 'Memories at Old Ford Factory', www.tripadvisor.co.uk/Attraction_Review-g294265-d1583247 (2014). **66.** www.singapore-guide.com/attractions/changi-prison-chapel-museum.htm (2014). **67.** '15–Royston Tan', www.directorsnotes.com2006061715-royston-tan (2014). **68.** Singapore Cuisine, www.yoursingapore.com/dining-drinks.html (2013); www.internations.org/singapore … culture … dining-in-singapore.html (2013). **69.** 'How to Order Coffee like a Singaporean', www.travelfish.org/entertainment_profile/singapore/downtown-singapore2295 (2014). **70.** Raffles Hotel, http://en.wikipedia.org/wiki/Raffles_Hotel (2013); www.gourmetgetaways.com.auraffles-high-tea-singapore (2013). **71.** Singapore Sling, www.drinksmaster.com/drink526.html (2014). **72.** A. T. Kearney, 'The Globalization Index, 2007', *Foreign Policy Journal*: www.foreignpolicy.com/2009/10/12/the-globalization-index-2007 (2016). **73.** Manfred Steger, *Globalization: A Very Short Introduction* (Oxford, 2013). **74.** *Seawise Giant*, www.vesseltracking.net/article/seawise-giant (10 January 2017). **75.** Lord 'Jim' O'Neill, 'Fixing Globalisation', BBC Radio 4 (6 January 2017); also *The Growth Map: Economic Opportunities in the BRICs and Beyond* (London, 2011). **76.** Jurong Island, www.jtc.gov.sg/industrial-land-and-space/Pages/jurong-island.aspx?ref=search (2014). **77.** Tom Freyberg, 'Singapore to Build Third Desalination Plant', *WaterWorld* (13 March 2015). **78.** Azra Moiz, 'Singapore – Running Out of Water', www.worldwaterconservation.com/Singapore.html (2014). **79.** Association of Pacific Rim Universities (founded 1997), www.apru.org (2014). **80.** F. R. Dulles, *America in the Pacific: A Century* *of Expansion* (1932) (New York, 1969). 81. 'Guam', www.infoplease.com/coun try/guam.html (2014). 82. I. Parmar, *Obama and the World: New Directions in US Foreign Policy* (New York, 2014). 83. See I. P. Austin, ed., *Australia-Singapore Relations: Successful Bilateral Relations in a Historical and Contemporary Context* (Singapore, 2011). 84. K. Vasvania, 'Brexit: The Singapore Lesson', BBC News (25 February 2016); Chris Key, 'Modelling the British Economy on Singapore after Brexit is a Really Bad Idea', *The Independent* (19 January 2017).

INTERLUDE. ORIENS

1. Sebastian Münster, 'Europa Regina' (1537), in *Cosmographiae Universalis* (Basel, 1552), 6 vols.; Matthew McLean, *The Cosmographia of Sebastian Münster: Describing the World in the Reformation* (Aldershot, 2007). 2. Tony Judt (1948–2010). See Tony Judt and Timothy Snyder, *Thinking the Twentieth Century* (London, 2012). 3. L. Bagrow and R. A. Skelton, *History of Cartography*, 2nd edition (Oxford, 1985); Jerry Brotton, *A History of the World in Twelve Maps* (London, 2012). 4. *SOED*, toponomy, 1876. 5. Henry R. Schoolcraft, *The Indian Tribes of the USA* (Philadelphia, 1851–7), 6 vols. 6. American Heritage, *Dictionary of the English Language*, 5th edition (New York, 2011). 7. Percival Lowell, *Choson: The Land of Morning Calm* (London, 1885); *The Soul of the Far East* (London, 1907). 8. J. W. Hall, ed., *The Cambridge History of Japan* (Cambridge, 1993), vol. 1. 9. E. O. Reischauer and J. K. Fairbank, *East Asia: The Great Tradition* (London, 1960). 10. See Norman Davies, 'The Germano-Celtic Isles', in *The Isles: A History* (London, 1996). 11. Edith Hall, *Inventing the Barbarian: Greek Self-Definition through Tragedy* (Oxford, 1989). 12. Alexander Blok, from 'The Scythians' (January 1918), <http://allpoetry.com/ TheScythians>. 13. Lev N. Gumilëv, *Ethnogenesis and the Biosphere of Earth* (Moscow, 1990); *Otkrytie Khazarii* (Moscow, 1966); *Khunny v Kitae* (Moscow, 1974); L. Gumilev, 'Ethnogenesis and Biosphere', www.cossackweb.narod. rugumilevcontentshtm (2016). 14. Marlène Laruelle, *Russian Eurasianism: An Ideology of Empire* (London, 2012); Charles Clover, *Black Wind, White Snow: The Rise of Russia's Neo-Nationalism* (London and New York, 2016), 'Lev Gumilev: Passion, Putin and Power', *The Financial Times* (11 March 2016); Benjamin Nathan, 'The Real Power of Putin', *New York Review of Books*, vol. 63, no. 14 (September–October 2016). 15. 'Where Three is a Crowd: Introducing the Eurasian Economic Union', *The Economist* (30 May 2014). 16. L. N. Gumilyov Eurasian National University, www.enu.kz/en (9 November 2016). 17. S. Lee, ed., *The Travels of Ibn Batuta* (London, 1984); Richard Hall, *Empires of the Monsoon: A History of the Indian Ocean and its Invaders* (London, 1996). 18. Martín Ignacio de Loyola, *Viaje alredor del mundo* (Madrid, 1989). 19. 'The Epic Journey of Hasekura Tsunenaga', www.artsales.com/ARTistory/Xavier/Hasekura.html (2016). 20. Aphra Behn, from 'The Disappointment', www.poetry.foundation.org/poems-and-poets/ poems/detail/43639 (2014). 21. See Maureen Duffy, *The Passionate Shepherdess* (London, 1977). 22. Pedro Cubero Sebastián, *Peregrinación del mundo* (Madrid, 1993). 23. See John Gemelli Careri, *Tour du Monde* (Paris, 1704). 24. Nellie

Bly, www.biography.com/people/nellie-bly-9216680 (2014).   25. Charles Cogan, 'You Have to Understand, George', *Huffington Post* (17 March 2014).   26. See Roger Adelson, *London and the Invention of the Middle East: Money, Power and War, 1902–20* (New Haven, 1994).   27. *El-Masudi's Historical Encyclopaedia Entitled the Meadow of Gold and Mines of Gems*, trans. from the Arabic by Aloys Sprenger MD, vol. 1 (London, 1841), pp. 27–8.   28. Al-Masudi, *Les Prairies d'Or*, trans. C. Barbier de Meynard and Pavet de Courteille (Paris, 1861–77), 9 vols.   29. Al-Masudi, op. cit., pp. 262–3.   30. Al-Masudi, *The Meadows of Gold: The Abbasids*, trans. P. Lunde and C. Stone (London, 1989), paragraph 2370.   31. Ibid., 'In the Audience Hall'.   32. Ibid., paragraph 2374.   33. David Rees, *The Soviet Seizure of the Kuriles* (New York, 1985).   34. Lord Byron, from 'The Bride of Abydos' (1813).   35. Edward Said, *Orientalism* (London, 1978).   36. Robert Irwin, *For Lust of Knowing: The Orientalists and their Enemies* (London, 2008).   37. Maya Jasanoff, 'Before and After Said', *London Review of Books*, vol. 28, no. 11 (8 June 2008).   38. Talal Asad, *Anthropology and the Colonial Encounter* (New York, 1973); Suman Seth, 'Putting Knowledge in its Place: Science, Colonialism and the Postcolonial', *Postcolonial Studies*, vol. 12, no. 4 (2009), pp. 373–88.   39. Timothy Snyder, *Black Earth: The Holocaust as History and Warning* (London, 2015).   40. Norman Davies, 'Western Civilisation versus European History', *Europe: East and West* (London, 2006), pp. 46–60.   41. Norman Davies, 'Fair Comparisons, False Contrasts: East and West in European History', in ibid., pp. 22ff.   42. J. Wertheimer, *Unwelcome Strangers: East European Jews in Imperial Germany* (Oxford, 1989).   43. Norman Davies, 'Great Britain and the Polish Jews, 1918–21', *Journal of Contemporary History*, vol. 8, no. 2 (1973).   44. Yitsak Shamir, quoted in Alan Berger et al., *The Continuing Agony: From the Carmelite Convent to the Crosses at Auschwitz* (London, 2012), p. 139.   45. Menzies (27 April 1939); Alan Watt, *The Evolution of Australian Foreign Policy, 1938–1968* (Cambridge, 1968), p. 24.   46. G. Abbondanze, *The Geopolitics of Australia in the New Millennium: Asia-Pacific Context* (Aracne, 2013).   47. Eric Newby, *The Rand McNally World Atlas of Exploration* (London, 1975); www.lifeonperth.com/dutchshipwrecks.htm (2016).   48. Burke and Wills: Alan Moorhead, *Cooper's Creek: The Classic Account of the Burke and Wills Expedition across Australia* (London, 2001); Sarah Murgatroyd, *The Dig Tree: The Extraordinary Story of the Ill-Fated Burke and Wills Expedition* (London, 2003).   49. James Lister Cuthbertson, *Australian Sunrise* (1879), www.alldownunder.com/australian-authors/james-cuthbertson/australian-sunrise.htm (2014).

## CHAPTER 7. MORIS

1. C. Clement, J. Gresham and Hamish McGlashan, eds., *Kimberley History: People, Exploration, and Development* (Perth, 2012).   2. Willem Blaeu, *Indiae quae Orientalis dicitur* (1637), in *Le Grand Atlas*, facsimile edition (Paris, 1992).   3. www.earthobservatory.nasa.gov/IOTD/view.php?id=703 (2017).   4. Willem Blaeu, *Africae Nova Descriptio* (1617), in *Le Grand Atlas*, op. cit., pp.

59–60.  **5.** A. Tasman, *Abel Tasman's Journal . . .*, translated from the Dutch (Amsterdam, (1898).  **6.** Robert Hughes, *The Fatal Shore* (London, 1987), p. 82.  **7.** https://fr.wikipedia.org/wiki/Île_Maurice (2014).  **8.** See J. Addison and K. Hazareesingh, *A New History of Mauritius* (Rose-Hill, 1993); Sydney Silvon, *A Comprehensive History of Mauritius: From the Beginning to 2001* (Port-Louis, 2001).  **9.** Benjamin Moutou, 'Sommes-nous tous des métis ou des Sang-melés?', in *Pages d'Histoire d'Ici et d'Ailleurs* (Baie du Tombeau, Maurice, n.d.), pp. 225–31. **10.** Ibid., endnote, pp. 155–6.  **11.** Ibid., 'L'Évolution de la propriété foncière à Maurice', pp. 79–87.  **12.** 'Les Sino-mauriciens', www.hualienclub.com/index. php? (2015).  **13.** National Postal Museum, Port Louis; see also Penny Blue Museum, Caudon Waterfront, Port Louis, www.discovermauritiusisland.com/ discover/postal-museum (2015).  **14.** Georges Brunel, *Les Timbres-Poste de l'Ile de Maurice* (Paris, 1928).  **15.** Eugene Byrne, 'Some Damned Fool', *History Extra* (11 November 2011).  **16.** 'Rare British Guiana Stamp Set Record at New York Auction', BBC News (17 June 2014).  **17.** Economist Intelligence Unit, Democracy Index 2015, www.eiu.com/public/topical-report.aspx?campaignid=D emocracyIndex2015 (2017).  **18.** Letter from Dr S. Hazareesingh (December 2016).  **19.** David Vine, *Island of Shame: The Secret History of the US Military Base on Diego Garcia* (Princeton, 2008); John Madely, *Diego Garcia: A Contrast to the Falklands* (London, 1995).  **20.** BBC News (29 June 2016), 'Chagos Islanders Cannot Return Home, Says Supreme Court', <bbc.co.uk/news/uk-36659976> (12 January 2017).  **21.** Vel Mahalingum, 'How the Hindus of Mauritius Uplifted Themselves, Transformed their Nation, and Became Models for the World', *Hinduism Today* (July–September 2010).  **22.** www.mauritius.org.uk/ fauna.htm (2016); www.mauritian-wildlife.org (2016).  **23.** Moutou, op. cit., p. 152.  **24.** Eileen Cowper, *Blessed Jacques Laval: Apostle of Mauritius*, Catholic Truth Society (London, n.d); Monique Denan, *Sur les pas du bienheureux Père Laval* (Port Louis, 2014); 'Pour le Pèlerinage Père Laval 2014', *Le Mauricien* (20 April 2013).  **25.** Serge Lebrasse, 'Séga Père Laval', <fr.wikipedia.org/wiki-Jacques-D%C3%A9sir%C3%A9_Laval> (2016).  **26.** Henry Gilfond, *Voodoo: Its Origins and Practices* (New York, 1976).  **27.** voyance.magie@yahoo.fr (29 January 2016).  **28.** Education, http://countrystudies.us/mauritius/11.htm (2017).  **29.** www.uom.ac.mu (2017).  **30.** www.expat.com/en/nationalities/ mauritian (2017).  **31.** Auguste Toussaint, *Port-Louis: Deux siècles d'Histoire* (Port-Louis, 1936).  **32.** www.chateaulabourdonnais.com/en (2015).  **33.** Tom Masters, *Mauritius, Réunion, and Seychelles*, Lonely Planet Guide (London, 2007).  **34.** Richard Price, *Maroon Societies: Rebel Slave Communities in the Americas* (Baltimore, 1973, 1996).  **35.** Moutou, op. cit., 'L'inextricable Echeveau Linguistique Mauricien', pp. 214–19.  **36.** See J. A. Holm. *An Introduction to Pidgins and Creoles* (Cambridge, 2000).  **37.** Philip Baker, *Kreol: A Description of Mauritian Creole* (London, 1972).  **38.** Anthony Grant and Diana Guillemin, 'The Complex of Creole Typological Features; The Case of Mauritian Creole', *Journal of Pidgin and Creole Languages*, vol. 27, no. 1 (2012). www.academia.edu/11088555 (2015).  **39.** 'Queen Elizabeth II Visit to Mauritius', www.vintagemauritius.org/people/queen-elizabeth-mauritius-ssr-march-1972

(2016).  40. Grant and Guillemin, op. cit.  41. www.lyricstranslate.com/en/lords-prayer-nou-papa-mauritian-creole-lyrics.html (2015).  42. www.tourism-mauritius.mu/Culture/writers-a-artists.html (2015).  43. www.nobelprize.org/nobel_prizes/literature/laureates/2008 (2017).  44. Robert-Edward Hart, *Poèmes Choisis* (Port-Louis, 1930), pp. 67–8.  45. 'Sega Dance – Mauritian Folklore', <ravaton.tripod.com> (2015).  46. Henry Dimbleby, 'The Beet Goes On', *Gourmet Traveller*, n.d.  47. The website of *Aviation Herald* hosts a major article about MH370 that is constantly updated: www.avherald.com/h?article=4710c69b (2014–).  48. Keith Ledgerwood, 'Did MH370 Disappear Using SIA68/SQ86?' (17 March 2014), www.keithledgerwood.com/post/79738944823 (2014); DailyMail.com, 'Vladimir Putin Ordered Russian Special Forces to Steal MH370 and Secretly Landed it at Huge Space Port in Kazakhstan, Says Expert', *MailOnline* (25 February 2015); Jeff Wise, *The Plane that Wasn't There: Why We Haven't Found MH370* (New York, 2015).

CHAPTER 8. TASSIE

1. Michael Pearson, *The Great Southland: The Maritime Explorations of Terra Australis* (Canberra, 2005).  2. www.answers.com/Q/what_was_written_on_the_Hartog_Plate? (2014).  3. J. E. Heeres, *The Part Borne by the Dutch in the Discovery of Australia, 1601–1765* (London, 1899), p. 147.  4. Janine Roberts, ed., *Mapoon: The Cape York Aluminium Companies and the Native Peoples* (Fitzroy, Victoria, 1975), pp. 35–6.  5. http://en.wikipedia.org/wiki/Theory_of_the_Portuguese_discovery_of_Australia (2013).  6. See note 65 below; C. M. H. Clark, *A History of Australia* (London, 1962–87), 6 vols.; Michael Cathcart, *Manning Clark's History of Australia* (London, 1993).  7. MONA official website, www.mona.net.au (2013).  8. 'Mona – What a disgrace! – Trip Advisor', www.tripadvisor.co.uk/ShowUserReviews (6 December 2014).  9. Joseph Beuys and Judith Nesbitt, *Joseph Beuys: The Revolution is Us* (Liverpool, 1993); Alain Borer, *The Essential Joseph Beuys* (London, 1996).  10. Cary Lewincamp, www.cary.com.au (2014).  11. Keith Bowden, *George Bass: His Discoveries, his Romantic Life, and Tragic Disappearance* (Melbourne, 1952).  12. *Encyclopaedia Britannica*, 11th edition (1910–11), vol. 25, p. 447.  13. Henry Reynolds, *A History of Tasmania* (Cambridge, 2012), p. 5.  14. N. J. B. Plomley, ed., *The Baudin Expedition and Tasmanian Aboriginals* (Hobart, 1992), p. 890, quoted by Reynolds, op. cit.  15. Reynolds, op. cit., pp. 6–7.  16. Geoff Page, from 'The Relatives', *The Great Forgetting* (Canberra, 1996), p. 5.  17. Lloyd Robson, *A Short History of Tasmania* (Oxford, 1985), pp. 3–4.  18. Ibid., pp. 5–6.  19. 'Van Dieman's Land' [sic], www.musicnet.org/robokopp/eire/comeally.htm (2014).  20. W. Ullathorne, *The Catholic Mission in Australia* (1838), reprinted (Adelaide, 1963), pp. vff.  21. Alison Alexander, *Tasmania's Convicts: How Felons Built a Free Society* (Crows Nest, New South Wales, 2010), p. 126.  22. Ibid., pp. 14–33.  23. Ibid., p. 43.  24. Ibid., p. 29.  25. Ibid., pp. 28–9.  26. Ibid., p. 44.  27. Paul Collins, *Hell's Gates: The*

*Terrible Journey of Alexander Pearce, Van Diemen's Land's Cannibal* (South Yarra, 2002). **28.** http://folkstream.com/027.html (7 December 2014). **29.** Henry Reynolds, 'The Land Question: Are We a Community of Thieves?', *Dispossession: Black Australians and White Invaders* (St Leonards, New South Wales, 1989), p. 67. **30.** Quoted by Reynolds, op. cit. **31.** Terry Crowley, 'The Colonial Impact', in 'Tasmanian Aboriginal Language: Old and New Identities', in M. Walsh and C. Yallop, *Language and Culture in Aboriginal Australia* (Canberra, 1993), pp. 55–63. **32.** Ibid., pp. 59–61. **33.** N. J. B. Plomley, *Friendly Mission: The Tasmanian Journal of George Augustus Robinson, 1829–34* (Kingsgrove, New South Wales, 1996), quote by Crowley, op. cit., p. 65. **34.** Keith Windschuttle, *The Fabrication of Aboriginal History*, vols. 1 and 3 (Paddington, New South Wales, 2002). **35.** Lyndall Ryan, *The Aboriginal Tasmanians* (London, 1981), p. 143. **36.** Ibid. **37.** Quoted in Black War, https://en.wikipedia.org/Black_War (2014). **38.** <adb.anu.edu.au/biography.batman-john-1752>; see also the novel by Rohan Wilson, *The Roving Party* (London, 2002). **39.** N. J. B. Plomley, *Friendly Mission: The Tasmanian Journals and Papers of George Augustus Robinson, 1829–34* (Hobart, 2008); Anna Johnston, *Reading Robinson: Companion Essays to Friendly Mission* (Hobart, 2008). **40.** Ryan, op. cit.: also 2nd edition (London, 1996). **41.** Lyndall Ryan, *Tasmanian Aborigines: A History since 1803* (Crows Nest, New South Wales, 2012). **42.** Henry Reynolds, 'An Indelible Stain?', Chapter 4 of *A History of Tasmania*, op. cit. **43.** Alexander, op. cit., p. 109. **44.** Oline Keese (Caroline Leakey), *The Broad Arrow: Being the Story of Maida Gwynnham, a 'Lifer' in Van Diemen's Land* (North Ryde, New South Wales, 1988). **45.** Alexander, op. cit., p. 113. **46.** University of Tasmania Seminar, Parliament House, Hobart, 13 March 2014. **47.** From Giacomo Leopardi, *I Canti*, no. II, 'L'Infinito'. **48.** These pioneering philatelic masterpieces of 1899–1900 were engraved from pictures taken by the Scottish-born photographer John Watt Beattie (1859–1930). There were eight of them from the 1/2d green, 'Lake Marion', to the 6d lake, 'Dilston Falls'. Curiously enough, if one goes to Dilston near Launceston, there are no such waterfalls to be seen. The engravers were either playing games or, pressed for time, invented a non-existent beauty spot. In 1899, with no 'sat nav' and as yet no tourist trade, the risk of being found out was minimal. **49.** Michel Foucault, *Surveiller et punir: naissance de la prison* (Paris, 1975). **50.** Port Arthur Historic Sites, www.portarthur.org.au (2014). **51.** From Karen Brown, 'A Lesson in History', quoted by Crowley, op. cit., p. 51. **52.** Aboriginality Certificates, www.humanservices.gov.au/customer/forms/ra010 (2014). **53.** Tasmanian Aboriginal Corporation, www.tacinc.com.au (2014). **54.** 13 August 1997, <abc.net.au/photos/2013/02/07/3685152.htm> (2017). **55.** Anthony Mundine, www.anthonymundinebrody.weebly.com (2014). **56.** 'Parlevar, Moihernee and Dromerdeener', www.civicsandcitizenship.edu.au/verve/_resources/handout (2014). **57.** J. Harrington, et al., 'An Acoustic Phonetic Study of Broad, General and Cultivated Australian-English Vowels', *Australian Journal of Linguistics*, vol. 17 (1997), pp. 155–84. **58** Jonathan Pearlman, 'G'day, Mate: "Lazy" Australian Accent Caused by "Alcoholic Slur" of Heavy-Drinking Early Settlers', *The Telegraph*

(20 February 2017). 59. Hugh Finlay et al., 'Language', in *Australia: A Travel Survival Kit* (Hawthorn, Victoria, 1992), pp. 31–2. 60. From Kel Richards, *The Aussie Bible (Well, Bits of It Anyway)* (Glencroix, 2006). 61. Ibid. See 'And God said "Let's have some light, mate"', www.smh.com.au/national/and-God-said; www.wikidot.com/sample-aussiebible (20 February 2017). 62. Steve Colquhoun, 'Tassie Whisky Named World's Best Single Malt', *Sydney Morning Herald* (21 March 2014). 63. Peter Hruby, *Dangerous Dreamers: The Australian Anti-Democratic Left* (Bloomington, 2010), pp. 109–16. 64. J. and B. Emberg, *Ghostly Tales of Tasmania* (Launceston, 1991); M. Giordano, *Tasmanian Tales of the Supernatural* (Launceston, 1994); K. Gelder, *The Oxford Book of Australian Ghost Stories* (Melbourne, 1994); J. McCullough and A. Simmons, *Ghosts of Port Arthur* (Port Arthur, 1992). 65. L. J. Devon, 'GM Poppies and the Pharmaceutical Industry', *Natural News* (10 August 2014). 66. Terry Newman, 'Tasmania, the Name', <utas.edu.au/companion_to_tasmanian_history/T/Tasmania%20name.htm> (2014). 67. Robert Cox, *A Compulsion to Kill: Australia's Earliest Serial Killers* (Carringdale, 2014). 68. 'World's Weirdest', <video.nationalgeographic.com/video/weirdest-echidna> (2014). 69. 'Echidna', https://www.britannica.com/topic/Echidna-Greek-mythology (2014). 70. Manning Clark, *A Historian's Apprenticeship* (Carlton, Victoria, 1992). 71. Port Arthur Massacre, www.nbcnews.com/world/port-arthur-massacre-shooting-spree. 72. Quoted by Natasha Cica (University of Tasmania), 'Does Tasmania Need an Intervention?', *The Conversation* (3 February 2013). 73. Martin Flanagan, 'Tasmania Cast as Australia's Greece', *Sydney Morning Herald* (23 February 2013). 74. *The Hunter*, <theguardian.com/film/2012/jul/08/hunter-tasmania-daniel-nettheim-dafoe> (2014). 75. *Thylacinus cynacephalus*, <https:en.wikipedia.org/wiki/Thylacine> (22 February 2017). 76. Bowden, op. cit. 77. David Bret, *Errol Flynn: Satan's Angel* (London, 2000). 78. 'Valentich Disappearance', <csicop.org/si/show/the_valentich_disappearance_solved> (2017).

## CHAPTER 9. KIWILAND

1. www.wellingtonnz.com (2014). 2. <http//www.tepapa.govt.nz/WhatsOn/exhibitions/Pages/allexhibitions.aspx> (2014). 3. *Te Papa: Your Essential Guide* (Wellington, n.d.), p. 3. 4. Victoria University, www.victoria.ac.nz (2014). 5. Michael King, *The Penguin History of New Zealand* (Auckland, 2003); Patrick Evans, *Encounters: The Creation of New Zealand, a History* (Auckland, 2013). 6. P. Tapsell, *Ko Tawa: The Maori Ancestors of New Zealand* (Auckland, 2006). 7. www.survivalinternational.org (29 December 2014). 8. http://en.wiktionary.org/wiki/Kiwiland (31 December 2014). 9. http://www.nzflag.com/Petition_Form.cfm (31 December 2014); 'New Zealand Votes to Keep Flag in Referendum', BBC News (24 March 2016). 10. www.nzhistory.govt.nz/culture/history-of-the-maori-language (2014). 11. 'Tainui', https://en.wikipedia.org/wiki/Tainui (2014). 12. Alexander Shand, *The Moriori People of the Chatham Islands: Their Traditions and History* (Wellington, 1896). 13. 'Iwi – Tribes of

New Zealand', <nzte.govt.nz/en/how-nzte-can-help/te-kete-tikanga-maori-cultural-kit/iwi-tribes-of-new-zealand> (2014), with map: Reed, *The Maori Peoples of New Zealand* (Auckland, 2006); R. Macdonald, *The Maori of Aotearoa-New Zealand* (London, 1990). **14.** Margaret Orbell, *The Illustrated Encyclopaedia of Maori Myth and Legend* (Christchurch, 1995); Kiri Te Kanawa, *Land of the Long White Cloud: Maori Myths, Tales and Legends* (London, 1997). **15.** Mervyn McLean, *Maori Music* (Auckland, 1996); Margaret Orbell, *Waiata: Maori Songs in History* (Auckland, 2005), pp. 1–2. **16.** Orbell, ibid., pp. 67–8. **17.** Ibid., pp. 28–9. **18.** After ibid., pp. 98–100. **19.** www.brianharris.com/ka-mura-ka-muri-walking-backwards-into-the-future (2017). **20.** www.teara.govt.nz/biographies/1m13/marion-du-fresne-marc-joseph (2014). **21.** Philip Temple, *A Sort of Conscience: The Wakefields* (Auckland, 2002). **22.** Patricia Burns, *Fatal Success: A History of the New Zealand Company* (London, 2002). **23.** Claudia Orange, *The Treaty of Waitangi* (Wellington, 1982): I. H. Kawharu, *Waitangi: Māori and Pākehā Perspectives . . .* (Auckland, 1989). **24.** A. G. Flude, 'Our Early Settlers', http://homepages.ihug.co.nz/~tonyf (2014). **25.** D. Keenan, *Wars without End: The Land Wars in Nineteenth-Century New Zealand* (Auckland, 2009). **26.** www.britainssmallwars.co.uk/the-flagstaff-war-new-zealand-1845.html (2014). **27.** <nzhistory.govt.nz/politics/the-maori-king-movement> (2014). **28.** Rex Ahdar, *God and Government: The New Zealand Experience* (Dunedin, 2000). **29.** H. T. Purchas, *History of the English Church in New Zealand* (Christchurch, 1914), Chapter X. **30.** 'Dominion of New Zealand', in King, op. cit., Chapter XII. **31.** See EyeWitness Travel, *New Zealand* (London, 2014). **32.** www.atlasobscura.com/places/fred-and-myrtles-paua-shell-house (2014). **33.** Dunedin, www.dunedinnz.com (2014). **34.** Royal Albatross Centre, www.albatross.org.nz (2014). **35.** Christchurch, www.lonelyplanet.com/new-zealand/christchurch-and-canterbury (2014). **36.** Akaroa, https://en.wikipedia.org/wiki/akaroa (2014). **37.** Coastal Pacific, www.rail-newzealand.com (2014). **38.** Kaikoura, www.kaikoura.co.nz (2014). **39.** www.marlboroughnz.com (2014). **40.** 'Wine Marlborough: New Zealand's Premier Wine Region', www.winemarlborough.co.nz (2014). **41.** Cook Strait Ferry, www.interislander.co.nz (2014). **42.** www.hobbitontours.com. **43.** Christine Niven, *Auckland* (London, 2000). **44.** Waitangi Treaty Grounds and Museum, www.waitangi.org.nz (2014). **45.** www.topuniversities.com/universities/Auckland (2014). **46.** Auckland University Faculty of Arts, www.arts.auckland.ac.nz (2013). **47.** www.aucklandcouncil.gov.nz (28 December 2014). **48.** David Fingleton, *Kiri Te Kanawa: A Biography* (London, 1982); Alice Fowler, 'Dame Kiri Talks of her Heartache', *MailOnline* (2 February 2017). **49.** https://nzhistory.govt.nz/culture/nz-painting-history (2014). **50.** From Robert Pope, *Some New Zealand Lyrics* (Wellington, 1928). **51.** From V. O'Sullivan, ed., *An Anthology of Twentieth-Century New Zealand Poetry* (Wellington, 1979); Hone Tuwhare, 'Rain' (1970), by kind permission of the Hone Tuwhare Estate. **52.** K. Pfeiffer and P. Tapsell, *Te Ara: Pathways of Maori Leadership* (Auckland, 2010). **53.** R. J. Walker, *Struggle Without End* (Auckland, 1990); M. Belgrave et al., eds., *Waitangi Revisited: New Perspectives on the Treaty of*

*Waitangi* (Melbourne, 2005); P. Temm, *Waitangi Tribunal: Conscience of the Nation* (Auckland, 1990). **54.** 'God Defend New Zealand', www.nz.com/new-zealand/guide-book/music (2014). **55.** 'Kiwispeak', https://nzguide.newzealand. co.nz/kiwispeak; www.gotournz.com/kiwispeak (2014). **56.** Toponomy, <en. wikipedia.org/wiki/ New_Zealand_ place_ names> (7 March 2017).

## CHAPTER 10. OTAHEITI

**1.** 'International Date Line', www.timeanddate.com/time/dateline.html (18 April 2016). **2.** www.chabad.org/article/cdo/ai (2 January 2015). **3.** Umberto Eco, *The Island of the Day Before* (London, 1998), or *L'isola del giorno prima* (Rome, 1985). **4.** *Annuaire Polynésien 2011* (Paris–Papeete, 2010), www.facebook. com/Annuaire-/ /Polynesien-14104769292573388 (2012). **5.** Ibid., p. 336. **6.** From David Stanley, *Moon Handbook Tahiti* (Emeryville, CA, 2003). **7.** *Tahiti and Polynesia*, Lonely Planet Guides (London, 2012); David Howarth, *Tahiti: A Paradise Lost* (London, 1983); Lloyd Shepherd, *The Poisoned Island* (London, 2013). **8.** *Oxford English Dictionary*, Compact Edition (1971), vol. II, p. 1,092. **9.** Charles de Brosses, *Histoire des Navigations aux Terres Australes* (Paris, 1756), 2 vols. **10.** Ian Davidson, *Voltaire: A Life* (London, 2010), Chapter 23; J. T. Fosset, ed., *Voltaire et le President de Brosses: correspondence inedited* (Paris, 1858), p. 5. **11.** J. F. G. Stokes, *Hawaii's Discovery by Spaniards: Theories Traced and Refuted* (Honolulu, 1939); T. Lummis, *Pacific Paradises: The Discovery of Tahiti and Hawaii* (Stroud, 2005). **12.** De Brosses, op. cit., vol. II, p. 140. **13.** Alexander Dalrymple, *An Historical Collection of Several Voyages and Discoveries in the South Pacific Ocean* (London, 1770), 2 vols. **14.** De Brosses, op. cit., vol. I, p. 198. **15.** D. Howse, *Background to Discovery: Pacific Exploration from Dampier to Cook* (Berkeley, 1990), p. 16. **16.** John Callander, *Terra Australis Cognita, or Voyages to the Terra Australis or Southern Hemisphere* (Edinburgh, 1766–8), 3 vols.; see also James Burney, *Chronological History of the Voyages and Discoveries of the South Seas or Pacific Ocean* (London, 1803), 5 vols. **17.** John Hawkesworth, *An account in two volumes of the voyages . . . . in the southern hemisphere performed by Commodore Byron, Capt. Wallis, Capt. Carteret, and Capt. Cook* (London, 1773), p. 26. **18.** Ibid., pp. 22–3, 31–2. See also George Robertson, *The Discovery of Tahiti: A Journal of the Second Voyage of HMS Dolphin round the World* (London, 1948). **19.** Glynis Ridley, *The Discovery of Jeanne Baret* (New York, 2010). **20.** J. E. Martin-Allanic, *Bougainville, navigateur, et les découvertes de son temps* (Paris, 1964). **21.** Louis-Antoine de Bougainville, *Voyage autour du monde* (Paris, 1771), trans. *The Pacific Journal of Louis-Antoine de Bougainville* (London, 2002); Denis Diderot, *Supplément au voyage de Bougainville* (1772) (Paris, 2002). **22.** 'Captain Cook's Endeavour Journal', http://jamescookjournal.blogspot.co.uk/p/tahiti (December 2013). **23.** Ibid. **24.** Ibid. **25.** James Cook, *Captain Cook's Third and Last Voyage to the Pacific Ocean* (New York, 1796). **26.** Dava Sobel, *Longitude: The True Story of a Lone Genius who Solved the Greatest Scientific Problem of his Time*

(London, 1995).  **27.** J. Conrad, 'Geography and Some Explorers', *Last Essays* (London, 1926), p. 10: quoted by Howse, op. cit., Chapter 1.  **28.** Diderot's supplement, op. cit.  **29.** J. Dunmore, ed., *The Journal of Jean-François de Galaup de La Pérouse, 1785–88* (London, 1994), 2 vols.  **30.** J. Boyne, *The Mutiny on the Bounty* (London, 2008); William Bligh, *An Account of the Mutiny on the Bounty* (Oxford, 1989).  **31.** Geoffrey Rawson, *Pandora's Last Voyage* (London, 1963).  **32.** Frank Horner, *Looking for La Pérouse: D'Entrecasteaux in Australia and the South Pacific, 1792–93* (Carlton, Victoria, 1994).  **33.** Matthew Flinders, *Voyage to the Terra Australis* (London, 1814); *Australia Circumnavigated: Matthew Flinders in HMS Investigator, 1801–1803* (London, 2015) 2 vols.  **34.** Amasa Delano, *Voyages in the Northern and Southern Hemispheres* (Boston, 1817), p. 139.  **35.** Ibid.  **36.** Trevor Lummis, *Life and Death in Eden: Pitcairn Island and the Bounty Mutineers* (London, 2000).  **37.** Peter Dillon, *Narrative and Successful Result of a Voyage in the South Seas* (London, 1829); J. W. Davidson and O. H. K. Spate, *Peter Dillon of Vanikoro* (Oxford, 1975); Sven Wahlroos, *Mutiny and Romance in the South Seas* (Salem, MA, 1989).  **38.** Helen Roseman, ed., *An Account in Two Volumes of Two Voyages to the South Seas by Captain (later Rear-Admiral) Jules S.-C. Dumont d'Urville of the French Navy* (Melbourne, 1987); J. Dunmore, *From Venus to Antarctica: The Life of Dumont d'Urville* (Auckland, 2007).  **39.** Conrad Malte-Brun, *Universal Geography, or a Description of all Parts of the World* (Edinburgh, 1823), 4 vols.  **40.** Frank Debenham, *Antarctica: Story of a Continent* (London, 1959).  **41.** Dan Graves, 'Henry Nott in Savage Tahiti', www.christianity.com/church-history/tahiti.  **42.** Joyce Reason, *The Bricklayer and the King* (London, 1938).  **43.** *Encyclopaedia Britannica*, 11th edition (1910–11), vol. 26, p. 358.  **44.** Ibid.  **45.** Ibid.  **46.** Charles Darwin, *Narrative of the Surveying Voyages of His Majesty's Ships Adventure and Beagle, between the Years 1826 and 1836* (London, 1839), vol. III, p. 480.  **47.** W. T. Pritchard, *Polynesian Reminiscences* (London, 1866).  **48.** H. Parker, *Herman Melville: A Biography* (Berkeley, 1989), p. 222.  **49.** Scott's *Standard Postage Stamp Catalogue* (1984), vol. II, p. 1,035.  **50.** D. Sweetman, *Paul Gauguin: A Life* (New York, 1995).  **51.** R. L. Stevenson, *The Ebb-Tide* (London, 1894), p. 3.  **52.** A. Methuen ed., *An Anthology of Modern Verse* (London, 1921).  **53.** Thor Heyerdahl, *Hunt for Paradise* and *Green Was the Earth*, www.volnomuvoly.com/Thor_Heyerdahl_Fatu_Hiva_island.html (2013).  **54.** Stefan Kanfer, *The Reckless Life and Remarkable Career of Marlon Brando* (London, 2011); Tarita Teriipaia, *Marlon: My Life and My Torment* (New York, 2004); Naomi Leach, 'Inside Brando's 12-islet Polynesian Paradise', *Mail Online* (3 February 2016).  **55.** Jacques Brel, from 'Les Marquises', *Les Marquises* (1977).  **56.** Charles de Brosses, *Du culte des dieux fétiches: ou Parallèle de l'ancienne religion de l'Egypte avec la religion actuelle, de Nigritie* (Paris, 1760).  **57.** Bougainville, op. cit., vol. II, p. 434.  **58.** 'Vocabulaire de l'Île de Tahiti', in Bougainville, op. cit., pp. 357–68. The list starts with *abobo* = 'demain', and ends with *toroire* = 'heliotrope'.  **59.** Wilhelm von Humboldt, *Über die Kawi-Sprache auf der Insel Java* (Berlin, 1836–9), 3 vols.  **60.** Roff Smith, 'Beyond the Blue Horizon: How Ancient Voyagers

Settled the Far-Flung Islands of the Pacific', *National Geographic* (March 2008). 61. Edward Tregear, *The Aryan Maori* (Wellington, 1885). 62. A. Fornander, *An Account of the Polynesian Race: Its Origins and Migrations* (London, 1878–85), 3 vols. 63. Alfred Russel Wallace, *The Malay Archipelago* (1869) (Oxford, 2015). 64. R. H. Codrington, *The Melanesians: Studies in their Anthropology and Folklore* (Oxford, 1891); id., *The Melanesian Languages* (Oxford, 1885). 65. Ernest Brandewie, *When Giants Walked the Earth The Life and Times of Wilhelm Schmidt SVD* (Fribourg, 1990). 66. www.dempwolff.de; Sofia Ozols, 'Otto Dempwolff: Islands of Language', www.parrottime.com/index. php?i=1&a=51 (20 April 2016). 67. M. W. Young, *Malinowski: Odyssey of an Anthropologist* (New Haven, 2004); Michael Young, 'Writing his Life through the Other: The Anthropology of Malinowski', *The Public Domain Review* (22 January 2014). 68. Robert Blust, 'The Austronesian Homeland: A Linguistic Perspective', *Asian Perspectives*, vol. 26 (1985), pp. 46–67. 69. Robert Blust, *The Austronesian Languages* (Canberra, 2009). 70. Franz Steiner, *Taboo* (London, 1958); J. Adler and R. Fardon, 'An Oriental in the West: The Life of Franz Baermann Steiner', in *Franz Baermann Steiner: Selected Writings* (London, 1999). 71. Thor Heyerdahl, *The Kon Tiki Expedition: By Raft across the South Seas* (London, 1950). 72. Andrew Sharp, *Ancient Voyagers in the Pacific* (Wellington, 1956), and *Ancient Voyagers in Polynesia* (Auckland, 1963). 73. Robert C. Suggs, *The Island Civilizations of Polynesia* (New York, 1960); Wade Davis, *The Wayfinders: Why Ancient Wisdom Matters in the Modern World* (Toronto, 2009). 74. Brian Sykes et al., 'The Origin of the Polynesians: An Interpretation from Mitochondrial Lineage Analysis', *American Journal of Human Genetics*, vol. 57 (1995), pp. 1,463–75; B. Sykes, *The Seven Daughters of Eve* (London, 2001). 75. Pallab Ghosh, 'Ancient Humans, dubbed "Denisovans"', BBC News Online (22 December 2010). 76. R. Capper, 'The Search for a Polynesian Homeland', *E-Local* Blogspot (New Zealand) (January 2011). 77. Sindya Bhanoo, 'DNA Sheds New Light on Polynesian Migrations', *The New York Times* (7 February 2011). 78. M. Hertzberg et al., *American Journal of Human Genetics*, vol. 44 (1989), pp. 504–10. 79. Eric Powell, 'Polynesian Chickens in Chile', *Archaeology*, vol. 63, no. 1 (2008). 80. Sid Perkins, 'DNA Study Links Indigenous Brazilians with Polynesia', *Nature* (1 April 2013: April Fools' Day). 81. Polynesian Voyaging Society, www.hokulea.com (21 April 2016). 82. Peter Marsh, 'Polynesian Pathways', www.polynesian-prehistory.com, created 2002–8. 83. Bruno Saura, *Pouvanaa a Oopa: père de la culture politique tahitienne* (Papeete, 1997); 'L'Hommage de François Hollande à Pouvanaa a Oopa' (22 February 2016), www.la1ere.fran cetvinfo.fr/polynesie/tahiti/333945.html (10 February 2017). 84. Ivan Sache, 'Hau Repupirita Pakumotu (Self-proclaimed States: French Polynesia)', www.crwflags.com/fotw/flags/pf%7Dpakum.html (10 February 2017); 'Self-Styled King of Pakumotu Republic Jailed on Currency Charges', *Pacific Islands Report* (2 February 2017). 85. www.cantinlevoyageur.com/ . . . /chansons_tahiti.htm (5 January 2015). 86. Alfred Gell, *Wrapping in Images: Tattooing in Polynesia* (Oxford, 1993); 'Polynesian Tattoos', www.tattooers,net/; www.tattootemple.hk/history-of-tattooing (24 April 2016). 87. Pascal Nabet-Meyer, *Rapa Iti*, Triloka

Records (1992).   **88.** Célestine Hitiura Vaite, *Breadfruit* (New York, 2000). **89.** Université de la Polynésie Française, www.enseignementsup-recherche. gouv.fr/cid67201/universite-de-la-polynesie-francaise.html (2014).   **90.** Rebecca Fan, 'Indigenous Peoples of Taiwan', www.indigenouspeople.net/taiwan.htm. **91.** www.aviation-safety.net/database/record.php?id=20070809-0 (2014).   **92.** 'Te Vahine Tahiti', 'Paroles des Chansons Tahitiennes', www.paroles.webfenua. com/chanson.php?id=1603 (24 April 2016).

## CHAPTER 11. TEJAS

**1.** www.airport-houston.com (2013).   **2.** Tony Perrottet, 'What Makes Houston the Next Great American City?', *Smithsonian* (July 2013).   **3.** J. H. Williams, *Sam Houston: A Biography of the Father of Texas* (New York, 1993).   **4.** Odie B. Faulk, *The Last Years of Spanish Texas, 1778–1821* (The Hague, 1964). **5.** S. R. Burzynski Clinic website, www.burzynskiclinic.com/burzynski-clinic (15 January 2015).   **6.** Burzynski Clinic, http://en.wikipedia.org/wiki/Burzynski_ Clinic (15 January 2015).   **7.** The mortality rate for liver cancer in the UK is expected to rise by 58% by 2035, https://www.theguardian.com/society/2016/ dec/20/uk-cancer-deaths-to-fall-by-15-per-cent-by-2035 (15 January 2017). **8.** L. Szabo, 'FDA Issues Warning to Controversial Houston Cancer Doctor', *USA Today* (11 December 2013).   **9.** www.bbc.co.uk./news/health-22717245 (15 January 2015).   **10.** Burzynski Clinic, <rationalwiki.org/wiki/Burzynski_ clinic> (5 April 2016).   **11.** Petroleum Club, Houston, www.pcoh.com (2013).   **12.** Bryan Burrough, *The Big Rich: The Rise and Fall of the Greatest Texan Oil Fortunes* (London, 2009); J. W. Rogers, *The Lusty Texans of Dallas* (New York, 1960); George Fuermann, *Houston: Land of the Big Rich* (New York, 1951); James Presley, *Saga of Wealth: The Rise of the Texas Oilmen* (New York, 1978).   **13.** S. H. Brown, *H. L. Hunt* (Chicago, 1976).   **14.** Jane Wolfe, *The Murchisons: The Rise and Fall of a Texas Dynasty* (New York, 1989); Robert Dallek, *Lone Star Rising: LBJ and His Time* (Oxford, 1991).   **15.** Hugh Aynesworth, '"One-Man Truth Squad" Still Debunking JFK Conspiracy Theories', *Dallas Morning News* (17 November 2012).   **16.** D. D. Hinton and R. M. Olien, *Oil in Texas: The Gusher Age, 1895–1945* (Austin, 2002).   **17.** Craig Thompson, *Since Spindletop: A Human Story of Gulf's First Half-Century* (Pittsburgh, 1951); Anthony Sampson, *The Seven Sisters: The Great Oil Companies and the World They Made* (New York, 1975).   **18.** Patrick Chamoiseau, *Texaco* (London, 1997).   **19.** Houston Bicentenary, www.texasbest.com/houston/ history.html (2013).   **20.** Marguerite Johnston, *Houston, the Unknown City, 1836–1946* (College Station, TX, 1991).   **21.** Rice University, www.rice.edu (2013).   **22.** https://en.wikipedia.org/wiki/Texan_English (2013).   **23.** John Steinbeck, *Travels with Charley: In Search of America* (1962).   **24.** www.taste-oftexas.com/restaurant (2012).   **25.** www.metrolyrics.com/red-river-valley-lyrics-marty-robbins; www.metrolyrics.com/streets-of-laredo-lyrics-/marty-robbins (2013).   **26.** Diana Kennedy, *The Cuisines of Mexico* (London, 1972);

A. De León, *Ethnicity in the Sunbelt: A History of Mexican Americans in Houston* (Houston, 1989). 27. www.molinascantina.com (11 April 2016). 28. 'Terco Corazon', https://puroconjunto.com/Song%20L (16 January 2015). 29. H. E. Driver, *Indians of North America* (Chicago, 1969); C. Taylor and W. C. Sturtevant, *Native Americans: The Indigenous Peoples of North America* (London, 2000); Adele Nozedar, *The Element Encyclopedia of Native Americans* (London, 2012). 30. 'Indian Nations of Texas', http://tsl.texas.gov/exhibits/Indian (17 January 2015). 31. T. Biolsi, *A Companion to the Anthropology of American Indians* (Malden, MA, 2004); A. B. Kehoe, *North American Indians: A Comprehensive Account* (Upper Saddle River, NJ, 2006). 32. Ives Goddard, *Native Languages and Language Families of North America* (Lincoln, NB, 1996); Lyle Campbell, *American Indian Languages: The Historical Linguistics of Native America* (New York, 1997). 33. 'Hasinai Indians', Texas State Historical Association, https://tshaonline.org/hand book/online/articles/bmh08 (11 April 2016). 34. R. E. Moore, 'The Texas Comanches', www.texasindians.com/comanche.htm (11 April 2016); Carol Lipscomb, 'Comanche Indians', *Texas Handbook Online*, www.tshaonline.org/hand book/online/articles/bmc72 (23 December 2013). 35. J. F. de la Teja, *San Antonio de Béxar: A Community on New Spain's Northern Frontier* (Albuquerque, 1996). 36. Salvador de Madariaga, *The Fall of the Spanish American Empire* (London, 1947); W. S. Maltby, *The Rise and Fall of the Spanish Empire* (Basingstoke, 2009). 37. D. Holloway, *Lewis and Clark and the Crossing of North America* (London, 1974). 38. T. J. Henderson, *The Mexican Wars of Independence* (New York, 2009). 39. C. H. Brown, *Agents of Manifest Destiny: The Lives and Times of the Filibusters* (Chapel Hill, NC, 1980). 40. J. F. Dobie, *The Longhorns* (Boston, 1941); K. Ulyatt, *The Longhorn Trail* (London, 1961). 41. S. Hoig, 'Jesse Chisholm', in *Encyclopedia of Oklahoma History and Culture*, www.okhistory.org/publications/enc/entry.php?entry=CH067 (23 December 2013). 42. Carleton Beals, *Stephen F. Austin: Father of Texas* (New York, 1953); Greg Cantrell, *Stephen F. Austin: Empresario of Texas* (New Haven, CT, 1999). 43. Marquis James, *The Raven: A Biography of Sam Houston* (London, 1929). 44. R. Borroel, *The Texan Revolution of 1836* (East Chicago, IN, 1989); S. W. Haynes, *Contested Empire: Rethinking the Texan Revolution* (College Station, TX, 2015); D. J. Weber, *The Mexican Frontier: The American Southwest under Mexico, 1821–46* (Albuquerque, NM, 1982). 45. T. E. Anna, *The Mexican Empire of Iturbide* (Lincoln, NE, 1990). 46. Will Fowler, *Santa Anna of Mexico* (Norman, OK, and Lincoln, NE, 2007); Ruth Olivera, *Life in Mexico under Santa Anna, 1822–55* (Norman, OK, 1991). 47. After 'The Yellow Rose of Texas', from *Texas Handbook Online*, op. cit. 48. Sharon Wallingford, *Fort Bend County, Texas: A Pictorial History* (Sugar Land, TX, 1996). 49. Stephen F. Austin, 'An Explanation to the Public Concerning the Affairs of Texas' (1835), published in *Quarterly of the Texas State Historical Association*, vol. 8, no. 3 (1905), pp. 232–58. 50. D. F. Ericson, *Slavery in the American Republic, 1791–1861* (Lawrence, KS, 2011). 51. Daniel Howe, *What God Hath Wrought: The Transformation of America, 1815–48* (New York, 2007); Bill Kiernan, *Blood and*

*Soil: A World History of Genocide and Extermination from Sparta to Darfur* (New Haven, CT, 2007). **52.** Angie Debo, *And the Waters Still Run: The Betrayal of the Five Civilized Tribes* (Princeton, 1972); Duane King, *The Cherokee Indian Nation: A Troubled History* (Knoxville, TE, 1979); Daniel B. Smith, *An American Betrayal: Cherokee Patriots and the Trail of Tears* (New York, 2011). **53.** Declaration of Texan Independence, www.lsjunction.com/tdoi.htm (2013). **54.** P. J. Haythornthwaite, *The Alamo and the War of Texan Independence, 1835–36* (London, 1986). **55.** Stephen Moore, *Eighteen Minutes: The Battle of San Jacinto and the Texas Independence Campaign* (Plano, TX, 2004). **56.** 'The Treaties of Velasco', https://tshaonline.org/handbook/online/articles/mgt05 (12 April 2016). **57.** Lucia St. C. Robson, *Ride the Wind: The Story of Cynthia Ann Parker and the Last Days of the Comanche* (New York, 1985). **58.** Stanley Siegel, *A Political History of the Texas Republic, 1836–45* (Austin, 1957). **59.** Glen E. Lich, *The Texan Germans* (San Antonio, TX, 1981, rev. 1996). **60.** Carl Solms-Braunfels, *Voyage to North America, 1844–45: A Diary of People, Places and Events* (Denton, TX, 2000); Sheena Oommen, '"Hin nach Texas!" – "Off to Texas!"', www.houstonculture.org/cr/germans.html (14 February 2017). **61.** James Kearney, *Nassau Plantation: The Evolution of a Texas German Slave Plantation* (Denton, TX, 2010). **62.** www.en.wikipedia.org/wiki/Adelsverein (14 February 2017); **63.** Irene King and John O. Meusebach, *German Colonizers in Texas* (Austin, 1967); 'The Meusebach-Comanche Treaty', <en.wikipedia.org/wiki/Meusebach–Comanche_Treaty> (2014). **64.** Orlando Martinez, *The Great Landgrab: The Mexican-American War, 1846–1848* (London, 1975); Cecil Robinson, *The View from Chapultepec: Mexican Writers on the Mexican-American War* (Tucson, AZ, 1989). **65.** Richard Griswold del Castillo, *The Treaty of Guadalupe Hidalgo: Legacy of Conflict* (Norman, OK, 1990). **66.** T. Lindsay Baker, *The First Polish Americans: Silesian Settlements in Texas* (College Station, TX, 1979); Anna Musialik-Chmiel, *Amerykańscy Ślązacy: dziedzictwo, pamięć, tożsamość* (Katowice, 2010). **67.** A. Blasig, *The Wends of Texas* (San Antonio, 1954); L. Caldwell, *Texas Wends: Their First Half-Century* (Salado, TX, 1961). **68.** Sam Houston's grave, www.findagrave.com/cgi-bin/fg.cgi?page=cr&CRid=5692 (13 April 2016). **69.** www.elyrics.net/read/t/tennessee-ernie-ford-lyrics/the-bonnie-blue-flag-lyrics.html (2016). **70.** www.texashighways.com?blog/item/814-independence-trail (13 April 2016). **71.** 'Chisholm Trail History', www.vlib.us/old-west/trails.chist.html (13 April 2016). **72.** 'Marty Robbins – Ballad of the Alamo', www.lyricsmania.com/ballad_of_the_alamo_1257259.html (13 April 2016). **73.** 'Remember the Alamo' (1955), www.azlyrics.com/lyrics/donovan/rememberthealamo.html (13 April 2016). **74.** Latino Festivals, www.festivalsoftexas.com (13 April 2016). **75.** 'Indian Reservations', https://tshaonline.org/handbook/online/articles/bpi01 (13 April 2016). **76.** Comanche County Museum, www.texasforttrail.com (13 April 2016). **77.** 'Cowboy Country Museum', https://texashistoricalfoundation.org/projects/cowboy-country-museum (13 April 2016). **78.** Notes from a conversation with Hilmar G. Moore (22 May 2012). **79.** Hilmar Guenther

Moore (1920–2012) died on 4 December 2012, aged 92, and was succeeded as acting mayor of Richmond, TX, by his widow, Evelyn, www.legacy.com/obituaries/houstonchronicle/obituary.aspx?pid=161506538 (2013).

## CHAPTER 12. MANNAHATTA

1. www.panynj.gov/airports/jfk-history.html (2016). 2. 'New Netherland Placenames', www.en.wikipedia.org/wiki/list_of_New_Netherlands_placename_etymologies (2016). 3. Ronald Bayor, *Encountering Ellis Island: How European Immigrants Entered America* (Baltimore, 2014); Barbara Benton, *Ellis Island: A Pictorial History* (Oxford, 1987); www.archives.gov/research/immigration/index.html (15 May 2016). 4. www.ny.com/transportation/ellis.htm (15 May 2016). 5. 'The Melting Pot', text in www.robmacdougall.org/4301/4301.04.MeltingPot.pdf; see also J. H. Udelson, *Dreamer of the Ghetto: The Life of Israel Zangwill* (Tuscaloosa, 1990); Meri-Jane Rochelson, *A Jew in the Public Arena: The Career of Israel Zangwill* (Detroit, 2008). 6. http://www.lenapelifeways.org/heritage.htm, http://en.wikipedia.org/wiki/Lenape (23 February 2015). 7. Ibid. 8. Herbert Kraft, *The Religion of the Delaware Indians* (South Orange, NJ, 1968). 9. Ibid. 10. Bruce Trigger, ed., 'The North East', *Handbook of North American Indians* (Washington, 1978), vol. 15. 11. Robert Juet of Limehouse (see note 17). 12. Evan Pritchard, 'The Naming of Things', *Native New Yorkers: The Legacy of the Algonquin People of New York* (San Francisco, 2007) Chapter 1. 13. Ibid., p. 122. 14. Ibid., pp. 123–4. 15. L. Wroth, *The Voyages of Giovanni da Verrazzano, 1524–1528* (New Haven, 1970). 16. Estevao Gomes and Diogo Ribeiro, <en.wikipedia.org/wiki/Diogo_Ribeiro> (8 March 2017). 17. Robert Juet of Lime-house, 'The Third Voyage of Master Henrie Hudson', in Samuel Purchas, *Hakluytus Posthumus or Purchas His Pilgrimes: Contayning a History of the World in Sea Voyages and Lande Travells by Englishmen and Others* (1625), Facsimile Edition (Glasgow, 1905–7), vol. 13, pp. 362–3. See also Douglas Hunter, *Half Moon: The Voyage that Redrew the Map of the New World* (London, 2009). 18. Juet, op. cit., pp. 363–4, 366. 19. Ibid., pp. 573–4. 20. Peter Mancall, *Fatal Journey: The Final Voyage of Henry Hudson* (New York, 2004). 21. Simon Schama, *The Embarrassment of Riches: An Interpretation of Dutch Culture in the Golden Age* (London, 1987). 22. E. M. Bacon, *Henry Hudson: His Time and his Voyages* (New York, 1907). 23. Gerald F. De Jong, *The Dutch in America, 1609–74* (Boston, 1975). 24. www.en.wikipedia.org/wiki/Adraien_Block#/media/File:Wpdms_aq_block_1614.jpg. 25. Douglas Feiden, 'Who Was the First Non-Native American Settler on Manhattan?', *New York Daily News* (5 October 2012). 26. 'The Two Row Wampum Treaty of Alliance', www.tworowwampum.com, 2013; 'New York Scholars Claim Indian Treaty Document Is a Fake', *The Wall Street Journal* (1 January 2012); also www.iroquoisdemocracy.pdx.edu/html/covenantchain.htm (15 May 2016). 27. J. Broome, *In Search of Freedom: The Pilgrim Fathers and New England* (Harpenden, 2001). 28. 'Document: The Purchase of Manhattan, 1626', www.

thirteen.org/dutchny/interactives/manhattan-island (2013). **29.** Oscar Reiss, *Blacks in Colonial America* (Jefferson, NC, 1997), 'New York', pp. 79ff. **30.** Amandus Johnson, *The Swedes on the Delaware* (Philadelphia, 1927). **31.** www.en.wikipedia.org/wiki/Pavonia-New-Netherland (2013). **32.** Jonathan Gill, *Harlem: The Four-Hundred-Year History from Dutch Village to Capital of Black America* (New York, 2011). **33.** J. D. Goodfriend et al., eds., *Going Dutch: The Dutch Presence in America* (Leiden, 2009); R. P. Swierenga, *The Dutch in America* (New York, 1985); E. Nooter and P Bonomi, *Colonial Dutch Studies: An Interdisciplinary Approach* (New York, 1988). **34.** L. Ruby, 'Dutch Art and the Hudson Valley Patroon Painters', in Goodfriend et al., op. cit., pp. 27–58. **35.** Christine van Boheemen, 'Dutch American Poets of the 17th Century', in R. Kroes and H.-O. Neuschäfer, eds., *The Dutch in North America: Their Immigration and Cultural Continuity* (Amsterdam, 1991), pp. 114ff. **36.** Ibid., pp. 123–7. **37.** H. C. Murphy, *Jacob Steendam noch vaster: A memoir of the first poet in New Netherland* (The Hague, 1861). **38.** Adriaen van der Donck, *A Description of New Netherland (1655)* (Lincoln, NB, 2008). **39.** www.en.wikipedia.org/wiki/Adriaen_van_der_Donck#/media/File:Jansson-Visscher_map.jpg (2013). **40.** A. Van der Donck et al., *Remonstrance of New Netherland, and the Occurrences There*, trans. E. B. O'Callaghan (Albany, 1856), p. 13. **41.** John Brodhead, 'The English Conquest of New York, 1664', from his *History of New York* (1853), www.usgennet.org/usa/topic/preservation/epochs/vol2/pg153.htm (2016). **42.** 'A City Lost, a City Gained', in Edwin Burrows and Mike Wallace, *Gotham: A History of New York City to 1898* (Oxford, 1999), Chapter 5. **43.** Ibid., Chapter 6. **44.** Mary Lou Lustig, *The Imperial Executive in America: Sir Edmund Andros, 1637–1714* (London, 2002). **45.** www.en.wikipedia.org/wiki/Shackamaxon (2013). **46.** New Netherland Research Center, www.nysl.gov/newnetherland (2013). **47.** <Wpdms.aq.block.1614.jpg> (2013). **48.** Edward Van Winkel, *Manhattan, 1624–39* (New York, 1916). **49.** See Isaac Stokes, *The Iconography of Manhattan Island* (New York, 1915–28), vol. 2. **50.** Hugo Allard, 'Totius Neobelgii Nova et Accuratissima Tabula', see www.collections/mcny.org/Collection/Totius-Neobelgii-Nova-et. (16 May 2016). **51.** 'Maps of New Netherland, New Amsterdam and New England', www.library.fordham.edu/maps/maplisting.html (16 May 2016). **52.** Walking Purchase, Pennsylvania, www.britannica.com/event/Walking-Purchase (2013). **53.** Earl Olmstead, *Blackcoats among the Delaware: David Zeisberger on the Ohio Frontier* (Kent, OH, 1991); Elma Gray, *Wilderness Christians: The Moravian Mission to the Delaware Indians* (Toronto, 1956). **54.** John Zenger's Trial, www.nps.gov/feha/learn/historyculture/the-trial-of-john-peter-zenger.htm (8 March 2017). **55.** T. J. Davis, *A Rumor of Revolt: The 'Great Negro Plot' in Colonial New York* (New York, 1985). **56.** Johannes Oertel, *Pulling Down the Statue of King George III, New York City* (1852–3), www.nyhistory.org/exhibit/pulling-down-the-statue-of-King-George-iii. **57.** William Smith, *The History of the Province of New-York: From its Discovery to the Appointment of Governor Colden in 1762* (New York, 1829). **58.** Diedrich Knickerbocker, *A History of New York from the Beginning of the World to the End of the Dutch Dynasty*

(New York, 1809), Book I, Chapter V. 59. Ibid. 60. *New York: A Historical Sketch of the Rise and Progress of the Metropolitan City of America, by a New Yorker* (New York, 1853), p. 13. 61. Nicholas Falco, 'The Empire State's Search in European Archives', *American Archivist* (1969), vol. 69, pp. 109–23. 62. J. R. Brodhead, *A History of New York* (New York, 1853–71), 2 vols. 63. Edmund B. O'Callaghan, ed., *The Documentary History of New York* (Albany, 1849–51), 4 vols.; *Documents Relevant to the Colonial History of the State of New York* (Albany, 1856–87), 15 vols. 64. Theodore Roosevelt, *The Works of Theodore Roosevelt* (New York, 1926), 20 vols.; Edward Kohn, *Heir to the Empire City: New York and the Making of Theodore Roosevelt* (New York, 2014). 65. Theodore Roosevelt, *New York: A Sketch of the City's Progress from the First Dutch Settlement to Recent Times* (New York and London, 1891), p. 1. 66. Ibid., Chapter IV. 67. Pritchard, op. cit., pp. 19–20. 68. J. Fenimore Cooper, *The Last of the Mohicans: A Narrative of 1757* (London, 1826), vol. I, pp. 48–9. 69. Ibid, vol. II, pp. 294–5. 70. David Zeisberger, *Grammar of the Language of the Lenni-Lenape or Delaware Indians* (Philadelphia, 1827); id., *Zeisberger's Indian Dictionary* (Cambridge, MA, 1887). 71. D. G. Brinton, *A Lenape-English Dictionary from an Anonymous MS in the Archive of the Moravian Church in Bethlehem, Pennsylvania* (Philadelphia, 1888, reprint NY 2006). 72. Walt Whitman, 'Mannahatta', from *Leaves of Grass* (1855). 73. National Museum of the American Indian, www.nmai.si.edu/visit/newyork (2016). 74. Lenape Museum of Indian Culture, www.museumofindianculture. org (2015). 75. 'Nanticoke Indian Tribe', www.easternshore.com/esguide/hist_nanticoke.html (2013). 76. American Indian Community House, 134 W29th St., NYNY 10001, www.aich.org/contact (26 February 2015). 77. C. A. Weslager, *The Delaware Indians: A History* (New York, 1972); *Many Trails: Indians of the Lower Hudson Valley* (Katonah, 1983). 78. Herbert Kraft, *The Lenape Indians of New Jersey* (New York, 1987); *The Lenape or Delaware Indians: The Original People of New Jersey* (Stanhope, 1996); *The Lenape-Delaware Indian Heritage* (Stanhope, 2001). 79. 'Native American Movement', www.countrystudies.us/united-states/history_133.htm (2016). 80. J. George, see www.archebooks.com/Authors/George/jake-george.htm (15 May 2016). 81. Jack Forbes, 'Dream Words'; see www.poetryfoundation.org/poems-and-poets/poets/detail/jack-d-forbes (15 May 2016). 82. www.lenapelifeways.org/heritage.htm; the 'Lenape-English Dictionary', www.gilwell.com/lenape.htm (15 May 2016). 83. Howard B. Rock et al., *City of Promises: A History of the Jews of New York* (New York, 2012), 3 vols. 84. Dutch International Society, www.dutchinternationalsociety.org (2013). 85. Leslie Harris, *In the Shadow of Slavery: African Americans in New York City, 1626–1823* (Chicago, 2002). 86. African Burial Ground National Monument, www.nps.gov/afbg (25 February 2015). 87. Nick Paumgarten, 'Useless Beauty: What is to be Done with Governors Island?, *The New Yorker* (31 August 2009).

## CHAPTER 13. TRANSATLANTIC

1. Walter Munk et al., *The Rotation of the Earth: A Geophysical Discussion* (Cambridge, 1975); D. D. McCarthy, *Variations in the Earth's Rotation* (Washington DC, 1990); Robert Newton, *Mediaeval Chronicles on the Rotation of the Earth* (Baltimore, 1972). 2. Ivan Crowe, *Copernicus* (Stroud, 2003); J. Adamczewski and E. Piszek, *Nicolaus Copernicus and His Epoch* (Philadelphia, 1973). 3. Aristotle, *Meteorology*, Book I, ed. E. W. Webster (Blacksburg, VA, 2011); P. Lettinck, *Aristotle's Meteorology and its Reception in the Arab World* (Leiden, 1999). 4. John M. Dillon et al., *Theophrastus* (Bristol, 2012). 5. 'Weather Brains', www.weatheronline.co.uk/reports/weatherbrains/Teisserenc-de-Bort.htm (7 March 2017). 6. Jetstream, www.metoffice.gov.uk/learning/wind/what-is-the-jetstream (10 March 2017). 7. S. E. Bishop, 'The Equatorial Smoke-Stream from Krakatoa', *Hawaian Monthly*, vol. 1, no. 5 (May 1884), pp. 106–10. 8. Wasaburo Oishi, *Raporto de la Aerologia Observatorio de Tateno* (Tokyo, 1926). 9. Heinrich Seilkopf, *Maritime Meteorologie*, in R. Habermehl, ed., *Handbuch der Fliegerwetterkunde* (Berlin, 1939), vol. II, pp. 142–50. 10. Rob Crilly, 'Jet Stream Blasts BA Plane across Atlantic in Record Time, *Telegraph* (10 January 2015). 11. Alden Hatch, *Glen Curtiss: Pioneer of Aviation* (Guildford, CT, 2007). 12. John R. Bayer, 'The Forgotten Fliers of 1919: The First Successful Transatlantic Flight', www.aerofiles.com/nc4.html (10 March 2017). 13. Brendan Lynch, *Yesterday We Were in America: Alcock and Brown, First to Fly the Atlantic* (Haynes, 2009). 14. Peterhouse, www.pet.cam.ac.uk (2015). 15. Tom Sharpe, *Porterhouse Blue* (London, 1974); Mini-TV Series, www.imdb.com/title/tt0002428 (2015). 16. J. D. North, 'Monasticism and the First Mechanical Clocks', in *Stars, Mind and Fate: Essays in Ancient and Mediaeval Cosmology* (London, 1989), pp. 171–88. 17. Caius Sundial, www.cai.cam.ac.uk/pics/clock.jpg (11 March 2017). 18. 'Reading the Dial in Old Court', www.queens.cam.ac.uk/life-at-queens/about-the-college/college-facts/reading-the-dial-in-Old-Court (11 March 2017). 19. Frank King, 'The Sundial in Old Court' (Selwyn College) <cl.cam.ac.uk/~fhk1/Sundials/Selwyn/Selwyn.pdf> (11 March 2017). 20. Cambridge Sundials, https://sundials.co.uk/~cantab.htm (11 March 2017). 21. *Oxford English Dictionary* (Compact Edition) (Oxford, 1971), vol. II, p. 3,801. 22. *Dictionnaire Encyclopédique Quillet* (Paris, 1935), vol. VI, p. 4,373. 23. Regimental traditions; www.exeterflottila.org/history-misc/passing-port.htm (2015). 24. 'Madeira – Historical Overview', www.madeira-a-z.com/facts-and-essentials/history/historical-overview (12 March 2017). 25. Machico, <en.wikipedia.org/wiki/Robert_Machin> (2015). 26. Medici-Laurentian Atlas, 1351, www.wow.com/wiki/Medici_Laurentian_Atlas (2016). 27. Nossa Senhora do Monte, www.cm.funchal.pt/en/index.php?option=com_content&view=article&id=117%3A (2016). 28. John Hailman, *Thomas Jefferson on Wine* (Jackson, MI, 2006), p. 40. 29. 'Madeira Decanter', www.monticello.org/site/research-and-collections/madeira-decanter (24 February 2017). 30. Desmond Gregory, *The Beneficent Usurpers: A History of the British in Madeira* (London, 1988). 31. Blandy family, www.blandys.com/the-blandy-family.html

(2016).   32. Herbert Vivian, *The Life of the Emperor Charles of Austria* (London, 1932); H. K. Zessner-Spitzenberg and K. Rasinger, *The Emperor Charles I of Austria, a Great Christian Monarch* (London, 1963); Gordon Brook-Shepherd, *The Last Empress: The Life and Times of Zita of Austria-Hungary, 1892–1989* (London, 1991).   33. John Paul II's homily, 'The Beatification of Five Servants of God', BBC News (3 October 2004).   34. Madeira Airport, www.madeira-web.com/PagesUK/airport.html   (2016);   https://www.aeroportomadeira.pt (2015).   35. Norman Hull, *Aquila to Madeira: The Story of Flying Boats to Funchal* (Kettering, 2010).   36. Not mentioned in Celia Sandys, *Chasing Churchill: The Travels of Winston Churchill* (London, 2003).   37. J. R. Press and M. J. Short, *Flora of Madeira* (London, 1994).   38. Eratosthenes of Cyrene, the 'Father of Geography': 'The Measurement of the World's Circumference', www.juliantrubin.com/bigten/erastothenes.html (10 March 2017).   39. 'Ptolemy's World Map', www.bl.uk/learning/timeline/item126360.html (11 March 2017).   40. Dante Alighieri, *Purgatorio*, Canto IV, ll. 61–84.   41. See J. H. Parry, *The Age of Reconnaissance* (London, 1963), p. 141.   42. Laura Smoller, *History, Prophecy and the Stars: The Christian Astrology of Pierre D'Ailly, 1350–1420* (Princeton, 1994).   43. 'Stargazing Live Australia', <bbc.co.uk/iplayer/episode/b08162r4/stargazing-live-australia-episode-3> (30 March 2017).   44. 'Cape Cross Inscription', www.bing.com/images'q=Cape%20Cross%20inscription&qs=n&form=QBIR&pq (2016),   45. Fernando Pessoa, 'Padrão', from *Mar Português*, in *Mensagem* (Lisbon, 1934).

## CHAPTER 14. FRA

1. 'Frankfurt International Airport Guide', www.frankurt-airport.org (2015); Freddy Bullock, *Frankfurt Airport* (Shrewsbury, 2001).   2. G. W. Sante, *Hessen* (Stuttgart, 1960); C. W. Ingrao, *The Hessian Mercenary State: Ideas, Institutions and Reform under Frederick II, 1760–85* (Cambridge, 1987); Piotr Napierała, *Hesja-Darmstadt w XVIII stuleciu* (Poznan, 2009).   3. Wolfgang Mommsen, *1848: Die Ungewollte Revolution* (Frankfurt, 2000); Brian Vick, *Defining Germany: The 1848 Frankfurt Parliamentarians and National Identity* (Harvard, 2002); Jan Palmowski, *Urban Liberalism in Imperial Germany: Frankfurt am Main, 1866–1914* (Oxford, 1999); Municipal Historical Commission, *Frankfurt am Main: Die Geschichte der Stadt in neun Beitragen* (Sigmaringen, 1991).   4. <en.wikipedia.org/Frankfurt_Airport#History> (2015).   5. John Toland, *The Great Dirigibles: Their Triumphs and Disasters* (Boston, 1972); Shelley Tanaka, *The Disaster of the Hindenburg* (London, 1993); Jane Bingham, *The Hindenburg, 1937: A Huge Airship Destroyed by Fire* (Oxford, 2006); <en.wikipedia.org/wiki/Hindenburg_Disaster> (2015).   6. www.lufthansa.com (2015); <en.wikipedia.org/wiki/Lufthansa#History>   (2015).   7.   www.airporthotel steigenberger.de (2015).   8. J. W. R. Taylor and K. Munsen, *History of Aviation* (London, 1978); J. H. Batchelor, *Flight: The History of Aviation* (Limpsfield, 1990); Dennis Baldry, *The Hamlyn History of Aviation* (London, 1996).   9. *The*

*Shorter Oxford English Dictionary* (1973), vol. 1, p. 138.   10. G. de la Landelle, *Aviation ou Navigation Aérienne* (Paris, 1863).   11. Linda Serck, 'James Sadler, the Oxford Balloon Man whom History Forgot', BBC News (12 July 2014).   12. Gerard Fairlie and Elizabeth Cayley, *The Life of a Genius: Sir George Cayley, Pioneer of Modern Aviation* (London, 1965).   13. F. C. Kelly, *The Wright Brothers: A Biography* (New York, 1989).   14. National Geographic, Aircrash Investigation TV series, www.natgeotv.com/uk/shows/natgeo/air-crash-investigation (2016).   15. PRO (London), HQ RAF Casualty Reports (1–10 September 1918), AIR/1/858/204/5/418.   16. In family possession.   17. IATA Conference, Montreal, www.frmsforum.org/2016-conference-montreal (2016).   18. Air losses, <en.wikipedia.org/wiki/List_of_accidents_and_incidents_involving_commerical_aircraft> (2015).   19. See John Lazenby, *The First Punic War* (Stanford, 1996).   20. The Kamikaze of 1274, www.britannica.com/event/kamikaze-of-1274-and-1281 (2017).   21. Barratry, www.legal-dictionary.thefreedictionary.com/Barratry (2016).   22. Tom Clancy, *The Hunt for Red October* (London, 1984).   23. Penny Smith, *The Lost Ship Waratah: Searching for the Titanic of the South* (Stroud, 2009).   24. A. Conan Doyle, 'J. Habakuk Jephson's Statement', *Cornhill Magazine* (January 1884).   25. Charles Fay, *The Story of the Mary Celeste* (New York, 1988); Brian Hicks, *Ghost Ship: The Mysterious True Story of the Mary Celeste and its Missing Crew* (New York, 2004); Paul Begg, *The Mary Celeste: The Greatest Mystery of the Sea* (Harlow, 2007).   26. Chris Irvine, 'The Arctic Sea Mystery: More Unexplained Missing Ships and Crews', *The Daily Telegraph* (18 August 2009).   27. Alan Cass, 'The Schooner Jenny', *The Mariner's Mirror*, Society for Nautical Research (August 1996), www.snr.org.uk/schooner-jenny (2016).   28. Brian Dunning, 'The Legend of the Flying Dutchman', www.skeptoid.com/episodes/4427 (2015).   29. John Howison: A. L. Strout, *A Bibliography of Articles in Blackwood's Magazine, 1817–25* (Edinburgh, 1959), p. 78.   30. Pierre-Louis Dietsch, *Le Vaisseau Fantôme, ou Le Maudit des Mers* (Paris, 1842).   31. Heinrich Heine, *Aus den Memoiren des Herren von Schnabelewopski* (1833), ed. C. Tophoven-Triltsch (Berlin, 1986).   32. From *The Cruise of HMS Bacchante, 1879–82* (London, 1888), vol. II, quoted by Kenneth Rose, *King George V* (London, 1988).   33. Richard Wagner, *Der fliegende Holländer*, libretto, www.gutenberg.org/files/31963/31963 (3 February 2015).   34. Barratry, CNN wire (21 March 2014), www.fox13now.com/2014/03/21/from-ghostly-to-psychic (2014).   35. 'Global Re-insurance', www.globalreinsurance.com/1407586.article (2016); P. Greenberg and N. Rapp, 'The Big Money Surprise about MH370', <http://fortune.com/2014/05/01/the-big-money-surprise> (2015).   36. Vincent Loomis, *Amelia Earhart: The Final Story* (New York, 1985).   37. Richard Winer, *The Devil's Triangle* (New York, 1974).   38. Stratojet disappearance, www.military.wikia.com/wiki/1956_B-47_disappearance (2016).   39. 'Unsolved Aviation Mysteries', www.theflightblog.com/flying-tiger-flight-739 (2016).   40. Kay Olson, *D. B. Cooper Hijacking: Vanishing Act* (New York, 2010); Ross Richardson, *Still Missing: Re-thinking the D. B. Cooper Affair* (New York, 2015).   41. *Stardust* disaster, 'Vanished: The Plane that Disappeared', BBC 2 (2 November 2000), www.bbc.co.uk/science/

horizon/2000/vanished/shtml (2015).   42. Piotr Kraśko, *Smoleńsk: 10 Kwietnia 2010* (Warsaw, 2010); Teresa Torańska, *Smoleńsk* (Warsaw, 2013 ).   43. Russian MAK Report, *Findings of the Interstate Aviation Committee Safety Investigation of the Accident involving Tu-154M . . . in April 2010 near Smolensk* (Moscow, 12 January 2011), <mak.ru/English/info/tu-154m_101.html> (2013); Poland's *Final Report of the Committee for Investigation of National Aviation Accidents into the Causes and Circumstances of the Tu-154M Plane Crash (tail number 101) in Smolensk* (Warsaw, 29 July 2013), <mswia.datacenter-Poland.pl/Final_Report_Tu-154M.pdf> (2013).   44. Fergus Hunter, 'After Three Years, MH370 Search Ends with no Plane and Few Answers', *Stuff* (17 January 2017), www.stuff.co.nz/world/australia/88513975 (14 March 2017).   45. A. Jamieson, 'MH370 Flaperon on Reunion Island is Confirmed as First Debris from Missing Malaysia Flight', NBC News (3 September 2015).   46. 'Why is the South China Sea Contentious?', BBC News (12 July 2016).   47. P. Apps and T. Hepher, 'Analysis: Geopolitical Games Handicap Malaysia Jet Hunt', Reuters (UK) (28 March 2014),   48. Malaysia's War Crimes Commission.   49. MH370 Cargo Manifest, www.themalaysianinsider.com/. . ./mh370_cargo_manifest (21 May 2015).   50. USA National Reconnaissance Office, www.nro.gov; R. Guillemat, 'De-Classified US Spy Satellites Reveal Secret Cold War Space Program', www.space.com/12996-secret-spy-satellites-declassified-nro.html (2015).   51. MH17, 'The Latest News and Comment on the Shooting Down of MH17', *The Guardian* (29 September 2016).   52. Freescale Semiconductors, '20 Freescale Staff on Vanished MH370 Flight', www.theregister.co.uk/2014/03/09/20-freescale-employees-missing-on-mh370 (2015).   53. Operation Cope Tiger, www.globalsecurity.org/military/ops/cope-tiger.htm (2015).   54. Inmarsat: Sophie Curtis, 'MH370: How British Satellite Company Tracked Down Missing Malaysian Plane', *The Daily Telegraph* (24 Mar 2014); www.inmarsat.com, official site.   55. Indian Ocean Gyre, www.wow.com/wiki/Indian_Ocean_Gyre (2015).   56. Jonathan Pearlman, 'MH370 Latest: Malaysian Airlines "deliberately set to autopilot" over the Indian Ocean', *The Daily Telegraph* (26 June 2014), www.telegraph.co.uk/news/worldnews/asia/Malaysia/10927078 (2015).   57. Helios Flight 522, 'Ghost Flight Horror Crash Blamed on Pilots', *MailOnline* (10 October 2006).   58. BHUAP, https://en.wikipedia.org/wiki/Boeing_Honeywell_Uninterruptible_Autopilot; https://counterpsyops.com/tag/bhuap; 'Evidence of the Hijack of MH370', www.n8wachter.info/wp-content/uploads/2015/04/BUAP_May-2014_Folder3 (2015).   59. Cyber, www.rand.org/cyberwarfare; <en.wikipedia.org/wiki/cyberwarfare> (2015).   60. 'Voice 370': 'We do not accept that MH370 has crashed', www.malaysiandigest.com/news/544362; (Sarah Bajc), 'Girlfriend of MH370 Passenger: Something is being Covered up', NBC News (8 September 2014) (2015).   61. Megan Levy, 'Blogger who Found Plane Wreckage is Funding his Own Research for MH370', *Sydney Morning Herald* (3 March 2016).   62. 'Could a Jumbo Jet (747) glide if its engines stopped working?', <uk.answers.yahoo.com/question/index?qid=20060810054129AAnddHD> (2015).   63. Rosemary Dobson, from 'The Ship of Ice', in *The Ship of Ice and Other Poems* (1948), Australian Poetry Library, www.poetrylibrary.edu.au/poets/dobson/ship_of_ice

(4 February 2015). The poem was inspired by the fate of the schooner *Jenny*. **64.** Joseph, Count Von Eichendorff (1788–1857), lines from 'Abschied' ('Farewell'), in *The Penguin Book of German Verse* (Harmondsworth, 1959), pp. 311–17. **65.** Unterschweinstiege Restaurant, *Geniessen aus Tradtion* (Frankfurt am Main, nd). **66.** www.chefkoch.de/rs/sO/handkäse+mit+musik/Rezepte.html (3 March 2017). **67.** Pouria Nour Mehrdad: 'Missing Malaysia Plane: The Passengers on Board MH370', BBC News (17 January 2017). **68.** *Fraktur*, <en.wikipedia.org/wiki/Fraktur_(script) (2016). **69.** Frankfurt's old city was completely razed by an Allied air raid on 22 March 1944 – 112 years to the day after the death of the city's most famous son, Goethe, www.revisionist.net/bombed-cities-07.html (2016). **70.** Schweinsteiger, www.quora.com/what-is-the-origin-and-meaning-of-the-surname-of-Schweinsteiger? (2016). **71.** Dante Alighieri, *The Vision, or Hell, Purgatory and Paradise*, trans. H. F. Cary (London, 1844), p. 562.

## CHAPTER 15. IMPERIUM

**1.** The original version of this lecture was presented at the University of the Arab Emirates, Al Ain (11 April 2012). **2.** Arundhati Roy, from *War Talk* (2003). **3.** From William Golding, *Lord of the Flies* (London, 1954). **4.** Ibid., Chapter 12. **5.** Iqbal Ahmed, *Empire of the Mind: A Journey through Great Britain* (London, 2007), pp. 20–21. **6.** Ibid., *passim*. **7.** Kwasi Kwarteng, *Ghosts of Empire: Britain's Legacies in the Modern World* (London, 2011). **8.** It was enthusiastically recommended to me by our neighbour, Lord Ian Blair. **9.** Kwarteng, op. cit., pp. 11ff. **10.** Ibid., p. 19. See Josephine Kamm, *Daughter of the Desert: The Story of Gertrude Bell* (London, 1956); Georgina Howell, *Queen of the Desert: The Extraordinary Life of Gertrude Bell* (London, 2015); Gertrude Bell, *A Woman in Arabia: The Writings of the Queen of the Desert* (New York, 2015). **11.** Quoted by Kwarteng, op. cit., *passim*. **12.** Ibid., p. 21. **13.** H. St J. B. Philby, *Arabian Days: An Autobiography* (London, 1948); id., *Arabia of the Wahhabis* (London, 1977); id., *Arabian Oil Ventures* (Washington DC, 1964); Anthony Cave Brown, *Treason in the Blood* (London, 1995); Elizabeth Monroe, *Philby of Arabia* (Reading, 1998). **14.** Kwarteng, op. cit., p. 397. **15.** Norman Davies, *Europe: A History* (Oxford, 1996), pp. 1–46. **16.** Niall Ferguson, *Empire: How Britain Made the Modern World* (London, 2003); 'The Six Killer Apps of Prosperity', TED Conference (20 July 2011); www.ted.com/talks/niall_ferguson_the_6_killer_apps_of_prosperity (2016); and id., *Civilization: Is the West History?* (London, 2011). **17.** Jared Diamond, *The Third Chimpanzee: The Evolution and Future of the Human Animal* (New York, 1993); *Why Is Sex Fun? The Evolution of Human Sexuality* (London, 1997); *Guns, Germs and Steel: The Fates of Human Societies* (New York, 1997); *Collapse: How Societies Choose to Fail or Succeed* (New York, 2005); *The World Until Yesterday: What Can We Learn from Traditional Societies?* (New York, 2012). **18.** Diamond, *Guns, Germs and Steel*, op. cit., *passim*.

19. Norman Davies, *God's Playground: A History of Poland* (Oxford, 1981), 2 vols.   20. Sebastian Conrad, *German Colonialism: A Short History* (Cambridge, 2012).   21. Roy Foster, *The Oxford History of Ireland* (Oxford, 1992); John Kelly, *The Graves Are Walking: A History of the Great Irish Famine* (London, 2012).   22. A. J. P. Taylor, *The Habsburg Monarchy, 1809–1918* (Harmondsworth, 1990); Norman Davies, 'Galicia: The Kingdom of the Naked and Starving', *Vanished Kingdoms* (London, 2012), pp. 439–89; Larry Wolff, *The Idea of Galicia: History and Fantasy in Habsburg Political Culture* (Stanford, 2010); Noel Malcolm, *Bosnia: A Short History* (London, 2002).   23. Norman Davies, *The Isles: A History* (London, 1999), 'The British Imperial Isles', Chapter IX, pp. 661–870.   24. Pierre Goubert, *The Course of French History* (London, 1991); <en.wikipedia.org/wiki/Territorial_evolution_of_France> with mobile maps (2016).   25. Michael Rywkin, *Russian Colonial Expansion to 1917* (London, 1988); G. A. Lensen, *Russia's Eastward Expansion* (Englewood Cliffs, NJ, 1964); Martin Sicker, *The Strategy of Russian Imperialism* (New York, 1988).   26. Suraiya Faroqi, *The Ottoman Empire and the World Around It* (London, 2004); Eugene Rogan, *The Fall of the Ottomans: The Great War in the Middle East* (London, 2015).   27. Massimo Pallottino, *The Etruscans* (London, 1975); Michael Grant, *The Etruscans* (London, 1980); G. Barker and T. Rasmussen, *The Etruscans* (Oxford, 1998).   28. Eric Christiansen, *The Northern Crusades* (London, 1988).   29. T. G. R. Tsetskhladze, *Greek Colonisation: An Account of Greek Colonies and Other Settlements Overseas* (Leiden, 2006–8), 2 vols.; D. V. Grammenos and E. K. Petropoulos, *Ancient Greek Colonies in the Black Sea* (Thessaloniki, 2003), 2 vols.   30. D. J. Mattingly, *Imperialism, Power and Identity: Experiencing the Roman Empire* (Princeton, 2011).   31. J. F. O'Callaghan, *Reconquest and Crusade in Mediaeval Spain* (Philadelphia, 2015).   32. Herman Schreiber, *Teuton and Slav: The Struggle for Central Europe* (London, 1965); F. Dvornik, *The First Wave of the Drang nach Osten* (London, 1945).   33. Orest Subtelny, *Ukraine: A History* (Toronto, 1996); Anna Reid, *Borderland: A Journey Through the History of Ukraine* (London, 2013).   34. Natalya Polonska-Vasylenko, *The Settlement of Southern Ukraine, 1750–75* (New York, 1955); William Sunderland, *Taming the Wild Field: Colonialism and Empire on the Russian Steppe* (London, 2006).   35. John Prebble, *The Highland Clearances* (London, 1963).   36. R. A. Voeltz, *German Colonialism and the South-West African Company, 1884–1914* (Ohio, 1988); J. Sylvester and J.-B. Gewald, *Words Cannot Be Found: German Rule in Namibia* (Leiden, 2003).   37. Quoted by Ian Gilmour, 'Terrorism', *London Review of Books*, vol. 8, no. 8 (23 October 1986).   38. Peter Kolchin, *Unfree Labor: American Slavery and Russian Serfdom* (Cambridge, MA, 1987); M. L. Bush, *Serfdom and Slavery: Studies in Legal Bondage* (London, 1996).   39. Moshe Lewin, *Russian Peasants and Soviet Power: A Study in Collectivisation* (London, 1968); Robert Conquest, *The Harvest of Sorrow: Soviet Collectivisation and the Terror-Famine* (New York, 1986).   40. Larry Neal and J. G. Williamson, *The Cambridge History of Capitalism* (Cambridge, 2014).   41. Davies, *The Isles*, op. cit., pp. 345ff.   42. 'Sublimis Deus sic delexit humanum genus', in Joel S. Panzer, *The Popes and Slavery*

(New York, 1996), pp. 79–81.  **43.** Michael Burleigh, *The Racial State: Germany, 1933–45* (Cambridge, 1991).  **44.** Raymond Betts, *Europe Overseas: Phases of Imperialism* (New York, 1968).  **45.** Élie Halévy, *Histoire du Peuple Anglais au 19ème Siècle* (Paris, 1913–46), 6 vols., trans. as *A History of the English People* (London, 1949–52).  **46.** Raoul Mortier, ed., *Dictionnaire Encyclopédique Quillet* (Paris, 1926), vol. 4, p. 2,334.  **47.** *Encyclopaedia Britannica*, 11th edition (1910–11), vol. 9, p. 355 (article by Ernest Barker).  **48.** Ibid., vol. 9, pp. 355–6.  **49.** Ibid., vol. 4, p. 606.  **50.** Ibid., vol. 9, p. 356.  **51.** The British Empire and Commonwealth Museum, Temple Meads, Bristol, www.empiremuseum.co.uk (25 June 2017).  **52.** 'Colonialism: Britain Can Learn from Germany about Not Denying the Past', *The Guardian* (27 December 2016).  **53.** John Darwin, *After Tamerlane: The Global History of Empire since 1405* (London, 2007); *The Empire Project: The Rise and Fall of the British World-System, 1830–1970* (Cambridge, 2009); *Unfinished Empire: The Global Expansion of Britain* (London, 2012); *The End of the British Empire: The Historical Debate* (Oxford, 1991).  **54.** Karuna Mantena, 'Mill and the Imperial Predicament', in N. Urbinati and A. Zakaras, eds., *J. S. Mill's Political Thought* (Cambridge, 2007).  **55.** Gary Magee and Andrew Thompson, *Empire and Globalisation: Networks of People, Goods and Capital in the British World, c. 1850–1914* (Cambridge, 2010).  **56.** Dr Shashi Tharoor, Speech at the Oxford Union (28 May 2015); <youtube.com/watch?v=VcWc7WqcS5M> (2015); see also Shashi Tharoor, *Inglorious Empire: What the British Did to India* (London, 2017).

## AFTERWORD

**1.** Norman Davies, *Szlak Nadziei: Armia Andersa, marsz przez trzy kontynenty* (Izabelin, 2015), published in English as *Trail of Hope: The Anders Army, an Odyssey across Three Continents* (Oxford, 2016).

# Index